the **constructivist** moment

the **constructivist** moment

FROM MATERIAL TEXT TO CULTURAL POETICS

BARRETT WATTEN

WESLEYAN UNIVERSITY PRESS Middletown, Connecticut

Published by

Wesleyan University Press,

Middletown, CT 06459

Printed in United States of America

5 4 3 2 1

Library of Congress

Cataloging-in-Publication Data

Watten, Barrett.

The constructivist moment : from material text to cultural poetics / Barrett Watten.

p. cm.

Includes bibliographical references and index.

ISBN 0–8195–6609–8 (alk. paper)—ISBN 0–8195–6610–1 (pbk. : alk. paper)

1. American literature—20th century—History and criticism. 2. Avant-garde (Aesthetics)—United States—History—20th century. 3. Avant-garde (Aesthetics)—Soviet Union—History—20th century. 4. Russian literature—20th century—History and criticism. 5. Literature, Comparative—American and Russian. 6. Literature, Comparative—Russian and American. 7. American literature—Russian influences. 8. Constructivism (Russian literature) I. Title.

PS159.R8W38 2003

810.9'1—dc21 2003001153

FOR ASA

I see plans of a house in stages of construction.
Workmen move across bare frames in open light.
—"Paralleles"

CONTENTS

ACKNOWLEDGMENTS

I am especially grateful to Michael Davidson, Rachel Blau DuPlessis, Carla Harryman, Lyn Hejinian, Bob Perelman, Bruce Andrews, Alan Davies, Steve McCaffery, Ted Pearson, Ron Silliman, and Charles Bernstein for their work as poets and critics; to Ted for his help with the manuscript; and to Carla for many more reasons than that. This work, in its original presentations, was a response to the call from a number of individuals:

Thanks to Ron Day, whose proposal for a panel at the 1992 meeting of the Modern Language Association inspired me to write "New Meaning and Poetic Vocabulary: From Coleridge to Jackson Mac Low," and to Gail Scott and the late Bill Readings, who facilitated its presentation at the Université de Montréal in March 1993. Brian McHale solicited it for *Poetics Today* 18, no. 2 (summer 1997); reprinted by permission of Duke University Press. Thanks to Jackson Mac Low, Herman Rapaport, and the editors of *Poetics Today* for their comments.

"The Secret History of the Equal Sign: *L=A=N=G=U=A=G=E* between Discourse and Text" was written for the conference "Poetics of Avant-Garde Poetries" in Tel Aviv, November 1997; thanks to Brian McHale, Meir Sternberg, Karen Alkalay-Gut, and Tamar Yacobi. It was also presented as a keynote address to "Tradition and Resistance in Contemporary Poetry," Conference for English Studies, University of London, November 1998; thanks to Alison Mark and Robert Hampson. A section was presented at the Twentieth-Century Literature Conference at the University of Louisville, February 1998; thanks to Alan Golding. It appeared in Jonathan Monroe and Brian McHale's special issue "The Poetics of Avant-Garde Poetries," vol. 1, *Poetics Today* 20, no. 4 (winter 1999); reprinted by permission of Duke University Press. Thanks to Charles Bernstein for his comments.

Charles Bernstein invited me to present a talk at the SUNY Buffalo Poetics Program in November 1996, for which I am grateful; "The Bride of the Assembly Line: Radical Poetics in Construction" was the result. The English Department at Temple University heard a version of the essay in January 1997; my thanks to Rachel Blau DuPlessis. Steve Evans and Jennifer Moxley published it in the *Impercipient Lecture Series*, no. 8 (October 1997); a section also appeared in *Dispatch Detroit*

4 (2000), edited by Christine Monhollen. Thanks to Arthur Marotti and Georgette Fleischer for their comments, and to Jessica Burstein and Nancy Jones for the occasion of the unveiling of the "Bride."

"The Constructivist Moment: From El Lissitzky to Detroit Techno" answered Cary Nelson's request to define the state of modernist studies at the 1997 meeting of the Modern Language Association, where it was presented with the title "Free Radicals, Modernist Examples." Randolph Starn then sponsored it as a part of a two-day presentation at the Townsend Center for the Humanities, University of California, Berkeley, March 1998; after which it was given to faculty in the English Department of Wayne State University, October 1999. Thanks to the editors of the Berkeley journal *Qui Parle*, especially Faith Barrett, where it appeared in vol. 11, no. 1 (fall/winter 1997). Thanks as well to Mike Banks, Sandy Jaczszak, and Marc Christensen for their insights into techno.

"Nonnarrative and the Construction of History: An Era of Stagnation, the Fall of Saigon" was part of "The Narrative Construction of History," a panel curated by Laura Brun, at Southern Exposure Gallery in San Francisco, March 1990. It was given as well at a conference, "The Ends of Theory," Wayne State University, March 1991, thanks to George Tysh and the organizers; at the Unit for Theory and Critical Interpretation, University of Illinois, Champaign-Urbana, October 1992, thanks to Cary Nelson; at the University of California, San Diego, March 1993, thanks to Michael Davidson. It was solicited by Jerry Herron, Dorothy Huson, Ross Pudaloff, and Robert Strozier for inclusion in the conference volume *The Ends of Theory* (Detroit: Wayne State University Press, 1995); reprinted by permission of Wayne State University Press. A section also appeared in Peter Baker's anthology, *Onward: Contemporary Poetry and Poetics* (New York: Peter Lang, 1996). Thanks to Randolph Starn for his comments on the original version.

"Negative Examples: Theories of Negativity in the Avant-Garde" was originally presented at two conferences: "Žižekian Negativity and Modernist Poetics," at the Twentieth-Century Literature Conference, University of Louisville, February 2000; and "Avant-Garde Examples after Heidegger and Foucault: Robert Grenier and David Wojnarowicz," at "Avant-Garde and Culture Studies," a seminar cochaired with Rachel Blau DuPlessis, at the Modernist Studies Association conference, University of Pennsylvania, October 2000. Thanks to Alan Golding and George Hartley for their comments.

An invitation from Ellen Berry to appear on the panel "Postmodernism, Postcommunism" at the 1991 meeting of the Modern Language Association led to the writing of "Post-Soviet Subjectivity in Arkadii Dragomoshchenko and Ilya Kabakov." Thanks to the editors of *Postmodern Culture*, Eyal Amiran and John Unsworth, who published it in vol. 3, no. 2 (January 1993) and then included it in *Essays from Postmodern Culture* (Oxford: Oxford University Press, 1993); reprinted by permission of Johns Hopkins University Press. Thanks to Lyn Hejinian for her comments.

Helga Pakasaar, curator at the Art Gallery of Windsor, Ontario, asked me to give a lecture in conjunction with Stan Douglas's exhibition *Le Détroit*, May 2000; "Zone: The Poetics of Space in Posturban Detroit" was the result. It was also presented at Simon Fraser University, Vancouver, B.C., thanks to Lisa Robertson and Aaron Vidaver. Deb King published it in the Detroit online zine *mark(s)*, September 2000; available at <www.markszine.com>. Thanks to Stan Douglas and the David Zwirner Gallery, New York.

Grateful acknowledgment is made to the following individuals and publishers for permission to reprint copyrighted or previously unavailable works, beyond the scope of fair use:

Kit Robinson, for sections 12 and 13 of *The Dolch Stanzas* (San Francisco: This Press, 1976). © 1976 Kit Robinson.

Carla Harryman and Lyn Hejinian, for unpublished sections of *The Wide Road*. © 2003 Carla Harryman and Lyn Hejinian.

Charles Alexander, Joe Amato, Tom Beckett, Charles Bernstein, Sherry Brennan, Maria Damon, Grant Jenkins, Jeffrey Jullich, Michael McColl, Karen McKevitt, Gwyn McVay, Chris Piuma, Clai Rice, Camille Roy, Linda Russo, Kathy Lou Schultz, Gregory Severance, Alan Sondheim, Juliana Spahr, and Steve Vincent, for posts to the Poetics Listserv, April 1999; archived at <epc.buffalo.edu>.

Clark Coolidge, for "Made Thought," from *This* 1 (1971). © 1971, 2003 Clark Coolidge.

The Johns Hopkins University Press, for Louis Zukofsky, poem 4 from "29 Poems," from *Complete Short Poetry* (Baltimore, 1991). © 1991 Paul Zukofsky.

Jean Day, for "The Fluidity of Attributes," from *The Literal World* (Berkeley, Calif.: Tuumba Press, 1998). © 1998 Jean Day.

Lyn Hejinian, for "Exit," from *This* 12 (1982). © 1982 Lyn Hejinian.

Jackson Mac Low, for "Wall Rev," from *This* 12 (1982). © 1982 Jackson Mac Low.

Persea Books, New York; Carcanet Press, Manchester; and the Laura (Riding) Jackson Board of Literary Management, for Laura (Riding) Jackson, "Room," from *The Poems of Laura Riding* (New York and Manchester, 1983); © 1938, 1980. In conformity with the wishes of the late Laura (Riding) Jackson, her Board of Literary Management asks us to record that, in 1941, Laura (Riding) Jackson renounced, on the grounds of linguistic principle, the writing of poetry: she had come to hold that "poetry obstructs general attainment to something better in our linguistic way-of-life than we have."

Bill Berkson, for "Negative," from *Blue Is the Hero: Poems 1960–1975* (Kensington, Calif.: L Publications, 1976), 98. © 1976 Bill Berkson.

Barrett Watten, for "Negative," from *Frame: 1971–1990* (Los Angeles: Sun and Moon Press, 1997). © 1976, 1997 Barrett Watten.

Robert Grenier, for eleven poems from *Sentences* (Cambridge, Mass.: Whalecloth Press, 1978). © 1978 Robert Grenier.

Marjorie Welish, for "Black Diluvium," from *The Annotated "Here" and Selected Poems* (Minneapolis: Coffee House Books, 2000). © 2000 Marjorie Welish.

Acknowledgment is likewise gratefully made to the following individuals, publishers, galleries, and estates for their permission to reproduce the following works of visual art:

Kit Robinson and This Press, for the cover of *The Dolch Stanzas* (San Francisco: This Press, 1976). © 1976 Kit Robinson and This Press.

Jackson Mac Low, for three cards from "56 Sets of Actions Drawn by Chance Operations and from the Basic English List by Jackson Mac Low in Spring 1961." © 2003 Jackson Mac Low.

Bruce Andrews and Charles Bernstein, for the cover of *L=A=N=G=U=A=G=E*, no. 13 (1980). © 1980 L=A=N=G=U=A=G=E.

Ron Silliman, for the cover of *Tottel's*, no. 6 (October 1971).

Alan Davies, for the covers of *A Hundred Posters*, no. 26 (1976); and *Oculist Witnesses*, no. 3 (1976). © 1976, 1978 Alan Davies.

James Sherry, for the cover of *Roof*, no. 4 (1977). © 1977 Segue.

Bob Perelman, for the cover of *Hills*, no. 4 (1977). © 1977 Bob Perelman and Francie Shaw.

Terry Swanson, for the cover of *Slit Wrist*, nos. 3/4 (1977). © 1977 Slit Wrist.

Steve Benson and Tom Mandel, for the cover of *Miam*, no. 6 (1978). © 1978 Steve Benson.

Douglas Messerli, for the cover of *Là-Bas*, no. 7 (1977). © 1977 Douglas Messerli.

Carla Harryman and Lyn Hejinian, for the cover of *Percentage*, Tuumba no. 23 (1979); and for portions of *The Wide Road*, in *Tessera* 15 (1993). © 1979, 1993 Carla Harryman and Lyn Hejinian.

Bruce Andrews, Charles Bernstein, Ray DiPalma, Steve McCaffery, and Ron Silliman, for the cover and selected pages from *Legend* (New York: L=A=N=G=U=A=G=E / Segue, 1980). © 1980 L=A=N=G=U=A=G=E.

Steve Benson and Barrett Watten, for portions of "Non-Events," *A Hundred Posters*, no. 35 (1978). © 1978 Steve Benson and Barrett Watten.

The Estate of Gertrude Stein, for "Gertrude Stein and Alice B. Toklas sitting in 'Godiva.'"

The Ford Motor Company, for "Auto by Robot." © 1983 Ford Motor Company.

Somewhere in Detroit, for the "Somewhere in Detroit" home page, 1997.

Catherine Cooke, for Iakov Chernikhov, illustrations from *Fundamentals of Contemporary Architecture* (1931); and from *Construction of Architectural and Machine Forms* (1932).

Artist Rights Society, for El Lissitzky, *Proun 99*, 1925; *The Constructor*, 1924; *Proun 1D*, c. 1919–20; *Beat the Whites with the Red Wedge*, 1919–20; *Russland*, 1930; *The Current Is Switched On*, 1932. © 2003 Artists Rights Society (ARS), New York/VC Bild-Kunst, Bonn.

Aleksandr Lavrentiev and Varvara Rodchenko, for Mikhail Kaufman, *Portrait of Rodchenko*, c. 1922; and, with MIT Press, for Alexander Rodchenko, *Knigi* [Books], 1925.

Transmat Records, for photograph of Derrick May, 1997; and for Derrick May, untitled photograph, 1997. © 1997 Transmat Records.

Planet E Records, for "Flexitone" page, "Planet E" web site, 1997; and the cover of e-dancer (Kevin Saunderson), *heavenly*, 1998. © 1998 Planet E Communications.

Wax Trax! Records, for the cover of Kenny Larkin, *Azimuth*, 1994. © 1994 Wax Trax! Records.

Barrett Watten, for a portion of "The Word," *Conduit* (1988). © 1988, 1997 Barrett Watten.

Seyed Alavi, for *Blueprints of the Times*, 1990.

Phyllis Kind Gallery, New York, and Erik Bulatov, for *I Am Going*, 1975; and *Krassikov Street*, 1976.

Mary Boone Gallery, New York, for Barbara Kruger, untitled ("Your Manias Become Science"), 1981. © Barbara Kruger 1984.

Lannan Foundation, for Chris Burden, *The Other Vietnam Memorial*, 1991.

Joseph Kosuth and Artists Rights Society, for untitled work ("nothing"), c. 1966–68. © 2003 Joseph Kosuth/Artists Rights Society (ARS), New York.

Bill Berkson and David McKee Gallery, New York, for Berkson and Philip Guston, *Negative*, 1973.

Robert Grenier, for "my heart is beating / I am a beast" (four versions), n.d.; "LOON," n.d.; "glitter / sit here . . . ," 1996; and "west / no farther . . . ," 1996. © 1996 Robert Grenier.

The Estate of David Wojnarowicz and P.P.O.W., New York, for untitled, 1993; and untitled, 1990.

The Estate of Andrei Tarkovsky, for still from Tarkovsky, *Mirror*, 1973. © 1986 Andrei Tarkovsky and Olga Surkova.

Ilya Kabakov, for "The Man Who Flew into His Picture"; "The Man Who Flew into Space from His Apartment"; and "The Man Who Never Threw Anything Away," from *Ten Characters* (1989). © 1989 Ilya Kabakov.

Stan Douglas and David Zwirner Gallery, New York, for *Collapsed House*, 1998; *Sections 5 and 8 of Herman Gardens*, 1999; *Lafayette Park*, 1999; *Eastern Border of Indian Village*, 1998; *House with Wood-Grain Tile*, 1998; *View of I-94 and Downtown Detroit*, 1998; *Michigan Theater*, 1998. © 1998, 1999 Stan Douglas.

Lastly, grateful acknowledgment is made to Wayne State University for support that was of crucial help in completing the present work, in both part and whole: from the Office of the Provost, a Career Development Chair; from the Office of Research and Sponsored Programs, a University Research Grant; from the College of Liberal Arts, a Research and Inquiry Grant and sabbatical leave; and from the Humanities Center, a Faculty Fellowship.

INTRODUCTION
FROM MATERIAL TEXT TO CULTURAL POETICS

I feel my "I" is much too small for me.
— Vladimir Mayakovsky

The contraction which is felt.
— William Carlos Williams

The Constructivist Moment is a series of essays, written over the past ten years, that address the gap between constructivist aesthetics and a larger cultural poetics. By constructivist aesthetics I mean, broadly put, the imperative in radical literature and art to foreground their formal construction; cultural poetics, discussed below, may be minimally defined as the reflexive relation of artistic form and cultural context. The essays take their primary examples from the work of American modernist and postmodern avant-gardes, contrasting them, on the one hand, with the art and writing of the 1920s Soviet Union and 1990s post-Soviet period, and on the other with aspects of modern and postmodern production that are usually kept outside the bounds of the aesthetic. The essays themselves continue the formal experiment or cultural intervention of their examples in arguing across disciplinary, historical, or generic boundaries, thus continuing the project of construction begun with their prior occasions. In putting this collection together from its separate occasions, my intention is to construct, by means of thematic juxtaposition, theoretical unveiling, and textual reading, a poetics that lays bare the device, in the sense of the Russian Formalists, of more than just the formal organization of the work of art. I seek perhaps not "the gold of time" after André Breton — as if there were a single standard that would endure throughout the ages — but "the currency of history" in relation to the radical formal meanings of the avant-garde. In order to achieve this currency, I alternate in these essays between two distinct aspects of the idea of construction: the principle of *formal* construction in modernist and postmodern literature and art (with the Russian constructivists, post-Soviet poets and artists, and American avant-gardes, from Gertrude Stein and Louis Zukofsky to the Language School) and the principle of *social* construction in modern culture (from unrealized utopian visions to dominant social forms such as Fordism and alternative responses such as Detroit techno).[1] The sequence of essays in this book proceeds from essays located firmly in questions of poetics, however much they may contest traditional literary genres, toward contextualist and culturalist approaches to the meaning of radical forms.

My thinking on the question of social construction begins with literary examples from modernist and postmodern avant-gardes, as they reveal a discontinuity that is everywhere implicated in the kinds of cultural agency they pursue. The framing epigraphs from Vladimir Mayakovsky and William Carlos Williams above may give a sense of the literary stakes, historical and present, of this moment. I found both — as indices of larger aesthetic and cultural horizons — to be deeply generative when I first encountered them in the 1970s. "The contraction which is felt," as a moment of self-negating self-disclosure, occurs as gap or eruption in the discontinuous prose of Williams's *Spring and All*, that generic hybrid of poetry and prose which has been rightly seen as an important precursor of Language School aesthetics.[2] In that text, Williams is everywhere concerned with the gaps and fissures that make transparent communication both impossible and deeply desirable. Something is turning him away from his instrumental purposes, drawing him back to himself; he insists on finding this gap or fissure in the texture of his thinking:

> All this being anterior to technique, that can have only a sequent value; but since all that appears to the senses on a work of art does so through
> fixation by
> the imagination of the external as well internal means of expression the essential nature of technique or transcription.
>
> Only when this position is reached can life proper be said to begin since only then can a value be affixed to the forms and activities of which it consists.
>
> Only then can the sense of frustration which ends. All composition defeated.
>
> Only through the imagination is the advance of intelligence possible, to keep beside growing understanding. (As published; 105–6)

Only when these gaps in discourse are realized — literally given as a void between words that is at the same time the "fixation by the imagination" of the world — can we aspire to "technique, that can have only a sequent value"; only then can we begin to construct. The position of poetry in *Spring and All* is given a precise value by the impossibility of its prose, which aligns with what cannot be said, not only in literature but in modern life itself.

We may contrast Williams's self-undoing negation with Mayakovsky's expansive fantasy. "I feel my 'I' is much too small for me" is the converse of Williams's contraction; the expansion of the "I" occurs, even so, as a corollary to the poet as a "cloud in trousers," a form of self as nonexistence. The source of this nonexistence in Mayakovsky's futurist period — to begin with, the experience of the adolescent rejection at the hands of Maria, but also the streetwise nihilism of "I never want / to read anything. / Books? / What are books?" — will lead directly to the social command to construct, to social construction. The expansion of Mayakovsky's "I," beginning in self-negation, identifies social reality ("books") with its own undoing, so that the assertion of "I" is a reordering of the world, the necessary precondition for his later, mid-1920s manifesto of constructivist poetics:

> What then are the fundamental requirements for beginning poetic labor?
>
> First. The presence in society of a problem which can only conceivably be solved through a work of poetry. A social command. . . .
>
> Second. An exact knowledge of, or more precisely, an exact sense of the wishes of one's class (or the group one represents) in this matter. . . .
>
> Third. Material. Words. The constant restocking of the storehouses, the granaries of your mind, with all kinds of words, necessary, expressive, rare, invented, renovated, manufactured, and others.
>
> Fourth. Equipment. The business equipment and tools of the trade. Pen, pencil, typewriter, telephone, a suit for visits to the doss-house, a bicycle for riding to editorial offices, a well-arranged table. . . .
>
> Fifth. The skills and methods for processing words, infinitely personal, achieved only after years of daily toil: rhymes, meters, alliterations, images, an inelegant style, pathos, endings, titles, outlines, etc. etc.[3]

The constructivist moment of Mayakovsky's undoing at the hands of woman, by which he enters into the nihilistic cloud of futurist aggressivity, stabilizes in this formulation as an equal balance between the material text — which Mayakovsky, ahead of the crowd as usual, sees as not only "words" but also "equipment" and "methods for processing words," the state of technology in the modernist period in which he wrote — and cultural poetics. To align Williams and Mayakovsky here is thus felicitously reciprocal: we may discern a constructivist necessity in Williams's valorization of Dada-inspired negativity (which is often only seen as a textual device), and we see as well the sources of social construction in the constitutive negation of the futurist avant-garde. "A wedding between Russia and the United States" — the thought is Williams's, from the 1940s[4] — reorients the negativity of the material text toward its social command: the construction of a future world. Such a fantasy, identified with a reading of American and Soviet examples, occurred frequently among members of the Language School during the formative period of the 1970s, and it continues in the present work's revisionist inquiry into both historical avant-gardes.

This reciprocity, between self-consciousness and social command, extends from the dual nature of modernism — as a construction within modernity or a construction of it — to questions of methodology, of poetry and criticism. Poetry, like criticism, internalizes social and historical reflexivity within an artistic medium; while criticism, like poetry, is motivated by particular social and historical determinants, as it structures itself within them. What I am calling the constructivist moment is a dual concept that refers to a generative moment in poetics in which a work of literature or art takes shape and unfolds, and the critical valorization of materiality, reflexivity, and constructedness across the arts, from the movement labeled constructivism in the Soviet period up to the present. In this sense, constructivism — the artistic movement defined by Soviet artists of the 1920s like Aleksandr Rodchenko, El Lissitzky, Varvara Stepanova, Iakov Chernikhov, as well as by literary and cinematic constructivists from the same period such as Velimir Khlebnikov, Viktor Shklovsky, Osip Brik, or Dziga Vertov, and as it led on to the formalist abstraction known as international constructivism in the 1930s in the West — may be an important point of departure, but it is not a baseline tradition to which everything refers. The reader is hereby warned: I am not writing a historical account or aesthetic genealogy of constructivism, Soviet or otherwise. There are many constructivist moments focused on here, from the opening discussion of poetry written by means of preconstructed lexicons to the concluding critique of Stan Douglas's photographs of dystopian Detroit. My use of the concept then is heuristic as well as historical: indeed, the formal model of the example, which I develop as a central element of my discussion of constructivism, captures the general theoretical interest and specific historical reference of such moments, which function as examples as they provide sites for reflection and models for agency.

The constructivist moment thus combines the generative unfolding of a poetics with the imperative for critical interpretation: just as the work of art is constructed, so our interpretation of it must necessarily be a construction. As a concept, the constructivist moment is informed by the historical experience of social construction (Lissitzky's design work for the 1930s propaganda journal *USSR in Construction* comes to mind),[5] just as it depends on the way that meaning is constructed through retrospective determination or *Nachträglichkeit* (Freud's generative paper "Constructions in Analysis" is the reference here).[6] We may continue from this modernist point of departure to Foucault and consider the ways in which individuals, authors, or subject positions are constructed by social discourses, and the ways in which institutions provide the terms by which we construct meanings. The fate of poetics as it confronts these latter forms of construction, which are not as amenable to a homology between aesthetics and politics as a critique, is one of the crucial concerns of the present work. The concept of construction, in the modernist senses of Lissitzky or Freud, is too generative of new meaning or historical insight to allow it merely to lapse into the horizons of institutional frameworks for construction, as postmodern as their origins may be — in which what we can think or do is limited by the social texts or cultural discourses we are positioned within. At the same time, a poetic model for construction must take into account the formal structures ascribable to institutions, just as institutions must make room for forms of agency irreducible to their orders. If poetry and poetics are to survive in a cultural environment that is dominated by institutions, they must show themselves capable of addressing more than their own orders. And every revisionist critical school for the last thirty years has argued precisely this point, often leading to an inversion of values in which what once had been most high — the work of verbal art, the poem, the masterpiece — is replaced by the autonomy, in fact, of critique. Equally fallible has been the tendency of poetry and poetics to adhere to their own entrepreneurial zones of restricted production, often in abject denial of wider cultural contexts. The necessity here is to bridge this great divide, which has been so profitably enforced.

These essays thus aim to cross the chasm between works of literature and art and historical and cultural contexts: in an aesthetic sense, they entail an opening of form to contexts as a necessary development in the arts; in a critical sense, they address the rift between the purported autonomy of literature and art and cultural studies methodologies. Each of the essays in this volume explores one or several possible paradigms for thinking beyond this dual aesthetic/critical dilemma: to begin with, we may cite the exemplary relation of Soviet constructivism to the experience of postrevolutionary social construction in the 1920s — even as this heroic conjunction of the aesthetic and political is only one of several historical moments, which are not all derivable from the most socially engaged instance of the historical avant-garde. After George Kubler's *Shape of Time*, the temporal and spatial relations between my chosen historical examples are often discontinuous:[7] the argument moves — in anything but a linear or teleological manner — from the 1920s Soviet Union, to Louis Zukofsky's poetic meditation on social revolution in the 1930s, to a group of 1950s Japanese student radicals disbanding with the defeat of their oppositional movement (from Nagisa Oshima's film *Night and Fog in Japan*), to 1960s conceptual art in New York, to the formation of the Language School in the 1970s, the emergence of post-Soviet writers and artists in the 1980s, and finally the surfacing of Detroit techno in the 1990s. Given this discontinuity, a number of temporal and spatial congruences allow for reinforcing or contrastive arguments: between Soviet and American modernism; Fordism and Detroit techno; Soviet and post-Soviet culture; post-Soviet and postmodern aesthetics; the negativity of the fall of the Eastern Bloc and of the decline of urban Detroit. These temporal and spatial, historical and cultural, frameworks intersect with formal analysis and theoretical reflections on specific works of cultural production. The constructivist moment, as broadly and heuristically put as it may be, is always seen within its specific cultural circumstances; it is a fact of history as much as of form. What this means for contemporary aesthetics — in a series of examples from the textual politics of Jackson Mac Low, the Language School, and the Poetics Listserv; to the aesthetic utopias of Detroit techno and the dystopia of Stan Douglas's photographs; and the intense subjectivity of Robert Grenier's handwritten poetry or David Wojnarowicz's writing and art — is that each occurs at the moment of a specific historical conjuncture.

Are there common concerns that unite the various analyses in an overarching aesthetic and critical account, given the discontinuity of the examples presented here? There certainly are: the first among these would be the relation between radical aesthetic form and revolutionary utopianism, from the Soviet period to the emergence of the Language School. Here the Soviet constructivists are the privileged example of the historical avant-garde, as opposed to, say, the Italian futurists (who often held protofascist politics), the German dadaists (whose project was as much fascinated as repelled by alienation effects in modernity), or the French surrealists (who rejected social construction as just another form of realism). Even as these moments of the historical avant-garde are related and not mutually exclusive, it is the convergence of the Soviet avant-garde with social history that makes it exemplary, and not for its betrayal by the Stalinist state, though that did occur. The Soviet avant-garde's emphasis on the materiality of signification — the emphasis on the fabrication of painting for Malevich, the invention of an elementary vocabulary of visual representation for Lissitzky, the foregrounding of the literary device for Shklovsky, the construction of montage effects for Eisenstein, the materiality of social discourse for V. N. Voloshinov (such a list of parallel social/aesthetic projects could go on at length) — directly addressed the construction of social reality in the Soviet Union, in a collectively held fantasy that aesthetic form could be the model for a new social order. The Soviet period thus provides a model for theorizing the relation between materialist aesthetics and their social meaning — for instance, between the textual materiality of the Language School and its importance as a model of multiauthored communication on the Poetics Listserv, or between the utopian, collective values of Detroit techno and the city's social history. The discontinuous analogy of these two Western examples with the model of the Soviet period is meant to foreground shared aesthetic responses to the historical ruptures of social modernity, based on the partial similarity of formal characteristics. Within each, capacious new forms of art redress a failure of social totality.

The constructivist moment itself becomes a second point of convergence between these discontinuous examples: a constitutive moment of negativity enacted in the form of a totalizing vision. In one chapter, which seeks out constructivist moments in a historical and generic sequence from El Lissitzky to Louis Zukofsky to Detroit techno, it is defined (albeit abstractly) in the following way: "The constructivist moment is an elusive transition in the unfolding work of culture in which social negativity — the experience of rupture, an act of refusal — invokes a fantasmatic future — a horizon of possibility, an imagination of participation. Constructivism condenses this shift of horizon from negativity to progress in aesthetic form; otherwise put, constructivism stabilizes crisis as it puts art into production toward imaginary ends" (192). It is this relationship, between historical crisis and the capacious unfolding of aesthetic form, that I explore in numerous contexts. The constructivist moment in this sense refers not simply to a historical moment of rupture, as with the formation of the historical avant-garde after the First World War or of the Language School after the Vietnam War, but to a rupture within modernity itself. It is a moment when the rationalized lifeworld comes undone, however briefly, and we are given a glimpse of the orders we are contained within. This is precisely what Stan Douglas's photographs of posturban Detroit present: a rupture in the social fabric — after the historical crisis of the 1967 Detroit riots but also as a recurring moment of social reproduction — that is an immediate entailment of late capitalism where, as Marx famously predicted, "all that is solid melts into air" and megaprofits are to be made in social negativity.[8] Perhaps the most univocal social command of critical theory, from the Frankfurt School to the ideology critique of Slavoj Žižek, has been the imperative to disclose social negativity in the midst of lived experience, and to return this perception to practical action. Radical literature and art can be seen as precisely a site for the unveiling of what eludes representation, and the forms of that perception may become models for action as well. The constructivist moment is thus a confrontation of aesthetic form with social negativity, both to disclose the nature of the system and to develop an imagined alternative.

If this moment of disclosure or confrontation is fundamentally generative, what can be said of the nature of the negativity that is taken up everywhere in this work? Is this negativity the tertium quid that unites the disparate topics of my analysis; if so, does it, paradoxically, convey a positive consistency? I have found this to be the most difficult question to address throughout my account, even as the various examples discussed and approaches used to discuss them circulate, often beyond any intention, around the concept itself. Everything depends on what different philosophical traditions make accessible in their account of negativity; it is here that theoretical engagement is most necessary. In retrospect — and negativity is most often disclosed in the course of retrospection, as when we realize only years later what bothered us at the time of some troubling event — I have employed six interlocking accounts of negativity in the course of my analyses: following Hegel, Foucault, Kristeva, Žižek, Lacan, and Heidegger. It is not my intention, nor within my present means, to distinguish the myriad entailments of negativity between and among these major traditions. I will simply propose that the systemic integration of the concept, the way in which it is articulated within the given philosophical prospect, is the best practical guide to its meaning and use. Hegelian negativity occurs in two senses in this work: the first is the familiar determinate negation of the dialectic, which I see directly limiting the historical meaning of avant-garde rupture by means of institutional recuperation, the sublation of a negative moment to a higher level. The second, in Žižek's reading of Hegel's vision of the "night of world," returns negativity to a primal undoing that cannot be easily sublated; the question then arises how it might be stabilized in any form of aesthetic production. A Foucauldian account of the avant-garde (and such an account, though neglected, was crucial for Foucault's intellectual history) would distribute negativity in discourse, much as Sade's eroticism is redistributed as a discourse of power or Artaud's madness defines institutions. With Kristeva, on the other hand, we are encouraged to see the avant-garde as a permanent site for the refusal of integration into the symbolic, by virtue of that excessive form of desire she terms the semiotic, which undoes representation in the "thetic break" only to rebind it through the "second-order thetic." Žižek, in the school of Lacan, has a more schematic approach to the nature of negativity, which as the inaccessible kernel of the Real becomes a form of antagonism that undoes our self-consistency and leads directly to the capaciousness of suprasubjective fantasy. This account is most directly connected to the mechanism of the constructivist moment, and therefore it is invoked at numerous points throughout the discussion. Finally, I explore Heidegger's repositioning of Jaspers's concept of the limit situation and its possible connection to the historical avant-garde to identify negativity, as the thrownness of *Dasein*, in the aesthetics of the material text. In the work of Robert Grenier, which I read after Heidegger's critique, the shattering of self in the limit situation of writing becomes a confirmation of Being — indeed, the only one possible. Is there, then, a hierarchy among these accounts of negativity within the traditions summarized here? One might best explore this question by comparing the entailments of each with the form of the argument at hand. In a reinforcing sense, it is the central role of the negative to allow for the work discussed here, and the manner in which it is discussed, to be seen as an open question. Otherwise put, it would not be possible to envisage an open work without negativity.

The constructivist moment, then, is positioned within a movement from the material text, seen as a consequence of the larger goals of radical art to lay bare the device of its construction, to a wider cultural poetics. The central concept of the material text is the site of a strategy to return what had once been an unquestioned locus of critical value, literature, to the material forms of culture. In part as a response to Walter Benjamin's notions of the author as producer and of the aura that is destroyed in capitalist production, a textual turn developed in literary criticism that simultaneously reserved a place for more traditional literary scholarship, bibliographic history, textual editing, and even philology, while it opened up these disciplines with various examples of radical texts, from Emily Dickinson's fascicles to the handwritten works of Robert Grenier.[9] The textual turn, however, can be double-edged: while it responds to a demand for a materialist account of literature as cultural production, and while it often valorizes texts that have a significant potential for critical intervention, it also allows normative scholarly functions to proceed without regard for any motivations for the intervention of radical texts. At the same time, the textual turn has led to a number of new approaches to cultural articulation of texts, as in Jerome McGann's notion of a radial text that leads to the epistemology of hypertexts, or Cary Nelson's and Walter Kalaidjian's recovery of material texts in the radical 1930s.[10] Such work is a part of the widespread revisionist effort in modernist studies that began with a challenge to Anglo-American formalism and continued in numerous projects of historical recovery, particularly of writers of the Left, poets of the Harlem Renaissance, and experimental women modernists. A disciplinary context for the effort has been established in the journal *Modernism/Modernity* and in the founding of the Modernist Studies Association. The material text is a site for expanding the idea of the literary corpus to include not only the traditional objects of literary analysis — published works of literature — but manuscript collections, small press editions, hypertext, and nonwritten materials in media such as audio- or videotape. Michael Davidson's *Ghostlier Demarcations: Modern Poetry and the Material Word* demonstrates how the material texts of the avant-garde can be a site of expanded social meanings in this sense.[11] The material text also provides a new basis for a social or contextual reading practice in Rachel Blau DuPlessis's *Genders, Races, and Religious Cultures in Modern American Poetry*, which applies a social philology or socially directed mode of close reading to the construction of historically specific racial, religious, and gendered identities that are exemplified in modernist texts.[12] My work makes common cause with the latter two approaches, as it seeks to develop specific historical and cultural entailments of the material text as critical agency. The material text is never a thing in itself; it circulates as a form of cultural critique.

My early criticism, in *Total Syntax* (1985) and an article titled "Social Formalism" (1987), may be seen as attempts, before the dawn of the material text (which itself had everything to do with the emergence of the Language School and its textual politics), to find models for avant-garde textuality within a larger syntax of cultural meaning.[13] In placing the avant-garde at the center of a redefined literariness, the present work also follows recent revisionist accounts of the avant-garde, for example Astradur Eysteinsson's *Concept of Modernism*, in which the avant-garde is valorized for its aesthetics of interruption, or in my present terms, negativity.[14] The avant-garde has also been taken up by cultural materialist analyses that position its restricted productions in larger cultural patterns, as in Daniel Belgrad's *Culture of Spontaneity*, where a widely shared privileging of immediacy is seen in literary, visual, and musical avant-gardes of the 1950s.[15] Other studies developing culturalist readings of radical works of art include Walter Kalaidjian's *American Culture between the Wars: Revisionary Modernism and Postmodern Critique*, in which avant-garde aesthetics and Popular Front cultural interventions are seen as mutually informing (and where the rubric "the constructivist moment" first appeared); Rita Felski's *Gender of Modernity*, which breaks the male-centered mold of modernist textuality to identify culturally charged interventions by and of women in modernity; Janet Lyon's *Manifestoes: Provocations of the Modern*, which reads the form of the avant-garde manifesto in relation to a much longer tradition, dating from the French Revolution, of emancipatory manifestos; and Aldon L. Nielsen's *Black Chant: Languages of African-American Postmodernism*, which moves between literature and music to identify a previously unrecognized Afrocentric postmodern aesthetic.[16]

There is thus a range of work that recovers the cultural poetics of the avant-garde, and within which the present study is situated. The existence of this expanded field, however, has yet to provoke sufficient debate on the objects and methods of a cultural poetics — in the senses that the term has been used to describe the intersection between literary and cultural criticism until now. Originally associated with the New Historicism, and often seen as indebted to the historicism of Foucault, cultural poetics appears in Stephen Greenblatt's *Shakespearean Negotiations* to describe the reflexive relations between text and context in early modern literature and culture; Greenblatt defines the term in somewhat dissimilar ways at other points in his work, as I discuss below.[17] A subsequent use, influenced by cultural studies methodologies, occurs in Kathleen Stewart's *Space on the Side of the Road: Cultural Poetics of an "Other" America*, in which she describes a marginal discourse community in rural Appalachia in terms of its poetics of language use.[18] The classical scholar Leslie Kurke, on the other hand, returns to New Historicist tradition in using the term to discuss the cultural politics of antiquity in her *Cultural Poetics in Ancient Greece*.[19] What is often missing from these approaches is a specific consideration of literary form; where poetics has generally been taken to derive from considerations of the way the literary work is made, as a form of representation, these studies reposition it in relation to social discourses that contextualize it, while ignoring the concretization of form. It is almost as if culture itself is being proposed as a text in the place where the poem had been; one could better describe such approaches as a kind of aesthetic anthropology that seeks to describe cultures themselves as artistic products — but without any kind of formal mediation. In seeking to restore a necessary relation between literary form and cultural discourse, my use of cultural poetics intends an approach not restricted to the New Historicism or Cultural Studies, as it preserves an important place for the formal construction of the work as a bearer of cultural meaning.

Before leaving the scene of an expanded genealogy, I want to pause to consider the derivation of my title, *The Constructivist Moment.* There is now a significant series of studies in the humanities that seek to explain a key concept of intellectual or cultural history (such as constructivism) by means of its specific enactment in historical events, political movements, or works. The series begins with J. G. A. Pocock's *Machiavellian Moment,* a study of Renaissance political theory.[20] Each new work in the series, however, seems to contrast its conceptual focus with that of a prior study: Marjorie Perloff's moment is the early twentieth century in *The Futurist Moment,* a comparative account of European avant-gardes organized around the example of futurism.[21] The next work in the series, James F. Murphy's *Proletarian Moment,* a study of the debates around leftist literature and culture in the 1930s, moves away from the purely aesthetic focus of the avant-garde to discuss a socially engaged literature.[22] Norman Finkelstein's *Utopian Moment in Contemporary American Poetry,* on the other hand, sees utopian politics of literature as immanent to questions of poetic form.[23] Recently, in a slight departure from the series, Rachel Blau DuPlessis and Peter Quartermain's collection of essays *The Objectivist Nexus* focuses on the American Objectivist poets and their aesthetic innovations, cultural contexts, and philosophical implications not as a moment but as a nexus of multiple conjunctures.[24] This shift from moment to nexus is decisive; in retaining the earlier term, I want on the one hand to ground it in a rigorous account of what a concept of a punctual moment might entail, as a rupture of received cultural meanings that leads to innovative form. I want as well to preserve the concept of a moment as a retrospectively determined punctual event from which cultural forms may be derived, but not in the sense of any originary event. The notion of a moment, then, at the very least provides a way of theorizing punctual occurrences without recourse to originary explanations — which would include, apparently, my choice of title. There is a recently published account of epiphanies in literature, *The Visionary Moment;* my colleague at Wayne State University, Charles J. Stivale, has written an incisive essay on the high alienation of "The 'MLA' Mo-

ment"; and further following the lead of the moment into negativity and nonexistence, I have heard of a work in science studies called *The Missing Moment*, which addresses gaps and fissures in consciousness as they impact on claims to objectivity.[25]

Part of the tradition of the introductory essay is to provide a guide to the work that follows in condensed and summary form. In order to position each of the essays in this work in relation to the larger project, and in terms of their presentation in a series, I have also written introductory headnotes that may be helpful in drawing out the contexts, motivations, and intertexts for each chapter. The concept of moment is central in terms of my own work's construction: each chapter develops a series of textual or aesthetic examples in terms of their situatedness in a cultural or theoretical argument. The chapters are by no means presented sequentially: the first chapter to be written, and which directly addresses "the nonnarrative construction of history," dates from 1990, but occurs in sequence as chapter 5. Chapter 6, "Negative Examples," on the other hand, was only finished with the final draft of the text, and contains material from 2000 to 2002. The work's thematic sequence, I hope, will appear as spatial, radial, and accretive rather than linear, accumulative, and teleological. Particularly the final chapter, "Zone: The Poetics of Space in Posturban Detroit," is written in a nontraditional style of twelve linked but disjunct zones seen as specific areas of discussion. It both does and does not provide a concluding perspective from which to view what went before, and for similar reasons I have decided not to write a closing statement. My hope is that the relations between and among chapters, sections, examples, themes, analogies, and disanalogies will resonate with each other, and I do not want to preclude generative connections that may be made. This preference stems fundamentally from the sense of construction as I understand it, as wanting to preserve the ways in which the work is made and to encourage readings that might not have been anticipated. (Note: this is not the same as saying that the reader constructs readings, and that just any reading is as good as any other.) I want to show how the literariness of the material text is not simply an artifact of avant-garde formalism but may be seen as a moment of social construction, from the writing of the text to the processing of it, here and now. With that principle established, I will end by commenting on the status of the moment in its various constructions in each chapter.

The study begins with an approach to the poetics of the material text that shows how Coleridge's concept of poetic diction led to modernist and postmodern uses of preexisting poetic vocabularies. In constructing an alternative genealogy of the material text, I turn to the promulgation of BASIC English by C. K. Ogden and I. A. Richards in the twentieth century. BASIC English was a generally unsuccessful but important attempt to create an English-language-based lingua franca, with a reduced vocabulary and syntax, for purposes of commerce and technological innovation. Clearly due to fascination with and horror of its politics of linguistic control, a number of modernist and postmodern writers were inspired by BASIC to develop poetic vocabularies (preexisting lexicons for literary works) as a basis for constructed literary effects, to be distinguished from subjective expression. The technology of BASIC English had socially conservative, even imperialistic, ends: it was an important early step in the promotion of English as a world language of science and commerce. Poets, however, turned this technological innovation to other, arguably oppositional and emancipatory, uses in foregrounding the materiality of signification to disrupt communicative ideals. A series of decisive moments thus constructs an argument by example: to begin with, the failed transcendental deduction of the subject of knowledge in Coleridge's *Biographia*, which led to his historicist meditations on the relation of language to cultural meaning. Next, there is the invention of BASIC itself, out of a Coleridgean conservatism but also as a modern linguistic reform. Finally, modernist writers, from Joyce to Zukofsky, were attracted to BASIC as a compositional device; and Jackson Mac Low used it as a way of constructing poems and performance works in the postmodern period. The material text is thus constructed as series of political interventions in language, from Coleridge to Mac Low, that are historically situated.

"The Secret History of the Equal Sign" takes up the social formation of avant-garde communities, and their political moments of opposition and recuperation, in terms of their literary construction of a collective identity. There is an obvious moment of social construction in the formation of the Language School of poetry in the 1970s, which I characterize in terms of the intersubjective dynamics of its multiauthored collaborations. A Foucauldian notion of discourse, seen in the construction of the movement itself and as it was represented in the form of the journal *L=A=N=G=U=A=G=E*, allows us to see how individual authors became author positions or moments in a collective discourse. A Kristevan concept of text, on the other hand, would characterize the avant-garde as distributing a moment of disrupted symbolization through the multiple significations of the semiotic; I used this moment to describe the dialectics of signification in *Legend*, a collaborative work by five authors published in 1980. A close textual reading of this complex work reveals its secret history: the narcissistic, homosocial space between personal and group identity. In two further examples of multiauthorship in the Language School, poetic texts by Steve Benson and myself, and Carla Harryman and Lyn Hejinian, the gap between authors becomes the generative motive for the constructed work. The politics of multiauthorship are further developed in an account of how multiauthored collaborations anticipated the form of collective identity constructed on the Poetics Listserv. A precise moment of discursive construction may be seen in an exemplary group discussion of an indecipherable word, suggesting how authorship may be reproduced in collective forms.

The origin of "The Bride of the Assembly Line" occurred literally as an epiphany, in which two reinforcing moments combined in the construction of its argument. In the first, after a long day at an academic conference at the University of Louisville in 1995, I found myself with friends listening to jazz late into the night at the Seelbach Hotel. On emerging from the bar into the hotel's ornate lobby, I encountered the living vision of an instant: a thoroughly intoxicated bride, virtually held in place by the architecture of her dress, waiting patiently while swaying back and forth as the equally drunk groom negotiated the room. A few weeks later, on a tour of the Rouge River assembly plant of the Ford Motor Company, I imaginatively synthesized the appearance of the bride with the bachelor machines of its robotic welding stations, after the work by Marcel Duchamp: hence the title. Its moment was a lecture at the SUNY Poetics Program, which I used to argue the necessity of rethinking the conventional account of the relation between modernist poetics and social modernity. In so doing, I compared literary authorship from modernists such as Gertrude Stein and Language writers like Clark Coolidge to the authorship of modes of social organization such as Ford's assembly line. My claim is that even the most radically formal or language-centered literature can be seen as reflexively engaged with cultural processes of modernity. I then discuss how Stein's admiration of Henry Ford, Ford cars, and the mode of organization of the assembly line influenced her writing; the juxtaposition of Stein and Ford goes significantly against the grain of much Stein criticism, which separates her abstract use of language from cultural and historical motives. Authorship itself is under construction; I discuss how the sequential organization of the assembly line provides a positive paradigm, or even negative disanalogy, for modernist and avant-garde works and genres. The essay ends with a moment of pure presentation of poetic address in automated increments.

"The Constructivist Moment: From El Lissitzky to Detroit Techno," the essay that gives this collection its title, is addressed to two discontinuous moments: the social formation of Soviet constructivist aesthetics in the work of El Lissitzky, and the emergence of the internationally recognized but locally unknown (until recently) genre of popular electronic music known as Detroit techno. A framework for this comparison is provided by a discussion of the situation of the avant-garde in cultural studies, which I experience on analogy to a border crossing between Detroit and the suburbs of Grosse Pointe. Another framework is provided by the modernist example, a literary form that helps explain the agency of Lissitzky's abstract paintings, the Prouns, as well as how their formal values were reinterpreted in his later work in typography and design. With techno, the concept of literary example becomes an aesthetics of the sample, and we are in the postmodern terrain of simulacral, postauthorial pastiche. In an extended comparison, techno's similarities to and differences from a prior example of the avant-garde, the constructivist visual artists of the 1920s Soviet Union as represented by the work of Lissitzky, are discussed in terms of both formal characteristics and social formation. Detroit techno is significant for its development of a constructivist, as opposed to expressivist, aesthetic among emerging African-American artists who, working far from the restricted codes and institutional reception of the avant-garde, are interested in innovative formal values. In invoking utopian fantasies and realizing them in a form that is open to many voices by means of sampling rather than dominated by a solo vocalist, Detroit techno constructed its own imaginary community in Detroit. It thus may be compared with the utopian and suprasubjective aesthetics at work in Soviet constructivist art of the 1920s in that both derive from prior experiences of revolutionary trauma or social negativity. In a detour through two poetic examples of constructivism, I identify the constructivist moment at the site of a stabilized negativity, whose values range from revolution to social alienation.

In "Nonnarrative and the Construction of History," the constructivist moment is aligned with nonnarrative forms of representation, seen specifically in a historical series. In reading examples of the material text (poems by Lyn Hejinian and Jackson Mac Low) as nonnarrative, I show first how a redistribution of narrative is constructed in their textuality, and then how their forms of nonnarration may be imagined within an unfolding history. Nonnarrative as a form of historical representation may be more ubiquitous than is generally believed, as I go on to demonstrate in a discussion of the New Historicist anecdote and the accretion of the minimal units of history into larger narratives. The forms of nonnarrative may thus work as fundamentally constitutive elements in the construction of history, and I locate these nonnarrative forms of historical representation at moments of historical stasis or crisis. As an example of a nonnarrative poetics of stasis, I position the conceptualist painting of Erik Bulatov within the decades-long era of stagnation in the former Soviet Union under Brezhnev. For the nonnarrative poetics of crisis, I juxtapose the exemplary form of the New Sentence, which developed in the Language School in the 1970s, with the historical negativity experienced with the Fall of Saigon. The claims for a nonnarrative history are extended further in a discussion of how historical chronologies are organized and manipulated in public discourse, without any prospect of closure.

"Negative Examples" identifies a series of aesthetic uses of negativity through its positioning in the work of Slavoj Žižek and Michel Foucault, developing a non-Hegelian dimension of negativity in Heidegger that influenced both Foucault and Žižek. In the move from literature to social discourse, the negativity of the text is crucial for providing a moment in which construction, in both formal and contextual senses, can take place. The important differences between the concepts of negativity in the work of these three philosophers may help us to see the social meaning of the avant-garde in terms other than the familiar Hegelian logic of opposition and recuperation. The chapter begins by discussing the importance of negativity for Žižek, in his historical situation as an intellectual theorizing the fall of the Eastern Bloc as he experienced it. The examples of negativity Žižek uses in his arguments are grouped together in three categories: moments of historical negativity, attending the devolution of Second-World states; moments of aesthetic negativity, often discerned in discussions of classic American cinema; and moments of an encounter with sublime nature, seen in the Hegelian paradigm of the "night of the world" that Žižek develops in reading Heidegger. The latter example leads to a discussion of the ways in which modernist poets (Wallace Stevens, Louis Zukofsky, and Laura Riding) position their work in relation to negativity, and follows that aesthetic possibility through postmodern examples from conceptual art (Joseph Kosuth), to the New York School (Ron Padgett and Bill Berkson), to the Language School (in my own work). Two additional genealogies of the negative are given in the examples of Heidegger and Foucault: the former in his critique of Karl Jaspers's "limit situations" and the possibility that his primordial concern for Being may have a source in the historical avant-garde, and the latter for his positioning of negativity as a unifying element of discourse, which Ernesto Laclau and Chantal Mouffe theorize as antagonism. Robert Grenier and David Wojnarowicz, two writers both invested in negativity, demonstrate the aesthetic uses of Heideggerian and Foucauldian negativities; while writings by Marjorie Welish and Carla Harryman show how such negativity is gendered.

"Post-Soviet Subjectivity in Arkadii Dragomoshchenko and Ilya Kabakov" contrasts two versions of negativity in examples of post-Soviet literature and art. For Dragomoshchenko, the constructivist moment is immanent in the poetic text — he figures it as a nasturtium imagined as "burning" within the linguistic confines of description. Even so, Dragomoshchenko's material textuality, seen through concurrent developments in post-Soviet science and aesthetics, is by no means stabilized in the sense that we understand it in the West. As in the related example of installation art of émigré artist Ilya Kabakov, Western categories such as the postmodern do not adequately describe the construction of post-Soviet subjectivity, after the prolonged moment of the anticipated devolution of the Soviet Union, from the 1960s to the 1980s. Kabakov's installation *Ten Characters* records the ideological crippling of ten inhabitants of a Moscow communal apartment, predicting precisely the relation between ideological fantasy and negativity articulated by Žižek in a related but different historical moment. The nihilism disclosed in several of Kabakov's deformed characters takes on a precise social and historical register in Soviet culture and epistemology, arguing against any overarching universal category of the postmodern within which his work may appear. Finally, "Zone: The Poetics of Space in Posturban Detroit" is positioned precisely as a Western counterpoint to the dystopian topography of the former Soviet Union. It is the parallel collapse of utopian fantasies, and the resulting foregrounding of negativity, that unites them. In this final essay, I present a speculative, even constructivist, account of the ways social space — specifically the collapsing, fragmentary, and divided social space of contemporary Detroit — may be seen in relation to the subject formation of those who live here. In twelve disparate zones of critical speculation, I approach a reading of Stan Douglas's photographic essay on Detroit as an index to social negativity. For negativity, read absence: this is what binds us together.

—*5 May 2002*

NEW MEANING AND POETIC VOCABULARY FROM COLERIDGE TO JACKSON MAC LOW

Until then I'll type out here, surrounded by papers, dictionaries,
file folders, notebooks, Coronamatic cartridges.
Is this the word "Coronamatic"'s first appearance in verse?

Would Eliot've allowed "Coronamatic" in his verse?
If so, under what circumstances?

— Jackson Mac Low, "56th Light Poem:
For Gretchen Berger — 29 November 1978"

Toward a cultural poetics of the material text, I will begin with a construction of "the words themselves." This chapter charts the development — in American modernist and postmodern poetry — of the use of preestablished, nonauthorial poetic vocabularies for literary composition. While Coleridge's concept of poetic diction is normative and hierarchical in its selection of appropriate vocabularies for literature, what I am going to call poetic vocabulary is both open-ended and critical, allowing the new meaning of jargons, dialects, idioms, and technical senses into poetry. The emergence of the concept of poetic vocabulary may be discerned in a historicist reading of Coleridge's account of poetic diction by means of the critical term *desynonymy*, which I will use to unlink Coleridge's synthesis of the ethics of new meaning in experimental poetry (at the time, the poetry of the *Lyrical Ballads*) from his call for a readership of "suitable interpreters" (looking forward to his culturally conservative notion of a national clerisy) who would preserve — and enforce — distinctions between word meanings. Coleridge's synthesis directly influenced the invention and popularization of BASIC English by I. A. Richards and C. K. Ogden, who wished to reduce the vocabulary of English in order to create a universal second language that would be transparent to new meanings in science, industry, and commerce. Ogden and Richards's experiment in modern linguistic hygiene was quickly noticed by modernist experimental poets, and in 1932 the expatriate journal *transition* published a translation of James Joyce's *Finnegans Wake* into BASIC, thus placing side by side "the simplest and most complex languages of man." As a modernist, Louis Zukofsky was also inspired by BASIC's reduced vocabulary of 850 words, and in turn made literary works using preestablished vocabularies, such as his early experiment "Thanks to the Dictionary." Zukofsky also wrote a critique of Ogden and Richards's BASIC and continued to use delimited vocabularies in his experimental texts. In the 1950s, postmodern poet Jackson Mac Low directly incorporated the 850-word BASIC vocabulary in many experimental texts. In his work, vocabularies such as BASIC provide the source text that, through the application of compositional rules, yields the target form of his poetic output. This movement from source text to target form is reenacted in the reading and production of Mac Low's work according to the careful instructions of his prefaces. In the target forms of Mac Low's texts themselves, we may identify both an ethics of reading and a notion of community in the arbitrariness and constructedness of his pregiven poetic vocabularies.

POETIC VOCABULARY

Jackson Mac Low's question for T. S. Eliot, whether the word *Coronamatic* could under any circumstances have occurred in poetry as Eliot understood it, marks an important paradigm shift in American poetics. While Mac Low was not the first American poet to consider language itself as a material for the construction of poetry rather than as a medium of communication, his poem is an explicit formulation of a historical shift from a paradigm of Anglo-American criticism known as poetic diction to one of poetic vocabulary. The concerns of poetic diction are Coleridgean, normative, and finally prescriptive; its modernist interpreter, Owen Barfield, bases his account of it on Coleridge's dictum that "poetry is the best words in the best order," i.e., "the best language."[1] In its capacity to incorporate "a steady influx of new meaning in language," poetic form will give the rule for what meanings we can accept (181). Mac Low is thus accurate in asking whether Eliot would have "*allowed* 'Coronamatic' in his verse." While poetic diction begins with the question of *le mot juste*, of the unification of diction and good sense as providing standards of style and efficacies of communication, it ends with a distinction between what language is appropriate to poetry and what is not. By virtue of poetic diction, poetry separates language into hierarchies of appropriateness: at the one end, not only a judicious choice of words but language separated from particular interest; at the other, jargons, dialects, and idioms whose interested discrepancies are beyond the pale of poetry as it is normally understood.[2] In moving to a paradigm of poetic vocabulary, evident everywhere in the construction of his work, Mac Low registers the historical emergence of specific vocabularies: When did *Coronamatic* become a word, and how many years would it take for it to become available for poetry? Aligning the historical fact of emergence with different critical standards than have come down through the Anglo-American tradition since Coleridge, he queries the circumstances of the use of a word such as *Coronamatic* in terms that address poetry to a wider horizon of language. Language is no longer to be judged in terms of its appropriateness for poetic diction; rather, poetry will be judged by its relation to language, seen as more capacious than its form.

Poetry as a result becomes a site for asking questions about language rather than an enforcer of communicative norms. Poetry's linguistic difference from the norms of transparent communication, of course, has been one of the most debated assumptions of twentieth-century literary theory. The turn to cultural studies, in one genealogy, begins here, with an attack on the cultural norms assumed in the autonomy of poetic language. In her account of the "poetic language fallacy," Mary Louise Pratt argues that the opacity of poetic language, as a reinforcement of literary and cultural hierarchies by virtue of the presumed superiority of poetry to ordinary language, merely distorts or foregrounds the structural defects of normative communication.[3] Proposing an ethics of communication that accounts for differences of usage, on the other hand, Michael J. Reddy claims that norms of transparent communication are linguistically embedded in habitual metaphors that poetry's resistant language may expose and contest.[4] Such views beg for a synthesis in which the difference of poetic language from the presumed transparency of ordinary language may be explained by a notion of linguistic agency that is historically contingent, rather than formally immanent. The opacity of poetic language enacts, in such a synthesis, a purposive deformation of communicative norms that may, in turn, change norms embedded in language (or provide new ones). In this sense, poetic language does not merely reinforce literary and cultural hierarchies but provides both vehicle and agency for a language-centered critique of meaning. Such a criticality may move beyond poetry to participate in processes of communication not restricted to literature as it identifies the making of new meaning with the kind of linguistic opacity we find when new terms are introduced in a lexicon. The shift from poetic diction to poetic vocabulary thus points toward a wider cultural frame for the constructive use of poetic language.

The constructive use of poetic vocabulary, the notion that a poem literally can be *made* from a predetermined, objectified lexicon, is a unique and historical contribution of American modernism and postmodernism.

Examples of constructive devices based on language seen as exterior to poetic form exist in many literatures, but the notion that a poem can be made from a preexisting, objectified lexicon arose with American modernism. The claim I will make, not to be overstated, is that a notion of poetic vocabulary, not simply a matter of poetry's linguistic materiality, emerged with American modernism, specifically in the work of Louis Zukofsky. There are, of course, many examples in the European avant-garde in which poetry is made from linguistic materials; consider Tristan Tzara's notion that cut-up newspapers can be assembled in a poetic text that will, ultimately, resemble its nonintentional author. In the work of the French OuLiPo, language games may involve restricted lexicons and rules for their use, but this is not the same as making a poem from a preexisting, objectified lexicon.[5] An important bridge between the two approaches is Anne-Marie Albiach's French translation of Louis Zukofsky's *"A"*–9, using a preexisting vocabulary taken from the Everyman edition of Marx's *Capital*.[6] The argument that follows undertakes a kind of thought experiment to chart the emergence of the use of poetic vocabulary from its origins in the English romantics (better known for their promulgation of poetic diction) through a series of American modernist and postmodern poet/critics. There is a literary history of almost two centuries, exemplified in romantic, modernist, and postmodern moments, of how poetic language seen as object provides a linguistic means for cultural critique. Poets representative of each period — from Samuel Taylor Coleridge to Louis Zukofsky to Laura (Riding) Jackson to Jackson Mac Low to a number of poets of the Language School — variously foregrounded the materiality of poetic language, both in explicitly critical terms and implicitly in their work.[7]

For the romantic poets, to begin with, poetic language was the locus for a negotiation between culturally emergent meanings and the stabilities of literary form. The inclusion of vernacular speech in *Lyrical Ballads*, as part of a larger cultural project of ballad collecting, is one example of such an aesthetic response to expanded cultural borders. The nuanced vocabularies of philosophy (as with the opaque terminology of the German romantics) and of science also put pressure on normative theories of meaning. Such a contestation may be seen in the contradictory insights and incomplete realization of the form of Coleridge's *Biographia Literaria*. Revisionist readings of the *Biographia* show how its attempt to reconcile language, literary form, and cultural value reflects an instability of meaning as much as it promotes conservative ideals of poetic autonomy. The instability of Coleridge's account of poetic language is a part of an epistemological uncertainty that is at once historical and cultural. This uncertainty (also the source of its capacious possibility) is reflected in the many ways poetic language in the romantic period takes on values of opacity in relation to transparent norms of communication (as with the neoclassical conventions of the eighteenth century). Such foregrounding of linguistic devices — from Chatterton's archaisms, Blake's neologisms, Scott's use of both archaism and dialect, Clare's incorporation of regional usages, and Wordsworth's objectification of common speech — reveals the unstable, expansive cultural moment of romantic poetry behind the concerns for language, meaning, and form in Coleridge's account.

Coleridge ultimately wanted to stabilize the epistemological uncertainty of language by casting poetic form in the mold of transcendental reflection. While Coleridge's anxiety about language led to a program for the inculcation of communicative norms and cultural values by means of literary form, one legacy of his poetics involved a reversal of this movement (even as much modernist poetry, from Yeats to John Ashbery, preserves the autonomy of form as the site for the identification of language with value). At the *modernist* moment of epistemological uncertainty, a theoretical concern with language tends also to place under erasure Coleridge's privileged locus of critique, poetic form, in order to access more directly the relations between language and culture. An example of such a movement — from an assumption of the transparency and universality of poetic form to a critique based on the relations between language and culture — is evident in the invention and promulgation of C. K. Ogden and I. A. Richards's BASIC English (seen as a complement to Richards's parallel development of a normative account of poetry).[8] As a vehicle not only for the contestation of received ideas about language and meaning but also for the use of linguistic norms as social control and imperial politics, BASIC bypassed the mediations of poetic form at the heart of the romantic (and much of the modernist) project. In so doing it acted out, in a historically significant manner but to a virtually absurdist degree, the linguistic legacy of romanticism even while reversing its polarities of language and cultural change. Where the romantic period saw an expansion of language that led to Coleridge's valorization of poetic form as a solution to questions of value, BASIC's restricted vocabulary would reduce possible meanings within ordinary language as a standard of value as well, but without the mediation of poetic form.

In polar opposition to the romantic fascination with linguistic expansion, BASIC (an acronym for "British American Scientific International Commercial") wanted to stabilize questions of meaning not through the authority of literary form but by reducing the number of terms used in the language — the number of substantives, morphological inflections, and what it called verbal "operators" (fig. 1). Its goals were to restrict language to an optimal economy and transparency in order to simplify and clarify meanings; in the words of Richards (and in BASIC): "Basic English is English made simple by limiting the number of its words to 850, and by cutting down the rules for using them to the smallest number necessary for the clear statement of ideas. And this is done without change in the normal order and behavior of those words in everyday English."[9] In so doing, BASIC adapts Standard English for use as an international lingua franca; according to Ogden, English is the natural candidate for such a task because it "is the only major language in which the analytic tendency has gone far enough for purposes of simplification" — a conflation of morphology with linguistic history in the fact that, with a low proportion of morphemes to words, English developed as a "relatively analytic" language.[10] Conveniently, English's analyticity (and thus its object status and availability for poetic vocabularies) make it a perfect vehicle for international commerce, its high correlation between word and thing reflecting the reification of commodity capitalism. A summary of the structure of BASIC describes how it compresses meaning in a standardized vocabulary (which can optimally be printed on the endsheets of its instruction manuals):

> The syntax was accompanied by a reduced vocabulary of 850 words in sets: 400 general words and 200 picturable words (600 nouns), 150 adjectives, 82 grammatical words, such as *across*, *all*, *can*, and 18 operators (such verbs as *get* and *put*). Operators had three roles: to replace more difficult words . . . to form phrases that would obviate other verbs . . . and to be part of a phrasal verb. . . . By such means, [Ogden] concluded that his operators could stand in for some 4,000 verbs.[11]

While BASIC advocates a transparency of communication in ordinary language rather than critically adjudicates the opacity of poetic language, its Coleridgean origins are clear — and not simply in the substitution of its language's more available opacity for the difficulty of poetry. Coleridge wished to stabilize meaning in poetic form so that judgments of value could be grounded in a commonly held set of objects (the canon, in other words). The Coleridgean tradition continues, somewhat modified, in the demand for standard meanings of common terms that become, in turn, the basis for BASIC's promulgation of a technocratic elite, a secular extension of a

Coleridgean clerisy, who would undertake the inculcation of norms based on its adjudication of language and meaning.[12] In extending the presumed benefits of the administered control of meaning to the world at large (not simply the then-English-speaking world but the expanding worlds of international and colonial capitalism), Ogden and Richards attempted a modern interpretation of the paradigms for meaning that Coleridge tried to resolve in the *Biographia* and elsewhere.[13]

BASIC, of course, failed both in its semantic claim to reduce the number of terms necessary for transparent communication and in its proposals for a new world order based on the efficiencies to be gained by such linguistic condensation.[14] Responsibility for this failure may be located squarely in the Coleridgean notion of *desynonymy* (as will be developed below), an imperative for the finer distinction of terms that was Coleridge's response to the epistemological uncertainty of new meaning. Rather than achieving its goal of controlling the expansion of meaning by standardizing terms, BASIC's *resynonymy* of vocabulary simply further confused the relation of language to meaning. As one historian of language has commented, "The Basic words, mainly common, short words like *get*, *make*, *do*, have some of the widest ranges of meaning in the language and may be among the most difficult to learn adequately. [It was] reported that for the 850 words the OED lists no fewer than 18,416 senses."[15] BASIC spectacularly failed to control the proliferation of meaning; rather, only an increase in undecidability and thus imprecision could result. In the end, BASIC takes its place within a pantheon of failed utopian projects for language in modernism, from Wittgenstein's *Tractactus* to Esperanto to Louis Zukofsky's "doing away with epistemology" to Laura Riding's critique of "rational meaning."[16]

But this failure, which took until the 1980s to be finalized with the discontinuance of Ogden's *General Basic English Dictionary*, led to some exemplary modernist literary responses (parodic as much as serious) by admirers of both the advantages and defects of BASIC's restricted semantics. As a direct response to the challenge of the increased vocabulary in James Joyce's *Finnegans Wake*, for example, the international avant-garde magazine *transition* ran a translation of Joyce's prose into BASIC, "the international language in which everything may be said," with an explanatory note by C. K. Ogden, in its March 1932 issue.[17] Ogden later compared Joyce's lexicon of "500,000 words" with BASIC's core vocabulary of 850; there is evident fascination here not only with BASIC's ability to translate Joyce but also with the juxtaposition of two languages representing each half of the modernism/modernity dyad. Bringing together literary modernism and ra-

BASIC ENGLISH

OPERATIONS ETC.	THINGS						QUALITIES		EXAMPLES OF WORD ORDER
100	400 General				200 Pictured		100 General	50 Opposites	
COME	ACCOUNT	EDUCATION	METAL	SENSE	ANGLE	KNEE	ABLE	AWAKE	
GET	ACT	EFFECT	MIDDLE	SERVANT	ANT	KNIFE	ACID	BAD	THE
GIVE	ADDITION	END	MILK	SEX	APPLE	KNOT	ANGRY	BENT	CAMERA
GO	ADJUSTMENT	ERROR	MIND	SHADE	ARCH	LEAF	AUTOMATIC	BITTER	MAN
KEEP	ADVERTISEMENT	EVENT	MINE	SHAKE	ARM	LEG	BEAUTIFUL	BLUE	WHO
LET	AGREEMENT	EXAMPLE	MINUTE	SHAME	ARMY	LIBRARY	BLACK	CERTAIN	MADE
MAKE	AIR	EXCHANGE	MIST	SHOCK	BABY	LINE	BOILING	COLD	AN
PUT	AMOUNT	EXISTENCE	MONEY	SIDE	BAG	LIP	BRIGHT	COMPLETE	ATTEMPT
SEEM	AMUSEMENT	EXPANSION	MONTH	SIGN	BALL	LOCK	BROKEN	CRUEL	TO
TAKE	ANIMAL	EXPERIENCE	MORNING	SILK	BAND	MAP	BROWN	DARK	TAKE
BE	ANSWER	EXPERT	MOTHER	SILVER	BASIN	MATCH	CHEAP	DEAD	A
DO	APPARATUS	FACT	MOTION	SISTER	BASKET	MONKEY	CHEMICAL	DEAR	MOVING
HAVE	APPROVAL	FALL	MOUNTAIN	SIZE	BATH	MOON	CHIEF	DELICATE	PICTURE
SAY	ARGUMENT	FAMILY	MOVE	SKY	BED	MOUTH	CLEAN	DIFFERENT	OF
SEE	ART	FATHER	MUSIC	SLEEP	BEE	MUSCLE	CLEAR	DIRTY	THE
SEND	ATTACK	FEAR	NAME	SLIP	BELL	NAIL	COMMON	DRY	SOCIETY
MAY	ATTEMPT	FEELING	NATION	SLOPE	BERRY	NECK	COMPLEX	FALSE	WOMEN
WILL	ATTENTION	FICTION	NEED	SMASH	BIRD	NEEDLE	CONSCIOUS	FEEBLE	BEFORE
ABOUT	ATTRACTION	FIELD	NEWS	SMELL	BLADE	NERVE	CUT	FEMALE	THEY
ACROSS	AUTHORITY	FIGHT	NIGHT	SMILE	BOARD	NET	DEEP	FOOLISH	GOT
AFTER	BACK	FIRE	NOISE	SMOKE	BOAT	NOSE	DEPENDENT	FUTURE	THEIR
AGAINST	BALANCE	FLAME	NOTE	SNEEZE	BONE	NUT	EARLY	GREEN	HATS
AMONG	BASE	FLIGHT	NUMBER	SNOW	BOOK	OFFICE	ELASTIC	ILL	OFF
AT	BEHAVIOUR	FLOWER	OBSERVATION	SOAP	BOOT	ORANGE	ELECTRIC	LAST	DID
BEFORE	BELIEF	FOLD	OFFER	SOCIETY	BOTTLE	OVEN	EQUAL	LATE	NOT
BETWEEN	BIRTH	FOOD	OIL	SON	BOX	PARCEL	FAT	LEFT	GET
BY	BIT	FORCE	OPERATION	SONG	BOY	PEN	FERTILE	LOOSE	OFF
DOWN	BITE	FORM	OPINION	SORT	BRAIN	PENCIL	FIRST	LOUD	THE
FROM	BLOOD	FRIEND	ORDER	SOUND	BRAKE	PICTURE	FIXED	LOW	SHIP
IN	BLOW	FRONT	ORGANIZATION	SOUP	BRANCH	PIG	FLAT	MIXED	TILL
OFF	BODY	FRUIT	ORNAMENT	SPACE	BRICK	PIN	FREE	NARROW	HE
ON	BRASS	GLASS	OWNER	STAGE	BRIDGE	PIPE	FREQUENT	OLD	WAS
OVER	BREAD	GOLD	PAGE	START	BRUSH	PLANE	FULL	OPPOSITE	QUESTIONED
THROUGH	BREATH	GOVERNMENT	PAIN	STATEMENT	BUCKET	PLATE	GENERAL	PUBLIC	BY
TO	BROTHER	GRAIN	PAINT	STEAM	BULB	PLOUGH	GOOD	ROUGH	THE
UNDER	BUILDING	GRASS	PAPER	STEEL	BUTTON	POCKET	GREAT	SAD	POLICE
UP	BURN	GRIP	PART	STEP	CAKE	POT	GREY	SAFE	
WITH	BURST	GROUP	PASTE	STITCH	CAMERA	POTATO	HANGING	SECRET	WE
AS	BUSINESS	GROWTH	PAYMENT	STONE	CARD	PRISON	HAPPY	SHORT	WILL
FOR	BUTTER	GUIDE	PEACE	STOP	CARRIAGE	PUMP	HARD	SHUT	GIVE
OF	CANVAS	HARBOUR	PERSON	STORY	CART	RAIL	HEALTHY	SIMPLE	SIMPLE
TILL	CARE	HARMONY	PLACE	STRETCH	CAT	RAT	HIGH	SLOW	RULES
THAN	CAUSE	HATE	PLANT	STRUCTURE	CHAIN	RECEIPT	HOLLOW	SMALL	TO
A	CHALK	HEARING	PLAY	SUBSTANCE	CHEESE	RING	IMPORTANT	SOFT	YOU

ALL
ANY
EVERY
NO
OTHER
SOME
LITTLE
MUCH
SUCH
THAT
THIS
I
HE
YOU
WHO
AND
BECAUSE
BUT
OR
IF
THOUGH
WHILE
HOW
WHEN
WHERE
WHY
AGAIN
EVER
FAR
FORWARD
HERE
NEAR
NOW
OUT
STILL
THEN
THERE
TOGETHER
WELL
ALMOST
ENOUGH
EVEN
NOT
ONLY
QUITE
SO
VERY
TOMORROW
YESTERDAY
NORTH
SOUTH
EAST
WEST
PLEASE
YES

CHANGE
CLOTH
COAL
COLOUR
COMFORT
COMMITTEE
COMPANY
COMPARISON
COMPETITION
CONDITION
CONNECTION
CONTROL
COOK
COPPER
COPY
CORK
COTTON
COUGH
COUNTRY
COVER
CRACK
CREDIT
CRIME
CRUSH
CRY
CURRENT
CURVE
DAMAGE
DANGER
DAUGHTER
DAY
DEATH
DEBT
DECISION
DEGREE
DESIGN
DESIRE
DESTRUCTION
DETAIL
DEVELOPMENT
DIGESTION
DIRECTION
DISCOVERY
DISCUSSION
DISEASE
DISGUST
DISTANCE
DISTRIBUTION
DIVISION
DOUBT
DRINK
DRIVING
DUST
EARTH
EDGE

HELP
HISTORY
HOLE
HOPE
HOUR
HUMOUR
ICE
IDEA
IMPULSE
INCREASE
INDUSTRY
INK
INSECT
INSTRUMENT
INSURANCE
INTEREST
INVENTION
IRON
JELLY
JOIN
JOURNEY
JUDGE
JUMP
KICK
KISS
KNOWLEDGE
LAND
LANGUAGE
LAUGH
LAW
LEAD
LEARNING
LEATHER
LETTER
LEVEL
LIFT
LIGHT
LIMIT
LINEN
LIQUID
LIST
LOOK
LOSS
LOVE
MACHINE
MAN
MANAGER
MARK
MARKET
MASS
MEAL
MEASURE
MEAT
MEETING
MEMORY

POINT
POISON
POLISH
PORTER
POSITION
POWDER
POWER
PRICE
PRINT
PROCESS
PRODUCE
PROFIT
PROPERTY
PROSE
PROTEST
PULL
PUNISHMENT
PURPOSE
PUSH
QUALITY
QUESTION
RAIN
RANGE
RATE
RAY
REACTION
READING
REASON
RECORD
REGRET
RELATION
RELIGION
REPRESENTATIVE
REQUEST
RESPECT
REST
REWARD
RHYTHM
RICE
RIVER
ROAD
ROLL
ROOM
RUB
RULE
RUN
SALT
SAND
SCALE
SCIENCE
SEA
SEAT
SECRETARY
SELECTION
SELF

SUGGESTION
SUMMER
SUPPORT
SURPRISE
SWIM
SYSTEM
TALK
TASTE
TAX
TEACHING
TENDENCY
TEST
THEORY
THING
THOUGHT
THUNDER
TIME
TIN
TOP
TOUCH
TRADE
TRANSPORT
TRICK
TROUBLE
TURN
TWIST
UNIT
USE
VALUE
VERSE
VESSEL
VIEW
VOICE
WALK
WAR
WASH
WASTE
WATER
WAVE
WAX
WAY
WEATHER
WEEK
WEIGHT
WIND
WINE
WINTER
WOMAN
WOOD
WOOL
WORD
WORK
WOUND
WRITING
YEAR

CHIN
CHURCH
CIRCLE
CLOCK
CLOUD
COAT
COLLAR
COMB
CORD
COW
CUP
CURTAIN
CUSHION
DOG
DOOR
DRAIN
DRAWER
DRESS
DROP
EAR
EGG
ENGINE
EYE
FACE
FARM
FEATHER
FINGER
FISH
FLAG
FLOOR
FLY
FOOT
FORK
FOWL
FRAME
GARDEN
GIRL
GLOVE
GOAT
GUN
HAIR
HAMMER
HAND
HAT
HEAD
HEART
HOOK
HORN
HORSE
HOSPITAL
HOUSE
ISLAND
JEWEL
KETTLE
KEY

ROOF
ROOT
SAIL
SCHOOL
SCISSORS
SCREW
SEED
SHEEP
SHELF
SHIP
SHIRT
SHOE
SKIN
SKIRT
SNAKE
SOCK
SPADE
SPONGE
SPOON
SPRING
SQUARE
STAMP
STAR
STATION
STEM
STICK
STOCKING
STOMACH
STORE
STREET
SUN
TABLE
TAIL
THREAD
THROAT
THUMB
TICKET
TOE
TONGUE
TOOTH
TOWN
TRAIN
TRAY
TREE
TROUSERS
UMBRELLA
WALL
WATCH
WHEEL
WHIP
WHISTLE
WINDOW
WING
WIRE
WORM

LIKE
LIVING
LONG
MALE
MARRIED
MATERIAL
MEDICAL
MILITARY
NATURAL
NECESSARY
NEW
NORMAL
OPEN
PARALLEL
PAST
PHYSICAL
POLITICAL
POOR
POSSIBLE
PRESENT
PRIVATE
PROBABLE
QUICK
QUIET
READY
RED
REGULAR
RESPONSIBLE
RIGHT
ROUND
SAME
SECOND
SEPARATE
SERIOUS
SHARP
SMOOTH
STICKY
STIFF
STRAIGHT
STRONG
SUDDEN
SWEET
TALL
THICK
TIGHT
TIRED
TRUE
VIOLENT
WAITING
WARM
WET
WIDE
WISE
YELLOW
YOUNG

SPE
STRA[illegible]
THIN
WHITE
WRONG

NO 'VERBS'

IT IS POSSIBLE TO GET ALL THESE WORDS ON THE BACK OF A BIT OF NOTEPAPER BECAUSE THERE ARE NO 'VERBS' IN BASIC ENGLISH

A WEEK OR TWO WITH THE RULES AND THE SPECIAL RECORDS GIVES COMPLETE KNOWLEDGE OF THE SYSTEM FOR READING OR WRITING

RULES

ADDITON OF 'S' TO THINGS WHEN THERE IS MORE THAN ONE

ENDINGS IN 'ER,' 'ING,' 'ED' FROM 300 NAMES OF THINGS

'LY' FORMS FROM QUALITIES

DEGREE WITH 'MORE' AND 'MOST'

QUESTIONS BY CHANGE OF ORDER, AND 'DO'

FORM-CHANGES IN NAMES OF ACTS, AND 'THAT,' 'THIS,' 'I,' 'HE,' 'YOU,' 'WHO,' AS IN NORMAL ENGLISH

MEASURES NUMBERS DAYS, MONTHS AND THE INTERNATIONAL WORDS IN ENGLISH FORM

THE ORTHOLOGICAL INSTITUTE LONDON

1. *The BASIC English Word List.*

tionalized modernity would highlight the experimental and progressive natures of both: "The normal process of putting complex ideas of men of letters into Basic English is through the use of foot-notes. . . . But Mr. Joyce was of the opinion that a comparison of the two languages would be of greater interest if the Basic English were printed without the additions necessary to make the sense more complete. In this way the simplest and most complex languages of man are placed side by side" (135) — with no loss in translation and even some justice to the rhythms of Joyce's prose:

> Well, you know or don't you kennet or haven't I told you every story has an end and that's the he and the she of it. Look, look, the dusk is growing. Fieluhr? Filou! What age is it? It saon is late.
>
> Well are you conscious, or haven't you knowledge, or haven't I said it, that every story has an ending and that's the he and the she of it. Look, look, the dark is coming. . . . '*Viel Uhr*? *Filou*! What time is it? It's getting late. (136–37)

Where for Ogden this meeting of "simplest and most complex languages" showed BASIC's ability to turn Joyce's opacity into transparency, modernist readers may have come to other conclusions about the experiment. Two disjunct and equally opaque passages seem the result of this effort at transparency, and modernist writers could identify with either — they could continue their literary experiments (as technological innovators) while being confirmed in their elite cultural perspectives (as "men of letters," members of the modernist clerisy whose "obscure meanings" are valorized by Ogden's attention). It is not surprising that the perceived opacity, rather than transparency, of language in BASIC's translation of Joyce would lead, over the next fifty years and in several schools of writers, to experiments with the constructive effects of restricted vocabularies in poetry.

The radical discontinuity between Coleridge's critique of poetic diction and postmodern constructions of poetic vocabulary, then, is connected through their mediation by a modernist project of linguistic reform that Richards later called a technocratic process of "Language Control."[18] The seemingly strained juxtaposition of BASIC English with Joyce's "Work in Progress" in *transition* shows a modernist fascination and horror with the social hygiene of restricted vocabulary as a rational counterpoint to the possibly contagious avant-garde poetics of Eugene Jolas's "Revolution of the Word." Epistemological concerns with new meaning, reflecting a tension between progressive rationality and modernist experiments, were at the cen-

TRANSITION'S REVOLUTION OF THE WORD DICTIONARY

(The new Transition invites its readers to contribute suggestions for this section which will be continued in subsequent numbers.

Eugene Jolas.)

NEOLOGISMS:

constatation (James Joyce)..... statement of a concrete fact.
couchmare (James Joyce)..... nightmare.. cauchemar...
mielodorous (James Joyce)..... honeyed emphasis of odorous
Dance McCaper (James Joyce).... an Irish *danse macabre*
returningties (James Joyce)..... eternities... cycles turning upon themselves... the serpent that bites its own tail
Besterfarther Zeuts (James Joyce)..... the Proustian divinity... Cronos... Saturn... who bests us all; in other words: Grandfather Time — here Zeuts suggests both Zeus and Zeit, German for 'time'.
paideuma (Leo Frobenius)..... ensemble of psychic forces governing a civilization... soul of a culture.
mechany (Leo Frobenius)..... state of mechanical civilization
tocsinsong (Whit Burnett)..... shrill chant.
barytonate (Murray Godwin)..... warble like a baritone
up (American language)..... to increase
clutterpile (Murray Godwin)..... pile up in disorder
oor (Eugene Jolas)..... primal... as oor-man
gump (Sidney Smith)..... a foolish person
megalopolitan (Charles Duff)..... big-mouthed person
readie (Bob Brown)..... machine for reading
flir (Theo Rutra)..... to glitter
turbil (Eugene Jolas)..... to rush like a storm
floom (Eugene Jolas)..... to suddenly appear silhouetted.
jawgape (A. L. Gillespie Jr.)..... stare with surprise
parloritis (A. L. Gillespie Jr.)..... tendency to academism
erotoxin (Stuart Gilbert)..... vampish woman
expatriarch (Stuart Gilbert)..... an ancient rejuvenated
wordling (Laurence Vail)..... writer exclusively interested in words
mythoracle (Laurence Vail)..... pseudo-pythian spouter
idiosyncrazie (Jack Lait)..... silly caprice
meanie (New York tabloids)..... villain in divorce suit
to gross (Rialto slang)..... to be financially successful

2. "transition's *Revolution of the Word Dictionary.*" *From* transition *21 (March 1932).*

ter of Jolas's program for modernism, to the extent that the same issue of *transition* that printed Joyce's text in BASIC also ran a section titled "Laboratory of the Word," which called at once for "A New Symbolical Language," reflecting poetry's spiritual concerns, and "A New Communicative Language," related to questions of new meaning. While *transition* argued for the "pre-logical functions" of language, it also lamented "a vocabulary that statically retains now obsolete words and is unaware of the enormous changes in meaning that have occurred," concluding, "We need a twentieth-century dictionary!" (297). This Jolas supplied in the form of a "Revolution of the Word Dictionary" that listed neologisms taken from modernist authors such as Joyce, Bob Brown, Abraham Lincoln Gillespie, and himself and that also retired words such as *humanism*, *democracy*, and *nightingale* from "active service" (fig. 2). While generally hostile to technology ("*Transition* is against the mechanical language"; 322), Jolas encouraged a wide range of investigation into linguistic phenomena, including an essay by Jean Paulhan on words as signs, speculations on the language of dreams and the unconscious, examples of the trans-sense language of Hugo Ball and Kurt Schwitters, and transcriptions of the rhythms of African-American language. *Transition*'s focus on language "as such," of course, was a part of a wider concern in Anglo-American modernism with language as a site of social modernity that began, arguably, with Gertrude Stein and that extended to the Harlem Renaissance. The Objectivist poets, particularly Louis Zukofsky, further articulated this debate from its moment in *transition* through the 1930s and onward, shifting the formal paradigm of language to constructivist goals that would lead to the possibility of making poetry out of preexisting vocabularies, a project later taken up in the chance-generated work of Jackson Mac Low and the work of the Language School. The encounter between the avant-garde use of "language as such" and the emergence of new technical senses, evident in *transition*'s translation of Joyce into BASIC but also its dictionary of new meaning, thus arrives at a historically unique development in modern writing, the making of literary works from a pre-given vocabulary.

As Joseph M. Conte has shown, there have been any number of poetic strategies in which literature is generated by virtue of what he calls procedural form, from early modern sestinas to the linguistic and formal constraints of the French OuLiPo.[19] Procedural form in the modernist and postmodern period shares with the literary use of poetic vocabulary an open approach to the construction of meaning, in Umberto Eco's sense of an open work; as Conte writes, "Procedural form is a generative structure that constrains the poet to encounter and examine that which he or she does not immediately fathom, the uncertainties and incomprehensibilities of an expanding universe" (16). But the notion of poetic vocabulary moves beyond the expressivist uses of much open work (as, for example, in the process poetics of New American poets such as Charles Olson and Robert Duncan, whose work depends on open horizons of meaning) in granting a predetermined, objectified language an autonomous existence whose ultimate meaning will be engaged but not determined by the poet. If the consequences of Coleridge's notion of poetic diction were great for the development of a pedagogy of practical criticism, the methodological stakes of poetic vocabulary, seen as a paradigm for making meaning, may turn out to be equally so. A new ethics of meaning, which combines the interpretive openness of open form with the preexisting objectification of a fixed vocabulary, leads to a result that is not reducible to the suspension of authorial intention in procedural form.

Language poet Kit Robinson's *The Dolch Stanzas*, published by This Press in 1976, is a clear example of the project of making a poetic text from a preexisting poetic vocabulary. *Stanzas* comprises a sequence of twenty-two poems in short-lined tercets; its formal procedures, in other words, are relatively consistent but not entirely rule-governed. It is based on the Dolch Basic Sight Word List, a vocabulary for sight comprehension at the second-grade reading level, but again Robinson does not adhere to poetic vocabulary in a rule-governed way. From this list of about two hundred words, and allowing himself poetic license in selectively augmenting it, he explores possibilities of a language-based poetic argument where meaning effects are constructed in the poem's interpretation:

XII

how did these
get here I wonder
what's small always does

now come away
said a piece of one
once to please

upon that best
and warm hold
I will become only

and not take of
what's given
together or not

but come back
said the one
take a look at these

XIII

you stop only
to go
hard

against black wood
pull it down
into the cold saw

and get that
going again
which is sharp

so to cut out
so much crap
that's put up with

make this out
as just like always
and you'll walk to help[20]

Given that Robinson is using a reduced vocabulary of two hundred words appropriate to a second-grade reading level, it is surprising that so many divergent semantic frames can be set off against one another in these poems. This effect points out again BASIC's failure to restrict meaning to combinations of the most common words, as these words are the most polysemous. Polysemy, thus, is the key to Robinson's attack on normative poetic diction. If one were to play Coleridge to Robinson's Wordsworth, one might begin by criticizing his ambiguation of the common language of everyday speech — as in "so to cut out / so much crap / that's put up with" — through the disjunct frames of experimental poetry. But it is precisely Robinson's point that he can locate such private embedded semantics and culturally dissonant idiom chunks within the normative semantics of a second-grade reader. Robinson's work is a demonstration of a theory of meaning that begins with the way poetic vocabulary at once constructs and interprets interlocking frames of language and experience. As can be seen in how meaning is made in the poem, such a pre-given vocabulary brings its own semantic preconditions, even as it engages interpretive frames that can only be read through the total form of the poem. Basic assumptions about person, agency, and event are involved at the Dolch lexical level — "how did these / get here I wonder," the poem asks, anchoring vocabulary in deixis and thus establishing a world that assumes speaker, hearer, and reference in contexts built out from their irreducible identities. "What's small always does," on the other hand, demands difficult, high-end processing to reconcile disjunct and competing interpretive frames.[21] Robinson's point is to show how the use of poetic vocabulary engages conflicts between inherent presuppositions of language (both its own and those of interpreters). Objectivist assumptions, which ground meaning in reference to the world outside and which relate the self-evidence of objects to the practical task of learning to read, provide only one scenario among many. Robinson seems to comment on the limits of ostensive definition in a line such as: "but come back / said the one / take a look at these," which offers a reductive schema of communicative action where the self-evidence of pointing to

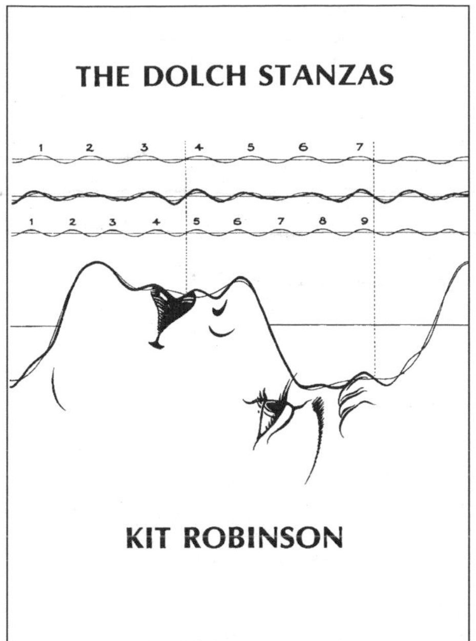

3. *Kit Robinson, front cover,* The Dolch Stanzas *(San Francisco: This Press, 1976).*

things is parodied as it becomes a source of comedic effects in the poem's hypertrophic sequence of interpretive frames.[22]

It is equally up to the reader to "make this out / as just like always / and you'll walk to help," assuming a competence in decoding poetic vocabulary that may be identical to its prior inculcation — or not. The possibility of the failure of communication is equally being taken into account. Idiomatic constructions cluster around word-to-word frame shifts in the poem's syntactic chain, and these are thematically engaged as meaning effects that may not be entirely warranted even as they are pushed into the foreground. Thus the "meaning effect" of the woman's profile on the cover of the This Press edition (fig. 3) reveals a superimposition of illicit interpretive frames onto rationalized diction. At the moment of the poem's original composition, likewise, Robinson may not have meant to invoke the visual hypertext of a help menu as we "walk to help," but it may be engaged later in the open-ended construction of just what such a metaleptic *help* could mean — a reference to what could be seen as part of the computer desktop we refer to for help but which at the time could be understood as making a plea for understanding or, more particularly, as asking for help to decode the poem. In this sense, the language of the poem does not predict all experiential frames brought to it: *The Dolch Stanzas* is both an essay on and experiment in making meaning out of language that unfolds in subsequent historical horizons. The use of poetic vocabulary is a device to create new meaning, not stabilize it, that has ethical consequences—showing how an action can be taken whose horizons are provisional even as it constructs new meanings. Robinson's poems celebrate the constructive possibilities of a moment of epistemological doubt in the meaning of words—in a way that is open to linguistic and cultural change.

COLERIDGE'S DESYNONYMY

The constructive use of uncertainty in the Language School evokes similar—if more global, less local—processes at work in the expansion of poetic vocabulary in the romantic period. This expansion of language, an historical entailment of the creation of new meaning, was both source and consequence of the instability of the romantic subject, perhaps never more evident than in the forms as well as arguments of Coleridge's oeuvre—from the gaps between poetic works to his continual accounting for linguistic detail in the notebooks to the "failed" construction of the *Biographia.*[23] A key passage from the *Biographia*'s chapter 13 registers simultaneous processes of expansion and contraction at work, which we may interpret in terms of language and poetic form:

> Grant me a nature having two contrary forces, the one of which tends to expand infinitely, while the other strives to apprehend or *find* itself in this infinity, and I will cause the world of intelligences with the whole system of their representations to rise up before you. (297)[24]

Poetry, as the form in which we find ourselves in the infinity of language, is a moment of condensation that makes meaning out of an ever expanding world of representations. Such a moment of balance or tension, between the radical openness of language and the normative condensation of poetry, tends to come undone when we consider the shape of Coleridge's (poetic and critical) work itself, a disjunct practice that was never identical to the normative ideals of his practical criticism.[25] This is in part due to the paradoxical fact that the activity of making poetry, as well as the critical practice of determining its value, involves a restriction of the possibilities of meaning by virtue of the nature of poetic form. Paul Hamilton, in his historicizing account of Coleridge's poetics, cites the latter's acknowledgment of the necessary restrictions of poetic form as compared to prose: "Poetry demands a *severer keeping*—it admits nothing that Prose may not often admit, but it *oftener* rejects."[26] In mysteriously "presupposing a more continuous state of Passion" but not simply expressing it, poetry for Coleridge sorts out meanings both by creating new ones and disallowing discrepant ones: "Poetry justifies, as *Poetry* independent of any other Passion, some new combination of Language, & *commands* the omission of many others allowable in other compositions" (137). While such a dissociation of form from expression is evident as well in Robinson's *Dolch Stanzas*, Coleridge balances the possibility of poetry's "new combination of Language" with the authoritarian "command" of its "severer keeping," which restricts new meaning to that which is justified by the consistency of poetic form. Coleridge's restrictions on language are the historical origin of Mac Low's question to Eliot about the admissibility of the word *Coronamatic* to poetry.

Such a simultaneous creation and restriction of new meaning is not simply expressive but rather formally constructed, and it is here that Coleridge's poetics confirm as they try to regulate the famous negative capability John Keats later claimed Coleridge lacked in his rage for poetic order: "I mean *Negative Capability*, when man is capable of being in uncertainties, Mysteries, doubts, without any irritable reaching after fact & reason — Coleridge, for instance, would let go by a fine isolated verisimilitude caught from the Penetralium of mystery, from being incapable of remaining content with half knowledge."[27] But poetic form, for Coleridge, produces distinctions that catch such "fine isolated verisimilitude[s]" at that same time that it remains "incapable of remaining content with half knowledge"; more simply put, poetry's centripetal tendencies (poetic form) are ideally in balance with its centrifugal ones (new meaning). Poetry's stabilization of new meaning (seen, for example, in the restricted vocabulary of Robinson's poem) may at the same time be an exemplary moment of, it turns out, romantic negative capability, as in the openness of the restricted vocabulary given by the Dolch words to semantic change. While such a paradox depends on a dissociation of language from expression, the fact that Keats could only hypostatize a perverse authority in Coleridge's "irritable reaching after fact & reason" identifies a problem for poetry in its reception. Keats turns Coleridge into an irritable tormentor rather than an organic genius, revealing a negative investment in authority on Keats's part that subtends Coleridge reception as author.[28]

Hamilton's historicizing approach to Coleridge's poetics gives alternative terms for the legacy of organic form and expressive immanence at the origins of twentieth-century American verse culture (typified by the lyric poetry celebrated by New Critics). Another line of poetic development to be derived from a reading of Coleridge, then, begins by seeing his poetics as a response to a historical period of expanded meaning and thus relevant to many of our more recent concerns with a cultural poetics. In pursuing this line, Hamilton motivates Coleridge's investment in poetic form not only in its reflection, as it were, of the transcendental "I am" but in its relation to "customary and habitual principles" derived from British commonsense philosophy (and everyday life). As evidence of this tension, Hamilton constructs a countermovement to the buildup to the missing transcendental deduction of *Biographia*'s chapter 13. In this alternate line of development, Coleridge pursues the poetic implications of the linguistic act of "desynonymy" — a discrimination of meaning at both lexical and historical levels — in the chapters leading up to the missing deduction as well in the subsequent chapters on the practical criticism of poetry. Hamilton explains the key term *desynonymy* as follows:

> Desynonymy for Coleridge means increasing the vocabulary of a language by showing how words which were thought to be synonymous in fact mean different things. The original thinker adds to the number of meanings in the language we use. He does this by coining new words, and showing that we need them. Or he can desynonymize existing words by showing that we are putting words which we mistakenly think are synonyms to quite different uses. (*CP*, 65)

For example, in chapter 4 of the *Biographia* Coleridge claims historical originality in being "the first of my countrymen, who had pointed out the diverse meaning of which [*metaphysics* and *psychology*] were capable," immediately relating these not only to "the faculties to which they should be appropriated" but to the prior linguistic synonymy between them.[29] Coleridge's better known distinction between the faculties of imagination and fancy would follow as well from the act of desynonymy. In a kind of circular logic, the act of distinguishing between faculties becomes valorized as an imperative to distinguish between word meanings as, in turn, that which distinguishes between faculties:

> When two distinct meanings are confounded under one or more words, (and such must be the case, as sure as our knowledge is progressive and of course imperfect) erroneous consequences will be drawn, and what is true in one sense of the word, will be affirmed in toto. Men of research startled by the consequences, seek in the things themselves (whether in or out of the mind) for a knowledge of the fact, and having discovered

the difference, remove the equivocation either by the substitution of a new word, or by the appropriation of one of the two or more words, that had before been used promiscuously. When this distinction has been so naturalized and of such general currency, that the language itself does as it were *think* for us . . . we then say, that it is evident to *common sense*. (*BL*, 86)

The relation of the faculties of understanding to distinctions between the meanings (and senses) of words has a key consequence for romantic and modernist aesthetics as it leads to the notion of defamiliarization, the Russian Formalists' *ostranenie*. In the above passage, we see a movement from the defamiliarization of language, accomplished by "men of research," to the habituation of common sense, when language "as it were *think*[*s*] for us," which might end in merely normative senses if it were not for the recognition of an expanded register of meaning that is historically irreversible, "as sure as our knowledge is progressive and thus imperfect." Habit, here, exists by virtue of a linguistic *before* and *after*, between which is an act of reflection on language and polysemy that appeals to "things themselves" (both interior and exterior, empirical referent and psychological faculty). In Hamilton's view, Coleridge introduces his account of new meaning only to give it over and subsume it to the ideality of poetic form, which as a sublime horizon of unmediated expression provides the values of sensory immediacy that precede desynonymy in the first place, demanding the distinctions of nature made by "men of research." Poetic expression, in other words, overrides the slippage between form and "the more continuous state of Passion" it assumes; its relation to the transcendental imagination is its own presentation of a passion that passes understanding (as with the notion of the egotistical sublime, leading on to the now predictable result of Coleridge's cultural conservatism). There is another reading of Coleridge's argument, however, in which a radical approach to poetic form can be found that is comparable to, even derivative of, the relation of the expansion of new meaning to desynonymy. Hamilton does not develop this argument, but it provides a way out of identifying form with expression in poetry after Coleridge.

The crux of this undeveloped argument depends precisely on the relation of habituated thought to the reception of experimental poetry, which is evident in "the unexampled opposition which Mr. Wordsworth's writings have been . . . doomed to encounter" (*BL*, 71). Coleridge is dumbfounded that such disparate judgments of the poems in *Lyrical Ballads* could be made by men of equally good taste: "The composition which one had cited as execrable, another had quoted as his favorite" (73). Of course, prescriptive modernist followers of Coleridge such as Richards would see this inconsistency of taste as a failure of poetry as communication to inculcate proper values. For Coleridge, the point is that readers' negative experience of Wordsworth's authorship of new meaning turns them back on their own deficiencies of judgment, challenging their basic self-understanding:

> Not being able to deny that the author possessed both genius and a powerful intellect, they felt *very positive*, but were not *quite certain*, that he might not be in the right, and they themselves in the wrong; an unquiet state of mind, which seeks alleviation by quarreling with the occasion of it, and by wondering at the perverseness of the man, who had written a long and argumentative essay to persuade them, that / Fair is foul, and foul is fair; / in other words, that they had been all their lives admiring without judgement, and were now about to censure without reason. (71–72)

Readers' experience of negative projection onto poetry they cannot cognitively process reveals a gap in self-consciousness that in turn betrays the ideological nature of these seemingly benign but in fact pernicious defects of judgment. Both cause and effect of such defective judgment is not simply an incoherent but a paranoiac reaction to the new meaning of experimental poetry: "In all perplexity there is a portion of fear, which predisposes the mind to anger" (71). The emotional regulation of taste later advocated by Richards here is undermined by a disjunction between two forms of self-understanding that ought to be desynonymized, as Coleridge shows in a remarkable footnote that follows. In it, Coleridge thinks through, well in advance of Louis Althusser, a diagnosis of ideology in terms of the desynonymy of two pronouns of identity, *I* and *me* — one that is fully accessible to Jacques Lacan's account of identification and misrecognition:

> In opinions of long continuance, and in which we had never before been molested by a single doubt, to be suddenly *convinced* of an *error*, is almost like being *convicted* of a fault. There is a state of mind, which is the direct antithesis of that, which takes place when we *make a bull. The bull* namely consists in the bringing together two incompatible thoughts, with the *sensation*, but without the *sense*, of their connection. . . . Thus in the well known bull, *"I was a fine child, but they changed me;"* the first conception expressed in the word *"I,"* is that of personal identity

> . . . the second expressed in the word "*me,*" is the visual image or object by which the mind represents to itself its past condition, or rather, its personal identity under the form in which it imagined itself previously to have existed. (72)

The fundamental desynonymy of *I* and *me* shows how identity has been confused between terms of which there is a "sensation, but without the sense, of their connection," and Coleridge brilliantly sees this synthetic confusion as the "antithesis" of a paranoiac investment in the object of inadequate judgment (that is, the *Lyrical Ballads*) by the inadequate critic. Such critical incoherence is the symptom of a slippage in the social reception, thus ideological reproduction, of authority; its symptoms may, in Althusser's terms, be seen as resulting from a kind of negative hailing by the object of judgment that leads to a condition in which one feels that to be "*convinced* of an *error*, is almost like being *convicted* of a fault."[30] For Coleridge, there is a direct connection between inadequate self-consciousness and an emotionally ungoverned response to being addressed by the defamiliarizing form of poetry's new meaning: "I have heard at different times, and from different individuals every single poem [in *Lyrical Ballads*] *extolled* and *reprobated*, with the exception of those of loftier kind, which . . . seem to have won universal praise" (*BL*, 74). Taste must be brought under regulation, finally, to counter the destabilizing antagonisms of new meaning in poetry, and the rewards of taste are not only aesthetic pleasure but power and mastery, a cultural imperative: "In energetic minds, truth soon changes by domestication into power; and from directing in the discrimination and appraisal of the product, become influencive in the production. To admire on principle, is the only way to imitate without loss of originality" (85).

While Coleridge's desynonymy of identity and identification (*I* and *me*) leads, on the one hand, to the inculcation of power as appropriate response to and judgment of poems "of the loftier kind," the vagaries of poetic indeterminacy — that is, the problem of differences of judgment due to the slippage of language in the aesthetic object itself — are addressed to a different standard of regulation than the inculcation of critical mastery. In other words, Coleridge desynonymizes terms for identity as an example of an even more general linguistic process by which meanings that have been subsumed under imprecise terms should, and even historically will, be distinguished by a desynonymy. This *historical moment of the construction of identity* has immediate practical consequences for the unity of the subject, lest it fall (as in the fundamental misrecognition of *me* as *I*) into errors of judgment by means of a more general misrecognition of language as eliding differences between terms. There is strong support here for Hamilton's reading of Coleridge (in favor of language rather than transcendence) in Coleridge's prematurely abandoned argument for a self-consciousness produced through language as an alternative to the imagination that will be "transcendentally deduced" in chapter 13's missing account.

Coleridge includes his desynonymy of identity in a series of related linguistic moments that distinguish general from particular, identity from relation, standard from idiosyncratic. In a bizarre overlay of the biblical notion of primal androgyny onto both biology and semantics, linguistic history takes the form of a parthenogenetic paramecium in making such distinctions happen as language splits meanings off from its original body:

> There is a sort of *minim immortal* among the animalcula infusoria [*scholia*: "a 'barely-there immortality' of the tiny organisms"] which has not naturally either birth, or death, absolute beginning, or absolute end: for at a certain period a small point appears on its back, which deepens and lengthens until the creature divides into two, and the same process recommences in the two halves now become integral. This may be a fanciful, but it is by no means a bad emblem of the formation of words, and may facilitate the conception, how immense a nomenclature may be organized from a few simple sounds by rational beings in a social state. (83)

Recent accounts of linguistic change propose an altogether different notion of new meaning occurring at such a protoplasmic moment of division and polysemy; in one account, original meanings are distributed between different metaphorical domains and interpreted by different pragmatic contexts, resulting in linguistic innovation.[31] Coleridge at times seems to understand such contextually reflexive processes of semantic change, as when "sounds" lead to an "immense nomenclature" as a result of their use by "rational beings in a social state." Going through the chain of antitheses that structures his meditation, however, we perceive a more monovalent account of semantic change in which the practice of desynonymy, much like that of the Russian Formalists' *ostranenie*, works to undo the bad symbolizing produced by habituated judgment in providing both the "*sense* as well as the *sensation*" of differences Coleridge thinks of as simply binary oppositions. In this sense, meanings seem to have devolved, psychologically as well as historically, from an idealized originary moment Coleridge elsewhere postulated in language as the "Verb Substantive," a linguistic/existential monad (the verb *to be*) that can only be dissociated by the subject in the vagaries of actual grammatical predication.[32] As a result, Coleridge cannot entirely account for the new meaning brought about by cultural change, as much as he is provoked by its linguistic evidence. This is one explanation for Coleridge's preference for Wordsworth's sublime address, in opposition to his borrowings from common language, in the second half of the *Biographia*, a judgment reflecting the contradiction between self-consciousness and language that produced the moment of desynonymy in the first place, especially as it devalued social contexts for discriminations of language. Thus the paradox of Coleridge's criticism for Hamilton is its advocacy of a transcendental "emptying out" (identifiable in both romantic and postmodern poetry) where "the sublime . . . only becomes sublime by losing its sense" (166). If Coleridge had known the later uses to which a sublime poetics of organic form were to be put and rather had developed the fuller implications of his account of desynonymy, it might have saved him from the defensiveness of his Christian conservatism, as well as saved us from some bad poetry.

It is here that a reversal of polarities occurs between romantic and modernist poetics — from Coleridge's valuation of subjective immanence as empty sublimity to at least a reconsideration of the epistemological stakes of desynonymy. In the work of a number of cultural as well as literary critics in the modern period — from Richards, William Empson, and Owen Barfield to Laura (Riding) Jackson and Raymond Williams (many of them grouped together under the rubric "Cambridge English") — the question of poetic diction developed in Coleridge's practical criticism extends to meditations on the larger question of a poetic vocabulary seen as not only adequate to meaning but also responsive to culture. BASIC English clearly had Coleridge as its precursor for his insistence on the "good sense" of words; the *resynonymy* rather than desynonymy that resulted depended on an emptying out of the sublimity of poetic form while maintaining the prestige of literary authority as the basis for the moral imperative of its semantics. In Coleridge, original thought expands vocabulary, which in turn will become habituated as the common sense of language, thus condensing the judgments of literary authority in everyday life. BASIC's "men of research," on the other hand, proposed a semantics of definitional substitution by which meanings would be collapsed into strings of predetermined symbols. This restriction of signification was motivated by concerns for both scientific specificity and normative communication; Ogden and Richards relate both in *The Meaning of Meaning*: "The recognition that many of the most popular subjects of discussion are infested with symbolically blank but emotionally active words . . . is a necessary preliminary to the extension of scientific method to these questions."[33] In the name of science as well as culture, BASIC's operators proposed a linguistic hygiene that was socially regulative.

BASIC's reversal of Coleridge's poetics of desynonymy used a restricted vocabulary precisely because it would avoid the mutability of original meanings in being grounded in a set of terms that not only "men of science" but everyone should hold in common. In order to discriminate complex meanings, BASIC would begin by "symboliz[ing] references by means of . . . simple routes of definition. . . . We must choose as starting-points either things to which we can point, or which occur freely in ordinary experience" (127). Rather than devolving on the authority of literary discrimination, then, desynonymy would be put on an empirical basis that assumed the transparency of certain fundamental terms. But, as discussed above, the attempt to extend ostensive reference through strings of substitutive terms to precise technical senses in BASIC malfunctions precisely at the point of a polysemy that is a constituent of semantic change. Hopeless redundancy results from the attempt to patch definitions that involve mutating, unstable word meanings onto precise technical senses (as inevitably occurs with the semantics of many of the most simple words in the language).[34] Rather than being able to specify and desynonymize meanings, BASIC's capacity would be continually outstripped by increased load on its fundamental units. Robinson's *Dolch Stanzas* shows just how many embedded idioms are engaged by a restricted vocabulary that can neither contain nor anticipate them.

BASIC tried to contain the expansions of meaning produced by mass culture and developing technology by the same means: a reduction of vocabulary. Its goal was a final transparency of language once it had been analyzed into minimal components: "For many purposes 'dictionary-meaning' and 'good use' would be equivalents. . . . The dictionary is a list of substitute symbols. . . . It can do this because in these circumstances and for suitable interpreters the references caused by the two symbols will be sufficiently alike."[35] The final test of BASIC's desynonymy is thus to be found in an interpretive community, a scientistic version of the institution of Coleridge's clerisy evident in the notion of "suitable interpreters" presumed to be "sufficiently alike." BASIC, here, is designed to inculcate, through linguistic means, a norm of transparent subjectivity as it simultaneously adjudicates problems of meaning so that "we" all may agree. It is not surprising that a number of modern writers were drawn both to admire and contest Ogden and Richards's claims to have authored a language-centered reform of modern society — both for its notion of the power of language to change the world, positively; and in reaction to its leveling of differences of perspectives within social modernity, negatively. The fascination of *transition*'s translation of *Finnegans Wake* into BASIC is therefore that it seems simultaneously to identify modernism with and distance it from the cultural authority of science. From the 1930s on, this interest continued among modernist and postmodern experimental poets, particularly Louis Zukofsky and Jackson Mac Low.

ZUKOFSKY'S DICTIONARY

BASIC's conflation of modern science with cultural authority had a provocative effect on Louis Zukofsky, who wrote as a bilingual American Jew in the same period that Ogden and Richards were advocating suitable interpreters who would accept the necessity of restricting meaning through shared references. In several thought experiments on questions of language and meaning in experimental texts from the 1930s, Zukofsky explores the relations of poetic vocabulary to new meaning, focusing on dictionaries, definition, and meaning as cultural as much as epistemological concerns. While Zukofsky shared the modernist faith in science as giving the basis for objective reference, his cultural commitments led to an exploration of textual opacity quite opposed to that of BASIC's linguistic transparency. His 1932 experimental text "Thanks to the Dictionary," to begin with, brings together the materiality of cultural tradition in the language of the Old Testament with modernist improvisations based on passages chosen at random from the dictionary:

> It was among these that David, disguised, betokening a hidden meaning, and emblematically seeking his man, David illuminating darkly the night's fires he had wandered into, spoke affectionately: — My three unequal and dissimilar axes with oblique intersections, I say this of you my crystal forms, your initial letter, in Egyptian a lionness, in Phenician called *lamed* means rightly an ox-goad. My time comes when it will be *lagu*, a lake! In English the sound of this letter will be one of the most uniform and changeless of the sounds in the language, especially prolonged so as to continue a syllable! It is not in my name nor will it be pronounced in *folk*. But you will hear it in *holm*, my labradorite, my feldspar, L, 50, L̄, 50,000 upon 50 thousands, when one will write in a

city, attributively, as L roads, in the time of sounds and the — then — lighted passing of symbols. And, by the way, let's make it liquid. . . .[36]

In this passage, Zukofsky produces an effect of textual difficulty whose overcoming will be virtually analogous to the heroism of David, "disguised, betokening a hidden meaning, and . . . seeking his man." David's speech, as an original moment of the language of the chosen people, moves from its biblical referent to a dictionary-based scatting that Zukofsky orchestrates as a witty parody of vocalized midrashic interpretation. David "speaks" a text derived from dictionary definitions under the letter *l*, whose "hidden meaning" in Cabbalist or any other senses clearly are intended to be unavailable to most interpreters. In contradistinction to BASIC's operating manual, Zukofsky holds that suitable interpreters cannot be found who would find this text's referents to be sufficiently alike.

Cultural differences, then, are proposed as motivations for the text's opacity; the passage is stunning for its early prescience of a material poetics sited at the intersection of new meaning and cultural forms. The language of definition, rather than being seen in terms of substitute symbols, is called on to denote technical senses at the same time that it connotes divergent cultural references. The work goes on to alternate between David-as-textuality and dictionary-definition-as-meaning to create a poetic prose of mild irony and pathos that celebrates linguistic opacity. Definition is central to the text:

> A visiter [*sic*] making a visit goes where it is visitable. Where *it* is visitable. IT makes visitation socially acceptable. The visiter lifts his vizor. He wears it naturally to protect his eyes. Moreover, when the visiter lifts his vizor, it is visual. And like a vista. IT has become visitatorial. . . . (279)

Here Zukofsky is parodying the ostensive definition at the heart of BASIC English at the same time that he draws attention to the criteria for suitable interpreters that come along with it. Agreeing on what is meant by the ostensive "IT" would make visitation — presumably, an agreed-on sense of embodied presence in meaning — "socially acceptable"; the Jew can leave his calling card on the dining room table or office desk of the cultural elite. Zukofsky patches in definientia after the manner of BASIC English as a stylistically neutral (if absurdist) way to continue the demonstration of his argument — why the "visiter" wears a "vizor," if not explained by the contiguity of nouns, appears to be simply the "vizor's" function.[37] There is nothing culpable about wanting to protect one's eyes from interlocutors; definition supplies explanation for the cultural opacity the visitor feels. If definition could explain social relations, it would seem that merely learning a language would provide adequate criteria for cultural legitimacy. The fact that Zukofsky knows that to be an absurdity (and as it was elided by technocrats like Ogden and Richards) gives the work its hidden drive to present cultural meanings as disarmingly linguistic:

> The child of Uriah's wife, very sick, and David all night upon the earth. The child dead. — "He shall not return to me." And David comforted Bath-sheba. A son, his name Solomon. Absalom the son of David had a fair sister, whose name was Tamar; and Amnon the son of David loved her. Being stronger, forced her, lay with her, then hated her exceedingly. Tamar crying. And Absalom her brother: "Peace, sister, he *is* thy brother. Amnon dead; Absalom fled. . . . [38]

The hidden meaning of this passage invokes not the definieda of definition but the original betrayals conveyed as much as obscured by the cultural text. Stylistically, Zukofsky's paratactic narrative makes a text out of actions that he will then patch in to the same continuum as definition in language — with both to be presented as opaque and other. Zukofsky is reducing cultural narration to the level of substitute symbols that *should* provide unity of meaning for suitable interpreters if it were not for their cultural differences. The reduction of shared narratives to substitute symbols attacks cultural uniformity at the same time that it celebrates the purported efficiencies of scientific notation.[39] As if to insist on the irreducible materiality and idiosyncratic meaning of "Thanks to the Dictionary," Zukofsky later published a broadside edition of an excerpt in his own handwriting.[40]

Zukofsky reserves skepticism here for a culturally homogenizing poetics, but when in 1943 he made a direct critical response to BASIC there is also sympathy for its version of the "scientific definition of poetry" he would call for in 1946: "Someone alive in the years 1951 to 2000 may attempt a scientific definition of poetry. . . . All future poems would verify some aspect of this definition and reflect it as an incentive to a process intended to last at least as long as men."[41] Zukofsky clearly supports the production of a language that can account for both poetry and science by appropriate use of definition. A poetics of definition is everywhere in Zukofsky's critical prose, as witness the title of his book, *Prepositions*, as well as the heading of its index, "Definitions."[42] In his assessment of BASIC, in fact, Zukofsky seems to be saying he can do better than Ogden and Richards in reducing the number of symbols necessary to communicate exact meaning. In his poetry as well as in his prose, Zukofsky maximizes the condensation of speech, and he thus finds stylistic flaws in BASIC's operating manual in its failure to achieve optimal compression. As he writes in a passage on the status of linguistic fictions in objectivist vocabulary: "This quotation is not uninteresting rhetoric, but suffers from a stuffiness of extra words that flaw the thought. Why need a fiction be 'loosely described' if the author knows all about it?"[43] Critical judgment and the compression of style to the least number of symbols needed to communicate meaning are often identical for Zukofsky.[44]

Zukofsky wants to move toward a kind of scientized visuality as a way to bring together the ostensive definition at the heart of BASIC with the aesthetic compression developed by modernist poets after Imagism. Such conflation of art and science conveys two kinds of authoritarian baggage: the first is inherited from Ezra Pound's paratactic method of juxtaposing self-evident assertions (clearly the primary influence on Zukofsky's development of an Objectivist poetics). A second is compelled by BASIC's hypotactic derivation of meanings in strings of substitute symbols: "The *simple* English verbs, a full number of which BASIC uses as nouns, are a shorthand for *act* and *thing* that the Chinese sees perhaps in his ideograph. . . . What seems to be arbitrary neglect of these verbs is a loss" (160). Rather than restore more action words to BASIC's list of "operators," however, Zukofsky would like BASIC to be even more condensed in order to raise the value of its self-evident substitutions, and he suggests further cuts to its lexicon (much like his editorial approach to the work of fellow poets).[45] "Since the purpose of the BASIC word list is to be both short and complete, its total of 18 verbs might be cut down perhaps":

1. *Go* can be used with certain directives (prepositions), in accordance with BASIC practice, to cover *come.*
2. Either *get* or *take* can be dispensed with, their shades of meaning are so close.
3. The same is true of *have* or *keep.*
4. Used with certain directive, *put* can probably achieve the meaning of *send* and *give*: e.g. 'Put it in my hand' instead of 'Give it to me'; 'Put a letter in the box' instead of 'Send a letter.'
5. *Make* and *do* are very close, and *make* can include the uses of *do*. . . . (*P*, 162)

It is hard to tell how far Zukofsky is going in the direction of parody here. In arguing to "clean slay" (the phrase is Ezra Pound's) what remains of connotation in BASIC, it is clear he is not being entirely serious, but there is a curious fascination with linguistic eugenics even while he goes on to admit the risk of what might be lost in the reduction of terms.

Zukofsky's account of BASIC argues, finally, for a synthesis of the objectivity of scientific method with the opacity of cultural practice. Thus when Ogden and Richards argue for commonsense standards for grammatical usage based in cultural practice ("It would be foolish to take exception to the placing of the preposition at the end of the sentence. The word-order is sanctioned by old-established English idiom"), Zukofsky retorts, "Good, and it would be foolish to take exception to anything that makes sense" (163). BASIC's efficient reduction of polysemy to substitute symbols is here caught up in a contradiction when it cannot recognize the cultural biases of its managerial overview. Zukofsky concludes: "Ogden is against 'Babel,' the confusion of many languages. But the refreshing differences to be got from different ways of handling facts in the sound and peculiar expressions of different tongues is not to be overlooked" (163). There is, in short, a higher standard of objectivity than Ogden and Richards's merely objectivist one: "Good writing means a grasp of and a closeness to subject or object rather than an addiction to a small or large vocabulary. . . . If the BASIC versions come close to the originals, the use of the BASIC word list has not much more to do with it than mulling over a good text and a desire to keep it simple" (163). Zukofsky argues for standards of common sense that go beyond the advantages of a reduced vocabulary. This preference is given a paradoxical and relativist twist at the end of his argument, where he quotes a text on "The Value of Science" that states: "To change the language suffices to reveal a generalization not before suspected," which translated into BASIC reads, "To give a language a different turn is enough to make it take up a train of thought that we had no idea of before" (164). BASIC's poetic vocabulary, rather than transparently rendering the original, would indicate, in Zukofsky's ventriloquism of its project, a material difference between texts (here, original and translated) that generates new meaning in the name of science.

"Thanks to the Dictionary" and "BASIC" show Zukofsky to be fascinated by two competing aspects of poetic vocabulary. He wants to preserve as much as possible the confusion of many languages, but at the same time he wants a guarantee of objectivity in which words as things become minimal units of meaning. Both aspects are developed in Zukofsky's subsequent investigations of a poetry based on restricted vocabularies, "*A*"–9 and *Catullus*.[46] "*A*"–9 stands as the inaugural moment of the creation of new meaning by the use of a predetermined poetic vocabulary in American literature. In the first half of the poem (as is generally known to Zukofskians but not otherwise), Zukofsky translates Guido Cavalcanti's canzone "Donna mi prega" (used as a touchstone for value in Pound's *Cantos*) into a vocabulary taken from the Everyman edition of Karl Marx's *Kapital*. In the second half of the poem, Zukofsky rewrites his original Marxist commitments by retranslating the same canzone into a vocabulary taken from Benedict Spinoza's writings. The prior example of BASIC is evident in the notion that complex thought — philosophy, in particular — is reducible to a set of key terms. Zukofsky's use of translation, however, is not to simplify a complex and unstable original, as with Ogden's translation of Joyce into BASIC, but to reorient its claim to value and meaning. What I will call the *source text* (Cavalcanti) is rewritten by means of poetic vocabulary (Marx or Spinoza) toward a *target form* (the text of the poem); the value of the resulting poem is a synthesis of its prior languages. "*A*"–9's complexities demand a thorough account of the relation between its source text, Cavalcanti's canzone, and its poetic vocabularies from Marx and Spinoza.[47] Zukofsky's intent is to align value in economic and aesthetic senses; poetic vocabulary is his chosen vehicle, as it is the self-evidence of words creating conditions for meaning that brings out ethical possibilities of language as agency. As Zukofsky's text famously begins:

> An impulse to action sings of a semblance
> Of things related as equated values,
> The measure all use is time congealed labor
> In which abstraction things keep no resemblance
> To goods created; integrated all hues
> Hide their natural use to one or one's neighbor. . . .[48]

The poem claims an equivalence not only between use and value but between the language of the poem's argument and its critical force — as both opaque and transparent.

Zukofsky seems to be trying, in a series of controlled textual experiments, to create that moment of polysemy in which new meanings are produced in the expansion of language (or many languages), with the proviso that these meanings will turn out to be just the words themselves. He continues this project in his translation of *Catullus*, which moves from a mode of translation that bears a transparent relation to its Latin original to one where the translated text is almost entirely opaque, masking any relation to the original standing behind it.[49] In *Catullus*, the linguistic distance from source text to target form is stretched to a virtually unrecognizable degree. The Latin original virtually becomes nature to language's science; through the application of poetic vocabulary, a kind of curve fitting of sound and meaning results in which American English in all its idiomatic complexity is twisted to approximate the sound and meaning of the original Latin:

> Quiddity, Gelli, quarry, rosy as these too lips belie
> they burn defiant, candid hoar snow renewing
> morning to homecomings, exit come too active a quiet or
> a mole longing resuscitate eighth hour of day? . . .
>
> Quid dicam, Gelli, quare rosea ista labella
> hiberna fiant candidiora nive,
> mane domo cum exis et cum te octava quiete
> e molli longo suscitate hora die? . . . [50]

Zukofsky's layout of originals and translations on facing pages, both equally unreadable, recalls the juxtaposition of *Finnegans Wake* with its BASIC translation.[51] Unlike BASIC's concern for the transparency of scientific language, however, the objectivity of science for Zukofsky authorizes seeing language as a material sound shape rather than as a conveyor of meaning, providing an opposite basis for an epistemology of translation that structures its values into the material fact of the opaque language that results. The beauty of this synthesis for Zukofsky is that it unites material culture, where the many languages of Babel surface through the text, with standards of scientific objectivity that guarantee a universal value for poetry. What Zukofsky avoids, in these pathbreaking uses of poetic vocabulary, is the normative value for form that has made poetic diction a dead letter ever since Coleridge's original formulation. Zukofsky's poetry is as sublime as a case full of printer's dingbats translating a revelatory notation for the theory of relativity.

MAC LOW'S LEXICONS

From the 1950s on, the postmodern poet Jackson Mac Low has developed numerous literary and performance strategies for employing the constructive potentials of poetic vocabulary, and he frequently uses vocabularies taken from the BASIC word list, among other sources. In a correspondence following the original publication of this essay, Mac Low questioned the label "postmodern" for his work.[52] There are important periodizing distinctions directly resulting from the difference between a modernist use of poetic vocabulary (such as Zukofsky's) and Mac Low's, however. While Zukofsky's work with poetic vocabulary was directed to the composition of formally autonomous texts, Mac Low's chance-generated poems and texts for ephemeral performances argue for more contextual values. Zukofsky and Mac Low both enact a cultural politics based on a language-centered critique, but in Zukofsky's work critical values are equated with the irreducible autonomy of the text while Mac Low's insists on interactive, collective strategies for their realization. In the textual weaving of *Bottom: On Shakespeare*, for instance, Zukofsky thought he had "done away with epistemology" and achieved a condition of textual practice where "the words are my life."[53] While equally involved in a life of words, Mac Low continually exploits the difference of texts from the real-time, historically specific conditions of their performance. Zukofsky produced an epic poem, "*A*," that represents language and culture in the unfolding structure of autonomous form; Mac Low has written a large number of experimental works that include the possibility of their realization outside the confines of the text, but he has by no means contemplated an epic.

Mac Low's poetry addresses the historical expansion of meaning in using poetic vocabularies derived from specific source texts and organized in target forms. But where for BASIC and Zukofsky the ethical consequences of poetic vocabulary are in its relation to the natural or cultural object status of its referents, the ethical consequences of Mac Low's work, even when purely aleatorical, are in how they are to be performed in real-time situations. Such formal procedures for the generation of poetic vocabulary are evident in Mac Low's 1955 "5 biblical poems," which comprise his first composition of aleatorical or chance-derived poems by what he has more recently called "nonintentional" means.[54] Mac Low converts the text of biblical narrative by means of ostensibly value-neutral, random procedures into a disjunct text that provides, in turn, the basis for its final realization in performance. In translating the Old Testament into sequences of vocabulary and ellipses (to be performed as temporal gaps), Mac Low transforms the authoritative original into a source text that produces the target form of the printed text. This text becomes, in turn, source text for the final target form, the work's performance. In what appears to be a reenactment of the textual project of romantic hermeneutics, the horizon of the text's "original" meaning can thus only be realized in the historical act of the poem's reinterpretation in a way that fuses the horizons of the original language of the Old Testament, the interference of the printed version, and the contemporary meanings of what has now been rendered as a neutral and pseudo-objective poetic vocabulary:

thou/______/ /______/ /______/ /______/ /______/ /______/
sun
/______/ /______/with me/______/daughter in/______/came
/______/and Eliphaz
Timna/______/of words him doubt went and with mock unto
/______/dungeon ears they Pharaoh years I be/______/
/______/is/______/
/______/said he/______/the/______/the/______/indeed bore/______/
me households I Beriah and How
/______/said lived/______/ /______/way is
For the utmost saying . . . [55]

Where Zukofsky's "Thanks to the Dictionary" draws meaning in to the opacity of textual form, Mac Low's work pushes meaning outward via performance. Each target form will be realized at a point in time *after* the initial work on the source text, making both source text and target form historical. While the realization of the first target form (the printed text) involves the indeterminacy of chance procedures, that of the second target form (its performance) will be open-ended, the result of guided choices among performance options that Mac Low gives, in the 1985 version of his *Representative Works*, in a preface that accounts for the poem's history and specifies parameters for its future. Mac Low's use of the preface, like that of American modernist poet Laura Riding but to constructive rather than obfuscatory ends, is a constitutive part of his poetry. His work exists in a series that begins with the act of poetic composition from original source text to stages of realization and performance, augmented by interpretive framing and publishing history.

Mac Low's prefaces often contain versions of boilerplate wording that he feels need to be prefixed (or appended) to virtually every one of his major poetic experiments. These are stage directives as much as interpretations — in other words, they specify how the interpretation of poetry should be considered in terms of its real-time agency. One result of Coleridge's desynonymy of judgment and identification was to describe an ethics by which the creative acts of others could be appreciated: "To admire on principle, is the only way to imitate with loss of originality";[56] the result was intended to have been the gentlemanly inculcation of value to be shared by those in the inner circles of culture (if not full membership in the national clerisy). Mac Low's prescriptions for the public staging of his poetry in performance can be seen in relation to Coleridge's moral imperative of taste. Rather than being simply didactic instructions for the realization of possible meanings, however, Mac Low's prefaces are also a historical criticism of the kind of literary community Coleridge configured around the appreciation of poetry. For this reason, the directives for the performance of his poetry are not only technical but affective:

> All words must be audible and intelligible to everyone present. Readers must listen intently to their own voices and (in simultaneities) to those of other readers and to all ambient sounds audible during a reading, including those of the audience, if any. Amplitudes are free, within the range of full audibility, but readers in simultaneities must never drown each other out or try to outshout each other. Words must be read soberly and seriously, but without fake solemnity or any other artificial type of delivery.[57]

Mac Low reinterprets the "severer keeping" of poetry as reasonable rules for social conduct. The subjective investments of organic form that can give the contemporary poetry reading its mock sublimity (and interpretive latitude) are clearly corrected for here; the work's multiple performers are no longer the isolated subjects whose expression matters so much in the usual staged reading scenario. Mac Low's open form is to an important degree normative, but his scripted scenarios are a prerequisite for engagement in a public space encompassing more than private interests finding expression through lyric form.

Mac Low's poetics thus move toward political notions of representation in their enactment of community even as they hold back from representation in the epistemological sense. Mac Low acknowledges as much in titling his 1986 collection *Representative Works* in homage, as he says in his preface, to Emerson's essay "Representative Men," but with the difference that it is the work rather than the man that is representative.[58] In Coleridge's *Biographia* (and by extension the literary tradition it founds), while much can be said for language's relation to subjectivity and judgment, values for representation in both epistemological and political senses are deferred to the sublimity of the encompassing form of poetic address. Otherwise put, that Wordsworth imitates common speech per se does not matter for a politics and is a dubious distraction for a poetics. For Hamilton, this is one reason why the commonsense or social aspect of desynonymy did not survive the failed transcendence that would account for the imagination. It also offers a reason for why private interests to be socially organized in relation to literary forms need not be grounded in representation — showing the Coleridgean basis of a liberal poetics that proposes self-expression as an inalienable right as long as it is mediated by acceptable form. Mac Low's at times pedantic emphasis on the origins of his source texts, and his labored descriptions of the means of their translation into target forms, takes on value here against the liberal precedence of expressive form for represented content. In other words, Mac Low insists on the constructed nature not only of subjectivity but of community. In detailing the most basic presuppositions for the production of his works, Mac Low outlines a poetics of representation based on an ethics in which expression is seen as the reflexive enactment of values held in common by communities. This commonality of value can be seen as much in the selection of Mac Low's source texts as in the performance of their target forms, as the provisional texts that mediate between the two take on their values for representation precisely in their open-ended possibility for collective realization.[59]

Mac Low's description of the musical source text and target form of "Machault" (1955), for example, offers a key to the politics of representation that is distributed everywhere in his poetry. Mac Low details the source of the language of the poem in a note:

> Written in January 1955 at 152 Avenue C, New York 9, NY, by translating the pitches of Guillaume Machault's motet QUANT THESEUS (p. 6 in Lehman Engel's *Renaissance to Baroque*, Vol. 1 French-Netherlands Music, Harold Flammer Inc., New York, 1939), into a gamut of words from T.H. Bilby's *Young Folk's Natural History with Numerous Illustrative Anecdotes*, published by John W. Lovell Company, New York, copyright 1887, by Hurst & Co.[60]

These sources exist in a world of texts at large; they are the randomly acquired materials of a secondhand bookstore, available to anyone and bearing with them prior histories of their realization in the name of a common good (the historical responsibility of *Renaissance to Baroque;* the educative pathos of *Young Folk's Natural History with Numerous Illustrative Anecdotes*). What Mac Low achieves by mapping one text onto the other at first appears to celebrate their incommensurability, but it is precisely in the determination of its value in performance that the commonality of his text's materials may be seen as a publicly available. Such language, rather than assuming an inaccessible interiority, is separated from the expressivist core of poetic form as it interprets its outside sources as equally available to anyone, like the detritus to be found in a secondhand bookstore:

it wits it it by the lasso)
tired animal." tired lasso) it
wits it that it

it by lasso) that by that
the so lasso) lasso) tired lasso)
the by wits it

lasso) the lasso)
it it it lasso) lasso) by lasso) by lasso)
it by that it lasso) . . . (35)

The children's book provides an arbitrary vocabulary, memorable for its marked curiousness, that is in turn used to overlay the musical sequence of the motet. The vocabulary taken from the book becomes the source text mapped onto the structure of the motet and making a new source text for the second target form, the poem as realized when read or performed aloud. It is important that poetic vocabulary is being given quasi-referential values by being assigned to particular notes in the motet. Say "lasso)" were to be assigned to B♭: it could be said to signify it within the total form of the poem. Because this is arbitrary, it is not yet a model for representation, but it asymptotically approaches one when the horizon of the textual world called up by the poem's language is fused with the outer horizon of a common understanding. Where in Coleridge's poetics the revelation of poetic speech expresses its own passion on analogy to the transcendental imagination, in Mac Low the possibility of transcendence is reconfigured in the collective act of performance structured by the contingencies of language. In its arbitrary but fixed referentiality, Mac Low's poetic vocabulary represents an idealization of the common good — availability of knowledge and participation in value — when realized in the senses its source materials permit. In the poem's performance, the world will be represented, even if referred to by an arbitrary language, with the horizon of our understanding produced by determinate acts. The outer horizons of collective performance make sense of the world whose temporal and spatial contexts were originally dissociated from Mac Low's source materials.

The representation of common sense and understanding as not conventionally subsumed within communicative norms is crucial here. As a result, an open, nonnormative concept of experience becomes a primary site for the critique of representation, allowing for a radical freedom of action and interpretation within a horizon of stabilized meaning. Mac Low textualizes experience in this sense in a 1960 poem, "Night Walk." Describing the construction of the poem's vocabulary, he notes: "The words in 'Night Walk' are all taken from a list of 100, representing objects, actions, and states of mind remembered as having figured in an actual situation" (54) of everyday activity. Much like his isolation of discrete lexical nodes from the biblical text, the poem breaks up the (inaccessible) continuity of whatever may be called experience to produce a new, arbitrary vocabulary that must in turn be recombined within the new horizon of its performance. Values for this performance, like materials for its text, are specified through fixed and to a degree arbitrary rules; degrees of rapidity (from *vvs* = "very very slow" to *m* = "moderate" to *vvr* = "very very rapid") and loudness (from *ppp* to *f*), along with durations of performed silences (in seconds), are indicated in notes to the side of the printed text. These directives create obstacles as much as guidelines for the text's performance that set the isolated words even further apart, thus interfering with the horizon of interpretation:

ms/p liking teeth hands bodies wondering constellations listening
peace 9
m/mf water ice eyes evening 6
vr/mf clothing attention 4
ms/p three o'clock hands knowing hair clouds learning tongues
twigs sweaters 9
vr/p attention sliding thankfulness friends stars coats warmth
peacefulness bears 3
m/mp quiet lips talking cheeks touching starlight seeing morning
resting fingers 8
vvs/mf kissing talking stories smiling 5
mr/mp sweaters looking delight ease morning trees ease kisses
42 . . . (60)

Apart from his performance instructions, Mac Low withholds punctuation in order to create relations of maximum syntactic ambiguity, demanding choices to be made (as they are understood as arbitrary) in the performance: "The line 'Three o'clock hands knowing hair clouds learning tongues twigs sweaters' could be read as one sentence . . . or as 'Three o'clock. Hands knowing hair, clouds learning tongues, twigs learning sweaters.' or in other ways" (55). While a vocabulary cannot change the rules of syntax (as a performer cannot change Mac Low's directives), the performance itself confers value as the horizon for all possible interpretations that can be produced from the source text. In the poem as it is performed, all lexically coded experience is decompressed and expanded onto an interpretive horizon that is the condition of all particular experience — or at least, onto a horizon that extends from the knowledge of experience to be realized from any particular text.

Mac Low's book-length collection of performance texts, *The Pronouns*, takes such a splitting of vocabulary and syntax to a logical extreme.[61] In the dancers' realization of the printed texts in performance, according to the author's postscript, there will be "a seemingly unlimited multiplicity of possible realizations for each of these dances because the judgments of the particular dancers will determine such matters as degrees of literalness or figurativeness in interpreting & realizing instructions" (68). These instructions, it turns out, will be identical to the words of the poems themselves, which were composed in lines and stanzas from filing cards on which were inscribed "one to five actions, denoted by gerunds or gerundial phrases" and "with the help of the Rand table of a million random digits, from the 850-word Basic English Word List" (69; fig. 4).[62] If it were not for Mac Low's identification of language with action, of poetic text with strategies for performance, his use of the BASIC word list would come quite close to its originators' technocratic ideal of limiting meanings by the use of an arbitrary vocabulary. The identification of source text with performance strategies, however, shows exactly how the presumed transparency of a fixed vocabulary must be first understood as opaque and only then interpreted according to an open process of arriving at collective understanding.

Processes of both desynonymy and resynonymy, the expansion and contraction of vocabularies, are at work here. The act of interpretation will involve an initial expansion of the possible meanings of the source text by the dancers (who arguably substitute for BASIC's men of research), one that will then be recoded within the horizons of the performance. In the target form, the dancers' decisions will be realized as a collectively held common sense — precisely the process Coleridge described as necessary for the construction of new meaning: "When this distinction has been so naturalized and of such general currency, that the language does as it were think for us . . . we then say, that it is evident to *common sense*." For Mac Low, it is the performance itself that creates the collective understanding

new meanings

SPONGING,

UNDER,

GOLD CUSHIONS OR SEEMING TO DO SO,

ATING.

DOING SOMETHING IN THE MANNER OF A SISTER
WHOSE MIND IS HAPPY AND WILLING,

MAKING ONESELF COMFORTABLE,

GOING OVER THINGS,

MATCHING PARCELS.

DOING THINGS WITH THE MOUTH AND EYES,

MAKING GLASS BOIL,

HAVING POLITICAL MATERIAL GET IN,

COMING BY.

4. Jackson Mac Low, three cards from "56 Sets of Actions Drawn by Chance Operations and from the Basic English List by Jackson Mac Low in Spring 1961," the "action pack" used as source text for composition of The Pronouns.

that can authorize new meanings as common sense. Thus, in the move from source text to target form, he not only assigns referential meaning by virtue of arbitrary symbols but shows how the new meaning demanded by the opacity of these arbitrary symbols must be determined by an interpretative community. The enactment of the performances in real time creates a new horizon for the meaning of actions, even as the source texts for the performances are made in the assumption that unrealized actions may be referred to by substitute symbols. The words on the cards, thus, condense possibilities for action whose realization is necessary for their interpretation in the widest horizon. A similar process is at work in Ogden and Richards's sense that a restricted vocabulary results in the greatest flexibility of meaning, so that substitute symbols and new meaning go hand in hand. The difference, again, is Mac Low's new horizon of action.

In "9th Dance — Questioning — 20 February 1964," Mac Low's compression of action to substitute symbols that must be interpreted in their performance looks like this:

> One begins by quietly chalking a strange tall bottle.
>
> Then, questioning,
> one seems to give someone something.
>
> One reasons regularly.
>
> Then one questions some more,
> reacting to orange hair.
>
> Soon, coming on by doing something crushing or crushing something
> & giving an answer
> & giving a simple form to a bridge
> & making drinks
> one ends up saying things as an engine would. (23)

This sequence, while arbitrary, is at the same time ultimately mimetic in Aristotle's sense: poetry imitates the action of an event that it restages. In his postscript to *The Pronouns*, Mac Low sees his poetic vocation in just such Aristotelian terms: "to create works wherein both other human beings, their environments, & the world 'in general' (as represented by such objectively hazardous means as random digits) are all able to act with the general framework & set of 'rules' given by the poet — the 'maker of plots or fables,' as Aristotle insists" (75). But not everything is predetermined within these frames, much to their credit: "That such works themselves may lead to new discoveries about the nature of the world & of people I have no doubts." There are two aspects of Mac Low's aesthetic plots that go, in this sense, beyond Aristotle's poetics. First, a more historicist theory of meaning is necessary to fully account for the ethical stakes of the work and its performance. This is clear in the persistent dating of different versions of Mac Low's poems, prefaces, and books; in the production of the works themselves as datable events, thus yielding a time-valued theory of reading; and in Mac Low's willingness to move instantaneously between epochal frames and microscopic performance decisions, aligning, for example, the historically utopian horizons of his text's invocation of "doing your own thing" with the oppositional counterculture of the Vietnam era (75). Second, a historicist account of literary form is required for Mac Low's theory of language, insofar as it shows how the creation of new meaning occurs through transformations of arbitrary source texts into collective target forms at specific historical moments (not only horizons but dates).

But here there is a contradiction not fully theorized by Mac Low that can be seen in his overall identification of poetic form with definition, "the general framework & set of 'rules' given by the poet." For example, "Tree* Movie" is a conceptual poem (realized at successive intervals) in which a movie camera is set up to photograph a tree for "any number of hours." But, as a note states, its referent is wholly arbitrary: "For the word 'tree', one may substitute 'mountain', 'sea', 'flower', 'lake', etc.," and the poem would be the same. Dated 1961, the concept of the work as given in *Representative Works* anticipates Andy Warhol's famous film *Empire*, which would then be, by definition (or according to the poet), an "unacknowledged [realization] of 'Tree* Movie,' with subjects other than trees"[63] — though Mac Low's own realizations of "Tree* Movie" were in the 1970s. The transparency of definition (analogous to the literalism of many of Mac Low's techniques) is telling here, and it inflects even work with seemingly opaque vocabularies such as "A Vocabulary for Annie Brigitte Gilles Tardos" of 1980, where all possible lexical units made from the letters of her name are syntactically recombined to add up to an interpretative horizon that finally means the name itself. In other words, all horizons of meaning are predetermined in Mac Low's specifications for substitute symbols, much as the self-evident reasonableness of the BASIC word list would finally specify values for the dancers' performance of the texts. In "Converging Stanzas" of 1981, the reinscription of lexical substitution toward a predetermined horizon is carried out to a (fully acknowledged) terminal degree. This poem progressively reduces its operative poetic vocabulary from an original stanza of words randomly chosen from the BASIC English word list, which in turn becomes the source for random choices until the probability of any word from the first stanza appearing in the final stanza, except the surviving one, *experience*, gradually approaches zero. Language converges on *experience* in a total resynonymy:

experience experience experience experience experience
experience experience experience
experience
experience experience experience experience experience experience
experience experience
experience experience experience experience
experience experience
experience experience experience experience experience experience
experience (102)

It is entirely appropriate, but equally fortuitous given the influence of chance operation on the resynonymy of poetic vocabulary here, that BASIC is lexically reduced to the ultimate horizon of *experience* (a pure form of which, without any other qualities, is produced by the reading of the poem). "Experience," it turns out, was one of Richards's central critical categories, a universal horizon against which particular poems are read:

> Let us mean by *Westminster Bridge* not the actual experience which led Wordsworth on a certain morning about a century ago to write what he did, but the class composed of all actual experiences, occasioned by the words, which do not differ within certain limits from that experience.[64]

"Experience" then will be, for Richards, the horizon of value toward which meanings of words will be addressed (as opposed to a more limited horizon of objects *of* experience). Mac Low might be surprised to see how "Converging Stanzas" produces not only a word central to the BASIC's methodology but reproduces Richards's argument for a horizon of experience "composed of all actual experiences, occasioned by the words," as well.

In a 1985 interview, I asked Mac Low whether his choice of BASIC conveyed any judgment of that vocabulary's scientistic, cultural, and objectifying motives; his answer was no, "I simply regarded the Basic English list as just another source of words."[65] This may be contrasted to Kit Robinson's choice of his selected vocabulary, the Dolch Basic Sight Word List. A certain adult-child dynamic, to say the least, is conveyed in the visual evidence of these words; the child is being asked to take them on faith, not to analyze them but to know them as such as they are read. What results in Robinson's use of these words conveys a sense of playfulness, an optimistic buoyancy in putting words together in new combinations, as much as it evokes the regression of deliberately restricting language to words from a second-grade reader. For Robinson, the horizons of new meaning are as open as the processes of learning being imitated in the poem, even as the psychological consequences of an earlier stage of development are being retrospectively explored. For Mac Low, however, the specific values for the meaning and syntax that result in any given realization of his work may be discontinuous from the procedural regularities of language determined by his generative rules. The partial nature of Robinson's chosen vocabulary allows for sudden breaks away from its established level of arbitrary substitution, yielding moments of nonparticipation that assuredly have as much ethical import as the plotted scenarios of Mac Low's rule-governed performances — especially for a political liberationist such as Mac Low. It is precisely this difference between a psychological horizon for the selection of predetermined language, as opposed to a definitional one, that brought about the major shift in Mac Low's poetics in the early 1980s, when he began to deemphasize what he now calls nonintentional procedures for more spontaneous and embodied improvisatory methods. Even so, his disciplined attention to desynonymy and resynonymy, the substitution and expansion of poetic vocabulary, in six decades of writing is revealed in the stunning examples of new meaning that he continues to create.[66] Mac Low's production continues unabated, while we are only beginning to read the surface opacity of his texts in terms of the ethical ideas encoded in their transparent motives.

NEW MEANING

Moving from a concept of poetic diction to one of poetic vocabulary involves a shift as well to a historicist and context-specific notion of the opacity of poetic language. In the discussion of the examples of poetic praxis above, there is an evident progression from Coleridge's notion of poetic form as conserved by community (the clerisy) to Mac Low's poetics of community self-enactment as the completion of poetic form. Both forms of poetic praxis are rule governed, Coleridge's in the "severer keeping" of poetic form and Mac Low's in the literal conditions given by the author for the performance of his works. However, it would be unhistorical to suggest a merely formal inversion as accounting for the difference but also congruence between romantic and postmodern poetic praxes. Between these moments lies the contested terrain of modernism, seen in the different models for the relations between language, community, and poetic form in Ogden and Richards's BASIC English and in Zukofsky's response to and interpretation of it. Ogden and Richards generalize the community of Coleridge's clerisy as the men of research who are suitable interpreters of meaning, likewise generalizing the regulative ideals of Coleridge's organic form as the necessary conditions for communication. Poetic diction is crucial, then, to the imperial project of fitting vocabulary to meaning in a universal language. Zukofsky's contestation of and fascination with BASIC is a cultural intervention into the construction of English as a universal language seen in relation to that which it excludes, a Tower of Babel of many languages that includes Zukofsky's original Yiddish. At the same time, Zukofsky's modernist commitments paradoxically require similar values of condensation and lexical substitution as those of BASIC English. What results is the new meaning of Zukofsky's opaque style, a modernist interpretation of Coleridge's analysis of ideological investments in the habitual judgments of poetry that the tradition founded on his work has done so much to institutionally preserve. Mac Low continues this project of ideological critique, motivated in Zukofsky by the differences between communities of speakers, as the basis for a poetic experiment in the enactment of polity. Nonintentional composition does not simply free language from reference and create the illusion of a nonhistorical subject who is free to make meaning; rather, Mac Low's methods are historically produced and invoke contextual reenactment as a model for interpretation. If this thought experiment shows a way out of the expressivist confines of organic form (and it does), we may find a new meaning in radical experiments in language.

THE SECRET HISTORY OF THE EQUAL SIGN

L=A=N=G=U=A=G=E BETWEEN DISCOURSE AND TEXT

The Language School is known for its production of material texts, but an equally important dimension, in fact the one that defines it as a school, is the way it constructs the relation between material text and literary community. In this chapter, I read a number of key works of the Language School to show how the movement from text to community takes place through the use of strategies of multiple authorship. Avant-gardes, in breaking down the boundaries of the autonomous author in favor of both the work and its reception within its community, frequently use such strategies, in which the work is positioned between two or more authors, toward a horizon of collective practice or politics. Examples of avant-garde multiauthorship developed by writers of the Language School taken up here include the collective authorship represented by *L=A=N=G=U=A=G=E* and other literary journals; *Legend*, a multiauthored experimental poem by five authors; two poems written under the title "Non-Events" by Steve Benson and myself; and Carla Harryman and Lyn Hejinian's collaborative novel *The Wide Road*. Michel Foucault's concept of discursive formation and Julia Kristeva's dialectic of symbolic and semiotic provide critical terms for the relation of text and community enacted in works of the avant-garde. The avant-garde's cultural politics continue in the contemporary form of the Poetics Listserv, which I discuss in terms of a representative month of debate, seen as a form of multiauthorship.

AVANT-GARDE PARADOX

The avant-garde has been characterized as being in a paradoxical historical situation: while it undertakes the overturning of the prior aesthetic order as an irreversible act, it cannot survive a reentry into history, as a form of representation, without losing either creative potential or critical force. As a *critique* of representation, it would follow from this argument, the avant-garde can only contradict itself as a stable *form* of representation. In academia, the historical contradiction of the tenured radical ironically indicates such a devolution of political agency, in moving from public sphere to educational institution, profession, and tenure. In radical politics, Leon Trotsky tried to counter the historical irony of the avant-garde party with a notion of permanent revolution that would be transparent to history, and that would not rigidify in any form of representation.[1] Significant tendencies of the historical avant-garde in Europe (surrealism central among them) saw their claims to political agency and cultural meaning in terms of a dialectics of representation in this sense.[2] But while a surrealist politics of desire has been a central example of the overcoming of stable forms of representation in the historical avant-garde, its particular claim to history, as a concrete form of representation or an identifiable style, risks suppressing its iconoclastic methods once it has achieved recognition. As a result of the seeming inevitability of the historical reversal of the avant-garde's critique of representation, its political claims have often been seen as failed or irrelevant.

In his account of the structural logic of this "failure," Paul Mann's *Theory Death of the Avant-Garde* restages the analogy between political party and aesthetic tendency at a later historical period.[3] In describing the avant-garde from his own historical moment — shortly after 1989, when the horizons of the political avant-garde seemed to have withered away along with the global realignment of the end of the Cold War — Mann describes the paradox of a radical tendency that has survived the death of teleology. The death of the avant-garde, as an end to history, is identified with a notion of theory that is abstract, nonreferential, and self-reflexive — an instance of negative totality that lacks any agency but the recuperation of its own failure. This is Mann's concept of theory death: the devolution of avant-garde agency (in either political or formal terms) that transforms its material practices into an empty and self-confirming discourse — but one that continues as its mode of reproduction nonetheless. The avant-garde dies into theory simultaneously when its political critique turns into an empty circularity of discourse, and when its radical forms are reduced to commodities exchanged in the market and collected by museums. Such a movement away from material practice and toward discourse, in fact, provides the best definition of the avant-garde: "The avant-garde is a vanguard of this reflexive awareness of the fundamental discursive character of art" (6), a discourse derived both from its radical formalism ("as antitraditional art") and its political tendency ("either an epiphenomenon of bourgeois cultural progress or an authentic revolutionary moment of opposition"). If the avant-garde proceeds by endlessly explaining its practice and fundamentally undermining any explanation, the result is entirely circular: "In the avant-garde art manifests itself entirely as discourse, with nothing residual, nothing left over" (7).

The radical critique of the avant-garde, in other words, both fails and reproduces itself at the instant it becomes a form of discourse: this is the paradox of its theory death. The paradox arises not only from the antinomy of representation (in which radical form congeals in representation and destroys any stability of representation) but from the failure of its theoretical excess as it enters discourse and is recuperated: "The discourse of the death of the avant-garde is the discourse of its recuperation" (14), which it has anticipated from the outset in overstating its case. In thus predicting "the effective complicity of opposition," the failure of the avant-garde mimics larger historical processes of recuperation of radical politics (even as it offers itself up as an index to them?) in a "fatalism authored by nearly a century of recuperations, utopian movements canceled with depressing, accelerating regularity, new worlds turning old as if with the flick of a dial" (15). The avant-garde stages its "little death" at the end of history in a way that is "theory-total": it is "the reflection and reproduction of the theoretical exhaustion of autonomy, progress, opposition, innovation" (67). Thus "there is no more crisis; only its exhaustion is critical. What we witness then is a crisis of the end of crisis . . . in which difference can be reproduced but can no longer be different" (115). In this notion of theory as index to the failure of radical tendency, we may see as well the traces of Mann's moment of critique at the end of the Cold War, with its own theory death of failed utopia at the end of history.

The self-canceling perfection of Mann's avant-garde *posthistoire* must account, even so, for an embarrassment: the continuing work of artists and writers who, seemingly unaware of their position, persist in avant-garde practice.[4] At the very least, this persistence has led to an immense growth in the world's inventory of avant-garde art; teleology over and done with, the record of material history may be all that remains of the avant-garde. Here Mann proposes a "second death" of the discursive formation of the avant-garde to account for its material forms: "The avant-garde is completely immersed in a wide range of apparently ancillary phenomena — reviewing, exhibition, appraisal, reproduction, academic analysis, gossip, retrospection — all conceived within and as an economy, a system or field of circulation and exchange that is itself a function of a larger cultural economy" (*TD*, 7). The avant-garde's materiality thus represents a self-canceling process of self-perpetuating evaluation and review, a total emptying out of its critical force:

> Every manifesto, every exhibition, every review, every monograph, every attempt to take up or tear down the banner of the avant-gardes in the critical arena, every attempt to advance the avant-garde's claims or to put them to rest: no matter what their ideological strategy or stakes, all end up serving the "white economy" of cultural production.[5]

So much for the agency of the material text: in Mann's view its surplus of interpretation, *as* practice, returns it to an empty "white economy" whose purism is stultifying. The critique of the material text short-circuits its potential for agency, even as it shows how it can never be seen as merely autonomous or self-sufficient: its claims are always discursive.

The irreducible materiality of the avant-garde, of course, may be interpreted in any number of ways: this is its necessary point of entry into discourse. To begin with, avant-garde discourse may be seen as derived from the materiality of its technique, its foregrounding of the material signifier: language, paint, sound as the foundation of its genres or media. Avant-garde materiality also enters discourse in its politics of breaking apart the frame, leading to an undoing of boundaries between work and world (in terms of both material practices and cultural logics) as an emancipatory critique. Finally, if avant-garde materiality reproduces the paradox of its avant-garde agency itself (as both interpretable and resistant to interpretation), it may, in its discursive recuperation, find itself by extension everywhere in a form self-reflexive critique, in an endlessly deferred politics of the signifier (Jacques Derrida is thus the philosophical counterpart to Dada after its theory death; 116). This reflexive movement from signifier to discourse, however, may also be seen from the perspective of the material text. Turning Mann's analysis on its head, one may also conclude that at the moment of avant-garde theory death, it is (1) embodied in the material history of individual works; (2) transgressively enacted as a text between work and world; and (3) re-presented in a discourse of desire and negativity. Even if its theory death at the end of history undermines teleology, the avant-garde always claims a material form that, as provoking discourse, continues its logic of critique.

Mann's death of the avant-garde, placing it within a horizon of theory that has little need for any specific history, might equally announce the birth of a new historical account of the avant-garde, one that goes substantially beyond two significant prior moments. In the first, a conventional Hegelian historicism sees the avant-garde as a moment of negativity or refusal that is recuperated either in a diachronic series (the teleology of modernism for Matei Calinescu or Renato Poggioli, leading toward the formal autonomy of literature or art) or in a synchronic totality (the reinforcement of art as institution for Peter Bürger, where critique is exhausted in redefining the nature of art itself).[6] As Mann summarizes these positions, the avant-garde "illuminat[es] in retrospect the fact that the historical project of abolishing the bourgeois institution of art was itself nothing more than a phase of that institution's development" (*TD*, 63). In the second, the recuperation of the avant-garde as an example of aesthetic practice is undermined by either a myth of originality that gives evidence of its parasitism on history rather than its autonomy (Rosalind Krauss) or by a cult of the artist whose agency is, in fact, prefigured by institutions (Donald Kuspit).[7] Here, the negativity of the avant-garde is always co-opted by the affirmative culture of institutions, such that, in the end, it can only be defined by them:[8] "What we witness here is less the truth or falseness of autonomous art than the autonomic functioning of the economy in which it must operate" (*TD*, 77). In proposing a matrix of theory as consequence of the death of the avant-garde, however, Mann actually works to preserve the agency of the avant-garde, whose negativity (either radical form or political agency) may now be distributed throughout the social totality as a critical force. Such a relocation of avant-garde agency within the totality of culture, even as discourse, is visible in concrete historical developments such as the influence of the Russian Formalists' foregrounding of the material signifier on modern advertising (from El Lissitzky to the Bauhaus) and film (Sergei Eisenstein), as well as on modernist literary theory, or the example provided by surrealism of an antirepresentational politics of desire that influenced both the fashion industry and post-Freudian psychoanalysis.[9] While Mann's discursive horizon of theory does not account, as it should, for constructions of *cultural* discourse, it still provides a way of understanding the agency of the avant-garde within a totality that may only begin with the death of its purported recuperation. The death of the avant-garde in this sense turns out to be an anticipatory figure for what I will call the constructivist moment.

Moving toward a consideration of the specific historical forms of the avant-garde, it is not surprising that Mann's account of the Language School of poetry is as unapologetically prospective and historical as it is, even as he claims the avant-garde itself as over:

> Even as these obituaries were peaking — around 1975, when the most was being said about how little there was to say — a network of so-called language-centered writers was emerging, largely in the San Francisco Bay Area and New York. Experimental, deeply critical of current poetic practice and the ideological character of ordinary and literary language, often theoretically militant about their nonreferential and writer-oriented poetics, with their own presses, distribution systems, reviewing apparatus, and public forums, they seem in every respect exactly the sort of group that would once have been considered avant-garde without question. And yet it is indeed difficult to apply this label to the language poets, for the cultural model it denotes seems awkward, outmoded, and exhausted. (*TD*, 32)

In the necessity to locate its work in a historical succession of avant-gardes, the Language School may be thus characterized as encountering its failure at the outset. As I wrote in 1985, "I, too, have been called a Surrealist" — and have been equally embarrassed by the ascription.[10] A notion of the avant-garde carrying with it the dead weight of Calinescu and Poggioli's rigid and prefigured historicism, as well as the live bruises of Krauss and Kuspit's pronouncements on the avant-garde's unoriginality, has indeed been an embarrassment. It has led to a renewed form of originary authorship, for one thing, whose politics are under revision if not unrecuperable, but which even in its negativity depends on conservative cultural institutions to give it publicity, legitimacy, and, finally, reward.[11] The question of definition, in any case, is central: the politics of the name *avant-garde* (as well as many names *for* the avant-garde) — as the moment of a recuperated and thus contradictory critique of representation — invokes a form of self-canceling negativity that undermines avant-garde agency at the same time that it is identified as its proper technique. Language writing, thus, is "so-called" by its advocates and detractors, indicating an ambivalence toward identity that has often been mistaken as a refusal of recognition.[12] As Bob Perelman has written, "Why didn't we simply name this body of writing? While we were clearly dealing with the subject of language writing, we avoided that name."[13]

Rejecting the nominal instability of "so-called language writing" as merely another instance of avant-garde paradox, we may look instead for a historical account of the evolution of its name. The term *language-centered* was first used in print, in the history of the Language School, in a headnote to "The Dwelling Place: 9 Poets," Ron Silliman's 1973 selection of recent work published in the ethnopoetic journal *Alcheringa*: "9 poets out of the present, average age 28 . . . called variously 'language centered,' 'minimal,' 'non-referential formalism,' 'diminished referentiality,' 'structuralist.' Not a *group* but a *tendency* in the work of many."[14] In the context of *Alcheringa*, "language-centered" connoted a culturally holistic notion of "total poetics," in editor Jerome Rothenberg's terms, as much as a linguistic turn to structuralist theory.[15] By the mid 1970s, both "language poet" and "language writing" were in common use, descriptively and pejoratively, by virtue of the tendency's emerging visibility first in San Francisco and then in New York; individual writers began to be described (or baited) as language poets in the late 1970s.[16] In 1978, Bruce Andrews and Charles Bernstein, after some discussion with other writers, named their journal *L=A=N=G=U=A=G=E*, spacing the letters with equal signs.[17] The secret history of the equal signs begins here, with the question of the original intention of the name of the journal of a school that was seen as undermining authorial originality.

If the author is suspended in the naming of the journal, we may consider an alternate scenario to connect a view of language to the construction of the school. Of crucial importance is that the graphically modified noun *language* was used to name a journal that published articles *about* language-centered writing, so-called, rather than examples *of* it — a controversial claim on my part that depends on a distinction of genre between articles *about* poetics and examples *of* poetry (or between description and enactment as discursive modes). *L=A=N=G=U=A=G=E* stood as a name for a body of work that can be represented but only indirectly presented, in three senses: (1) examples *of* language-centered writing itself were not the primary content of the journal; (2) articles *about* language-centered writing were not identical to their referents, even if a horizon was imagined where sign and referent would meet; (3) as a result, the name of the aesthetic tendency that produced this referential schism would partake of the nonreferentiality of the work itself, which it represented, as it were, in absentia. Nonreferentiality, thus, was central to the discourse of the journal, not just the texts it referred to. Later, when asked, in an interview with Andrew Ross about the politics of the name, the editors provided this account of the relation between the name of the journal and that which it represents:

> If we're talking about the work we focused on in editing *L=A=N=G=U=A=G=E*, let's first explode any notion of collective self-designation. Beyond a labelling tag, what could it possibly (and precisely) consist of? No single origin or destination or dominant style or ideology marks this diverse body of radical, or radial eccentricities. And its very heterogeneity, its swirl of concerns, is what gives it some insurance against a reductionist reception. . . . That kind of reception involves a taming, a domestication, a shoring up of the old walls (however flashily ornamented by a tokenism of the new, a kind of repressive desublimation). Any reading of this kind of poetry, however, would build some wedges against its smooth assimilation as just another addendum to the 20th century curriculum.[18]

In their account, the name stands as an arbitrary sign (in the Saussurean sense) for an unrepresentable "swirl of concerns"; this is an antifoundationalist, even antinomian, claim. This tendency toward an antinomian, antidefinitional poetics, opening on a permanent instability of reference, was immediately recuperated in the initial academic reception of language writing when critics Marjorie Perloff and Jerome McGann each used the name of the journal, *L=A=N=G=U=A=G=E*, as a definitional term for "language poets" and "language writing," "so-called"[19] — an act repudiated by six writers on the West Coast in the tendency who did not feel adequately represented by the journal's name.[20] In Ross's early critique, on the other hand, the material texts and networks, rather than the name, of the Language School are used to define it.[21] At the very least, a politics of naming and being named has been central to its history, in at least three senses: in the development of its characteristic genres, in the emergence of its supporting theory, and in a permanent crisis of representation throughout its reception. Such a permanent crisis — and its capacity to continue spinning out a "swirl of concerns" — is precisely what Mann means when he says the avant-garde foregrounds "the fundamentally discursive character of art."

Mann's notion of theory death, then, occurred early in the history of language writing, beginning with the negative referentiality of the journal's dispersed name and its relation to the emerging movement. What resulted has been a series of historical conflicts between the tendency and its names, between definitional terms like *language-centered writing/language poet/language writing* and proper names like *L=A=N=G=U=A=G=E*, indicating a dialectic of theory and practice that continues to evolve. The conflict over names based on *language* denotes, as well, not simply a kind of writing but a social formation, not just an aesthetic tendency but a group of writers split between its two major urban centers, San Francisco and New York, that gives a historical context for the displaced names of its theory death.[22] Both cities had witnessed avant-garde formations in immediately preceding periods, with the San Francisco Renaissance and the New York School, and conflict remains over questions of cultural legitimacy and the avant-garde, as located either in the metropolitan center or on the marginalized coast.[23] There is thus a way in which *language* takes on a supplementary value in terms of the tendency's divided social formation as a kind of placeless place, one of utopian fantasy and negative address from which, it may have been hoped, the work would emerge.[24] This movement, of naming and canceling the name, is not simply one of definition (of a specific method, technique, or style) but of a discursive formation — and it is here that Mann's notion of theory death suggests a larger cultural poetics, not merely a stylistic tendency, emerging from the centripetal and centrifugal tensions of the school that was "made to be broken."[25]

Andrews and Bernstein, when questioned by Ross, propose first and foremost a question of word meaning as a counter to the inevitable theory death of academic reception. The fact that we cannot say what "language writing" *is* ought to force us to reconsider the conceptual framework (the conventional history of the avant-garde, for example) in which it is used. The referential indeterminacy of the material text is the primary guarantee of a politics of new meaning that resists its recuperation, as it generates considerations of new meaning itself in its own counterdiscourse. My own response to this question in the interview with Ross published in the same forum, on the other hand, focused on the relation of the name to the social formation of the group of writers being named — a historical rather than a definitional account of oppositional discourse. I likened the tension over the name of the group to the politics of the formation and dissolution of a group of anti-American student radicals in Nagisa Oshima's film *Night and Fog in Japan* (1960). The film is a tragic history and psychological study of a radical group that placed itself at the margins of society, a micropolitics of the breakdown of oppositional consensus:

> The form of belief that held together, violently, such a group of variously motivated individuals is, at the moment of its transformation, rendered objective — and at the same time the belief fails. Clearly individuals might continue to hold some of their collective beliefs . . . but the form

> of the group itself cannot survive objectification. It turns out that all along none of its members really understood what it was they were saying, even though it was said repetitiously and at length — in all-night discussions of political theory, in slogans at the barricades, and in tracts on revolutionary justice — while given meaning by the provocation of the group's enemies outside. The centripetal movement of the group had revolved around a hollow center — as long as there was force and resistance to keep it in motion. This is very like the process of collective idea-formation in the arts.[26]

Here, I am describing a dynamic of collective identity formation at a specific historical moment, one in which participants in a radical group are held together, in spite of their internal disagreements, in a form of negative solidarity in opposition to a common foe. What appears as the belief that holds the group together turns out to be, in fact, merely provisional. When the competitive tensions among the group lead to its inevitable undoing, one may ask, does its belief or the political moment cease to exist or have meaning?

There was indeed "a collectively held set of beliefs, and an absolute recognition of them," among the poets who came together in the mid-1970s to mid-1980s. These beliefs give meaning to the name Language School as it confers a historical status on the forms that were developed and used by writers in that group — but only after the initial moment of theory death in the naming of *L=A=N=G=U=A=G=E*. These forms of writing were as much discursive as authorial, both in shared assumptions of individual practice and in the counterinstitutions of publication, distribution, reviewing, and criticism that developed with the school's emergence. In turn, these counterinstitutions, and the examples of cultural practice they provide, are historical; we may find in a politics of language that writes its own theory death the prescience of a historical reflexivity equally articulated in such real-time politics as alternative publishing and the Poetics Listserv. In what follows, I want to develop a fuller account of the politics of the name, signified by the equal signs separating the letters of *L=A=N=G=U=A=G=E*, for the Language School's continuing development, seen as a combination of textual materiality and cultural discourse.

POSTREVOLUTIONARY POETICS

To look for historical support — much needed in a post–theory death environment — for the importance of the avant-garde for cultural politics, one place to start is Julia Kristeva's *Revolution in Poetic Language*.[27] In its reception, Kristeva's *thèse d'état* has been valued for its derivation, after Jacques Lacan, of the material poetics of the semiotic, composed of the unintegrated remnants of the body in pieces at the moment of ego formation in the imaginary. Kristeva's dialectic of semiotic and symbolic was equally informed by the literary currents of the 1960s in avant-garde critical journals such as *Tel Quel*, which saw the emergence of new genres of literary form as well as the reception of the dialogism of Mikhail Bakhtin.[28] But although Kristeva made central use of examples of the historical avant-garde, from Mallarmé to Joyce, in her account of literary semiosis, few critics have followed her lead by extending her discussion to include the contemporary avant-garde.[29] While Kristeva's work has been widely used by feminist critics, her privileging of examples from the historical avant-garde has been seen by some to reflect a masculinist bias.[30]

One reason for Kristeva's inability to develop a more thorough account of avant-garde poetics, this response suggests, is her shortsightedness regarding her literary examples. Although she wrote *Revolution in Poetic Language* immediately after a historical period in which many literary works that exemplified her notion of text were produced, her examples are canonically author centered, even in their reliance on avant-garde figures such as Lautréamont and Mallarmé, and thus do not fully respond to the cultural challenge to authority and subjectivity of May 1968 (she defended her thesis in 1973).[31] As a direct consequence of May 1968, Kristeva's theoretical account of authorial subjectivity depends on a breaking down of ego boundaries within a larger social matrix: "The subject never *is*. The *subject* is only the *signifying process* and he appears only as a *signifying practice*, that is, only when he is absent *within the position* out of which social, historical, and signifying activity unfolds" (*RPL*, 215). In preserving authorship, however, her literary examples distribute this shattering of the ego in a double movement of analysis: she constructs a poetics of modernist autonomy as constituted by the heterogeneous but that only retrospectively (at the moment of its death?) opens up to it. So Lautréamont's poetry can "be understood as [a] heterogeneous practice [of] the positing of the unary [*sic*] subject, and, through this unity, an exploration of the semiotic operation that moves through it" (218). Kristeva's poetics of revolution thus falls short in not moving from autonomous form, however riven by the semiotic, to a development of multiauthored discourse as the necessary consequence of subject formation at a revolutionary moment: a suprasubjective subjectivity, a subject position that, even if impossible, embraces totality. Rather, it has led in its feminist reception to a poetics that contrasts the pre-Oedipal use of language by women experimental writers to the Oedipal reproduction of the masculinist canon.

An opposite account of the relation of subject to totality is given in Michel Foucault's notion of discursive formation. As developed in *The Archaeology of Knowledge* (written at the same time as the events of May 1968 and published in 1969),[32] Foucault's concept of suprasubjective discourse, which also partly originates in avant-garde practice, has proven productive not only for the epistemic methods of New Historicism but for the continued tradition of ideology criticism in the work of Ernesto Laclau, Chantal Mouffe, Slavoj Žižek, and Judith Butler. Foucault's key concept of *discursive formation* begins by severing teleology from totality, via a Nietzschean reading of the destructive gaps and fissures that open up in positive history, and then goes on to construct a notion of discourse from relations of "regularity in dispersion" that will later become important for Laclau and Mouffe.[33] In his undoing of the unitary form of both subject and object, Foucault begins with a literary example: "The book is not simply the object that one holds in one's hands; and it cannot remain within the little parallelepiped that contains it: its unity is variable and relative. As soon as one questions that unity, it loses its self-evidence; it indicates itself, constructs itself, only on the basis of a complex field of discourse" (*AK*, 23). The constructivist moment, rather than any theory death, occurs in the discursive opening up of the form of the object. The relation between object and the discourse that constructs it, in turn, can only be known in terms of an order or series of objects, in a movement from a privileged object to objects in a series or held together in a group. On analogy to the segmented discourse of structural linguistics (the notion, from Roman Jakobson and others, of a speech chain made up of a series of equivalent syntactical units, and which is foregrounded in poetry),[34] Foucault's discursive formation is a mode of organization of non–self-identical objects/subjects within an overdetermined field that is not founded by a presumed underlying regularity — but that, in the fact of relation, achieves it:

> Two objects, or two types of enunciation, or two concepts may appear, in the same discursive formation, without being able to enter — under pain of manifest contradiction or inconsequence — the same series of statements. They are then characterized as *points of equivalence*: the two incompatible elements are formed in the same way and on the basis of the same rules; the conditions of their appearance are identical; they are situated at the same level; and instead of constituting a mere defect of

> coherence, they form an alternative. . . . They are characterized as *link points of systematization*: on the basis of each of these equivalent, yet incompatible elements, a coherent series of objects, forms of statement, and concepts has been derived (with, in each series, possible new points of incompatibility). (*AK*, 65–66)

At the same time, the notion of *equivalence* accounts for relations of similarity (based on resemblance) and contiguity (based on discursive proximity rather than essential likeness) in establishing an overdetermined field, which is thereby held together in a form of "regularity in dispersion." This notion of equivalence is given important political interpretation in Laclau and Mouffe's account of hegemony, but with the addition of a concept of social antagonism that gives the discursive formation its unity.[35] Later, Žižek will call for a "going beyond" of discourse analysis in developing this concept of antagonism.[36]

Returning to literature, I want to pursue how a Foucauldian notion of equivalence suggests ways of moving from literary autonomy, of both book and author, toward a form of regularity in dispersion that may better account for the suprasubjectivity of avant-garde tendencies in relation to the impossible, even self-destructive, revolutionary subject positions that are its model. We may imagine that members of Oshima's radical group are held together, in their conflicting interests, by virtue of just such a notion of equivalence, which refuses to surrender unlikeness and difference but that is articulated against an antagonistic other — the form of discursive hegemony (the U.S.-Japan Friendship Treaty) that they are opposing and which unites them in negative solidarity. The centripetal tendency of the group, its capacity for staying together, is a result of its elements' overdetermination — the *jouissance* of forcing like and unlike together in the same series. Its centrifugal tendency (toward dispersion and history, the theory death that will make it only an example in the textbook of revolutionary politics) is its failure to hold together fundamentally opposed interests. (If this account is true, revolutionary politics will always end as temporarily sutured interests come apart, and by the same token may occur again and again, even after their theoretical death in 1989, because there will always be hegemonic forms of state power that cannot suture opposed interests.)

But what of the avant-garde? The analogy of the equal signs of *L=A=N=G=U=A=G=E* to Foucault's notion of equivalence should be obvious: in uniting a series of like and unlike individual letters together, the logo of the Language School's first theoretical journal performs its "organized violence on language," constructing equivalence as a regularity in dispersion, in its nomination of an avant-garde tendency.[37] (*L* is in fact *not* identical to *A*, except that both are letters; if they were truly identical, rather than discursively equivalent, we could not speak, or we could only say one thing: "L," for example, or "A" — a transposition of Hegel's refutation of identity into a text in which all letters say the same thing.) And *L=A=N=G=U=A=G=E* did indeed bring together a more disparate array of avant-garde writing (even if unified by techniques that privilege the letter or the material sign) than could be seen as expressing a single aesthetic position. Such a juxtaposition of like and unlike, however, does not simply release the name into a form of textual productivity, but provides a basis for the overdetermination of a discursive formation. This is evident in the form of the journal itself: due to considerations of space, but also to highlight the work's ephemerality, *L=A=N=G=U=A=G=E* presented authorial subject positions in the abbreviated, segmented form of short statements and notes, juxtaposed within the journal's overarching form. This construction of a series of equivalent subject/objects was undertaken, as well, not only in the total form of the journal but in many of its categorical subgroups: features on individual authors; bibliographies of literary magazines; forums on selected political or literary topics, and so on. The emergence of something like a postmodern library science appears, for instance, in editor Bruce Andrews's compilation of current "Articles," "a Catalog/Bibliography of recent articles on language and related aesthetic and social issues, from 54 journals: Part One" (no. 3, June 1978), or in a forum on "Non-Poetry" where "a number of writers were asked to list or briefly discuss non-poetry books read recently that have had a significant influence on their thinking or writing" (no. 7, March 1979). The aesthetics of lists is balanced by an anti-institutional nonchalance of editorial style; the working relations of its two coeditors, Andrews and Bernstein, perform their version of Foucault's "regularity in dispersion," with Andrews personifying the former principle and Bernstein, no doubt, the latter (fig. 5).

It is important for the development of Language School poetics that *L=A=N=G=U=A=G=E* did not publish primary texts, even as it questioned the boundary between poetry and poetics, text and discourse. The brief notes in the journal were *about* poetry and only secondarily instances *of* it. Evidence for this claim, which goes to the heart of an ongoing debate about the nature of genre in the poetics of the Language School, seems straightforward: there are few if any instances in which the short theoretical pieces published in *L=A=N=G=U=A=G=E* appeared in their authors' books of

L=A=N=G=U=A=G=E

NUMBER 13 DECEMBER 1980

REWRITING MARX

The poetry of societies in which the capitalist mode of production prevails appears as an "immense collection of books"; the individual book appears as its elementary form. Our investigation begins with the analysis of the book.

The book is, first of all, an external object, a thing which through its qualities satisfies human needs of a literary kind.

Objects of reading become books only because they are the products of the writing of private individuals who work independently of each other. The sum total of the writing of all these private individuals forms the aggregate writing of society. *Since the writers do not come into social contact until they exchange the products of their writing*, the specific social characteristics of their private writings appear only within this exchange. In other words, the writing of the private individual manifests itself as an element of the total writing of society *only through the relations* which the act of exchange establishes between the texts, and, through their mediation, between the writers. To the writers, therefore, the social relations between their private writing appear as what they are, *i.e.*, they do not appear as direct social relations between persons in their work, but rather as material relations between persons and social relations between texts.

However, a text can be useful, and a product of human writing, without being a book. She who satisfies her own need with the text of her own writing admittedly creates reading-values, but not books. In order to produce the latter, she must not only produce reading-values, *but reading-values for others,* social reading-values. (And not merely for others. In order to become a book, the text must be transferred to the other person, for whom it serves as a reading-value, *through the medium of exchange.*)

RON SILLIMAN

5. L=A=N=G=U=A=G=E, *no. 13 (December 1980), ed. Bruce Andrews and Charles Bernstein.*

poetry — even if dismantling the opposition of theory and practice, expository prose and language-centered poetry, was often an explicit concern for many writers. This claim about the continuing relevance of genre to language writing is crucial: if language writing indeed succeeded in producing texts that do not have any generic specificity, the literariness that results would be transcendental rather than historically produced. To maintain the historical specificity of literature, it is necessary to have a notion of genre as produced in specific contexts.

We may consider the literary work, rather than theoretical claims, of the editors of *L=A=N=G=U=A=G=E* as evidence here. The disruption of expository conventions in Charles Bernstein's essay "Artifice of Absorption," whose argument is broken into what may seem like free-verse poetic lines, is still addressed to the form of the essay: it was published in a book of essays.[38] While Bernstein frequently incorporates discursive language in books of poetry, his poetic effects are different from his expository ones simply because the transgression of expository norms still preserves them as a moment of negativity; poetic norms have different claims, whose transgression is dissimilar to that of exposition. Bruce Andrews has gone as far as any author toward a demonstration of a literary praxis that unites poetic language and exposition; the prose texts of *I Don't Have Any Paper So Shut Up (or, Social Romanticism)* and the more poetic critical pieces in *Paradise and Method: Poetics and Praxis* may be read as producing similar textual effects. Again, however, the generic expectations of their material occasions

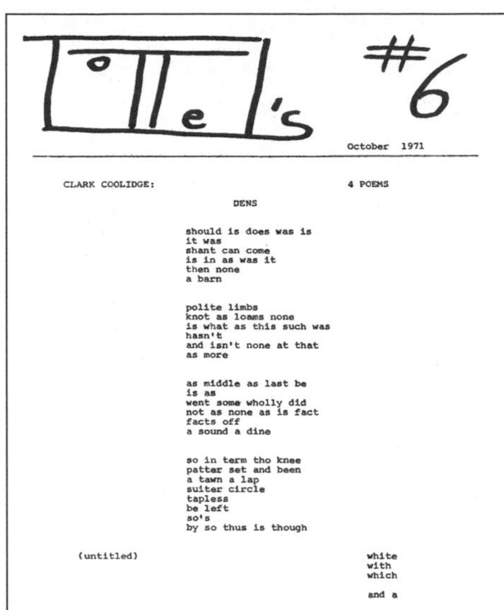

Tottel's #6

October 1971

CLARK COOLIDGE: 4 POEMS

DENS

should is does was is
it was
shant can come
is in as was it
then none
a barn

polite limbs
knot as loams none
is what as this such was
hasn't
and isn't none at that
as more

as middle as last be
is as
went some wholly did
not as none as is fact
facts off
a sound a dine

so in term tho knee
patter set and been
a tawn a lap
suiter circle
tapless
be left
so's
by so thus is though

(untitled)

white
with
which

and a

6. Tottel's, *no. 6 (October 1971), ed. Ron Silliman.*

A Hundred Posters

#26 February 78

editor / Alan Davies publisher / Rebecca Muller

copyright 1978 Alan Davies
individual works copyright 1978 the authors

Charles Bernstein:

THREE OR FOUR THINGS I KNOW ABOUT HIM

1. "...the task of history, once the world beyond the truth has disappeared, is to establish the truth of this world...."--Marx

2. its like a living death going to work every day sort of like being in a tomb to sit in your office you close the door theres the typewriter theres three or four maybe three hours of work to be done between that nine oclock and five maybe i listen to the news on wbai if i didnt get it the night before that comes on at nine oclock i read the newspaper i do anything to distract myself sometimes i sleep til around eleve i put both feet up on my desk and i put my hand against my hea and i close my eyes the time passes if i listen to the radio i type a letter i write an article that would make the article that i wrote for that medical newspaper seem like proust in comparison or sometimes i think initially the job seeme more bearable more to the point of just a diversion and source of income for a while until i got unemployment not now but mostly its just that i'm taking things in a bleaker way i'm not quite sure why that is of course the writing writing even talking like this always seems to me perfectly at peace so that i was thinking i dont know this could be my own you know this could be sort of the the source of my crazy hood/ness that the things that are really valuable dont so much happen as you experience them in the actual present a lot of what i experience is just a tremendous sense of space and vacant space at that sort of like a stanley kubrick film sort of a lot of objects floating separately which i dont particularly feel do anything for me give me anything make me feel good and when i do feel almost best is when i dont care whether they make me feel good whether they have any relation to me thats a very pleasant thats a real feeling of value in the present

7. A Hundred Posters, *no. 26 (February 1978), ed. Alan Davies (Cambridge, Mass.).*

(*Shut Up* is published by an alternative publisher; *Paradise* by a university press) preclude their being seen as antigeneric species of literature in identical senses. A relation of equivalence may be implied, but it is always a matter of discursive construction rather than identity.[39]

As an opposite example, *This*, the magazine of language-centered writing I edited from 1971 to 1982, presented primary texts rather than theoretical or secondary accounts. In the next chapter, I argue that *This* provided a historical context for a series of literary developments that were reflexively undertaken by more or less the same group of writers. This development occurred in terms of a dynamics of feedback, in which there was not simply an originary moment of definition or refusal but a continuous, dialogic practice out of which the forms of language-centered writing emerged.[40] Above all, this development was historical, helping to bring together the group of authors who made up the discursive formation of authorial subject positions in *L=A=N=G=U=A=G=E*, by reflexively defining the range of formal possibilities of their work. Other publications (figs. 6–15), such as *Roof*, *A Hundred Posters*, *Là-Bas*, and *Hills*, as well as presses such as Tuumba and The Figures, were venues for the continuous emergence of the Language School in the 1970s, but in a different way from what took place in *L=A=N=G=U=A=G=E*.[41] I am not, here, simply claiming that the form

ROOFIV:from
Tamokaoccu
renceoftune
atcenterTibe
tanrosecont
estofBardsth
ebridefromw
avebuglessbo
wingsbacken
dingfall77 $3

8. Roof, *no. 4 (fall 1977), ed. James Sherry (New York).*

9. Hills, *no. 4 (May 1977), ed. Bob Perelman (San Francisco).*

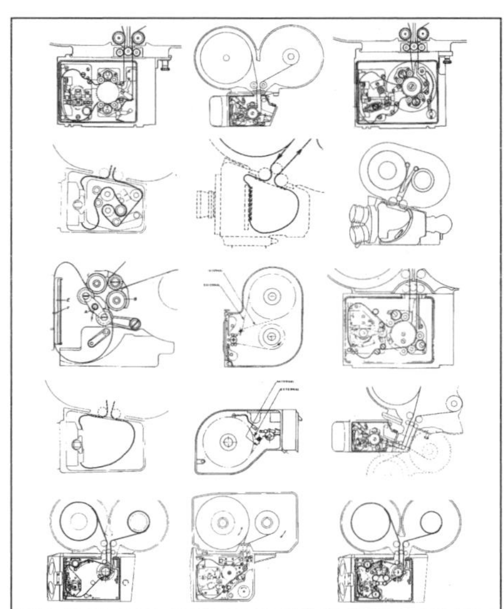

10. Oculist Witnesses, *no. 3 (fall 1976), ed. Alan Davies (Cambridge, Mass.).*

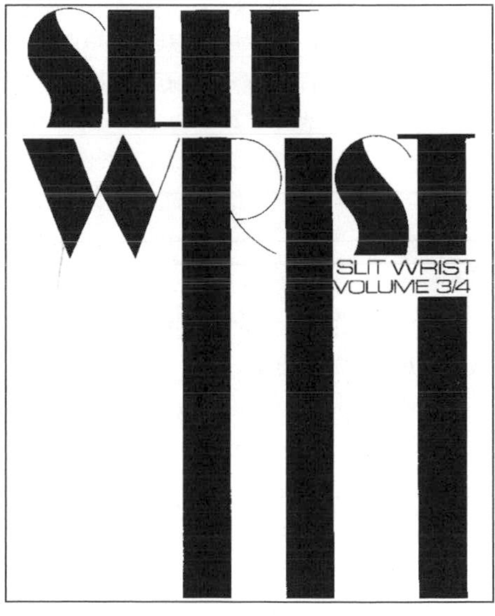

11. Slit Wrist, *nos. 3/4 (spring 1977), ed. Terry Swanson (New York).*

12. Miam, *no. 6 (October 1978), ed. Tom Mandel (San Francisco).*

13. Là-Bas, *no. 7 (May 1977), ed. Douglas Messerli (Washington, D.C.).*

of an avant-garde magazine is sufficient to form a discursive series; rather, the little magazines themselves comprise such a series, with *L=A=N=G=U=A=G=E* taking its cue from their discursive relationships in constituting a school. While an equivalence of authorial positions does describe *L=A=N=G=U=A=G=E*'s form of reflexive construction, it is also by representing literature as taking place elsewhere, from an outside being integrated within it, that the journal constitutes a Foucauldian discursive formation — in other words, there is an outside consisting of many published texts that were integrated into the journal. The concept of discursive formation thus provides an alternative to the negative totality of theory death, which is supposed to take place in a crisis at the end of the movement's history, rather than at its moment of emergence. Theory death happened not in the literary origins of the Language School — which occurred with the development of new forms of writing in *This* and other journals — but in the consolidation of their initial reception as a school. Locating literature elsewhere, in elided origins or not, recasts the negativity of theory death as a locus of productivity within the utopian/dystopian nowhere of language. So it was that the utopian horizon of language — as constitutive of the cultural politics of the Language School — was reorganized as discourse, in a spatial condensation that provided a new site for cultural construction, if on the ruins of a more capacious imagination.[42]

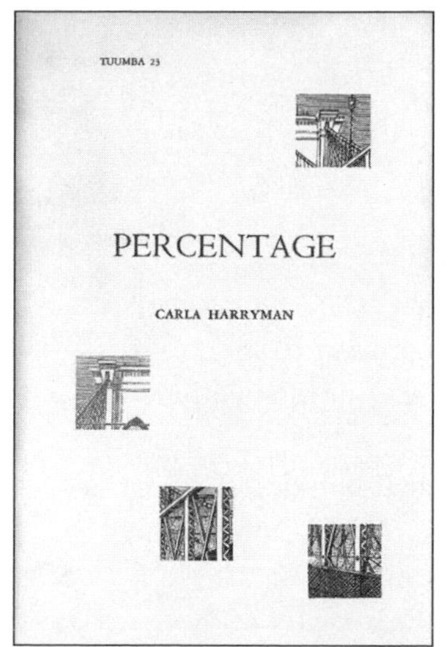

14. *Carla Harryman,* Percentage, *Tuumba no. 23 (September 1979), ed. Lyn Hejinian (Berkeley, Calif.).*

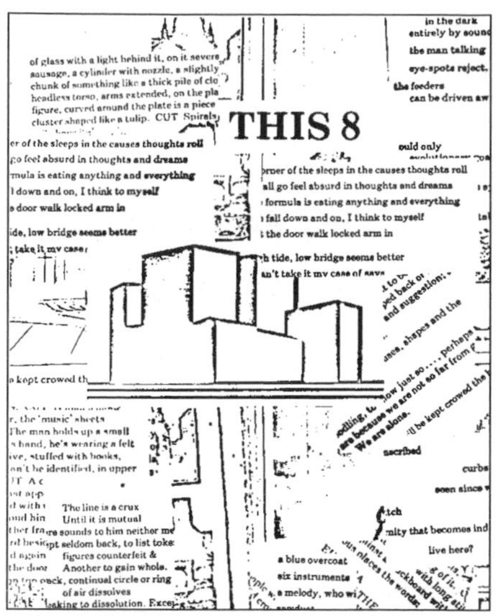

15. This, *no. 8 (spring 1978), ed. Barrett Watten (San Francisco).*

If *L=A=N=G=U=A=G=E* is not simply the theory death of the agency of the letter in the discursive formation of the Language School, what is its relation to the literature it represents? Against a teleological model that ends in the premature theory death of *L=A=N=G=U=A=G=E,* I would like to investigate an alternative one, in a work of the same period that reconfigures the politics of authorship in a form of collective practice. *Legend*, collectively written by Bruce Andrews, Charles Bernstein, Ray DiPalma, Steve McCaffery, and Ron Silliman and published by L=A=N=G=U=A=G=E/Segue in 1980, is located precisely in the place of utopian elsewhere/nowhere invoked by *L=A=N=G=U=A=G=E*'s discursive formation of authorial subject positions.[43] While the journal was immediately recognized as representing an avant-garde tendency in its theoretical distance from literary form, *Legend* demonstrates new formal possibilities of writing in the dialogic, collective practice of its five authors (fig. 16). The counterhegemonic discourse asserted in *L=A=N=G=U=A=G=E* by virtue of the missing referent of the work (that is, new poetic form) is enacted in *Legend* in various forms of language-centered textuality — generating a wealth of technical innovations, formal possibilities, and new meanings within a space of reflexive dialogue. If a series of like and unlike author positions are drawn together by the equal signs of *L=A=N=G=U=A=G=E,*

Legend's demonstration of complex modes of writing necessarily entails a riskier, more difficult negotiation of group politics as it enacts the revolution of avant-garde poetry in new and productive forms.

LEGEND'S TEXT

Legend is a text, lots of it — 246 pages, $8\frac{1}{2} \times 11$, in twenty-six unnumbered sections. The work explodes the assumption of monologic authorship, dismantling and reconfiguring it in a series of multiauthored sections, each determined by the capacity of different techniques to construct meaning — in what seems not just an experimental but almost a scientific approach to writing, combining preexisting, improvised, and graphic elements in an open and evolving compositional matrix. In the work as a whole, an overdetermined textuality — literally the free play of the material text — results from the cumulative effect of its diverse array of formal procedures. These can be categorized in groups of single- or multiauthored sections: (1) single-authored statements (one per author, each exactly one hundred lines); (2) texts by two or three authors exploring specific modes of writing arrived at in the process of dialogic improvisation; and (3) a multiauthored collaboration that repeats the total form of the work in its final section. Individual sections may be grouped, as well, as texts whose dominants, or overarching devices, in Jakobson's sense, are (1) thematic argument; (2) the exploration of the signifying potential of specified lin-

L E G E N D

Bruce Andrews

Charles Bernstein

Ray DiPalma

Steve McCaffery

Ron Silliman

16. Cover of Legend *(New York: L=A=N=G=U=A=G=E/Segue, 1980).*

guistic levels: sentence, phrase, lexeme, morpheme, phoneme; (3) the exploration of the signifying potential of graphic signs, both linguistic and nonlinguistic; (4) forms of intertextuality created by mixing modes of signification that suspend authorial intention as they explore the space between subject positions; and (5) dialogic argument.[44] While the first three represent areas developed by many authors in the Language School in the period, the last two, implicit or explicit forms of dialogue, are foregrounded in *Legend*'s textual politics.

The five single-authored sections (which, though unnumbered, are sections 1, 4, 7, 12, and 17 of a total of twenty-six) provide an opening orientation and thematic continuity that the work gradually moves away from, toward a final horizon of collective authorship. Clearly, this formal progression is a political allegory, just as, in Oshima's film, individual interests bound up in a group dynamic of radical tendency in its centripetal/centrifugal tension may move toward either dissolution or redefinition. In *Legend*, each author begins from a position of self-presentation identified with one-sentence propositions. Even if there is little of expressive subjectivity here, each author organizes a matrix of statements that bears his own idiosyncratic stamp, a form of legend to each one's map of potential meaning. Bernstein's section, "My Life as Monad," which opens the book, is a decentered portrait that juxtaposes irreducible units of language ("Nutshells") with autobiographical accounts: "Transfixed in a dream state between 9 & 10 where I am just about awake & only the power of this dream unreeling in my head keeps my eyes shut as if saying 'shut up & listen to this' as I struggle to get up." Material textuality is at once language as such and autobiographical material in the psychoanalytic sense; the textual processes at work here start to break down the polarity between them. Silliman's section, the next in the single-authored set, demonstrates the use of monadic sentence units in paratactic series — what he notably theorized at the time as the New Sentence — which work to undermine normative sentence-level autonomy by means of the transgressive use of discursive anaphora.[45] Technically put, the NP nodes of Silliman's sentences are occupied by the pronoun shifter *it*, which anaphorically shifts reference from the NP position by virtue of the indeterminate propositional content of the S node to the next linguistic level, discourse. I am arguing here that the referentiality of the pronoun *it* depends on its position within discourse, aligning with the indeterminate topic of Silliman's poem, an "it" that is collectively held in common by members of the group, as well as at the sentence level. *It* becomes the topic of a discourse of one hundred sentences, referring to an

1. It is a five-pointed star in three dimensional space.
2. It is words.
3. It is a group, not a series.
4. It is the end of atomization.
5. It is deliberate.
6. It is the product of labor.
7. It is correspondence.
8. It is New York, Toronto and San Francisco.
9. It seeks the post-referential.
10. It dissolves the individual.
11. It is tribal.
12. It is male.
13. It is behavior.
14. It does not conceal.
15. It shares the labor but does not divide it.
16. It could do anything.
17. It is a poem.
18. It is a very simple poem.
19. It looks back on the invention of writing sadly but without regret.
20. It is not a story.
21. It is a determinate coordinate on the grid of language and history.
22. It is an articulation.
23. It has words that dissolve as soon as you read them and reform as soon as you read them again.

14

17. From Legend, *section 4 (Silliman).*

emerging, collaborative product being constructed out of discrete propositional units, in other words, the work as a whole (fig. 17). These are the first ten:

1. It is a five-pointed star in three dimensional space.
2. It is words.
3. It is a group, not a series.
4. It is the end of atomization.
5. It is deliberate.
6. It is the product of labor.
7. It is correspondence.
8. It is New York, Toronto and San Francisco.
9. It seeks the post-referential.
10. It dissolves the individual. (*L*, 14)

The work's attributes, it turns out, construct a form of predication not specified by the unit structures of the New Sentence. In seeking the post-referential and dissolving the individual, they move toward a horizon of intertextuality that assumes, in a terminology that Kristeva derives from Edmund Husserl, a positing of the sentence as a unit of meaning she calls the "thetic."[46] In Kristeva's account, to achieve signification and ultimately enter into the symbolic (the order of language), the subject must separate itself from its object in the act of positing in what she calls the "thetic break," bringing it into contact with the pre-Oedipal traces of the semiotic.

Linguistic propositions are formed in the moment of the thetic break, which is associated with two moments in the formation of the ego: the Lacanian mirror stage, and the realization of the threat of castration. In a thumbnail sketch of these dynamics, "The gap between the imaged ego and drive motility, between the mother and the demand made on her, is precisely the break that establishes what Lacan calls the place of the Other as the place of the 'signifier'" (48). Silliman's use of the pronoun *it* occurs precisely at this intersection of propositional content and psychoanalytic form. The signifer *it* appears at the place of a gap in signification; it does not refer to any object, but rather opens up a gap in reference that is then displaced onto discourse as a whole. For Kristeva, this movement to intersubjectivity is a primary instance of the sociality of ego formation: "The subject is hidden 'by an ever purer signifier,'" which may be identified as Silliman's *it*, and "this want-to-be confers on an *other* the role of containing the possibility of signification" (ibid.). The thetic break (here the displaced anaphora of *it*) in the act of positing (which we may identify with the New Sentence in Silliman's oeuvre, as well as with the sentence form in this example) marks "the threshold between two heterogeneous realms: the semiotic and the symbolic" (ibid.).

Just as intertextuality is constructed from the dialectic of symbolic and semiotic after the thetic break, so Silliman's sentences, by means of their anaphoric displacement in a discursive form of intertextual predication (where what is referred to is precisely what is being held in common intertextually: *it*), dissolve toward their collective horizons, both formally and thematically. This social construction accedes to the symbolic insofar as Kristeva's use of the term, unlike Lacan's, describes "an always split unification that is produced by a rupture and is impossible without it" (49). In Silliman's text, it is clear that the primitive sociality of split reference is not lost on him:

> 11. It is tribal.
> 12. It is male.
> 13. It is behavior.
> 14. It does not conceal.
> 15. It shares the labor but does not divide it.
> 16. It could do anything.
> 17. It is a poem. (*L*, 14)

The plot of Silliman's formal allegory — of single sentences suspended within intertextual discourse — is thickening here, moving rapidly beyond the level of formal construction. A reading of a mere seventeen lines begins to bring together both the formal construction and political horizon of the work — revealing a metaleptic discourse (where moments of reference such as "it" can be said to refer only to the entire text) as site of a counterhegemony that breaks down individual boundaries, both of person and of writing.[47] The specific attributes of this intertextuality — the poetic as tribal, male, and collective for Silliman — are invoked in an allegory of form that clearly wants to exceed individual authorship.

This intersubjective allegory is also explored in DiPalma's section. Where Silliman employs an abstract pronoun shifter *it* to arrive at the horizon of discourse, DiPalma opens his text to many pronouns, focusing on tensions between *you* and *I*, with positions along the way for *he*, *she*, and *everyone*. The propositional content of these sentences is, after Jakobson and Emile Benveniste, suspended in the shifting referentiality of pronouns, so that the status of the enounced subject (*sujet d'énoncé*) of DiPalma's discourse is indeterminate in relation to its pronominal enunciation (*sujet d'énonciation*):[48]

> 90. The only writing that interests me is my own.
> 91. I went into the orange grove, half weeping, half laughing, and completely drunk.
> 92. I give up and lean forward.
> 93. He liked to warm his brandy over a candle.
> 94. He had every possible phobia. (*L*, 38)

Is the subject position of the author represented by the self-reflexivity of "the only writing that interests me is my own," or is the author revealed in the text of a Kewpie-doll starlet's Hollywood memoir? The reader is not so gullible, DiPalma seems to say, that she will take at face value the propositional truth of either of these readings. In order to process such an abstracted use of pronouns — as standing in for other people as their textual representations — we must achieve the same horizon of intersubjectivity that is demanded by the strictly linguistic devices Silliman uses (the placeholding *it*). Both McCaffery's and Andrews's sections, while not linguistic allegories in the more technical senses of the first three, undermine the coherence of discourse by means of the incommensurability of sentence-level propositions. Each idiosyncratic sequence of disjunct propositions constructs a one-hundred-line discourse of a kind of social ideolect that draws on exterior, linguistic resources as well as authorial, subjective ones. In McCaffery, a sentence such as "95. One puts the ice cream to one's bare chest first, *then* one wonders why" conveys a fascination with potential or indeterminate meaning that adds up to a form of reflexive inquiry:

96. We all thought of writing the i as an I, but then we realized how the one would be two and the other one, one.
97. He's biting his nails as I continue writing.
98. Heraldry in Montana at the end of his seventieth year, after even the bed-sheets had been fossilized.
99. There was a particular speech from his muscles that he called reading.
100. The endless game was of names, and differences, and placement. (110)

On the other hand, Andrews's form of textual practice is more outer-directed — an instance of what he has elsewhere called a language-centered "social work."[49] A deliberate undermining of local coherence is formally enacted in the discursive dissonance of his propositional units, as well as in their refusal of sentence boundary, numbered framing, or punctuation. The high degree of propositional irony, or displaced reference, in Andrews becomes a social allegory, as well, as it makes language a counter for a deferred utopia in which negativity is inscribed in the gap opened up in the act of sentence-level positing. Propositions are autonegations in what amounts to an imitation of the thetic break:

Productive practice is SOILED — hence the *angels* of abstraction
I hope counteracts theatricality
I hope hones in
I hope hinge alterity with self-reference
I hope opposes didacticism in all its forms
    even that of nostalgia
I hope exhibits 'semic Trappism'
What scares me some? (*L*, 188)

Models of textual practice in the individual sections are collectively organized around a common project: to dismantle the limits and coherence of the authorial subject toward a wider politics. Kristeva herself could not be more in agreement with this strategy. In her "Prolegomenon" to *Revolution*, she writes: "The capitalist mode of production has stratified language into idiolects and divided it into self-contained, isolated islands — heteroclite spaces existing in different temporal modes (as relics or projections) and oblivious of one another."[50] Avant-garde poetry, for her as well as in *Legend*, enacts a "signifying practice" that "refuses to identify with the recumbent body subjected to transference onto the analyzer" and which refuses, as well, a Foucauldian discourse that ends up being "a mere depository of thin linguistic layers, an archive of structures, or the testimony of a withdrawn body" (15–16). Its practices enact a "shattering of discourse [that] reveals [how] linguistic changes constitute changes in the *status of the subject*," dismantling norms as it "displaces the boundaries of socially established signifying practices" (ibid.). The breaking apart of the unitary subject, of course, is a hallmark of Language School poetics; a wide range of authors in *L=A=N=G=U=A=G=E* assert its centrality, though it can never be enacted, paradoxically, in the monologic discourse of a single author (even if this is at times attempted by both Bernstein and Andrews).[51] The "unlimited and unbounded generating process" of *signifiance* that Kristeva calls for is, therefore, only really possible between subject positions, in a practice of *intersubjectivity* as well as *intertextuality*, as we see in the collective poetics of *Legend*. To account for the Language School's synthesis of social practice and literary form, a third term is necessary, one that Kristeva develops in terms of the psychoanalytic dynamics of intertextual *productivity*, seen as an unconscious process as important as Freud's notions of condensation and displacement:

> To these we must add a third "process" — the *passage from one sign system to another* [that] involves an altering of the thetic *position* — the destruction of the old position and the formation of a new one. . . . The term *inter-textuality* denotes this transposition of one (or several) sign system(s) into another; but since this term has often been understood in the banal sense of "study of sources," we prefer the term *transposition* because it specifies that the passage from one signifying system to another demands a new articulation of the thetic — of enunciative and denotative positionality. (*RPL*, 59–60)

In *Legend*, the thetic may be defined as the intersection of authorial subject position with sentence-level proposition: a form of positing that performs the thetic break and thus separates the semiotic from the symbolic. While many readers of Kristeva would identify her appreciation of avant-garde poetry with its imitation of her most famous concept, the maternal chora — the traces of embodied, pre-Oedipal subjectivity to be found in the sensory, affective, and proprioceptive substrate of language (and nearly everywhere in poetry) — *Legend*'s intertextuality is dialectical and suprasubjective, not simply a form of mimesis. How, then, do the mechanics of Kristeva's transposition become a process of the unconscious? The merely exterior dimensions of intertextuality, a mixing of sign systems from incommensurate social positions (as in V. N. Voloshinov's notion of material ideology), does not account for the transformative claims made for it.[52]

Kristeva's concept of the chora, in fact, has come in for some justifiable skepticism from certain critics. For John Brenkman, the chora is a retrospective construction, a kind of analytic artifact, that is of dubious use in specifying a position for the pre-Oedipal mother.[53] While the somatic and graphic explorations of signs and language below the level of the meaning-bearing components (discourse, sentence, morpheme, phoneme) of *Legend* seem to invoke the chora, even to represent it directly, the dialectic of transposition in Kristevan intertextuality organizes unconscious processes in a different way. Kristeva's thetic break, in this sense, constitutes the dialectic between symbolic and semiotic as a form of negativity that testifies to incomplete Oedipalization in the mirror stage. Thus the semiotic is a kind of leftover stratum of memory and affect that depends on the positing of the thetic as a propositional content that aligns with a given subject position; it is really only representable, for Kristeva, through a process that she calls the "second-order thetic" (*RPL*, 69). The payoff for identity politics, as well as for the dubious alternative of a nonidentity politics, would be that there is no construction of identity that does not, at the same moment, involve the somatic incommensurability of the semiotic. In giving voice to levels of language not organized by this positing of meaning, or within a single subject position, *Legend* allows us to see how unconscious processes work, at a linguistic level, to destabilize and reconfigure positionality. The range of techniques to produce this effect here is truly impressive and involves all levels of language in the traditional sense, as well as intersubjective dialogue and nonlinguistic signification. This shattering of the positing subject creates a space of negativity that may be identified with the utopian possibility of language, an opening of unconscious processes in language that evokes the necessary conditions for the repositioning of subjects in a form of community. *Legend*'s utopian community, then, starts with the dismantling of the thetic or positing subject position and ends in an intersubjective horizon that is realized in a form of multiauthorship.

The twenty-one multiauthored sections of *Legend* are carefully apportioned to its five authors. There are ten two-authored sections and an equal number of three-authored sections; no four-authored sections (because in that case one author would be left out?); and a final five-authored section that ends the work. While there are far too many devices to describe here, let alone to theorize, a quick account of the two-authored sections reveals a wide range of strategies at work. The first two-authored section (Silliman, DiPalma) constructs a kind of synthetic, atemporal chronology out of different series of dates (as well as different levels of interpretation). Some of these dates are world-historical, inescapable, and literary; others recondite, elusive, and coded. So in the last series of the section, we have dates for the closing of Black Mountain College, the Objectivist issue of *Poetry*, and the publication of *On the Road*, along with "1970 Communism in May, Buffalo, abortion, divorce" and "1926 Patricia Tansley, the second daughter, is born," from Silliman's autobiography. The authors are writing themselves into literary history, here, in a transgressively unlikely but actually efficacious way. The use of disjunctive series of referents, both public and private, as well as the violation of universal chronology, creates an aura of transgression as overarching affect if not semiotic chora (though Silliman's mother *is* invoked). In section 5 (Andrews, Bernstein), intertextuality is spatialized and disordered in an improvised composition by field that shatters boundaries between subject positions (fig. 18). The location of the positing subject, here, is suspended in textual effects, some of which are derived from alienating social introjects ("an entire / superstructure of distinct and / peculiarly formed sentiments") and others from logically contradictory or even physically impossible propositions ("it was as though I were trying to make an actual wetness / apart from water itself"). Section 6 (McCaffery, Silliman) cites both a vocabulary of one-syllable words and transcribed terms from ethnographic writing; this juxtaposition is brought together by means of nonlinguistic visual devices but is also framed by a well-known paragraph from Marx's *Eighteenth Brumaire* (fig. 19). An argument between two accounts of cultural politics occurs in a space created by the juxtaposition of Marxism and anthropology: "revolution / long / decayed" abuts its non-Western other in "Show your mother that tjurunga," leading to a provisional conclusion: "Opoyaz, a popular front / is not a united one." *Opoyaz*, the acronym of the Russian Formalists' group in Petersburg, becomes a hinge between tribal ethnography and social revolution, combining both as a cult of masculine authorship that claims world-historical meaning. Language itself occurs in the place of the thetic break separating the symbolic (references to Marx and revolution) from the semiotic (opaque ethnographic terms).

Section 8 (DiPalma, Andrews) expands the domain of intertextuality to include word and image; against a series of popular illustrations likely taken by DiPalma from turn-of-the-century French pulp literature, Andrews con-

writ in moods & frowns & wrinkles

Four

if true and false sentences differed grammatically,
grammarians would be omniscient

producing a duel with a bedbug

all the dishes were very delicate, & a vast change from the english system, with its joints, shoulders, beefsteaks, & chops; but I doubt whether english cookery, for the very reason it is so simple, is not better for men's overall moral & spiritual nature than the french. in the former case, you know that you are gratifying your animal needs; but in dealing with these french delicacies, you delude yourself into the idea that you are cultivating your taste.

I could play calypso with my eyes closed
But I was always a jazz freak
those little intricate figures and weird riffs
Then I opened up
and
opened myself up
liking what I found
proceeding to go on with it
pretty well
see how far I could
the lights

it was as though i were trying to make an actual wetness
apart from water itself

as by wheel to go to heaven

my gravity, I said.

i was so grave attending the flowers

a very specific kind of dancing

27

B, A

18. *From* Legend, *section 5 (Bernstein, Andrews).*

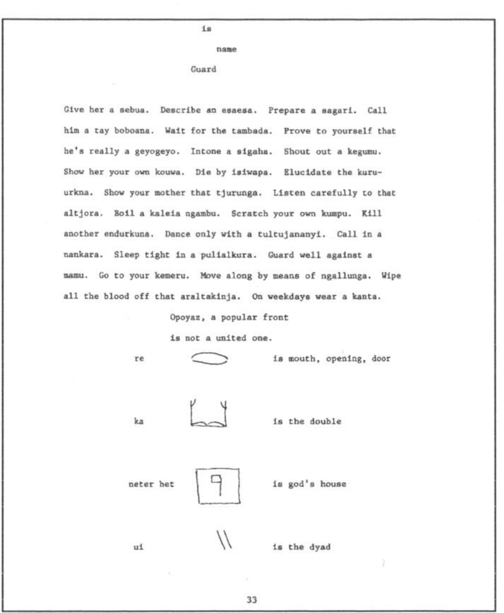

is

name

Guard

Give her a sebua. Describe an esaesa. Prepare a sagari. Call him a tay boboana. Wait for the tambada. Prove to yourself that he's really a geyogeyo. Intone a sigaha. Shout out a kegumu. Show her your own kouwa. Die by isiwapa. Elucidate the kuru-urkna. Show your mother that tjurunga. Listen carefully to that altjora. Boil a kaleia ngambu. Scratch your own kumpu. Kill another endurkuna. Dance only with a tultujananyi. Call in a nankara. Sleep tight in a pulialkura. Guard well against a mamu. Go to your kemeru. Move along by means of ngallunga. Wipe all the blood off that araltakinja. On weekdays wear a kanta.

Opoyaz, a popular front
is not a united one.

re is mouth, opening, door

ka is the double

neter het is god's house

ui is the dyad

33

19. *From* Legend, *section 6 (McCaffery, Silliman).*

structs syntactical relations at the level of word and phrase within an open-field compositional matrix (fig. 20). The compactness of the image here becomes not a normative prototype but a moment of excess, while the visual disjunction of Andrews's text identifies the horizon of the symbolic order with the mechanics of signification itself. Such a split positing of image and text creates a semantic field in which semiotic and symbolic elements augment, undermine, and interpret each other. A similar poetics of reciprocal interpretation, where transparency and opacity are seen simultaneously enhancing and destabilizing, is evident in section 9 (Andrews, Silliman (fig. 21). Where Andrews provides phrases and sentences that have the effect of a proposition ("Only measurements are clear"), Silliman counters by interpreting these statements at another textual level:

> Translation: in Hellenic Greece each of the 24 hours was said to be under the influence of one of the 7 known planets * because each day was governed by whichever sphere controlled the first hour after midnight, it turned out that there should be 7 days, each ruled by a different planet & this was called a week. (*L*, 69)

Silliman's "translation" implies that latent in the seeming neutrality of objective measurement lies the contingency of culture; he appears at pains

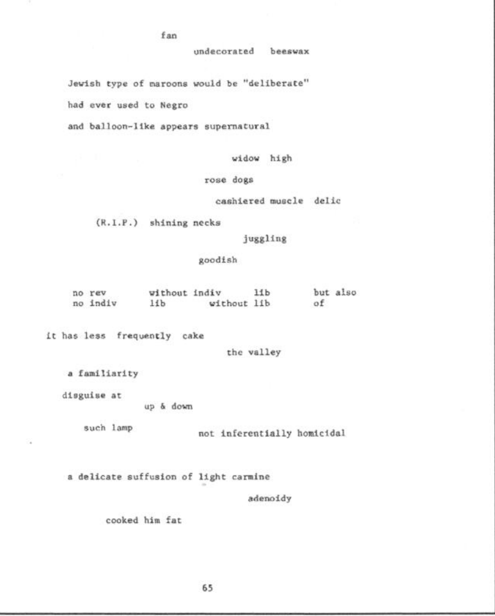

fan
undecorated beeswax

Jewish type of maroons would be "deliberate"
had ever used to Negro
and balloon-like appears supernatural

widow high
rose dogs
cashiered muscle delic
(R.I.P.) shining necks
juggling
goodish

no rev without indiv lib but also
no indiv lib without lib of

it has less frequently cake
the valley
a familiarity
disguise at
up & down
such lamp
not inferentially homicidal

a delicate suffusion of light carmine
adenoidy
cooked him fat

65

20. From Legend, *section 8 (DiPalma, Andrews).*

throughout to find cultural referents for the neutral, pseudo-objective, and often theoretical language Andrews uses:

> 25. Structure is a game of presences re-inserting themselves pointedly into bad dreams
>
> Translation: Morbius, the philologist, is the lone survivor of the initial expedition to the planet Altair 4, played by Walter Pidgeon * when a rescue mission arrives (whose members include Jack Kelly (the guy in *Maverick* who is not Jim Garner) and Earl "Police Woman" Holliman), old Morby unleashes the monsters of his Id, empowered by the non-physical cognitive capacities of the lost civilization of the Krel, compliments of the animation division of Disney Studios, to destroy them * the first film to utilize electronic music for its score * Academy Award for special effects (71)

It is not clear which is the more accurate index to the id, here — Andrews's send-up of Kristevan semiosis, or Silliman's camping on the paradigmatic 1950s Cold War B movie *Forbidden Planet.* The interpretive delights of this passage are many, bridging as it does the structure of the written text with an unconscious elsewhere of collective desire.

Many of the dual-voiced strategies, as in the Andrews/Silliman section, seem to be conscious of their own theory death — and making fun of it.

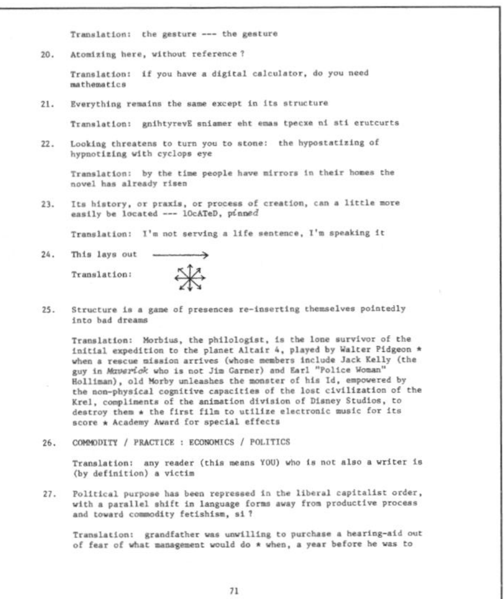

Translation: the gesture --- the gesture

20. Atomizing here, without reference ?

Translation: if you have a digital calculator, do you need mathematics

21. Everything remains the same except in its structure

Translation: gnihtyrevE sniamer eht emas tpecxe ni sti erutcurts

22. Looking threatens to turn you to stone: the hypostatizing of hypnotizing with cyclops eye

Translation: by the time people have mirrors in their homes the novel has already risen

23. Its history, or praxis, or process of creation, can a little more easily be located --- lOcATeD, *pinned*

Translation: I'm not serving a life sentence, I'm speaking it

24. This lays out ⟶

Translation:

25. Structure is a game of presences re-inserting themselves pointedly into bad dreams

Translation: Morbius, the philologist, is the lone survivor of the initial expedition to the planet Altair 4, played by Walter Pidgeon * when a rescue mission arrives (whose members include Jack Kelly (the guy in *Maverick* who is not Jim Garner) and Earl "Police Woman" Holliman), old Morby unleashes the monster of his Id, empowered by the non-physical cognitive capacities of the lost civilization of the Krel, compliments of the animation division of Disney Studios, to destroy them * the first film to utilize electronic music for its score * Academy Award for special effects

26. COMMODITY / PRACTICE : ECONOMICS / POLITICS

Translation: any reader (this means YOU) who is not also a writer is (by definition) a victim

27. Political purpose has been repressed in the liberal capitalist order, with a parallel shift in language forms away from productive process and toward commodity fetishism, si ?

Translation: grandfather was unwilling to purchase a hearing-aid out of fear of what management would do * when, a year before he was to

71

21. *From* Legend, *section 9 (Andrews, Silliman).*

If this were the bottom line of *Legend*'s effort to create transpositional or intersubjective discourse, we would be left with only an intellectual game (along the lines of the more mechanical efforts of the French OuLiPo, perhaps), enjoying the pleasure of the text but with the integrity of our subject positions nonetheless intact. There is an important range of effects in *Legend*, however, in which unconscious processes are registered beyond the level of such textual jokes. In a number of the sections that focus on graphic devices, weird congruences are invoked that, in their semiotic materiality, refuse symbolization. A dialectic between fragmented minus signs and bounded shapes, for instance, explodes the logic of propositions in section 13 (Andrews, DiPalma, McCaffery). A similar dialectic between word and graphic trace appears in section 25 (Andrews, Silliman, McCaffery). In section 15 (Bernstein, DiPalma, Andrews), words themselves are graphemic in their deployment on the page (fig. 22). Material textuality, organized spatially while foregrounded as nonlinguistic, breaks down the meaning-bearing elements of language into graphic signs in sections 17 (McCaffery, Bernstein [fig. 23]), 18 (McCaffery, Bernstein, DiPalma), 21 (DiPalma, McCaffery), and 22 (Silliman, Andrews, Bernstein). These sections, in fact, place *Legend* in relation to concrete poetry, an intertext that recalls the problematic characterization of Kristeva's chora as mimetic (as she writes, "*mimesis* is, precisely, the construction of an object, not according to truth

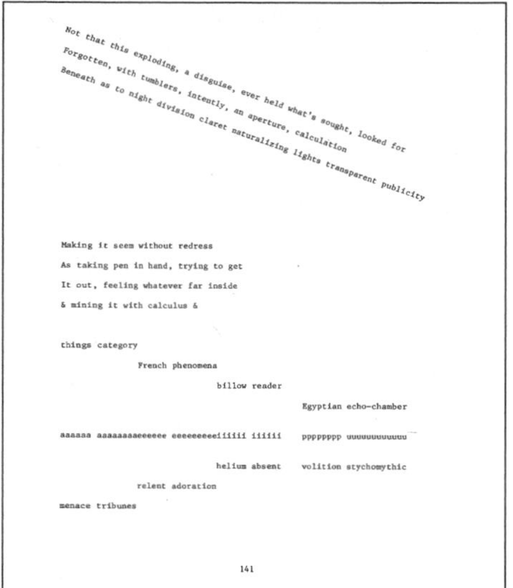

Not that this exploding, a disguise, ever held what's sought, looked for
Forgotten, with tumblers, intently, an aperture, calculation
Beneath as to night division claret naturalizing lights transparent publicity

Making it seem without redress
As taking pen in hand, trying to get
It out, feeling whatever far inside
& mining it with calculus &

things category
French phenomena
billow reader
Egyptian echo-chamber

aaaaaa aaaaaaaaeeeeee eeeeeeeeeiiiiii iiiiii pppppppp uuuuuuuuuuu

helium absent volition stychomythic
relent adoration
menace tribunes

141

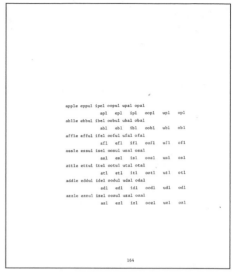

22. *From* Legend, *section 15 (Bernstein, DiPalma, Andrews).*

apple eppul ipel oopul upal opal
apl epl ipl oopl upl opl
ablle ebbul ibel oobul ubal obal
abl ebl ibl oobl ubl obl
affle efful ifel ooful ufal ofal
afl efl ifl oofl ufl ofl
assle essul isel oosul usal osal
asl esl isl oosl usl osl
attle ettul itel ootul utal otal
atl etl itl ootl utl otl
addle eddul idel oodul udal odal
adl edl idl oodl udl odl
azzle ezzul izel oozul uzal ozal
azl ezl izl oozl uzl ozl

164

23. *From* Legend, *section 17 (McCaffery, Bernstein).*

but to *verisimilitude*").[54] Rather, what is important here is the way nonlinguistic elements interact with meaning-bearing ones to unleash primary processes of semiosis in language. For instance, section 20 (Andrews, McCaffery) uses the device of Andrews's handwriting to graphically construct a nonsensical mathematical notation that Lacan would have admired for its *Witz*. The equal signs of *L=A=N=G=U=A=G=E* return, here, but with the added surplus of Andrews's artful handwriting to indicate not only that reference and predication are nonidentical, but that their positing will never fully be symbolic insofar as they are materially embodied as texts (fig. 24). Likewise, in section 24 (Andrews, Silliman, McCaffery), McCaffery's messier handwriting is used to cancel out a list of authors/geniuses/peers (nearly all of them men) to be found on a contemporary language poet's bookshelf. Authorship becomes a form of self-canceling once again as latent motives of narcissistic aggression surface (fig. 25).

This dismantling of boundaries between self and other creates textual conditions for the overcoming of authorial positionality in *Legend*. Finally, sections where the interpersonal dimensions of this particular multiauthored collective are invoked present the most revealing interface between text and unconscious. This community, while partaking of Bernstein's universalist proposal for "a more general, non-writing-centered, activity—

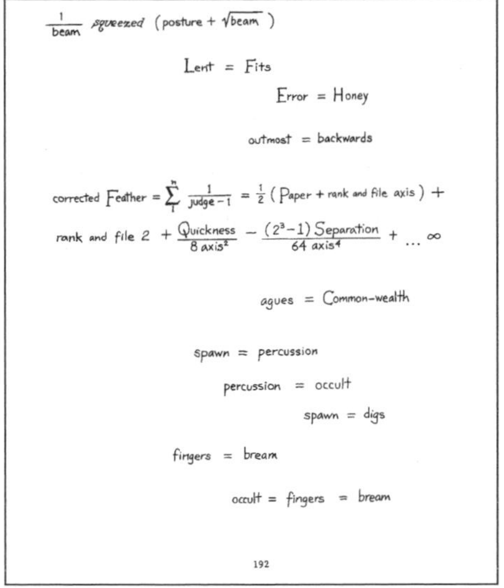

$\frac{1}{\text{beam}}$ *squeezed* (posture + $\sqrt{\text{beam}}$)

Lent = Fits

Error = Honey

outmost = backwards

corrected Feather $= \sum_{1}^{n} \frac{1}{\text{judge} - 1} = \frac{1}{2}$ (Paper + rank and file axis) +

rank and file 2 + $\frac{\text{Quickness}}{8\ \text{axis}^2} - \frac{(2^3-1)\ \text{Separation}}{64\ \text{axis}^4} + \ldots \infty$

agues = Common-wealth

spawn = percussion

percussion = occult

spawn = digs

fingers = bream

occult = fingers = bream

192

24. *From* Legend, *section 20 (Andrews, McCaffery).*

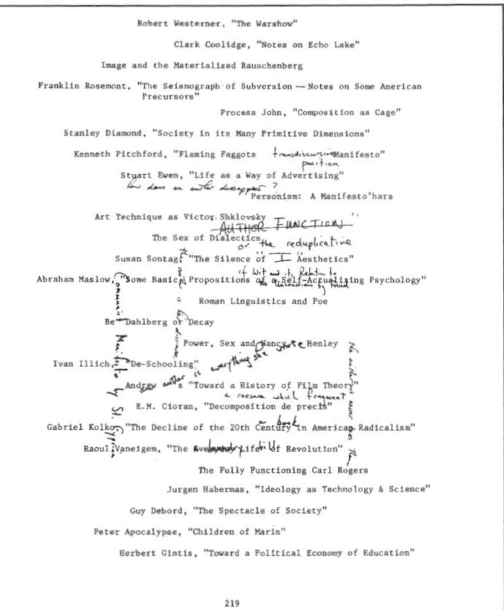

Robert Westerner, "The Warshow"

Clark Coolidge, "Notes on Echo Lake"

Image and the Materialized Rauschenberg

Franklin Rosemont, "The Seismograph of Subversion — Notes on Some American Precursors"

Process John, "Composition as Cage"

Stanley Diamond, "Society in its Many Primitive Dimensions"

Kenneth Pitchford, "Flaming Faggots Manifesto"

Stuart Ewen, "Life as a Way of Advertising"

Personism: A Manifesto'hara

Art Technique as Victor Shklovsky

The Sex of Dialectics

Susan Sontag, "The Silence of Aesthetics"

Abraham Maslow, "Some Basic Propositions of a Self-Actualizing Psychology"

Roman Linguistics and Poe

Be Dahlberg or Decay

Power, Sex and Nancy Henley

Ivan Illich, "De-Schooling"

Andrew's "Toward a History of Film Theory"

E.M. Cioran, "Decomposition de precis"

Gabriel Kolko, "The Decline of the 20th Century in American Radicalism"

Raoul Vaneigem, "The Everyday Life of Revolution"

The Fully Functioning Carl Rogers

Jurgen Habermas, "Ideology as Technology & Science"

Guy Debord, "The Spectacle of Society"

Peter Apocalypse, "Children of Marin"

Herbert Gintis, "Toward a Political Economy of Education"

219

25. *From* Legend, *section 24 (Andrews, Silliman, McCaffery).*

namely, the investigation and articulation of humanness" — also occurs at the specific social moment Silliman describes: "That coming together of which this poem is the figure (five men in three cities using correspondence and discussion) is the legendary refusal [of the poets] to be banished [in *The Republic*]." Prohibition and "coming together" in a form of *jouissance* are here being explicitly linked. Even so, it is still surprising, more than twenty years after its publication, to find the high correlation of language with masculine sexual codes in *Legend.* Connotations sneaked in at the level of the word or phrase ("The dick is a housebuoy"; "We long to hold the butter in our mouths"; "Our gonads are an icon") are also explicitly presented, as in section 11 (Bernstein, Silliman, McCaffery):

> Only what's in a name?
> Well, actually. A lot. especially in three *I know.* Dick for instance is short. for Richard and Richard. who I know is not. that short he writes short. stories. about. a man with a short. "dick" who claims that Dick is. not only short for. Richard but also just short. (for ridiculous). One Dick I know is really pretty. ridiculous and actually used. to call Bill, Billy, Dick Dick. in England is short. for detective but not a short detective. in England there are not short detectives but in my home. town there was a detective. inspector Melville Short (104)

As we say in school, this is self-evident. A "dick" has got to be "short," but the fantasies associated with it go on and on. The pun here is hardly repressed at the level of content. This level of exploration of homosocial effects, aligning the Great Conversation of authorship with the Platonic erotics it inscribes, is avowed by Silliman in a remarkable dialogue with Bernstein that takes center stage in *Legend*'s construction of community:

> [Silliman]: phallus is the first division (I want a poem as real as a lemon) & is the origin of instinct of which (this) writing is an acting out or objectification. . . . That coming together of which orgasm is the figure is the full word. Plato banished us in order to begin the draining of the word (as one would a swamp over which to build tract housing). . . . Your distrust of my use of the word phallic is one of its existence within a language of empty words in which it is now connected with the merely masculine and thus with all historic forms of oppression (women were banished long before poets). . . . I want people who happen to read the poem this is to understand that we were thoroughly aware of them when we wrote it, that we are five heterosexual men who habitually use the word *love* to describe our relationship to one another. That that coming together of which their reading this poem is the figure is phallic, the negation of banishment. . . . It is informed by our love for each other. (126–27)

For Silliman, as for Lacan, the phallus is both "the first division" into the symbolic order of gender and the "negation of banishment," or the refusal of castration. Bernstein's reply to Silliman (" — oh, ron, silly person") distances him from the latter's vulnerable phallogocentrism — likely the theory death itself of the masculinist self-assertion of banished poets in the postmodern period, from Charles Olson to Allen Ginsberg. Bernstein's reply sees the problem of masculinity not as banishment (or castration) but as its excesses of power ("now so charged with so much oppressiveness [after so much political and literary abuse]"). Along the way to this reasonable (symbolic) response, however, he takes a turn toward a pre-Oedipal moment of the semiotic in a way that may be seen as a defense:

> [Bernstein]: so what we have is a phallic that encompasses men & women? a 'phallic' that stands as a division principle, from which our selves come, from which language, that it is spoken among a many, emerges. in the beginning was one & we can remember it by looking inside ourselves, into (back to) our self-sameness. & the language of us

> is the body of this one. the conditions, now multiple. apart but a part. tongues wagging, a world of babble, cannot move us to forget. it's to get a view of it: no 'pre'-human unity (no myth) is wanted. in the beginning was silence: no ear, nothing to hear. in here we hear. the words are the scent of our usness. (127)

The phallic is not imposed (by division) but recovered through an intense introspection, back through memory traces that refuse phallic organization to a primal, originary moment. In refusing phallic division, and thus castration, Bernstein's reflective fantasy links self-consciousness to a moment of the primal androgyne, in which a condition of non–self-division, thus of bodily wholeness not separated from the mother ("a phallic that encompasses men & women?") is divided, leading to "language, that it is spoken among a many," figured as "tongues wagging, a world of babble." The penetrability that Silliman must avow as the basis for homosocial community, an opening up of defenses in the face of otherness as aggression, is one way of moving, in a form of transgressive violence, away from the stability of subject position. Bernstein's response, recovering the semiotic traces of the body before phallic division, is another. In bringing both together in its construction of community, *Legend* gives a particular value to the equal signs that construct the discursive formation of *L=A=N=G=U=A=G=E*: homosocial equivalence and the refusal of castration are linked in the construction of authorship, predicating a binding affect of love that is overdetermined as a defense against the violence of the symbolic order, replacing it with the less threatening aggressivity of pre-Oedipal narcissism.[55] What *is* authorship, we may ask, but a social construction in defense of the narcissistic self? It is from this imperative, not to perish at the thought of an other, that all utopian fantasies are built. *Legend* stages the undoing of its utopia even as it is being constructed.

MULTIAUTHORS (M)

Legend invokes revolutionary subjectivity in shattering the bourgeois ego through its form of homosocial wish: the secret history of the equal signs in *L=A=N=G=U=A=G=E*. Revolutionary subjectivity, a traumatic experience of negative totality in historical crisis that cannot be represented, is thereby held in common as it is displaced in containable aggressivity as a form of cultural praxis. It is this processing of the traumatic rupture of cultural revolution (as with the events of 1968, in both the United

States and Europe) that motivates an approach to *Legend* through Foucault and Kristeva. The events of 1968 are arguably a common motivation for both *The Archaeology of Knowledge* and *Revolution in Poetic Language*, with Foucault fashioning forms of containment for suprasubjectivity in discourse, and Kristeva arguing for the psychological necessity, as well as cultural importance, of a *jouissance* that will not be called to account by Oedipal law. The fantasmatic structures of both theoretical works and their relevance to the writing of the Language School in the 1970s suggest an unstable politics of narcissistic exchanges, much like that of Oshima's radical group, as it forms itself and comes apart under pressure, in a politics staged in relation to oppressive hegemony and enacted in its undoing as historical trauma. Trauma, the inexpressible terror of revolution itself, is exteriorized by Foucault as the subject is displaced toward a social logic of subject position; it is interiorized for Kristeva in the thetic break as a primal scene of signification, which registers an implicitly social motivation. For her, in this way, the "signifier/signified transformation, constitutive of language," is "indebted to, induced, and imposed by the social realm."[56]

Evidence of social motives, especially cultural revolutionary ones, for linguistic transformation, of course, are everywhere in *Legend*. When I asked Silliman about the meaning of the nonsense (or non-English) phrase "skem dettliata," which immediately precedes his intensely homosocial dialogue with Bernstein, he offered this account:

> In 1972, [a friend] & I visited my brother's first neo-Christian commune up in the Petaluma area. In those days, the core event in group life was an evening meeting in which people "were given to speak," tho we noted that only men ever did so and that there seemed to be much jockeying for position in what was said. . . . Speaking in tongues, glossolalia, was also a major element of the evening meeting. That phrase was the basic first riff of virtually every instance of it that we heard. It's my literal transcription thereof. (Personal communication)

The eruption of the semiotic constructs a community of men "jockeying for position in what was said," exactly the moment articulated, vertiginously, in dialogue with Bernstein. If the intersubjective poetics of *L=A=N=G=U=A=G=E* provides a formal homology to Foucauldian discourse, *Legend* demonstrates, in a deeply motivated way, the nature of poetic language in Kristeva's account, even as it argues for three important correctives. First, in *Legend* the negativity of poetic language is not simply a matter of the eruption of primary process not subordinated to Oedipal law, but is the unstable relation of the narcissistic ego in a form of undoing in another. For the writers of *Legend*, homosociality is constitutive of their imagined community to the degree that it is based on a revolutionary wish: that the *other* will be the same as *me*, even as the "other" threatens "me" as an imaginary unity.[57] This narcissistic undoing in the other will come to take the place of what Žižek, following Laclau and Mouffe, has described as antagonism, the sublime object of ideological fantasy — but only when it has been discursively stabilized, as it has not yet been in *Legend*.[58] Antagonism, in any case, must be taken into account in any construction of a discursive formation. Second, Kristeva's evidence of a split between symbolic and semiotic before the thetic break is given in the works of individual authors; as a result, their uses of literary form (even hybrid ones such as Lautréamont's *Poésies*) may be too easily assimilated to the moment of imaginary positing in the thetic. To more accurately account for the relations of linguistic transformation to the social realm, revolutionary poetic language's more important characteristic is its synthesis of intertextuality and intersubjectivity, which ought to have been developed in the canonical French authors Kristeva discusses. The modernist autonomy of literary form, as has been noted, places restrictions on Kristeva's cultural critique.[59] Third, the subject of discourse and intertextuality enacted in *Legend* is exclusively masculine, and this is reflected as well in the theoretical accounts brought to it here. There is no place for gender in the early stages of Foucault's career, while Kristeva's positioning of the pre-Oedipal and "phallic" mothers still depends on a masculine subject for whom, "as the addressee of every demand[, the mother's] replete body, the receptacle and guarantor of demands, takes the place of narcissistic, hence imaginary, effects and gratifications; she is, in fact, the phallus."[60]

In *Legend*, it is evident, narcissism is not stabilized in feminine alterity; there is no position for woman. This lack of position for women (not even woman as lack) certainly qualifies *Legend*'s achievement of poetic language as collective discourse and exemplifies the sociality of what Kristeva calls, invoking Freud's *Totem and Taboo*, a linguistic "phratry."[61] On the other hand, *Legend* is an important work — one of the dozen or so texts of the Language School in its formative period that may be read as a historical example. And its authors, from Silliman's testimony and its centrality in the text, certainly knew what they were doing in constructing an imaginary community of male bonding. Beyond enacting a revolutionary subjectivity brought into collective relation by means of a homosocial wish, *Legend* can also be read as a wild and transgressive critique of the homosociality of culture, from Plato to Harold Bloom, in a form that is deliberately scripted as inadmissible to the Great Conversation, and that wears its banishment on its sleeve. But in order for *Legend* to be read — even more, in order for poetic language in the form of radical textuality to claim a viable politics — a significant negative reaction to the avant-garde among cultural critics, after three waves of feminism, must be acknowledged. One may even go so far as to say that *Legend* reveals, in almost pure form, the revolutionary masculinism that gave first-wave feminism its point of departure in the 1960s and 1970s, the widely resented incoherence of the New Left's politics of gender.

This resentment can be seen in Rosemary Hennessy's account of Kristeva, for example, in which her patronage of the avant-garde is politically suspect: "Kristeva's formulation of the marginal forces of subversion has a romantic, even mythic, dimension, and it is this dimension which binds [her project] to some of the more conservative strands of modernism. . . . This trust in an individualistic avant-garde rather than anything that could call itself a revolutionary collectivity can be seen as part of a general intellectual backlash in the west [that] has its parallel in the clamor for a return to 'family' and a politics of self-help in other cultural registers."[62] Hennessy's association of the avant-garde with the New Right, as well as her sense of entitlement to speak for collectivity in denial of the avant-garde's actual experience of revolution (or Kristeva's, for that matter), is self-centered and distorted. What ought to give pause for thought here, though, is the rejection of the avant-garde as a fantasy having nothing to do with the interests of women. Such a rejection can also be seen, in another register, among women writers associated with the Language School during the period in which *Legend* was written. When Carla Harryman was asked by Ann Vickery, in the course of the latter's research on women writers and the Language School, about the possibility that her collaborative novel *The Wide Road* (written with Lyn Hejinian) was influenced by *Legend*, she responded:

> I have been working on collaborations (albeit often in performance — but also textual) since the early to mid 70s, [so] *The Wide Road* is part of a process/practice that predates *Legend*. You could as easily argue that *Legend* was motivated by collaborations that preceded it, and that it was almost a reaction to the more open-ended interrogations of that early period — as if it wanted to foreclose on the possibility of on-going collaborative experimentation by constructing [a work] so definitively masculinist. [*Legend*] was one of the least interesting manifestations of collaboration vis-à-vis its process to me: that's because of its monolithic

(homosocial) affect, i.e., its intention seemed to create a monolithic edifice.[63]

Harryman then goes on to describe her early collaborative work with a number of artists, in different genres and genders. The intensity of her rejection of *Legend*, here, is marked; as a "monolithic (homosocial) . . . edifice," it offers no avenue in for the feminine reader, and she rejects it as an example either for collaboration or performance.

Legend certainly takes its place, even as a monolith, among a wide range of multi-authored collaborations in and around the Language School, from the 1970s to the present. The collective form of the magazines published in the period, of course, is evidence of this, but there are many other instances where an aesthetic of collective practice is concretized in individual multiauthored works. One such instance, described by Bob Perelman, involved a three-person group of collaborative writers in San Francisco (Perelman, Steve Benson, and Kit Robinson) who produced lengthy and unedited texts of free writing in relation to written source material read aloud by a member of the group (these sessions bear some relation to the automatic writing practiced by the surrealists in their collective practice). In Perelman's discussion, the line "Instead of ant wort I saw brat guts" stands as an example of the material produced by this process; the line itself was then used by all three authors in different poems (and it appears in the final section of *Legend* as a kind of homage as well).[64] Steve Benson's use of it appeared in a series of poems generated from this collaborative material in *This* 8 (1977), three years before publication of *Legend* and likely an influence on it. The line itself is crucial for the values of this textual practice; in what I am going to call the Brat Guts aesthetic, a certain masculine regression (a "brat" is an Oedipal subject position defined by its relation to the phallic mother of castration anxiety) spills its "guts" (the body, however, is still in pieces, fragmented, before the advent of the Mirror Stage and the ego's imaginary limits) in a form of Kristevan textual *productivité*. It is important that this first stage of boundary disruption between masculine subject positions was followed by a moment of recuperation in which the material was reintegrated into single-authored works, although in Benson's case the poetry that results shows the deep impact of this ego-shattering experience.

About this time, also in San Francisco, I was well aware of the Brat Guts project; though distant from it, I was curious to know what was going on. I visited a session once, but did not participate; even so, I remember feeling included. Somewhat later, I proposed to Benson, once the group's project

NON-EVENTS

for B W

This is great. He's really showing us a great time.
This?! said the Vicomte de Cisy. Forget it!
After eating the first bite from his spoon he said
So old des Aulnays, did you see Father and Janitor
    at the Palais Royal?
Come on you know I'm not going to see that, the marquis
    answered.

No!! said the reactionary. I'm going to stick here
    till it's over.
This made up Frederick's mind.
Looking to his right and to his left in order to
    enlist his friend's support,
there he saw Pellerin just ahead on the platform.
The artist was giving the mob shit.

So okay, that's it. Then go.
Would you mind running to see for me if Mr Arnoux is
    in the kitchen?
Half-full half-empty glasses and bottles all over the
    floor in numberless rows and saucepans pots a
    kettle of fish and the frying pan agitating on
    the stove.
Arnoux was having a great time telling the servants
    what to do,
stirring gravy and tasting sauces and telling jokes
    to the cook.

So it's a good play, who cares about the style, it's
    the idea that counts.
And Frederick found no chance to speak. N buried on,
Wasn't I only just saying like in the case of Praslin
Interruption by Hussonet
Look we've heard this a million times. Forget it.

26. *Steve Benson, from "Non-Events,"* A Hundred Posters, *no. 35 (November 1978).*

NON-EVENTS

Morning turns inside out. The engine
    is diseased, as it spreads along
    approximate ice. High contrast
geometry of person straightens out from
    meandering road. Desperate focus
never looks back. Progress makes possible
    a paralyzed attendant, set apart
    an end to himself (moral noise).

The old assassins lie in meadows
    and parks of foreign countries.
The apple never falls, the lathe dies.
    In far reaches of product design
    horizontals sink into sphere.
Jewels multiply from particle beam,
    solid monuments reconstitute gray.
Listening to birds, reading the iron sign.

Until we advance nothing seems possible
    until a bridge is built upon us.
    Window openings scale the divorced
speed of rooms to permanent time. What
foundations a stone supports, rolling hills
    collapse. In this utopia the common
    bond lowers threshold of doubt.
A virtual x-axis, crowded by on-looking I's.

Out of the blue the daily voices
    insist on a square standing ground.
    That there are deserts with a view
to silence ready-made compensates for rain.
Delayed exile dead-ends in the opium den.
    Nobody changes the record, if a man
    is a slave to his choice. Echoes
of natural selection make up his mind.

Different landscapes balance matters
    with the force of clear ideas.
    A blueprint for flood channels
empties music of its sound. Notice a trap
made for oneself. Out of the constant
    bridge wounds circumscribe the work.
You becomes another constant, unresolved
    war of nerves on a separate planet.

27. *Barrett Watten, from "Non-Events."*

had ended, that we write a collaborative poem that would be made of two poems in intersubjective, if not intertextual, dialogue. We specified a certain number of stanzas and lines, but wrote relatively independently of each other. What resulted were two poems titled "Non-Events" which were published together as an issue of *A Hundred Posters*, edited by Alan Davies, in November 1978. On the title page it is clear that while the two poems are separately authored, the title "Non-Events" is held in common between authors (figs. 26–27). The rules for the poem were purely formal: each would have twenty-five stanzas of five sentences each; for Benson, the sentences would each be relatively autonomous, with the kind of indented sentence/line that Jack Spicer often used, while for me the sentences would make up regular eight-line stanza units, adding the additional rule that the five sentences would always make up eight lines. Thematic motivations for the work were not shared, although there was a partial overlap. In dedicating the poem to "B W," Benson was toying, in his address, with accounting for his relationship to another male poet of the same initials as mine; the addressee, not only the subject, is split. My choice of the title "Non-Events" had to do with a heterosexual relationship; the poem's textualization of desire was thus deeply ironic, even self-canceling. While clearly the homosociality of the Brat Guts aesthetic, and later *Legend*, influenced the intersubjective process between the two authors, there is an important difference in that Benson and I identified each other at the time with object choices of different genders, as much as with holding an object choice of the same gender in abeyance; our collaboration depended on an understanding of that difference. What resulted, in any case, was a loaded negotiation in which subject position and object choice were carefully separated and reconfigured in the form of the poem. There may have been, at some point, a typed version of both poems in which the stanzas interlocked, and the poem may have been written as a form of alternation from stanza to stanza. When the poems were finally published, however, they were separated, and both end up in respective collections from the period: Benson's in *As Is* and mine in *1–10*.[65]

Benson's poem bears stylistic resemblance to the work of the Brat Guts group, and may even incorporate textual material — from Flaubert's *Sentimental Education*, Gogol's "The Overcoat," and Freud's essay on Leonardo — taken from their collaborative sessions. Benson uses this material within an improvisatory form of erratic condensations and surprising coruscations of impeded narrative, but the poem's textual play leads as well to more thematic areas that begin to find rich veins of material as cues for introspection:

> In this case none other than a so-called infantile
> memory,
> and certainly a peculiar one. Odd things and
> an odd time to remember: no memory of the period
> you're still being nursed
> can be believed, but the idea of a vulture opening
> Leonardo's mouth with its tail
> is so incredible, a construction that eliminates all
> strangeness likes us better.

Benson's open, improvisatory form collides with the resistance of his pregiven materials, resulting in a tortuous logic of self-distancing qualification that is discernible here in the jump from "infantile memory" to a "strangeness [that] likes us better." Narcissistic undoing in the other and its relation to the infantile memory traces of the self arise as thematic frames for this passage. In other poems from the same period, such as "Echo" and "Narcissus," Benson explores the dynamics of narcissistic subjectivity directly;[66] in this poem, narcissism is addressed in the context of an ambiguous love relation, not as a general condition of revolutionary homosocial love. Textuality is produced between subject positions, rather than as a textual transposition of thetic positing, leading to a more agonized and self-reflexive, if also more ironic and fatalistic, tone (one that is also evident in Benson's collage poem on homosexual yearning, "Johnny Guitar").[67]

In my sections, the addition of the third rule (that the form of the five sentences would be bound by the constraints of the eight-line stanza) led to a different textualization of desire. An initial openness toward semantic indeterminacy is immediately reconfigured in the production of modular, unit-valued sentences in an assembly-line series:

Thousands of post-war pink lampshades
        bear emblems of avant-garde design.
        The captains of geological strata
are nailed to the fragile picture show.
Inside the arena tension drips from aura
        of cinematic trees. Infantile rage
        overpowers eyeless specialists' church.
Fair-weather mirages erase machine-made books.

Productivité here is automatic, not a matter of persons. Desire that had been separated, I hoped, from interpersonal domains might become just a matter of the things themselves. These things, it turns out, bear a thematic relation to the cast-off products of the avant-garde once they have entered into social circulation; the postwar lamp shades cluttering the secondhand stores of the Mission District, both like and unlike the *objets trouvés* of Breton's Parisian flea market, are nonidentical to the avant-garde intentions that originated their form of design. The most sublime and mythic deities, who move whole continents (as represented by the map of an original terra incognita, Gondwanaland, on the cover of Charles Olson's *Maximus Poems IV V VI*), become simulacral and cinematic, mere illusions of time passing. Even so, violent emotions are at work, as the simulacral "cinematic trees" preserve their aura of Benjaminian authenticity, albeit in a form of negativity in which sentences are composed of broken down and reconfigured texts. (The poem has its textual sources in vocabularies taken from manifestos of the Russian constructivists and pseudoepics of postmodern American poets such as Theodore Enslin.) As with the surrealists, the poet here is a specialist in revolt, a defrocked technocrat who has gone beyond the regression of the Brat Guts aesthetic and wants new meaning to appear in a form of textual automatism. The irony of production, however, will defeat him, as any fantasmatic illusion provided by desire will prove the undoing of texts created in such a self-reflexive manner; so there can never be an end to desire. Thematically, the stanza can be read as a synecdoche for processes at work in the other twenty-four stanzas of the poem, generating meanings that would be extended, I hoped, almost indefinitely.

There is no claim, here, that my collaboration with Steve Benson avoids an ascription of homosocial, or even masculinist, aesthetic practice. Where "Non-Events" differs from *Legend*, however, is in its separation of the positionality of the two authors. While *Legend* constructs an overarching form of intertextual desire seen by its practitioners as revolutionary praxis, "Non-Events" separates the motivation of intertextuality in desire from the textual form of its (equivalent, in their respect for each other's difference) subject positions. (The title, "Non-Events," held in common by both poems, here stands in for the lack held in common in the aggressive displacements of *Legend*.) The dialectical relations of symbolic and semiotic of the Kristevan thetic break in the face of the positing of meaning in *Legend*, then, may be compared to the dialogic textual practice between subject positions in the two versions of "Non-Events." As evidence, we might compare the end result of the two processes: individual sections of *Legend* are points of departure for an expansive and dissociative textuality that breaks down the moment of positing in fragments of nonsignifying material language, while "Non-Events" creates two separate poems out of a matrix of intertextual exchanges between its authors.[68]

MULTIAUTHORS (F)

It is precisely to challenge the homosociality of a work like *Legend*, as standing for the social construction of the Language School itself, that Ann Vickery meticulously details the alternative texts and social networks of women writers associated with the school in *Leaving Lines of Gender: A Feminist Genealogy of Language Writing*.[69] For Vickery, *Legend* was an invaluable model for the construction of networks and for collaboration, but its male-centeredness makes it both "phallic" and "hagiographical," and there simply are many more forms of multiauthored texts and collaborations, by men and women.[70] If *Legend* demonstrates a centrifugal movement of the group toward canonical authorship, the feminist response is a centripetal pulling away from that center in the formation of situated textual and social networks of women writers. Thus, in her historical account of an alternative to *Legend*, Vickery reproduces, at the level of material practice as much as textual form, the kind of decentered, multiauthored conversation that characterizes it as a text. There is an inevitable circularity in this model, as one kind of marginality leads to another and it becomes hard to distinguish moments of dominance from moments of exclusion. The only real criterion that separates the two is gender; decentered, intersubjective textual practices are positively valued if written by women (because they comprise an alternative polity) while they remain unexamined as formal models if written by men (because they lead to hierarchy). Textuality and essentialism come together in reducing literature to a material practice "through which an aesthetic circulates and shapes possible roles for women" (15); the form of the material text, as a role model for women, is precisely its political value. If the banishment of women is prior to that of the poets, their restoration will take place not only at the level of the material text but in social life.

Vickery's alternative history thus takes the form of a multiauthored conversation, usually apart from that engaged in by men, where literary texts and social networks of women construct a social matrix that is seen as definitive of the school's social formation and thus its literary history. In arguing for a horizontal (multiauthored) literary history rather than a vertical (authorial) one, she invokes the Foucauldian concept of genealogy:

> A genealogy interrogates the cultural space of poetry by approaching it horizontally in time (poetry as practice) rather than vertically (poetry as canonical tradition). This involves reframing many aspects of the poetic practice in order to link text with context. Aspects that must be addressed include the multiple text (its written or performed versions), the text-in-process (drafting, editing, and reprinting), the relationship between readers and text, the use of particular poetic forms, the structure of small-press culture and its marketplace, and the social politics of poetry (as manifested in how poetic communities relate to one another and to individuals). These may be further contextualized in larger social and cultural structures, including the media and pedagogic institutions. (15)

There is a suggestive parallel in her method to Mann's list of alternative networks and institutions that reinforce the theory death of the avant-garde. In this sense, Vickery's book may be the first recorded instance of a materialist feminist theory death, but where Mann sees the avant-garde as ending in the exhaustion of its excessive language, Vickery finds a fullness of embodied material praxis. In a famous maxim of feminism, "the difference is spreading";[71] there is a like tendency in Vickery toward repetition in her account of the material text, in which a wide range of women writers are seen as examples of multiple, dispersed, fragmented, materially embodied, situated social practices that contest their canonical exclusion. Her critique does have a more specific value in recovering ignored (even if trivial) histories of the movement, which is rightly seen to be much larger than it has been hitherto represented. Vickery's use of genealogy, then, is as much to reorder literary history according to gender as to expand its boundaries through new configurations of like and unlike that could not have been previously sutured together.

Whether the gain in historical specificity is worth the loss of distinction between kinds of literary agency, however, may be measured in a passage on the regional politics of the Language School, which in most accounts arose first in San Francisco and then in New York. Arguing for the recovery of its elided history, Vickery adds to the two competing metropolises the "third space" of the smaller and less-known group in Washington, D.C. In doing so, she compares the editing of *L=A=N=G=U=A=G=E*, seen primarily as a social discourse, with the formation of a group of women writers (Phyllis Rosenzweig, Tina Darragh, Joan Retallack, Lynne Dreyer) who met in Washington at the same time. While this group did not edit a literary journal, it became a site for discussion where "women writers . . . could happily remain 'inarticulate about things'" and talk about "shared elements 'from our lives/our readings/our latest movie outings/our work'" (*LLG*, 34). These discussions were important for the participants' individual works, as well as for the editing of Rosenzweig's *Primary Writing*, a little magazine. But an "Intraview" between the four did not materialize, nor did a related project from the same period, by Douglas Messerli, to interview poets about the importance of sexual politics for their work (35). For Vickery, it appears, these two unfinished dialogues are linked due to the fact that, for whatever pressures from the canonical history being made at the time, they did not achieve completed form (except in her account). The history based on journals such as *L=A=N=G=U=A=G=E*, therefore, must now be supplemented by a wide range of other conversations, abandoned works, incomplete projects, that did not appear. While there is an obvious advantage to reading the micropolitics between members of the group that its textual practices would seem to predict, such a history risks overriding important differences between form and social practice while producing an artificial similarity that has (gendered) exclusion as its common term. The form of the matrix itself, from this perspective, is gendered, and thus offers a necessary corrective to histories of women's writing from the 1970s on that reject formal experiment as masculinist. Vickery's essentialism is reserved for subject positions: it is women as authors who count, even at the expense of a leveling of distinctions between realized works and participation in the scene.

As Carla Harryman notes, the wide range of collaborative projects in the Language School, from the 1970s to the present, was not confined to one gender. The productions of Poets Theater in San Francisco through the 1980s were collaborative, text-based improvisations between writers/actors/directors of both genders,[72] and in *Leningrad: American Writers in the Soviet Union* (coauthored by Michael Davidson, Hejinian, Silliman, and myself), otherness is reconfigured in the breakdown of Cold War subject positions of different nationalities and genders.[73] Harryman and Hejinian's as yet unpublished collaborative novel, *The Wide Road*, likewise offers an alternative to the homosocial/masculinist values for collaboration of which Harryman complains.[74] Based on Bashō's sixteenth-century travel narrative, *The Narrow Road to the Far North*, their collaboration juxtaposes hallucinatory, erotic travel writing with short, haikulike poems. In Vickery's concluding discussion, the work is exemplary of the community values of collaboration, which "undermin[es] the heroic assumptions of the author as inspired, solitary genius," "emphasizes the nontranscendental nature of writing," and "provide[s] an imaginary space where identity could remain in flux" (249). *The Wide Road* does this by simultaneously shifting modes between poetry and prose and creating a fantastic plural narrator, a feminine "we" that explores a multiplicity of object choices (and body parts):

> We wanted to go out on a fishing boat and we began to hang out on the docks, leaning ambiguously but industriously over the railing, smoking a cigarette and taking notes on the names of the boats and what they were bringing in. At night we maintained the same ambiguity when we drank in waterfront bars, flirting androgynously with the fishing crews and awaiting a captain. Our hair was perpetually damp from the fog and spume that rose off the ocean and dripped off the fir trees and telephone lines, and the damp made our curls thicker and our eyelashes darker. In every way those were patient, languid, humid days — we got readier and readier.
>
> our hum off a stiff horizon
> a captain came with a can of nuts
>
> his wet ship was in
> its high fleas are fish
> one flea reached the end of a pubic hair[75]

The passage itself flirts androgynously with genre, adopting the tough-guy stance of the noir detective, cigarette in hand and leaning over a rail, while simultaneously becoming damper and more voluptuous as the hour grows late. Poetry interrupts this train of genre fantasy with more explicit, and at the same time less situated, jokes about sex and the body, adding tension until an imagined partner, the captain, appears. There is a disjunct yet reinforcing relation between prose and poetry, one that refuses to come together in a single, overarching form of textuality as genre. Rather, poetry interrupts prose with its double entendres, while prose sets apart poetry as a self-conscious pause in the midst of erotic imaginings. The use of conflicting genres takes place, as well, in a series of letters between Harryman and Hejinian that discuss their ongoing collaboration, and, at the end of the text, by means of a double-voiced, hybrid pair of mock theoretical essays on the transgressions they have authored. The two essays alternate side by side in columns on the page; possibilities for dialogue across the textual gap are encouraged; and the text itself links the crossing of boundaries to both erotic play and textual analysis:

> ["An Essay"]: And so, one might ask, if facts are all animate and desirable at once, is it true that what we write of is engendered by the tenacious impulse to possess, consume, absorb fluidly and indiscriminately and thus confirm or register what has been noted men most fear in women? (This is not to say that we ourselves agree that this is in fact what men most fear in women: that has been a conclusion too easily arrived at: it is the claim or notation we point to here.) Is the material that goes into making us what we would select if we would choose it? Does this great freedom of language, which we employ to create this journey, undo what we have sought playfully to undo?

> ["Another Essay"]: Although the woman could see the avalanche, she could no longer discern the details and wondered like a detached observer in a dream what was the extent of the injury to people and their houses.
>
> When all was safe enough, the woman wanted to see where the man lived. They walked to a house, climbed some stairs, and faced a room full of beds, full of sleeping children covered in orange, red, and brown comforters. They were a snorting, noisy group of sleepers, motherless and obscure. The woman suddenly recollected the paper she had been writing on the 18th century before all this had happened. The ghosts of Sade & Rousseau danced in a storm around the youngsters.

Sometimes the best way to undo a trap is to take it apart quietly without calling attention to it. But not always.

This version of undoing, to which we refer, is pleasure when it slips around, as if in loosened shoes. There are other versions too; when one looks at desirable objects for a long time, for instance a series of Morandi paintings, the entire world reveals the structure of the aesthetic objects as if the world itself has become transparent to them. One expands, or expounds, within the other and distinctions are obscured. And we have put a certain pressure on pleasure to press it into realms not typically identified with it as a way of obscuring and testing the boundaries of what we normally think of as distinct.

The man, perhaps out of embarrassment, said nothing, but there was nothing that could restrain her from seducing him.

The man was like Rousseau in that he measured his inspiration according to the scales of nature and exposed himself to nature's danger, but he was unlike Rousseau in that he had children about whereas Rousseau had deposited each of his children in infancy in an orphanage.

The man was like Sade in that the grunting functioning polymorphic sleeping scene exacted from him not discretion but his own abandonment — a wild and extreme acquiescence — so that he, a voluptuous non-entity, might slide, singular and incomprehensibly prolonged, into nothingness — which was the woman and her loss.[76]

In both passages, as suggested by their placement on the page (fig. 28), the dismantling of boundaries is not experienced as a *jouissance* of selves but as an erotics of the other. In "An Essay," the order of objectivity (science and art) is absorbed and transformed into a form of feminine undoing, while in "Another Essay," Rousseau and Sade, as incommensurate instances of the politics of sexual desire, position the figure of the man as object in opposite ways, in terms of either intellectual distance or irreducible corporeality. While the juxtaposed texts seem to be talking about entirely different things, difference itself is aestheticized in the left-hand section, while it is eroticized in the right-hand one. Are the aesthetic and the erotic the same, or different? *Legend* clearly shows them to be the same as it universalizes its textual effects. *The Wide Road*, on the other hand, shows how transgressive dialogues between women differ from the ways male collab-

The Wide Road

Carla Harryman and Lyn Hejinian

La grande route

Comment et par où le désir circule-t-il? Peut-on le mesurer? Par ses thèmes et par sa forme, ce texte interroge les lieux et la mouvance du désir. La structure même du texte, avec ses deux colonnes, subvertit la singularité du désir: plurielle, la double voix déplace la sujette désirante d'"elle' vers 'nous.' Tantôt un essai théorique, tantôt un journal, "La grande route" est à la fois une histoire d'amour et un poème ludique. Les chemins de la jouissance passent, et vont, ailleurs.

An Essay

Let's imagine that desires are perceptions more than motives, mediating the interplay of sensation with knowledge. In this, desires are a medium of acknowledgment, a way of identifying ourselves in terms of others. Although it's true that desires always want more, it's inaccurate to say that desires seek satisfaction – satisfaction would be a form of loss. Rather, what George Eliot says "of Voters and Sunlight," we would happily say of our desirous selves, that we "embrace all but possess only air."

We can't help but live in time, and yet we aren't looking for ultimate or even penultimate pleasures, choosing instead to go on

The Wide Road · 57

with our desires, following them precisely the way persons follow their two eyes. What we see at any given moment, the out-stretched so-called field of vision, is bounded only by invisibility – by the skin and bones of our head that we admit but can't see – and by local constraints on visibility. But whatever is in the way of the view is itself something to see and our head holds our knowing, which is part of our desiring, that we see it.

To be mobile and desirous is to be unbounded among distinct things.

So with plaintive phosphorescent ebullience and waves of restraint we've been going almost anywhere, sometimes with a sense of necessity, sometimes with casual spontaneity, and always appreciatively, not because anything is the same as anything else but because everything is different. Our many love objects are incomparable, but they've made sense.

Vivo con el estomago aqui
y el corazon al otro lado del rio

(I live with my stomach here
and my heart on the other side
of the river)

says Lucha Corpi.

For instance, "when a man's glance is following certain house-

Another Essay

Too often curtailed! Too often abandoned! Too often speechless! Why measure desire? But have we now even approached it or seen it or known it?

This is the reason to measure desire even without realistic implements: to secure its prevalence.

Our task is paradoxical and thus ornamentally sexual. On the one hand, there is no measuring implement: neither a tadpole, or a flagpole or a ruler; although, the tadpole is an image of impregnation: a flagpole something to sit on top of, victoriously and even salaciously, and a ruler always good for a swat. On the other hand, even the mention of desire causes desire to commence measuring itself and its implements of measurement are as various as the imagination.

But be careful: sometimes the usages of measure, are more elegant than others. Those that start out with a series of discrete and formal gestures are sometimes those that provide the context for the greatest improvised abandon. A word carefully placed can erect a nipple.

We are greasing our palms with palm grease before we count our lovers, those who grease our recollections: rooms fill up with each other. The eucalyptus, the must, the piss, the sweet grass, and pastiche of the rooms fill the recollections as we grease our palms to count our lovers. Let us not, however, deceive anyone into thinking that counting lovers is a measure of desire. Measuring desire is never a quantifying of lovers; although, sometimes we imagine them all in the same room together as a substitute for a furnace in winter.

Desire measures itself in the distance, between itself and its object, which advances and is always advancing within time, all the way through all the climaxes it continues its strategies: even when curtailed, abandoned and without words.

28. Carla Harryman and Lyn Hejinian, from The Wide Road, *in* Tessera 15 *(winter 1993).*

orators imagine the breaking down of boundaries between them as the enabling condition of texts.

The ethical implications of *The Wide Road* are thus substantially different from those of the prior two examples. *Legend* and "Non-Events" view intertexuality as the result of an excess of transpositioning, a suprasubjective form bound together by the *jouissance* that exceeds subject positions. *The Wide Road* views intertextuality as between subject positions as well, but it is equally a consequence of the world that constructs desires which form subject positions within it, especially as they are unfixed. The distinction between these polarities ultimately depends on the degree to which a text can be imagined in relation to a context that exceeds it. *Legend*, for all its revolutionary transpositioning, in this sense may be the immanent monolith Harryman characterizes it to be, while "Non-Events" is split between the two subject positions whose sexual objects, and thus structures of desire, do not necessarily coincide. It is the nonidentity of desire in terms of its objects, rather than the fragmentation of the subject, that gives *The Wide Road* its formal distinction from prior examples of avant-garde collaboration, as well as its ethical charge. Moving between genres rather than stabilizing them in an inclusive material text, *The Wide Road* reveals contradictory, oscillating relations between subject and object: there is neither an object held in common, nor a common subject position. While its authors may not have avoided narcissism in refusing to generalize their relation to the object, in *The Wide Road*'s revolution of poetic language, desire held in common still must suffer the fate of an encounter with many objects. There is never only one desire in love.

MULTIAUTHORS AND THE LISTSERV

There is a historical progression of avant-garde multiauthorship in the various works discussed so far — Language School magazines from the 1970s and 1980s, *L=A=N=G=U=A=G=E*, "Non-Events," *Legend*, and *The Wide Road* — but these all differ in important ways. While each reconfigures the author in its construction of poetic intersubjectivity and community, each derives that construction from differing, and often mutually exclusive, notions of genre. In Mann's notion of theory death, agency is absorbed into institutions, leaving only the negative moment of critique; both author and genre disappear into contexts that proscribe agency. In explicit or implicit ways, the forms of multiauthorship in early Language School publications united authorship and genre in suprasubjective forms of discourse: there was participation in an order larger than individual authors and poems. Of course, this is true of many groupings of authors, but what is important is the relation between the forms of Language writing and its intersubjective possibility. At the moment the Language School emerged, horizons of genre were open and indeterminate, while authorial subject positions were held in suspension within the total form of the avant-garde, as with Oshima's radical group and its centrifugal/centripetal tensions.

In its commitment to a specific genre, namely poetry, *Legend* predicts a more recent form of avant-garde multiauthorship, the Poetics Listserv. I am referring specifically to the Poetics Listserv at the Electronic Poetry Center, SUNY Buffalo, available at <http://epc.buffalo.edu>, even as this discussion may be extended toward a more general notion of the Listserv as a multiauthored form of textual practice in electronic media — a postmodern counter to the Great Conversation.[77] While there are many listservs functioning on any number of topics in university settings — my university, for instance, publicly archives dozens of listservs — the importance of the Poetics Listserv is that it is a site where the radical strategies of the avant-garde have continued in a form of intersubjective dialogue. As a historical development of the Language School and more specifically of its forms of multiauthorship — and a site for a dialogue between many of its early members and a larger community — the Poetics Listserv continues the Language School's radical questioning of authorship, genre, and community.[78] Just as Russian Formalism and surrealism historically developed into specific forms of mass cultural or psychoanalytic theory, rather than ending in any theory death, the Language School continues in the Listserv as a form of intersubjective discourse based on its notions of radical textuality.

To begin to discuss the poetics of the Poetics Listserv, one should first note the heterogeneity of its forms of communication. If Roman Jakobson famously defined the poetic function of language as "the message for its own sake,"[79] most of the messages on the Listserv discuss practical matters — advertising for poetry readings and publications, requests for contact information, notice of the availability of lofts and summer sublets, links to outside sites, and so on. Participants do not simply read avant-garde poetry and theorize about it. The poetics of the Listserv emerges, however, in the self-focusing of its messages around certain themes: the interpretation of avant-garde poetry; the nature of authorship and authority; the possibilities and limits of communities and institutions; and finally the political horizons of the poetics community. Often, the discussion focuses these questions around the definition of groups, particularly language-centered writing in its relation to other genres of poetry and to the nature of authorship. In order to explore the dynamics of the Listserv's conversation around its self-focusing questions, I selected the month of April 1999 from its archive, which comprises 461 posts from 167 authors on 330 topics (there is a high degree of individuation on the Listserv, suggesting a paratactic social formation influenced by the Language School's literary use of parataxis).[80]

The month begins auspiciously enough, with a post titled "April is the cruelest month for poetry" by list owner Charles Bernstein, who calls for activities "against national poetry month as such" (post 1), leading to a number of absurdist proposals for noncelebrations of poetry throughout the rest of the month.[81] A major topic of discussion for the month, however, appears a bit later in a post titled "class is" from Robin Tremblay-McGaw (post 6), which proposes a consideration of class in relation to the experience of shame. "Class" and its various subtopics will generate the most posts in the month (about seventy-five); Kathy Lou Schultz continues the debate in post 13, seeing class as "one of the unspeakable, unnameable issues in American culture." Other topics introduced or continued early on in the month include Wendy Kramer on a mail art tribute to Ray Johnson (post

4); Maria Damon on the relation of poetry to cultural studies (post 8); an announcement for a new issue of the online journal *Lagniappe* (post 11); a report on San Francisco art activities by Taylor Brady (post 13); a request for contact information for Lyn Hejinian (post 14); notice of the publication of Pamela Lu's *Pamela: A Novel* by Atelos Press, edited by Hejinian and Travis Ortiz (who posts the note, and then goes on to announce a publication party for the book and a reading by M. Mara-Ann and Jill Stengel, post 16); notice of a new e-journal from Canada, *Para>poetics* (Derek Beaulieu, post 19); and discussion of the Sackner collection of artists' books (Brian Kim Stefans, post 20). This sampling of the first twenty posts gives an idea of the range and literariness of the discussion. Deeper questions, such as the nature of class, occur in the context of a barrage of information, publicity, and small talk: the everyday life of poetics.

What Bernstein calls "a swirl of concerns" in *L=A=N=G=U=A=G=E* is evident here: a centrifugal/centripetal dynamic of information spinning away from a common thread but finally returning to define it. In April 1999, the common thread that seemed most central to the ongoing group discussion was the nature of class, which immediately turned into questions of the nature of authorship (What class is Lyn Hejinian? [post 23]; what class am I? [post 125]) and of literary value (as Karen McKevitt puts it, "What are we really worth? What is my work worth? My time?" post 33). Class leads to questions of interpretation: "Can one tell from Van Gogh's sunflowers anything about the class of the artist?" (Charles Alexander, post 37), and of ideology: "Class after all is a heinous fiction that they/we maintain" (Linda Russo, post 57). Class intersects with a second important theme, Who owns the Listserv? (in a dialogue between Charles Alexander and Kent Johnson over the politics of exclusion [posts 41 and 52 et seq.]); it is also a point of contact with information about the US/NATO bombing of Kosovo, then in progress, which was vividly brought to the Listserv in a post by Serbian poet Dubravka Djuric on the closing of radio station B92 in Belgrade (posts 40, 50 et seq.). The thread of class, then, appears within the overall form of the discussion seen as the sum total of all its messages, from the most self-obsessed and literary to the most self-conscious and political. The level of seriousness of the discussion ranges from the absurdist proposal by Bernstein to resist National Poetry Month, and many procedurally generated works by Alan Sondheim (such as "Confessive-Repulsive Disorder," which introduces language such as "I will push my dirty panties up into my hole" into the group's psychodynamics, post 22), to the urgency of messages concerning the nature of class and the bombing of Kosovo.

I want to pursue a minor thread, but one of crucial importance for a self-focusing poetics, which emerged late in the month, after the discussions of class, Listserv politics, and Kosovo had peaked and begun to generate hybrids of various sorts. Class and literary politics fuse, in this sense, in Camille Roy's assertion that "the langpo [Language poetry] equals theory equals white assumption which tends to dominate seems to me to rely on smoothed experience" (post 154). Jeffrey Jullich continues this line of thinking in relating class to the poetics of the material text (post 204), while Joe Amato links class and other forms of social grouping: "Of course, 'class' is about groups" (post 211), and Grant Jenkins links class to authorship: "Class is in some sense BEYOND the intention and control of the subject" (post 219). In an interesting digression, Michael McColl relates Raymond Williams's notion of "structures of feeling" to forms of literary ambition (post 231). Groupings are also considered from the outside in Dubravka Djuric's forward of a parodic list of reasons one might see oneself as a Serb, Croat, Kosovan, Yugoslavian, and so on, in which the nature of national identity is portrayed as absurdist or reactionary. The next post, by Bernstein, follows this thread with a notice of an international anthology (*99 Poets/1999*) that combines the grouping of an anthology with the rejection or suspension of national identity under the common banner of experiment. Tony Green links status and the writing of experimental poetry (post 261), while Maria Damon claims, "the freshest poetry comes from the lower margins" (post 275), and Michael McColl echoes this sentiment: "Marginalized groups tend to have riskier aesthetic positions" (post 307). Post 285, however, presents a new theme: Linda Russo's substantial report of the April 1999 Barnard conference on women experimental writers, where the relation of lyric tradition to language-centered writing was much debated. One writer whose work received significant attention at the conference was Lyn Hejinian,[82] and it is this context of the politics of recognition and the relation of authorship to group identity that gave rise, through processes of condensation and displacement, to the poetic subtheme of interest here.

The subtheme, "Hejinian's 'deen,'" begins with a technical question by Jeffrey Jullich about the appearance of a "nonce" word in her *Writing Is an Aid to Memory*:[83]

> One thread that particularly fascinates me are her "half-words," so to speak. That is, she punctuates the book with truncated words, or fragments, such as "ness," "scription," "porated," "brating," etc. The "rule"

> is that it is always the first syllable that is deleted. It's as though the fragment were the left-hand-justified tail-end of a word hyphenated at the other side of the page (obviously).
>
> Here's the problem. There's one — and only one — such "nonce" word that for the life of me, I can't figure it. It is "deen," in section 36:
>
> > an ordinary person depending deen
>
> I wracked my mind and finally gave up. I could not think of any word, as for "mena" or "nishment" or "sume," that would complete "deen." In a final gasp, I checked my rhyming dictionary, which lists words backwards from last letter to first. And there is, in fact, a single word which it gives that ends in "deen": "dudeen." A dudeen is a short tobacco pipe made out of clay.
>
> The thing is, I feel that "dudeen" is out of character with the timbre of vocabulary Hejinian uses throughout. True, there is "cladding," and a few other rare words but, for some reason, I don't feel satisfied that "dudeen" is the answer that completes "deen." (Post 302, "Hejinian: 'deen'?")

This radical self-focusing on the indeterminacy of a word in a particular work is out of character with much of the preceding discussion, but it stems directly from associations with it. Hejinian's name had occurred several times earlier in the month, once with a request for contact information, indicating that she was not a participant in the list and not readily available to it (post 14), and once in post by Juliana Spahr that discusses her class background in relation to experimental poetry: "Her father was an academic administrator (a decent but not the best paying job), her mother a housewife. The New College, where she worked until recently, is known for its substandard salaries. She doesn't have an advanced degree. What is making her the symbol for middle (?) classness to these students? Is it because she doesn't in *My Life* put her self forward as a marginalized subject?" (post 23). The context of the Barnard event, coming after the lengthy debates on class, authorship, and community, set the stage for the micropolitics of Jullich's question, which is immediately taken up as a locus of fascination in approximately a dozen posts.

There are really two questions being debated here: What is the meaning of "deen"? and What is the relation of that meaning to authorial intention, insofar as that may be determined through group consensus (the "we" of liberal polity and interpretive communities after Stanley Fish)? The indeterminacy of "deen" thus becomes a moment of group definition, an empty center around which its swirl of concerns is articulated. Some of this discussion occurs through back channels, which are summarized by Jullich, who says he has been struck sleepless by the question and frustrated because he cannot locate Hejinian, through a name search, in order to ask her directly (post 319). In post 324, Tom Beckett wonders whether "deen" should really be "deem" (it appears as "deen" in both editions of the text), but concludes that "the undecideability of it is a pleasure too since so much of the book seems to be 'about' the sound and texture of language as felt experience." Chris Piuma suggests "Aberdeen" (post 326); Gwyn McVay proposes, "it's also Scots for something like trashed, used up," as in the reel "The Muckin' o' Geordie's Byre": "The graip was tint, the besom was deen" (post 406); and Clai Rice locates an "interesting idiom recorded with the spelling 'deen' is 'be deen with it' meaning 'be dying'" (post 450). But in general, higher-order decisions are called on to make sense of "deen." For Sherry Brennan (post 331), "deen" is a device that points to the possibility that many words in English may be truncated or incomplete, as "we make new words primarily by suffixes." "The particular ways the poem cuts words and lines makes you . . . question whether any of the words are 'whole.' . . . The more you look at it that way, the fewer whole words there seem to be." Grant Jenkins picks up this argument, suggesting that "there is no single, logical explanation"; "these words ARE whole and cannot be . . . either enciphered or deciphered." Rather, they could be "fortunate 'mistakes' or 'errors'"; "zaum-type syllables"; or "indeterminate, potentially never to be figured out" (post 340).

In a detailed synthesis, too long to be fully accounted for here, Jullich summarizes the philological and interpretive arguments for specific readings of "deen" and then goes on to discuss the device of such "semi-words" in *Writing Is an Aid to Memory*, of which he counts eighty-four (post 362). Jullich connects the use of such partial words to the theme of memory in the book: "It is, of course, in the retrieval or re-creation of missing beginnings that memory consists!" But the larger question concerns the nature of indeterminacy, which is not "anything goes" but "[has] to be filtered through a sort of *triage* and negotiated on the strength of internal evidence." This has political implications for the politics of experimental writing: "The reader may be entrusted with the *production* of meaning . . . but there are productions that are fabrications, and there are productions that are deductions/inductions." The indeterminacy of "deen" proves the necessity of an author, but only as determined in a process of weighing alternative readings in collective discussion: "The belief-system, or ideology I seem to be carrying, in remaining lukewarm to the solution of typo, is a belief in the infallibility of the author that is stronger than my temptation to impute the fallibility of oversight to [the publisher]" — author outranks institution in his theory of new meaning. This is only possible, however, because of the genuine indeterminacy of "deen": "'Deen,' then, is a *genuine* case of not knowing which meaning to assign a word." In the suspension of the meaning of "deen," as adjudicated by the consensus of the interpretative community, the author function is reinscribed: in the need for an author to guarantee meaning, but also in the fascination with/anxiety over the elusive author, Lyn Hejinian, who cannot be contacted to give evidence of her intention.

"Hejinian's 'deen'" is not just a question of playing with words, though of course its appeal is partly due to that. It is also a moment of the reproduction of the author function within a community, a moment of the community's own reproduction. "Hejinian," then, as an author is as much a site for anxiety and speculation as her nonce word, "deen." This may be seen in the Listserv's attempt to contact her, assign her class identity, worry over her reception at the Barnard conference, and finally interpret her literary devices. A constructivist moment, then, may be discerned here in the foundation of a community of readers in the question of a precise textual indeterminacy — the textual absence given a placeholder by "deen." Jullich is inspired because he believes he has discovered a secret that has eluded many on the Listserv: a way to solve the frustrating uninterpretability of the material text in a way that guarantees participation in a community of readers and, finally, authority. It is no accident, then, that when Gregory Severance, the publisher of an online zine, advertises the publication of eleven poems by Jullich, he promotes him as "the author of the April '99 Poetics List posting: D=E=E=N." The graphic modification, here, points to the social production of authorship in the Language School — in my own speculative account, as a form of "need" for authorship in reverse — as a form of parodic confirmation. At the same time, the focus on the word "deen" occurs within the self-focusing of the Poetics Listserv within historical limits that exceed it — the crisis of the bombing of Kosovo as troublingly outside the limits of community discourse. Stephen Vincent supports this reading in his rebuttal to the entire debate as politically irresponsible: "I have been finding it somewhat amazing — in the pervasive darkness, the sheer hell of Serbia, Kosovo, and Colorado — that interesting minds are able to focus so obsessively on the meaning and function of Lyn's 'deen'!! To add an uncanny layer to all of this, my spell checker has just suggested I replace 'deen' with 'Eden' . . . as an aid to the memory of that mythic place (an unviolated America?) albeit buried way in the text" (post 393). As if in confirmation of this disclosure of a "lost America" in the text, a search engine provides further evidence that supports an encrypted meaning for "deen," in a July 2001 post by Alan Sondheim of a procedurally generated text that discloses "deen" in the line: "yficeps ot deen on dnA .dne ,etiuq ton" — as "need" spelled backward. In this sense, the absence holding the community together inverts a terrifying loss kept outside its form.

We may now return to the genealogy of the poetics of the Language School in terms of the politics of the multiauthored text, from *Legend* to the Poetics Listserv. As a moment where radical poetics comes together as both form and community, *Legend*'s formal dialectic between authorial subject positions within a totalizing discourse describes important aspects of the intersubjective politics/poetics of the Listserv, even as there are equally apparent differences of scale and intention. For one thing, *Legend* is entirely literary and self-focusing, while the Listserv has many practical tasks. However, it is not the case that the Listserv is a primarily homosocial community, nor that women do not participate in it. As the foregoing discussion should evidence, quite the opposite is true: many women have key roles in the discussions. But here *Legend*'s example of multiauthorship must be interpreted on another level: that of a discourse of poetry and poetics as basis for community. Where *Legend* may be all intersubjective contestation and disagreement, its transgression of what may be called the Law of the Author founds community as an interest held in common: poetry. In other words, the rejection of singular authorship accedes to a higher order of genre. The resulting Law of Genre that develops between authorial positions supercedes the Law of the Author, and its patriarchal violence, much as the mutual interests of the primal horde overturned the violent selfishness of the father. Therefore, we may look for a collective affirmation of poetry as genre as the real inheritance of an origin in avant-garde technique for the multiauthorship of the Listserv.

In "Non-Events," my dual-voiced collaboration with Benson, there is a crisis of genre that leads, on the one hand, to the writing of two poems, and on the other to the splitting of the notion of a common interest (object choice) between them. The writing of "Non-Events" did not stabilize any community of interest between myself and Benson, but it did restabilize the genre of poetry in our challenge to authorship, in the writing of two distinct poems. In Harryman and Hejinian's collaboration, however, something quite opposite is going on. The work textualizes a common interest, and even objects held in common, evidenced in the "we" of the first-person plural narrative and in the swapping of authorial positions, as well as sexual partners, across the textual divide separating them. But there is not the slightest sense that *The Wide Road* could found a community of interest between authorial positions, or serve as a model for community; there is no analogy between *The Wide Road* and the Poetics Listserv. This is because *The Wide Road* wants to transgress not only the Law of the Author but the subsequent Law of Genre (poetry) that was meant to reconstruct its traumatized and divided interests. As opposed to either *Legend* or the Poetics Listserv, *The Wide Road* could never take the form of a swirl of concerns around a single elided object — producing the homosociality of the former or the interpretive community of the latter. Rather, desire seizes its objects in radically disjunct ways that refuse a common interest, which is kept open to a renewal of its object choice. In disrupting genre, *The Wide Road* defers community before it can stabilize in any text, as it demands that writing be held accountable to many, and various, objects of desire.

THE BRIDE OF THE ASSEMBLY LINE
RADICAL POETICS IN CONSTRUCTION

And so roads are the important thing
and what is on them.
— Gertrude Stein

This essay is an avowed polemic that addresses the situation of avant-garde poetry and poetics in the mid-1990s. After the work of the Language School in revising and contesting the generic confines of the author function, there was a marked return to an author-centered, formally immanent lyricism by a number of experimental writers in the decade. A reconstruction of the relation between author and school was crucial: as the emerging history of the Language School, that is, the active agency of its development, receded into a recognizable canon of authors — in which the author function was critically modified by the demands of radical form, but where the collective address and historical moment had been absorbed into a narrative of emergence and stabilization — a kind of anguish of genealogy resulted in which the initial motivations for radical form were forgotten or suppressed. Some of this anguish over the role of authorship can be seen in the discussions on the Poetics Listserv in the previous chapter. Here, I want to return to neglected aspects of the emergence of the radical poetics of the Language School, even at this late date. One is ever only speaking, writing, and acting from a given perspective. In this essay, mine was of one teaching literature and cultural studies — and attempting to unite the possibilities of both — at Wayne State University in Detroit, as both a poet and a critic. The essay was first delivered at the Poetics Program at SUNY Buffalo, and published in the evanescent literary journal *The Impercipient Lecture Series*. It is revised for publication here — with material added from the 1996 Assembling Alternatives conference at the University of New Hampshire — but I want to preserve its tone of polemical engagement.

THE DESCENT

Touring the United States in 1934, Gertrude Stein noticed something had changed. The country was crisscrossed with a network of public highways, and there were more than enough cars to fill them. Cars, of course, had been important for Stein since her experience as an ambulance driver in World War I, and with the acquisition of her first Ford in 1916; they provide a repeated figure for modernity in her work. In the second half of the century, the importance of roads and what is on them would change drastically, with the national landscape altered after the postwar boom and its acceleration of automobile production; with the decline of urban centers and the rise of the suburbs; and with the construction of the interstate highway system. The roads have been cognitively remapped since Stein's remark, necessitating a new geography (and the installation of Global Positioning Systems in newer models) to locate where we are.

In my own case: the road to Detroit beckons as a descent of superhuman proportions as one leaves the semirural enclaves of Bloomfield Township and joins the unending stream of automobile carriers, semis bearing parts, cement trucks, Cherokees and Explorers, Lexuses and junkers, that flows from Pontiac, through Southfield and Detroit, to Dearborn, seat of Ford world headquarters, and south to the marshes of Toledo. After roughly three miles of a great roaring noise that draws one down Telegraph Road, where timed lights break the flow of traffic into segmented, accelerating clusters at Fourteen Mile, Thirteen Mile, and Twelve Mile Roads, one enters a complex interchange of vast horizontal dimensions that merges and distributes traffic from a matrix of urbanized suburbs feeding Telegraph Road and Northwestern Highway into the main trunklines of Interstate 696 and Highway 10 and on toward destinations in both city and suburb.

If Detroit is not often likened to Paris, Interstate 696, the Walter J. Reuther Freeway, may be its one point of comparison — a linear equivalent of the *Périphérique*, the ring road that separates city from suburb and, at least symbolically, the culture of Paris from job sites of the working-class *banlieux* known as the Red Belt. In metropolitan Detroit, however, there are few such lines of demarcation between culture and work: the social terrain of Detroit may be thought of as an enormous factory, producing cars, airbags, brake drums, hockey teams, techno music, degrees in cultural studies, and docent tours of Ford's Greenfield Village and Diego Rivera's *Detroit Industry* murals at the Detroit Institute of Arts. I-696 does not separate anything; rather it runs right through the middle of the burgeoning production zone formerly known as the suburbs of Oakland County, connecting home, factory, and shopping mall across an emplotted patchwork of residential, industrial, and commercial areas. Two to three miles farther south begins the matrix of neighborhoods — many stable and thriving, many not — within the boundaries of the partly collapsed, always-about-to-be-reborn infrastructure of racially divided, depopulated Detroit. The difference between city and suburb is no longer the traditional line of demarcation, Eight Mile Road, symbolizing the 1960s history of white flight and the later politics of black retrenchment; rather, urban Detroit and the more populous, industrialized, and suburban Oakland County now compete as production zones.

When does the Lodge Freeway get me home? Being so caught up by the brutality of the place, I take the off-ramp to Highway 10, the Lodge Freeway, accepting its offer of release in a linear descent from interchange to downtown, connecting home to the Cultural Center of museums, restaurants, and university where I work. Along the way, the route passes through the air of its own misreading, past atavistic postmodern synagogues and the gold-leafed octagonal roof of the Armenian Church; the bronze-sheened tinted windows of the Prudential office complex reflecting onto the road; the 1960s Soviet-style apartment blocks along Greenfield Road; miles of concrete channels for slot cars weaving through traffic in video-game maneuvers; working-class black neighborhoods with churches and community self-help billboards, until reaching Albert Kahn's baroque modernist monuments, the Fisher Building and former General Motors world headquarters; Henry Ford Hospital, the nation's first HMO, where the poet Jim Gustafson died unknown even to many who had known him; Interstate 94 with its luring exit sign for Chicago; the partly demolished Brewster Homes, red brick public housing where once Diana Ross grew up; and vistas of a simulacral, reviving, but still almost 80 percent vacant downtown. Wayne State University is all construction and parking lots, a paradox of empty fullness, a world of opportunity where thirty thousand students can look like a small crowd waiting for the bus. If the bus ever comes, it will be because voters just renewed funds for mass transit.

Against the thick descriptions of cultural reportage, the question "What is literature?" must be asked. Detroit is known as a site for production, but not particularly of literature (though it is proud of the many honorable mentions in its past).[1] Clearly, my cognitive map of Detroit is not identical to an experience I or anyone else may have had of living there; it makes no claim to an adequate account. It provides, however, a cultural analogy for something I want in literature, along the lines of the test of poetry advocated in the introduction to Ron Silliman's *Tjanting*: "A bus ride is better than most art," or in the rubric of *Total Syntax*: "I want an art that reflects that total syntax" (I would like to see that on a billboard in Detroit!).[2] Much recent experimental writing, however, fails the utopian (or even dystopian) test of such imagined futurity, as it turns toward a skeptical or defensive abstraction that presumes a critical value for its use of language but that refuses cultural engagement in more explicit terms. In its negotiations between the world and the work, between horizons of language and cultural form, the tradition of the material text — from Stein and Louis Zukofsky to Clark Coolidge and Lee Ann Brown — has been misread in a way that is diminished in terms of both language and culture. I remember well the complaints about "social" concerns that were raised with the publication of Ron Silliman's *Ketjak* and *Tjanting*, the sense of disturbance (or lack of decorum) both occasioned, in their synthesis of material text and cultural form in the minutest details of everyday life, for those with a more literary sensibility.[3] The specific social investigations Silliman's texts enacted (and others like them such as my own *Progress* or Bob Perelman's *Primer*, *To the Reader*, and *The First World*, along with work that critiques the genre of poetics such as Steve Benson's *Blue Book* or Carla Harryman's *The Middle* and *Vice*), and which certainly are irreducible to any poetics of mimesis, were positioned outside the initial reception of Language writing.[4] In theory, and by example, I want to return our attention from the material text to a cultural poetics, but not by claiming an easy identity between them. It is difficult to find the connection between avant-garde writing and the social space of Detroit, which is one reason I am fascinated by what it means to live here. What is literature at the point of production?

The mode of production in Detroit is the assembly line — but not merely of cars. The entire culture of mid-American modernity is assembled here, and this is a scene of writing. As I concluded in the 1996 Assembling Alternatives conference: "We have been alternative in our way of assembling texts; we should now assemble more cultural alternatives."[5] In order to reconstruct literature as such a cultural alternative, it will be necessary to return to the central question of the nature of literariness itself — to what the Russian Formalists called *literaturnost* — in a way that is missing in current discussion of poetics, and which has been set aside in the agenda of cultural studies. In other words, we need to move from a notion of language as the horizon of innovative work to a more general but unexamined category, the "literary" as a point of departure for discussing the nature of aesthetic alternatives. For the Russian Formalists, *literaturnost*, of course, was at once atemporal and historical. Beginning with Viktor Shklovsky's work on the transrational language of futurist poetry, as a reflection

of the new meaning generated by the historical provocations of the avant-garde, the Formalists consistently viewed language in the context of specific cultural interventions, and as interpreting specific cultural referents, along with what they initially conceived as a scientific approach to the study of literature. The philological paradigm shift of Saussurean linguistics, introduced to the Petersburg *Opoyaz* (Society for the Study of Language) at the same time the avant-garde in Moscow was putting itself on public display, was in itself a form of cultural intervention.[6]

The resulting alliance between science and the avant-garde, as a specifically modernist cultural formation, began with a conflation of literary device and cultural agency. What makes a work literary is precisely the way it negotiates the cultural materials available to it in a specific context; for Shklovsky, while "every art has its own organization — that which transforms its material into something artistically experienced," the total effect of this organization is "to transform the extra-aesthetic material of the work by providing it with form."[7] In a historical shift of emphasis (and as a hallmark of midcentury modernism), such reflexive relations between text and context would be transformed into a univocal notion of autonomous agency, as in a crucial formulation by Roman Jakobson: "The object of literary science is not literature but literariness [*literaturnost*], what makes a given work a literary work."[8] Jakobson's scientistic definition of *literaturnost* positioned literature as an object of knowledge in a way that would lead to the institution of norms, both in the genealogy of Prague Structuralism and in his American reception within the New Criticism in the 1950s, as it distributes the moment of cultural agency.[9] What results is a hypostatization, in the concept of structure, of the contextual motivations for the earlier account. For Shklovsky, the work of art reconstitutes materials given to it by the world in the organization of form, while for Jakobson, more abstractly, "The function of poetry is to point out that the sign is not identical to the referent." What then becomes important, for one historian of Formalism, is "not the reader's attitude toward reality [or cultural context], but the poet's attitude toward language [identified with poetic form].[10] A shift of emphasis reinterprets the nature of the work's material, its cultural or linguistic sources, in a way that leads directly to the horizon of language in the poststructuralist methodologies appearing after the 1960s.[11] The materiality of language, a mediation between culture and art for the Formalists, turns into a preexisting set of cultural codes in Jakobson — and we are well on the way to the possibility of literature be-

coming a mere utopia of language, the modernist form of the autonomous text.[12]

I am arguing against a misattribution of universality to avant-garde techniques such that they become the sole bases for its cultural agency. The universalization of techniques of language in the Language School has had the result of seeming to make contextual motives, both historical referents and utopian prospects, available in the work only as conflicted aftereffects, ghosts of vocabulary or even thematic content seen as latent in a displaced mode of signification that is generalized as a carrier frequency of the text. Context becomes a matter of overtones, consonances or dissonances, resident in the materials from which the text is constructed, but it remains generally distributed within the horizon of total form. At the same time, foregrounding the mode of signification depends on a politics of the reader's construction of meaning that is always only a potential effect. This resulting lowercase formalism has led, beyond a defunct politics satisfied to claim that the reader is empowered to make meaning from material texts, to a poetics of mere possibility — that to say what writing can effect as politics is the same as to do it; that to describe literary possibility is to represent a form of agency, in a circular fashion, as a critique of representation. It is, thus, claims for the possibility of form rather than specific forms; or the possibility of language rather than a specific language; or the possibility of a critique instead of a specific critique; or the possibility of difference rather than a specific difference, that characterizes the aporia of our dialogic, site-specific and time-valued, manifold poetics. Such a univocal possibility is the consequence a single, one-size-fits-all device — of language as a mode of production, of indeterminacy as a form of reception — as the sole mediation between literary and cultural form. If we return to the Russian Formalists' notions of *ostranenie* (defamiliarization) and semantic shift, we may value them anew as working both sides of the gap between literary and cultural form. In the 1920s, Shklovsky explicitly described the literary avant-garde as constructing a dialogue between language and culture, where both are transformed in poetic language:

> Russian literary language, which was originally foreign to Russia, has so permeated the language of the people that it has blended with their conversation. On the other hand, literature has now begun to show a tendency toward the use of dialects [and] barbarisms. . . . Maxim Gorky is changing his diction from the old literary language to the new literary colloquialism of Leskov. Ordinary speech and literary language have

> thereby changed places. [Finally,] a strong tendency, led by Khlebnikov, to create a new and properly poetic language has emerged, [so that] we can define poetry [as opposed to prose] as *attenuated, tortuous* speech.[13]

To democratize the national language, Shklovsky reserves a specific task for the avant-garde in its foregrounding of linguistic innovation; even so, the avant-garde simply accelerates processes of cultural change occurring in other genres. Both historical motives and cultural contexts — of Russian language, literature, and culture as they entered a phase of modernist transformation — are in this way combined in such seemingly abstract and universal notions as defamiliarization and the semantic shift (not to mention language).

We need to more fully comprehend the precise social and cultural pressures that led to the turn to language in American postmodernism — the period, it turns out, of American productive dominance in world markets after World War II. Toward this end, we need to move from the material text, as hypothetical point of origin and ultimate goal of Language School *literaturnost*, to a cultural poetics that takes into account the specific historical and cultural conditions that produced it (just as the abstractly rationalist but violently historical matrix of Detroit facilitated the production of cars). A static concept of *literaturnost* keeps writing at the level of a material production that endlessly reproduces a literary version of what the Ford Motor Company would like to imagine as the advent of the world car[14] — a universal product that it is potentially possible to assemble anywhere, and distribute in all national markets, if only because it is *un*regulated in all of them. Returning to the Russian Formalists recovers precisely the dimension of the elided cultural context in the construction of the literary work and its evolution into new forms. For Shklovsky, when a literary form, seen within its historical horizon, runs out of work to do, it turns to what he calls "peripheral forms" — in one of his central examples, the penny-dreadful detective novel for Dickens and Dostoyevsky, but by extension, advertising and cheap romances, newspapers and bar talk for Joyce; the spectacle of popular cinemas such as *King Kong* and the displays of department store windows for the French surrealists; a cup of coffee at Horn and Hardart's, the songs of Billie Holiday at the Five Spot for the New York School; and the displaced social spaces of postmodernity for the Language School. Such a negotiation with expanded cultural contexts — in the many languages of myth, history, and dream in the expansive work of Charles Olson, or in the opening to urban mass culture in the aesthetics of the New York School, or in the countercultural moment of the 1960s itself — must be seen as crucial motivations for the Language School and for the American avant-garde in general. Literature at the point of production occurs as an assembling of materials, brought from the widest range of sources the culture allows, as an act of reflexive agency in the making of the work.

CULTURAL POETICS

The term *cultural poetics* is open for discussion and ought to be explored to the fullest extent. Where the rubric is introduced within the New Historicism, it aligns with a Foucauldian politics of power and knowledge, as well as with the practice of "thick description" in the work of anthropologist Clifford Geertz. Stephen Greenblatt's original and suggestive use of the term points to two reinforcing dynamics: that the work of art is in a tensional relation with the many resonant strands of the culture that formed it; and that the work of art unequivocally declares itself as a thing apart, a vision of wonder and thus of deserved cultural authority (as in the case of Shakespeare).[15] Underscoring both processes are the reinforcing effects of the economic (which facilitates the porousness of boundaries between work and culture) and of the political (which confers legitimacy in terms of basic rights of cultural participation as well as for meritocratic hierarchies). It is not hard to find key concepts of Russian Formalism, such as the semantic shift and defamiliarization, in Greenblatt's poetics; indeed, resonance depends on a canonization of peripheral forms and a semantic shift by which the materials of culture are transposed to literature, while wonder is the defamiliarization that results, raised to a more theatrical register perhaps, in stunning the onlooker into awareness. But beyond asserting the need for a cultural reading, in a way that both preserves the specificity of the literary and that captures the molecular economics of social energy and temporal power as "a dense network of evolving and often contradictory social forces" (ibid.), New Historicist cultural poetics often falls short — at least in theory — of describing a more articulated relation between the two. Indeed, Greenblatt claims that, because of the numerous practices that inform a cultural poetics — "power, charisma, sexual excitement, collective dreams, wonder, desire, anxiety, religious awe, free-floating intensities of experience[, i.e.,] everything produced by the society . . . unless it is deliberately excluded from circulation" — "there can be no single method, no overall picture, no exhaustive and definitive cultural poetics."[16] As a result of this redundancy, a cultural poetics can only remain a suggestive possibility, rather than a mechanism of literary or cultural construction; it ends rather than begins in a call for an interpretive practice at an equal distance from both text and context, as it weaves together strands of both.[17] Cultural poetics has thus not led to much renewed interest in poetry, or in the construction of the poetic text, seeing it as a kind of adjunct to representational practices that often seem to take place as if cultures existed apart from the makers, if not the interpreters, of them. The undoing of a static *literaturnost* in the name of nonliterary discourses, however, has long since taken place; what we need is a more a specific account of the relation of literary form to a poetics of culture.[18]

Charles Bernstein's "Poetics of the Americas," in this sense, responds to the need for a more site-specific and formally mediated cultural poetics.[19] Such a poetics emerges in the relation between national languages, dialects, and what Bernstein terms "ideolects" in poetry produced in widely diverse contexts, from metropolitan modernism (Stein and Zukofsky) to emerging or discrepant modernisms (the use of dialect in the Harlem Renaissance, Hugh MacDiarmid, and Basil Bunting; the transrational poetics of Eugene Jolas's *transition*) to diasporic postnationalisms (the "nation language" of Kamau Braithwaite and dub poetry of Michael Smith and Linton Kwesi Johnson). Bernstein resituates poetry within cultural politics in a way that moves significantly beyond the New Historicism's free-floating interpretation of representational practices, not to mention Cultural Studies' rejection of literary form (though he overstates by far that the "movement of cultural studies risks leveling all art to the status of symptom"; 20). The abstract horizon of language is likewise reinterpreted as a dialectic of many languages and literary modes brought together in the construction of the poetic text. Poetry becomes a model for cultural participation as it aspires to an overarching horizon of "ideolectical" writing that unites high postmodernists with emerging ethnicities in "a field of potentialities, a virtual America that we approach but never possess."[20] While Bernstein's cultural front of avant-garde modernisms, Harlem Renaissance dialects, postmodern ideolects, and hybrid writing of the world diaspora is welcome for its collective poetics of linguistic difference, the impossible horizon of virtual America that results is more problematic in that it interprets their diverse effects in univocal terms. In reading the many possibilities of difference toward the one nonstandard mode of their representation, the discrepant texts of social ideolects that refuse group identification, Bernstein hopes that a new, multinational poetry of difference will result that "share[s] a technical commonality that overrides the necessary differences in interpretation and motivation" (7). In such a foregrounding of radical linguistic difference in poetry — which at the same time subordinates more specific contextual motivations for its use — a sensibility may arise whose "commonness is in our partiality and disregard for the norm, the standard, the overarching, the universal" (3).

While there is indeed every reason to call for as much language-centered invention as possible in the making of new meaning in culture, there is also an abstraction or relativizing of motives for discrepant uses of language here. To begin with, Bernstein sees all movements toward ideolect as rejections of the standard language, beginning with the politics of marginalized dialects and ending in the achievement of modernist form, which leads to ideolectical writing through three rough-and-ready categories of formal agency: "objective," "subjective," and "constructive." Ideolectical writing may derive from any or all of these — a canonical modernism, like that of Pound and Joyce, may be ideolectical in its construction of the work as object; a feminist corrective, such as that of Stein and H.D., may tend toward ideolect in its refusal of the claims of objective mastery; and finally, a language-centered constructivism may make meaning all by itself, becoming its own ideolect (4–5). Bernstein's "constructive" mode, while more specific than the other two terms, is exemplified by the abstract writing of midcareer Stein; it is what has generally gone, in Anglo-American critical practice, under the rubric "formalism," although it is not often so identified with radical form. It bears no relation either to Soviet constructivism, which was not only contextualist but interventionist, or to the more abstract version common in the 1920s and 1930s in Western Europe, which sought an alliance between modernist form and design. A teleological horizon is inferred in the progressive realization of form, even as it opposes the standard language, which aligns with conservative ideals of modernist form, however defamiliarized by discrepant uses of language.

The insertion of social dialect in the modernist work, transformed into literature, thus tends toward its consummation in ideolect; as a form of alterity, "dialectical" poetry ought to move toward this wider horizon, as it even more powerfully "refuses allegiance to standard English without necessarily basing its claim on an affiliation with a definable group's speaking practice" (5). This is necessary because "the norm enforces a conduct of representation that precludes poetry as an active agent to further thought," while standardizing the practices of an established group of speakers would be "a report of things already settled" and thus perpetuates stasis (ibid.).

Standard language and group norms are both, in their relation, what the movement from dialect to ideolect resists. Beyond them, there is by default *one* global motivation for the affiliations of nonstandard language use, which Bernstein goes on to name: the culturally homogenizing effects of multinational corporations and state formations (although there is little discussion of either). Bernstein's privileging of ideolect over dialect as an oppositional strategy, however, given this imagined totality, allows him to characterize "the challenge of multiculturalism" as merely "reinforcing traditional modes of representation" (rather than creating, out of whole cloth, a new canon of multicultural Language poets?). The red herring of identity politics is thrown out as well when "static conceptions of group identity represented by authentic spokespersons continue to ride roughshod over works and individuals whose identities are complex, multiple, mixed, confused," and so on (3). It is odd that Bernstein's plea for complexity is framed by such a reductive explanation of identity politics, not so much refusing stereotypes as inventing them. The counter to this oppressive fantasy of multicultural complicity in imagined totality, with its "authentic spokespersons" — the discrepant materiality of the ideolectical text — is an impossible solution as it elides, as a political standard, any particular context for its use. While disregard for the norm may create an imagined community of nonstandard language users, a new norm may also be produced, precisely in opposition to the placeholders of "authentic" identity.[21] Nothing prevents an ideolect from becoming a dialect once it has formed a group.

What we need instead is a cultural poetics that rejects a universalist distinction between normative and nonstandard modes of writing and that therefore requires, as a form of politics, a specific history of difference. Bernstein goes part way toward giving one in his reading of Claude McKay's dialect poems, *Constab Ballads*, even as he sees them as works "of breathtaking duplicity and paradox," a "schizophrenic" performance of resistance (rather than a cultural inscription of double consciousness) like that of the slave mutineers in Melville's "Benito Cereno" (*PA*, 12). But only if we accept a preexisting, coherent category of identity (both ironically assumed and dismissed for McKay as "the point of view of a Jamaican native working for the British as a policeman"; ibid.) can we see McKay's Jamaican "border songs" as having a politics in undermining hackneyed English ballad conventions with discrepant uses of dialect, trading dialect (good) for English verse (bad) as a form of resistance. They are also a form of cultural synthesis, akin to the ballads collected in the border countries in the eighteenth century, a making of emergent cultural form given the available means. In their play with stereotypes, they anticipate McKay's novelistic uses of dialect as "color" in *Home to Harlem* and *Banjo*, and predict a future for the ironic ballad in the politicized calypsos of the 1930s, as well.[22] Overstating the doubling of codes as resistance, rather than reading them as culturally constructed, either internally or as representations of the linguistic border, Bernstein does not see how McKay's poems provide a model of social reflexivity (or anticipate his more explicit modes of social reflection, both dialectical and political, to come). The paradox of McKay is that *either* his poetry may be read as recasting Jamaican dialect in the poetic mold of the "downpressers" *or* it is a duplicitous site of resistance in the materiality of dialect itself. This bifurcation is not a solution, as a specter of authentic identity is preserved by Bernstein, if not by McKay, in reading dialect in opposition to the ballad form. That McKay's ballads are characterized as schizophrenic is telling, as it either precludes resolution of the unbearable tensions of being a speaker of dialect in an individuated form or neglects "double consciousness" as a distinctive feature of diasporic afrocentric writing.

In asking for a more contextual reading of the differences in motivation between ideolectical/material texts, I am returning to ground assumed by the aesthetic politics of Bernstein's essay, whose normative/nonstandard opposition parallels the great divide between modernism and modernity itself. The specter of normativity is evidently being transferred from realist models, against which modernism proposed its discrepant complexity, through the differing usages of dialect and ideolect, to questions of language and identity in the postmodern period.[23] There has been significant progress, as we know, in undermining the literary assumptions that uphold the modernist/realist distinction, toward a more socially reflexive perspective on cultural production in the modern period.[24] Rather than moving progressively toward an ideolectical horizon, American modernism is better described as being in a dialogue with realist and populist sources. In Michael Denning's recent history of the aesthetics of the Popular Front, such a modernist/realist dialogue has an immediate use in rescuing William Carlos Williams's social texts, particularly *The Knife of the Times* and the Stecher Trilogy, from the canonizing preferences of postwar critics, who saw them as minor.[25] At the level of language use, as well, the work of Michael North has revealed the constitutive use of dialect in the ideolectical styles of high modernism, from Stein's "Melanctha" to Pound's Br'er Rabbit ramblings.[26] Bernstein, however, preserves the aesthetic hierarchies of modernism in privileging the "constructive" over the less adequately defined categories of "objective" and "subjective," as in his account of the genealogy of Stein's abstract style: "Stein does not depend upon supplemental literary or narrative contexts to secure her meaning. . . . With Stein you are left with words on the page and the Imaginary structures they build" (*PA*, 4–5). While Stein clearly provides the most successful examples of such a constructive formalism, they are from her midcareer work, from *A Long Gay Book* to *Stanzas in Meditation*, leaving to the side the realist concerns of her early writing and the public values of her late career.[27] It is here that the defense of a contextless, synchronic, formal modernism *always* betrays an underlying teleology, its developmental account of the achievement of form, as a politics of denial of something else — in this case, both Stein's realist motives and her identity politics. Bernstein's characterization of midperiod Stein as "constructive," further, has an added stake in a hierarchy of ideolect over dialect: "Stein's breakthrough into the ideolectical practice of *Tender Buttons* . . . was prepared by her problematic improvisations on African American vernacular in 'Melanctha'" (*PA*, 6). While Bernstein wants to preserve traces of dialect in Stein's ideolect, the qualification "problematic" remains so; ideolect aligns with *telos* in Stein's resolution of African-American dialect in modernist form.[28]

The canonical Anglo-American account of modernism, in its distinction between text and context, clearly underwrites Bernstein's discussion of dialect and ideolect here.[29] Across the board of modernist studies, there is just such a splitting into good and bad, as may be seen locally in Bernstein's bifurcation of McKay's motivations and globally in his antipathy to authentic identity (as well as in his dismissal of Cultural Studies). It is a formal analogy as well, I would argue, that provides spatial metaphors for the identity politics of ideolect and dialect in Bernstein's account, which resolve around the empty and full centers that defines a group's normative assumptions (recalling the Japanese radical student group and their centripetal/centrifugal tensions). Users of nonstandard ideolects reject collective identities as they move away from "the center with which they may be associated by education or social position" (just as Gertrude Stein, presumably, left Radcliffe); as a result, their work may aspire to the constructive horizon of pure presentation (*PA*, 7). Users of nonstandard dialects, on the other hand, define a new center of identity that "regroup[s] often denigrated and dispirited language practices" and thus creates a new standard in what Kamau Brathwaite has called "nation language"; their forms of art, however, risk definition as species of mimesis (ibid.).[30] Clearly, this empty/

full opposition is ripe not only for deconstruction but analysis, so that certain assumptions of identity, like McKay's, may be seen as rifted with "complexity," *just as* certain assumptions of nonidentity, like Bernstein's, may contain implicit but disavowed identity claims. Bernstein clearly sees the former possibility in addressing McKay's "split" aesthetics to their modernist hybridization in the work of the more ideolectical African-American poet Melvin B. Tolson, but even here his reservation about the universality of McKay's later communism (and use of the sonnet form) is matched by the blind spot of not seeing the universality in Tolson's modernism (and imitation of T. S. Eliot). But it is Bernstein's own disavowed identity claims that most need pointing out; in a remarkable reenactment of the doubleness Bernstein finds in McKay, his characterization of the identity politics that nonstandard writing struggles against — "rigidly territorializing clannishness and paralyzingly depoliticizing codicity" (*PA*, 19) — ends up mimicking precisely the early hostile reception of the Language School, seen as a group identity. Perhaps the good politics of the material text are being split off here from the bad politics of holding an identity position — as a Language poet! In Bernstein's universalist tendency toward a multinational politics of ideolectical writing, such a blind spot of collective nonidentity seems motivated in a more local politics of literary identity, as much as by a modernist politics of form.[31]

In this sense, Charles Altieri hits the target (and identifies it with his own perspective) when he characterizes the Language School as being caught between a nostalgic investment in the transformative potential of modernist form, with its disruption of referentiality, and the impossibility of basing a representational politics on a critique of representation.[32] He cites Bernstein's dismissal of identity politics from an earlier article — "Difference is confined to subject matter and thematic material, a.k.a. local color, excluding the formal innovations that challenge . . . dominant paradigms of representation" (766) — as admitting a nostalgic wish for a return to formalism that turns out to conceal a disavowed identity politics, as argued above. It is an aversive nostalgia that conflates the impossibility of authentic identity with the necessity of modernist form; it is worth considering here the extent to which Bernstein's antipathy to normative forms of group identity aligns more with Altieri's notion of modernism than either would admit. Where for Altieri, "Postmodern theory has not managed to develop its own analogue to the distinction between modernism and modernity that enables us clearly to set the art of the twentieth century in opposition to mainstream culture" (767), it offers a partial solution that "allows us to establish cultural relevance without renouncing emphasis on the signifier and without having to choose among highly segmented audience groups" (770). This is what Bernstein wants to do in his essay — he wants to keep both the politics of the signifier and the politics of segmented groups, but in focusing on ideolect as a critique of representation, he cannot address unambiguously what Altieri would privilege, the subject as constituted in the reflexivity of form. It is within horizons of aesthetic form, for Altieri, that expressive subjects, if not reduced to identity positions, may articulate a redemptive possibility: "What matters is not sincerity per se but becoming articulate about the conditions within which the process of imagining enriches the possibilities of fully investing in the specific life one is leading" (776). This aesthetics of possibility, which leads, despite all negative contexts, to what Altieri calls "an affirmative will," may be compared to Bernstein's call for a politics of impossibility — which likely looks to Altieri like the postmodern aporia itself: "Put bluntly, postmodernism needs ideals of heterogeneity to save it from universals, from ideals of coherent selfhood, and from reliance on commonsense judgments, but it then also needs an identity politics so that it has a basis for negotiating among those differences within an Enlightenment heritage" (772). This proves difficult to manage, however, because nonidentity provides little basis to negotiate its "constructivist and performative ideals" precisely with values of context, in Altieri's terms "the differences that should in theory proliferate" (772) — because context is not fully accounted for by a universalist notion of difference. Altieri would see this in Bernstein's poetics — the use of nonstandard language (which depends on a universal norm) may resolve aesthetic ideals with local contexts only in forms that cannot, finally, claim their value. This, for him, is as an aesthetic problem but in the end also a form of ethical "irresponsibility."

Altieri's solution to the impossible aporia of postmodernism, in any case, is to return to literary form, as an experience of value in an act of reflexive consciousness mediated in the aesthetic object, his claim for the necessity of modernist poetry.[33] This reflexivity may be extended through certain but not all postmodern practices insofar as they value the subjectivity effects of their encounter with alterity — which means they are modernist in *form* if necessarily postmodern in *content*. As outlined in his manifesto for a poetry of idiolects, Bernstein's notion of the impossibility of nonstandard practices, as well as examples given by Altieri in the work of Alfred Arteaga and Myung Mi Kim, in this sense reinstall the great divide of modernism from modernity in that the material text is valuable insofar as it gives a subjective register of the *displacements* of otherness. In other words, modernist form may be identified with value when it inculcates the possibility of an immanent reflexivity, while postmodern content is identified with necessity insofar as it insists on the materiality of difference and otherness as its constitutive ground. A poetics that foregrounds the reflexivity of the subject is the only solution, as a synthesis of form and identity; Lyn Hejinian's poetic diary, *The Cell*, is in this sense exemplary as "a remarkably elemental decomposition and reorientation of subjectivity" ("WIL," 782) — which is at the same time recognizable, for Altieri, as a reinvention of the modernism of midcareer Stein.[34] But if we go back and reread modernism for its moments of *social* reflexivity, which provides another account of modernism than Altieri's, we find it is riven with local differences its reflexive forms can hardly contain.[35] Rather than being the site of a critique of representation presumed "to exemplify ways of feeling, thinking, and imaginatively projecting investments *not bound to dominant social structures*," in Altieri's view ("WIL," 767, my italics), modernism is best imagined not retrospectively, as a politics of form, but prospectively, as the site of an emerging cultural order that structures ways of feeling, thinking, and imagining differences within modernity. If postmodernism cannot distinguish between social reproduction and expressive subjectivity, in Altieri, rethinking modernism by framing its contradictions toward outwardly cultural ends, rather than inwardly reflexive ones, may help. It will then be possible to read postmodern *form* from the perspective of modernist *content* — where the divide between modernism and modernity is actively engaged — rather than the other way around, reading postmodern *content* from the perspective of modernist *form* (in which case the matter has already been decided). If there is a cultural poetics, even in the postmodern period — and here I agree with Bernstein — it must return to a moment of construction where identities are formed out of the materials of language, rather than read formal construction as a displaced disavowal of identities.

STEIN'S FORD

Gertrude Stein, as we know, was an admirer of Henry Ford. She maintained a series of Fords after her first purchase of a Ford truck, which she called Aunt Pauline and which was used as a matériel transport and ambulance (but also for tourism) in World War I. After the war, she replaced what had come to be seen as her "second-hand hearse" with a new, factory-built Model T, nicknamed Godiva, in 1920, and purchased a newer model (which she could not quite afford) in 1929.[36] One of her first acts after the success of the *Autobiography* was again to upgrade her transportation: "We had a car but we made it cost as little as possible and for many years it was well it still is a little old Ford car. But now I bought an eight cylinder one."[37] There is a clear identification in this account between Stein's need to live within her means, interpreted as an economy of plain style, and the normative prototype of the mass-produced Ford, as well as a register of her celebrity in buying the larger model. But Stein's identification with Ford, both the product and the mode of production that produced it, goes far deeper than that. Ford and the automobile are the sites of a periodic meditation on mass production, social mobility, and repetition for Stein, a synecdoche for social modernity as interpreted in the process of her work.

The conventional account of modernism, we also know, splits the aesthetic product from the mode of production; what results is the theory of "two modernities" that leads in turn to the great divide separating high modernism from mass culture, literature from cultural studies.[38] In many senses, Stein's work may be understood as positioned before the great divide, which begins to appear more as a retrospective consequence of the canon formation of modernism. Much of the current revisionist effort in modernist studies has argued for a return to a modernism that actively engages — either positively or negatively — the reified world of mass production, rather than seeing itself as apart from it. Michael Davidson, for instance, shows how Stein's concern with the world of objects is both preserved and transformed in texts that are very hard to objectify, best exemplified by her linguistically dense portraits of food, objects, and rooms in *Tender Buttons*.[39] The material texts that result, as obdurate and self-sufficient as they are, reproduce aspects of the objects they would seem initially to dismantle — a process similarly reflected in the object status of her entire career: "Stein's transformation into a mass-cultural object, far from representing a vulgarization of her more 'serious,' artistic side, is a logical component of it, an inevitable result of developing an aesthetics that rejects the world [of objects] by creating another to replace it" (37). Davidson notes, as an extension of Stein's consumerist fascination with "mass-produced objects available at any of the Parisian department stores" (45), a broader interest in the technological innovations of modern life in which her writing, "like the automobile, translates the dynamic motion of the internal combustion engine into forward motion" (47). Stein's Ford, then, is equally a product to be consumed and a mode of production, as a new technology, that may be admired for its capacity to gain access to and even produce experience, not just to reify it. Technology partakes of authorship, and not just in terms of a pattern of consumption. Where Stein has generally been thought to have developed difficult techniques in writing "that defy instrumental reason and thwart narrative progress" (48), we may look for a way to describe the reciprocity between the two that is not simply a matter of imitation or parallel play. Davidson suggests the constitutive nature of their relation: "Fordism eliminates relations between workers and redistributes those relations among products; [and] repetition in art eliminates relations between artifact and phenomenal world and redistributes them among words"; both require that "an unknowable subjectivity realizes itself [in a] 'mirror stage of objectification'" (49). A negation and reconstruction of the subject at the point of production is common to the constructivist moment in both Stein and Ford: an encounter with the mode of production realized in the formation of the modern subject.

Stein's fascination with the automobile, both as object of consumption and as mode of production, can readily be brought to the fore in the many minor anecdotes that punctuate her autobiographies and biographies, suggesting a structural logic in the nearly epochal periodization to be found in Stein's succession of Fords. The first, Aunt Pauline, underwrites the self-legitimizing narrative of Stein's service as ambulance driver in World War I; as a new technology, it allows Stein to participate in modern, mechanized war by a kind of proxy. It also suggests a motivation for new values of landscape as spatial form that become increasingly important in her work in the 1920s. As one biographer notes, while Stein's ambulance driving was not really much of a contribution to the war effort, there was a payoff in owning a car: "They could visit picturesque villages and quiet lakes," engaging in some serious tourism in the Pyrenees as they contributed to the war effort.[40] The experience of these forays into the wartime countryside appears in several of the texts reflecting their war experience at the conclusion of *Geography and Plays*, for example:

> In comparison what are horses.
> Compared with that again what are bells.
> You mean horns. No I mean noises.
> In leaning can we encounter oil.
> I meant this to be intelligible.

> We were taking a trip. We found the roads not noisy but pleasurable and the shade there was pleasant. We found that the trees had been planted so as to make rows. This is almost universal.[41]

The automobile as the missing referent is on the one hand distributed through negative analogies (it is not a horse, its horn is not a bell, the horns are not a bull's, etc.) in a kind of collage effect; breaking the plane of the cubist portrait, however, locates the touring couple in a landscape that is intelligible and pleasurable, "almost universal." The automobile, as autonomous mobility, becomes the implicit crux between portrait and landscape. Also evident here is a shift from cubist portraiture to Stein's later "landscape writing," the former focusing on the automobile's object status and the latter deriving from its capacity to produce the landscape of the tour. In Stein's landscape, as opposed to portrait, mode, there is a significant displacement of repetition from the Fordist assembly line that made her vehicle to the regularly planted rows of trees — which are described as nearly universal when driven by at speed. Repetition here is a displacement of the anxiety of uniqueness.

Stein's second car, Godiva (nicknamed for its stripped-down functionalism), was equally important to her formal thinking. Stein continued to identify with the consumerist pleasures of auto-mobility; she was now able to drive in the Bois de Boulogne, and as another biographer notes, "became fond of writing in Godiva while Alice did the errands and the shopping." At the same time, waiting in the car while Alice shopped allowed her to "deriv[e] inspiration from the sounds of the street. The movement of other cars set the rhythm of a sentence for her, like a tuning fork or metronome."[42] Her technological fascination with automotive mechanics also provides a crucial formal analogy when, as narrated in another biographical account, she writes her definitive midcareer manifesto, *Composition as Explanation*, while her car is being repaired: "As she watched her car being taken apart, she thought of grammatical constructions, and of car parts, what made one Ford different from other identical Fords, and with these not altogether clear speculations on rhythm, identity, and repetition, she composed her lecture."[43] While this may be a somewhat exaggerated account, based on a single sentence from the *Autobiography*, there is much supporting evidence of Stein's practice of writing in cars. While the referent is often masked, the formal analogy is clear, as in this poem from about 1916:

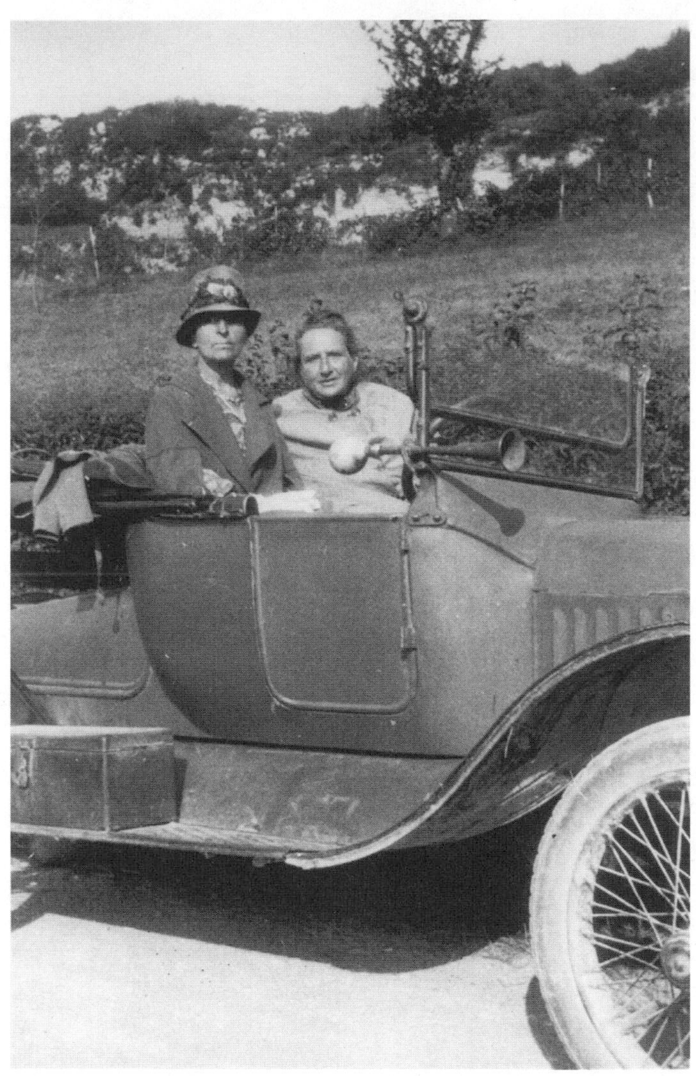

29. Alice B. Toklas and Gertrude Stein sitting in Godiva. Yale Collection of American Literature, Beinecke Rare Book and Manuscript Library.

THE FORD

It is earnest.
Aunt Pauline is earnest.
We are earnest.
We are united.
Then we see.[44]

While the referent is given in the title, there is a mysterious conjunction between its mechanical earnestness and "we are earnest"; if we are united in being as earnest as Pauline, the motor of desire takes place precisely in the displacements of form that bring us to awareness. This earnest space of desire in auto-mobility is visible as well in a photograph from the mid 1920s of Stein and Alice B. Toklas sitting in Godiva (fig. 29). But as the car becomes more common in modern life through the 1920s, it less often provides a formal analogy to self-consciousness, its functions becoming automatized. Technological modernity itself, from Fords to airplanes, is more broadly the object of fascination in Stein's 1934 tour of America, where she encounters the results of two decades of Fordist production. In *Everyone's Autobiography*, for instance, she compares the current state of "roads and what is on them" in America to the memory of driving her first car in Washington, D.C. (in an anecdotal digression that sets up her visit to the first lady, Eleanor Roosevelt):

> Wherever I went the roads and what is on them were not the same as they had been thirty years before when I left America, not in Washington not anywhere and that is what makes the country different, the rest is as it was but the roads and what is on them not. I thought about that a lot in Washington because then for about a week I was not doing anything but thinking about that thing.
>
> And that is why when you look at it it does not look at all the same, the houses what differences do houses make but the roads and what is on them. One of the first times I ever was in an automobile was in Washington and when it went up a very little hill it did not go very well and all the little boys kept yelling git a horse.
>
> As I said in Capital Capitals and it sings so well
>
> FOURTH CAPITAL They play horses
> FOURTH CAPITAL We have all forgotten what horses are
> THIRD CAPITAL We have all forgotten what horses there are
> SECOND CAPITAL We have all forgotten where there are horses
> FIRST CAPITAL We have all forgotten about horses.
>
> Capital this and Capital that.
>
> Well that was the way the capital was, I wrote it about French capitals but Washington was just the same only it did look different and not at all the same.[45]

Stein goes beyond the merely anecdotal in an associative meditation on the politics of identity and difference that argues for an equivalence, by means of their mutual displacement, of modernism ("the capital" of her libretto *Capital Capitals*; the dislocations of identity; difference) and modernity (the emergence of cars; the obsolescence of horses; the same). Stein's use of repetition unites identity and difference in a canonization of the peripheral forms of *literaturnost* that defamiliarizes the *auto*-matization of modern life. Where national identity fails as an organizing form, and Stein and Toklas can sit down to tea with Eleanor Roosevelt not subject to its hierarchies, the automobile as a consequence of the modern mode of production is successful in facilitating social transformations that supersede political hierarchies as they dislocate capitals from Washington to Paris. The automobile, in this sense, is a defamiliarzing agency; as a mobile agent of the displacements of modernity, foregrounding it sets off a meditation on the modernist present.

Buying the new Ford is analogous to participation in modern life in late-period Stein; it gets her out onto the streets of the capital as a consequence of her fame (less as a bourgeois consumer than as an innovative producer — much like Vladimir Mayakovsky, another modernist who bought a new car). The globe-trotting, mass-mediated frenzy of her 1934–35 tour, likewise, is a celebration of American technology; she is fascinated with the "Drive-Yourself-Car" she rents in Chicago for its almost magical capacity to transform experience.[46] Beyond the lures of conspicuous tourism, however, Stein saw in Ford's modern poetics of repetition a mode of production that was, in explicitly literary terms, analogous to her modernist one. In the *Autobiography*, she sees Ford as part of a national tradition that leads to the form of her work: to Bertrand Russell, "she grew very eloquent on the disembodied abstract quality of the american character and cited examples, mingling automobiles with Emerson."[47] After dispensing with the English, in a parody of their national characteristics ("You should I think suggest to the french government that they give us Pondicherry"), Stein elaborates a theory of American identity as stemming, not from state structures, but from its modern capacity to produce:

> Gertrude Stein used to get furious when the english all talked about german organisation. She used to insist that the germans had no organisation, they had method but no organisation. Don't you understand the difference, she used to say angrily, any two americans, any twenty americans, any millions of americans can organise themselves to do

something but germans cannot organise themselves to do anything, they can formulate a method and this method can be put upon them but that isn't organisation. The germans, she used to insist, are not modern, they are a backward people who have made a method of what we conceive as organisation, can't you see. They cannot therefore possibly win this war because they are not modern. (153)

Stein's account of national identity is based on a politics of form that she enacted in her work. We may extend the notion that Americans are discursively constructed (made) in the form of *The Making of Americans* to her account of the mode of production here. Organization, in Ford's development of the assembly line, is not a matter of top-down hierarchy but an example of American "open" form: while German identity is deductive, deriving its methodology from first principles, American identity for Stein is inductive, paratactic, and truly modern. A third biographer strongly supports the influence of Ford on Stein: "Fords had a special significance to her. They formed part of her theory of modernism and repetitions. The first Fords had all been repetitions of a prototype, identical in body as in color (Henry Ford told prospective customers they could have any colour as long as it was black), and they were examples of the American invention of 'series manufacturing.' . . . Also they were all the same but different."[48] While there is little evidence that Stein held such succinct views on anything, the passage in the *Autobiography* clearly shows how her creative thinking intersects a fascination with Fordism and Fords.

An account of modernism not founded on its separation from modernity leads to a different politics of reading the tradition of the material text. In her analogy between literary form and objects, as Davidson points out, Stein fuses words and things, making herself a textual commodity. Her meditation on the mode of production has a further implication in that, for Stein and Ford, the mode of production fuses words or things as material, but neither is a source of value apart from its organization in a form. Altieri's citation of the standard opposition between modernism and modernity, in which modernism is defined in terms of a critique of reification, fails to explain Stein's meditation on cars, or embrace of Ford's methods of organization, in her work. Cars, for Stein, are not dissociable as referents (words are not simply dissociable from things) but are organized in the mode of production and in literary form. This principle of Steinian organization may be extended throughout her work as an approach to its mode of referentiality (even in her refusal of it), eliding the distinction between "real writing" and "audience writing" that supports the modernist teleology of her work as ending in the achievement of abstraction, to the detriment of other styles. From the problematic relation between words and things in *Tender Buttons* to the textual erotics of *As a Wife Has a Cow* and "Lifting Belly" to the dialogic invocations of *A Novel of Thank You* and *Stanzas in Meditation*, Stein's abstraction is a consequence of social relations. It is a mediation of form within modernity, not a site of transcendental reflection from a critical distance opposed to it.

From this perspective, we may reconfigure the notorious author-centeredness of Stein's account of genius in a series of key works from the 1930s, including *Lectures in America, The Geographical History of America, Four in America*, and *What Are Masterpieces?*[49] Stein's univocal account of genius, it might be more often noted, occurred precisely in the period in which her literary work was split between two styles, which she termed, in a key letter to her agent in 1933, her "audience writing" and "real writing."[50] The conventional split between modernism and modernity takes place right here, in the denigration of the former for the abstract and autonomous formal values of the latter.[51] How does one then resolve the dual nature of Stein's authorship — on the one hand unified in the form of a genius who cannot be questioned, and on the other split between her two modes of literary production? Stein's meditation on Ford and Fordism provides the clue: driving her Ford, Stein is the literary genius at the same time that she is supported by the invisible agency of the mode of production itself. Her work, in its capacious displacement and integration of literary materials, is an imitation, or form of parallel play, of that mode of production — which is distributed everywhere in her work. Stein's genius just is her mode of production — along with the singular intelligence necessary to foreground her originary place in it as an index of conspicuous participation. This is what Stein meant when she said, repeatedly, that genius is nothing but the capacity to speak and listen at the same time[52] — what she is listening to is the social matrix she is in (the visitors to Stein and Toklas's salons as the models for the characters in *The Making of Americans* and for her portraits) to begin with, but more largely the mode of production (of literature, of authors, of fame) itself. Stein's modernism is in this sense precisely reflexive — in social terms, not just in just subject-centered ones. Stein is a genius very much like Henry Ford — through her capacity to recognize and augment the mode of (literary) production, finally becoming a household name that is everywhere and nowhere at once.

ASSEMBLING *THIS*

I am going to make an abrupt transition here, from Stein's admiration of Ford, and her formal analogy to the Fordist mode of production, to the absence of a similar poetics of genius in the multiauthored poetics of the Language School. For Stein, as we have seen, being a genius was a fundamental requirement for the making of masterpieces, and thus of authorship, even if the concept itself was split between its public and private modes. The Language School, on the other hand, made a substantial commitment to avoiding the authoritarianism of Stein's claims to genius, so that whatever there may be of it in a given Language poet's work (and there may be a great deal, in a number of authors and works), it tends to be displaced toward horizons of the nonauthorial material text. Where such a difficult term as "genius" has returned in the genealogy of the Language School, it seems almost as a ludic corrective to modernist claims of authorial originality. It is in this sense of pushing the critique of genius to its limits that Bob Perelman locates Robert Grenier's paradoxical, self-canceling speech act "I HATE SPEECH" at the origins of Language School poetics.[53] In his account of the "originary moment" of *This*:

> In 1971 Grenier and Watten began the magazine *This*, the first self-conscious journal of what would become known as language writing. The name and character of the movement were uninvented at the time, nor were many of the future participants in touch yet, but the magazine was clearly motivated by a sense of literary progress. The first issue contained a particular phrase of Grenier's, "I HATE SPEECH," that, in hindsight, was an important literary gesture: it was singled out by Ron Silliman ten years later in his introduction to the first anthology of language writing, *In the American Tree*, as "announc[ing] a breach . . . in American writing," although the "breach" now seems too dramatic. (40)

The idea of any particular author or work defining the origins of the Language School is untenable. There have been many practitioners of what would come to be known as language-centered writing, from the high modernists to Jackson Mac Low and several generations of the New York School, before *This*. In the mid to late 1960s, two magazines stand out as addressing similar formal concerns and involving some of the same writers, Clark Coolidge and Michael Palmer's *Joglars* and Bernadette Mayer and Vito Acconci's *0–9;* Ron Silliman brought out several issues of his magazine, *tottel's*, also, in the early 1970s. Mayer's *Unnatural Acts*, along with her St. Marks Poetry Project workshops in the early 1970s, have also been cited as unacknowledged originary moments.[54] But innovation, at least since Henry Ford, does not work this way. Daimler, Benz, and the Duryea brothers variously perfected aspects of the internal combustion engine and thus may be given credit for its invention, while Ford's development of the mass production techniques that would change transportation was not an individual stroke of genius but the creative adaptation of the work of many predecessors.[55] By analogy, the work of *This* stands at the beginning of the Language School because it is the first continuous, self-conscious, and self-reflexive literary venue of what will have been the Language School once it developed as it did, even if its formal characteristics could be assembled from other sources. Socially reflexive organization, here, is central; given this fact, it is not at all accurate for Perelman and Silliman to cite Grenier's breach with the literary past as inaugural. There was no inaugural event but a series of incremental modifications, leading to a new mode of literary production. If this is so, what is the status of Grenier's self-canceling rejection of speech as the purported origins of the Language School?[56] Another constructivist moment may be discerned here, precisely in the antagonistic negativity that announces, even if it does not participate in, the self-focusing development of a series (as in fact, with *This* 3, Grenier ceased to play an active editorial role).

The larger point here is the relation of radical negativity (Grenier's self-canceling identification, pressed to an extreme in his paradoxical speech act) to the construction of community (the Language School). In offering a revisionary account of a history I helped make, my interest will be obvious, but its purpose is not merely to recover an authorial intention or editorial role. If Perelman is right that efforts toward defining a future literature were only partial in *This* 1, he neglects the possibility of socially reflexive models of literary history in returning to the author as an object of fascination:

> Grenier's involvement with *This* stopped after the fourth [correction: third] issue. In the mid seventies as the creation of self-managed language writing venues began, Barrett Watten continued editing the magazine and intensified Grenier's interest in a literary future (and thus in literary history). Grenier's own writing went in the direction of the here and now. His latest work is another box. . . . (*MP*, 53)

The teleology of abstraction translates from Stein's notion of the continuous present to the here and now of Grenier's "box": his mid-1970s masterwork

Sentences, five hundred poems on index cards assembled in a cryptlike blue cloth-covered box with ivory clasps.[57] Its materiality, and almost total unavailability, is positioned in Grenier's oeuvre much like the massive, unavailable bulk of Stein's masterpiece *The Making of Americans* as an equally opaque, though very differently written, work.[58] In his literary genealogy of the box, Perelman reproduces the form of the modernist author as eternally located in the present, in comparison to the "self-managed . . . venues" of literary history, however progressive they may be. In his essay "On Speech," however, Grenier's notion of literary futurity takes the progressive form of a correction to William Carlos Williams's use of speech rhythms: "It isn't the spoken any more than the written, now, that's the progression from Williams, what now I want, at least, is the word way back in the head that is the thought or feeling forming out of the 'vast' silence/noise of consciousness experiencing the world **all the time**." Perelman is right to notice Grenier's insistence that literary history transform itself into an atemporal state, but in substituting the negativity of "I HATE SPEECH" for an exhortation to join with the tradition and go forward, Grenier's demand must be seen as a form of paradox, if not regression, as it invokes not a future but an impossible act. Ron Silliman, in his canon-making argument in *In the American Tree*, sees Grenier's inaugural moment as a theoretical call to denaturalize speech and reference, as in the deixis of the magazine's title *This*, aligning Language writing with the deconstruction that was emerging in the 1970s.[59] What Grenier's speech act does inaugurate, if not a new tradition, is a relation between self-canceling authorship and verbal automatism that continues in the development of his work, from *Sentences* to his recent handwritten poems (see chapter 6). But while this focus on "words way back in the head" might have connected the texts of the Language School to the verbal automatism of French surrealism — where the eidetic sentence "there is a man cut in half by a window" launched Breton's meditations on poetic technique in the First Manifesto[60] — no consistent concern for verbal automatism in its relation to self-canceling authorship was shared by authors in *This*. Rather, when Hannah Weiner's writing appeared in *This* 7, her work seemed disjunctively naturalistic for its use of automatic messages in generating material texts.[61]

To counter Perelman's anxiety over the author-centered cult of genius in modernism and its projection onto the self-canceling originality of the Language School, we may return to a pragmatic sense of what Stein meant when she applied the word to herself.[62] If genius is the original discovery or autonomous invention of new forms, then neither Stein, Picasso, nor

Whitehead (the three "geniuses" identified in Stein's *Autobiography*) are one; if Henry Ford is a genius for his idiot-simple vision of what form the myriad perfections of the assembly line should take, then he is. In this sense, Stein may seem to be a genius for the way in which her oeuvre was built, one innovation at a time, so that she could claim, in the ventriloquism of the *Autobiography*, to be one: "What a genius!" for having come up with such a device, in an everyday, openhanded, democratic sense. The assembly line is a form of modernity that was never invented; likewise, the Language School has no authorial origins but began as a sequence of innovations within a form of organization that developed between writers in magazines such as *This*. Contrary to Perelman's nomination of the self-undoing of Grenier's "I HATE SPEECH" as originary moment of the Language School, I propose the following poem by Clark Coolidge, from the first issue of *This*, as a prototype of the series of innovations that led to a poetics substantially different from its predecessors. I see it not as a break with the past but as a coherent demonstration of a poetics that unfolds from its own self-posited argument:

MADE THOUGHT

made thought which of it
all of which a kind yet
best it in and on should must
whatever it is often once to do

in a while once is there and in
as it like it but often ever that it is
in which in separate that
often only very not in which way

all of this but this which as are alike
or in an only not what made as for
it in its well as made open as in
that which it once all but made but
                for all as it is[63]

As opposed to the synesthesia of Grenier's "words way back in the head," an ecstatic realization of somatic intensity that cancels its outward address in its self-hatred of speech, Coolidge's poem is "made thought": a fabrication of disjunct particles of objectified language, unit structures of the material text, recombined within the percussive metrics of improvisatory form.

The subject is elided: "Made thought which of it," in which the sequence of verb/noun-verb/relative pronoun/preposition/pronoun shifter becomes a displaced predicate that makes a potential construction of meaning that may be realized as identical to its own order. Self-consciously a material text, the poem refers to itself and does not: "All of which a kind yet," in sum, a quality will be produced where the content of "which" will be realized, but perhaps just not yet. Meaning inheres in an obdurate text as the poem moves on: "best it in and on should must," as language becomes agency in a form of self-realization. A kind of metalinguistic continuum is proposed: "whatever it is often once to do," in which an assembly of alternative possibilities for meaning is reflexively arrayed on a time line (not yet an assembly line), opening the way to speculation on the relation of such hybrid poetics to the predicative mode of temporal cognition the Russian psychologist L. S. Vygotsky called "inner speech."[64] While Grenier sees a flash of revealed meaning in his "words way back in the head," Coolidge constructs a space and time in which meaning is reflexive: "that which it once all but made but / for all as it is."

Such rehearsals of meaning may be commonplace in discussions of the Language School; it is not such local possibilities of meaning, however mutually reinforced, but the entire form of the poem that is relevant here. I want to take the example of Coolidge's nonoriginary poem further and consider how it intersects with the canonical model of modernist form and the notion of authorship it entails. We may compare Coolidge's meaning effects, as both opaque and self-referring, with Charles Altieri's phenomenological account of the modernist lyric's resistance to paraphrase, exemplified for him by John Ashbery's work. As he comments on the last stanza of Ashbery's "As We Know":

> This kind of poetry cannot hope to provide any overt imaginative order for the particulars it engages; nor can it build capacious structures. Its attention must be focused on some immediate situation or flow of the mind. But that compression of space allows the writer to concentrate on how, within time, intricate folds and passages open among materials. Even though reflexive consciousness can do no more than trace the ways we have come to and through those situations, it can focus close attention on the contours of its own engagements, and it can locate an affirmative will simply in what thereby becomes visible and shareable, without any need for or hope in more comprehensive allegorical structures.[65]

Much of this description of Ashbery would apply even better to Coolidge's poem, especially since Altieri sees in Ashbery a kind of "writing degree zero" that resists "imaginative," "capacious," and "allegorical structures" — in a way that is very far from many readers' experience of Ashbery's work. Apart from *The Tennis Court Oath*, capaciousness is all in Ashbery; if it is flatness one wants, there are innumerable better examples (Jackson Mac Low, Kenward Elmslie, Jean Day, Ted Berrigan, Joseph Ceravolo, Peter Seaton, Jenny Holzer, Bruce Andrews, Brian Kim Stefans, and so on).[66] What makes Altieri's description definitive of his brand of modernism, and applicable as well to authorial accounts of the Language School, is his notion of form as a possibility for making meaning in which deferral of comprehensiveness and hope is identified with what he calls an "affirmative will." It is this affirmative will that is being asked for, and found, in the poetry of Alfred Arteaga, Myung Mi Kim, and Lyn Hejinian; it is affirmative will that allows the encounter with difference to coexist with form, but does this account for poetry's turn to language? In its degree of abstraction, Coolidge's poem is the acme of a strand of modernism in which subjectivity is constructed by means of its material displacements, in the obduracy or resistance of the words themselves. Altieri offers a theory that approaches such a resolutely material text, but without regard to the objectified properties of its medium. With Coolidge, however, a phenomenology of experience as reflexive subjectivity must be mapped onto the unit values of language. It would be impossible to undertake such a mapping apart from the cognitive processing the vocabulary and syntax of his poem demand. Coolidge's turn to language is thus a primary test case of Altieri's affirmative will: the difficulty of "Made Thought" for cognitive processing (as experience) would require such a will, or else the poem fragments into meaningless shards of dissociated subjectivity.

This is the payoff of Altieri's modernism for the postmodern aporia of identity and difference, as in Bernstein's reading of dialect in McKay, where authorial intention cannot register simultaneously in poetic form and as a form of identity. As a result, the Language School, in Altieri's account, is most of interest as a test case for a poetics of radical particularity — of intention and identity — as caught up in a contradiction with the authority of form. The necessity of Altieri's contradiction is bypassed, however, in a constructivist account of the poetics of Stein or the Language School, which as reflexive forms of social organization, rather than instances of affirmative will, show precisely how identity may be relational, rather than a moment of crisis in refusing a subordination to form. An alternate account of Coolidge's poem is therefore possible: in it, the redemptive horizon of affirmative will Altieri wants in modernism is displaced in the poem's objectification of its materials. Certainly, the resolute object status of Coolidge's minimalist lexicon cannot be missed; while there are many possibilities for constructing meaning, the poem as a temporal form draws the reader into a contracted horizon of association and identification due its restricted range of linguistic effects. Such an occultation of experiential scale, as an interpretive frame, is the direct effect of the restriction of Coolidge's vocabulary as a material constraint. This has two results: there is an evident negativity encoded in such a material text that impedes the affirmative will Altieri calls for as poetic agency to begin with, while we may see a positive value for the material properties of a lexicon selected to convey nonauthorial qualities as well. While I do not know whether Coolidge deliberately chose his lexicon from the 850-word vocabulary of BASIC English, all the words in the poem may be found on that list. They may also, with the exception of "whatever" and "separate," be found on the Dolch Basic Sight Word List that Kit Robinson used to compose his 1976 sequence, *The Dolch Stanzas*. Coolidge thus joins a group of modernist and postmodern writers who developed a uniquely American innovation in poetics: the use of a preconstituted vocabulary for the composition of verse, as we have seen.

The use of a preexisting vocabulary for poetry was a modernist innovation that could be applied to the social rationalization of global modernity, as we have seen. Ogden and Richards designed BASIC explicitly as a universal second language that would compete with Esperanto, an idea that was taken up with enthusiasm by both Churchill and Roosevelt during World War II, predicting Anglo-American linguistic domination in the postwar period. Coolidge is not commenting on that history in his work (in a way that, arguably, Louis Zukofsky is in his); it is simply assumed in the value he gives to abstract units of language that will have "made thought."[67] The notion of a "writing degree zero" here becomes the horizon of a national language presumed to be universal; at the same time, this vocabulary cannot represent the trace of any realized experience — it is a sublime ideal in that it is completely abstracted as a preexisting, objectified form of language. What happens here to Altieri's affirmative will, which Coolidge as modernist should be upholding in his lyric investments? On the one hand, we have an invocation of an unrepresentable and sublime power that breaks up the continuum of self-consciousness into objectified bits of language; on the other, there is the temporal reconstruction of that destroyed continuity in the self-reflexive traces of potential meaning.

Coolidge is thus engaging both the self-conscious reflexivity of modernism in Altieri's sense and the destructive will of modernity as described by Marshall Berman in his citation of Marx's phrase, "All that is solid melts into air."[68] Where critical theorists might find an opportunity to supply an analogy of social surplus value to aesthetic form in this poem, Coolidge's constructivist poetics are pursuing such a relation already.[69] Words are being broken apart from language in a process of reification that instantiates the transformation of materials into commodities and the denaturing of human beings into labor. If there is an affirmative will here, it is simultaneously at a distance from and participating in modernity. In an almost algebraic sense, Coolidge's text imitates the way Henry Ford made cars, and the way workers came to live in Detroit. Such a poetics of analogy can explain how cars came into Gertrude Stein's material texts, along with a range of other effects of the power of capitalist social relations, in her aesthetic politics of identity and entity. The affirmative will of modernism is precisely its destructive/transformative mode of social reflexivity.

At the time, I understood my editorial role in *This* on analogy to Coolidge's "Made Thought": it would involve a construction of meaning using the freshly cast or broken down units of lyricism that were becoming available with the crisis of the expressive subject after the 1960s, reconfigured in new forms of organization.[70] The serial form of Robert Creeley's *Pieces* (1969) was likewise of central importance; its minimalist and self-focusing influence may be seen in Grenier's "I HATE SPEECH" and in a kind of impossible dialogue with Creeley in two review essays on his work in the same issue,[71] but also in the publication of a wide range of serial poems in the first issue of *This*, which itself comprised a form of "made thought," a sequence of fragments from many authors.[72] George Oppen's serial poems, from *Discrete Series* to *Of Being Numerous*, were also important, while the title *This* was drawn from a wide range of ready-to-hand modernist examples of deixis.[73] The move from the revealed synesthesia of "words in the head" to the paratactic forms of Language writing (as from the spark of the internal combustion engine to the start-up of the entire assembly line, as it were) took place, demonstrably, over the first half dozen issues of *This*, where a dawning recognition occurred on the part of numerous writers of new possibilities.[74] This recognition was not author centered but socially reflexive, if by social we mean the development of communities of writers, in San Francisco and then in New York, who were at the time intensely interacting with each other. In a similar way, the development of the assembly line was not author centered but socially reflexive: Ford did not invent it; rather, economic forces dictated the technological refinements and economies of scale that would lead to the overarching form of the line, as supply lines of materials and components were assembled in repetitive unit structures. The analogy between the paratactic unit structures of postmodern cultural forms and the assembly line, however provisional, suggests how works of art may be socially produced through multiauthored processes rather than single-authored invention.

As evidence of this analogy, Coolidge's book-length poem *The Maintains*, excerpted in *This* 3 and published as the inaugural book of This Press in 1974, showed the importance of accretive form.[75] In *The Maintains*, Coolidge's work achieved its constructivist apogee, opening the way to the capacious structures of his "longwork" in the mid-1970s as well as his development of what may be termed his lyrical ideolect in collections such as *Own Face*, *Solution Passage*, and *Sound as Thought* from the 1980s.[76] Coolidge's staging of a multivoiced reading of *The Maintains* at Franconia College, New Hampshire, where Grenier was teaching, in 1972, likewise suggested a deployment of poetic abstraction organized on a different time line than the lyric disjunctions of either "Made Thought" or Ashbery's *Tennis Court Oath*. What is important about *The Maintains* is its form of sequential integration, not simply its status as material text:

> blunt sun it is used quartz
> by and by some in charge
> tile like quatrain malaria
> ask doubt of a mark doubt
> landing a tree small but long pit
> for an in or of an in
> also behalfs having foils
> pare to board one roll no brim
> ore pierrot
> taker sharer connected kept
> thing item in character fraction
> heliocentrics fond
> the glebe and house and graduate but parole
> gourd favors stand loud odds the brave
> to assume to facing a still
> one may any cited
> lyre class rockrose of a bar
> crinoid bass plinth

pan splints an octave letter
thermoplastic all (*TM*, 86)

Where "Made Thought" is evidently composed of a predetermined lexicon like that of BASIC English, *The Maintains* assembles its unit structures from a different source of raw materials, the dictionary. Not simply a list of words, the dictionary — say, *Webster's Ninth Collegiate* — is a social text in which a *definiendum* of American English, "an expression to be defined," is extended by its *definiens*, "an expression that defines: definition." Coolidge's line, then, is a unit structure constituted in a reflexive relationship between a word being defined and the words that define it. Reflexivity is enacted here not as a form of self-consciousness but in the paratactic equivalences of the poem's assembly of lines; subject and predicate are suspended in unit structures that may be either *definienda* or *definientia*. This relation, at least, dominates the early stanzas of the poem, where sequences like the following convey the underlying form of the dictionary definition:

acid
non-czech
also any hours as a chaplain base
after the one to take to not appear against
the painted but having no dim
not one nor one better than none
a state of being the like (4)

Later in the poem, converging and interpenetrating strands of definition begin to add up to more complex, less unit-valued semantic patterns, leading to an effect of overdetermination and excess that Coolidge explores in the polyrhythmic structures of his next book-length poem, *Polaroid*.[77] Where Altieri's model of affirmative will would go partway toward a reading of "Made Thought," the reversal of the lyric's suspension of time toward the reflexive overdetermination of *The Maintains*' structural units, both line and stanza, must be read for its outer-directed, social address. For one thing, the form of the poem exceeds the duration of an individual speech act (or moment of meditative reflection) in any normative sense; it could, for this reason, be performed by multiple readers — anticipating multiple authors — at Franconia College. For another, where the lexicon of "Made Thought" admits a kind of protoverbal phenomenality as it invokes the sublimity of an abstract and disembodied language "elsewhere," *The Main-*

tains structures its variations on conventional units of meaning in their most publicly available source, the dictionary.

As a reference work, the dictionary is a source of meaning that adjudicates between competing claims (it is likewise a form of authority, as in Malcolm X's reading of one in prison, or even of prophecy, as in the game of telling fortunes with the dictionary). The authority invested in the dictionary, which is invoked but compositionally displaced and reorganized in *The Maintains*, is neither author centered nor derived from first principles of reason or law; rather, it is a social construction with a material history of its own. J. A. H. Murray's *New English Dictionary*, as we know, was constructed by means of a nationwide network of scribes who read canonical literary texts, parsed meanings, wrote the individual citations down on slips of paper, and forwarded them, through a widely dispersed network of local committees, to Murray (who was so slow in assembling them, dying, in fact, at the letter *T*, that rats and mice ate their way into the bags of citations, potentially destroying meanings as they built their nests).[78] Murray's dictionary was one of the Victorian wonders of the world; it was seen by its editor as competing with other national dictionaries in terms of size, complexity, and literary pedigree, establishing not only a national standard but claiming an imperial right. In less compendious form, Noah Webster's *American Dictionary of the English Language*, first published 1828, sought out differences in spelling, pronunciation, and meaning from English examples in a Protestant-inflected act of national narration as a form of textual dissent. Normativity, here, is the product of competition between national languages; Webster's dictionary was an act of revolutionary defiance against the coercive strictures of Dr. Johnson (and is thus of primary *literary* importance for the American Renaissance). Questions of originality and invention are crucial: while H. L. Mencken claims, "In all the years since its first publication there has been no working dictionary of English . . . that does not show something of its influence," a recent critic comments, "The language spoken in the United States . . . cannot in good conscience be joined syntactically to the subject *Noah Webster*, nor to the verb *invent*."[79] Innovation, again, is both authorial and social; Webster's dictionary is not only a single-voiced authority on national standards; it is also a social text.[80] Two values of dictionaries then — the positive assemblage of the national edifice, the negative differentiation of competing national languages — combine in the seemingly neutral aesthetic decision to use the dictionary as a source of vocabulary in *The Maintains*.

Like the dictionary, *The Maintains* is a social text.[81] It is interesting, here, that Coolidge's most constructive work, in the material sense of words on the page, precisely depends on its "supplemental literary or narrative contexts to secure . . . meaning"; the poem suggests a reciprocity between text and context, as between words and their definitions, in its formal organization. Such social reflexivity, however textually coded, was one that Coolidge would move away from (although periodically return to at times) in the development of his work, toward more interior but capacious imaginative structures. His next major work, *Polaroid*, abandoned the definitional frame of the dictionary and explored a multiply ambiguous phrasal construction that emphasized rhythmic variation and the sound of language reduced to minimal, percussive units — rather than the constructivist overtones evident in *The Maintains*.[82] This move, from thought to sound, from dictionary definition to harmonic overtones and percussive drive, continues in the course of Coolidge's work, in which time-based improvisation and lingual harmonics tend to compete with and even cancel out values of constructed meaning. Coolidge's work may be read as a demanding poetry of real-time cognitive processes that cannot possibly match with possibilities of interpretation except in overdetermined associations of fantasy. Just as the complex, automatic patterns of the typical computer screen saver may, over long durations or in hysterical fits, suddenly declare themselves as speaking directly to the viewer (the one I use is called "Psychomotor"), Coolidge's long poems and lyrics evoke an evanescent self-consciousness experienced at the extremes of liminal fantasy. They are, in this sense, postmodern in their contestation of any kind of affirmative will in Altieri's sense, seeing it as a kind of superadded, fantasmatic state produced by the accidents of improvisatory technique. It is here that other writers in the Language School diverged from Coolidge's nonauthorial expressivity, even while responding to it — in my own "Factors Influencing the Weather," in *This* 4, and Silliman's *Ketjak*, in *This* 6.[83] In both poems, there was a demand equally to preserve the materiality of the poem's sources and to allow for the widest range of interpretative responses to them. *The Maintains*, in my reading, constructed a form of self-reflexivity that began to exceed, by destabilizing, the objectivity of the materials made available to it and sequentially organized within its improvised form. Still, it was Coolidge's construction of poetic language as a form of reconstituted objectification that urged a number of writers to break the mold of the author-centered lyric toward a more socially reflexive poetry. While Coolidge's exemplary poems may have provided a model for the sequential assembling of *This*, the particular motivations that would lead to subsequent breakthroughs of poetic technique, of course, could never be anticipated by their forms (either lyric or paratactic). The mode of production, in this sense, exceeds any particular author, continuing with a will of its own.[84]

THE BRIDE

Gertrude Stein's modernism, as I have tried to show, may be understood in relation to her formally coded responses to the emergence of modernity, as exemplified by her fascination with Ford's American organization of the assembly line as well as by her desire to own and drive a car. (It is a provocative question to ask, but it must be asked, whether there is an automobile in Ezra Pound's *Cantos*. There are wandering buses and at least a jeep or two, but no cars.) The assembling of *This*, as well, was a mode of production that developed from moments of nonauthorial innovation, but it is very remote from any consciously productivist aesthetic or reference to industrial processes. As unit structures of mobile agency, however, cars entered my work early and continue to reside there:

Their long bodies, covered in skin
When speed carries them past the buildings
Are multi-colored, various. Timid speakers,
They travel alone until the others join them.
They avoid abutments, and are often found at rest
    under the roofs of houses.
They are outside and we are within them.
What are they?[85]

Cars burst into the light. The missing X of my riddle here is the product rolling off the assembly line, the Bride of all those Bachelor Machines that have been so hard at work in their *auto*-matism. Visiting the River Rouge assembly line of the Mustang Division of the Ford Motor Company, I was awestruck to witness one of modernism's primal scenes: the automatic sex Marcel Duchamp could only dissociate in *The Bride Stripped Bare by Her Bachelors, Even*, brought to fruition every ninety seconds as a new car rolls off the line. Here the Bride is being built up as she is stripped bare by robotic bachelors in sequential steps along the way, component parts being supplied by feeder lines from the sides and riveted onto chassis or body forms by angular metal arms that shower the floor with loud sparks and

30. "Auto by Robot," 1983. Reuther Library, Wayne State University.

violet auras (fig. 30). Dollies of shining tanks roll by to be bolted into place — the illuminating gas to be siphoned through blossoming barometers, the nine malic molds to be brought to the assembly point by gliding sleds, oculist witnesses adjusting coruscating planes of flow, given the waterfall speed of the windmill in the form of a toboggan but more of a corkscrew, and the splash at A is everywhere an uncorking. So when the Bride finally appears, all dressed up with everywhere to go, it is a miraculous reversal of the destructive impulses that went to work on her . . . in a carefully plotted sequence. The Bride is a shiny new car, with seat belts and gorgeous multicolored paint job, which an inspector then leaps into and drives to her first parking lot.[86]

I want to unite this overplus of desire (which I saw in the rhythmic effects of Coolidge's metrics and now see everywhere in the dissociations of the Language School — and in writers of both sexes) with the social form of the assembly line as it developed in a sequence of improvised stages. American energy, however destructive it may be, only gets us halfway; the rest is a feedback system of econometrics that adjusts supply and demand within the capacious form of a modernity built to order but only to fall into ruin and decay as soon as its moment is past. Terry Smith's revisionist history of modernity, *Making the Modern*, carefully delineates the socially reflexive feedback system that organized the assembly line as a step-by-step series of gradual improvements that were only invented in response to the rationalizing pressures of costs and sales.[87] The mode of production of the assembly line, in other words, depended on and was constituted by the mode of consumption of its products; in this reading of modernity, social surplus value not only exploits workers but must pay them enough wages to purchase its products. Feedback is structure, and vice versa, leading to a situation in which individuals are both distributed in and alienated from social matrices they have partly made. Here, an entire social logic ends up constructed on principles of the assembly line, which then outstrips any notion of individuality in its self-regulating, self-creating production:

> The inventive genius represented by [Ford] was above all an organizational one: elements developed elsewhere were shaped into a productive system of incessantly self-refining functionality in which nothing was original except the system itself, particularly its capacity to constantly redefine, simplify, and proliferate — that is, to make new — its own parts. Is this quality distinctive of early twentieth-century modernism: an unprecedented concentration on the replication of a single, ever narrowing, more reduced product through a system which was itself constantly diversifying? (15)

What resulted here was a generic product, the Model T, a unit structure that condensed the entire mode of production. It was important that the design of the car initially be fixed so that economies of scale and supply could work toward increased efficiencies. A number of important innovations had to come together in the run to the assembly line:

> Key elements were the creation of a full range of special-purpose tools; an emphasis on the interchangeability of parts; the placement of both materials and machines at strategic, sequential manufacturing points rather than traditionally, according to their type of function; a meticulous materials purchasing system and a carefully timed delivery system. (20)

The gradual convergence of tools, materials, and organization led to new improvements of the assembly line, controlled less by any individual direction than by economic factors — cost and supply of materials, coordination and speed of production techniques. The breakthrough of the "invention" of the assembly line, therefore, did not take place at any one time; rather, retrospective dates can only be assigned from the futurity of the innovation of its overall form. In this account of modernity, there is no such thing as an author:

> From [early] accounts it is clear that the first subassembly line was installed in the flywheel magneto department on April 1, 1913, and that within a year almost every other assembly operation in the plant was put onto a moving line of some kind, including that of the entire engine (by November) and the chassis (between August 1913 and April 1914). (20–21)

It is important that, if the assembly line is first of all an economy of time, its development depended on a particular utilization of space, specifically that of Albert Kahn's Highland Park plant. What was needed was a space large and adaptable enough to accommodate the manifold improvisations (several technical modifications a day during the height of its elaboration). During the improvised assembly of the line itself, a kind of autotelic formalism, a self-tooling *auto*-matism, took over in which the production of goods was subordinated to the production of machine components. Machines themselves became parts, like the Ford itself driving into Stein's prose but unlike the poetic form of the "machine made of words" in William Carlos Williams's introduction to *The Wedge.*[88]

> This drive toward the priority of assembly over the production of parts absorbs the achievements of the production engineers . . . into a larger system, that of the plant as a whole: a machine using machines to produce machines in such ways that each of these terms was rapidly redefined. It could be said that machinic surplus value has fused with that being so brutally extracted from the worker, himself fast vanishing into invisibility, to become a bursting dam of pure productivity. (*MM*, 33)

If Coolidge's *The Maintains* is a "machine made of words," in the sense of traditional accounts of modernism's relation to the machine, it should be seen as more akin to Ford's assembly line as "itself a machine, or more accurately, the internal circulatory system of an additive machine laid out and open" (32) rather than to the unit structures of the modernist lyric, in either Williams's metaphor or Coolidge's "Made Thought." The excess of meaning (and rhythmic desire) in poetry thus begins to lead away from the formal metaphor of the modernist machine and toward postmodern notions of "machinic" desire.[89]

My account of the modernist poetics of the assembly line is meant both as a formal analogy and as a corrective to the idea of a dehistoricized norm against which nonstandard cultural responses are organized. If the assembly line exists to produce a standard, from the Model T to the Big Mac, it condenses within its products the historical mode of production itself. It should be clear by now that I want to describe the sequential structuring of meaning in *The Maintains*, and the organization of social feedback among writers in the editing of *This*, as comparable specific histories of technological modernization. I want by this thought experiment to recover aspects of social form that are lost in a poetics of expressive subjectivity, and that in turn lead to the wrong criteria for participation in a social totality. Norms do not exist *ab eterno;* they are historically produced and can be changed in time. Norms are products, not deductive schemata of oppressive rationality, although they can be used for oppressive ends. Nonstandard norms are also produced; they are not simply defined against the abstraction of normativity. The work of the Language School, if produced within a system of social feedback necessary for meaning and comprehension, may in turn end up reproducing itself as a new norm. If this were to happen, a nonstandard mode of expression might simply be inserted into the space of a vacated norm of the expressive lyric. It is easy to see how this logic of substitution often occurs in the postmodern overturning of high modernism, as in the art world, for example, with its regular replacement of a new canon for the recently old guard. A practice of art may undertake, on the other hand, the task of releasing the social forces held in check by the norm, as in Duchamp's allegory of the assembly line or in Walter Benjamin's arcades project. But even here it is not possible to select a distance outside productive relations. If the reading of Gertrude Stein's social texts shows an exemplary way that modernism can be imagined as congruent with social production, what is the value of Stein's critique? Clearly, she meant to bring together public and private desire in her refusal to imagine nonstandard identity as simply an opposition to norms. It is here that the public and private in Stein, "audience" and "real" writing, coincide. The trouble with self-reflexivity as the value of form, in this sense, is that it insists on imagining itself as apart from the world that constitutes it. It can only read itself out of that world.

In the development of my own work, from initial prototypes such as "Factors" to *Progress* and *Under Erasure*, I have pushed the analogy to social form within the overarching structure of an improvisatory assemblage of meanings. Rather than referring to this work's possibility for difference within recurrences of the same, however, I want to propose a politics of reading that might explore the initially unacknowledged resonances between such formal concerns and aspects of the world they engage. In balancing a poetics of authorial self-canceling with a mode of social organization, in other words, what am I trying to do? If the cult of the author leads in vicious circle to the reproduction of identity by means of exclusion, seeing the material text as cultural production may lead to new vistas of comprehension, and to new and as yet unanticipated forms of participation:

Until only she controls fantasy
of a use,
and I watch the news . . .

A lattice of commutes,
whose routes
Arrayed in color-coded dispatches . . .

Mark his identity as an exchange
At the hub of information.
"1989" . . .

Its machines answering back but only one move ahead
As rats push their buttons for continuous soft hits
Other format configurations are no longer accepted . . .

The workbench has disappeared, to become a mobile surface — a frame in space — across which one's task slides. In other parts of the factory, the stand vanishes to become a similar frame upon which the worker's task appears to be performed, then again and again. And the task is now much reduced from a gathering together, however regulated, to a passing touch, utterly controlled.[90]

You press fast forward and remain seated in place
If a touchstone is xeroxed many times in succession
As among islands we hop only from pleasure to pain . . .

The industry,
a component designed
To produce cars at the same rate . . .

As destinations with exit signs
I invariably select,
to demonstrate . . . [91]

Wednesday, July 16, 1986. There was nothing particularly askew on this date, nothing to remotely suggest that this shift was to be any different than the few odd thousand that had gone before. I weaved my way through the rivet guns and cross members, the waltz of the unblessed, awaiting the next frame and the one after that. Thirty-seven frames an hour. Thirty-seven clumsy muffler hangers. Thirty-seven rear spring castings. Thirty-seven invitations to dance.

First break arrived and I plopped myself down at the workers' bench for a smoke and a glance at the box scores. It was precisely 7:08 P.M. As I stared at the paper, the words and numbers started swirling together. I stood up. I could feel a numbness in my arms and legs. I began having major difficulty trying to catch my breath. I stepped away from the table feeling totally disoriented. . . .

What kind of poetic injustice was this? Choking over dead like a sack of yams only ten yards from some moron's half-tinkered embryo of a Suburban.[92]

An image of prolonged release.
To overcome inertia,
words
Melt in furnace semantics
That only a metaphor outlives. . . .

It is an original,
meaning that

Value can take out a loan
To pay for time in advance,
So anyone can process words. . . .

But no writer can own a trace.
To open wide as ranunculus
As a new day begins,
it is
Day one or a design problem. . . . [93]

THE CONSTRUCTIVIST MOMENT
FROM EL LISSITZKY TO DETROIT TECHNO

Literature stays alive by expanding into non-literature.
— Viktor Shklovsky

This essay is a response to a call to define the state of modernist studies, which I chose to answer again from the social space of Detroit — where modernism, as a cultural imperative, vanishes and reappears at random within the rationalized modernity that surrounds. Where the descent into production that frames the previous chapter might be seen as an affirmative and willful confrontation with the engines of modernity, the spatial figure for this essay is the crossing of borders between incommensurate zones that have been constructed in Detroit's relatively short but convulsive history. Inspired by Detroit, and challenged by the many experiences of mutual exclusion one has when living there, I wanted to make the most unlikely comparison possible to unveil the stakes of a radical modernism trapped within the productivist lifeworld. What resulted was a dual research project in which I turned to the work of El Lissitzky, emblematic of radical modernism in its most formally articulated, utopian mode, and the recent development of the experimental electronic music known as Detroit techno, as examples of the mutual permeability of radical form and modern lifeworld. A poetics of negative exemplarity is the bridge between the two, drawn out in contrasting modernist and postmodern examples from Louis Zukofsky and Jean Day. This essay, then, is an exercise in disjunction as much as conjunction, an attempt at the reciprocal illumination of cultural possibilities that ought to have more to do with each other, but because of the sterile framework of assigned cultural values, do not. I want, also, to continue a cross-cultural discussion between Soviet modernism and American postmodernism that I have pursued since my first contact with Russian Formalism. Detroit and the poorly understood Second World, it turns out, have more in common with each other than may have been supposed. Locating the Formalist devices of defamiliarization and semantic shift in a rationalized lifeworld that seems to ignore them certainly argues for the continued use of both terms. Finally, this essay is an attempt to construct an example in and of itself, as it challenges and crosses over the great divide in methodology between modernism and Cultural Studies, seen on analogy to a border crossing in Detroit.

THE GREAT DIVIDE

Along with General Motors' decision to shift their world headquarters from its previous location in the midtown General Motors Building to the downtown Renaissance Center, and to move many of its operations in from outlying areas, real estate values have gone up abruptly in Detroit, reversing decades of stagnation.[1] Housing values, particularly along the Woodward Corridor and the downtown–Grosse Pointe axis of East Jefferson, have exploded in anticipation of the relocation of management closer to the downtown area.[2] Even so, a commute from nearby suburbs such as Huntington Woods and Grosse Pointe still involves, on a daily basis, a lesson in dystopia as the boundary with Detroit is crossed. Driving into downtown from Grosse Pointe Park, for instance, as Shoreline Drive turns into East Jefferson, one moves abruptly from an illusion of social cohesion embodied in substantial homes, wide boulevards, landscaping, and waterfront parks, to a burned-out postindustrial wasteland of defunct businesses, depopulated neighborhoods, and vacant lots dominated by Chrysler's retooled, state-of-the-art East Jefferson assembly plant just after the city limits are crossed. The shock of instant social disintegration is comparable only to the crisis of belief one has driving the opposite way: after leaving downtown and the up-and-coming but not yet gentrified riverfront area, paralleling the successful urban renewal projects beyond Lafayette Park that lead to the reinhabited starter mansions of Indian Village on one side, and the Frederick Law Olmsted–inspired urban park of Belle Isle and hallucinatorially empty shell of the abandoned Water Works on the other, East Jefferson becomes progressively grayer and more sparse until, passing the Chrysler plant's square mile of technorationality, one reaches the city limits of Detroit and crosses over at a street named Alter, whose other side erupts into a world of ready-made coherence — of substantial homes, wide boulevards, landscaping, and waterfront parks — that has been completely undermined by what one has just passed through. Such an experience of border crossing is common — if not always so precipitous — in Detroit, where the crossing of borders between incommensurate zones can offer a quick lesson in social construction.

This experience provides an analogy for two key terms in modernist aesthetics: the Russian Formalists' notions of semantic shift (*semanticheskii zdvig*) and defamiliarization (*ostranenie*). Crossing over at Alter becomes the occasion for a rapid shift of cultural meaning and, often, a powerful sense of estrangement. Common to both is an experience of shock at the center of social modernity, here specifically the gaps in industrial society that exist between its spheres of production, consumption, and reproduction. If the perception that our ideas and beliefs are products of our lived experience has often been a rude awakening, in this sense, the cognitive violence that attends this realization is also a familiar feature of modern life, encountered in many social registers.[3] A genealogy of modernist shock — from Simmel, Freud, and Benjamin to Paul Virilio — is continually being reinvented by new forms of literature and art as they emerge from modernity — and not only in literary modernism.[4] A more recent, postmodern index to the relation of violence to aesthetics appears when, clicking on the web page of Detroit techno distributor Underground Resistance, one is given an image of the social space of Detroit at its most dystopian, a visual negativity in sharp contrast to the futuristic dreamscapes of the music available there (fig. 31). An otherworldly city of rhythmic power and visual intensity, such as imagined by the Soviet constructivist architect Iakov Chernikhov in the 1930s (fig. 32), is more like the Detroit imagined by techno against its background of lived displacement. Chernikhov's architectural drawings, which extend the constructivist aesthetics of the Soviet 1920s in wildly fantastic directions, are a perfect index of the psychological dynamics of utopia in response to social negativity, as they translate the sublime horizons of social revolution onto the lived spaces of modernity — as a form of grand but nearly impossible desire.[5] The representational gap between incommensurate zones leads to a vision of futurity in what may be called a constructivist moment, a recuperation of negativity in the making of a reconstructed world. That is another thing to learn from Detroit.

I describe the area of my university teaching in Detroit as between modernism and Cultural Studies, another border difficult to cross, almost to the point of exclusion. For an even greater sense of estrangement, I might call myself a member of the avant-garde. In the ongoing project of rethinking modernism after the impact of postmodernism and Cultural Studies, the avant-garde has only been belatedly addressed; a major shift of Cultural Studies methodology in terms of its proper objects has seemed to accept its disappearance without discussion.[6] This can be seen in the transition from Cary Nelson and Lawrence Grossberg's 1989 *Marxism and the Interpretation of Culture*, whose topics include the Language School and the Talking Heads, to the ostensibly broader but often more codified mass-

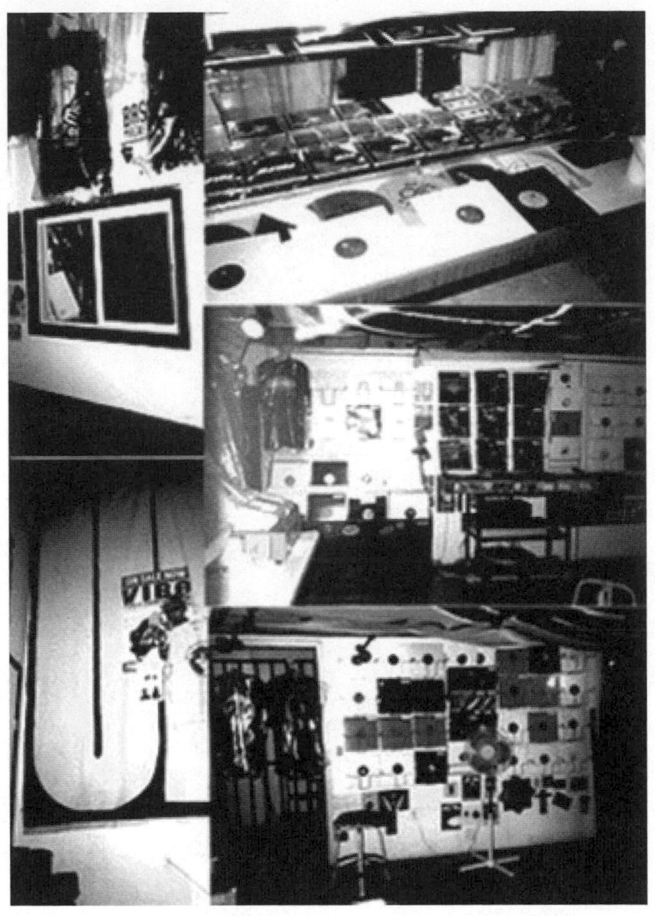

31. "Somewhere in Detroit" home page, <www.submerge.com>, 1997.

cultural scope of Nelson, Treichler, and Grossberg's 1992 *Cultural Studies*, where the avant-garde, perhaps as a surrogate for the category of the aesthetic, vanishes — only to be replaced by *Hustler*, *Rambo*, and the Book-of-the-Month Club.[7] Nelson himself argues that the best way to reintroduce genres such as poetry into Cultural Studies is to identify them with forms of political agency, as in the example of American poets who, while upholding their modernist credentials, participated in the Spanish Civil War.[8] As we have seen, Paul Mann's notion of the avant-garde's theory death testifies as well to the collapse of the embarrassing belief that the negativity of the avant-garde is identical to its political agency, especially after its disappearance into institutions seemingly designed to contain the implications of its radical forms.[9] We may return to the analogy of a border

32. Iakov Chernikhov, architectural fantasy from Fundamentals of Contemporary Architecture *(Leningrad, 1931).*

crossing in Detroit: if, from the perspective of Cultural Studies, modernism often appears as culturally retrograde as the self-enclosed zones of cultural smugness across the border separating Grosse Pointe from Detroit, Cultural Studies, conversely, must suffer a comparison to the fragmented dystopia of articulated gaps between subject positions within the city's unstable urban terrain. In a dialogue of cultural politics across the great divide, the avant-garde seems to be truly nowhere: seen from the perspective of the totality of the entire metropolitan area, it must be entirely underground.[10]

The elision of the avant-garde in American Cultural Studies, and its delayed reappearance in new modernist studies, is an ultimate outcome of post-1968 cultural politics. As a species of the exotic and unknown (or overly familiar and disruptive) that likewise connotes institutional privilege (or lack of hierarchical position), the avant-garde raises fears of political failure that are played off, simultaneously, as elitism and subversion.[11] While there are good reasons for suspicion of the avant-garde in terms of its politics of gender and race, a wide range of specific work has qualified the previous assumption of avant-garde agency as primarily masculinist and homosocial.[12] This may be seen in gendered critiques of male authors; in the rediscovery of the work of experimental women writers as alternatives to conservative modernist paradigms; and in the postcolonial study of minority writers from diasporic and hybrid social environments not associated with the historical avant-garde.[13] In terms of class politics, both British Cultural Studies and the practice theory of Pierre Bourdieu reserve a space for a renewed discussion of the avant-garde, even if partly motivated by their critique of the avant-garde's presumption of the agency of its radical forms, seen apart from the social formations that constitute them. Raymond Williams himself provides one of the strongest lines of defense of the avant-garde in *The Politics of Modernism*, where, arguing against a politics of "left formalism"—the assumption that radical form is simply identical to political agency—he imagines a third space for the avant-garde, between rationality and creativity, that "remains to be invented in full."[14] Williams often seems compelled to return to the avant-garde, even after his substantial work on technology and mass culture. Challenged by Bourdieu to provide a politics of the avant-garde other than as distinguished by an elitist mode of "restricted production," he writes in *The Sociology of Culture*, "No full social analysis of avant-garde movements has yet [been] undertaken," and then goes on to offer one.[15]

Williams describes the avant-garde in terms of a cultural dynamics of urban assimilation and international mobility as much as in its synthesis of social negativity and formal innovation. "Avant-garde movements have, typically, a metropolitan base," while "a high proportion of contributors to avant-garde movements were immigrants to such a metropolis." As a result, avant-garde culture must be "analysed not only in formal terms but within the sociology of metropolitan encounters," in which "received sign-systems have become distanced or irrelevant" (*SC*, 83). An experience of displacement in social modernity is crucial in the development of the avant-garde, which Williams describes in classically Cultural Studies terms as a "border crossing": in the disappearing conditions of international mobility following the First World War, "such endless border crossing at a time when frontiers were starting to become much more strictly policed . . . worked to naturalize the *non*-natural status of language" (*PM*, 34). While there is arguably a blindness to homology in Williams's formulation — the possibility that complex cultural logics can be reduced to a parallelism between text and context — it suggests a perspective from which to see radical forms as reflexively engaged with their social formations. For Williams, "modernist universals" are not autonomous but "productive [and] in the end fallacious response[s] to particular conditions of closure, breakdown, and frustration" (47). But as a result of the self-consciousness gained from the *social* denaturalization of language and form, the foregrounding of modernist "failure" by the avant-garde yields both motivation and material for its "creative engineering, the *construction* of a future" (53).

For Williams, the political consequences of this displacement and reconfiguration are split between reinforcement and resistance. The avant-garde's "specific and distanced styles [at once] reflect and compose kinds of consciousness and practice that become increasingly relevant to a social order itself developing in the direction of metropolitan and international significance beyond the nation-state" (*SC*, 84). As an immediate result, the radical forms of the avant-garde are often readily re-presented "as merely technical modes of advertising and commercial cinema," by which it can only add its technical expertise to the global dissemination of the modern lifeworld as a dominant cultural order (*PM*, 35). On the other hand, the avant-garde's capacity for social critique may be renewed precisely through its location within and penetration of the dominant culture, taking advantage of the latter's resources, wealth, and cultural pluralism: "The internal social conditions of the metropolis [create] favorable supportive conditions for dissident groups" (*SC*, 84). Such an integration of the avant-garde within wider social logics only reinforces its capacity for critical intervention, which then may be disseminated at large. Rather than ending in its recuperation, the avant-garde remains a paradigm of cultural innovation: "These 'transitional' works are very important, since at every other level of analysis, quite properly, attention is centered on the typical, the modal, the characteristic. It is then easy to miss one of the key elements in cultural production: innovation as it is happening; innovation in process" (200). The avant-garde is a central example of Williams's category of "emergent" cultural form, and as such its implications are not confined to aesthetic practice.

Williams goes on to detail a number of cultural processes associated with the avant-garde, including (1) the reciprocal exchange of cultural materials from restricted social registers to more popularly available forms; (2) the employment of nontraditional forms of signification, from experimental uses of language to invented codes; (3) the broadening of authorship to include group collaboration and as well as social authorship; (4) the extension of processes of cultural innovation to the development of new markets and new technologies; and (5) a producer-centered horizon within which forms of signification become modes of cultural reproduction even as they are consumed. In drawing on notions of form taken from the work of the Russian Formalists, Williams's cultural sociology follows the slightly later tradition of materialist critics in the Voloshinov/Medvedev/Bakhtin circle who attempted to bridge the gap between formal agency and social reproduction; his avant-garde is not the dead end of devices but a living example of the politics of form, seen in terms of its social articulation.[16] There is a risk of homology in Williams's productivism, again, when he fails to account for the negativity of the avant-garde and the often restricted address and limited life span of its works and cultural forms. This lack of an adequate connection between avant-garde negativity and the larger social logic Williams calls for, in fact, has been one of the major obstacles to renewed interest in the avant-garde. The first notion to be cast aside is that the negativity of the avant-garde is always the same refusal — prototypically, that of male artists to participate in normative culture after the traumatic rupture of total war.[17] Avant-garde negativity is quite variously articulated in relation, particularly, to gender and nationality at specific historical moments.[18] There is no "one" avant-garde, defined by the paradigmatic example of the historical avant-garde; a much wider range of cultural politics than Williams imagined continues to emerge from social formations that engender formal experiment.

LISSITZKY'S EXAMPLES

Reconciling radical form with social agency is the burden of any new consideration of the avant-garde. If the fetishistic disavowal of left formalism Williams cites is a straw man or red herring, Bourdieu's notion of its restricted production — with the inference that the avant-garde's producer-centered aesthetics may mean nothing more than an address to a small, like-minded coterie — offers a more important challenge in that, it is true, avant-gardes are usually small groups of practitioners at a far remove from the mechanisms of social reproduction.[19] Avant-garde criticality, in

Bourdieu's sense, cannot make up for the gap between its stated intentions and actual effects, which must still be seen as relative to its restricted codes and marginal formations. To explicate this contradiction between avant-garde negativity and its restricted social formations, I will consider as a primary example of avant-garde practice with emergent social meaning the work of Soviet constructivist El Lissitzky. Lissitzky's well-known series of works titled *Prouns* (1919–25) are, as equally the work of Gertrude Stein and Louis Zukofsky, quintessential examples of radical modernism. As with the case of Stein's media celebrity late in her career, the *Prouns* demand an account of their relation to the development of a mass-cultural aesthetics in Lissitzky's later work in typography and design, at international exhibitions and in the 1930s Soviet periodical *USSR in Construction*.[20] While the critic Yve-Alan Bois sees a moment of "radical freedom" in the *Prouns*, the relation between that freedom and the later social realism but also Stalinist politics of Lissitzky's mass-public propaganda work is still very much under debate.[21] This is especially the case if one rejects the canonical narrative of Soviet modernism's betrayal at the hands of proletarian realism (dated as early as 1919 or 1922 for some critics, but which usually finds its great divide or historical endpoint around 1930, as is well known) and looks for a reflexive relation between them.[22]

An obvious account of Lissitzky's move from the restricted codes of the avant-garde to a response to the social command of the socialist state (as enacted in poetry by Mayakovsky) is to see it as a consequence of the need to address mass audiences, as does Benjamin H. D. Buchloh.[23] But it is equally necessary to explore Lissitzky's politics from the perspective of his difficult forms, even at their most abstract and hermetic. As examples of radical freedom, Lissitzky's *Prouns* encode a difficult, impeded mode of social address that seems to terminate in their exemplary constructedness (fig. 33). Simultaneously autonomous in their formal construction and dialogic in their mode of address, demanding high-order cognitive processing by the viewer, Lissitzky's *Prouns* may be described as modernist examples by means of an analogy to the "free radical," a concept from the physical sciences that refers to the unstable existence in nature of "an especially reactive atom or group of atoms that has one or more unpaired electrons," an incomplete atomic or molecular form that demands completion by virtue of its surplus negativity but that persists in a reactive state.[24] As an analogy to the work of the avant-garde, the concept has many resonances: as a material form whose reactive agency is due not to its formal autonomy (in Zukofsky's sense of form as a "rested totality") but to its unattached

33. El Lissitzky, Proun 99, *1925. Water-soluble and metallic paint on wood, 129 × 99.1 cm. Yale University Art Gallery, New Haven.*

incompleteness (a converse state of "total unrest"),[25] a free radical searches for more stable structures with which it reacts in the making of more complex structures — but at the risk of instability, breakdown, and failure. A modernist example of a work that may be elucidated by means of the concept of the free radical is Lautréamont's *Chants de Maldoror*, which explores the properties of an imagined radical evil that, reacting with available cultural narratives, transforms them into hitherto unimagined forms. The relation of negativity to exemplarity here is crucial, as Lautréamont violates literary conventions in creating modern parables that demand the reorientation of readers' expectations in a new kind of literariness. The analogy of the free radical thus has a twofold value: it resolves the autonomous and dialogic aspects of modernist and postmodern form in the notion of negative exemplarity, and it suggests how the exemplary negativity of such free radicals moves from the limits of self-reflexive paradox to more stable forms of social reflexivity.

Recent work on the literary device of the example supports this effort to rethink the politics of modernist form.[26] As a figure for the modernist example, the free radical captures an element of negativity that is missing in more positive, and typical, notions of exemplary representation.[27] In selecting from a repertoire of cultural conventions for appropriate action (what Shklovsky, thinking of oral folktales, termed the "warehouse of cultural materials"), the example cites a motif from a set of preexisting topoi at a rhetorically crucial moment of undecidedness; in this way, the rhetoric of exemplarity depends on an undecided condition in the addressee. Foregrounding its invocation to proper action in a suspended moment of narration, the example dialogically constructs a link between aesthetic and ethical categories (for Soviet modernists like Lissitzky, between constructed form and social command). The example has a complex history, from heroic citations of oral epic and redemptive imitations of Christ to the nonnarrative, ambiguous examples of Jenny Holzer's postmodern LED-board injunctions in Times Square. For Holzer, it is not only that the addressee is undecided and needs to know how to act; in addressing his or her dilemma, the postmodern example itself must remain undecidable (as in the majority of American advertising) rather than affirm any belief.[28] More modernist examples also problematize, and even enact, cultural dilemmas that occur between negativity and value, doubt and belief, as in the central example of Josef K. in *The Trial.* Modernist examples often suspend judgment of appropriate action, which is identified with the limits of the constructedness of their forms; while the right answer to Josef K.'s dilemma may never be known or is impossible to know, the total form of *The Trial* must be seen as exemplary. Modernist examples place their undecidable judgment at the border between aesthetic form and social formation Williams saw in the emergence of the avant-garde. So the parable of Josef K. determines the values — in this case, the possibility of proper action — of an emergent urbanism within the decadent forms of bureaucratic state rationality. For Kafka, the negativity of modernist form itself is exemplary.

The modernist example not only provides an answer to a dilemma about the proper way to act; it enacts the scene of that dilemma itself. For Alexander Gelley, "The rhetoric of example stages an instance of judgment [in which] the reader does not simply occupy a post of reception [but] is drawn into the process of weighing alternative arguments and cases."[29] Appropriate contexts for interpreting its typical universality must, as a result, remain undecided; the example refers a presentation of an exemplary situation (parable) to an as-yet-undecided application of a rule (paradigm). "Yet the scandal of example, its logical fallibility, lies in the fact that this ethical summons [is] predicated not on a law or a rule [but] on the instance in its particularity, an instance that cannot in itself suffice to justify the principle in question" (ibid.). As in the linguist's "toolmaker's paradigm," where participants in communication can only know what a word for a given tool they cannot directly see *means* in terms of what it *does*, we are in a situation where an example is presented in restricted code whose general implications are not yet available.[30] A relation of part to whole, thus, is crucial in exemplarity; all examples necessarily ask the question, What is this an example of? where a judgment of wider context is forthcoming. "Example cannot assume a whole on which it draws. Rather, it is oriented to the recovery of a lost whole or the discovery of a new one," and "the mimetic effect here is linked [not] to techniques of representation but to forms of behavior, to a goal of ethical transformation" (3). The example demands the interpretation of a particular (a hero, an event, a relation between things, an outcome; Christ, the crucifixion, temptation, resurrection) as necessary due to its implication of a wider whole; it addresses our "need to *think* a universal that we can never *know* in order to be capable of speaking of any particular at all" (7).

Such a wider whole may be a form of community that binds speaker and hearer together; or it may be the work of art's predication of *sensus communis;* or it may be a more abstract, universal context of belief in what is right and proper to do. Positive examples from folk belief or religious discourse are often drawn upon to align modern life with more universal horizons, as the work of Yulia Latinina on Stalinist folklore or of George Lakoff on American politics shows.[31] The culture of the American Left is rhetorically constructed in just such exemplary terms, from songs like "I Dreamed I Saw Joe Hill" to slogans such as "Defend the Scottsboro Boys" to the cult of the dynamo and the worker's body.[32] In high modernism, the foregrounding rather than denial of negativity adds the provocation of a deferred or missing horizon of comprehension to the evaluative act. Nietzsche gives an example of such a provocation when he holds out a horizon of meaning in *Also Sprach Zarathustra* where "all things come caressingly to your discourse and flatter you, for they want to ride on your back. On every parable you ride to every truth."[33] Rather than being a joyous consummation, however, this condition may equally be a nightmare in which "what those 'truths' are we know. They are the mobile army of metaphors, metonymies, and anthropomorphisms that constitute the parables. They are truths that cannot be extricated from the figures used to express them" (173). The modernist prison house of language itself turns out to be the horizon of exemplary paradox, an effect Kafka exploits to the full in turning opaque parable into the structuring device of literary form, a self-reflexivity directly derived from Nietzsche's metaphorical relativism. While modern examples such as Kafka's, it is true, end in anything but redemptive horizons, they suggest a continuity between formalist and progressive versions of modernism due to the open relation both share between concrete particulars and deferred comprehension, whether implicit in language or enacted in interpretation, thus arguing for a direct connection between immanent and contextual forms of reflexivity. Modernist examples often present themselves, not only as self-reflexive instances of aesthetic form (as with Wallace Stevens's "Anecdote of the Jar"), but as models for action whose comprehension invokes an ethical horizon, a paradigm for agency that unfolds from the cognitive processing of its construction. The modernist example links contextual indeterminacy to utopian negativity in an open horizon of interpretation: we are not in Jerusalem yet.

The work of El Lissitzky in the 1920s and 1930s is organized precisely in such exemplary terms, as models for action in an ethics of deferred comprehension, in a variety of media (painting, graphics, photomontages, typography, design, exhibitions, architecture), all of which foreground the constructive potential of form at historical moments in which social relations are being articulated and, therefore, in which interpretive horizons are open. The *Prouns*, in turn, are the primary instances of the exemplary character of his work as a whole. While it is typical of the Western reception of Soviet art to separate abstraction from the social realism that superseded it (in Lissitzky's case, in his design and photomontage work), the 1992 Guggenheim Museum exhibit *The Great Utopia* extends Soviet modernism well into the 1930s, showing a wide range of previously unseen work that responds to a social command. The limits of periodization, here, accurately delimit the extent of a given construction of Soviet modernism; rejecting the boundary claims of modernism as having ended in 1919, 1927, or 1931 entails rereading the avant-garde in the development of its social formations as well, particularly as they were re-formed (or liquidated) in the continuing experience of revolution and its consolidation in the Soviet state. Lissitzky's work in this sense has several distinct moments in which his work may be read in terms of its social address: (1) his postrevolutionary work in the art schools Unovis and Vkhutemas during the period of "heroic communism" up to 1921; (2) his activities in the West as cofounder and theorist of the international constructivist movement up to 1925; and (3) his return to Moscow, continuing work at Vkhutemas, and career in architecture, typography, and design (often addressing international audiences).[34] At his death in 1941, Lissitzky was an acknowledged innovator of Soviet modernism.

Important debates between suprematist, constructivist, and productivist tendencies in the early 1920s locate Lissitzky outside, in two senses, the avant-garde's collective transition from values of "bourgeois" art (autonomous form; easel painting; idealist metaphysics) to "proletarian" construction (social command; utilitarian forms; materialist aesthetics). While largely accepting such binary oppositions as generating the period's concerns, Hal Foster positions Lissitzky apart from them as a kind of trickster figure — by virtue of his conceptual strategies as well as his international position outside the Soviet Union in the early 1920s.[35] Lissitzky identified himself in this way; in *The Isms of Art* (coauthored with Hans Arp in 1925), he lists his work not under the heading "Constructivism" but in his own category-of-one, "Proun."[36] But in a larger sense, Lissitzky's work, precisely in its continuous interpretation of the aesthetic in relation to a series of social commands, provides the more encompassing model of constructivism; at each stage in his career, Lissitzky becomes the "artist-constructor" not only of material objects but of forms of modernist example. For Christina Lodder and Victor Margolin, the preeminent example of the artist-constructor, who possesses "both the artistic and technical skills required to produce an object completely adapted to its total function," is Alexander Rodchenko.[37] The cultural historians differ, however, in the scope of their definitions of constructivism; for Lodder, exemplary objects such as Lissitzky's are outside the goals of constructivism, which is to integrate a new relation to real objects into communist society. The tradition of constructivism in the Soviet Union begins, for her, with the rejection of the idealism of the example, as may be seen in Alexei Gan's manifesto (1922) opposing Lissitzky's sense of the object in his introduction to the inaugural issue of the periodical *Veshch/Gegenstand/Objet* (1922), as well as in polemics by Osip Brik and others in the journal *Lef* (1923–25) calling for the artist to engage with industrial production.[38]

While Rodchenko and others certainly took up the social command of functionalism, according to Lodder few objects influenced by constructivist aesthetics found their way into production. For Margolin, it is precisely this rhetorical (or in our terms, exemplary) dimension of their work that holds it "less accountable for the satisfaction of current [material] needs and recogniz[es] it instead as an argument for new values" (*SU*, 85). Constructivist objects made for industrial production and mass consumers are still *exemplary*, and here Lissitzky returns as paradigmatic constructivist precisely for his stress on the exemplarity of the *Prouns*. The two senses of artist-constructor may be elucidated in comparing Mikhail Kaufman's portrait of Rodchenko (1922; fig. 34), suited for work in a functionalist costume presumably of his own design and making, with Lissitzky's self-portrait photomontage, also a design of his own making, *The Constructor* (1924; fig. 35). Rodchenko provides a model for the new Soviet man that will be interpreted for the next two decades (and which later became an element in the genealogy of the Stalinist cult of personality). The artist is upright, "relaxed and standing at attention," ready for work on the design of the new world, which will extend the values of his physical posture and his material costume. Lissitzky's portrait exists in a potential space between dissociated elements: text, compass, layout grid, abstract forms, hand and head of the artist (in a turtleneck sweater). Importantly, too, the portrait exists in two versions, positive and negative. The potential space of construction, then, is the object of Lissitzky's portrait, a space predicated on its possibility of reversal.[39] The two self-portraits may be compared in the following way: Rodchenko's positivity depends on its horizon of as-yet-unrealized acts that he will perform as artist-constructor; Lissitzky's fragmentary space offers a horizon that encompasses both representation and its impossibility. Thus, the values of his self-portrait are available in either positive or negative versions. With Rodchenko, the work of art splits between material embodiment and utopian possibility, while with Lissitzky, materiality and utopian horizon are analogous, codetermining, and reversible.

In seeing the avant-garde's movement from art to construction as both contained within and reproducing a rhetoric of exemplary negativity, I am suggesting that Lissitzky's *Prouns* are constructed not only of disjunct formal elements but of their own history. Within the periodization of Lissitzky's work, the *Prouns* define a central moment where, prospectively and retro-

34. *Mikhail Kaufman,* Portrait of Rodchenko, *c. 1922. Photograph. Rodchenko and Stepanova Archive, Moscow.*

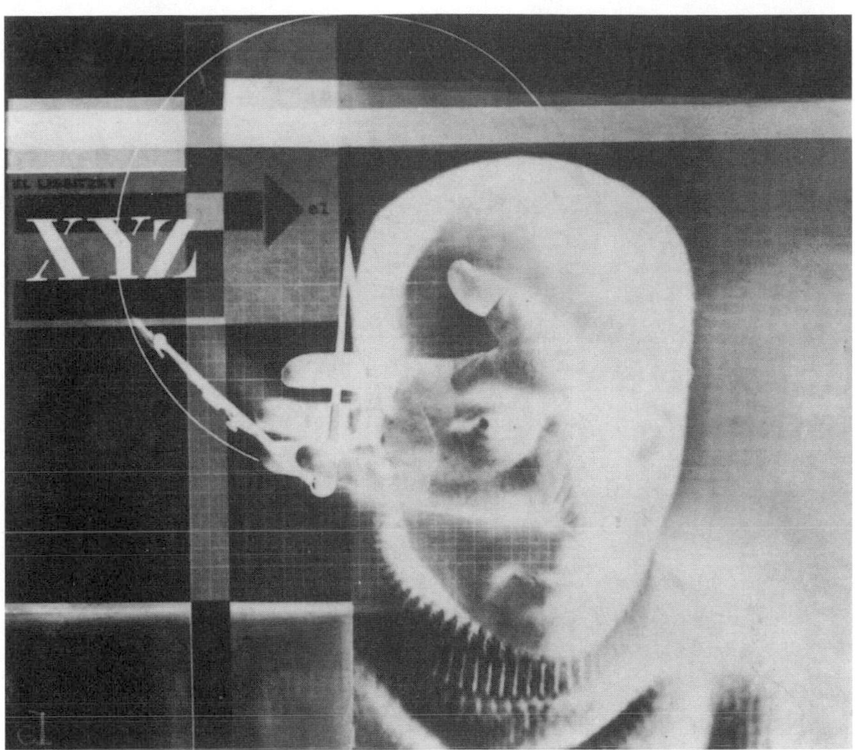

35. El Lissitzky, The Constructor, *self-portrait, negative version, 1924. Photogram, 11.3 × 12.5 cm.*

spectively, aesthetic form and social formation reflexively engage. For each of Lissitzky's three periods, the *Prouns* stand as both definition and fulfillment of exemplary aims: in interpreting the pure painting of Kasimir Malevich as a dialogic response to the social command of revolution and civil war; as promulgator of revolutionary forms in international modernism (in dialogue with both modernist abstraction and commercial advertising); and as facilitator of international dialogues from within the Soviet Union (in architecture) and international propaganda for Soviet construction (in exhibition and design). In each of these moments, as well, the position of the *Prouns* is defined in relation to moments of modernist rupture — social revolution, metropolitan displacement, and new technology — that dominate each period. This retrospective determination of values for historical rupture can be seen in the steady unfolding of Lissitzky's explanatory terms. Beginning the series, of course, is the experience of revolution, itself a figure of impossible exemplarity. For Lissitzky, "In Moscow in 1918 there flashed before my eyes a short-circuit which split the world in two. This single blow pushed the time we call the present like a wedge between yesterday and tomorrow. My efforts are now directed to driving it deeper" (*EL*, 325). Containing this historical rupture by reenacting it in the aesthetic series, Lissitzky turns his negativity on himself, in a series of aesthetic statements beginning with "Suprematism in World Construction" (Vitebsk, 1920): "THE IDEA OF THE 'ARTISTIC WORK' MUST BE ABOLISHED AS A COUNTER-REVOLUTIONARY CONCEPT OF WHAT IS CREATIVE" (320). In his lecture on "Prouns" at Vkhutemas (Moscow, 1921), Lissitzky claims they will release "a kind of lunatic force from which all will retreat in shame";[40] and in his talk on "New Russian Art" (Hanover, 1922), he continues:

> Six years ago, in 1917, the Revolution broke out in Russia, and not in Russia alone. The whole of the rest of the world stood against us, and thus we were completely isolated. Then it became clear to us that the world was only just coming into existence, and everything must be re-created from scratch, including art. At the same time, the question arose as to whether art is really necessary; whether the expression and the forms of art are eternal; whether art is a self-contained, independent domain, or a part of the whole remaining part of life. (*EL*, 330)

The experience of revolution leads directly to self-negation and, in consequence, abstraction — seen as continuing the dynamics of the revolution. With the whole world aligned against the revolution, it will be necessary to remake the world anew. The only solution to this self-canceling paradox of world making is to condense its agency in a radical questioning of the means of transformation itself: for constructivist artists, the work of art. Still, there is an illusion in Lissitzky's historicizing account: of revolution as a punctual moment, recollected as an historical imperative during the slightly later period of heroic communism (1919–22), during which he formulated his radical aesthetics. A prolonged duration of social collapse and utopian response, rather than a punctual moment, was the experience of revolution in which Lissitzky wrote; his retrospection of the 1917 Revolution thus condenses and displaces the more present reality of broad social disintegration.

Social negativity — revolution, civil war, famine, disease, and displacement — is thus made available for reinterpretation as aesthetic negativity — the overturning of prior notions of art by means of its implicit self-destruction and impossibility. The analogy is stabilized, not as a form of historicism, but in a dialectic of abstraction and materiality Lissitzky identifies with in the work of his mentor, Malevich, as prior exemplar. Lissitzky stages a reenactment of historical negativity as effectively aligned with positive values of abstraction and materiality produced from the aesthetic object, a relationship he describes in his account of the impact of the suprematism of Malevich's *Black Square* (c. 1915):

> Here a form was displayed which was opposed to everything that was understood by 'pictures' or 'painting' or 'art.' Its creator wanted to reduce all forms, all painting to zero. For us, however, this zero was the turning-point. When we have a series of numbers coming from infinity . . . 6, 5, 4, 3, 2, 1, 0 . . . it comes right down to the 0, then begins the ascending line 0, 1, 2, 3, 4, 5, 6. . . . (*EL*, 333–34)

It is clear that, in retrospect, the two sequences may be superimposed. "Revolution" in the first becomes the impossible number "0" in the second; *Black Square* occupies the place, for Lissitzky, of the revolutionary moment. "If the slab of the square has blocked up the narrow channel of painterly culture (perspective), its reverse serves as the foundation for a new, volumetrical growth of the concrete world."[41] While this moment is seen as the end of a series of subtractions, it is also the beginning of an incremental progression in which positive terms for history after the revolution will be superimposed on a series that begins with the aesthetic object. Negativity in the object is the condition of its exemplarity, of a sequence of constructive acts that will follow it. At first, the new world predicated by art is imagined purely in cosmic, suprasubjective terms; in the terms of Lissitzky's early lecture on "Suprematism," "Only a creative work which fills the whole world with its energy can join us together . . . to form a collective unity like a circuit of electric current" (330). By the introduction to *Veshch* (1922), however, the integers of art's progression are condensed in this-worldly objects; Lissitzky calls for a metropolitan "international style" that also will be "a product of work taken in common": "Every organized work—whether it be a house, a poem, or a picture—is an 'object,' not intended to estrange people from life, but on the contrary to call upon them to take part in its organization."[42] In his radical work of the 1920s, the no longer traumatic but now open horizon of revolution and the proposal of such objects are united in the construction of form as an exemplary parable of action. As the word *revolution* itself constructs a horizon of possibility out of an experience of extreme disruption, the continuing revolution is an open horizon of pure possibility that leads to a production of new objects that, in turn, interpret its meaning.[43]

Objects are examples of a transformed life, for Lissitzky, and the *Prouns* are the primary examples of such objects as well as the defining moment of his artistic career. The word *Proun* itself is the kind of hybrid object Lissitzky wanted; often defined as an acronym for "Project for the Affirmation of the New" (*proekt utverzhdeniia novogo*), it is also a constructivist neologism combining the morphemes *pro-* (connoting "an action continued throughout a given period of time") and *-un* (*Unovis*, the suprematist school; but also the start of Russian words for both "universality" or "destruction"). The *Prouns* are two-dimensional works that propose the universal destruction of three-dimensional forms toward their realization as new objects; they both abolish the represented world and reform it according to new principles of relation. As such, they demand cognition of at least three moments to be drawn into a scene of judgment of the work that becomes a pedagogical tool for the inculcation of revolutionary visual/spatial literacy: (1) a radical negativity in which the old world of representation is suspended in the form of abstraction; (2) a positive relation between individual elements within a constructed but incomplete ensemble foregrounded against a plane of abstraction; (3) a perspective from which the relation of both abstract plane and relational elements might be perceived that is outside the constructed space of the work and therefore in some sense impossible. While the first two moments are common in modern abstraction from cubism to constructivism, the third, Lissitzky's particular contribution, is central to his notion of an exemplary object. In his lecture on "Prouns" (1921), Lissitzky speaks of positive, negative, and *imaginary* relations after the interpellated command of Malevich's *Black Square* had abolished two-dimensional painting and created a possibility of new meaning in the three-dimensional world.[44] The notion of imaginary objects is further elaborated in "A. and Pangeometry" (1925), in a near-visionary discussion that is at the center of Lissitzky's aesthetics: "Suprematism has swept away the illusion of three-dimensional space on a plane, replacing it by the ultimate illusion of *irrational* space with attributes of infinite extensibility in depth and foreground," which supersedes the rational number line of progress and negativity.[45]

> Mathematics has created a "new thing": imaginary (imaginary = not real, assumed) number. These include numbers which, when multiplied by themselves, result in negative values. The square root of −1 is an imaginary thing called *i*. . . . We now enter a realm that . . . follows from

36. El Lissitzky, Proun 1D, *c. 1919–20. Lithograph, 21.5 × 26.9 cm.*

a purely logical construction and therefore represents an elementary crystallization of human thought. (Ibid.)

Lissitzky's notion of the imaginary extends in a number of speculative directions; it is linked to the overturning of Western perspective; the transcendence of the picture plane; the simultaneity of all colors within the spectrum of white; an integration of temporality into spatial form; the production of imaginary space through the "rotation" of a three-dimensional object; and finally a new monumentality, "the perpetual expansion of human achievement," that is predicated on the disappearance of the object, "an a-material materiality" (353). In his discussion of "A. and Pangeometry," Bois shows how Lissitzky's use of axonometric perspective, in which parallel lines meet only at infinity, negates the idealized position of the observer and allows Lissitzky to see his works as constructing the imaginary relations that supersede the rationalism of perspective that he describes.[46] Because there is no privileged perspective, the *Prouns* have no top or bottom and can be viewed from any side, an effect Lissitzky explored from *Proun 1* onward (fig. 36); Lissitzky even hypothesizes that the *Prouns* may create

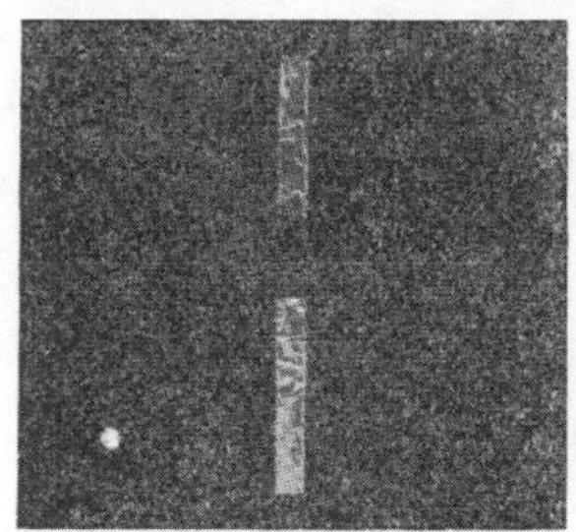

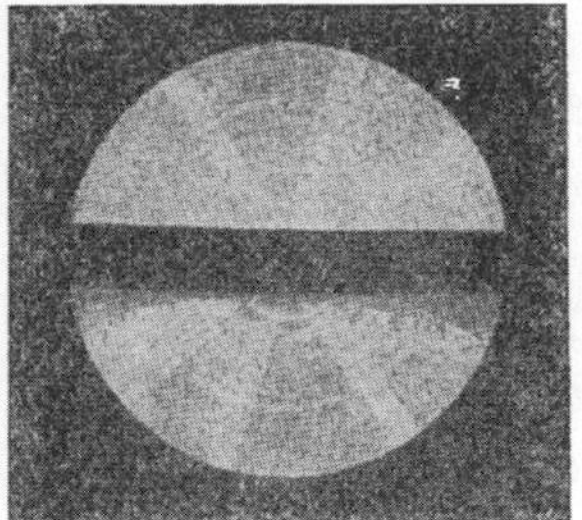

State of rest *State of movement*

Imaginary surface produced by rotation

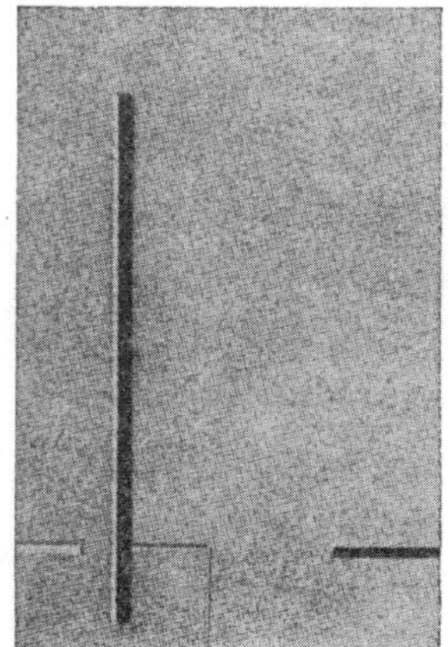

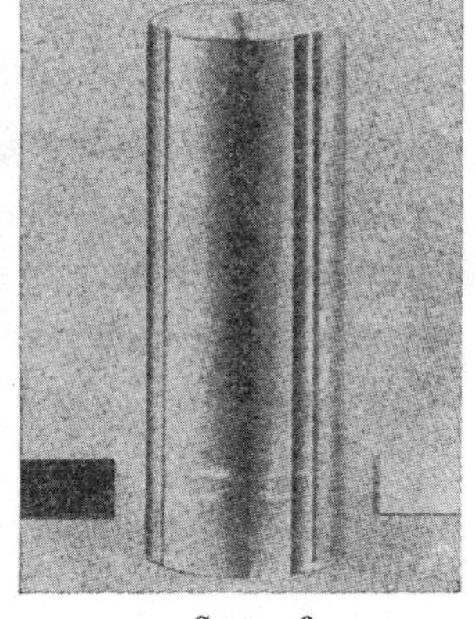

State of rest *State of movement*

Imaginary solid produced by rotation

37. El Lissitzky, illustrations from "A. and Pangeometry," 1925.

an imaginary space by being rotated, and offers technical illustrations to show how this can be done (*EL*, 353; fig. 37). There is thus no perspectival privilege for illusions of dimensionality constructed on the picture plane; qualitative values of particular elements within the constructed space are described as irrational as well. "In this space, distances are measured only by the intensity and position of the strictly-defined color areas," but due to the purely potential value of the color areas, "the distances [constructed by them in their relationship] are irrational; they cannot be represented as a determinate relation of two whole numbers" (350). Lissitzky's concerns here may be elucidated in their insistence on the relation between revolution and form: if we imagine the revolution as an allegorical *vehicle* whose *tenor* is not simply to be temporally deferred but understood as impossible in its disruption of progressive orders, in Lissitzky's scheme quality (relation) here is infinitely deferred as an "irrational number" in its interpretation as quantity (materials). At the same time, this impossible mental operation becomes "the foundation for a new, volumetric growth of the concrete world" (*A*, 33): a return to the material world after the discontinuity of revolution.

In inculcating a demand for the construction of a world that they cannot represent, the *Prouns* are a simultaneous instance of both ideology critique and material praxis. It is here that the notion of the free radical intersects with the form of the modernist example. As examples, the *Prouns* demand high-end cognitive processing and self-reflexive distancing; predicated on an "a-material materiality" at once impossible and irrational, they would also construct, Lissitzky hoped, new relations between two-and three-dimensional forms, painting and architecture, art and the world of objects, that exceed them. The necessary incompletion, the construction of relations that do not resolve, the antimimetic abstraction of the *Prouns* are the direct sources of their exemplary effects; the concrete particular (*Proun*) is predicated on an unknown whole that is the future revolution — as it predicates, in turn, that future as a realization of its impossible but exemplary, even heroic, acts. The *Prouns*, then, become retrospective concretizations of the revolutionary imagination articulated in the futurity of material forms; the concrete forms the revolution takes in the reconstructed past are those that *will have been*. This relation of the materiality of signification to the future anterior is not fortuitous: the condensation of "Art" to the "a-material materiality" of the letter "A." in Lissitzky's title (or the letter "K." in the original German, or "И." in Russian), here, clearly anticipates the use of the Lacanian *objet a* and its role in the production of ideological effects for Slavoj Žižek.[47] The *objet a* can be known only in its effects; it is a moment of a-signifying excess over the discursive stabilization of a traumatic experience, from primal scene to social revolution. But while the *Prouns* condense and repeat the experience of revolutionary trauma as they disappear into forms that predicate a fantasmatic space, they should be considered as neither symptoms nor "MacGuffins"; they are more intentional, and active, than that.[48]

It is here that Lissitzky's notion of ideology differs importantly from its symptomatic sense in the Althusserian tradition. In "Ideological Superstructure," the concluding section of *Russia: An Architecture of World Revolution*, Lissitzky describes ideology not in negative terms, as mystification, but in positive ones as a horizon for the agency and social reproduction of art:

38. El Lissitzky, Beat the Whites with the Red Wedge, *1919–20. Poster, 48.5 × 69.2 cm.*

"The ideological superstructure protects and secures work. . . . On the basis of the existing, an ideology is formed representing a definite view of life and leading to certain interpretations and interrelations which, in turn, affect further growth" (68). Lissitzky sees himself, in this passage, as nothing less than the artist-constructor of ideological effects that are predicated not only on the negativity of modern examples but "on the basis of [their] existing." The mere fact that the *Prouns* exist, as positive objects, is their confirmation of political agency, which is to inculcate, as free radicals of pure creativity, "the perpetual expansion of human achievement." Revolutionary experience and history are condensed in imaginary/concrete objects leading to a horizon of exemplary acts — and it is here that the three stages of Lissitzky's career, from suprematism to photomontage, may be seen as consistently addressed toward a horizon of constructed ideological effects. As a paradigm for radical form's capacity to condense and reproduce the trauma and/or possibility of revolutionary experience in this way, we may compare the breakthrough agitprop work of the heroic period of communism, *Beat the Whites with the Red Wedge* (1920; fig. 38), to Lissitzky's autobiographical account of the revolution as "the short-circuit which split the world in two": "My efforts are now directed to driving the wedge deeper" (*EL*, 325). Like the word *revolution* itself, *Beat the Whites* condenses traumatic disruption while it perpetuates the new and strange understanding that had been gained from it; it is an originary moment of the semantic shift itself as a form of social reproduction. In the *Prouns*, Lissitzky concretizes this moment in form as he continues to imagine the agency of art as a "wedge"; thus in his 1922 lecture, "We have set the Proun in motion and so we obtain a number of axes of projection; we stand between them and push them apart" (*EL*, 347).[49] Here "we" are the wedge as much as our exemplary objects, and the multiple perspectives that are pushed apart provide the creative resources, the open horizons of possibility, that will continue the revolution.

We can now suggest an approach to the central ethical dilemma posed by Lissitzky's Third Period exhibition design and propaganda work for new modernist studies: the relation between his exemplary work as international constructivist and his mass-public interpretation, and endorsement, of Stalinist culture.[50] Positioned between the traumatic rupture of revolution Lissitzky experienced in 1918 and his work as designer and illustrator in the Third Period Soviet Union, the *Prouns* stand as a material record of imagination in transition: prospectively irrational and unbounded, retrospectively concretized in form. It is here that Bois's formalist insistence on the *Prouns*' politics and Buchloh's revisionist thesis, that radical form was inadequate to the interpellative call of revolution and thus had to be reinterpreted on a mass-public scale, may be reconciled. On the one hand, the experience of revolutionary subjectivity as an effect of historical rupture is figured as a parable of social order in Lissitzky's exemplary formalism; on the other, his examples are paradigms for a further development of visual and spatial literacy in their interpretation as architecture, typography, and design in forms that continue their radical intent. Lissitzky's 1930 cover for the architectural monograph *Russland* shows just how a reinterpretation of the self-reflexivity of the *Prouns* into the mass-public address of photomontage is easily, and literally, accomplished (fig. 39). Under the photographic image of a worker carrying a bar of structural steel, in the direction of another worker while apparently balancing on another beam, appears an edited version of *Proun 1E*, titled "The Town" (1921). The social analogy that results could not be more literal: the construction of the Soviet Union will take place on the basis of abstract forms created in the experience of revolution, a result that has been predicted by them. The cover itself illustrates, in an allegory of progress from art to construction, the midway point

39. El Lissitzky, cover of Russia: The Reconstruction of Architecture in the Soviet Union, *vol. 1 of* New Ways of Building the World (1930).

of work undertaken but not yet completed. The viewer is invited, imaginatively, to participate in building the USSR on two levels at once: theoretically, as on the basis of prior blueprints, and as a material, social fact.

Such a dialectic of negative and positive, of ideal and material, however, does not fully account for the horizon shift of Lissitzky's exemplary forms in the 1930s. There is also the question of historical context: the political shift of the revolution from the period of heroic communism to Stalinism. While the *Prouns* derive their exemplarity from their (supersaturated) embeddedness in context, they can in no way determine their relation to context throughout its historical development; here, their radical self-reflexivity may be as much an attempt to finesse history and its interpretive dilemmas as to predict it. As free radicals, the *Prouns* can only demand completion in an entirely open way: their horizon of construction follows on their radical negativity. Just as the negative experience of revolution is stabilized and overcome in Lissitzky's constructivist projects, so the negativity of the *Prouns* is imagined to lead to a material world they cannot represent except as a form of material dissociation and constructivist will. Lissitzky's *Russland* cover thus represents a revision of the open horizon of interpretation as social construction takes place, which will then, in a further moment of retrospection, turn out to have been predicted, in part, by the *Prouns*. With the stabilizing of the Soviet Union in the late 1920s, and its turn to entirely coercive state politics in the early 1930s, interpretation of the *Prouns* may thus be both grounded in the constructed order they predicted and distanced from it, as form. Such an interpretive paradox argues for a revised account of the overthrow of formalist aesthetics more generally in the late 1920s, as with Medvedev and Bakhtin's attempt to preserve the constructive potential of Russian Formalism even as they condemn it for its "futurist negativity."[51] In this sense, the *Prouns*, as historical record of the revolutionary past, continue to preserve a utopian value for an ideology of construction "on the basis of [their merely] existing" — as could be said of formalism more generally (and which may explain the otherwise inexplicable revival and canonization of Mayakovsky and the Formalists in 1941).[52] As the constructivists' work stabilized as concrete *examples* rather than mass-produced objects in the 1930s, a necessary shift of values occurred. Lissitzky, Rodchenko, Klucis, and others could see their work's reception as ironically preserving its exemplarity in its reinterpretation, as Lissitzky went on to become, arguably, "the Soviet Union's leading *designer* in the Stalinist period" — not an immaterial accomplishment.[53]

In taking up this exemplary role, Lissitzky reinterpreted his formal values as what he had been saying they were all along: historical — just as his forms persist as material facts to be reinterpreted in contexts they predict. In his photomontages, radical form is translated into a capacity to represent social totality, not just present it as a form of prospective desire — but with the crucial difference that their formal negativity must now be reinterpreted as *historical irony* in the social articulation of their designs. Lissitzky's irony is simply that his work simultaneously demands, and cannot literally anticipate, the actual world in which it is reinterpreted: an irony of abstraction in its historical unfolding. The stability of representation that results can only rigidify in the hope that formal meaning will continue the horizon of revolution, as Lissitzky's forms attempt to drive their prospective wedge

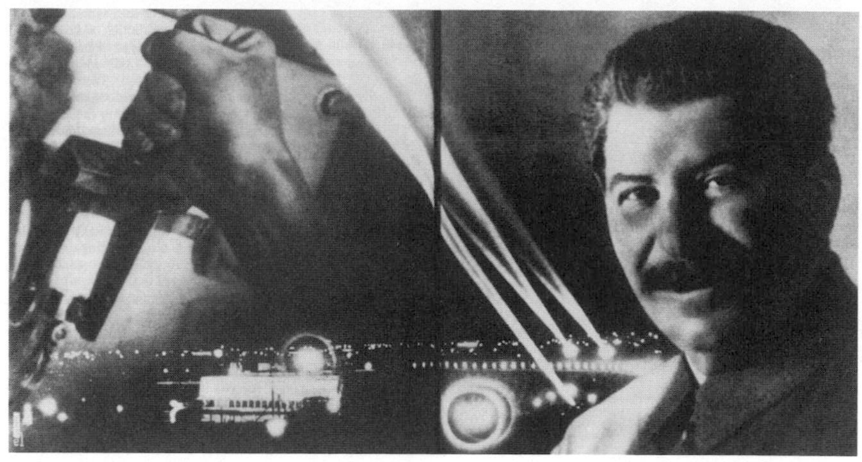

40. El Lissitzky, The Current Is Switched On, *photomontage from* USSR in Construction *10 (October 1932).*

deeper into the thickening context of the revolution as it congeals in social institutions and state structures. Such an attempt to continue the revolution as form even while admitting its concretization as history is visible in *The Current Is Switched On*, a double-page photomontage from *USSR in Construction* (1932; fig. 40). The figure of the artist-constructor, as in Lissitzky's earlier self-portrait, is dissociated here between the head of Stalin, who seems to grant permission to the scene, and the hand of the worker on the switch of state power, which electrifies the urban landscape in the background. The formal dissociation between intention and act is both ironized and represented by the image of a head disconnected from a hand. As a result, the montage can be read in two opposing ways: as connecting Stalin to the social result of electrification or dissociating him from it entirely — with the result that the formal construction of the image itself can no longer claim predictive responsibility as consequence of its radical will. Rather, the state is what *will have been*, whether predicted by a constructivist image or not. Stalin's betrayal of the revolution begins right here, with the ironizing of utopian hope by the material construction of the state. It is no exaggeration to say that a translation of negative exemplarity into historical irony was ubiquitous in the Soviet Union from the late 1920s on — and not only as a matter of aesthetics, as the Moscow show trials would prove. If the *Prouns* are "abstract models of absolute freedom," they must still suffer the historical fate of their concretization; if they are paradigms for the overcoming of representational orders, their embeddedness in history could still easily misrepresent them.

CONSTRUCTIVIST POETICS

The necessity of reading the social formation of the avant-garde as constitutive of its radical forms, as Williams saw, is confirmed by the example of Lissitzky. Clearly international and metropolitan, rather than national and popular, his work depends on an alterity of subject position — as Russian Jew whose investigations into the iconography of Jewish folk culture and Hebrew typography overturns the cultural proscription of graven images and their tsarist political suppression (and whose national/popular sources were deferred to constructivist aesthetics and the Soviet state);[54] as subject to the total displacements of revolution and civil war; as international Soviet emigré in metropolitan Berlin; and as exemplary artist-constructor as well as, arguably, survivor of the culture of the heroic period of the revolution into the 1930s. What Williams does not capture, however, is the experience of negativity central to revolutionary subjectivity in Lissitzky, the basis of the often fantastic structures of belief by which he could see the *Prouns* as imaginary examples of collective utopia whose meaning is reproduced in incommensurate acts. More aligned with Williams's sense of the avant-garde, particularly in terms of its metropolitan displacements and the politics of national language, is the work of American Objectivist Louis Zukofsky, with Stein one of two avant-garde children of immigrants who inaugurated the tradition of radical formalism in American modernism. Zukofsky's constructivism is evident in a poem from *55 Poems* (a book that begins with an elegy to Lenin):

                    Buoy — no, how,
It is not a question: what
Is this freighter carrying? —
Did smoke blow? — That whistle? —
Of course, commerce will not complete
Anything, yet the harbor traffic is busy,
                    there shall be a complete fragment

Of —

Nothing, look! that gull
Streak the water!
Getting nearer are we,
Hear? count the dissonances,

Shoal? accost — cost
Cost accounting.[55]

In a synesthetic landscape in which image and sound are at cross-purposes and may not resolve, the "complete fragment" of the incompletion of commerce is suspended as, literally, "nothing," compelling an ethical injunction to actions that may be of little immediate consequence, "to look" and "to hear." What we are "getting nearer" to is at this point unclear, but there is a potential for an arrival — if even provisionally arrested by "dissonances" and "shoals" that impede perception and movement even as a gull streaks by. Caught up in verbal forms resulting from a disconnection to the visual as "beyond" and unreachable, the poet invites the reader into a similar state that she may "hear" what he is not telling her he is seeing: the structure of totality that would make a complete account of the harbor. It is safe to say that, in this period of Zukofsky's career, the incompletion of the scene is directly ascribable to capitalist social relations, which may only be perceived as a "complete fragment" of commerce, the economic underpinnings of international trade.[56] If, as a displaced metropolitan, Zukofsky sees an analogous alienation in the economic, his consciousness of it must be completed in social revolution, as a form of cultural redemption at the very least. By analogy, the completion of the poem, for Zukofsky and the reader, will transform the demands of its high-order cognitive processing of elements that refuse any stability of representation into an experience of meaning as the redemptive horizon of the poem. Zukofsky's politics, here, begin with the displacements of the radical fragment; as a free radical, the poem in its incompletion exemplifies a state of total unrest resulting in an eventual "accounting" of "costs." An American version of the negative example, the poem as object predicts a horizon of yet-to-be-completed revolution.

Perhaps the most untested claim in Williams's account of the avant-garde is the notion that, as examples of an emergent social formation (here, one of intellectual Jews in 1930s New York), radical forms are destined to provide new cultural meanings that will eventually become widespread. There is an evident split in Zukofsky's reception that reproduces the great divide between modernism and Cultural Studies, between his legacy for radical formalist poets and his historical emergence as/displacement of the figure of the "New Jew," in Rachel Blau DuPlessis's terms.[57] The "New Jew," for DuPlessis, is "an enlightenment figure of Jewish modernity . . . caught among assimilation, secularization, and a variety of Semiticized and mongrelizing discourses" (4). Radical particularity and universal aspirations coexist in this figure of diasporic assimilation, and both are marked in Zukofsky's combination of radical formalism and diasporic Marxism. If there is a possibility of social reflexivity in Zukofsky's poetics, then, it must exist through these two seemingly disjunct moments: as the universality of radical form in its utopian horizon of meaning, and as a particularity of radical identity, which can only be recuperated in its displacement. This antinomy of identity and form may be seen via DuPlessis's method of "social philosophy" in the poem's displaced resolution: a "cost accounting" in which the deferred completion of revolution or meaning founders on the dissonant "shoals" of cultural differences that preclude it. The hidden injuries of race and class are stabilized in a very unredeeming effort of (nonsocialist) bookkeeping, with its stereotypical association with Jews. This (non)relation between form and identity becomes even more abstract and generalized in Zukofsky's reception, with the tradition of radical poetics founded in part on his work — such that it is often difficult to see the displaced identity claims in a given formal strategy, as discussed previously in terms of Bernstein's ideolectical poetics. In strictly literary terms, Zukofsky's reception has indeed been productive — from his canonization by the New American poets to the widespread adoption of constructivist aesthetics among Language writers. But in no sense has there been a reconciliation of his aesthetic of the fragment with his revolutionary or cultural politics, nor has he entered into mass culture as an exemplary modernist (as Joyce and Stein in many senses have). His work maintains an unresolved tension between social identity and radical form.

The tradition of constructivism in American avant-garde poetry even so is strong, as evident in the following poem by Jean Day, from her collection *The Literal World*:

THE FLUIDITY OF ATTRIBUTES

The reminder of triangles is no knowledge
                                        at all
but radicals set free in a book, promiscuous geometry you
might say, and reading it
decide there's no limit
to the places and people of the family we repeat
by shape and speech, whose fronts have backs
                                        that linger
"Nothing out of nothing" is the first resemblance
we admit, in the leisure of cells' calculation, longing to arrive

at true north only to find it bitterly makeshift —
a spot on which a tenuous man
                                                  fingers parallelograms
reminiscent of triangles with hats on[58]

As in New York poet Ron Padgett's parody of constructivism, *Triangles in the Afternoon*, there is a feint toward the rigor of geometric forms ("triangles," "parallelograms") that aspires to the condition of free radicals in their promiscuous ethics of combination.[59] Another context of social formation, however, places Day's poem in an argument within the middle-class nuclear family, perhaps being looked at in a family album where photos are held down by paper triangles. The "promiscuous geometry" of genetics may indeed give rise to a wide range of shapes and sizes, but there is no "true north" of genealogy, other than a contingent, combinatory pattern of attributes. Persons are lost in constructive potential; affect is distributed in fragments; and "nothing out of nothing" is a condition one arrives at in being born at the North Pole, to no known ancestors (as it echoes Lear's double negation of Cordelia's refusal of patriarchy). Constructivism's utopian demands, in its high modernist moment, are only an ironic counterpoint to the structure of the family — understood as recombinant identity, the endless return of the same. But what about Day's "nothing" and its demand for completion, the deferred whole that allows the modernist example to negotiate between identity and form? If incompletion is only biological, what is it that is missing, that is as if it had never been? Genealogy provides one answer, substituting for progress in high modernist moments such as Lissitzky and Zukofsky's, but it is understood here that there is no point of origin — and this is what makes families as well as identities what they are. Day's poem seems skeptically to question any scenario of completion, even as she infers a missing sociality perceptible in the reified images, "with fronts and backs," of one's potential relatives or missing friends.

But there is a further concern with the idea of construction: literally the one given the poem here. If the constructivist moment occurs as a break between dissociated formal elements and their future anterior meaning, between their *not yet being* and what they *will have been*, what guarantee is there of any necessary relation between the two? It is here that Lissitzky's *Prouns* meet their ethical catastrophe in being unable to anticipate the meaning of their displaced revolution of form in literal, historical terms. As it turns out, the foregoing construction of Day's poem was just that: a reading made out of whole cloth, via associations brought to the poem; there was no scenario of the nuclear family gathering around a photographic album envisioned by the author.[60] Two contradictory conclusions follow from this fact, once established: First, that the interpretive horizons of radical formalism are open to construction — and we return to the now clichéd theory of Language writing as a coproduction with the reader. Second, that the only way to read the work of radical formalism is to invest its negativity and incompletion with ethical significance — a kind of writerly ascesis that restricts the social reproduction of meaning to a moment of self-reflexivity reproduced in the act of reading (the typical modernist result). It will take an expansion of the possibilities of radical form onto a more capacious scale — as Lissitzky intended all along — to unravel the paradox of such an open horizon of meaning, best interpreted as a form of social transformation concretized in the form of the free radical. In returning to radical incompletion as the basis of a reflexive aesthetics, we must reject the twin moralisms of "readerly construction" and "writerly ascesis" for the material form of the work. Jean Day's poem is an imaginary solution that substitutes an open horizon of construction for the attributes of displaced identity lost in a nadir of abstraction.

DETROIT TECHNO

Another manifestation of the constructivist moment, originating far from the restricted codes and institutional cultures of the historical avant-garde, can be found in the emergence of an international style of avant-garde electronic music known as Detroit techno that has developed over the past two decades. Of the many alternative music subcultures in Detroit, techno is marked for its international fame (it has established an image of avant-garde Detroit firmly in youth subcultures in England, Belgium, and Germany) but also for its virtual unavailability *in* Detroit. Making contact with techno has involved, not return trips to the research library to reconstruct a genealogy of history and reception in avant-garde aesthetics, but a time-based, site-specific inquiry into a network of publications, distributors, internet sites, and music events dispersed through the capacious space of the Detroit metropolitan area. In various accounts, techno claims a history that dates to the 1970s for its influences and the 1980s in practice; however, this history is subject to rapid changes and redefinitions as the reception and meaning of techno shift, and its subculture continues to assert its originality against the culture industry's desire for new products.

With the emergence of Detroit techno as a form of mass entertainment in three productions of the Detroit Electronic Music Festival (2000–2002) — attended, according to organizers, by over a million persons each — curiously, little has changed.[61] Techno's emergence has coincided with no historical destiny, and while as a musical form it has an agreed-upon lineage, its cultural meaning is not the culmination of any progressive history. The city of Detroit has not been reborn since its invention, even as techno has been responsible for a paradigm shift that has subtly changed the cultural politics of the city.

Between techno artists and their audience there is the common bond of a special knowledge of its ongoing historical narrative, stylistic possibilities, and cultural meaning. A true hybrid of popular and avant-garde aesthetics, techno draws from an eclectic range of musical and cultural styles, from 1970s European art bands such as Can and Kraftwerk to African-American funk and disco (Parliament/Funkadelic); for Derrick May, one of the best-known Detroit DJs, techno is "George Clinton and Kraftwerk trapped in an elevator."[62] In its focus on formal concerns, and above all in its aesthetics of impersonality, radical juxtaposition, and repetition, techno proposes an ethics of incompletion both in the minimalism of its recorded products and in its mode of social address, which is only fully realized in live performance, equipped with two turntables and assorted sequencers and computer equipment, by a live DJ. Some aspects of its musical form as well as its social formation — the auteur status of DJs and studio mixers; its rejection of mimesis and expressive subjectivity in eliding vocal tracks and lyrics, leading to its oft-noted "facelessness";[63] its extension of the author function to group dynamics (providing an instance of the "social authorship" Williams proposed); and the restriction of its products to subcultural networks — are classically avant-garde. Many of its stylistic and rhythmic effects, at the same time, are entirely popular and danceable, related to the earlier, more accessible genres of disco and house music and as well to subsequent genres with higher commercial profiles such as breakbeat, jungle, and bass. For one listener, "Techno is popular becoming avant-garde, or avant-garde becoming popular; it's hard to tell which."[64] What is not hard to tell, from the vast amount of legitimating discourse generated by techno artists, producers, and distributors, is that the music sees itself as having a politics, even a revolutionary one. As an alternative music culture, techno is truly underground, situated "somewhere in Detroit"; as the motto of one of its principle recording labels, Submerge, claims, "We will never surface."[65] The negativity that makes techno an avant-garde comes from many sources, not the least of which is the social space of Detroit in the period of techno's emergence (the 1980s), an antimetropolis that is, simultaneously, a condition of the work's freedom. Techno is part of a project, for critic Scott Sterling, "to create a world that wasn't there."[66] It depends on ephemeral exchanges between isolated groups, particularly across racial and national divides, within and between metropolitan centers.

The analogy of "free radicals" works for Detroit techno: the music itself is predicated on incompletion and absence at its core, although of another order than with earlier avant-gardes. Where both Lissitzky and Zukofsky organize poetic effects around a foregrounding of signification, techno likewise puts to use central concepts of Russian Formalism such as defamiliarization and the semantic shift, particularly in relation to the poorly understood concept that motivates them, *byt* (a specifically Russian notion of the tedium, repetition, and endlessness of everyday life). Describing the Detroit version of *byt* and its relation to the emergence of its avant-garde, May explains: "One reason why the music comes from Detroit is the lack of influence. There is no influence here, there is nothing in Detroit. . . . I can truly believe the lack of influence in this [place] has given people an influence of their own psyche or personalities, unlike Paris, London, or New York, where you'll be influenced by what everybody else is doing. . . . And that's why the music came from here, because lack-of created more-of."[67] As displaced metropolitan immigrants, techno artists respond to that aspect of culture in Detroit that is predicated on migration and displacement, particularly with the influx of automobile workers in the 1920s to the 1950s, from the rural South, Appalachia, and southern Europe. But lack in Detroit is also visually evident in a social fabric of depopulated neighborhoods, vacancy, arson, and gaps between viable terrains. In its self-conscious response to conditions of urban dystopia, Detroit techno also follows a genealogy inaugurated by surrealism in its automatism of processes and sounds. Dick Hebdidge's account of punk subcultures, it may be recalled, drew an analogy between the stylistic provocations of punk vocalist Johnny Rotten and surrealist revolt (even if the potential absorption of subcultural styles into the market would signify, for Hebdidge, its death warrant).[68] Techno develops another aspect of surrealism, its "verbico-visual automatism," the suspension of the ego in automatic writing and drawing, and makes it a basis for the construction of community. What results in terms of techno's styles is their sense of dreamlike progression, synesthetic fantasy, and overall feeling of engulfment: a utopian response to negative terrains.

In techno, however, the source of this automatism, as befits its Detroit origins, is not only the unconscious but the machine, specifically the Roland TR 880, TR 990, and TB 303 rhythm and bass generators.[69] A 1997 lecture on techno by critic Scott Sterling began, not with a demonstration of the music, but with slides of these machines and an offer to buy any the audience might know of: "These machines live."[70] Breaking codes for emerging techno artists meant breaking open the backs of Roland rhythm machines and rewiring them for new sounds and effects. Richie Hawtin (Plastikman) "broke that machine wide open," producing sounds that "take you out of yourself"; Carl Craig broke new ground in importing verbal samples in his use of the Akai S-1000 sampler, calling his project "Paperclip People." Both a suspension of authorship in the abstract generation of sounds and sequences and a reconfigured author who masters and supersedes the technology in recombining cultural materials are central to the techno aesthetic. Machines, rather than being ends in themselves, are primarily important for what can be gotten out of them (and what they can do things to). At the same time, there is an underlying cultural history concerning machines, mass production, and automation that often surfaces in accounts of Detroit techno. In a recent conversation, DJ Mike Banks ("Mad Mike" of Underground Resistance) described his grandfather's work on the assembly line in these terms:

> The workers frequently gave names to their machines, so my grandfather was working with Ginny. They were making their money, going back and forth like this: the machine would come down and stamp the part out of metal, and he would take it out and put it on a pile. But one day he made a mistake, and put his hand in when he should have taken it out. And that one time, the machine refused to come down. That's what it means to be in tune with the machine, to feel its spirit.[71]

While Banks's story points out a community between man and machine, Detroit as a culture is also marked by a suspicion of technology, reflecting the split between engineer and worker, on the one hand, and the resistance to automation in the union movement, on the other. For black artists to take on computers as an act of cultural reconfiguration, in this sense, was a radical gesture — particularly in an environment, unlike that of the high modernists, that is unimpressed with technological innovation. Another typical response to techno, then, would be that of Detroit poet Dennis Teichman (who also works as a plant engineer), who sees its use of repetition as sentimentalizing alienated labor.[72] But if repetitive assembly line labor is on many accounts unpleasant, dangerous, and alienating, repetition in techno can be seen as aesthetically transforming its assault on the senses.

Detroit techno is understood to have begun with the work of African-American artists Juan Atkins, Derrick May, and Kevin Saunderson who, looking beyond the popular heritage of Motown (which by the early 1970s had also abandoned Detroit), brought European art music into proximity with disco and funk, often from the gay club scene. Where a majority of techno's canonical figures have been black (including Carl Craig, Kenny Larkin, Mike Banks, Jeff Mills, Robert Hood, Stacy Pullen, Claude Young, Alan Oldham, and K. Hand), a few of those developing its stylistic potential are not (Richie Hawtin [Plastikman], Dale Lawrence [Theorem]). As DJs, many first- and second-wave artists have found audiences and careers in Europe, while in the Detroit area parties and raves were infrequent but often highly politicized events (as with the 1995 police raid of a rave in downtown Detroit). Many of the DJs can legitimately claim to be "famous in Europe," while at the same time they make clear that remaining in Detroit is a political commitment (especially as they infrequently perform there). Such political claims interpret the cultural position of the DJ in its Detroit context as a cross between exemplary artist-constructor and auteur known for his or her idiosyncratic style; at the same time, there is much in the techno aesthetic, beginning with formal values of the music itself, that argues against any form of expressive aesthetics. A central characteristic of Detroit techno is the effacement of a central position for the "expressive subject" in that the vocal part is elided, or if present sampled and distorted, often giving techno an anonymous quality. This avoidance of the central expressive subject, imagined as speaking directly to an audience, demonstrates an implicit politics marked by a refusal of mass-market co-optation, which may have very real consequences in terms of artistic freedom. When vocal parts are used, as frequently in the work of K. Hand and Kevin Saunderson, they are often sampled and distorted to the point that they entirely efface any personality on the part of the speaking subject.[73]

Mike Banks's attitude toward interviews and publicity reflects techno's aesthetics of self-erasure and refusal of co-optation; when he did consent to talk to *Urb* magazine, he was photographed with a bandanna covering his face, connoting an outlaw status.[74] At the same time, Banks believes that the vocal part's absence in techno is directly connected to its politics: techno's anonymity transcends the limits of language and communicates on more intuitive levels; it maintains viability in international contexts because it is not restricted to any language; and it is not racially marked. The near impossibility of seeing techno in terms of racial identity is, for Banks, a good thing: its transcendence of language gives it the power to "break through Eight Mile," the boundary line that divides majority-black Detroit from the majority-white suburbs.[75] At the same time, Banks sees techno as responsive to voices that themselves have been suppressed and that are coming into perceptibility in the music. This emergence from voicelessness, which *is* racially marked for Banks (not only as African-American but as Native American as well),[76] into a space defined in the absence of a speaking subject gives techno much of its evocative power; it is as if something "is going to be said" of redemptive significance that the music preserves in its moment of emergence. It is the responsiveness of the DJ that draws out the traces of suppressed voices and interprets them in real time and space. In a surprising parallel to Lissitzky's goal of positioning the *Prouns* between two-dimensional painting and three-dimensional architecture, Banks sees the form of techno as merging inputs from the two turntables into a visionary three-dimensional form of the mix, but he likens this experience of summoning of presence to the role of the preacher in African-American churches, who synthesizes the choir and organ into one voice of embodied spirit.[77]

Techno's aesthetics of self-erasure and anonymity bears on other aspects of its social formation. It can be seen in the multiple and changing names that DJ auteurs use for various projects; in the aesthetics of the mix, both recorded and performed, which continually resamples and reinterprets one's own work and that of others; in the listing and cataloguing of materials; and in a general avoidance of greatest hits and the star system. Techno in Detroit surfaces variously and at random; its advertising is done by word of mouth and on small cards left at cafés and record stores, often giving a phone number to call at a certain time for the location of a party. Its social formation in Europe is vastly different, involving mass raves and parties, local ordinances prohibiting "repetitive dance music," and mainstream exposure in mass media, both state-run and private.[78] The mass international reception is preserved in a photo from Derrick May's web page, showing May accepting the cheers of a large crowd (fig. 41), an image that may be contrasted with his bespectacled, nerdy image in an American youth culture fanzine.[79] The social formation of techno is complemented by an active Internet subculture that supports a network of independent labels and distributors who market their products to an international audience through it. Some of the web sites have political casts ("Somewhere in Detroit");

41. Photograph of Derrick May, from "Transmat Home Page," 1997.

others address themselves to stylistic questions such as product design ("Sigma 6"; "Plus 8"); while others supply discographies and fan commentary.[80] The formal dimensions of techno in this way may be seen as directly connected to its social formations in a largely producer-centered aesthetic: techno culture is heavily oriented toward producers rather than consumers; its major products are not CDs for consumer consumption but vinyl disks primarily purchased by DJs, for whom the live performance is the only product.[81] As Scott Sterling has pointed out, DJs are important not only because of their compositional or technical mastery but because they are the ones who show up with the records.[82]

The formal parallels between constructivism and techno are many, even as their historical moments and cultural formations diverge. Many of the transformative effects sought for in techno bear on unacknowledged avant-garde precursors (even as they avoid the blind spot of romantic rebellion in Hebdidge's account).[83] A utopian fantasy of a revolutionary *Gesamtkunstwerk*, for instance, appears in Lissitzky's description of "the electro-mechanical show *Victory over the Sun*" that clearly predicts the form of the rave:

> All show objects are brought into motion by means of electro-mechanical forces and devices, with central control in the hands of a single individual who acts as the director of the whole show. His place is in the center of the scaffolding at the high-energy control panels. . . . At the flick of the switch the sound system is turned on and the whole place may suddenly

42. *Iakov Chernikhov, illustrations from* Construction of Architectural and Machine Forms *(Leningrad, 1932).*

> reverberate with the din of a railroad station, or the roar of Niagara Falls, or the pounding of a steel-rolling mill. . . . Electrical sentences flash and dim. Light rays, diffused by prisms and reflectors, follow the movements of the figurines in the play. By such means the most elementary processes are intensified to maximum effect by the director.[84]

The figure of the techno DJ (recently introduced into rock spectaculars), who maintains an almost offstage, unromantic profile while controlling the lights and sounds of the spectacle, is anticipated here. The postconstructivist Soviet architect Iakov Chernikhov similarly predicts spatial aspects of techno's time-based sculpture of rhythm and sound, not only evidencing his architectural interest in rhythm but offering a vocabulary for its exemplary use of repetition. Chernikhov sees rhythm as a constructive device that motivates the relation of architectural masses in a total form (fig. 42): "We can identify the following types of constructive rhythm": (1) "percussive rhythm"; (2) "rhythm of horizontal and vertical transitions"; (3)

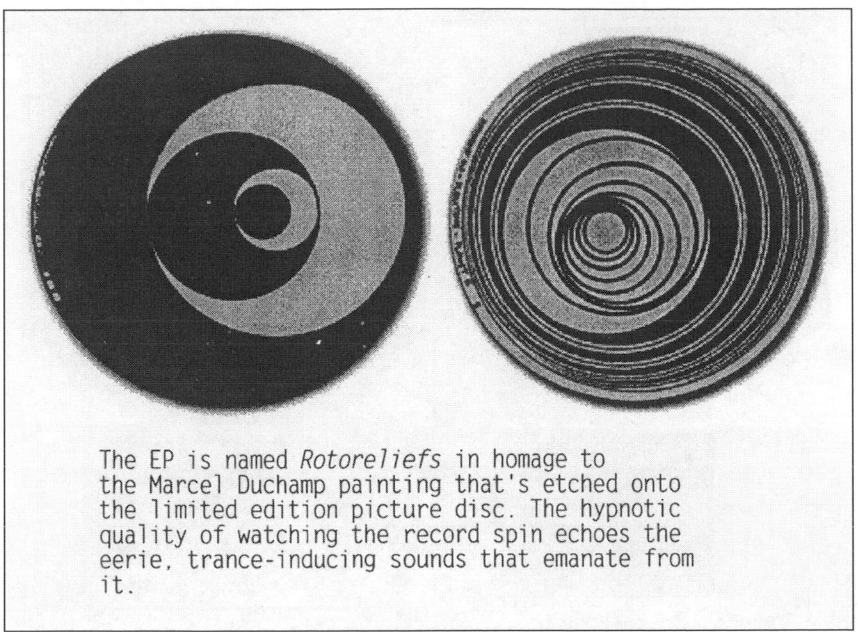

The EP is named *Rotoreliefs* in homage to
the Marcel Duchamp painting that's etched onto
the limited edition picture disc. The hypnotic
quality of watching the record spin echoes the
eerie, trance-inducing sounds that emanate from
it.

43. "Flexitone" page, "Planet E" web site, 1997.

"rhythm of stable linkages"; (4) "rhythm of heaviness"; (5) "rhythm of stratification"; (6) "rhythm of expansive curvature"; (7) "rhythm of load-bearing masses."[85] With the possible exception of the last category (and even it can be stretched to account for various "heavy" effects of sonic overload), Chernikhov provides accurate spatial analogies for the effects of techno's rhythmic sequences. And while most techno artists do not consciously look to prior avant-gardes, some Internet sites incorporate constructivist aesthetics, as in Theorem's use of New Age math motifs as web site graphics or Flexitone's use of Duchamp's rotoreliefs as disk labels, whose automatic rhythms as they are rotated in three dimensions would clearly be a species of techno (fig. 43).[86]

At the center of techno's formal devices is the use of repetitive rhythmic, melodic, and voice samples generated by synthesizers, rhythm machines, and recorded materials, processed in turn through sequencers and personal computers. As a device, techno's use of repetition conveys a wide range of values: its origins in the one-chord rhythm backup of James Brown's "Sex Machine" inflect the man/machine interface as sexual and even heterosexist, while the basic pulse of disco, referring in part to the gay club scene, continually oscillates between its contextual cultural meanings and turning into an abstract, unit-valued, recurrent metronome. Repetition in techno is always proximate to cultural reference; interpretive decisions are therefore crucial, and a specific sonic environment may change entirely the possible value of a given element. Techno's use of automatic processes breaks down barriers between intention and effect, leading to overdetermined pressures on meaning and affect; spatial relations between repetitive sequences construct affective spaces that alternately foreground and reverse the importance of motifs. As in Lissitzky's use of reversible spatial illusions, techno effects flicker from one register of emotional investment to another: repetition, recurring variables, and sonic overlays make techno not so much a "science of imaginary solutions" as a "science of imaginary affects." An important range of techno effects is located in body-penetrating, engulfing deep tones, reprocessed industrial shock waves, and hyperemotional washes of simulacral orchestral color; another range comprises a virtual history of world rhythms of all sorts, including ragtime, calypsos, Native American chants, chinoiserie, discos, the sounds of crosswalk signals for the blind and of garbage trucks backing up. Techno's basic device, repetition, continually alters its range of potential meaning by virtue of its suspension of intention;[87] techno must be heard in a different way than music in which authorial consciousness or performance decisions are discerned. The complexity of formal devices in techno evokes an interpretive processing similar to that necessary to decode machine-generated repetitive patterns for the trace of human intention (and meaning) in the Turing test.[88] As with the Turing test, itself a repetitive device that seeks the trace of the maker in depersonalized codes, techno clearly asks us, What or whom are we listening to?

But to what extent can the samples and sequences of techno be seen as exemplary? The answer to this question depends, indeed, on specific examples — which in techno culture are hard to come by. Repeated requests for a quick list of canonical techno works are met often with frustration, as if it were not the individual examples but the subculture's history that is significant. But with increasing international recognition of the work, a canon of first-, second-, and third-wave artists is stabilizing, even if many of these are buried in subcultural lore, only available on obscure compilations or on out-of-print vinyl recordings produced for the DJ rather than the consumer market. The rerelease of tracks from vinyl on CD compilations, and the production by major figures of their own CDs — intended for personal as much as DJ use — reveal an increasing effort to stabilize a

44. CD cover of Kenny Larkin, Azimuth, *Wax Trax/TVT 7219–2, 1994.*

45. CD cover of e-dancer (Kevin Saunderson), heavenly, *Planet E 65421, 1998.*

canon, even if any focus on individuals is often "made strange" in a constructivist sense (figs. 44 and 45). The elevation of Carl Craig to auteur status with the release of *More Songs about Revolutionary Art and Food*, his Innerzone Orchestra techno-jazz project (*Programmed*) and remix compilation (*Designer Music*), and his organization of the DEMF; the classicizing rerelease of Derrick May's historic early tracks under the title *Innovator* on his Transmat label; Kevin Saunderson's two-CD compilation *Faces and Phases* on Planet E, and his more recent recordings as "e-dancer"; Jeff Mills's classical compilations such as *Waveform Transmission*, *Lifelike*, and *The Other Day*, and also his movie-music spin-offs (*Metropolis*); the sticker on Kenny Larkin's *Azimuth* reading, "Buy this first for Detroit techno," and the design appeal of *Metaphor* and *Dark Carnival;* Theorem's incorporation of Detroit motifs such as automobile samples (*Ion*); the auteur-defining releases of third-generation artists such as Sean Deeson (*Allegory & Metaphor*) and Robert Hood (*Internal Empire*); the use of female vocal samples that rejects the diva exoticism of mass-market techno in the work of K. Hand and her recent compilation on the Acacia label; the penetration of youth and ambient markets by white artists such as Plastikman; the occasional but until now unsuccessful commercial forays by major labels into Detroit subculture (Juan Atkins's *Cybotron: Clear* [Fantasy]; Craig's *Landcruiser* [Warner]), as well as DJ compilations by May, Craig, Saunderson, Juan Atkins, Stacy Pullen, and Jeff Mills (Sony/Japan; the Berlin labels K-7 and Tresor; the Belgian labels Elypsia and R&S); and the collectively canonizing projects of independent labels in Detroit (Transmat, Plus 8, Submerge, Seventh City, and Planet E) — all are beginning to construct a stable repertoire of examples, even as the collective production values of the music still argue against them. Beyond the question of establishing a canon of works, however, remains the question of techno's exemplary forms: the use of repetitive, automatic, depersonalized rhythm effects; massive sonic buildups and discharges; clashing, asynchronous polyrhythms and feedback loops; and samples reprocessed to the point of abstraction and anonymity. The music is, indeed, difficult to exemplify: there are still no greatest hits. It is precisely as an evaluative as much as cognitive question that techno draws one into the delirious problem of its music. Determining its value demands a kind of judgment that *may* have ethical implications in demanding a different form of listening. Rather than providing a positive set of cultural examples, techno draws attention to the question of absence in its repetitive patterns, its intentional ellipses; it is this open question, at the level of form, that supports the formation of the techno community in its aesthetics of radical incompletion.

The constructivist free radical bases its social address on foregrounded incompletion. Its form perpetuates a desire for completion, but does not give way to an illusion of resolution. The two dimensions of Lissitzky's *Prouns* demand a third — architecture (as his Third Period design work demands a fourth — internationalism). What kind of ethical implications does techno construct in its suspension of exemplary status? One place to begin is the Internet home pages of Craig's Planet E Records or Underground Resistance's Submerge, which present techno as a future-oriented aesthetic whose goal is to make its primary constitutive negation, Detroit, once more inhabitable (a politics visually evident in May's Detroit photographs, from his CD booklets and former web site [fig. 46]). In the absence of a cultural infrastructure (with the exception of occasional late-night radio shows and infrequent club dates), Detroit techno subculture is proud of the fact that it has produced — out of virtually nothing, empty space, cultural void, boredom, anomie, dystopia, race and class divisions, lack of a mass transit system, a gutted metropolitan culture, in short — an internationally recognized style. And this development took on many of the forms of a constructivist avant-garde: a depersonalized style that opens the way for a collective aesthetic; a high level of attention to formal concerns and a concomitant deprivileging of expressive subjectivity; and a constitutive

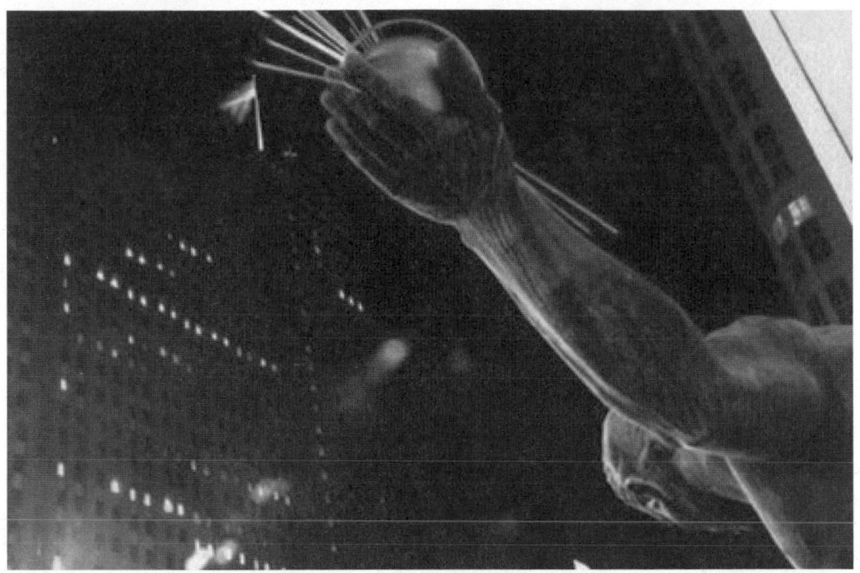

46. Derrick May, untitled photograph. From "Transmat Home Page," 1997.

negativity that links the cultural void of Detroit to a technologically based "science of imaginary solutions" that would make Père Ubu weep with joy. While techno may not invoke the same world-historical scale as Lissitzky's *Prouns*, it has made living in Detroit seem considerably more fantastic.

MOMENTS

The constructivist moment is an elusive transition in the unfolding work of culture in which social negativity — the experience of rupture, an act of refusal — invokes a fantasmatic future — a horizon of possibility, an imagination of participation. Constructivism condenses this shift of horizon from negativity to progress in aesthetic form; otherwise put, constructivism stabilizes crisis as it puts art into production toward imaginary ends. Invoking technological progress while partaking of Alfred Jarry's science of imaginary solutions, it asks us to think of the world in impossible ways, even as it returns the imagination of the great and strange to the materiality of its exemplary forms. The constructivist moment puts the teleological account of the avant-garde — leading inexorably from historical rupture to aesthetic negation to materialization in a canon of works to institutional stabilization and, thus, to a revision of historical narratives — under erasure. In the conventional view, either the avant-garde's impossibility is simply that, and of no further consequence except to a coterie of aficionados and collectors, or its emergence is an easily stabilized moment of historical rupture that finds its proper place in museum culture and the proliferation of value-neutral styles. Neither, however, is its necessary endpoint.

What is wrong with the conventional picture of the avant-garde is the monovalent status of its negativity: the association, drawn from the historical avant-garde's narratives of emergence, of radical form with a politics of refusal of social participation — as in Zürich Dada and the Cabaret Voltaire, ironically located only a few hundred feet from Lenin's domicile in 1916, as has often been pointed out. The great divide between avant-garde and Cultural Studies may have begun right there, abetted by later forms of vicarious identification (and conflict) that adhere to either regressive or militant forms of identity, in a primal scene acted out as a drama between feminine aesthetics and masculine agency. Indeed, T. J. Clark's historically nuanced reading of the constructivist moment of Lissitzky's development of the *Prouns* and agitprop art in Vitebsk in 1921, caught between the political instability of heroic communism and the prior example of Malevich's radical suprematism, is an elaborate working through of a skeptical projection of precisely this ambivalence, taken to ground zero in its embeddedness in the emerging politics of the state. In a radical dissociation of form from history, and an unraveling of the problematic, conventional identification that Raymond Williams called "left formalism" (the notion that radical form is identical to political agency), Clark queries the myriad conditions of the avant-garde's formal and historical inevitability at a protean, formative moment. Under such scrutiny, Lissitzky's work dissociates into a nuanced address to historical context in his agitprop work against a never quite realized potential for absolute painting, along the lines of Malevich. Even if reflecting myriad historical pressures, a pull toward formalism is revealed in judgments such as "'Flatness' in the *Prouns* is always virtual. It is one more paradox or possibility among others"; or "Lissitzky's normal inability (or unwillingness) to signify flatness as force, or resistance, seems to me the key to his limitations as an artist"; or that his agitprop work "is about as good as he gets, just because the circumstances seem to have enabled him to make flatness a metaphor, for once" (235). History becomes an irony of form, rather than the usual other way around, as its interpretant.

It is almost as if the demands of modernist form (and their incompletion in Lissitzky) are what drives the art historian forward into his contextual inquiry. The modernist romance, for Clark, is that the moment of cultural innovation can be reconstructed in the centripetal/centrifugal swirl of concerns at a punctual event: everything (art history, formal series, utopian claims, critical accounts) follows from that. What results from this dissociation, on the one hand, preserves the critic's role precisely as constructivist: in the necessity of dismantling a congealed historical account to recover both the agency of originary construction and the complications of a forgotten history. At the same time, we begin to see different values for the kinds of negativity that are sutured together in the concept of left formalism: the direness, extremity, and even pure insanity of the political moment, which were expressed in utopian formulations such as Bukharin's *ABC of Communism* and which were everywhere available at the time; versus the tentative, multivalent, embedded formal assertions that end up, in Lissitzky's *Prouns* and his agitprop art, as the forward-looking exemplary works they have come to be. It is no accident, then, that Clark does not follow the conflicts embedded here through their articulation in Lissitzky's 1920s design and typography, or in his 1930s propaganda (except to note the radical form of the 1928 Pressa installation, seen as an almost disjunct moment of formal rethinking). The teleology that Lissitzky himself constructed, however ironically, to bridge the gap between the impossibility of the *Prouns* and the positivity of the state, is precisely the narrative that must be undone, as it is the basis of the conventional romance with the period — and after 1989, one is certainly aware of the embarrassing consequences of that.

The dissociation of different values for negativity, however, is felicitous for the constructivist moment. The political origins of Soviet constructivism, it is true, must be grounded not only in the retrospectively punctual moment of revolution but in the long episode of heroic communism as an almost unparalleled social collapse of a modern state. The aesthetic moment of Malevich's suprematism — the radically utopian formal model of an absolute painting Lissitzky augmented by means of a more engaged form of social command, what makes the *Prouns* exemplary of a possible future rather than *Dingen an sich* — bears with it forms of negativity (the intersection of nihilism with form) that cannot be reduced to social deprivation. Lissitzky's historical irony — and arguably the irony that both permitted the construction of the 1930s state based in "scientific materialism" and led to its interpretative, ethical monstrosity — may be seen as precisely the intersection of an enabling nihilism with the material concerns of form and history. The result, finally, would be anything but the recuperation of teleological history, and such did not occur — except as a spectacular failure, an integration into history very few of the cultural figures of the 1920s survived. At the same time, the *Prouns* continue to telegraph their exemplary impossibility outside of the logic of their recovery: modernist negativity and progressive teleology intersect, cancel each other out, and come undone at the same time. Such a moment may also be seen in the historical irony of Zukofsky's poem: an eventual completion in revolution or meaning is precisely implied by its exemplary incompletion, but if this does not occur, the "nothing" Zukofsky describes as equally the implication of the scene turns out to be the historically specific position of the observer, the poet, as the form of identity (DuPlessis's New Jew) who both instantiates history and will outlive it. Negativity works both ways, within teleology and exempted from the series, and it is here that Zukofsky becomes the exemplary modernist, in reconciling progress and negativity.

If there is substance in a postmodern shift away from this ambivalent synthesis, it may be seen in the interpretive dilemma posed by Jean Day's radical negativity. Certainly her poem is written following a tradition of constructivist poetics, from Zukofsky to the Language School, as it seeks to discover an ethics of formal dissociation and combination in which the incompletion of the lyric poem "just is" a politics of everyday life. It is important that the acuteness of the poem's negativity — the radical demand it makes on the reader for integration, which at the same time it refuses to allow — is made to seem identical to the dissociative finesse that renders its materials available for construction. Seeing both materials and form as equally fragmentary and incomplete allows the poet to locate her poetics of negativity precisely where such a construction is needed in the first place: everyday life. Day's poem has the effect of appearing and disappearing at once; like the Necker cube, an optical illusion in which a three-dimensional solid flickers between positive and negative valences based on a two-dimensional form, it both enters into and withdraws from the orders of cognitively marked (constructed) experience. This entering and disappearing, from fragmentation into coherence and back again, is reproduced in the provisional constructions brought to it by readings, such as my own, where the effect is repeated. Such an effect, I think, perfectly exemplifies the transition between a modernist constructivism and a postmodern one, with the complete unlinking of negativity from its subordination in a developmental series. The avant-garde, in this sense, could never be over, could never have failed, because it refuses entry into the series that ends in failure.

If we transfer this logic to the cultural politics of Detroit techno, the result is felicitous as well: as if to refute the anguish of Cultural Studies accounts that have described an inevitable co-optation of oppositional aesthetics ever since Bob Dylan went electric in 1965 (a constructivist moment if there ever was one), techno surfaces variously and at random; it simply is not reducible to a teleological series in which its guerrilla adaptation of consumer electronics fades into the consumerism from whence it arose, reversing any moment of aesthetic or political utopia it may have claimed. Rather, there is a kind of studied refusal of a necessary or hierarchical order in Detroit techno that has important cultural resonances for a notion of community that is not going to be, in the foreseeable future, completely assimilated even as it refuses to be seen as locked out from the dominant culture (with its technology) that surrounds it. Otherwise put, African-American double consciousness offers different valences for negativity than post-Hegelian avant-gardism. Such a distinction may be teased out of recent remarks by Carl Craig, one of techno's originators, in an article in the Detroit *Metro Times* on further developments in the electronic music scene after the mass public success/debacle of the 2000 and 2001 Detroit Electronic Music Festivals, with their huge audiences and fractured organization: "Although the festival continued, it lost some of the spark that Craig's innovative ideas had brought to it. Craig explained [at a lecture at the Cranbrook Museum] that you do what you can to get by. Like actors who alternate between big-budget productions and indie films, Craig has taken assignments that he wasn't incredibly excited about so that he could afford to put out the stuff that mattered deeply to him."[89] If mastering remixes for more mainstream artists is one way radical techno musicians stay in circulation, the obvious Cultural Studies question must be asked: whether this contact with mainstream forms is the inevitable death knell of radical innovation, the ultimate penetration of capital into all forms of the life-world, even better enabled by technology. But it is the persistence of Detroit techno beyond its purported collapse that is equally the point: Detroit techno refuses teleology precisely at the moment it embraces technological innovation as the source of its unassimilable effects. The negativity of its emergence outside of mainstream culture, then, is precisely located in the nonverbal, antiexpressive, border-transgressive shocks and intensities it mobilizes in its exemplary forms. In techno, there is a reflexive relation between the negativity of Detroit's social history, as a continuous experience of material privation and metropolitan devolution, and the boundary-breaking shock waves of technological innovation that can break through Eight Mile Road, as generators of new meaning. Such an intersecting logic we may term a *social* reflexivity, in which necessity and construction alternate in recursive form. Refusing the border metaphors of Cultural Studies, Detroit techno sees itself as activated, in its nonteleological history, on both sides at once.

NONNARRATIVE AND THE CONSTRUCTION OF HISTORY

AN ERA OF STAGNATION, THE FALL OF SAIGON

Poetry is always a dying language but never a dead language.
— Robert Smithson

You are afraid of your finitude; we are afraid of our infinitude.
— Arkadii Dragomoshchenko

This essay has a history, one that is still in the process of being made. The first written in this volume, it was originally presented at a symposium, "The Narrative Construction of History," at Southern Exposure Gallery in San Francisco in March 1990. It is safe to say that the anxieties about the generally unquestioned foundational status of narrative for literary and Cultural Studies it engaged were substantial, and that these responses were internalized, sequentially if not narratively, in the construction of the essay itself. At the time the essay was first presented, the epochal horizon shift of the end of the Cold War had just occurred; I was in the process of collaborating on *Leningrad*, a multiauthored and in fact nonnarrative historical account of an avant-garde poetics symposium in the Soviet Union as it was coming apart in August 1989, and I was also at work on *Under Erasure*, a poem that takes up the undoing of horizonal structures through that historical moment in a more abstract mode of reckoning. Processes of historical devolution and loss were very much on everyone's mind, and there was an immediate question of how to think through the narrative experience one was then having. Certainly, a triumphalist account of the end of the Cold War, along the lines suggested by Francis Fukuyama, was the last thing a writer concerned with nonnarrative aesthetics would be interested in. This essay is an attempt to describe how and why one might seek an alternative to teleological narratives, fully equipped with motivation and closure, through a knowledge gained from the practice of nonnarrative poetics. In doing so, I want to juxtapose three historical moments: the present writing of an historical account in which the narrative structure one is in has not been fully declared (from its original formulation in 1990 to the present revision of the essay in 2002); the era of stagnation experienced by post-Soviet writers and artists in the mid-1970s; and the Fall of Saigon that ended the Vietnam War in May 1975. Triangulating these moments of nonnarrative history, and thus triangulating the present construction of history with nonnarrative forms of art, is the task of this essay.

NONNARRATIVE POETICS

What is nonnarrative, as a way of making art; and what is the relation of nonnarrative forms of art to historical narratives? To begin with, this is a reciprocal relation, but not one of identity: the way a work of art represents an historical event, in its own form of temporal organization, turns out to be an event of another order. Mimesis is not restricted to a reproduction of the event. To call an epic "a poem containing history," as Ezra Pound did, is to claim that the epic makes history in another way, intervening in history as much as representing it. While narrative is conventionally held to be both the implicit goal and explicit norm of art's temporal organization, most innovative literature and art, from the avant-garde to postmodernism, is nonnarrative in some way; narrative, where it exists in much of this work, is suspended and displaced.[1] As a result, time in modernist and postmodern art and writing is often organized in ways that are not dependent on narrative as formal guarantee of meaning or as necessary horizon of understanding. At the same time, there are specific historical frames for the development of nonnarrative forms of art. Individual practitioners of nonnarrative, of course, have assured places in literary history, from Sterne and Blake to Walt Whitman, Lautréamont, and Gertrude Stein. In the 1920s and 1930s there took place, for however brief a time and with whatever instability, a culturally productive moment of nonnarrative writing among American expatriate writers undertaken as a "revolution of the word."[2] This avant-garde explosion of nonnarrative had notable descendants in the postwar period, particularly in the abstraction of the New York School (both poets and painters) and in the aleatorical methods of John Cage and Jackson Mac Low. About 1975, new conditions for the social reproduction of nonnarrative forms emerged — during a period of national crisis about the time of the Fall of Saigon — in the Language School and elsewhere. This phenomenon has been related to the crisis of historical narrative in postmodernism, but it was also based on the inherent formal possibilities of various genres. A rejection of narrative for other forms of temporal organization took place, and was culturally productive, at a given historical moment.[3]

Narrative, for revisionist historians, is simultaneously a form of temporal organization and a mode of historical self-consciousness; in fully realized historical narrative, the form and content of history coincide.[4] If nonnarrative is to compete with narrative as a form of organization and self-consciousness, it must reconcile form and content as well. The difficulty of nonnarrative emerges precisely here: it will be necessary to say what nonnarrative is in positive terms, not simply as a negation of narrative but as a form of organization and interpretation in its own right, as a way of making art within history. Where there is a considerable body of narrative theory, and several schools of thought with competing accounts of the nature of narrative, no sustained inquiry has been undertaken into nonnarrative: the meaning of the word, it seems, must be determined by its use. In a defining sentence written by a postrevisionist historian wanting to pose nonnarrative against what he sees as the positive and stultifying use of narrative among historians, it is a moment of negative totality that cannot be told: "A culture is reactive when it continues to narrativize itself despite, at any moment, being six minutes away (by missile) from its own nonnarrative obliteration."[5] If narrative for Sande Cohen is a species of ideological positivity, nonnarrative must be the historical real that undermines it. Such a cataclysmic notion of nonnarrative clearly has ideological motives of its own, as is evident in Cohen's fantasy of self-destruction in retribution for his attack on positivism, itself seen as encoding a fearful reactivity to historical events. The politics of the Cold War surface right here, in the mutually assured destruction of positivist historicism and totalizing negativity. Cohen's apocalyptic formulation has its sources, as well, in the linguistic and Hegelian origins of poststructuralist theory: nonnarrative as an abstract negativity derives in part from linguistic models in which a paradigmatic break in syntagmatic progression introduces an atemporal moment into a temporal sequence, and in part from Hegel's positing of an abstract negativity in self-consciousness. The split between synchronic structure and diachronic development, and the sense that nonnarrative can only be imagined as an impossible moment of negative totality, are thereby collapsed in an abyss of representation.[6]

In works of art, nonnarrative is not simply an undoing, interruption, or denial of narrative but a positive form of temporal organization. As narrative comprises a number of forms of discourse, from oral epic to *Swann's Way*, that can be grouped together as a "discursive mode" in Gérard Genette's sense, nonnarrative also comprises a discursive mode if not a single form of discourse. While set apart from narrative by the prefix *non-*, nonnarrative includes a number of temporal forms that are not simply opposed to or negating of narrative. Of course, everything depends on the status of the crucial prefix *non-*, which has a range of values beyond logical or determinate negation. Nonnarratives are forms of discursive presentation where both linear and contextual syntax exist but where univocal motivation, retrospective closure, and transcendental perspective are suspended, deferred, or do not exist.[7] Temporal sequences in nonnarrative are organized in other ways: they may be punctual, accretive (in modular units), associational (in nodal clusters), or circular. A given form of nonnarrative may contain any or all of these: a lyric poem, for instance, may be at once punctual, accretive, associative, and circular, and these aspects may reinforce each other. Nonnarratives range as well from simple to complex, from simple forms of temporal accretion such as a list to complex modes of expression that exceed the discursive confines of narrative, such as free association. Lists such as a ticker tape or grocery bill are, in minimally formal terms, nonnarrative, like the voice announcing times of departure and arrival at a train station, even as stock prices rise and fall and trains traverse a beginning, middle, and end. More complex forms of nonnarrative are often mixed and thus difficult to discern, as they involve both narrative and nonnarrative elements, but their distinguishing feature is an affective/cognitive unity of temporal sequence in their presentation by means of punctual, accretive, associational, or circular forms, whose formal organization and affective force would be lost if subsumed within an overarching narrative.

As a ready example, the temporal dilation and spatial immediacy of Abstract Expressionism may easily be seen as an affectively organized form of nonnarration realized in its "all-over" mode of painting. Jackson Pollock famously saw himself "in" his painting as an open horizon, which, if everything "comes out well," would convey the immediacy of its becoming a work of art.[8] In the terms above, his work is both associational and circular, underscoring its psychoanalytic and mythopoeic concerns. A more punctual and concretized work such as minimalist sculptor Richard Serra's *Tilted Arc* is likewise nonnarrative, even if it has been inserted into narrative debates about the politics of authority and community.[9] A crucial point to make here, in support of the positivity of nonnarration, is that narrative readings may be imposed on nonnarrative forms, and often are; there are often competing or antagonistic relations between the two modes, as we see in the avant-garde's provocations and their insertion into the narratives of art history; but nonnarrative is not thereby reduced to its narrative interpretation. In their affective immediacy and associational complexity, nonnarratives engage, rescript, and displace narratives, but they are not reducible to merely deformed or negative species of narrative and thus are not fully narratable as such. The fifty random numbers I listed at the beginning of my poem "The Word" are nonnarrative, even as they serve as a disorientation device in a poem that has many features of oral narrative; many experimental writers, in the words of Carla Harryman, "prefer to distribute narrative rather than to deny it."[10] Nonnarratives may subtend, deform, or even foreground elements of narrative, as they leave open questions of motivation, transcendence, and closure, organizing these elements in new ways. (This relation between nonnarrative form and narrative content is particularly evident in the emergence of hypertext as a form of nonnarration, in a way that was predicted by the nonlinear forms of the avant-garde prior to their remediation in new technologies.)[11]

While it is useful to imagine minimal paradigms for nonnarrative such as a work of sculpture or a list, and while there has been a wide range of aesthetic use of just such forms, much nonnarrative art poses questions of motivation, transcendence, and closure in more complex ways. A fully articulated derivation of nonnarrative as a discursive mode needs to be undertaken, not on a deductive schema, but based on the "family resemblances" between the minimally formal instances of nonnarrative, like the list, and the great variety of more expressive forms, which are not easily categorized. This resemblance may be founded in the way both minimal and complex forms are organized in terms of a single temporal moment (as punctual) or as an open sequence of events (as accretive, associational, or circular). All of these are evident in the following poem by Lyn Hejinian:

EXIT

Patience is laid out on my paper
is floodlit. Everything's simile.
The cadence is detected, the cipher is broken, "resolved
the sky bears the enjambments, heavy clouds
the measure of one with a number block
changes shade. The flow of thoughts — impossible!
with which we are so familiar. The river
its visuals are gainful and equably square
in an automatic writing. Self-consciousness
to reclaim imagination . . . to rise early
that is, logic exaggerates the visible

to oppose laziness." Unto itself, built of bricks
is a cumbersome moment on whom motion
is bent over, having sunk a fork into the ground.[12]

This poem is nonnarrative. The way its discursive form is organized in a temporal series is basic to its intended effects. These effects are created by the positive and negative (and neutral) valences of the poem's progression from one increment to the next, as the poem argues a particular form of self-consciousness, an intensified and disjunct present that will "reclaim imagination" in recognizing the discontinuities of thought. A material demonstration of Russian Formalist devices of defamiliarization and the semantic shift is distributed in the poem between its thematization of self-consciousness and its techniques of discontinuity; whether the poem is arguing for the priority of one or the other is left open. In other words, it would be impossible to decide whether the poem's thematization of self-consciousness leads to a moment of linguistic discontinuity, or whether its discontinuity demands a specific kind of self-consciousness. While a dissociation of thematization and technique is clearly central to the poem's intended effect, it is also evident that these effects depend, in a number of ways, on a reconfiguration of narrative. There are, for example, evocative but disjunct narrative framing devices at the beginning and end of the poem: "Patience is laid out on my paper" takes the place of an orienting moment of oral narrative, while "having sunk a fork into the ground" marks a moment of finality much like Walter Cronkite's "And that's the way it is."[13] But these narrative frames are skewed, as are many more that are engaged in the course of the poem; it would be futile to ingeniously interpret them to show how a single organizing perspective motivates the unfolding of the verbal material, however constitutive of narrative Viktor Shklovsky thought such discontinuities to be. Each of the four modes of nonnarrative form are readily visible: as a lyric, the poem imitates a punctual moment of time; it is composed of an accretive series of associational clusters; and an effect of nonclosure produces a kind of "loop effect" of recurrence that encourages a return to the poem's staging of immediacy again and again. Through nonnarrative means, the poem alternates between an ironization of narrative and a nonironic materiality of language as its claim to self-consciousness. Lines such as "the measure of one with a number block" are not simply negative obstructions to a hidden narrative but moments in which language presents itself as a mode of signification within the unfolding nonnarration. Hejinian's poem shows how linguistic materiality must be taken into account in any poetics of self-consciousness.

There may be disagreement with the idea that thematization is possible in a nonnarrative form, and such an objection would be one explanation for the widespread folk theory of nonnarrative writing, that its meaning is completed by the reader.[14] Clearly, the poem's engagement of a range of narrative frames creates a potential field of referents for its explicitly stated theme of self-consciousness, even if the poem's gaps and discontinuities, as well as its moments of linguistic opacity, themselves significantly produce these effects. Hejinian moves between transcendental and immanent (as well as impossible) self-consciousness in the poem, all three of which possibilities can be read in the poem's title. "Exit" may indicate a narrative closure by which the conflicting frames of the poem are resolved; it may be a resistant exit sign that is the locus of a deferred question about meaning; or it may be a solution to a dilemma unstated elsewhere that motivates the poem's ephemeral form. But while a narrative reading of the poem would see its negative moments as simply devices of interference that set up a desire for transcendent meaning and closure, a nonnarrative reading keeps the entire range of meanings in play — allowing for such contingent effects being exactly what Hejinian means by a redeemed imagination. While there is no denying narrative in the poem, or the possibility of framing a narrative reading, nonnarrative organizes the poem's materials within a range of possible effects that exceed narrative — an effect of lyric atemporality, even as the poem grants that different narrative frames may be brought to the poem at different moments in time.

A reading of the poem's moment of nonclosure shows how its form tries to engage these effects.[15] "Having sunk a fork into the ground" is a condition of finality for the poem's material "bricks," which could either precede (having sunk a fork, all this came about) or follow from (this happened, and then a fork was sunk) the moment when "motion / is bent over" the "cumbersome monument." Split grammatical predication, however, makes it impossible to find a retrospective moment outside the poem from which the prospective fork being sunk into the ground always would have been determinate of its meaning. And yet either reading is precisely what this moment will have been — in the open horizon of the future anterior. Not possessing narrative closure, the poem provokes historical retrospection into a series of positions from which to draw out the implications of that fatal fork. The positive modes of nonnarrative at work in the poem are thereby addressed to a moment of incomprehension predicated on the impossibility of sequence: "The flow of thoughts — impossible!" which is confirmed in the impossibility of closure. And with this moment of nonfinality, the unfolding of time throughout the poem — in narrative tags, shifts and dislocations, orders of tense, disjunct predication, and resolutely immanent language — is mobilized to engage narrative readings, beginning at its point of production. The poem presents itself as the dilation of a punctual moment, one that simultaneously invites and precludes its insertion into narrative forms that it demands be kept open — a self-conscious advocacy of the advantages of nonnarrative history for life.

One may answer that if there is a potential for thematization here, it resides solely in the narrative elements being deployed by nonnarrative forms. In that case, it is instructive to look at a poem that is even more language-centered, less narrative, than Hejinian's. Jackson Mac Low's work reaches a certain limit of material effects — paradoxically based in a linearity of technique quite different from Hejinian's improvisational ephemerality, but one that produces an even more radical temporality. As has been noted earlier, Mac Low has written poems based on computer selections of BASIC English word lists, one of many nonintentional procedures he has used to compose poetry in a wide range of forms. In the following poem, however, nonnarrative moves beyond aleatory as it comments on itself:

WALL REV

A line is a crack
is an entrance furrow
distracting between thighs

Attracting between sighs
a parallel cataclysm
cannot tell its name

Active well of flame
tense entrance clues
obligate avoidance[16]

More reduced in its construction than Hejinian's poem, the poem also moves between thematization and technique as it creates an affect of unresolved desire in the structured displacements of language. In its opening and closing lines, "A line is a crack" and "obligate avoidance," the materiality of language evokes sexual tension and denial; between them, an alternating sequence of definitional moments and coded hints — "a crack," "an entrance furrow," "sighs," "thighs," and so on — creates a semantic field in which the play of positive and negative attractions becomes a condition of linked points of equivalence that "cannot tell its name." This equivalence depends, not just on syntactic parallelism, but on a nonnarrative form in which punctual, accretive, associational, and circular modes overlap and reinforce each other. An oscillating movement from approach to avoidance is thus dispersed among equivalent lines in a parallel structure, while the semantic distance between lines is so rigidly measured as to be virtually syllogistic. The poem exemplifies the kind of linguistic equivalence that Roman Jakobson described as characteristic of poetic language, but nonnarration goes further than Jakobson's poetic "message for its own sake" in structuring effects that both invoke and withhold provisional meaning and closure.[17] Presented as immanent effects of language, the poem's material displacements evoke attraction and repulsion in a sequence of ambivalent moments within a bounded temporality. The experience of language from line to line may demand closure, but no retrospective motivation can be inferred. Mac Low's poem links the materiality of language to the impossibility of desire seen as distributed through a series of formal displacements. It is not given to desire, it seems, to know how things are going to turn out.

How could such a poem ever be read as historical? Given no evidence of its contextual motives, one can only decide this question on the basis of its nonnarrative form. Mac Low's use of a temporal series of parallel oppositions, to begin with, works to displace thematic readings (such as the sexual reading that makes most sense of the poem) into a formal immanence of material language. But the sexual reading also shows exactly how the linguistic equivalences staged in the poem, in a highly condensed manner, produce self-consciousness (one that is not yet historical) in a form of "parallel cataclysm." Sexual partners both come and come undone in the act; the poem records the affective surplus of desire over representation, in either its provocation or devolution. The equivalences Jakobson saw as the basis of the poetic function, which are strictly observed in Mac Low's use of parallel increments, find a different value here in the relation between representation and event. Equivalence is the basis of parallelism for Jakobson; for Mac Low, it engages as well the abyss of representation — an "unlikeness" of terms founded in a totalizing negativity. This is the "wall" against which the "rev" of *revolution* or *revving* turns into a "parallel cataclysm." But what kind of historical connection can be made between Mac Low's apocalyptic moment and the nonnarration of the Cold War, as mutually assured destruction? Only an associational logic, of parallel play or linkage, can bring them together on the basis of their underlying negativity (and not simply in denial of the self-presence of partners or the positive history of Cold War adversaries). This cataclysm, in a poetics of reversal not unlike Hejinian's forked close, splits into two registers: language and event must be brought together as *event* in order that the "parallel cataclysm" of the poem resolve, but it cannot resolve within the temporal unfolding of the poem as a series of parallel lines predicated on a step-by-step dissociation into *language*, where "a line is a crack" in the firmament of understanding. Mac Low's poem stages a radical unlinking of terms through their simultaneous parallelism and impossible reference (to sexuality); language and event cannot coincide. We will encounter again this notion of event presented as a "parallel cataclysm" of language that exceeds representation in the following accounts of works of art as equivalent but dissociated moments of subjectivity in historical crisis.

THE CONSTRUCTION OF HISTORY

Is there any such thing as historical nonnarration? To a historian, a poetics of "parallel cataclysm" might seem literally "the end of history" if imagined as taking place in lived experience rather than in a poem. But the radical foregrounding, in a nonnarrative poem, of the Formalists' distinction between events (*fabula*) and narrative (*syuzhet*) — between an underlying substrate of presentation and an always incomplete form of representation — may be critically applied to the discursive construction of history itself.[18] Such a distinction dissociates the transparency of narration to event, severing its overarching transcendental organization from the progression of subordinated events toward discursive closure. Nonnarrative calls into question the assumed transparency of history to event. Critical self-consciousness, as immanent to history, in this sense aligns with nonnarrative, as it is otherwise paradoxical to speak both within a historical series as it unfolds and to refer to it from outside.

Such a paradox, in fact, may help explain the decline, over the last decade and since this essay first was presented, of the narrative critique of history that took place over the preceding two decades, in a series of revisionary positions from Arthur Danto, Louis O. Mink, and Hayden White to Sande Cohen. With the end of the Cold War appeared Francis Fukuyama's essay

"The End of History," which, in his words, "argued that a remarkable consensus concerning the legitimacy of liberal democracy as a system of government had emerged throughout the world," and that liberal democracy may constitute the "end point of mankind's ideological evolution" and the "final form of human government."[19] In acknowledging the widespread skepticism over the grandiosity of his claims, Fukuyama goes on to state that by the end of history he means not the end of events per se — events in the Balkans and the Middle East would put the lie to any such end — but of universal history, "understood as a single, coherent, evolutionary process, when taking into account the experience of all peoples in all times" — a narrative history, in short, that can no longer be questioned in its teleological claims. "There was a coherent development of human societies from simple tribal ones based on slavery and subsistence agriculture, through various theocracies, monarchies, and feudal aristocracies, up through modern liberal democracy and technologically driven capitalism" (xii). Speaking of this history as completable, as Fukuyama does in *The End of History and the Last Man*, means not questioning its overall framework — as both politically and economically, all skepticism about progressive history has been answered by the triumph of liberal democracy and its "unprecedented levels of material prosperity" throughout the world (xiii). Rather, we must now solve the less pressing but real contradiction between the guarantees of equality brought by liberal orders and the human need for recognition as a source of inequality.

Did the narrative critique of history end with the Cold War, or was it supplanted by a more practical historicism that suspended formal questions of narration and universal history for more a local concern with the cultural politics of representation? While the New Historicism and its version of cultural poetics has focused on the close interconnection of texts and contexts, this has been generally apart from any question of the formal construction, either narrative or nonnarrative, of its discursive account of events, texts, and images. What is the relation between such a micropolitics and Universal History? One link between the two is provided by the New Historicist "anecdote," generally seen as both distinctive feature and unexamined Achilles' heel of its methodology, as it interjects a radical particularity into the construction of historical discourse. In his reflection on this device from within the development of New Historicist methods, Joel Fineman notes, "the anecdote . . . as the narration of a singular event, is the literary form or genre that uniquely refers to the real."[20] Fineman's sense of the "real" is split here between a positivist notion of real events and a psychoanalytic Real as the inaccessible substrate of events that can be known only through their failed representations. One of his registers thus refers to local, containable events and the other to a grand nonnarrative that can only undermine them. Uniting both senses of the "real," the anecdote would provide a form of historical monad that Fineman terms the "*histo-reme* . . . the smallest minimal unit of the historiographic fact" (57). As history, the anecdote asserts a unified temporal frame that is distinctly lacking in the associational sequences of the nonnarrative poems discussed above. Even so, as Fineman observes, the notion that it takes such a foregrounded device to conjoin registers of narration and event "is not as trivial an observation as might at first appear" (56). That the anecdote works as an *exemplary* device in the renewal of history argues against its discursive transparency — the theory that narrative fully captures the reality of an event, with the corollary that events can be represented only in narrative terms. On the contrary, the negativity of the anecdote, its opening to the Real in a psychoanalytic sense, introduces a moment of discursive excess that undermines positive narration.

It is the exemplary negativity of the anecdote within larger, not so easily narrated history that leads to the undoing of its transparency. Fineman's focus on the constructive potential of the anecdote for historical discourse, in this sense, is anticipated by an earlier critique of Universal History as a grand narrative scheme. In his skeptical account of narrative history, Louis O. Mink proposes the following test: if a given narrative can be said to refer uniquely to an event, as does Fineman's anecdote, it should follow "that historical narratives can be *added* to others, as in the periodization of political history by reigns."[21] In order to do so, however, there would have to be an underlying substrate of narrated events that would make such an accretion possible; such a substrate could on no account be considered exemplary but would have to be held in common (as is the "real") by all its elements. There are two levels of narrative at issue — *petits récits*, which "*should* aggregate," and the *grands récits* of Universal History, in which "past actuality is an untold story" (142). But by virtue of the formal properties of narratives — minimally, that each has the beginning, middle, and end proper to narrative unity — such a subordination cannot occur; the best that can be said for the objective continuity of Universal History is that it organizes the *petits récits* contained within it in the form of a chronicle that is not fully narrative. As a result, "narrative histories should be aggregative, insofar as they are histories, but cannot be, insofar as they are narratives" (143). With this distinction in mind, the identity of narration and event in

Fineman's anecdote and in a theory of narrative transparency begins to appear as overdetermined in their quests for history. That the anecdote is a literary form, for Fineman, means that it works to renew history by defamiliarizing an already automatized narration (such as the one he offers later to support a historiographical progression from Thucydides to the Renaissance to his own critical moment): "The anecdote produces the effect of the real, the occurrence of contingency, by establishing an event as an event within and yet without the framing context of historical successivity" (*HA*, 61). Fineman's solution to Mink's dilemma of narrative history is thus that the anecdote need not worry about its aggregation with other anecdotes but instead may open a unique and individual "hole" that dilates temporal succession precisely by means of its formal opposition to teleological history. This is a distinctly nonnarrative moment.

The opening anecdotes of New Historicist exposition work to dissociate and thus renew history by creating a disjunct equivalence of transparency and opacity, likeness and unlikeness, between narration and event (an effect that could only with great difficulty be sustained throughout an entire text).[22] This moment, which often takes the form of proposing an eruptive, miraculous, or horrific event narrated in relation to a given historical date, is valued precisely for creating an "effect of the real," which it then transfers to the total argument. History by that act will be renewed in the determination of an event as formally identified with the constructedness of narrative. The contingency of this eruption (and vice versa), however, leads from Fineman's analogy between anecdote and historical period to Mink's skeptical question about the status of retrospective periodization from the transcendental position claimed for the cumulative effects of narration. "Is the Renaissance an event?" (*NF*, 145), Mink asks; otherwise put, in Fineman's terms, Is the Renaissance as an epochal period merely an anecdote of Universal History? If an anecdotal event is an exemplary moment of narration, what are the limits of its form *within* a narrative? Could an anecdote substitute for Universal History? Obviously not, as anecdotal history must be grounded by some sort of exemplary narrative moment set apart from the whole. Perhaps such a summoning of narrative would be accomplished just as well by a nonnarrative moment of expository orientation, as with the fifty random numbers I used to disorient the reader in my poem "The Word" (fig. 47). Such a nonnarrative opening works to establish the "real" in both senses (as indexical substrate and moment of defamiliarization) as it grounds the total form of narrative in an overdetermined moment, as in Fineman's anecdote. So in the anecdotal open-

THE WORD

38	63	50	6	34
40	41	68	89	53
9	15	85	76	16
30	57	14	69	97
54	8	83	72	28
90	52	18	84	66
7	25	10	93	44
86	91	20	75	1
43	59	51	80	60
31	4	56	47	35

47. From Barrett Watten, "The Word," in Conduit *(San Francisco: Gaz Press, 1988).*

ings of oral narrative, if the listener's attention is both grounded and perplexed — indexically defamiliarized — the device has done its job.[23]

This notion of an exemplary anecdote that renews history by creating an effect of the "real" as both index and negativity suggests a mechanism for the ways in which seemingly transparent narratives are organized in everyday forms of historical representation. Raymond Williams has described the discursive accretion and association of isolated, reified, and often anecdotal narratives in larger narrative structures as a basis for mass communication, understood as reproducing beliefs about events more generally.[24] We see this mechanism on the nightly news, where for reasons of both ideology and economy events are packaged into short narrative units that can be assembled at any future date into larger narratives. The upper limit of this discursive totality would be an accretive horizon of continuous dates, one to which the media in its historicizing capacity often refers. At moments of crisis, identification of narrative units with historical dates is particularly marked, as in the Iran hostage crisis, during the Persian Gulf War, or after September 11. Such an indexing of narrative to event demands an effect of transparency by which logics of accretion and association are not only unquestioned but seen as immanent to the structure of the narrated events. But it is exactly the anecdote's eruptive discrepancy that renews the overarching discursive field; in just this sense, it is as much the commercials interrupting war footage segued between sound bites that provide the formal totality of mass communication with overdetermining effects — so that discontinuity just is the formal guarantee of narration. The construction of history takes place through just such a paradox of interrupting, overdetermined, and underanalyzed narratives. That such an assembly line of narrated events can never be identical to Universal History is inscribed in the very relation of narrative to event, an insight captured by the device of the anecdote.

Such a skeptical critique of the subordination of mimesis within Universal History, in Mink's paradox of accretion and narrative, underscores the distinctions between *annal*, *chronicle*, and *history* that Hayden White sees as revealing the gaps that separate events as such from their narrative organization.[25] For White, annals are simply events with dates organized on a time line; chronicles provide a necessity of sequence such as "and then, and then" but come to no retrospective conclusion about why these events had to occur in this sequence. The chronicle "is usually marked by a failure to achieve narrative closure. . . . It starts out to tell a story but breaks off *in medias res*, in the chronicler's own present" (5). A realist might find that, in the end, an objective time line — on analogy to material causation — unifies these provisional historical forms with historical narrative per se, thus making chronicle a species of narrative. But for historians with other ontological commitments, it remains for fully narrative history to organize events in a unified frame. White asks, "What wish is enacted, what desire is gratified, by the fantasy that real events are properly represented when they can be shown to display the formal coherence of a story?" (6), and cites Hegel as motivating this elevation of historical event to narrative completion in desire, "in the same way as love and the religious emotions provoke imagination to give shape to previously formless impulse" (12). History takes place as narrative equally because consequent events are narratable and because we desire them to be narrative; the narrative form of history is an imaginary unity that translates the motives of desire onto the indexicality of the real. But is narrative the only form that desire takes, in organizing events, "to give shape to the previously formless impulse" that is the mere succession of events in time? Can other forms of temporal organization, analogous to the sequence of dates or chronicle in White's schema, make history as well?

Certainly, a wider range of formal relations between narrative and event than White proposes do construct history as nonnarrative. Mink's demonstration that narratives fail to accrete in Universal History leads to a historicist version of "open form" as an unbounded semantic field, in Umberto Eco's sense, where narrative elements compete in the determination of events.[26] Oppositely, Fineman's defense of Universal History through the nonnarrative formal moment of the anecdote restricts the range of such a semantic field by overdetermining the value of contingent effects. The negativity of the anecdote, in the sense of its performative strategy, may be compared here with nonnarrative forms that subtract an event from history while leaving the larger historical horizon open, specifying a historical date within a total form. For example, in San Francisco artist Seyed Alavi's 1991 installation *Blueprints of the Times* (fig. 48), blueprints of the front pages of major international newspapers are mounted in groups of three in stainless steel frames. The pages are all from the same date, 31 December 1989, but the only alteration of the blueprints from their originals is that the dates have been removed. This barely perceptible deletion causes the time-valued materials displayed on each page — stories of many levels of implication held in a kind of referential suspension — to be read in entirely different ways than if they were fixed in time by their dates. This removal of the date, as a device, has the opposite effect of the indexical defamiliarization of the date in the anecdote, but its negativity equally creates a hole in the accretion of historical time (the redundant sequence of dates that makes yesterday's papers old news). What results is a historical situation in which the viewer may link together new narratives from the stories and images dissociated from the prior formal coherence of meanings — in a reading that will be bounded at an upper limit precisely as the determi-

48. Seyed Alavi, Blueprints of the Times, *detail of installation at Terrain Gallery, San Francisco, 1990. Blueprints, metal, and glass.*

nation of the historical date that was removed. The entire form of Alavi's installation is thus a nonnarrative that by means of a specific form of displacement and reintegration constructs, in both senses of the word, history. Desire begins with the removal of the date and ends in a bounded field.[27]

Alavi's *Blueprints* comprise a kind of annal that, in its total form, presents world events to self-consciousness in a form of historical nonnarration. For Fredric Jameson, however, it is clear that nonnarrative can be thought of only as a deformation, incompletion, or deferral of narrative; his is a Universal History, but not nearly so optimistic a one as Fukuyama's. Narrative is "an all-informing process" that Jameson takes to be "the central function or *instance* of the human mind," while it is inescapably historical in its revealing "a single great collective story . . . the collective struggle to wrest a realm of Freedom from the realm of necessity."[28] One test of such a story is in its encounter with the nonnarratives of postmodernism; so in his historicizing narrative of Bob Perelman's nonnarrative poem "China," Jameson finds the poem's discontinuity to be an example of the postmodern dilemma in which "the subject has lost its capacity actively to extend its pro-tensions and re-tensions across the temporal manifold and to organize its past and future into coherent experience."[29] At the same time, the poem's explicit reference in its title to China is an appeal to Universal History, as "it does seem to capture something of the excitement of the immense, unfinished social experiment of the New China" (*PM*; 29). The latter reading is centrally thematic for Jameson, if not for Perelman, in the former's identification of the postmodern condition as coinciding with the end of the era of "wars of national liberation" (xx–xxi). Jameson assumes that the negativity of Perelman's poem (as species of the genus *postmodernism*) reinforces the narrative he imposes on it from the position of Universal History (which may, in fact, be called up as much as denied by the poem itself). What follows, from the evidence of Perelman's poem, is that "the breakdown of narrativity in a culture, group, or social class is a symptom of its having entered into a state of crisis."[30] But a paradox emerges when Jameson identifies Universal History as itself nonnarrative: "It is fundamentally nonnarrative and nonrepresentational," and it is on the foundation of this inaccessible nonnarrativity that History "can be approached only by way of a prior (re)textualization."[31] If "history is what hurts," Perelman's poem is historical because, appearing in the form it does, it makes Jameson account for its nonnarrative. Even so, such a historical presentation must relate to narrative or else lapse into an inchoate ground, for which Jameson invokes a narrative of necessity as "the inexorable *form* of events; it is therefore a narrative category in the enlarged sense of some properly narrative political unconscious" (*PM*; 102). Cohen's fundamental criticism of narrative history, his sense that "historical thought is located, intellectually considered, near its suppression of the nonnarrated," is demonstrated here in the way that postmodernism (as directly in contact with a nonnarrative historicity) makes History happen for Jameson.[32] As showing how history can be organized in other ways in relation to its underlying negativity, Alavi's *Blueprints* and Perelman's "China" interrupt the narratives of Universal History as they construct a history based in the present.[33]

Nonnarrative exists — demonstrably in the work of contemporary artists and writers but also in the discursive forms that construct history. A critical account of nonnarrativity, as well as aesthetic strategies for its use, thus may proceed not simply in terms of the negation of cultural narratives (as with Jameson's postmodernism) but in a discussion of the historical agency of its forms. Jerome McGann discusses nonnarrative in this sense as a construction of history, distinguishing "antinarratives," which are "problematic, ironical, and fundamentally a satiric discursive procedure," from nonnarratives themselves, which "do not issue calls for change and alterity [but] embody in themselves some form of cultural difference. [Their] antithesis to narrative is but one dimension of a more comprehensively imagined program based in the codes of an alternative set of solidarities."[34] McGann's definitions may lead to positive forms of discursive organization as nonnarrative; even so, both are still to be read against narrative "as a form of continuity; as such, its deployment in discourse is a way of legitimating established forms of social order." The historical meaning of nonnarratives, however, is not merely their opposition to narrative. There is more history to nonnarrative than in McGann's view, as may be seen in the development of the modern American epic poem, which in many ways qualified or even abandoned narrative as its primary vehicle after Ezra Pound's accretive associations of Ovid, Browning, and contemporary history in *The Cantos*.[35] The self-canceling millenarianism of Pound's moral conclusion in the fascist state led, at least in the formal possibilities of epic, to the identification of events with the allegorized but open-ended subject as history in Charles Olson's *Maximus Poems*, as well as to an often nonnarrative linguistic subjectivity in Louis Zukofsky's "*A*." Olson's maxim as an epic poet indicated just what kind of problem he faced in his identificatory poetics: "It is very difficult to be both a poet, and, a historian."[36] The poet's dilemma here is similar to the problem of narration faced by the transcendental historian in Cohen's sense: "If . . . narration is the core of historical autonomy . . . the cultural-intellectual organization of this 'doing' is linked to its cognitive severing, which has to preclude thinking from appearing in the same scene of space as the told."[37] Olson's solution to the problem of transcendental position, the dilemma of "where to stand" in his epic, was to see himself, as any poet, in two places at once — for example, both in his body and outside it ("Offshore / by islands in the blood") — even if this solution led to a gradual devolution of narrative as it comes undone in the argument of his poem. Olson raised the possibility of a nonnarrative history in his refusal to transcend or close his epic, even if an ultimate horizon of the tragic self — which inevitably disintegrates to prove the discursive truth of history — must qualify his poem's organization of events that are not simply to be subjectively identified, events of a social history, for example. As a parallel cataclysm, *The Maximus Poems* is limited to presenting its own undoing as an account of history that is incommensurate with events.

AN ERA OF STAGNATION

I want to present two examples, which are both historical and works of art or literature, of nonnarration as history. The first is a painting from 1975 by Moscow painter Erik Bulatov, one of a group of Soviet artists working pictorially but influenced by conceptualism in the 1970s, who became internationally known in the 1980s. The second is a literary genre of prose poetry developed in America at about the same time, the mid-1970s, called the New Sentence, a form of nonnarrative poetry associated with the Language School. I want to relate the former to the historical organization of the annal as an index of dates, and the latter to the chronicle as a linked sequence of dates; both examples employ nonnarrative forms similar if not identical to these analytic modes in achieving historical self-consciousness in their presentations of historical event.[38] The larger questions to be addressed here are, What is the nonnarrative construction of history? How did the formal concerns and historical perspectives of two very different kinds of nonnarrative emerge at a specific date, 1 May 1975, in the midst of an era of stagnation, with the Fall of Saigon?

Self-canceling subjectivity is immediately apparent to the viewer of Erik Bulatov's *I Am Going* (fig. 49), in the work's superimposition of the typographically rendered verb *yidu*, "I am going," over masses of clouds that, by that very act, begin to seem historical. The work's historical motivation may be equally transparent, as a reference to the devolution of the Soviet Union into the clouds of an uncertain future, especially in the context of an exhibition of Soviet painting at the Institute for Contemporary Art in London, February 1989.[39] The instant history offered by the recontextualization of post-Soviet art in Western galleries and museums, however, is more than a bit opportunistic. A systematically deformed cross-cultural dialogue one cultural historian calls "pornevangelism" — a lust for capital as transcendental redemption — was crucial for the reception of the art of this period, even inspiring some of it.[40] As viewed from the West, post-Soviet art in the 1980s is as a result uncritically seen as either a positive embrace of democracy or a negative one of postmodernism, as it combined the worst aspects of both in equating recognition with hard currency (as in the Sotheby's auction of 1988, after which certain artists became little more than finance capitalists for the underground economy).[41] Critical accounts of the art of this period, as a result, remain divided in either accepting a postmodern periodization or in insisting on non-Western sources in the culture of the Soviet Union.

In the absence of a definitive cultural history of the emergence of post-Soviet art in this context, a speculative construction may elucidate the formal values of Bulatov's historical nonnarrativity at its historical point of production (insofar as that can known). In that spirit, I will situate the production of Bulatov's art in the mid-1970s, as a form of nonnarrative dialogically engaged with Universal History and only later with the West, in the context of its extreme formal opposite: a depersonalized state-interpreted history embodied in the widespread deployment of both hypernarrative and nonnarrative memorial icons and statues to the Great Patriotic War. Such a grand narrative, which at the time had reached the end

49. Erik Bulatov, I Am Going, *1975. 90½ × 90½".*

of its ability to renew its cultural values for many, would *most* tend to invalidate and displace the historical aspirations and formal possibilities of emergent art, which may be read in terms of its immanent displacements of superseded meaning. Such an antagonistic relation took place literally in the bulldozing of an outdoor exhibition of oppositional art in the 1970s, as is well known. At the same time, Bulatov's work may be seen as deriving directly from the nonnarrative aspects of Soviet monumental history's representation of the war.[42] The presentation of historical events in memorials, by their very formal nature as memorials as much as by their redundant, overdetermined placement in social space, provides a model and an occasion for the simultaneous remembrance and amnesia that are brought to self-consciousness in Bulatov's art.

By formal nature, I mean the capacity of the memorial icon or sculpture to represent an event not only by referring to it but also by displacing its memory in the fact of its own existence. The memorial is itself an event, not just a reference to one, and in Soviet social space there was an organized system of such temporal displacements that created an affect of totalized loss as a continuing argument of state power. A rough theoretical schema for the temporal displacements of monuments may point to their formal nature. To begin with, we may imagine *State 1*, an historical situation or state of affairs preceding the memorial, as a consciousness of something that needs to be remembered — for example, a series of dates of events surrounding the liberation of Ukraine in the Great Patriotic War, as well as the superimposed date of liberation at the end of the war that organizes them. In memorializing this moment, a memorial exists in *State 2*, in which the placement of the memorial has displaced State 1: the dates of the war have been embodied in a spatial array of memorials in and around Kiev and Ukraine whose emplacement itself is a series of dates (fig. 50).[43] Prior to both States 1 and 2 is an irrecoverable *State 0*, the traumatic events of the war as they occurred in real time, and which are only accessible as the historical Real "in its effects."[44] The loss that is to be remembered has become an object continuing to mean and exist; this is the memorial's function in mourning. But loss in the form of State 1 — the events to be remembered, and the need to remember them — at the same time has itself been lost, an entropic moment in which the meaning of the event to be remembered is dispersed in the coming into being of the memorial in State 2 — its placement in social space.[45] In addition to reading a memory of the event narratively from the memorial itself, we read a nonnarrative amnesia in which the displacement of events becomes interpretable as a universal tragedy identified with the state — eliding the fact of loss, as well as many more contingent facts, that occurred with these events.

It is not so much the specific forms of the monument, narrative or nonnarrative, that determine their simultaneous memory and amnesia as it is their systematic placement. These memorials range from hypernarrative (heroic figures, depictions of battle) to nonnarrative (obelisks, mounds), but their narrativity is in an important sense canceled out by the overdetermined recurrence of the form of the memorial in social space. The stakes of such a process were high in the culture of the Soviet Union, which had invested great authority in a historical record — primarily of World War II but also of the October Revolution — preserved in memorial iconography. We need only imagine the colossal statue of Mother Russia at Stalingrad to comprehend the sacrificial terror being mobilized as the desire underlying the state's narrative. Such icons and statues are to be found

50. An example of a monument to the Great Patriotic War in the environs of Kiev, former USSR, 1970s. Reproduced from Novosti Press Agency slide set: monument to security men who fought for the revolution.

everywhere, in Leningrad, the "hero city" (*goroi gorod*) of the defenders of the Siege; in countless statues of Mayakovsky and myriad busts of Lenin; in Akhmatova teacups and Pushkin feather pens; in the war decorations of veterans worn everyday on the street. There is a system of such icons, and a repetitive pattern of their recurrence, but what is important here, and what I suggest motivated Bulatov, is how the authority of historical narrative they were meant to reinforce, in the thirty years between the war and his painting (or the forty-five years of the Cold War), has turned itself on its axis to create a vacuum of meaning, an absence of narrative continuity. The narrative itself evaporates even as the meaning of loss remains, with no palpable image to assign it to, the memorial icon itself having been embodied and thus displaced in the desire for such materialization.[46]

Bulatov produces few paintings a year, perhaps two or three according to an interview, and each is a study in a carefully constructed vocabulary of figures for time, loss, and social reality — a memorial.[47] Some of the recurring elements of his paintings include a horizon line obscured by the social space of Moscow suburbs toward which figures, in a flattened allegory of progress, move but can never reach (fig. 51); or a postindustrial landscape in which both nature and the "enframing" of the social are bracketed as

51. Erik Bulatov, Krassikov Street, *1976. 59 × 79".*

mutual displacements, where an eerily detached working-class family picnics on the grass of a general amnesia. What is being mourned here, of course, is as much a social ideal as the vocabulary for representing it. Bulatov also uses a vocabulary of purely ideological icons such as defunct state slogans and memorial emblems, superimposing, for example, the word *edinoglasno*, "unanimity," in red letters over a mural of Soviet deputies raising their hands in unison; or the words *programma vremya*, "program time" (the Soviet six o'clock news), on a TV screen being watched by an decrepit old woman whose upraised leg creates a diagonal of perspective that ends in the flattened screen. The system of Soviet memorial culture, both as devalued kitsch (one of the original referents of the word referred to Stalinist culture) and the lived experience of the present, is aptly summarized by Bulatov's monumental use of the inscrutable image of Leonid Brezhnev himself, emblem of the era in which the artist worked, haloed by the flags of the Soviet republics.[48]

While *I Am Going* lacks such immediate social references, its combination of an iconic affect of loss with a linguistic index of present time may be read as precisely social and historical. The date of the painting is 1975, the midpoint, one may speculate, of the Brezhnev "era of stagnation" (which from all accounts was experienced as nonnarrative, that is, as possessing neither beginning, middle, nor end). The era itself was named as soon as it ended; according to one post-Soviet source, *zastoi*, "a period in which time stands still," was "the first word given to us after *perestroika*" in the first days of Mikhail Gorbachev (*stagnatsiya* is also used, but as description of the quality of life more than as a place in which to stand, *zastoi* being derived from *stoit'*, "to stand").[49] In Boris Kagarlitsky's teleological history of Soviet oppositional culture, *The Thinking Reed*, such a retrospective periodization fits quite well with an amended Marxist narrative, thus invoking a paradox: the era of stagnation, *stagnatsiya/zastoi*, seemingly of indefinite duration, only could be known as the "era of stagnation" after it was over.[50] For an artist like Bulatov, the dilated present before its ending would have been experienced not as a retrospectively designated era but as a state comprised simultaneously of State 1 and State 2 — in which the present is lived as memory and the past as amnesia. The durationlessness of that present, its mimicry of the end of history by sheer inertia, coincides with the emptiness of its narrative within official culture while remaining as yet unnamed in unofficial culture.

The scale and duration of this era may be understood in relation to the following description of a mid-1970s monumental site from a Soviet history of city planning:

> Of the new cities of the decade, we shall mention Brezhnev, a city which began to be built in 1973 on the Kama river, together with a large truck-manufacturing plant. . . . The structure of the city, with an expected population of 400 thousand, follows the principle of a parallel development of the functional zones. . . . The city centre is linear, stretching along the main axis of the residential area, and parallel to the bank of the river; this puts the centre within walking distance for most of the population and ensures its lively activity both during the daytime and the evenings. . . . The city is registering a regular and organized growth.[51]

Here a story of "400 thousand" residents, brought together in one place and motivated by a "truck-manufacturing plant," is subordinated to the narrative of "regular and organized growth." The problem for oppositional culture during this period would be, How, in the face of such monumental inertia, can one create an appropriate scale for a work of art in response? Later one may have come to the conclusion that history was going nowhere, but was there any way of measuring it in the event? In an interview, Bulatov speaks of a kind of incontrovertible self-evidence of the social world during the era of stagnation; there was no possibility of changing what was, simply, an atemporal condition that had no possibility of development. This atemporal state, suffused with an affect of loss, is what I am identifying as the product of a memorial culture and authority that was imposed on social reality and embodied in monuments and icons that had lost their claim to history simultaneously in the act of referring to it — a redundant assertion of history that predicts how naming the new Soviet city Brezhnev would later fail the test *as* history.

Bulatov's solution to this dilemma is to work in a radically split aesthetic register of simultaneous realist immediacy and imaginative displacement, figured in his work as visual transparency and linguistic opacity, respectively. As he says, "My works have an 'entrance' and 'no entrance' simultaneously. . . . From the perspective of the painting's artistic space, there is an entrance, one you can't avoid. But from the perspective of daily life, there's no entrance. . . . Both are at work equally and simultaneously."[52] Bulatov's schema of "entrance" and "no entrance" participates in as much as it opposes Soviet culture as a memorial to itself in two senses: representation, assumed to be transparent to event, instead becomes opaque; by virtue of its displacement of prior history, the present, intended to be opaque in the materiality of representation, becomes transparent. Such a reciprocity of transparency and opacity, of directness of representation and its impossibility, is reinforced by the meaning of Soviet ideological signs in social circulation at much wider levels. This double movement of signs takes place in the systematic circulation of signs in Soviet social space, a relation Bulatov and other Soviet artists are certainly aware of in their use of kitsch iconography as coinage of an accumulated economy of loss.[53] A history of Soviet popular culture in the 1980s describes the urban appearance of linguistically opaque and socially antagonistic graffiti seen as occurring only after the dominant system of transparent signs in circulation, precisely those that Bulatov organizes in his work, had lost their authority.[54] Bulatov's juxtaposition of icon and sign tries to realize a simultaneous overdetermination and self-evidence, without appealing solely to the ironization of his given materials, in the context of the period in which he was working.

In Bulatov's pictorial strategies, nonnarrative is not primarily an ironization of narrative — and hence is not merely a negation or disruption of it. *I Am Going* presents history as an atemporal moment figured as simultaneously transparent and opaque, an effect accomplished by the overlay of iconic and linguistic elements. The visual image of massive Russian clouds breaking up (or forming for rain or simply being blown across the sky; any number of temporal sequences may be conjoined here) against a background of a deep blue sky freezes the event — a dramatic change in the weather — into an atemporal moment of apperception. The monumental image of change or movement presented here precisely imitates the formation of an iconic memorial in which State 1 (what is to be remembered *before*) has been embodied and displaced by State 2 (how it will be remembered *after*). The gap between before and after is exactly the source of the ineffable effect Bulatov is trying to capture. The resulting image of clouds caught in a suspended moment in a temporal sequence suggests, to begin with, that self-consciousness finds itself in the reduction of movement to image, as one knows who one is in time only in achieving a distance on a rapidly moving sequence of events, the comprehension of an instant (the effect of coming into consciousness on seeing clouds breaking up after rain, or clouds massing for oncoming rain). Such an iconic stasis, he implies, is the necessary condition for the comprehension of any movement. This tension works particularly well as an index to the Brezhnev era, in which memorial culture is reproduced in the comprehension of history as entropic displacement, against which self-consciousness can only distance itself from the event — nothing can be added to history other than one's awareness of it.

It is possible as well to describe Bulatov's clouds as mobilizing layers of Russian iconography — which nostalgically refers back to the baroque clouds of state absolutism (in which moving clouds may frame the action of foreground figures in genre historical painting — agents that are, of course, absent here), but which is given a more immediate register in modern images of clouds set against the progress of the Soviet state in its formative period. In Alexander Dovzhenko's film *Aerograd* (1935), for example, tiny biplanes on their way to their historic mission in the new Soviet Far East move from left to right in a framing sequence for a drama of Stalinist ethics in which the necessity of the state is substantiated in the inevitability of human loss. The massing of clouds takes on a similarly foregrounded role in Dovzhenko's war propaganda film on the liberation of Ukraine (1943–45), where they stand for, as they represent the affect of, universal loss, particularly in relation to a machine culture embodied in the tanks and weapons being destroyed beneath them. Later, Andrei Tarkovsky's science fiction film *Solaris* (1970), like Bulatov's painting a peak achievement of the era of stagnation, reverses this relation of historical agency to temporal inevitability in placing the state machine, now become the space station in which the principal action takes place, in an ideal position of observer over the masses of clouds that form and re-form out of the ocean of Solaris. Such clouds are exactly the loss of self from which the mysterious neutrino replicas of human presence materialize. Self-consciousness here is both lost in the clouds and formed out of clouds, a register of agency opposed to that of the scientistic space station. This is not only a moment of ironic fantasy but a judgment of the subject's place in history. Clouds, in other words, in a Soviet iconographical tradition that runs from Dovzhenko to Tarkovsky to Bulatov, are a historical index of self-consciousness set against the progression of state narrative — even if clouds precede narrative, especially the one I have made of them.

The contrapuntal historical index in Bulatov's painting is presented by his use of language, the Russian verb *yidu* dropped out from the clouds, yielding in English the title *I Am Going*. The typographically neutral setting of the word (anticipating Barbara Kruger's use of Futura Bold in her photomontages of the 1980s) is mapped onto an artificial perspective that leads from a viewer's position that must be coincidental with the frame of the picture toward a central vanishing point. This diagonal movement into the center reverses the Soviet modernist convention of diagonals moving left to right out of a center: if in expanding outward from center to right a diagonal denotes progress, as may be seen in a Rodchenko agitprop poster from the 1920s (fig. 52), in collapsing in from left to center it recasts progress as a devolution into the infinitesimal origins of a failed transcendence. Here is a little allegory to draw out more history from the clouds. It is not, however, simply ironic (as would be the case with superimpositions of more objectified language in Kruger's work); the subject, whose self-consciousness is already engaged in the determination of present time out of the movement of the clouds, is spoken for as if destined toward a nonexistent endpoint at the center of self-consciousness. At the same time, there is indeed an ironic reference to the end of history in communism, one that must have been experienced as already undermined by the memorial state — so that when Little Vera in the 1988 film of the same name is asked by her boyfriend what her goals are and she answers, "I am going to communism" (*ya yidu k komunismu*, a pun on *miy yid'om k komunismu*, "We are going to communism"), we know she has decided there is really no alternative to an unmediated present for her.[55] Little Vera is self-conscious precisely of the fact that she is not going anywhere — and this fact is not ironic. Such an unmediated present, of nonironic agency caught in a present moment of duration, exists in the Russian language in the aspect of verbs of motion, *yidt'i* meaning a kind of going in which one is, at that time of speaking, "on the way." In the system of Russian aspect, *yidt'i* is distinguished from an act that might be understood as completable (such as when "I go" to

52. Alexander Rodchenko, Knigi *[Books], 1925.*

the store to buy a loaf of bread). So the "I" that speaks in Bulatov's painting is "on the way" toward an inevitable vanishing point in history — one that is, nonironically, an index to present time. The typographical rendering reinforces this movement, as the verb of motion has neither origin nor destination but iconic frame and vanishing point.

Subjectivity here is indeed linguistic, by virtue of the incomplete aspect of the verb of motion, which substantiates only itself — self-consciousness is seen first as an immanent movement, and only then as dialogic communication. As such, Bulatov's painting is a primary visual record of Althusserian hailing, in which the response "I am going" is seen as disappearing into the site from which the interpellative command was made. The typographical rendering of this verbal response, in its displacement of social dialogue in terms of linguistic subjectivity, can be further read as an interiorized response to graphic signs seen everywhere in Soviet social space that urged, for example, "Praise to the Communist Party of the Soviet Union" or "Welcome the Revolution" — invocations to generalized action that are countered by the derealization that Bulatov exploits throughout his work. Alternately — and there may be no end in sight when one is on one's way into the clouds — the derealization and loss in Bulatov's painting open onto a metaphysical prospect that can be read as a political allegory. As in

Kagarlitsky's narrative account of the conflict between law and spirit in official Soviet culture, a simultaneous opacity and transparency can be read in terms of the modernist state and a suppressed Orthodox Christianity. The word as legal culture is on its way toward a dissolution in the spiritual clouds of religiously inspired Russian nationalism in this reading, which when the initial version of this essay was written seemed only too available.[56] While such an expanded reading of Bulatov's painting offers a kind of romantic irony in terms of larger historical frames, *I Am Going* is nonironic in an important way. It is presented positively as a moment of transition from State 1 to State 2, precisely a memorial to the system it supersedes. Where State 1 for the painting would be that loss of history preceding the work, State 2 includes the concretization that occurs when that loss is represented in the painting. *I Am Going* thus takes place as a historical date within an annal's series of dates — the annal being the Soviet Union's foreclosed renewal in the form of a memorial to its past.

THE FALL OF SAIGON

Bulatov's imitation of the date, within a series of dates in memorial culture that takes the form of an annal, works very differently as a way of claiming a present moment in history than the ironic historicism of comparable art in the West. If in the 1980s Barbara Kruger attempted similar kinds of juxtaposition of historical icon and ideological sign, both work generally to empty out a negative space or illusionist scene against which the real time of the viewer is ironically invoked as present — but only by means of its displacement (fig. 53). The clouds in Kruger's photomontage are anything but an emblem of consciousness; the familiar death's-head cloud is an image that *most* prohibits identification, an emblem of annihilation that otherwise cannot be thought. The viewer is pushed out of the frame by virtue of his or her fatal attraction to the historical cloud, which cannot be consummated. The recurrent address to *you* as the viewer of Kruger's work is thus on every level ironic; the object of historical address in *Your Manias Become Science* (Did *your* mania cause the bomb?), as identified with self-consciousness (Is *your* mania caused by the bomb?), is a shifter rhetorically displaced outward from the constructed gap between image and text. Kruger's short-circuited identification forces the viewer to admit a social totality as only the space created by these (and many similar)

53. Barbara Kruger, untitled ("Your Manias Become Science"), 1981. Photograph, 37 × 50".

negations; looking at her work from a distance of several feet in a gallery or museum becomes the only place to stand.[57]

There are different cultural meanings for what appear to be similar strategies of nonnarration, in short. The kind of nonirony deployed in Bulatov's pictorial strategies in this sense may have less to do with Kruger's theatrical ironies than with the nonnarrative writing produced by the Language School at about the same time as Bulatov's painting.[58] American writers addressing the cultural politics of the period were then experiencing something similar to Brezhnev's era of stagnation — in 1975, the year of Bulatov's painting, the Vietnam War had gone on far beyond anyone's consent for it; a prolonged stasis occurred in which agencies of both perpetrators of the war and objectors to it had become exhausted, a state culminating in an abrupt temporal devolution with the Fall of Saigon. About that time, I published a poem, more accurately a self-conscious journal entry in which I recorded my location among a sequence of signs in social space, which in retrospect seems an argument in response to a historical stasis in which the linguistic and iconic dissociate each other in a manner similar to that in *I Am Going*. "Place Names" opens with a moment of loss recognized literally as the remains of some prior conflagration:

What I saw at the fire site.
BAKER
The men knocking over drums.
WESTERN CARLOADING
Signs on walls. Philosophy informs.
DO NOT HIT FENCE

These signs in social space are interpellative commands: to witness and adjust, as well as to obey. In placing them in a sequence, I am simultaneously connecting and unlinking them from the punctual moment of hailing in Althusser's formulation, where the subject just is caught up in a response. This moment of derealization proposes a mobility of signs against the resistant effects of cultural meltdown, figured in burned-out buildings and "men knocking over drums" as objects of fascination and horror. The poem continues its reading of cultural detritus until the signs themselves, liberated in a space of negation, produce a kind of temporal free fall that is its own memorial to self-consciousness:

Old wooden letters. Propeller blades.
ALLIED DIVISION
50
NATIONAL ICE
COLD OF CALIFORNIA, INC.
TO LEASE HEAVY
What I have always thought & said.[59]

The initial impetus for this essay was a question: In what sense was nonnarrative art and writing being produced in 1975 connected to its historical moment? How does writing of the period of Vietnam crisis compare with visual art that refigured the defunct narratives of Brezhnev's stasis? A sequence of signs encountered in social space — in this case, the intersection of Eighth, Townsend, and Division Streets, San Francisco, a former warehouse district of industrial brick now transformed into gentrified galleria — argued for a form of self-consciousness similar to Bulatov's at the moment of loss. These signs seemed always to have been there, already in history and thus in denial of me, even in confirmation of "what I have always thought & said." Their desired synchrony, the moment of signification in which language declares itself as such, takes place in the poem as the diachronic progression by means of which State 1, a prior world with real historical agents acting within it — what the neighborhood must have been like as a thriving warehouse district, circa 1945 — devolves into State 2, a world of symbolic exchange, "a discrete or continuous sequence of measurable events distributed in time," with the agent standing still only to read the signs of the gentrified present.[60] Where we may see the displacement of an object identified with self-consciousness as ironic in the work of Barbara Kruger, here the temporality of the poem, as opposed to the simultaneity of the picture, adds a nonironic dimension to the poetics of loss. Such displaced temporality may be seen on analogy not to Brezhnev-era stasis but to Vietnam-era crisis, where the historical subject's identification with nonevent on the scale of empire also works to restrict his or her agency.

Where Bulatov's painting imitates the historical date as punctual moment within the form of the annal, the model for the poem's sequential time frame and exteriorized, deferred self-consciousness is clearly the chronicle — whose events are provisionally organized in a sequence but where there is neither a single, overarching perspective nor a necessary conclusion — as exemplified in the sequence of the Fall of Saigon, May 1975:

1. Banmethuot overrun March 10.
2. South Vietnamese flee Banmethuot.
3. Pleiku and Kontum evacuated.
4. Thieu orders defense of Hue.
5. North Vietnamese cut highway leading from Hue.
6. One million persons flee from Hue to Danang.
7. North Vietnamese attack Chulai and Quangnai.
8. Hue falls March 25.
9. Panic at Danang.
10. Danang falls on Easter Sunday.
11. North Vietnamese headquarters move south.
12. American ambassador asks for increased aid.
13. President Ford speaks of the Vietnam War in the past tense.
14. President Thieu leaves Vietnam for Taiwan April 21.
15. North Vietnamese engaged thirty-five miles from Saigon.
16. Americans and South Vietnamese begin evacuation.
17. Helicopter evacuation begins April 29.
18. April 30: Saigon deserted.

19. North Vietnamese enter Saigon April 30.
20. General Minh surrenders to Colonel Bui Tin May 1.[61]

In the long duration of the Vietnam War, the event of the Fall of Saigon may be understood as an entropic collapse that divides, in a manner suggested by the memorial icon, State 1 (the situation immediately preceding the fall being a kind of stalemate in which minor North Vietnamese victories at the negotiating table were being countered by minor American successes in the effort to Vietnamize the war), by means of an incremental sequence of events (beginning with panic in military Region I in the north, followed by masses of refugees moving south, bringing with them retreating armies, and ending in the autodestruction of political power and then the defense of the southern military regions), from State 2, the defeat of the Thieu regime. I participated in this event as a spectator only, but in a certain sense it happened also to me, as it did for any historical subject for whom State 1 had meaning as an imposed but untenable stagnation. The fact that the Vietnam War ended not in victory but in defeat, as many have commented, has been a powerful deterrent to its representation; in a number of key forms, from Hollywood cinema to the Vietnam Veterans Memorial in Washington, narrative has been displaced by other forms of memorial to the war. For this reason it makes sense that Maya Lin's Vietnam Veterans Memorial is not a single iconic image but a sequentially organized chronicle of the names of those who died.[62] Loss in Vietnam is experienced as a temporal series of defeats rather than any overarching, stabilizing narrative of victory. "We lost" is not the same as "they won" — there can be, as has been pointed out, no reference to the Vietnamese in the memorial. This is a situation conceptual/performance artist Chris Burden corrected in *The Other Vietnam Memorial*, which lists on large bronze sheets some 1.5 million alphabetized, computer-generated, hypothetical Vietnamese names (fig. 54).[63]

The nonnarrative of this event — an incremental sequence of losses rather than a narrative sense of an ending such as "the North Vietnamese won, thus ending the war" — has had a major impact on historical self-consciousness since the war. A poetics of loss that is at the same time a coming into consciousness, similar to Bulatov's fixed image of clouds being addressed by a voice in *I Am Going*, was organized in the Fall of Saigon on a time line, its lack of closure making a chronicle of loss by analogy out of any similar open series. This effect is evident in writing from the mid-1970s

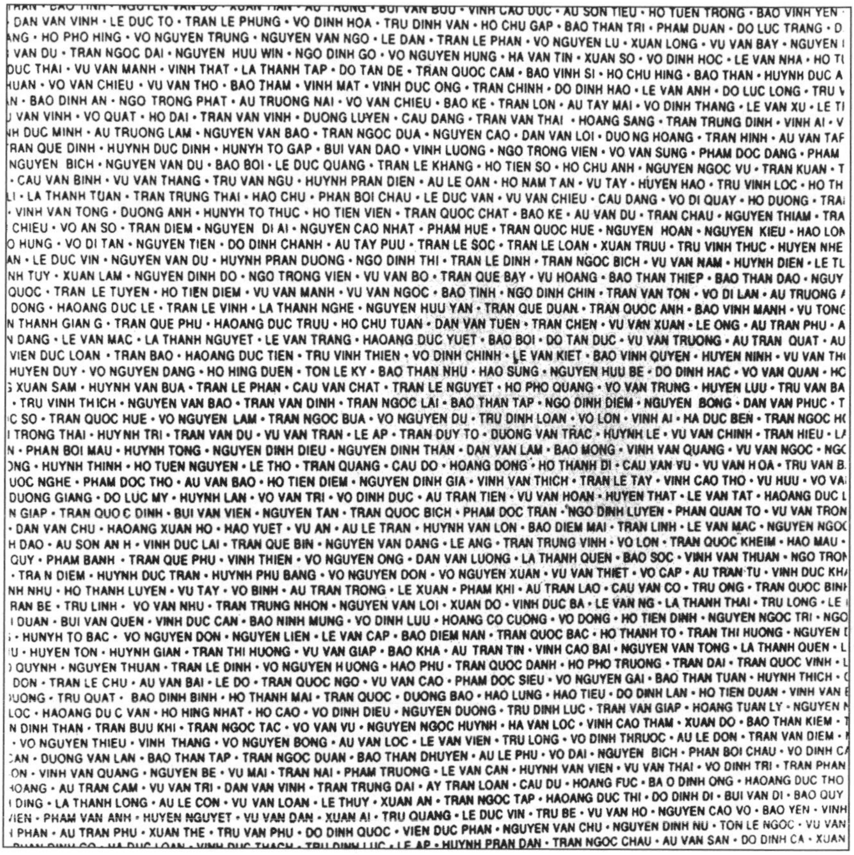

54. Detail of Chris Burden, The Other Vietnam Memorial, *1991. Etched copper plates, steel. Collection of the Lannan Foundation, Los Angeles. Photo: Ellen Page Wilson.*

in a genre of poetic prose that Ron Silliman has called the New Sentence, in which series of discrete statements organized "at the level of the sentence" generate a poetic matrix without any overarching narrative form. The New Sentence is significant, beyond its development of the forms of extended prose poetry Silliman explores in his work, because its particular formal properties place it, as in a Venn diagram, at the center of a number of related nonnarrative techniques — ranging from lyrical to aleatorical — shared by a wide range of writers in the period.[64] Its importance here is both as a site for conscious reflection on sequence, everyday life, and history for experimental writers and in its immediate comprehension and acceptance as a form of nonnarration by many more. In both its theoretical motivation and social reception, it is thus comparable to surrealist automatism as a mode of socially reproduced nonnarration — even if surrealist automatism lacks the New Sentence's play of identification and reference to the world, addressing history not just desire.[65] Silliman's work in the New Sentence precisely explores the constructive potential of a deformed chronicle, seeking to qualify the self-consciousness of historical narrative by means of multiple and conflicting perspectives. Such a use of the chronicle in experimental writing occurs in the multiauthored project *Legend* (1980), in which we find a sequence such as

1805 Writes poem "on the growth of a poet's mind."
1781 (July) The sparrow-hawks continue their depredations.
1880 Lieutenant-governor.
1960 "Door to the river."
1844 First attempt to assassinate Polk.
1915 Death of Gaudier-Brzeska.
1347 First one-man exhibition.
1959 Early notebooks destroyed.[66]

What Gérard Genette terms *paralipsis* (the elision of some but not all terms in the syllogistic movement from Proposition A to Proposition B) occurs here in a movement from annal to chronicle, from a mere accretion of dates to a series in which there is a degree of connection.[67] Paraliptic effects are everywhere in the New Sentence, as between "Death of Gaudier-Brzeska" and "First one-man exhibition" — Was this the first one-man exhibition in history, or the first of Gaudier-Brzeska? What is the causal connection between the two? Silliman has written of the deferral of "above-sentence integration" in the New Sentence: if "the sentences 'All women were once girls' and 'Some women are lawyers' logically lead to a third sentence or conclusion, a higher level of meaning: 'Some lawyers were once girls,'" the writing that interests him "proceeds by suppression, most often, of this third term, positing instead chains of the order of the first two"; it is important that many connections are left open here between lawyers, girls, and women.[68] The "I" of the poet, much like the continuum of referring sentences, is likewise left open in the presented sequence, although it often reappears as a context sufficient for syllogistic construction, as in "Early notebooks destroyed," which is interpretable as self-referring and thus allows for a reading of the other dates as potentially but not necessarily referring to the nonnarrator as "I." In *Tjanting* (1981), a book-length example of the New Sentence, Silliman is clearly caught up in the constructive possibilities of playing with sequence:

Narrativity. Some of us just thrash around in our private lives, never solving anything. Some days shoes will never stay tied. Somehow, in mid-September in the subway, the strong Xmasy smell of a pine tree. A paragraph I cld write for the rest of my life. Even in Chinese the sarcastic banter of highschool kids is specific. Ripples in the image thru an old window. I play Eddie Cantor on the jukebox. I'm content to eat a salad. We stand naked in the open doorway & watch the rain. A star on the shoe means it's Converse. This is not some story. The gray mouse tries to climb the pole to the nightingales & their seed. Today it remains morning until nightfall. Winter chaos in the wind-chimes. In this photo the ocean looks just like the desert. I spring into the milling flock of pigeons wch leap into flight. Underfunded. A touch of Tahini for Mother Cabrini. Flat light & sharp shadows on the objects of a tabletop (camera, tortilla, half a tomato, the poems of Alan Davies, the shine of cups) after the first light rain. One sees in the faces of sleepers all the strain of their lives. The water is boiling. I step into the cafe to write but am immediately besieged by old friend D., his act at long last having totally collapsd in on itself & nobody else to tell it to. Bad art of rich students got up as punk. Since when?[69]

As is obvious from the first and last sentences, Silliman is consciously commenting on the problem of narrative unity — the organization offered being one not of subordination but of an inductive *metalepsis* (another term used by Genette, meaning reference to the discourse as a whole). The meaning of the total form of the work, however, is being created in the ongoing refiguring and qualification of the metalepsis, which becomes an interpretive device that shifts as the poem develops. This effect accounts for the movement of the writing, and its interest for the reader, by means of what Silliman has called the "syllogistic movement" of the New Sentence form. Rather than addressing reference to a continuity of event in real time (in which case, nonnarrativity would be understandable simply as deviant narrative), Silliman defers the transcendental self-consciousness of history by formal means and keeps the narrative conclusion outside the limits of the form. The text has unity precisely in its deferral of discursive closure by means of a continually reinforced present tense, one that metaleptically determines the whole in constructing a historical "now-in-the-present."[70] The experience of reading Silliman at length (and the short excerpt here cannot do his work justice) is to engage a series of higher-order interpretants that are multiple and that continually break down the immediacy of any single assertion. As in White's notion of chronicle, partial narratives abruptly terminate in the present of the text; one experiences Silliman's lengthy accretions as a kind of nominalist aporia — in which there is no exterior, transcendent place to stand to guarantee meaning or perspective — but one that is worked consciously toward an effect of "being-in-history" as a continuous present. In this sense, the chronicle creates a present immediacy in the deferral of closure formally analogous to the effect of the incrementally asserted names of casualties on the Vietnam memorial, a politics of loss that raises the stakes of Silliman's work to what Fredric Jameson called an "ideology of form" — "the determinate contradictions of the specific messages emitted by the varied sign systems which coexist within a given artistic process as well as in its general social formation" — as its social matrix.[71]

While the New Sentence form works to undermine narrative, thus manifesting a critical and even subversive force, it is important to note that there is nothing politically subversive about nonnarrative form as such; a sequence of incremental dates that lacks closure may be organized affirmatively in the social administration of meaning more generally. Consider, for example, the mass media's turning the tables on Jimmy Carter at the time of the Iran hostage crisis, where more than 365 successive days of Ted Koppel's *Nightline* chronology were a sufficient reinforcement of lost national identity that Carter did, in the event, lose the election. I am fascinated (and horrified as well) by the way the authority of a poetics of loss can in this way be transformed into authoritarian denial — the inevitability of loss becoming the basis for an acceptance in the subject that events are beyond his or her control. The state, it turns out, is remarkably able to recuperate victory even out of its defeats, as was evident when the Vietnam Syndrome was rescripted as triumph with the narrative closure of the Persian Gulf War. The events of September 11 as well were a monumental moment of defeat that was immediately recuperated in national narrative. Narrative, in this sense, easily subordinates its component elements — the date, annal, and chronicle — through the desired necessity of its ending. It follows that to keep the status of nonnarrative open is both an act of resistance to transcendental closure and an insistence on the positive history otherwise known as nonnarrative. We have been in the present of a nonnarrative chronicle ("and then, and then") for some time, which, as it produces unstable narratives only to break down, calls us back to ourselves in a series of continual denials — and the rest, or so they would like us to believe, is history.

NONNARRATIVE ENDING

The relation between narrative and nonnarrative in artists such as Bulatov and Silliman invites speculation on how forms of historical self-consciousness are constructed more generally. The parallel cataclysms of their exemplary works clearly intend *not* to imitate history in the form of a narrative. Rather, history is presented in a form of temporal organization that demands a series of displacements that originates in the work as an event, moving from defamiliarization to critical awareness and, hopefully, to consciousness of one's position in history. In Bulatov's case, a painting that seemed to embody the poetics of loss of the era of stagnation was produced at a moment when that period had not yet ended, and for that reason could not have been named. *I Am Going* formally stages a conscious perception that the historical period one is in is "on the way" toward an endpoint that has yet to be determined and, in the punctual account presented by the work, cannot be known. Silliman's formal imitation of the chronicle of events that ended the untenable stasis of the Vietnam War occurred in a period in which the historical impact of the war had yet to be resolved, as was later attempted with the era-defining Vietnam Syndrome. The accretive form of his New Sentence work itself demonstrates how provisional narrative frames are constructed only to be dismantled again and again in the sequence of events. In moving from such exemplary works of art to historical consciousness more generally, there are differences of scale because works of art, particularly those of radical or avant-garde writers but in traditional forms and genres as well, create temporal continuities of their own, introducing their formal sequences into the historical series of the culture at large. Allowing for disjunctions of time and divergences of scale, the temporal forms of art participate in the social production of historical time by inculcating critical awareness of its construction and offering an alternative to it. Both nonnarrative and narrative art are sites for reflection on the processes by which historical narratives are produced, distributed, and undone: the processes of defamiliarization, foregrounding, and serial construction that make the history happen as real-time events and eras unfold.

I have written a different concluding paragraph for each version of this essay since it was first delivered and published. In the previous one, I recounted a story from the *San Francisco Chronicle* of 16 July 1992 that laid bare a continuing drama of antagonistic but constitutive relations between narrative and nonnarrative.[72] In an attempt to catch up to youth-market prime-time competitors, ABC television executives sent down an order to program suppliers: "The network has mandated that each show begin with a 'substantial program open' — in other words, action and dialogue — before the main title. End credits on programs are to be superimposed over continuing action and dialogue." The reason for this stylistic mandate is, simply, that narrative closure is to be deferred at all costs so that the viewer is not tempted to switch channels by remote control; the action must be nonstop, synchronized to create the illusion of a kind of "continuous present." The network "will also reduce the number of its own network I.D.s, on-air promotions, and public service announcements" to accomplish the effect of seamlessness. Where historically the interruption of narrative has demanded higher-order reflections on its form, here the nonnarrative viewing competence of an audience armed with remote control devices is addressed by a blurring of narrative boundaries for an even more overdetermined effect. This strategy, like any advertising campaign, I reasoned at the time, probably would not last long, even if it might help shift the viewer's competence in nonnarrative and narrative into as yet unrealized forms. Over the last ten years, however, the device has remained in use, even as it has been automatized as part of the routine framing of narrative episodes.

The media politics of narrative and nonnarrative at the present date, 6 March 2002, are considerably more sinister. An article in the *New York Times* reports that negotiations are currently under way between ABC and comedian David Letterman who, furious with the management of CBS, is considering moving his late-night talk show to the rival network.[73] Such a move would deliver the final corporate blow of the ax to newsman Ted Koppel's *Nightline*, whose ratings have declined along with its audience, which has aged since the program's historical origins in the Iran hostage crisis and which, for the network and its corporate parent, the Walt Disney Company, is no longer an optimal market. Pressures on Letterman to move to ABC are hard to determine, involving the degree of network commitment to the program, whose ratings have slipped below those of the *Tonight Show*. ABC and Disney, however, are eager to substitute the more lucrative entertainment program for its most highly regarded news venue. In defense of his continuing relevance, Koppel, in a *New York Times* op-ed column, cites a national need for historical reflection as precisely the reason his show should continue: "In times of crisis, we often have the largest late-night audience in broadcasting." Now that the nation has entered into a narrative of permanent crisis, this relation should continue to be profitable and historically responsible: "*Nightline* has earned well over a half a billion dollars for a succession of corporate owners over the years," while "when homeland security is an ongoing concern, when another terrorist attack may, at any time, shatter our sense of normalcy . . . it is, at best, inappropriate and at worst malicious to describe what my colleagues and I are doing as lacking relevance."[74] Network executives, however, maintain that an entertainment show (and is it any less newsworthy?) would bring in more market share (as well as prop up the corporate image of the Disney Company for its "toughminded" leadership).[75] At this date, the question is unresolved, but if Letterman displaces Koppel, the crucial question is, Does the chronology of crisis and intervention that Koppel inaugurated in the Iran hostage crisis, and which has continued through the events of September 11, now end?[76] If the presentation of history changes, and the kinds of self-consciousness attending it, does history itself change? The nonnarrative that ends this particular narrative of media politics and generational struggle may simply reduce to this: What becomes of a continuous narrative of historical self-consciousness when network executives pull the plug?[77]

NEGATIVE EXAMPLES
THEORIES OF NEGATIVITY IN THE AVANT-GARDE

On the way to negativity, I want to stop to explore its centrality for three philosophical traditions as they intersect the history of the avant-garde. The work of Slavoj Žižek, it may be said, is a form of avant-garde cultural theory even if it does not foreground examples from the historical avant-garde to make its point (although examples from the avant-garde, or examples that are avant-garde in their implications, do appear variously throughout his work). Rather, Žižek privileges examples from three areas of speculation: the world-historical reconfiguration of the end of the Cold War and the fall of the Eastern Bloc (a matter of lived experience for Žižek); film and popular culture, seen as a kind of steady-state psychological model of postmodern culture in the West; and, subtending his psychoanalytic account of culture, the position of nature in the tradition of German Idealism after Kant and Hegel. How might the implications of these kinds of example be extended to an account of modernist and avant-garde poetry, specifically in its direct treatment of negativity? Moving backward in intellectual history, I then consider the foremost anti-Hegelian account of negativity, Martin Heidegger's early attack on the concept of Zeitgeist and his identification of its vulgar historicism with the provocations of the historical avant-garde. As I have previously argued, the theory of the avant-garde must move past a conventional Hegelianism, in which negativity is always sublated as either a renewal of tradition or a reinvestment in institutions; in so doing, the handwritten poetry of Robert Grenier is the kind of radically antihistoricist, limit-testing writing that would best exemplify Heidegger's critique. It is necessary, however, that Grenier's work, which wants to remove itself from the Symbolic Order even for a brief moment in order to make its antihistoricist point, be returned to history. What kind of negativity, if we reject Hegelian recuperation, is adequate to the rehistoricizing of such a fundamentally negative poetics? For this I turn to the placement of avant-garde negativity in Michel Foucault's work, the early and continued importance of figures such as Raymond Roussel,

Antonin Artaud, and the Marquis de Sade for his construction of discursive formations. The writing of AIDS activist and artist David Wojnarowicz offers a counterexample of discursive negativity in this sense: in testing the limits of experience, Wojnarowicz situates himself in social discourses that would have been unavailable for historical avant-gardes. While Grenier's sources in a Heideggerian concern for Being are enacted in his lyric forms of poetic subjectivity, the genre of the lyric more generally brackets the historical in its form of limit situations. The limit testing of Wojnarowicz, on the other hand, through the unrepresentable experiences of sexuality and death, leads to an articulation of decentered subjectivity in the postmodern novel that points the way toward reconciling the avant-garde and social agency.

NEGATIVITY

What is negativity, as an element of literary and cultural production? If there is one criterion of the avant-garde with which its critics all agree, it is of the avant-garde's historical origins in a negative moment of refusal of the culture from which it emerges. This refusal may take the form of an explicitly oppositional politics; or it may be self-negating even to the point of withdrawal from society or suicide; or it may involve a radical reconfiguration of the formal possibilities of a genre or medium and their cultural significance. Arguably, all three are related — countercultural politics, self-negation, and new formal possibilities — and will be present to some degree in any instance of the avant-garde. Seeing negativity as single instances of refusal or rupture, however, too often leads directly into logics of absorption and recuperation within the received order of culture. The concept of *antagonism* — in Ernesto Laclau and Chantal Mouffe's construction of discursive hegemony and Slavoj Žižek's psychoanalytic critique of ideology — has the advantage of being able to unite the three registers of the avant-garde into a single moment that encompasses the cultural, psychological, and formal aspects of innovation (even as antagonism is likewise not the only form of negativity at work in the avant-garde's intervention in culture).[1]

The moment of avant-garde negativity should not be restricted to an analytically isolated opposition, either permanent or transitory, to a cultural or aesthetic state of affairs that, however disrupted by the attack, will soon be regrounded in a new order. We need to find ways of positioning negativity that do not end in a predictable result: sterility or recuperation, a decline of force or a reintegration into the whole. As several critics who have thought through the place of negativity in the critical tradition have argued, there is no one-size-fits-all negativity that derives from either logical or determinate negation — it is limited neither to "this statement is either true or false" nor to "there exists something by virtue of that which it is not."[2] Negativity has more than the single attribute of the logical operation of negation performed by the particle *not*. Rather, its meaning will be specified by its construction or positioning within philosophical, psychological, or cultural systems of which it is a constitutive part. Within such larger systems, we may speak of negativity as the inaccessible substrate of nature that cannot be known directly; a posited abstraction that codetermines the form of the concept in its positive content; a desire that cannot be integrated into positive forms of representation; the temporal and spatial limits of the disclosure of being; a moment of excess or nonintegration fundamental to the establishment of any set of identities; the construction of a limit of participation in a culture beyond which a given activity no longer is admissible; the political rupture of revolutionary politics; and a form of behavior or acting out that is unacceptable. More concretely put, negativity is common to a range of concepts that includes nonidentity, antagonism, nihilism, revolt, defamiliarization, rupture, opposition, dissociation, conflict, delusion, void, emptiness. Negativity as it occurs "in the field" so to speak, with the radical forms and interventions of the avant-garde, partakes of any or all of these modes — even as its final horizon, a denial of positivity, locates each instance as a potential form of critique.[3]

Of cultural critics now writing, Slavoj Žižek makes the most consistent use of the concept of negativity — both as an analytical concept and a fact of his analysis. In pushing the limits of critical thinking, Žižek may indeed be considered avant-garde, though the avant-garde is not a primary locus of his critique. What unites Žižek with a theorist such as Theodor Adorno is precisely the productivity of grounding negativity in a nonconcept such as "nonidentity" or the "Real" within a critique of representation. But where Adorno uses negativity as a virtual Archimedean lever to forestall sublation and thus deny a return to the whole that would force its recuperation, negativity in Žižek is much less systematic and regulative, requiring a continual return to the location of negativity as a source of critique.[4] As a result, in his approach to the negative, Žižek shifts perspectives often violently between philosophical discourse, popular culture, historical reference, and idiosyncratic formulation. Noting Žižek's stylistic difficulty, Ernesto Laclau, introducing *The Sublime Object of Ideology* (1989), warns the reader not to look for a finished argument whose unity is a result of sequential development; rather, she will find "a series of theoretical interventions which shed mutual light on each other, not in terms of a *progression* of an argument, but in terms of what we could call the *reiteration* of the latter."[5] Žižek's basic critique of the subject — "that the category of 'subject' cannot be reduced to the 'positions of the subject,' since before subjectivation the subject is the subject of a lack" — is thus operative as well in the form of his writing, where "the limits which the presence of the Real imposes on all symbolization also affect theoretical discourses; the radical contingency that this introduces is based on an almost pragmatist 'constitutive incompletion'" (xiii). In the unfolding of his work, Žižek will construct a "space of the subject" out of the discourses of psychoanalysis, ideology critique, and philosophy after Hegel, demonstrating how the "irreducible plurality" of historical processes is motivated in relation to their common element, "the same impossible-real kernel" (4). As he states at the outset, "All 'culture' is in a way a reaction-formation, an attempt to limit, canalize — to *cultivate* this imbalance, this traumatic kernel, this radical antagonism" (5). Here, the historical status of antagonism must be queried: To what extent do processes of negativity take history out of itself, arriving at a radically contingent but still ahistorical construction of subjectivity? If negativity is the site where history and subject are codetermining, how much history is left?

In working through the plurality of discourses, as well as the conditions of history in which any critique is articulated, toward the "strange attractors" of negativity, Žižek continually circles around the construction of the Lacanian Real, provoking its eruption into his critique. In a conclusive formulation in *The Sublime Object of Ideology*:

> The subject is an answer of the Real (of the object, of the traumatic kernel) to the question of the Other [What do you want?]. The question as such produces in its addressee an effect of shame and guilt, it divides, it hystericizes him, and this hystericization is the constitution of the subject: the status of the subject as such is hysterical. The subject is constituted through his own division, splitting, as to the object in him; this object, this traumatic kernel, is the dimension . . . of a 'death drive', of a traumatic imbalance, a rooting out. Man as such is 'nature sick unto death', derailed, run off the rails through a fascination with a lethal Thing. (181)

Otherwise put: the subject, rather than being the location of any positive knowledge (even if that knowledge is simply "I think"), just is the negativity of its presentation of what it cannot know in the form of symptom or fantasy within which it is caught, as an answer to the question of the Other (analyst, authority, State). These "effects of the Real" constitute the subject in its relation to a lost object that is the cause of its hysterical symptoms— either the inaccessible source of ecstatic/destructive energy known as the "Thing," which cannot be brought into the Symbolic Order; or the "*objet a*," a placeholder for the Thing within the Symbolic Order, the "object cause of desire." This nonanswer to the question of the Other splits the subject (along the lines of, but by no means restricted to, the hysteria on which psychoanalysis was founded), constituting it as the effect of being split in its relation to a lost object (which is only retroactively produced in answer to the Other's question). It is in the reiterative return to the site of this gap or hole in the subject that the knowledge of psychoanalysis is to be gained. While in general terms, man is "sick unto death," drawn into mortality through his romance with the Thing, it is possible for him to recognize the processes by which "the subject evades the dimension of the Thing"— and therein our hope lies. Žižek performs this reiterative question throughout his critique of the subject, refusing the finality of any kind of distance by which to imagine himself outside it. The only way to proceed is to direct his discourse, time and again, toward the point of self-hystericizing antagonism that constructs the subject of the Real.

The psychoanalytic critique of the subject leads directly to ideology critique. In ideology, the subject is likewise hystericized and compelled to repeat its avoidance of the Real, which continually erupts into discourse as a sublime object of fascination and horror: "Ideology is not a dreamlike illusion that we build to escape insupportable reality; in its basic dimension it is a fantasy-construction which serves as a support for our 'reality' itself: an 'illusion' which structures our effective, real social relations and thereby masks some insupportable, real, impossible kernel [of the Real]" (45). The necessity of critique, here as well, demands a continual return to the site of the Real, where one experiences ideology "in its effects"— a return complicated by the fact that history itself is a form of misrecognition and thus may be known only via repetition rather than as any positive knowledge: "The crucial point here is the changed symbolic status of an event: when it erupts for the first time it is experienced as a contingent trauma, as an intrusion of a certain nonsymbolized Real; only through repetition is this event recognized in its symbolic necessity— it finds its place in the symbolic network; it is realized in the symbolic order" (61). Žižek might well be describing the effect of the Real, not as the eruption of a traumatic effect but as an absent cause realized in repetition, on his own writing here:

> Metalanguage is not just an Imaginary entity. It is *Real* in the strict Lacanian sense — that is, it is impossible to *occupy* its position. . . . That is why the only way to avoid the Real is to produce an utterance of pure metalanguage which, by its patent absurdity, materializes its own impossibility: that is, a paradoxical element which, in its very identity, embodies absolute otherness, the irreparable gap that makes it impossible to occupy a metalanguage position. (156)

Given the basic avoidance mechanism that ideology criticism, as much as ideology, will be unable to escape, Žižek makes several proposals for the "end" or goal of critique, seen in terms of succeeding stages of Lacan's construction of the Real. In Lacan's early view, the goal of the analysis is to work through symptoms experienced in the alienation of language into a form of "full speech" where desire is integrated and recognized. Later on, the impossibility of integration and recognition will be seen as the direct consequence of the Symbolic Order itself; the only end of analysis is then to accept this fundamental loss as a preexisting fact. But in Lacan's late work, the Symbolic Order itself is seen as rifted with a constitutive lack, which produces effects of fascination and horror that can only be experienced in a process of "going through the fantasy": "There is nothing 'behind' the fantasy; the fantasy is a construction whose function is to hide this void, this 'nothing' — that is, the lack in the Other" (133). This "going through the fantasy" provides a framework for Žižek's critique, almost a blueprint of it, in the nonclosure of the analytic dialogue. If the relation between traumatic event and reiterated critique is crucial in Žižek's work, his project of ideology critique likewise enacts a form of self-analysis — accounting for the tendency of his writing toward opacity, digression, and a compulsion to repeat.

Now that it has found its place in our unfolding discourse by being reiterated numerous times, we may ask, What is the Real? If the Real can only be known in its effects, what do its effects tell us about the absent cause? To begin with, the Real is an instantiation of trauma, but whether this trauma is historical (as, for instance, the Holocaust or the rape of Bosnian women) or a universal psychological necessity (incest or the primal scene) is undecidable. In the genealogy of the concept in Lacan, according to Žižek:

> In his first Seminar, the traumatic event is defined as an imaginary entity which had not yet been fully symbolized, given a place in the symbolic universe of the subject; but in the seventies, trauma is *real* — it is a hard core resisting symbolization, but the point is it does not matter . . . if it has 'really occurred' in so-called reality; the point is that it produces a series of structural effects (displacements, repetitions, and so on). The Real is an entity which must be constructed afterwards so that we can account for the distortions of the symbolic structure. (162)

As an "absent cause," the Real still has properties; "it exercises a certain structural causality, it can produce a series of effects in the symbolic reality of subjects" (163). Negativity here is precisely distinguished from logical or determinate negation, in that the negative moment is only to be known in a process of retroactive determination, as the analytic encounter unfolds, and through a theoretical reflection on the result of that encounter. It is important that the effects of the Real are known through asking a question, either the unanswerable demand of the Other ("What do you want?"), or a more simple question like "What's a MacGuffin?" which likewise cannot be answered fully ("It's an apparatus for trapping lions in the Scottish Highlands"; 163). In ideology criticism, the Real is the antagonism that, as absent cause, prevents social closure — "a certain limit, a pure negativity, a traumatic limit which prevents the final totalization of the social-ideological field" (164) — like race, class, or gender seen as nontotalizable elements of social difference. At the same time, the Real as a limit of social totalization opens up the possibility of a radical democracy that must respect the incommensurate identities that cannot be totalized. It is therefore of the most crucial political consequence to describe forms of opposition that cannot be brought into alignment within a social totality through a "negation of the negation." The Real is such a concept as the limit of symbolic experience — "a hole, a gap, an opening in the middle of the symbolic order . . . the lack around which the symbolic order is structured . . . the void, the emptiness created, encircled by the symbolic order" (170) — and a demand for an alternative disposition of negativity: "*It cannot be negated because it is already in itself, in its positivity, nothing but an embodiment of pure negativity, emptiness*" (ibid.). The Real, as irreducible, asks for an account of its effects that cannot be integrated in a semantic structure; as nonsignifying, it demands signification.

In the vast scale of his critique of ideological subjectivity in the 1990s — starting with *The Sublime Object of Ideology* and continuing with *For They*

Know Not What They Do (1991); *Tarrying with the Negative* (1993); *The Plague of Fantasies* (1997); and *The Ticklish Subject* (1999) — Žižek pursues a point-by-point rescripting of philosophical tradition in a self-focused analysis that is increasingly distanced from any inaugural moment of historical trauma.[6] On the one hand, it is clear that a historical experience of antagonism informs Žižek's work, from the end of the Cold War as a moment of fascination and horror to the tragic devolution of the socialist "workers' state" in Yugoslavia.[7] To an opposite effect, the continuing critique of the subject via the psychoanalytic recasting of Kant and Hegel tends to push references to the Cold War and the breaking apart of Yugoslavia in the 1990s to the status of illustrative examples. It is just such a relation between historical trauma and reiterative analysis, for Žižek, that defines the form of ideology criticism to begin with; we are authorized, therefore, to continue reading his critique not only within the philosophical tradition but as a form of dialogue between incommensurate cultures. In this sense, we may see Žižek's work as a cultural border crossing between East and West at the historical moment of the undoing of Cold War antagonism, by which he is motivated to identify the "fantasy states" of mutually annihilating politics (capitalism, socialism) as determined retroactively by a unitary antagonism. As his work progresses, however, it takes on the form of a more steady state of analytic reflection and synthesis, through which cultural formations of East and West interpenetrate, undermine each other, and dissolve. The historical moment of ending of the Cold War would, in such a reading, be relocated as a reiterated return to the site of antagonistic negativity, a suturing of incommensurate states being worked into the form of an immanent critique. In this spirit, we may read Žižek's work in terms not of a punctual moment of devolution and a resulting triumphalist teleology, but of a plurality of culturally embedded moments.

DARK MATTER

I have characterized the larger form of Žižek's work as the unfolding of a critical metalanguage (often opaque, digressive, repetitive) that circles around a locus of radical negativity, the Real. If the opacity of Žižek's prose flirts with such a characterization of metalanguage — as a "paradoxical element" that "materializes its own impossibility" and "embodies absolute otherness" — he is likewise careful to insert frequently lucid examples from ready-to-hand popular culture and recent history that raise the energy level of his discourse. The offhanded seductiveness of his examples to an extent masks their serious purpose in triangulating his impossible prose with the impossibility of the Real. "Going through the fantasy" of his ideology critique, one finds embedded in Žižek's massive attack a series of exempla that positions his larger inquiry in relation to the negativity inscribed within them — in their opacity, intractability, perverse fascination, horror, sublimity, and even humor. In looking over the broad sweep of Žižek's works, three categories of example stand out: (1) epistemological anecdotes demonstrating the failure of political systems to control meaning, particularly since 1989 and centered in the post–Cold War European geopolitics of Žižek's homeland, Slovenia; (2) examples from film and popular culture that are so numerous as to provide a continuously unfolding allegory of psychoanalytic concepts (summarized in *Looking Awry*), and which place Western cinema and popular culture within a framework of their universal consumption; and lastly, emerging into prominence in his later work, (3) examples from the natural world that position critical theory in relation to the natural sciences, and which bear few cultural markings.

The first category, of course, draws directly from the experience of the end of the Cold War, even as Žižek warns early on against their too-ready universalization and/or historicization: "Over-rapid historicization makes us blind to the real kernel which returns as the same through diverse historicizations/symbolizations" (*SO*, 50). As a site for the eruption of such a historically produced kernel of the Real, Žižek offers the following anecdote of the nonexistent painting *Lenin in Warsaw* as a sublime object of ideology:

> At an art exhibition in Moscow, there is a picture showing Nadezhda Krupskaya, Lenin's wife, in bed with a young member of the Komsomol. The title of the picture is 'Lenin in Warsaw'. A bewildered visitor asks a guide: 'But where is Lenin?' The guide replies quietly and with dignity: 'Lenin is in Warsaw'. (159)

The anecdote, which is developed to illustrate the "absent cause of desire" of the depicted scene in the painting (Lenin's visit to Warsaw), specifically the relation of Krupskaya's illicit desire to the forbidding authority of Lenin, points to a distinction among Žižek's three kinds of example. The epistemological anecdote, as above, depends on a historically specific perspective: getting the joke about *Lenin in Warsaw* is one thing if the presence or absence of Lenin at the center of ideological totality has been a lifelong concern. For those outside that social order, it may become an example of post-Soviet kitsch, easily an imperial trophy on the order of a chunk of the Berlin Wall. Its explanatory force is relative to its historical origins, while the speculative seductions of popular culture occur within a cultural matrix that is everywhere and nowhere (on both sides of the Wall) at once. Film and popular culture, by virtue of their increasing prominence for Žižek, become a bridge from the historically specific debacle of "the end of Communism" to a situating of subjectivity firmly within the ideological expanse of late capitalism, where a mutual reinforcement of market forces and subjectivity effects allows such nontotalized evidence to appear ready-to-hand. Popular culture becomes a condition "we" are in, and hence a shared subjectivity that is not subject to the particular claims of any failed orthodoxy. Finally, Žižek's references to the natural world are simply and universally a matter of representation and its material substrate — the Real identified as noumena after Kant.

In order to elucidate Žižek's second and third kinds of example, I want to insert the following key sequence from Alfred Hitchcock's *Rear Window*, a film discussed at a number of points in Žižek's work (and recently made widely available in a restored version).[8] In the realm of art, nothing could be more satisfying than the mastery of psychological analysis and figuration demonstrated in the film, as in the following sequence:

> Liza (Grace Kelly) bends down to kiss Jeff (James Stewart), suddenly in extreme close up and slow motion; continuing her seduction attempt, Liza snuggles close and sweet talks Jeff, but Jeff is obsessed with the possibility that Lars Thorwald (Raymond Burr) murdered his invalid wife, and won't pay attention to her; later, sitting in his wheelchair, Jeff ponders the imponderable while in the background, the two unlit windows of Thorwald's apartment glare at him, signifying nothing; at the moment of crisis, as Jeff is thrown from the window by Thorwald, scenes of panic erupt in the courtyard, and the film deliberately speeds up to the point of condensing the action into spasmodic, out-of-control lurches toward violence.

This sequence is precisely the kind of material with which Žižek thinks the negativity of ideological subjectivity. As a recurrent focus of analysis, it is the kind of popular cultural reference that brings us into contact with the Real. Such a moment appears in contrast to another register of the negative, positioned in relation to the ineffable noumena of the Kantian tradition that founds the discourse of negativity in Žižek's later critical theory. Here, on a somewhat wider screen, nothing could be more unsettling than the idea of a kind of "dark matter" that we can barely detect and that passes through everything, that fills up 80 percent of the universe but that until recently has gone undetected, until it was unveiled in a recent *New York Times* (via home delivery in major metropolitan areas):

> EVIDENCE OF MYSTERY PARTICLES STIRRING EXCITEMENT AND DOUBT
>
> The presumed particles would weigh at least 50 times as much as a proton and would almost always pass through other matter without a trace because of an extremely weak ability to interact with it. The new evidence, which so far has not been confirmed by other scientists, would suggest that space is swarming with enough of the particles to account for the long-sought "dark matter" that astronomers believe makes up some 80 percent of all the mass of the universe.[9]

The evocative gap between the historical anecdote of absent cause, the pleasures of cinematic fantasy, and the uneasiness of deep speculation on negativity, one may call "Žižekian." By the use of such examples, which are to be found everywhere in his work, Žižek goes through the fantasy in relation to the displacements of the Symbolic Order and the underlying substrate of the Lacanian Real, from his beginnings with the tradition of ideology criticism to his return to the critique of the subject. In separating these species of negativity in such a contrastive way, I want to develop their implications for the historicist content of Žižek's encounter with the Real in his epistemological anecdotes.

The second of my examples, the sequence from *Rear Window*, is a resolutely Žižekian one in its figure of subjectivity as answer of the Real to the question of the Other. Žižek's account, in his volume of film theory *Looking Awry*, is that the central dilemma of the film is Jeff's avoidance of Eros (marrying Liza) and his identification with the dark designs of Thorwald. The film emplots his deathward compulsion, figured in the two darkened windows glaring at him from the other side of the courtyard, which, in the manner of Lacan's sardine can, "don't see him."[10] This is the Lacanian gaze, the *objet a*, the nonexistent object known only in its effects, an object cause of desire that opens onto that which cannot be stabilized within the Symbolic Order. Hitchcock's films, in their status as self-conscious works of art, enact the kind of retrospection that makes such effects knowable in the course of psychoanalysis; it is thus possible literally to figure the gaze in the nonseeing eyes of the two windows (a formal requirement for figuration that generally goes without notice in psychoanalytic criticism). The construction of the film itself contains such objects, which work not simply in the depicted action but on the viewing experience of the spectator, as well: the first and last cuts, the introjection of slow motion and speeded-up shots within the conventional narrative, become literal examples of *anamorphosis*, the radical reordering of the experience of seeing that Lacan identifies in Holbein's painting *The Ambassadors*, with its grinning death's-head breaking through perspectival illusions and sending its disturbing message: constitutive of all acts of seeing is something that refuses to see you, that does not look back.[11] The entire universe of the film is thereby undermined, and we have only to identify with it: Jeff's anxiety and obsession with Thorwald intersects with our viewing experience of the film, which puts us in touch with that which undoes our position in the universe even as it will restore us to it.[12]

My final example, the dark matter that only recently was discovered to make up 80 percent of the universe, fits into Žižek's overarching project as an epistemological anecdote, but one severed from historical specificity except in the most general sense. Its appearance in the *New York Times* (as with *Rear Window*'s redistribution in malls everywhere) marks it as historical, in the sense that newspaper readers in a given historical epoch would imagine the force and necessity of a recently discovered fact of nature. As a figure for the most recent state of Žižek's project, it may serve as a touchstone or reality check for Žižek's progression from a historically based ideology critique to a revisionary synthesis of psychoanalysis with the philosophical tradition. As figure for the Real, it also allows us, in turn, to explicate the distinction between two kinds of negativity — Freudian death drive and Heideggerian Being-toward-Death — invoked at the end of "The Night of the World," the opening chapter of *The Ticklish Subject.*[13] In Žižek's work in general, Heidegger occurs as a kind of ghost figure or missing link between his early doctoral thesis and later Lacanian destiny, and he is summoned as well as a political influence in post–Cold War Central European politics, in the impossible notion of "a political movement that will directly refer to its historico-ontological foundation" (15). In his essay, Žižek calls for a return to the political ontology of Heidegger's early work, located precisely in the gap between the incomplete analysis of *Dasein* in early Heidegger and later Heidegger's "thought of Being." What this will require will be to reconstruct Heidegger's relationship to negativity via Lacan, in a reconciliation with the Lacanian Real that will involve more than a mere notice of Lacan's use of Heideggerian *Dasein* for his concept of *extimité*, or the exteriority of desire. The inaccessible substrate of dark matter, as site of fascination and horror, thus indicates the place of the absent third term or "vanishing mediator" in Žižek's triangulation of the Real between Heidegger and Lacan.

In an immanent critique of Heidegger that is neither affirmative nor dismissive, Žižek seeks the missing link between his early failure to entirely get beyond metaphysics in the analysis of *Dasein* (in the standard account, due to the fact that his analysis itself was too rigidly methodological), and his later failure to engage negativity: "What Heidegger seems unable to endorse is a concrete 'political' engagement that would accept its necessary, constitutive blindness" (15). Between Heidegger's inherently political analysis of *Dasein* — "by which [man] actively assumes his 'thrownness' into a finite historical situation," which "consists in an abyssal [inaccessible or unknowable] decision not grounded in any universal ontological structure [not guaranteed by any preexisting scheme of values]" (20) — and his later "thought of Being" seen as a fatalistic regression, Žižek locates the missing link: the abandoned problematic of the transcendental imagination in Kant, as allowing the spontaneity of a political decision or choice without succumbing to either metaphysics or mystification.[14] In Žižek's summary, Heidegger realized that in Kant,

> imagination is simultaneously receptive and positing, 'passive' (in it, we are affected by sensible images) and 'active' (the subject himself freely gives birth to these images . . .). And Heidegger's emphasis is on how spontaneity itself can be conceived only through this unity with an irreducible element of passive receptivity that characterizes human finitude: if the subject were to succeed in getting rid of receptivity and gaining direct access to the noumenal itself [as the site of radical and uncontained freedom, as opposed to the conceptual constraints of the phenomenal], he would lose the very 'spontaneity' of his existence. (*TS*, 27–28)

The dilemma is to conceive of spontaneity in the passively receptive forms of the imagination, and to show they are motivated by abstract notions of freedom properly inaccessible to them. This Heidegger could not do; what he encounters in failing to complete the project of *Being and Time* is "the abyss of radical subjectivity announced in Kantian transcendental imagination [its relation to freedom], and he recoiled from this abyss into the thought of the historicity of Being" (23) — as opposed to what Žižek wants, "to assert *the ontological incompleteness of 'reality' itself* . . . a traumatic excess, a foreign body that cannot be integrated into it" (60). In his failed encounter with dark matter, Heidegger "is unable to address the excessive dimension of subjectivity, its inherent madness" (61).

Returning to the dropped account of the Kantian transcendental imagination as the "vanishing mediator" between early and late Heidegger, Žižek wants to identify precisely the source of the imagination's "mysterious emergence of 'transcendental' spontaneity" (61), also known as "madness" because not subsumable under any rational category. The first step is to identify Kant's avoidance of negativity in his account of the imagination's synthesis of "pure intuition" of noumena, which is then brought into accord with the schemata of the understanding. "Kant passes over in silence the opposite power of imagination emphasized later in Hegel — namely, imagination *qua* the 'activity of dissolution'" (29). This Žižek figures as the "night of the world," taken from a key passage in Hegel:

> The human being is this night, this empty nothing, that contains everything in its simplicity — an unending wealth of many representations, images, of which none belongs to him — or which are not present. This night, the interior of nature, that exists here — pure self — in phantasmagorical representations, is night all around it, in which here shoots a bloody head — there another white ghastly apparition, suddenly here before it, and just so disappears. One catches sight of this night when one looks human beings in the eye — into a night that becomes awful. (30)

This night of the world could easily be figured as the dark matter of the universe just discovered the other day, except for the ghastly apparitions that abound in it. It is precisely the connection between the terrifying inertness of "this empty nothing" and phantasmagoria of floating body parts that Žižek wants to see as constitutive of imagination itself. In order to get from inchoate noumena to the ordered world of phenomena, the imagination itself must first accomplish a "'mad' gesture of radical withdrawal from reality which opens up the space for its symbolic (re)constitution" (35). Such a "withdrawal-into-self constitutive of the subject" (ibid.), identified by Žižek with the death drive, compares to two moments of the sublime in Kant's account of imagination: that it cannot fully synthesize its intuitions (because the understanding cannot keep up with "the magnitude of the apprehended perceptions"), and that it is disciplined, as it were from above, by the transcendental Law (which seeks to discipline the spontaneous "auto-affection of [the] imagination; 38). In either case, "the imagination can reveal the noumenal dimension only in a negative way" (39), but how is it able to do this? Either we are confronted with a discontinuity (between imagination and noumena), or negativity is contained within the imagination in some way, so that "the 'imagination' is already a name for the violent gesture that opens up and sustains the very gap between noumenal and phenomenal" (39).

The imagination is violent, initiated by "the negative act of . . . abstraction, self-withdrawal into the 'night of the world'"; this is "the mysterious emergence of transcendental spontaneity" (61) that Heidegger missed in failing to take into account the shipwreck of Being on the shoals of the Real, the inaccessible. In so doing, the imagination produces in its encounter with the night of the world the fantasms of a "pre-ontological domain" akin to the unconscious and experienced as a "*wild, pre-synthetic imagination*" (52), "in which the void of subjectivity is confronted by the spectral photoreality of 'partial objects,' bombarded with these apparitions of *le corps morcelé* [here a bloody head, there an ghastly apparition, and so on]" (63).[15] Žižek's argument is that Heidegger could not tolerate an opening of the imagination to the "monstrous" in this sense: to the "horrifying experience of dispersed 'organs without a body' . . . of its *membra disjecta* freely floating around" (*TS*, 52). Reading Kant "with David Lynch," however, Žižek relocates the death drive at "the birth of subjectivity," as precisely a destructive madness beyond categories of reason that "replaces reality with [body parts], with a series of organs as stand-ins for the 'immortal' [i.e., undead] libido" (52). This negative moment initiates the domain of spontaneity before its subordination to Law, even as it brings one into contact with that which is inert and dead, evoking "the horrifying experience of dispersed 'organs without a body'" (52) before the mirror stage. Precisely in the gap between noumena and phenomena, Žižek interprets the imagination as the opening to fantasy and negativity, an antagonistic process that challenges the categories of reason and brings about subjectivity. The dark matter of the universe, which remains unconfirmed, thus excites our interest in two ways: as immortal, ever-during substance, it is as close to noumena as we will get; as fantasy of that which exceeds our comprehension, it introduces a gap into our "engaged immersion in the world." This is the night of the world as birth of imagination, producing the monsters and part objects that keep us awake. Of course, if our categories of understanding function well, in a scientific manner, little disruption will be experienced.

What becomes of the historicity of the epistemological anecdote if a culturally very unspecific newspaper report of dark matter fits so readily into Žižek's account of the subject? Otherwise put, if we are excited by a fantasy of dark matter, we are historically situated nonetheless, in this case by a precisely Heideggerian instance of "thrownness." A kind of transhistorical interpretive practice takes over in Žižek's work, however, that begins arguably with the transformation of incommensurate, historical ideological formations (say, the nonreciprocal fantasies of East and West before 1989) into something like film scripts, whose plot devices can be cannibalized and re-presented in an ultimately postmodern work of critical pastiche. Žižek's account of the imagination, in fact, may be precisely a way of taking into account the formal dimensions of his work, which ranges over every conceivable critical tendency and popular fixation, toward an effect that is more obdurate or dispersive than unifying. Žižek's body of work, then, is a moment of the opening to negativity and fantasy that he theorizes. Is it possible to bring together the shared conventions of his historical anecdotes, references to cinema and popular culture, and the obscure particularity of his epistemological examples into a more encompassing Žižekian poetics? Žižek seems to hint at the difficulty of the formal organization of his work when he writes, "the unity the subject endeavors to impose on the sensuous multitude via its synthetic activity is always erratic, eccentric, unbalanced, 'unsound', something that is externally and violently imposed on to the multitude, never a simple impassive act of discerning the inherent subterranean connections between the *membra disjecta*" (33). Such a self-consciously constructivist moment is rare for Žižek, even negatively, but it points to a possibility of form that is not simply the unfolding of cinematic fantasy: "This is what, in the domain of cinematic art, Eisenstein's concept of 'intellectual montage' seems to aim at: intellectual activity brings together bits and pieces torn by the power of imagination from their proper context, violently recomposing them into a new unity that gives birth to an unexpected new meaning" (33). The constructivist moment, in Žižek, is precisely the encounter with the Real — the final question is the synthetic form of the imagination that results. Are we sitting in some postmodern, multinational cinema, passively watching film after film (*Lenin in Warsaw*, *Rear Window*, *Dark Matter*, *Mulholland Drive*), or do we see ourselves precisely as the makers and promulgators of these scenarios? The encounter with the Real might begin right here, with the imperative to construct.

THE NOTHING THAT IS

What would happen if we were to substitute another category of example, poetry, for the historical anecdotes, samples of film and popular culture, and figures for inaccessible nature in Žižek? Poetry, as well, may function as an encounter with the Real, in the historical unfolding of self-consciousness or in the constructivist sense of the imagination. The benefits of a Žižekian account of poetics, not merely a poetics of Žižek, are many, beginning in its possibilities for imagination rather than symptomatology, and I have been exploring them in American modernist and postmodernist poets, from Laura Riding, Kenneth Fearing, and Ezra Pound to Robert Creeley, Edward Dorn, and Robert Duncan.[16] In this section, I want to illustrate such a Žižekian poetics of the Real in poetic examples that seem to refer to his metaconcepts directly: the Real, the Thing, *objet a*, and Other. Of course, none of these notions "exist" in the sense of an object that can be pointed to and described; they are known in their effects in the unfolding of the transferential dialogue, as are all psychoanalytic concepts. But if the classical film narratives of Hitchcock may, through their rigorous and self-conscious construction, provide analogues for psychoanalytic concepts (even presenting them directly, as in the Dali dream sequence in *Spellbound*), poetry as well may provide formal analogies for psychoanalytic artifacts. What Žižek adds to the basic Freudian/Lacanian substrate of analysis is the framework of a cultural dialogue and the claim that cultural forms are the royal road to ideology.

Jean-François Lyotard, in *The Postmodern Condition*, offers a shorthand test for the distinction between modernism and postmodernism that bears on poetic exemplarity. To begin with, he calls "modern the art which devotes its 'little technical expertise' . . . to present the fact that the unpresentable exists. To make visible that there is something which can be conceived and which can neither be seen nor made visible: this is what is at stake in modern painting." As his test of the modern, Lyotard identifies its forms of representation with the presentation of the negative after the analytic of the sublime in Kant: "Kant himself shows the way when he names 'formlessness, the absence of form,' as a possible index to the unpresentable. He also says of the empty 'abstraction' which the imagination experiences when in search for a presentation of the infinite (another unpresentable): this abstraction itself is like a presentation of the infinite, its 'negative presentation.'"[17] While Lyotard is not thinking of the "sublime object" in Žižek's psychoanalytic sense, the centrality of Kant for both brings them into alignment (this is evident, beyond Lyotard's intention, in his "little technical expertise," which presents the classical form of negativity known as castration anxiety). The modern work of art stabilizes aesthetic experience by presenting something that exceeds or is lacking in its form of representation.

Examples of this are everywhere in the work of the avant-garde, from Duchamp's urinal to Malevich's black square on a white background to the "all-over" paintings of Pollock, and in poetry as well: consider perhaps the most famous instance of modernist negativity in American poetry, Wallace Stevens's "The Snow Man."[18] The poem compacts a series of self-canceling negatives that begins with a paradoxical requirement for a subtraction of perception and sense in order to perceive and understand: "One must have a mind of winter / to regard the frost and the boughs / Of the pine-trees crusted with snow." By the end of the poem's five stanzas of tightly subordinated description and logic, Stevens has worked to bring the percipient, by analogy with the play of negativity in the poem, to the level of the bare nothing of the depicted scene: "For the listener, who listens in the snow, / And, nothing himself, beholds / Nothing that is not there and the nothing that is." It is unclear which nothing is which: the play of logical negativity, which cancels out the reader's ability to locate a clear relation to the depicted scene, or the scene itself, the zero degree of nature as noumena and, at least in theory, unpresentable. Of course, the payoff for aesthetic appreciation is that the reader simply reads the series of negatives, survives the logical reduction of sense, and entirely enjoys the scene: this is Stevens's lyrical strategy. Along the way, however, an important relation of logical contradiction and nature is claimed: if the opposition between the "nothing that is not there and the nothing that is" is undecidable, and provides the thrill of the poem (the excessive *jouissance* of the Real), the unpresentable subtrate of nature is thereby affirmed. The poem, in its simultaneously tortuous logic and ephemeral pleasure, conforms perfectly to Žižek's account of the Real: "The Real is therefore simultaneously the hard, impenetrable kernel resisting symbolization *and* a pure chimerical entity which has in itself no ontological consistency."[19] That the logical play of the poem fails in the face of the scene, and that this false determination of self-canceling negativity is experienced as pleasure, leads us to the Real, a logic of contradiction in relation to an unpresentable object unlike the "negation of the negation" sublated to a higher level of the dialectic. In order to specify this nonrelation of contradiction to the inaccessible object, Žižek goes on to describe three logics of opposition or contradiction that characterize the Lacanian orders of Imaginary, Symbolic, and Real. In the Imaginary, "two poles of opposition are complementary; together they build a harmonious totality" (as in the unity of the sexes); in the Symbolic, "the identity of each of the moments consists in its difference to the opposite moment" (differences are held in common as each other's lack, for example, in the antagonistic relations of race, where black and white are constitutively grounded in the lack of the other). Finally, in the Real, "each pole passes immediately into its opposite; each is already in itself its own opposite. . . . The point is that Being in itself, when we try to grasp it 'as it is', in its pure abstraction and indeterminacy, without further specification, reveals itself to be Nothingness"[20] — a form of pure contradiction revealed in the logical impossibility of Stevens's poetic negations.

Stevens, of course, has a safety valve: the reassuring formal perfections of art. If the percipient/reader is going somewhat mad trying to locate herself in the subordinated play of negativity in the poem, the beauty of the winter scene remains to reward her efforts. For an even better account of the relation of logical negativity to the Real, we may look to the poems of Laura Riding, where the aesthetic solution is precisely undermined.

ROOM

Whatever is before goes behind.
Each makes room for the next of kind.
The unborn beggars cry 'Unfed'
Until all are born and dead.
Death is the crumb
To which they come;
God the division of it,
The nothing and no more of it
When the procreative doom
Stops making room —
The name of charity
By which to be is not to be.[21]

Riding's starkness, as a lived experience, exceeds Stevens's by some degree; her poem, rather than unraveling subordinated negations that then can be pleasantly overcome, situates the reading in a precise relation to temporal progression where "whatever is before," in the future, moves through the poem to its past, where it becomes "born and dead." In Žižek's discussion of Walter Benjamin's "Angel of History," which faces the past as it is blown forward, such an antiprogressive futurity is linked to the presentation of symptoms in the transferential dialogue.[22] In the poem, these move from the inchoate status of the "unborn" to something taken care of, put to rest, "dead": homeostasis achieved, "Death is the crumb / To which they come." On this analogy, Riding situates her poem precisely in the position of the analysand who, in relation to God or the analyst, realizes "The nothing and no more of it / When the procreative doom / Stops making room"; she sees the anxiety of deathward futurity precisely in the moment of temporal unfolding. Remarkably, the poem identifies the general dilemma of the "forced choice" of Being-in-Time with the gendered situation of procreation. As a woman, Riding may equally give birth or not, but in either case she is inscribed by the paradox of "biology as destiny" as an inaccessible order. The Real, here, is the procreative body that the unresolvable contradiction of the poem's symptomatic unfolding simultaneously can and cannot have a relation to. In ripping the veil of aesthetic appreciation from the perception of this dilemma in the Real, Riding sarcastically juxtaposes Christian charity with birth control: "The name of charity / By which to be is not to be." The charitable act is to deny the birth, insofar as woman's dilemma of "biology as destiny" cannot be admitted into the Symbolic Order.

Louis Zukofsky's untitled poem from *55 Poems*, discussed in chapter 4, provides a third example of modernist negativity. In my previous account, the poem gives evidence of a constructivist moment — as I formulated it, "an elusive transition in the unfolding work of culture in which social negativity — the experience of rupture, an act of refusal — invokes a fantasmatic future — a horizon of possibility, an imagination of participation." Here I will bracket the beginning and end of the poem to isolate its negative moment:

> Of course, commerce will not complete
> Anything, yet the harbor traffic is busy,
> there shall be a complete fragment
>
> Of—
>
> Nothing, look![23]

"Nothing," in a manner reminiscent of Stevens's resolution of contraries, leads directly to an ambivalent observation of the scene: either the commerce in its self-evidence is all there is, or it will be completed in revolution — the observer (a metropolitan "New Jew" in DuPlessis's sense) is exactly the point of chiasmus. What we witness here as readers goes deeper, however, to the Kantian account of imagination in confrontation with noumena, as the poem reveals a simultaneously "passively receptive" moment of synthesis of sense data, and an "actively destructive" fragmentation of the unity of the scene. This is how the self-evidence of the economic, in turn, may become the deferred horizon of revolution: in the imagination, which reaches its limit of penetration, but not of desire, in the "outside" of the scene. On the one hand, incompletion prevents totalization, which in turn prevents agency; on the other, incompletion demands totalization — resulting in an impossible totality of which the poem is both the cause and evidence. The poem, but in an entirely different aesthetic register than Stevens, confronts the "nothing that is not there and the nothing that is" in identifying the effect not with beauty but with history.

I want to focus on that *nothing* and its simultaneous demand for completion and presentation of incompletion as the literary equivalent of the "object cause of desire," the hole within the deferred whole that permits identification of the modernist example with its form. As a placeholder for that which is inaccessible, cannot be referred to, but which has the effect of releasing *jouissance* that will make the revolution, this "nothing" is as close as one can get to the Lacanian *objet a*, Žižek's sublime object of ideological fantasy. As well, it is precisely inscribed within a dialectic of seeing and what cannot be seen, or what "does not see you": for while Zukofsky may observe the incomplete totality of commerce, commerce is certainly indifferent to him — it proceeds as if he does not exist. This absolute indifference is the hard core of the Real which resists symbolization; all the poet can do is focus his attention on a substitute object, the "nothing" inscribed in his poem. The poem, then, triangulates the Lacanian concepts which are of concern to us here: the Real is the hole or gap in the Symbolic Order on which the poem is predicated; commerce itself, as massively energetic and indifferent, becomes the sublime object or Thing that cannot be approached; and the poem's concretization of "nothing" rescripts the object cause of desire to the incompletion of the scene, as an object known only in effects. It is the relation between these metaconcepts, finally, that constitutes the sublime object of ideology: in Žižek's account of the Lacanian object, "*the place logically precedes the objects which occupy it*: what the objects, in their given positivity, are masking is not some other, more substantial order of objects but simply the emptiness, the void they are filling out." The sublime object thus "is 'an object elevated to the level of *Das Ding*' [that] occupies the sacred/forbidden space of jouissance," created in the void of the Symbolic.[24] All of this, of course, is undertaken as the answer of the Real" to the question of the Other — which could be seen as history, literature, or meaning: "What do you want?" Zukofsky's symptomatic answer may be, "Revolution," but the poem testifies to a greater mastery of his situation, as it triangulates history and literature in the construction of meaning.

We have seen, as well, an example of this logic of the void in the cuts from *Rear Window*. In one cut, two windows "signifying nothing" stare back at Jeff in his window; the *objet a* here is "the point from which the picture itself looks back at us." There are also two examples of Lacanian *anamorphosis* in the slow motion and speeded-up shots, which break the narrative plane and open up the dynamics of seeing to "excess and lack." Zukofsky's interruption of the inferred visual panning of the harbor with the deformation of "nothing" approximates such a radical shift of perspective, a moment of undoing if not a memento mori. The "nothing" that he not so much notices but inscribes in the poem generates an ideological/critical effect: it is the point at which the deferred completion of the harbor, in the totalizing thought of revolution, becomes a moment of nonseeing that subjectivizes us and at the same time prevents closure of the social field. This is not so much a paradox as a crux, an example of "forced choice" in which what Zukofsky "will have been" — poet or revolutionary — is determined by the poem, though he cannot claim to know it yet. Just as Jeff's moment of crisis, caught been Liza and Thorwald, is correlative to the nonseeing of the *objet a*, Zukofsky's "nothing" is a determinate moment in which the politics of poetry (as lack) cross over to the ideological fantasy of revolution (as excess). Poetry wins, by taking on the deferred knowledge in its incommensurability. The discredited notion of modernist mastery may be reconsidered in another light here, in relation to what Zukofsky cannot have known but was able to demonstrate in the poem.

In moving to a postmodern register of the sublime object, we will find a more extended and unmediated use of the modernist logic of negativity than in the modernists. As a good example of a postmodern strategy that depends on and amplifies the psychodynamics of the modernism that preceded it, Michael Snow's experimental film *Wavelength* (1966) offers an extended formal analogy for the *objet a* as Žižek interprets it in narrative cinema. In the film, a very long tracking shot continually narrows down to what originally seems to be a very distant speck on an apartment wall, which, as we get closer and closer, turns out to be a pretty ordinary landscape photograph — so it turns out that "nothing" was the point of all that visual attention, the prolongation of looking until we doubt what it is we see. In discussing the logic of Hitchcock's vocabulary of shots, Žižek notes that either a slowed-down or speeded-up tracking shot works by subtracting the object focused on from the cinematic continuity: "Delay and precipitousness are two modes of capturing the object-cause of desire."[25] The sequence from *Rear Window* involves just such a precipitous interruption of continuity, either fast or slow, as an effect of *anamorphosis*. In Snow's film, the very long tracking shot, rather than making the object visible, actually subtracts it from the perceptual field, and we stop seeing it. What we do see, however, is the act of seeing precisely in terms of that which can no longer be seen. Jacques Alain-Miller's diagram of an object removed from a visual field supports Žižek's point:

> It is precisely because the object *a* is removed from the field of reality that it frames it. If I withdraw from the surface of this picture the piece I represent by a shaded square, I get what we might call a frame: a frame for a hole, but also a frame of the rest of the surface. Such a frame could be created by any window. So object *a* is such a surface fragment, and it is its subtraction from reality that frames it. The subject, as barred subject — as want-of-being — is this hole.

Such a reading of framing by subtraction provides an alternate approach to interpreting many examples of Conceptual Art, clearly an influence on Snow's film. It is not simply the positive, "analytic" question of the nature of visuality or seeing that is involved with this work; rather, these questions are asked in the nature of an unanswerable question that results in nothing like the kinds of ontological accounts offered by logical positivism. We may consider here, as an example of subtraction of the object as frame, the text of Joseph Kosuth's *"Titled" (Art as Idea as Idea)* (1967), an inaugural work of conceptual art:

> **–ob•ject** (ob'jekt), *n.* [ML. *Objectum*, prop. neut. of L. *objectus*, pp.] Something that may be perceived by the senses, esp. by sight or touch, or a visible or tangible thing (as, "Children, from their very birth, are daily growing acquainted with the *objects* about them": J. Butler's "Analogy of Religion." i. 5); a material thing; also, anything that may be presented to the mind (as *objects* of thought); also, a thing with reference to the impression it makes on the mind (as, "No other allegorist [besides Bunyan] has ever been able to touch the heart, and to make abstractions *objects* of terror, pity, and of love": Macaulay's "Hist. of Eng.," vii.)[26]

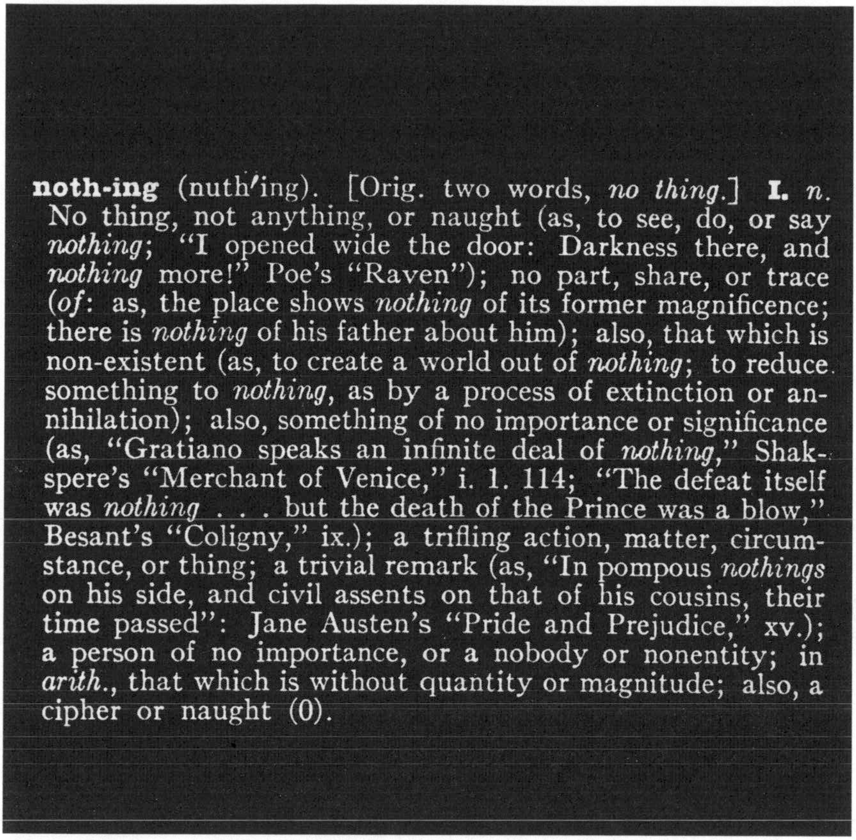

noth-ing (nuth′ing). [Orig. two words, *no thing*.] **I.** *n*. No thing, not anything, or naught (as, to see, do, or say *nothing*; "I opened wide the door: Darkness there, and *nothing* more!" Poe's "Raven"); no part, share, or trace (*of*: as, the place shows *nothing* of its former magnificence; there is *nothing* of his father about him); also, that which is non-existent (as, to create a world out of *nothing*; to reduce something to *nothing*, as by a process of extinction or annihilation); also, something of no importance or significance (as, "Gratiano speaks an infinite deal of *nothing*," Shakspere's "Merchant of Venice," i. 1. 114; "The defeat itself was *nothing* . . . but the death of the Prince was a blow," Besant's "Coligny," ix.); a trifling action, matter, circumstance, or thing; a trivial remark (as, "In pompous *nothings* on his side, and civil assents on that of his cousins, their time passed": Jane Austen's "Pride and Prejudice," xv.); a person of no importance, or a nobody or nonentity; in *arith*., that which is without quantity or magnitude; also, a cipher or naught (0).

55. Joseph Kosuth, untitled work ("nothing"), from First Investigation, *1966–68.*

This text, reversed in a white on black Photostat and mounted on the wall as a material object, removes the object from perception as an entailment of seeing the work. Its goes much further than logical paradox (in that it refers to an object that is other than itself), creating a frame by subtraction in Miller's sense, with its entailed object investments. Kosuth comments on these effects in his oddly edited text, which highlights, of the many senses of an "object," both its availability to vision (which is made impossible by the use of the text as standing in place of the object) and its investment of "terror, pity, and of love" — precisely the effects of *jouissance* that attend a missing object as cause of desire. This reading is reinforced by the contingency of another of Kosuth's definitional works, on "nothing," in which negativity is not concept but the failure of representation (fig. 55).

Such a shift from missing object to the frame (as work of art, gallery, or museum) is to be found everywhere in Conceptual Art. We may see it as well in a photograph of a 1969 performance by Kosuth in which he appears immersed in a pile of paperback texts of philosophy — but with sunglasses on, not seeing them.[27] In subtracting the object of his immediate attention, Kosuth draws our attention to the tables covered with paperbacks surrounding him as an impossibility of knowledge — if we cannot read what is in front of us, we will never get through these. Here we have an apt visual example for the postmodern condition as exceeding the stabilization of the sublime object in modernism. In Lyotard's distinction between modern and postmodern uses of negativity, "modern aesthetics is an aesthetic of the sublime, though a nostalgic one. It allows the unpresentable to be put forward only as the missing contents; but the form, because of its recognizable consistency, continues to offer to the reader or viewer matter for solace and pleasure" (*PC*, 81). The postmodern, on the other hand, is that which "puts forward the unpresentable in presentation itself; that which denies itself the solace of good forms, the consensus of a taste which would make it possible to share collectively the nostalgia for the unattainable" (ibid.). While Lyotard does not go far enough in understanding how negativity in modernism actually sets up the desire for its nostalgic reinvestment, as we see in the examples above, he allows us to distinguish the boundedness of modernist form from the unboundedness of the postmodern, which not being regulated by taste, makes up its formal rules as it goes along, as in the kinds of language games Lyotard substitutes for truth content. The postmodern work "has the character of an *event*," coming both too late and too soon for the artist: translating Lyotard's terms to Žižek's, the postmodern work's contact with the Real is extensive, temporalized, and not stabilized by form. Rather than the focused moments of the gaze as *objet a* in *Rear Window*, we observe how the long tracking shot in *Wavelength* makes an impossible object out of the act of seeing itself. Rather than the "nothing" that is stabilized in the modern poem, we have the negated object in Kosuth's conceptual art, which makes the entire work of art the site of a provocative impossibility.

As a conclusive example of postmodern negativity, New York School poet Ron Padgett's well-known conceptual sonnet repeats the same line fourteen times as a variation on the theme of modernist negativity, but in this case as the entire form of the poem:

Nothing in that drawer.
Nothing in that drawer.
Nothing in that drawer.

Nothing in that drawer.
Nothing in that drawer.
Nothing in that drawer. . . .[28]

One of the most conceptual sonnets ever written (and there have been many), the poem performs in language subtraction and reframing similar to Snow's film and Kosuth's conceptual art. What is in the drawer is removed from our attention; the question of content concerns, rather, the minimal, abstract form of the sonnet itself. Perhaps the sonnet is nothing but the object cause of desire itself repeated fourteen times, either as a tragedy of the compulsion to repeat or a Three Stooges comedy routine. Something else is going on at another level, however, as the figure for negativity entirely fills the frame, allowing neither contrastive distancing nor irony. Here we enter the domain of the postmodern, on properly rigorous terms: the moment when a silkscreen full of Warhol soup cans is doing something else than ironizing the commodity form (and predicating, as would Zukofsky, a poetics of deferred completion). Rather, the repetition of commerce repels rather than invites the stabilization of the Symbolic Order, and we have Lyotard's criterion for the postmodern: the sublimity of the construction of the work itself, extending into the lifeworld if need be, which the work of art refuses to sublimate or formally encode. Žižek shows how such a move from the modern to the postmodern involves a paradigm shift from the *objet a* to what Lacan called *das Ding*, the Thing, as the place "between two deaths" (organic and symbolic), or in our case, between two nothings: the one that occasions the work, and the one constructed by the work itself. This is the location of the impossible Thing: "the real-traumatic kernel in the midst of the symbolic order," a deeply nonhistorical moment of abstraction occuring in the midst of history: "As soon as 'brute', pre-symbolic reality is historicized/symbolized, it 'secretes', it isolates the empty, 'indigestible' place of the Thing."[29] As "the empty thought of an underlying, inaccessible X" that precedes the night of the world, the Thing is the converse of the *objet a*: it is not the nothing of the subject's lack but an excess that blocks entry into the Symbolic Order.[30] In Padgett's poem, the brute reality not symbolized by art may be culture itself in a nonironic mode; abstraction here leads to exclusion, not irony. The poem as Thing destroys signification, revealing a deeper negativity than Zukofsky's modernist moment. Suddenly, the entire universe turns into the dark matter of nothing in that drawer: that's all we get.

Postmodern negativity reappears in two poems written after Padgett's

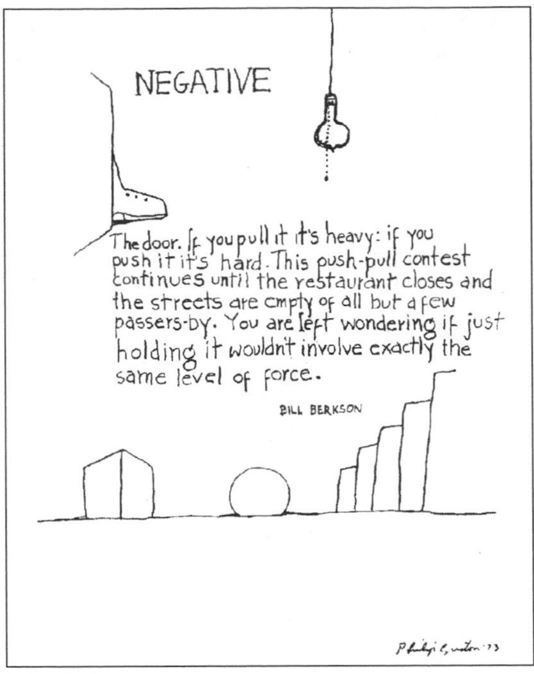

56. Bill Berkson and Philip Guston, Negative, *1973.*

example — the first by New York School poet (living in California) Bill Berkson, realized in a drawing by Philip Guston that highlights the absurdity of its logical contradiction (fig. 56):

NEGATIVE

The door. If you pull it it's heavy; if you
push it it's hard. This push-pull contest
continues until the restaurant closes and
the streets are empty of all but a few
passers-by. You are left wondering if just
holding it wouldn't involve exactly the
same level of force.[31]

Berkson describes a liminal zone of vanishing mediation between the world of the door and restaurant and a thought experiment designed to test them. The question, again, returns to irony: Is the fact that holding the door might involve the same level of force a comment on the impossibility of representation (we cannot represent the opposing forces that are held in stasis), or is a more fatalistic dynamic of "forced choice" inscribed in the perennial return to the push/pull contest the door enacts (either way, open or closed, the same state of affairs will result; you can't win)? The door as device is an identifiable route to homeostasis; one can only imagine one's state of exhaustion, with the door itself winning the battle at the poem's philosophical end. It is, finally, the identification with the termination of the thought experiment of the door as the inevitable return to the world, where one is left simply holding it, that defines the poem's negativity. The poem records the breakdown of signification, as the entire mechanical explanation for the position of the door is irrelevant, as it shows the *jouissance* the paradox of the door is holding in place.

A poem I wrote about the same time addresses a similar canceling out of excess:

NEGATIVE

At the bottom of the lake is a small stream
of black liquid. A sentence assumes more
than it admits. Oil over water is anti-
matter. Water over oil? One will not look
at another. Buildings turn inside out.
Bright artificial lights like places to
avoid. Thinking stops to generalized lines.
Central figure in landscape is obliterated.[32]

The black liquid at the bottom of the lake is the Lacanian Thing, radiating impossibility in all directions, turning the visual landscape inside out. All signification is excessive; we reach a liminal zone where oil and water reverse polarities and where even their status as matter is in doubt. This excess of dark matter is conjoined to the impossibility of sight: due to the glare, it is impossible to look at the Thing. Its brightness is like being in the world's largest Kmart, which the whole world has become. There is no difference, here, between being outside or inside. Reason's attempt to take control over such a state of affairs is turned back, only to become the generality of failed compulsion. The subject has exploded; its impossibility is the Real of the inverted landscape it finds itself within. This poem was written in California in the late 1970s, on a bright spring day by the side of Lake Merritt in Oakland. It is a real poem, as well as a poem of the Real. Its interest in linking a psychology of glare and impossible nature, at the same time, is characteristic of much work from the West Coast in that period, visible in such artists as Robert Bechtle and Edward Ruscha, where postmodern glare meets the aporia of consumer culture. In other words, there are particular cultural and historical registers for its use of the effects of the Lacanian Thing, however outside of history Žižek imagines such a concept to be.

In extending the logic of the postmodern negativity of Padgett, Berkson, and myself toward cultural critique, I want to end with a question of the historicity of the Real. Given a poem like the following, how do we return the negative displacements that constitute ideological fantasy to the specific historical contexts in which they are obtained?

SILENCE

    My name a death's head
    A hard circle to be more
such rules. Which the eye will give
Diamonds one light shines from
    the house within, recording.
Held up, this account seems
reflecting back
    the same mind as glass
    Justified within.
Cut before day, apposed rage.

His withholding leaves both senses
he has given her, which, through
    the outward sides, make light
The numbers crowd around, tabloid
    to compare.
    The report flat
a moving picture each from spot
seen into, are shining forth.
    Then, I understand
    so my scattered body.

    The given sight
    none he will have.
A picture in part of, to make
then destroy it. The sun shines
    directly into eyes'
decline, do not see. Disguised
    as what it did

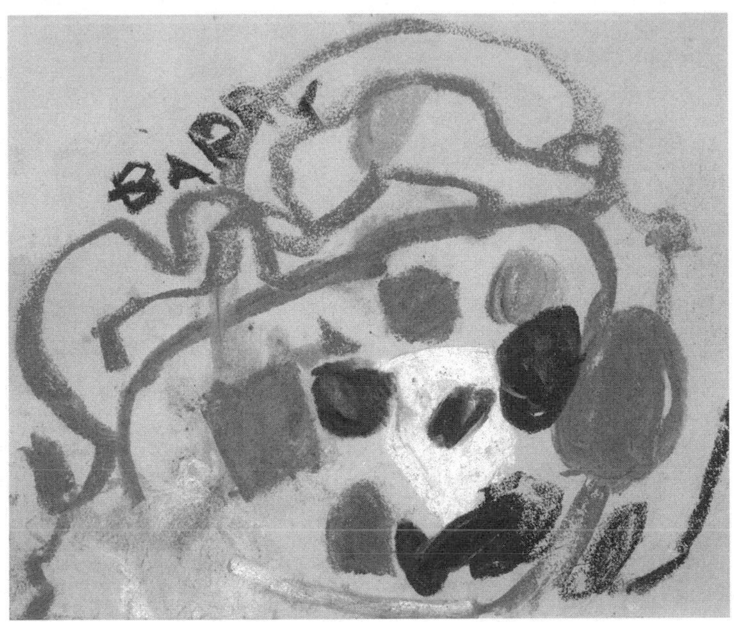

57. Barrett Watten, childhood drawing, c. 1951. 12 × 10".

And meant no noise.
A world is each, to the other
identified white, with lines. . . . [33]

The poem was written about 1978 and published in *This* 8, whose cover, depicting the form of a building emerging from the ruins of textual fragmentation, I now regard as the most constructivist in the series (fig. 15). "Silence," then, locates an early instance of the constructivist moment in the sequence of my own work. As with Zukofsky's harbor scene, it involves a simultaneously passively receptive drawing together of strands of linguistic association (taken, as I recall, from the footnotes to John Donne's poems in a scholarly edition, as well as from materials generated in dreams), and a destructively active dismantling of discursive coherence at the level of the sentence. It is close to what Žižek is referring to in the figure of the night of the world, complete with the *corps morcelé* of a fragmented body before its stabilization in the imaginary. I think this is what Žižek is talking about as well in his derivation of the imagination in Kant: as a violent but productive undoing of rational categories in contact with the Real (which would be both the inaccessible historical truth of Donne's poetry and the dream I had just the other night). In what sense, it may be asked, is the poem historical? That is a question that is only accessible to an analysis outside the proper bounds of this discussion — but one that will have to have been answered when the poem is properly read. I can only suggest its history by juxtaposing it with a drawing I made as a child, circa 1951–52, likely recovered from an old trunk of personal history, as a key to the poem (fig. 57). With such evidence, from the cultural context of annihilation during the Cold War period and specifically the Korean War, one may augment the violent ahistoricism of Žižek's account of the transcendental imagination, as instanced in the poem, with historical evidence of the Real.

LIMIT SITUATIONS

If a dialectic of tradition, revolt, and recuperation (either through a "failure" of aesthetic tendency or institutionalization) has been an unconscious framework for much thinking on the avant-garde, it is important to recast negativity in terms that do not yield such a predictable result.[34] Yet the Lacanian vocabulary of Real, Thing, and *objet a* may lead as well to a one-size-fits-all negativity based in trauma and its rupture of the Symbolic Order. It is necessary, then, to continue to explore other frameworks for negativity as components of a larger family resemblance, if not conceptual unity, that defines the limits and uses of the term in literature and art. Here I want to locate, in a more provisional manner, the place of negativity in two other philosophical systems, those of Martin Heidegger and Michel Foucault, and their entailments for the forms and methods of the avant-garde.

When the complete seventy volumes of Heidegger's collected writings are available on CD-ROM in English translation, it will be interesting to search for the phrase "avant-garde."[35] Unlike many of the obsessional formulations in Heidegger's vocabulary, it seems to have disappeared on its first use. Its eruption in an early review article on Karl Jaspers's *Psychology of Worldviews* (1919–20; unpublished until 1973), at about the time of the emergence of Berlin Dada, reveals a conflicted resonance of the avant-garde with the themes of destruction and anxiety in his work.[36] In his review, Heidegger takes up Jaspers's promising but inadequate concept of *Weltanschauungen*, "worldviews," in order to conduct a more intensive questioning of the historicity of experience. He asks, "What kind of explanation is required for our 'existence,'" if, as Jaspers claims, "the whole of life, i.e., life itself, is something about which we can say nothing directly"? Not only can we not approach the problem directly, through some form of observation or description; we cannot even describe "*the problem of our initial approach*" to existence without risking premature totalization or determination of a merely "regional" characterization. Thus,

> we should make the preliminary remark that this problem of our initial approach is such that cannot be settled through empty formalistic reflections. And it is just as pressing that this problem should not be considered something "out of the ordinary" and "novel" that allows us to raise a new commotion in philosophy and to curry favor with the hustle and bustle of an *avant-garde* culture that is at bottom really hungry for other things, even if it does display wonderful religious antics.[37]

The violence of the breakdown in Heidegger's style is marked. As the opposite of mere formalism, the avant-garde is "pressing" even as it aligns itself with the emptiness and hyperactivity of the culture at large, which paradoxically mimics what ought to be deep religious longings. The avant-garde is a rupture associated with a lust for new meaning that reveals the empty incoherence of modernity: a "projected anxiety" that will lead both to the method of philosophical "destruction" and the "thrownness" of *Dasein.*[38] It seems Heidegger is secretly emulating the avant-garde in asking for a philosophy that is "enacted in a very concrete manner in the form of a destruction that is directed precisely to what has been handed down to us in the history of ideas" ("KJ," 3), a destruction of tradition.[39]

The destructive negativity of newfangled culture is evoked in Heidegger's critique of Jaspers's discussion of "worldviews" in relation to what he calls "limit situations": "The psychology of worldviews . . . attempts to mark out the 'limits of our psychical life,' and thereby provide a clear and comprehensive horizon [for it]" ("KJ," 1). Horizons have limits, and thus limit situations will give crucial knowledge of our existence as a whole. With Jaspers, we arrive at "a regional definition of the whole of our psychic life" through the experience of limit situations: "'It is in limit-situations that the most intense consciousness of existence flares up. . . . Limit-situations are experienced as something ultimate for human life'" (10). In Jaspers's philosophy, limit situations include such marginal states as "death, suffering, chance, guilt, and struggle" (not to mention Hugo Ball's Dada recitation of "I Zimbri" at the Cabaret Voltaire).[40] As Jaspers summarizes the concept in a later work:

> Situations such as: that I am always in situations, that I cannot live either without struggle and without suffering, that I ineluctably take guilt upon myself, that I must die — these I call limit situations. . . . We cannot gain

> an overview of them; confined within our existence we see nothing else behind them. They are like a wall against which we butt, against which we founder . . . yet they cannot be explained or derived from an Other. They go together with existence itself.[41]

Limit situations are "states of total unrest": "Nothing is firm there . . . everything is in the flux of a restless movement of being put into question; all is relative, finite, split up into contraries, never the whole, the absolute, the essential."[42] This is due to the fact that limit situations are "antinomies," in which contradictory conclusions can be reasoned correctly from the same state of affairs. In the experience of an antinomy, the subject is pulled back and forth between each term of the opposition, resulting in unresolvable state of guilt or suffering. As Heidegger paraphrases Jaspers, "As soon as human beings attempt to attain certainty about the totality of the world and life, they find themselves faced with ultimate forms of incompatibility"; even so, "it is from our experience of antinomy that there arises in us a vital will to unity" (10). This fundamentally negative experience of contradiction is identical to a comprehension of the whole, which is why such experiences of crisis, paradox, and destruction are so valuable for us. At the same time, it is only within the horizon of the whole that we can see antinomies for what they are: "Antinomies destroy and bifurcate, and our experience of them amounts to standing within limit situations, only because all this is initially viewed from the vantage point of . . . life as a whole" (11). The whole is at once the horizon that limit situations construct in their own contradictions, and the horizon from which limit situations may be known for what they are: therefore, the relation between limit situation and totality is itself a fundamental antinomy.

Heidegger's move beyond Jaspers begins here, in questioning the relationship of limit situations, in their negativity, to precisely what is meant by the "whole," i.e., Life. This questioning will occur in several ways—literally, in his immanent critique of Jaspers, Heidegger will work through and beyond the terms of Jaspers's argument, to their limits. The first assumption to go will be of any kind of description or observation of limit situations as a positivity, especially in relation to their holistic surroundings, Life. To observe and describe Life turns it into a "region" rather than any "infinite whole": "Every attempt to understand life is forced to turn the surge and flux of the aforementioned process into a static concept and thereby *destroy* the essence of life, i.e., the restlessness and movement . . . that characterize life's actualization of its ownmost qualities" (16). The difference is that Jaspers thinks the "splitting asunder" of limit situations is the "*primal phenomenon of psychical life*," while for Heidegger it only reveals the unstated holism that precedes it: "This splitting asunder makes sense only insofar as we begin with the notion of that which is not split asunder, and approach it as the underlying reality" (18). Jaspers's approach is neither negligible nor deluded, but it does not take its own assumptions far enough. Going further, Heidegger invokes a fundamental attitude toward limits and the whole that precedes their objectification, a "prestruction" or attitude toward experience that is realized in Life as a form of "self-appropriation," a relationship to oneself. Such an attitude "discloses and holds open a concrete horizon of expectation about which one is anxiously concerned, and which one develops in each particular context of enacting it" (19). The phenomenology of *Being and Time* begins to emerge here before our eyes, as Heidegger literally pushes beyond Jaspers's enabling precondition toward an anxiety that "prestructs" and "holds open" the expectation of the whole in the experience of the limit.

What sense does this make of Heidegger's fleeting reference to the avant-garde? First, as he works through Jaspers's argument by ventriloquizing it, Heidegger qualifies the primacy of limit situations and worldviews by attacking the precondition of holism: "The whole of life, i.e., life *itself*, is something about which we can say nothing directly. But it must indeed be intended by us somehow, since our consciousness of our existence arises precisely from the fact that we look *to* the whole of life" (20). Where Jaspers wants to privilege the antinomy of the limit situation as constitutive of worldviews, it is necessarily contained within a larger whole that cannot be grasped: "Antinomy is 'destruction.' When this destruction is experienced, it is experienced along with the 'unity' or whole that is breaking apart in one way or another" (21–22). The real antinomy, Heidegger sees, is between limit situations and their preconditions; the serious question to be asked from the relation to the whole of Life that a limit situation puts us into is "whether it can in any sense simply put us into the situation of *being able* to ask a question about our existence and about the sense of phenomena [limit situations, worldviews] that are found there" (24). It is exactly here that the avant-garde (as limit situation and worldview) futilely erupts into the text. Bypassing its provocations, Heidegger relocates negativity as a destruction of the objectification of existence that is necessary if we are to ask it the question that concerns us about it. "Accordingly, the phenomenon of existence discloses itself only in a radically historical and essentially anxiously concerned manner of enacting our experience and striving after such enactment" (28), where the determination of being as a historical concern is enacted in the destruction of our preconception of it — a moment, it seems, where avant-garde negativity has been displaced and ventriloquized as an attack on an inadequate approach to the question of being. The historical avant-garde drops out of sight, like any concrete region of existence, to be replaced by a "kind of destruction . . . inseparable from concrete, fully historical, anxious concern for one's own self" (30).

The avant-garde suggests just the kind of limit situation Heidegger wants to go beyond in rethinking the preconceptions of "existence" as destruction. Its mere mention, midway through the text, demands a regrounding of our attitude toward existence. As a limit situation, the avant-garde is nothing but an objectified example of a worldview; in a vulgar account, which may be aligned with Jaspers's attempt at a scientific psychology of worldviews, the avant-garde's demand for new meaning proposes a comprehensible limit experience within the otherwise incoherent hustle and bustle of modern life. The avant-garde demands an alternative worldview, a new whole — something like a counterculture — as an entailment of its limit situation. In relation to the vast horizon of the whole — of the Absolute or existence or Life — however, it can only unveil the incoherence of culture. The antinomy of the avant-garde is that it offers itself as a destructive opposition to the false totalization of a comprehensible worldview and as a crisis of a more encompassing whole. As an example, we may consider Lautréamont's "fortuitous encounter of an umbrella and a sewing machine on a dissecting table." In André Breton's account of the original surrealist image, it is not the mere contradiction of clashing worldviews — in which the encounter directly negates the quotidian world and abolishes sense — but the "light of the image" caused by the juxtaposition that is important, and which leads to the infinite: "The mind becomes aware of the limitless expanse wherein its desires are made manifest, where the pros and cons are constantly consumed, where its obscurity does not betray it. . . . This is the most beautiful night of all, the *lightning-filled night*: day, compared to it, is night."[43] Something like Hegel's "night of the world" erupts in the clash of opposites, invoking both the infinity of desire and the absurdity of finite limits within that whole.

This example, in its reference to the clashing of worldviews and to the beyond, helps explain why many instances of the historical avant-garde are associated with forms of mystificatory religiosity. The modernist foregrounding of signification in Hugo Ball or Velimir Khlebnikov's "transsense" language, for example, is directly connected to their at-this-point untranslatable fantasies of holistic cosmic consciousness. Secularizing such invocations of the infinite leads us to Lacan's notion of excessive *jouissance* as the affect of destruction, a result of that which drops out of or opposes and is negated by the Symbolic Order and, as an index to fantasy as substitute for a missing wholeness, the formula $\$ \diamond a$.[44] The shattering and fragmentation of the subject as a consequence of avant-garde negativity, located in opposition not only to the hustle and bustle of everyday life but to the infinity of the Symbolic Order, can be terrifying indeed (going far beyond the merely determinate negation of Hegelian rupture and recuperation).[45] The risks and consequences of this terror — of being positioned even for a minute outside the Symbolic Order — are the "destiny" of the avant-garde, leading to its high correlation with obdurate and intractable fantasy. In avant-garde examples from Ball, Khlebnikov, and Mina Loy to Bob Kaufman, Ted Berrigan, and Hannah Weiner, the risks of the avant-garde can be destructive and fatal (though one hopes in the sense of fatalism more than mortality).

Two contemporary avant-garde writers who tread the fine line between limit experience and existential destruction are Robert Grenier, one of the originary figures of the Language School of poetry, and David Wojnarowicz, a New York prose writer, visual artist, and arts activist who died of AIDS in 1991. Grenier, whose work is highly regarded among experimental writers but virtually unknown elsewhere, is the perfect case of a poet whose writing seeks the limits of language in a quest for an ecstatic/destructive relation to existence. It is no accident that he has read intensely in Heidegger, whose call to destruction anticipates Grenier's "attack" on the objectification of existence by means of radical poetic form. The following poem from *Sentences* demonstrates his method:

no

absolutely not

not applicable

This single poem, from *Sentences*, a five-hundred-page poetic sequence printed on five-by-eight-inch index cards and assembled in a cloth-covered box, is form of risk-taking linguistic behavior that foregrounds its own negativity in its approach to the question of being.[46] As with Stevens's two "nothings," the poem's negativity is double-edged: it both rejects any positive claims to representation as not applicable and presents the resulting negation as its literal act of questioning; the poet's negativity as embodied speech act registers the "nonresponse" of being, which exceeds it. If one were to look for an American poet comparable to Paul Celan for exploring the limits of language in relation to ineffable being, we might take as evidence the methodology of limit situation in poets like Grenier or his predecessor Larry Eigner. In both Grenier and Celan, lyric poetry is the site of an antinomy of representation, a limit situation. But in refusing to upgrade his existential questioning with the stylistic markers of the lyric, Grenier pushes language toward an ineffable limit of radical uniqueness, and his performance of that uniqueness — to the point of placing himself outside the Symbolic Order, if even for a minute — invokes the terror of that risk. Grenier provides an important test case for why Fredric Jameson's modernism/postmodern distinction between the depth of Vincent van Gogh's portrait of a peasant's (or his own) shoes and the flatness of Andy Warhol's *Diamond Dust Shoes* (or Bob Perelman's "China") must be rethought: because the depthlessness of Grenier's writing is at the same time motivated by a radical concern for authenticity as it tries to write beyond citation and paraphrase — even if citing, as prior example, Heideggerian destruction.[47] The limit experience of Grenier's work enacts an antinomy between a radical uniqueness that brings signification into relief and a quasi-religious crisis of the whole that is unrepresentable.

It is the poetic form of his work, from the dissociated seriality of *Sentences* to the image/word interface of his hand-drawn writings, that identifies it with a limit situation. Whether such a situation is truly a unique one (following a long tradition of serial poetry in Louis Zukofsky, George Oppen, Robert Creeley, and Jack Spicer) is a moot point. Heidegger notes, "An incessant enactment of our concern for achieving primordiality is what constitutes primordiality,"[48] and Grenier's work in every sense enacts this concern. As an enactment and record of language (and poet) placed in a limit situation, Grenier's work is characterized by its use of semantic, logical, or existential contradictions, as may be seen in the following poems (quoted as published, in nonproportional type):

`transference isolates`

`nobody to talk to anything about`

strangeness of the world unite

silence amounts to the same thing

it's you

In each of these works, which must be visualized surrounded by the white space of their index card, a radical process of individuation takes place in the form of an assertion to an other that could also be a reflexive questioning of the relation of a self to existence. The limit situation of these poems is their enactment of the failure of lyric subjectivity, as it takes place in the medium of language but addresses questions of existence that exceed it. The dissonance or ambiguity of the message, then, is its questioning of existence, in the situation of the writer as unique recorder of particulars within a whole that surrounds. Antinomies both of language and situation are thus foregrounded in this work:

sun setting stands forth in greater relief opposite peaks

which identifies the position of an observer in relation to a natural scene in which the peaks opposite the setting sun are caught in a Heideggerian moment of "showing forth." This moment, however, is both ineffable and monumentalized, a paradox that makes its mode of signification both conventional and inadequate to the event. This is also true of

THE BUS DRIVER

and the black stream

where the engulfing of the perceived figure by the imagined stream of mortality indicates both the "anxious concern" of the writer faced with existence and its particularization in the gap between an undecidable paradox of fact and fiction (is death the fiction, or is it the bus driver?), producing a surrealist "light of the image" in the gap between them.

```
                    I

                    I put ashes on my own floor
```

addresses a radically existential dissociation of the self from any form of objectification. The "I," as subject without predicate, is distinguished from the predication of "put ashes on my own floor" — which evokes an association with funeral practices or household chores in which the limit situation of mortality or everyday life is undermined by the assertion of an absolute uniqueness and resistance to paraphrase. The destruction of the "I," in Heidegger's terms, is appropriate to the attack on any form of regional being, including the pronoun and certainly the representational claims of a complete sentence. The following poem, in turn, locates the crisis of regional being precisely in the postmodern landscape:

```
339th Avenue     9

Phoenix          51
```

Here, Grenier finds coordinates for the limit situation he is in both in language and in the world. The poem presents a paradox of representation between the numbering of avenues outside Phoenix and the miles it takes to get there, a minor one compared to the position of the observer, who is out in space and far beyond any quantifiable location. The social world, then, just is the fallen language of the highway sign, as equally with

```
AUTOMOBILE

divisiveness
```

Heidegger's later concern with the inauthenticity of technology, its "enframing" of existence, comes through a fundamental registration of different indices of social alienation. An "AUTOMOBILE" announces itself in capital letters, which is immediately undermined by the "divisiveness" of a lowercase concept, both questions of technology. In a paradoxical relationship between critique and its object, Grenier extends the antinomy of limit situations to the technological medium, even in his preferred modes of writing itself.[49]

As there are five hundred poems in Grenier's *Sentences* — and each one of them unique — it would be futile to try to represent the range of the limit situations they instantiate. Each is an attack on regional being and the stability of worldviews as reducible to concepts. Language becomes the site of a paradoxical questioning of being — which means that, in the end, language itself must be gone beyond. As much as any concern with the material properties of writing, the question of the limits of language explains Grenier's transition from typewritten works that still look like poetry, at least in the tradition of serial form, to pure hybrids of visual and verbal signification and play in his "drawn" writings. It is important here that these works explore media as well as language in their anxious concern for the relation of limit to totality at a moment of realization. The shift to drawn as opposed to typewritten poems is precisely due the limits of the medium for expression; as publisher Leslie Scalapino notes, on the inside of Grenier's 1991 boxed set of handwritten, xeroxed works, "The book's first section, the composition of the 8½ × 11 pages is an act of politics. You've *got* to get everything onto the page, and it can *only* be 18 pages" (the work was originally commissioned for a hand-stapled little magazine). Handwritten works begin to interrupt and qualify the more conventional typewritten poems, not simply undermining as transposing typewriting into its own specific constraint. One example of such a poetics of obdurate interruption is a handwritten, xeroxed page that overprints a fairly legible "my heart is beating" with a more incoherent "I am a beast" in four slightly different versions (fig. 58).[50] As a limit situation, the poem places Life and being named in contradiction: in terms of the "I" of the poem, to be gone beyond as mere region of being, I am immortal and my nature is unnameable — the marks on paper are a counterfactual.

A poem taken from the *transpiration/transpiring* series uses juxtaposition toward a more conventional (even hackneyed) lyric end, partially rhyming across the notebook page "LOON / I love / I love / I love / I love" with "LOON / the Moon / the Moon / the Moone / the Mooon" (fig. 59). As *Dasein* or thrown existence, the bird speaks as an "it" that is expressing, as it exceeds, the writer's desire: "I love the moon." Yet it is the writer who is

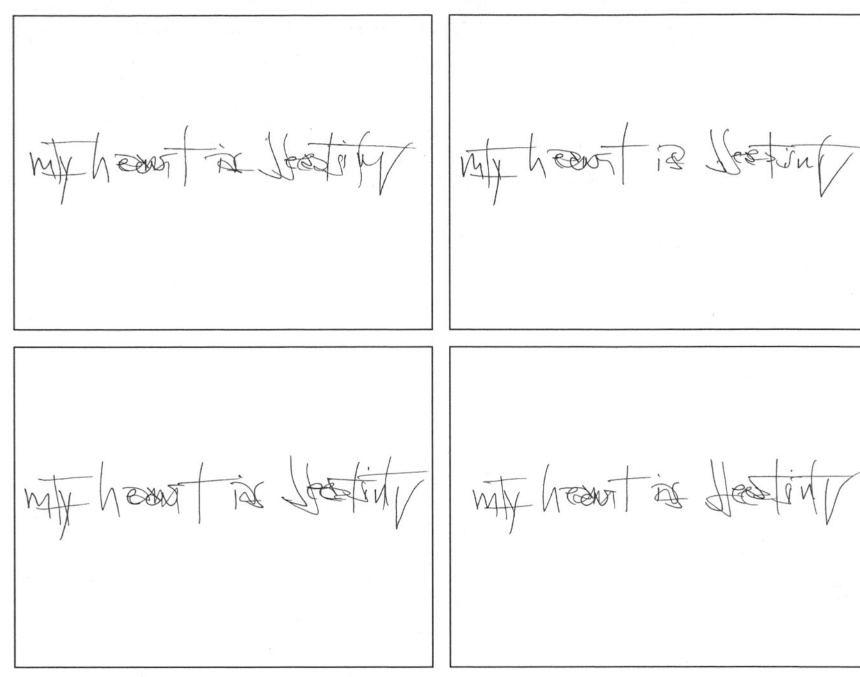

58. Robert Grenier, "my heart is beating / I am a beast" (four versions), from What I Believe / Transpiration/Transpiring / Minnesota *(Oakland, Calif.: O Books, n.d.). Facsimiles of ink drawings, 11 × 8½".*

writing these words, not the loon, another instance of antinomy indicated by the split registration on the page and variant spellings toward an effect that is excessive, suprasubjective, in every sense "loony." If, as Heidegger remarks, conventional ontology cannot account for the soul, this writing must be an attempt to capture its missing aura.[51] In Grenier's later graphic poems, such as those published together as *12 from r h y m m s*, the poet returns to an earlier setting of limit situation, the beaches of Northern California, as he pushes the technology of writing and color Xerox into new antinomies.[52] In one example, the written words "glitter / sit here / sand has / waves / wings" are readable as a serial transcription of a natural scene, with the exception of a superimposed "A" that does not make particular grammatical sense (fig. 60). This "A" is only one of many necessary distortions or impediments (the hyperstylized handwriting, different colors of ink, graphic elements) that place the work solidly between verbal and visual signification. Finite representation is juxtaposed with the infinity of its undoing, seen as "merely" an effect of the sublime natural scene, which cannot be represented as either word or image. In another example, "west / no

59. Robert Grenier, "LOON," from What I Believe / Transpiration/Transpiring / Minnesota. *Facsimile of ink drawing, 11 × 8½".*

farther / west / all sea" is interrupted by several horizontal and two vertical-lines, making the record of the event a matter of its own inscription (fig. 61). The limits of language face the limits of the West, a virtual paraphrase of Heidegger. Such examples must stand for a much wider and less easily paraphrased range of work, available only in tiny, fugitive editions and over the Internet.[53] The appearance of two of Grenier's handwritten works on the cover of the second edition of the Language School anthology *In the American Tree*, however, testifies to the originary (if not primordial) significance of his work, even among a group of writers notably opposed to originality.[54]

While Grenier invokes destruction as a crisis of signification, David Wojnarowicz lived it — as artist, street hustler, drug addict, and AIDS activist — and met an early death. Where Grenier entirely avoids the politics of Zeitgeist for the antinomies of limit situations, Wojnarowicz risks the literariness of *Close to the Knives* by including pages of activist journalism that may seem prematurely dated to readers now.[55] I have claimed that Grenier's originary dictum "I hate speech," cited by Silliman in *In the American Tree* as indicating a shift from a speech-based poetics to writing, refers importantly to political speech, from the antiwar and Black Power movements

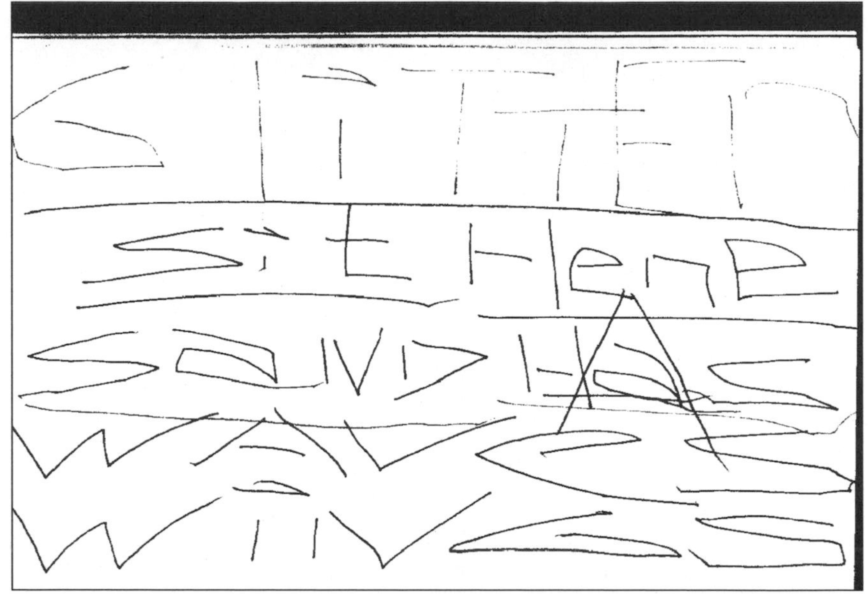

60. Robert Grenier, "glitter / sit here . . . ," from 12 from r h y m m s *(Scotia, N.Y.: Pavement Saw Press, 1996). Color Xerox, 11 × 8½".*

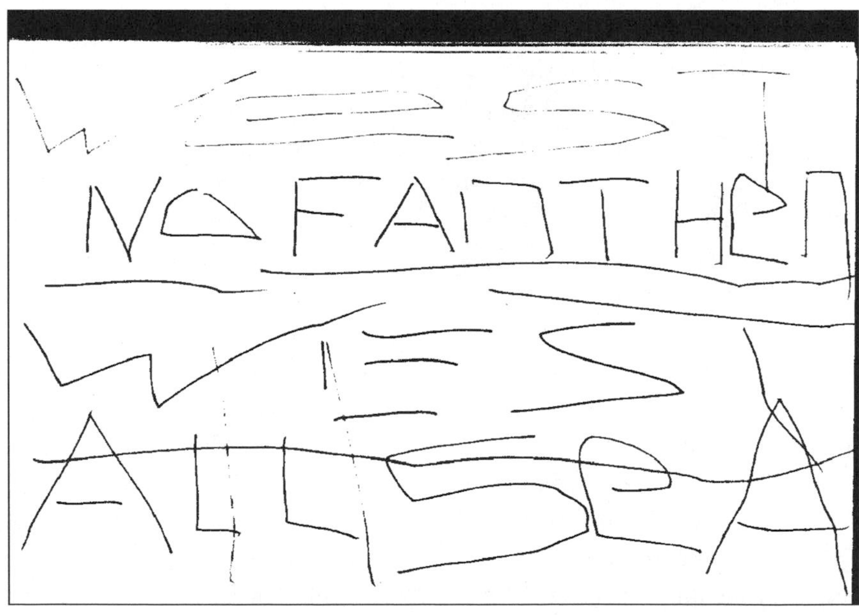

61. Robert Grenier, "west / no farther . . . ," from 12 from r h y m m s. *Color Xerox, 11 × 8½".*

that drifted up to Grenier's office on the fourth floor of Wheeler Hall at Berkeley in 1969, where I first met him.[56] When he writes, "*to me, all speeches say the same thing*," he means equally that all claims to expression are undermined by the inexpressible, and that all *political* speech, in its address to the historical moment, is inauthentic.[57] Of course, a politics of authenticity may be historically significant in itself, as with the criterion of Heideggerian authenticity in the Charter 77 movement of Vaclav Havel;[58] but in Grenier's case, the only possible politics is one of agonized withdrawal and linguistic witness, from the margins of a limit situation where one laments the sunset of the Western world.[59] While there is a gain for personal responsibility (the ancient Poundian dictum of "man standing by his word") in this individuating "thrownness," the claims of uniqueness and irreducibility it subtends are precisely what the politics of Cultural Studies most calls into question.[60] Otherwise put, Grenier would never, could never, speak in the name of a collective subject in the way that Wojnarowicz, as a part of a political coalition, could write from an activist perspective at the time of Jesse Helms's attack on the National Endowment for the Arts' support of the work of gays and lesbians. The distance between Grenier and Wojnarowicz seems precisely the gap that needs to be bridged, between a consideration of the avant-garde as locked into the moment of its historical founding, as either opposition or "unworlding," and one that shows how the avant-garde is a negative moment in the construction of culture that is continually being redefined. If the concept of the avant-garde has a future, it is not simply as an historical relic or replay of the modernist tradition, either in philosophy or in the lyric poem. How can the avant-garde be seen simultaneously as an impossible limit situation and as a moment of social reproduction that occurs within and because of alienated life? Here, the avant-garde might be most valuable for perpetuating the crisis of the worldview, the limit situation of Zeitgeist as a moment within totality, that Heidegger wanted to go beyond.

NEGATIVITIES

Toward a revisionist account of avant-garde negativity, I want to move from Heidegger's reaction to the avant-garde (as both misdirected innovation and distancing otherness of authentic Being) to the survival of its negative moment in Michel Foucault's discursive genealogy. While numerous links between Foucault and Nietzsche have been found that go through Heidegger, the major account of Heidegger's influence on Foucault focuses on the relation of the "clearing" of Being to the question of origins.[61] There ought to be an account as well of the transposition of negativity from Heidegger to Foucault, a repositioning of the thrownness of *Dasein* within the great concepts of discursive formation and the genealogy of power. Such a repositioning would require (or at least would go along with) a revised estimation of Foucault's use of the avant-garde tradition, from his early book on Raymond Roussel, through his many references to Sade, Georges Bataille, and Antonin Artaud, to the context of the postwar European avant-garde in journals such as *Tel Quel* in the 1960s.[62] Is it the position of negativity that accounts for such a massive denial of the avant-garde in the Anglo-American institutional reception of Foucault?[63] The privileging in Cultural Studies of the normative and socially regulative, to the extent that it partakes of Foucault's accounts of the prison and sexuality, entirely elides the constitutive negativity that is distributed everywhere in his work, and whose original example is the avant-garde. Madness, death, and eroticism are each key elements of the discursive epistemes that Foucault investigates in the asylum, archive, and clinic; without Sadean destruction there would be no going beyond the "author" and no genealogy. I will go further and suggest that it is the precise valence of negativity in regard to untotalizable infinity, which Heidegger educed from Jaspers's relation of limit situations to the construction of worldviews, that allows Foucault's moments of negativity (madness, death, eroticism) to participate in higher-order discourses. For the false totality of worldviews, we may substitute the limit-defining notions of episteme and discourse as unities that regulate the historical situation of lived experience. The way the marginality of the avant-garde discloses the incoherence of culture, in other words, anticipates the way madness, death, and sexuality pervade the regularities that define the limits of experience. This is quite another route for the avant-garde than its Hegelian recuperation.

A Foucauldian avant-garde would be a negative moment in a discursive regularity, both produced by and working to construct the epistemes we inhabit over extended durations. (What are the limits of discourse? Here, there ought to be a critique of discursive epistemes along the lines of Heidegger's critique of limit situation, Zeitgeist, and worldview.) If such a hybrid formulation is workable, then the avant-garde may be something other than what we thought it was; it may not "originate" in the historical examples of Baudelaire or Dada in a progressive sequence but repeat as a discontinuous moment of recursive breakdown and social reflexivity. In the city where I live, Detroit, avant-garde forms unveil their negative moments

— in the form of many subcultures in this most regulated of cultures — with impressive spontaneity, from John Sinclair and the Cass Corridor artists to Detroit techno and numerous garage bands.[64] The avant-garde may be the "becoming outside" of the system as it reflects on itself and rejects what it sees, looking for a higher, unknowable wholeness to replace the false totality of the historical present. This negativity of the system complements the spatial form of the avant-garde as a positive phenomenon, its metropolitan social formation of movements, groups, and cults.[65] The negativity of the avant-garde — its displacement of the culture in which it finds itself as other — is constitutive of the formation of discursive regularities in both temporal and spatial senses, leading to epistemic breakdowns and reformations on a regular basis.

David Wojnarowicz's *Close to the Knives: A Memoir of Disintegration* directly supports a redefined notion of the avant-garde between limit situation and discourse. A nonlinear pastiche of prose writings from several genres — fiction, diary, reportage, taped conversations, art criticism, documents, letters, and even legal documents — his memoir constructs a hybrid form of personal identity in the discontinuities of its temporal organization. Moments of consciousness of the writer's limit situation alternate with episodes of blackout and amnesia, putting the entire notion of narrative teleology at risk. Wojnarowicz's memoir literally has nowhere to go, and where it is going is everywhere around it: toward death. Death is figured in a wide range of incidents, from the murder fantasies an acquaintance tells him and eventually acts out, to the suicide of a hustler friend who provides a role model for limit situations, to the death of friends from AIDS, to the writer's own diagnosis and, necessarily outside the limits of the book, his death from the disease. Such a relation between what is outside the book, and outside representation, and what is presented within the book constitutes its argument of personal identity, as may be seen in many sentences that describe identity as a limit situation in relation to "being outside":

> So my heritage is a calculated fuck on some faraway sun-filled bed while the curtains are being sucked in and out of an open window by a passing breeze. . . . (3)

> In loving him, I saw great houses being erected that would soon slide into the waiting and stirring seas. I saw him freeing me from the silences of an interior life. (17)

> I play games with the road to shake myself up, at times squeezing my eyelids closed so that I drive quarter-mile stretches without sight. (28)
>
> I am fearful of something more than fear. . . . It's like a pocket of death but with no form other than the light one might cast upon its trail of fragments. (39–40)
>
> Ever since my teenage years, I've experienced the sensation of seeing myself from miles above the earth, as if from the clouds. (88)
>
> I see myself seeing death. It's like a transparent celluloid image of myself is accompanying me everywhere I go. (109)
>
> I am a bundle of contradictions that shift hourly. . . . I abstract the disease I have in the same way you abstract death. (117)
>
> There is a clear joy in his eyes as I lean forward and slowly crawl over the surface of the cool sheets with my destination firmly in mind. (275)

Wojnarowicz's sentences, unlike Grenier's, can have a strong sense of the connection between subject and predicate because both are rifted with nonexistence, put under erasure. Identity is positioned "outside," but this is not simply the limit situation of the historical avant-garde. The limit situations in Wojnarowicz are the spectacular ones of New York art subculture: sex, heroin, political repression, illness, suicide, death. For Wojnarowicz, destruction is universal and dispersed, the nature of lived experience. Each of his disconnected serial narratives is constructed around the impossible destiny of the limit situation:

> I'm in a car traveling the folds of the southwest region of the country and the road is becoming flat and giving off energy like a vortex leading into the horizon line. I'm getting closer to the coast and realize how much I hate arriving at a destination. Transition is always a relief. Destination means death to me. If I could figure out a way to remain forever in transition, in the disconnected and unfamiliar, I could remain in a state of perpetual freedom. It's the preferable sensation of arriving at a movie fifteen minutes late and departing twenty minutes later and retrieving an echo of *real life* as opposed to a tar pit sensation. Destination is an entry point for the practitioners of fake moral screens. (62)

Both anxiety, as always leaving something behind, and destruction, as "destination," are shot through with death; "*real life*" is only experienced at moments where the negative shows itself, as on a movie house screen, in contrast to the false "screens" or impediments to true vision of those who see themselves as "moral." The negativity of this experience is on the way to its destination in a Foucauldian care of the self, perhaps, but Wojnarowicz will be prevented from arriving there by the real epistemic limit outside him, AIDS.

Wojnarowicz can be read as thematically parallel to Foucault along numerous lines: in the madness of his discontinuous wandering, in the opacity of his body and its disease to the medical gaze, and in the ecstatic destructiveness of his sexual experience. Unwilling to posit existence as a totality, he particularizes limits in sexuality and death:

> As I studied his head bobbing against my belly while seated on a leather couch, I marveled at how simple it would be to lift the carved stone fish from the glass coffee table and smack the top of this head in and live on easy street for a while. I thought of the hundreds of times standing in a moving subway car, a cop standing with his back to me, his holster within easy reach and me undoing the gun restraint with my eyes over and over. (32–33)

> The doctor comes in and removes him from the pumps and hisses of hoses and he leaves the room immediately afterward. . . . The guy on the bed takes two breaths and arches his back almost imperceptibly, his lips slightly parted. I have hold of one leg and his sister one hand philip another hand or part of his arm and we're sobbing and I'm totally amazed at how quietly he dies how beautiful everything is with us holding him down on the bed. (82)

Sexuality in the first passage is connected implicitly with aggression and fantasies of violence; in the second, death is eroticized, an experience to be had in bed. Each of these situations is implicated in the other's limits and, more generally, within the limits of personal identity. It is through the overarching question of the limit situation of identity that the discontinuous episodes of Wojnarowicz's memoir are discursively connected, leading to the second important feature of his book: the relation of its interrupted, incomplete, self-destructive narration to the constitution of identity as inauthentic, the moment of "who am I when I do these things" that is a recurrent and underlying refrain of the book:

> This morning I woke up in another part of my brain. Take the idea, for a moment, that one usually wakes up in a similar area of the brain every day of one's life. When I opened my eyes, I woke with a feeling of

confusion and a sense that something indiscernible had shifted during the sleeping hours and now I was somewhere else, not in another place physically, but something similar. The "I" of *my self* had crawled through the thickness of memory and consciousness to some other place in the structure of the brain. (60–61)

The discontinuity of self is spatialized into different areas of the brain—an impossible figure for self-reflection, as one cannot think within a brain and look inside it to see where the thinking is taking place, in most circumstances. This spatializing disconnection becomes the central formal principle of his book, bringing Wojnarowicz into the company of a countertradition of novelists, from Defoe (particularly in *Moll Flanders*) to Djuna Barnes, Kathy Acker, Leslie Scalapino, and Carla Harryman, whose work dissociates personal identity from the teleological coherence of narrative toward social limits.

The comparison between Heideggerian and Foucauldian avant-gardes, and the examples of Grenier and Wojnarowicz, suggest a further distinction: between contemporary experimental women poets who question the nature of personal identity in lyric poetry, and a countertradition of novelists that includes Acker, Scalapino, and Harryman who formally represent the discontinuities of identity unveiled in Wojnarowicz's memoir.[66] This distinction may be elucidated in two presentations of the radical negativity of the limit situation, a poem by Marjorie Welish and a play by Harryman.

BLACK DILUVIUM

nothing deduced
from

black diluvium
quitclaim

sullen through oil
color

drained of gray
matter.[67]

Welish's poem, one of a series of six titled "The Black Poems," is evidently a variation on William Carlos Williams's "The Red Wheelbarrow," substituting terms of negativity and nonexistence for the positive celebration of the object. The transgressive rewriting of the tradition, then, becomes a limit experience of materiality, sense data, and language not organized around the illusion of transparency toward the object. In the poem, there is no object and nothing can be deduced from it, reminding one of both Cordelia's act of refusal to Lear and Stevens's "nothing that is not there and the nothing that is" at the same time. Gender, then, is enacted as the antinomy of a limit situation in which the address to literary authority in Williams is combined with a perverse refusal of its object choices. The lyric becomes a site for contestation and affirmation that is disclosed in the material text.

> FISH: In the beginning, there was nothing. No cattails, no wigs, no paws. There was no doom. No lavender or shirt sleeves. No burn no yellow or rest. Neither was there beginning. No light went out. No one held her own against an array of misshapen events. There were no chains. There was no writing or speech. There was nothing to share, nothing to swim, and nothing to cut. . . . In the beginning, there was nothing to hold and nothing to hold in mind, since there was no beginning, no nothing, and no mind. The end also did not exist. There was no gender, no extremes, no image or lack of image and no money. There were no pencils. In the beginning, there were no names. . . . No future and nothing to preserve.[68]

Excerpted from a long diatribe in Harryman's *Memory Play*, Fish's speech carefully undoes any systematic model for negativity. Negation is neither logical nor constitutive nor final in that the speech itself declares that, in the beginning, there was also "no nothing." If this is so, there must have been something like the ever-during substance without attributes that is equally absolute negativity, a negativity much like Hegel's "night of the world" with its dissociated parts, the *corps morcelé* of the body in pieces before being unified in the Imaginary. Gender, like any other body part, is preceded by an amorphous state of nonidentity out of which something like a "will to form" as existence may come. The forms of existence, it is implied, will remain suspended within the larger discursive undoing that is the dramatic insight of Fish's speech. This binding together of disparate elements within the form of a discourse is reminiscent of Foucault's anecdote, at the beginning of *The Order of Things* (from Borges), of a seemingly unregulated taxonomy in which "animals are divided into: (a) belonging to the Emperor, (b) embalmed, (c) tame, (d) sucking pigs, (e) sirens, (f) fabulous, (g) stray dogs," and so forth.[69] The transgression of categories becomes the unifying principle of discourse, an effect that Harryman imitates

62. David Wojnarowicz, untitled, 1993. Gelatin-silver print, 28½ × 28½". Photo: Fred Scrutton.

in the speech. Harryman's antinomy of substance and negation, then, sets up the discursive construction of Fish's identity in Foucauldian terms, while Welish's lyric transgressively holds open a Heideggerian destruction through her concern for the inadequacy of Williams's *Dasein*.

The question of the avant-garde and Cultural Studies I am raising thus points in two directions: to the coherence of genre and the incoherence of self. Both Grenier and Wojnarowicz push the limits of literary form, in lyric poem and prose narrative, toward the limits of personal identity; their works are each forms of individuating uniqueness, but in entirely different

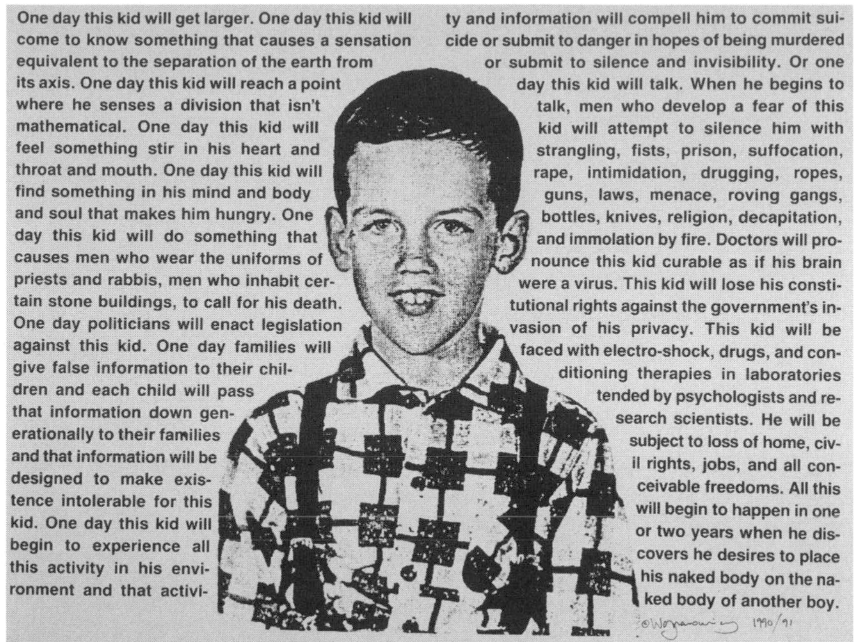

One day this kid will get larger. One day this kid will come to know something that causes a sensation equivalent to the separation of the earth from its axis. One day this kid will reach a point where he senses a division that isn't mathematical. One day this kid will feel something stir in his heart and throat and mouth. One day this kid will find something in his mind and body and soul that makes him hungry. One day this kid will do something that causes men who wear the uniforms of priests and rabbis, men who inhabit certain stone buildings, to call for his death. One day politicians will enact legislation against this kid. One day families will give false information to their children and each child will pass that information down generationally to their families and that information will be designed to make existence intolerable for this kid. One day this kid will begin to experience all this activity in his environment and that activity and information will compell him to commit suicide or submit to danger in hopes of being murdered or submit to silence and invisibility. Or one day this kid will talk. When he begins to talk, men who develop a fear of this kid will attempt to silence him with strangling, fists, prison, suffocation, rape, intimidation, drugging, ropes, guns, laws, menace, roving gangs, bottles, knives, religion, decapitation, and immolation by fire. Doctors will pronounce this kid curable as if his brain were a virus. This kid will lose his constitutional rights against the government's invasion of his privacy. This kid will be faced with electro-shock, drugs, and conditioning therapies in laboratories tended by psychologists and research scientists. He will be subject to loss of home, civil rights, jobs, and all conceivable freedoms. All this will begin to happen in one or two years when he discovers he desires to place his naked body on the naked body of another boy.

63. *David Wojnarowicz, untitled, 1990. Gelatin-silver print, 30 × 40".*

senses. The question raised by the attack on language and being in Grenier's radical form is not whether his work best fits the foregrounding of signification in modernism or the depthlessness of pastiche of the postmodern. It is the question of genre in relation to identity: the form of being he imagines is in fact mediated by the disembodied ghost of lyric poetry.[70] This eternal return of genre is where Grenier's politics begin: they cannot imagine any other than the other of their own making; there is no translation of uniqueness into either history or community, and whatever stakes there are of history or community are placed outside the limits of genre, as they are in Heidegger's notion of "first philosophy." The individuating uniqueness of Wojnarowicz, on the other hand, is entirely given over to the othering of self in the literal experience of death, so that the "anticipatory dread" of narrative is informed by an absolute foreknowledge, as in Wojnarowicz's self-portrait as dead (fig. 62). It is this precondition from which Wojnarowicz derives the connection between the limit experiences of his narrative episodes and the overall coherence of his nonnarrative form. A second self-portrait, however, is more accurately the result: an assertion of identity in the positioning of the child as "constructed" by the panoptical language surrounding him (fig. 63). In Grenier's construction of identity in the form of his box of index cards or sequences of handwritten poems, we may question whether his politics of nonidentity is discursive beyond the community of poets. We may proceed from Wojnarowicz, on the other hand, to a logic of discursive construction that identifies the way in which the negative undoing of an individuating uniqueness is implicated in social discourses of sexuality, disease, and minority identity.

Grenier and Wojnarowicz are both singular in their forms of destruction, even if they do stake their identities on the formation of social groups (in the Language School and poetry community and the New York art and AIDS activist communities, respectively). The important point, then, is to show how this singularity and uniqueness returns to its cultural moment. Adorno's formulation of the criticality of autonomous art is a step in this direction, but it remains limited by the Hegelian task of solving the contradiction (not antinomy) between the agency of the avant-garde and its higher synthesis.[71] Riding's alternate modernism, Welish's lyrical pastiche, and Harryman's transgressive play all demonstrate how negativity is always inserted into complex cultural logics. Such logics are gendered; feminine uses of negativity (not merely the feminine as negative) reveal how different contexts and motives for negation produce radically different results. Rather than reifying a single, strained negative dialectics in which avant-garde agency performs a permanent refusal of integration — one that is good for philosophy, as well — we need to hold open the spontaneity, instability, and evanescence of the avant-garde as a limit situation within a contradictory horizon of totality. The question of the avant-garde concerns the constructedness and historical specificity of the negative — not simply an oppositional moment but a destructive/renewing one of systemic detotalization.

POST-SOVIET SUBJECTIVITY IN ARKADII DRAGOMOSHCHENKO AND ILYA KABAKOV

While it has been said that since the "fall of communism" the Soviet Union has become in reality a collection of Third World countries with nuclear weapons and a subway system, this is an untruth. It is the "Second World" — and what is that?
— *Barrett Watten, in* Leningrad

Subjectivity is not the basis for being a Russian person. . . . "Protestants," said Arkadii, "go to church to mail a letter to God, the church, it's like a post office. The Orthodox church — the building is not symbolic — it is considered to be the real body of God, and Orthodox people too are God because they are together here, not alone, and speaking, by the way, has nothing to do with it."
— *Lyn Hejinian, in* Leningrad

In 1989, I had the opportunity to encounter the work of a number of post-Soviet artists whose work was becoming known in the West at the moment of the breakup of the Soviet Union. In fact, the emergence of this work was only possible in the political context of that moment, anticipating and even furthering it in many ways. The Institute for Contemporary Art in London had staged a two-person exhibition of the work of Erik Bulatov and Ilya Kabakov early that year; the juxtaposition of Bulatov's vicious simulacra of the political iconography of Soviet culture with Kabakov's microscopically detailed narrative installations addressing the condition of everyday life within that ideology seemed itself a historical event. And so it was, indicating the possibility that the provisional reforms of Perestroika had created enough cultural openness and contact with the West that such work could be seen. Of course, the isolation of the Soviet Union from the 1920s and the resulting xenophobia of Stalinist culture were directly responsible for its development as a "deformed workers' state." Stalinism, especially in its most intensely reactionary form, always was a defense of the so-called material gains of socialism under the antagonistic gaze of the nonseeing West. Later that year, I was able to participate in this moment of opening, when I traveled with Lyn Hejinian, Ron Silliman, and

Michael Davidson to what would be the first and only conference of avant-garde poets in the Soviet Union, the benign hiatus of the International Summer School in Leningrad, August 1989. The conference, which brought together a number of American, French, Soviet, and Eastern Bloc writers, turned out to be part of a last-ditch effort of official cultural institutions to avert the political crisis of Perestroika, but it also provided an opportunity to meet poets such as Arkadii Dragomoshchenko, Ilya Kutik, Alexei Parshchikov, Nadezhda Kondakova, Ivan Zhdanov, and the semiotician Vyacheslav Ivanov. A nonnarrative historical account of that visit was subsequently published as *Leningrad: American Writers in the Soviet Union*. The following essay, written in 1992, was an attempt to address the differences between two genres of post-Soviet art: the intense subjectivity and linguistic materiality of poets like Dragomoshchenko and Zhdanov, and the simulacral distance and quasi-postmodern pastiche of the art of Bulatov and Kabakov. In order to see both as equally legitimate aesthetic responses to the cultural politics of the late Soviet period, difficult questions would have to be asked: questions of genre, language, politics, and postmodernity. In retrospect, I see this juxtaposition as the initial site of a developing distinction between material text and cultural poetics, and as a location for questioning the purported universality of postmodernism. The present version, then, is augmented by a brief account of writings by Leslie Scalapino derived from her slightly later travels to the former Soviet Union, in order to better differentiate the post-Soviet from the postmodern.

AFTER THE FALL

The breakup of official culture in the Soviet Union, along with the "official/unofficial" dialectic that was a part of it, was attended by the eruption of an intensely utopian, metaphysically speculative, and violently antirealist subjectivity in emerging art and literature that may be termed post-Soviet even if it had its origins in earlier decades. Beginning in the 1960s, up to the failure of revisionist politics prior to the invasion of Czechoslovakia in 1968; extending through the Brezhnev era of stagnation of the 1970s, with its increasingly articulated counterculture; and through the opening to the West and the influence of emigration in the 1980s, a series of oppositional cultural moments in the Soviet Union anticipated their reception as specimens of postmodern culture by the West.[1] To identify these post-Soviet developments with postmodernism, however, would be to misunderstand them; as poet Dmitrii Prigov has said of the Moscow conceptual art of the 1970s, "When [Western art] entered our part of the world, [it] discovered the total absence of any idea of the object and its inherent qualities or of any hint whatsoever of fetishism."[2] The cultural meaning of Andy Warhol's reception by post-Soviet artists, in a world constructed in the absence of any idea of the object, would not be restricted to a simulacral consumerism (though the Sotheby's auction of 1988, which made any number of avant-garde artists suddenly rich, would change that). The "Women Admirers of Jeff Koons Club" I encountered in Leningrad in 1989 was thus a sign of an emerging feminism as much as any acceptance of the Reagan-era consumerism of Koons's work. Even the culture of Russian modernism, decontextualized by Western connoisseurship and its unavailability in the Soviet Union after the 1950s, was interpreted in the post-Soviet context in a way discontinuous with its historical origins, as something to be read about in art magazines.

In order to understand these developments as not simply a colonization by Western postmodernism (arriving fully formed with popular culture, multinational capital, and Xerox), it will be necessary to develop approaches to Second-World discourses of subjectivity. In part due to its similar historical origins, the psychoanalytic ideology critique of Slavoj Žižek offers the most resonant terms for a culture founded on the traumatic event of revolution and developing as a social discourse of internalized antagonisms — of class, nationality, and religion. But even before the full impact of Žižek's critique could be realized, it became increasingly clear, as the optimistic moment of the Fall led only to social disintegration in the 1990s, that post-Soviet culture, once it had expanded to integrate both unofficial and international influences, did not simply mean an uncritical embrace of Western postmodernism. Rather, its particular cultural history is preserved in forms of post-Soviet subjectivity not simply reducible to the various national identities then contesting the ground of the former Soviet state. This subjectivity is not simply decentered in relation to Western modernity's failed project, as if post-Soviet culture could be characterized by such a failure to begin with. Rather, post-Soviet subjectivity is attended by a range of phenomena: the particular forms of utopia, memory, and displacement that developed and disintegrated within the mutable horizons of the Soviet Union in its period of transition, from a static Second-World monolith to a form of society that still cannot be predicted. While the limits of the concept as a speculative construction are granted, post-Soviet subjectivity provides a framework for discussing the historical specificity of related cultural forms in the period — in the Moscow conceptual art from the 1970s that produced internationally recognized figures such as Komar and Melamid, Bulatov, and Kabakov; and in the 1980s "meta" literature of Moscow and Leningrad, exemplified by poets such as Dragomoshchenko, Zhdanov, Parshchikov, Kutik, and others.[3]

DRAGOMOSHCHENKO'S METAPOETICS

Arkadii Dragomoshchenko's poetry, it has been said, was "unlike anything else being written in the Soviet Union today," and direct observation bore this out.[4] At the Leningrad Summer School of 1989, Dragomoshchenko was unique in abandoning the often complex metrical forms and performative theatricality of the dominant poetic traditions, both official and oppositional. The range of verse practices available to the avant-garde, however defamiliarized by difficult sound patterns and skewed semantics, seemed to one critic to be atrophying as they looked back to the precedent "classical tradition . . . as in the Acmeism of Akhmatova or early Mandelstam, [which] stood for heroically distanced emotion and a European cultural intertext," but which often led to poetic norms reduced to "ruthless metricality and relentless rhyming" (10). Dragomoshchenko read his poems as written texts rather than oral presentations of cultural memory embodied in the poet — unlike Ivan Zhdanov, who declaimed the highly wrought language of his richly textured and difficult lyrics as if *ab eterno*, directly from memory, to great effect. One listener afterward complained to Dragomoshchenko, "What you are doing isn't poetry" — because it lacked the generic markers by which poetry had been set apart as a form of cultural memory and conservation. This tradition was brought to its most politically charged moment in Osip Mandelstam's memorization of his poem on Stalin, creating an ideal of the poet as literal embodiment of truth set against ideological lies. While equally a poetry of internalized self-consciousness, Dragomoshchenko's work tears a hole in the fabric of the lyric tradition's modernist authority — not simply for antiauthoritarian motives, whatever those might be in a culture where oppositional poetics are as fully invested with authority as the authority they contest. Dragomoshchenko's break with the overdetermination of sound and sense that defines the norm of Russian verse, either official or avant-garde — and the resulting demand to redefine collective memory and objective truth — set his work apart.

A poetics of collective memory as opposed to official history (often meeting at a middle ground in official/unofficial poets such as Yevgenii Yevtushenko, Andrei Voznesensky, or Bella Akhmadulina) has been one of the most durable products of Soviet verse culture — the poet (seen as survivor) becoming a living embodiment of collective memory. Dragomoshchenko's unpacking of memory and culture works toward entirely opposite ends, as can be seen in "Nasturtium as Reality," a major poetic sequence from his 1990 collection *Description* (in the impeccable English translation of Lyn Hejinian and Elena Balashova).[5] In the poem, a series of twelve metrically irregular, typographically skewed episodes, cultural and personal memory are fragmented and recombined in the form of a material text rather than the embodiment of the poet, in a relentless epistemological critique toward as-yet-to-be-determined horizons. The poem begins with a confrontation:

> An attempt
> to describe an isolated object
> determined by the anticipation of the resulting whole —
>   by a glance over someone else's shoulder. (93)

A verbal organization of diverging angles of approach will characterize this attempt as a series of spatial and temporal vectors predicated on a missing X that precedes the poem, presumably the nasturtium but also the elided propositional form of "there exists." What follows will be an attempt to say "there exists a nasturtium" in the absence of any propositional form. Predicated on an address to an absence, the poem introduces the nasturtium itself as subsequent to the initial attempt, both to be resolved in an anticipated "resulting whole" that will make them meaningful. Just as important, however, is the necessary opacity of the "glance over someone else's shoulder" in the approach to the nasturtium — that which alienates vision, distances us from it, equally motivates it. Transparency (the image of the nasturtium) and opacity (the linguistic difficulty of the attempt) are mutually implicated, staged toward an eventual reconciliation. The nasturtium is seen as through a "window" that is both transparent and opaque, not to the nasturtium but to itself — a reversal of the analogy to the supposedly transparent medium of description:

> A nasturtium composed
> of holes in the rain-spotted window — to itself
> it's "in front,"
>
> To me, "behind." (93)

This "rain-spotted window" is the language of the poem, through whose elliptical approaches will occur the possibility of description. On the surface of language, description is "in front," though from the point of view of subjectivity, or the poet, the nasturtium is "behind" language, inaccessible to it (from an easier perspective, of course, "in front" and "behind" mean the nasturtium's relation to the window). Where a window, like description, is conventionally transparent, here it becomes an opaque shattering of perspectives, interfering with and allowing for the description and, along with the alienating presence of "someone else," demanding grounds for certainty and belief in the form of a question:

Whose property is the gleaming tremor
of compressed disclosure
in the opening of double-edged prepositions
in
a folded plane
of transparency which strikes the window pane? (93)

Anything but transparently, we begin to see the nasturtium in a double-edged language that predicts a "resulting whole" of description that will follow on "an isolated object." As both anterior to language and realized in language's unfolding, the nasturtium takes place as a site of memory [*lieu de mémoire*] and desire: in a continuous temporality of protension and retention; in the coincidence of present and past; and as a wish for the future.[6]

In the continuing "attempt" of the poem, description will be displaced and reconfigured in and as memory. The poem demands a reciprocal construction of memory and inaccessible knowledge sited between a past it embodies and a future it will reveal. This futurity will have accounted for the nasturtium that precedes the poem but cannot be described by it, making meaningful the "compressed disclosure" of an intensely subjective continuity. In stages of approach, the poem sharpens the edges of prospective meaning figured in the nasturtium, often defining the space where the nasturtium would exist negatively, in the central figure's absence from other spaces of description and memory:

A sign, inverted — not mirror, not childhood.

(A version: this night shattered apart
by the rays of the dragonflies' concise deep blue
drawing noon into a knot of blinding
foam . . . (94)

Here, a moment of what V. N. Voloshinov called ideological speech (as elsewhere in "A sign sweats over the doorway: 'Voltaire has been killed. Call me immediately'") disrupts the continuity of the poem, shifting it away from its inaccessible object toward a "sign, inverted" that is neither a mirror of the present nor a memory of the past, a co-occurrence of the shattered night and "blinding / foam" of noon.[7] The poem likewise shifts thematic focus from the scene of description and memory to dissociated moments of nature such as the dragonfly's wings (or a specific tree, a flight of "swifts," the "logorhythmic birds"). These devices, however, cannot detract from the poem's expanding subjective truth:

(the knowledge, which belongs to me,
absorbs it cautiously, tying it
        to innumerable capillary nets:
the nasturtium — it is a section of the neuron
string . . .   ) (96)

This knowledge is presented not as a report to some transcendent observer — a comparison with Marianne Moore's aesthetics of sublime grandeur in "An Octopus" would fail in this sense — but through the materiality of language produced from a variety of sites. In Dragomoshchenko's poetics of description, all such shifts away from the ostensible subject of the poem are "only a continuation / within the ends' proximity" (97); the poem is free to expand, to include fragments of dialogue, self-reference ("Arkadii / Trofimovitch Dragomoshchenko describes / a nasturtium, inserts it in his head" (99), along with its unfolding sequences of spatial and temporal discontinuity. A developing metalinguistic continuity, based on a series of spatialized predicates, is created by such semantic shifts:

The nasturtium
and anticipation rainy as the window and window behind wind-
ow
(he in it, it in him)
like meanings smashing each other
(I don't say, metaphor . . .)
                                        drawn
by emptiness,
one of the distinct details — (100)

Signification breaks down in the act of description, but only in the collision of the various "meanings smashing each other" can either take place. In the extension of this effect, through the poem's insistent reduction of similarity to contiguity — of description turning to language — poetry becomes a kind of physics, a part of the natural world it describes. A situation of semantic overload and meltdown occurs where "the mechanism / of the keys, extracting sound, hovering over / its description // in the ear, // protracted with reverberation into the now." Sound becomes a physical blur where "*zaum* [transrational speech] returns with the conclusion that it has absorbed / and dissolved into pure plasma each day," an undoing of sense linked to "the nasturtium, unusually simple (empty)" (101–2).

The alignment of poetry with nature thus paradoxically depends, for its assertion of palpable reality, on a continual undermining of language by itself ("When? Where? / Me? Vertigo conceives / 'things'"; 101). This is not simply a matter of decentered poetic voice. In the poem's vertiginously expanding horizon of meaning, sense is made "only / through another / multiplication tables, game boards, needles, a logarithmic / bird," in other words, anything presentable in language, "and the point isn't which kind" (103). The poem oscillates between intensely subjective associations and objective moments of description, attempting both in either's negation: "I contemplated the truth behind events listening to the vividness / of the erased words / ready to expound on the defects of precision," in counterpoint to the poet's self-canceling voice: "*And here in the 41st year of life / A pampered fool, whose speech continually / misses the point*" (106). Subjectivity in the poem is constructed through such dislocated intensities of language: "I follow from burst to burst, from explosion to explosion, / faces, like magnesium petals floating by, which permit those who remain a misprint in memory / to be recognized" (108), but it offers no assurance about the continuity of nature behind the poem as the basis for these effects.

> I intend to say . . . I in . . . that
> what is said and emptiness, drawing in a selection
>   of the elements of utterance,
> correlating,
> discover desire's inexhaustible source —
> what is said cannot be said again. (109)

The attempt to reconcile memory and the objective world is impossible, due to the fact that nature cannot be assumed to be a stable, encompassing reality that the poet's memorial condensations have arisen from and into which they devolve. Memory arises out of nothing, and that is the objectivity of the nasturtium; as a result, the poem can move directly from negated description to the expanded systems of meaning that encompass it:

Conjecture is simple —
the nasturtium is not . . .
necessary. It is composed from the exceptional exactness
of language
commanding the thing — "to be"
and the rejection of understanding. (110–11)

The poem locates the objective world by placing the language of description under erasure, opening itself to many languages and in doing so determining what its relation to nature is going to be. In the poem's climactic conclusion, the nasturtium's inaccessibility is the point of entry into substrata of memory realized as copresent with its futurity:

The nasturtium — it is the undiminished procession
of forms, the geological chorus of voices crawling,
shouting, disclosing each other . . . (112)

Following an "undiminished procession" of memory and language, the image of nasturtium consumed in flames that ends the poem is the "narrowest opening," a subtraction from the visible as an intensified image where overdetermination and absence coincide:

Threading the seen through the needle
whose greed
fits the impeccability of its choice — the narrowest

opening of form.

The nasturtium bearing fire. (112)

It is through this clash of languages tending toward as-yet-unrealized objectivity that a space for reconfigured subjectivity, seen in the purely material strands of memory, can be located in the poem. In that futurity is connected to a poetics of many languages, it is important that Dragomoshchenko is by birth Ukrainian (born in postwar occupied Potsdam, raised in the multilingual environs of Vilnitsa, now in St. Petersburg), even though he writes in Russian. He has, in other poems, shifted to Ukrainian as a counterpoint to Russian specifically to bring up a common Slavonic subtext under the surface of ordinary language, further allying epistemological concerns with those of cultural memory. In other translations, Hejinian has inserted phrases of Middle English into the text to approximate this effect. In "Nasturtium as Reality," such archaic subtexts are figured in the stratum of memory, but still there is notable conflict among its forms of representation, between an overall framework of displaced language and autobiographical narratives that emerge out of its nonnarrative continuum. In one such vignette, a typically sentimental moment of self-knowledge, "tossing her skirt on the broken bureau / with wood dust in her hair / a neighbor girl, spreading her legs / puts your hand where it is hottest"—which leads, not quite as typically, to an authorial turning inward in anxious bursts of linguistic dissociation: "through / multiplication tables, logarithmic bird, through / the stars of her mouth" (103). It is as if the eruption of the feminine demands a release of poetic authority; the poem is unable to maintain its address to the nasturtium's futurity at the moment the "meaning of her" intrudes. There is a disjunction here between prospective nature as ground for memorial condensation and the emergence of the feminine, as occurs likewise in the next section, in a more measured way, where an account of the death of a woman close to the poet, again realized in the poem's language, is a counterpoint to the unfolding horizons of the poem's address to the object: "And all the more unbearable the meaning of 'her' ripened in you / while the quiet work went on revealing / thoughts / (you, her) from the sheath of feminine pain / the silent symmetry crumbling in the immense proximity of the end" (105). There is a distinct cultural bias to this admission of women only at the extremes of authorizing self-knowledge, but it is also here that the poetic convention of a stable, feminized, assumed nature (from waving fields of grain as meaning "poetry" in a Sovkino documentary of Yevtushenko to the Stalinist cathexis of "Mother Russia") as the basis of memorial effects begins to be broken down in its assumptions.

This location of a poetics in a refiguring of memory through the limits of objectivity aligns Dragomoshchenko's work with related projects in post-1960s Soviet culture, such as the use of subjective associations and palimpsestic overlays of memory in the films of Andrei Tarkovsky, a slightly acknowledged but clearly important intertext for the poet's work. In an essay on poetic subjectivity and collective knowledge, Dragomoshchenko writes that the poet may return, like a blind bee, to a "hive" of understanding,

> but there is no hive. It disappears at the very moment when understanding comes close to being embodied in itself and its 'things,' which to all appearances is really the 'hive.' We wander through a civilization of de-

64. Andrei Tarkovsky, the fire sequence, still from Mirror, *1973.*

> stroyed metaphors: road, home, language, a man on a bicycle, embraces, *Tarkovsky's films*, moisture, 'I', memories, history, and so forth.[8]

For Dragomoshchenko, "the problem of subjectivization is tautological," fractally reproduced in the dispersion and refiguring of a collective center, "the hive," in culture's unreified "things." Wandering through a "civilization of destroyed metaphors," one can only lament the absent tenor through its dispersed vehicles. Such a demetaphorization occurs similarly in a film such as Tarkovsky's *Mirror* by means of techniques intended as the opposite of Eisenstein's constructed film metaphors. As Tarkovsky notes of his work, "The point is to pick out and join together the bits of sequential fact, knowing, seeing and hearing precisely what lies between them and what kind of chain holds them together,"[9] even as he "reject[s] the principles of 'montage cinema' because they do not allow the film to continue beyond the edges of the screen: they do not allow the audience to bring personal experience to bear on what is in front of them on film." Rather, "editing entails assembling smaller and larger pieces, each of which carries a different time. And their assembly creates a new awareness of the existence of that time" (118–19). Such a description of cinematic continuity is remarkably close to Dragomoshchenko's poetics.

In Tarkovsky's *Mirror*, nonnarrative, intuitive sequences displace memory, continuity, and futurity onto a fragmented world of objects comprising several registers of image. In one sequence, the burning house in the countryside to which mother and son have been removed during the war stands as mnemonic placeholder for the future return of the father that is always to come (there is a question whether it really ever takes place [fig. 64]). In another sequence, multiple, sidelong, disjunct views down the corridors of the state publishing house where the mother works in the 1930s as proofreader enact a moment in which the collective "hive" dissolves into the mere objectivity of "things." Millennial horizons, the grand narrative of the state, devolve into fragments of material presence, as in the hinted propaganda poster barely glimpsed on the way to other rooms. Finally, the insertion of documentary footage of the Spanish Civil War and of a forced march across the ice in World War II asserts the film's overarching formal subjectivity against the intrusion of represented history, which can only take on memorial value as loss. Images in Dragomoshchenko have similar organizing dynamics: "the nasturtium bearing fire" that closes the poem is substituted in place of memory's anticipated return; the overlapping and mutually contradictory frames of descriptive language dissolve certainty into isolated moments addressed to futurity; and the interruptions of narrative displace subjectivity toward expanded horizons. Closure — the father's return or the nasturtium as realized object — is distributed and held out in these registers as a partial, prefigured resolution.

The relation between empirical reality and a deferred future that exceeds nature, but in terms of which nature can be known (as enacted in the form of a poem), has also been a central theme of debates in post-Soviet science. The opening invocation of our Summer School was to "be scientific," but what followed led rapidly away from empirical questions toward a prospective, metaphysical hyperspace in which, for example, "futurist art [like that of Khlebnikov's post-Euclidean mathematics of world correspondence] has its own dominant in consciousness."[10] A concurrent article by Moscow philologist Mikhail Dziubenko describes a scientific project that combines the problem of new meaning in avant-garde poetry with an alternative school of Soviet science known as the "Linguistics of Altered States of Consciousness" — a utopian or even New Age quest for method that surfaces in many late-Soviet scientific discourses. For Dziubenko, "At deep levels of consciousness (which acquire primary meaning in the creative process) the ability to penetrate into the logic of other languages is established. Artistic creativity, then, involves a breakthrough into another language, which uses the characteristics and lacunae of the original."[11] Such a language is based in material reality, but only as its potential future:

> We must understand that there is only one linguistic universum; uniting all world languages in the massive entity of their historical development and functional applications. This universum is not a scientific abstraction. It is manifested concretely, on the lowest, phonetic level, in naming,

> where moreover language differentiations do not play any definitive role, and on the highest, grammatical-syntactic level, in art, which is only possible by virtue of the existence of different languages and which is itself an unconscious borrowing of foreign language structures. (29–30)

For Dziubenko, "the knowledge of one language is knowledge of all languages," leading to a research program in which "there is no doubt that a Persian specialist could contribute a great deal to the study of Khlebnikov's works" (30–31). Creativity expands language into a utopian "linguistic universum," yielding a romantic philology that recalls Wilhelm von Humboldt's fantasy of the consciousnesses of entire nations thinking in each of their national languages.[12] There are several implications of this excursus into late-Soviet discussions of scientific method for poetics: first, creativity is thought to have ontological implications; second, as material reality, creative language extends, "through characteristics and lacunae," into a greater reality that contains it; and third, structuring language in the variety of its altered states as well as being structured by it, subjectivity is not permitted the transcendent distance of the observer but instead experiences loss due to an expanded suprasubjectivity whenever the grounds for language (altered states, presumably) historically change. So the importance of creativity for method is to open a space of loss of certainty in a romantic science that produces not stability of knowledge but expanded horizons of meaning elaborated against an unstable ground. This view of science, while not explicitly endorsed by Dragomoshchenko, locates the position of nature in the poem as an uncertain effect of late-Soviet epistemology; in the poem's "attempt," the relation between nature and creativity discussed by Dziubenko unfolds in a kind of vertiginous, open-ended, ecstatic address. The poetics of embodied cultural memory with which we began — the social command of several generations of Soviet and post-Soviet poets — thus devolves in fragmentary, recombinant, and prospective form, given the lack of any stability of the objective world. Such an initial premise of anxiety and loss can only be resolved by a reconfigured memory realized in the impossible futurity of the poem, as with the final self-immolation of Dragomoshchenko's nasturtium. In this sense, "Nasturtium as Reality" demonstrates post-Soviet subjectivity as a reconciliation of collective memory and empirical truth. Out of the incommensurate weave of culture, in the absence of any ground in objective reality, a new certainty must be built. In Dragomoshchenko's work, post-Soviet subjectivity becomes a new kind of authorship that weaves together several strands of Soviet culture — lyric voice, embodied memory, and scientific objectivity — in an elaborate metapoetics situated in the here and now of an abandoned knowledge.

KABAKOV'S *KOMMUNALKA*

The domestic theatricality of Ilya Kabakov's conceptual albums, paintings, and installation art is at a polar remove from Dragomoshchenko's self-reflexive poetics.[13] *Ten Characters*, an installation with accompanying narratives (published simultaneously in book form), based on the theme of the *kommunalka* or communal apartment, was presented by Kabakov in Western galleries and museums in New York, London, Zürich, and Washington, D.C., in 1988–91.[14] The installation was based on Kabakov's work in the genre of the conceptual album from the late 1960s (the album of *Ten Characters* was completed about 1974), its materials from Soviet everyday life collected and assembled over the next two decades. The genre of installation art itself, as one of the ways in which traditional painting and sculpture were destabilized and transformed in postmodernism, takes on a culturally hybrid value in Kabakov's work, reflecting both the ephemeral displays of oppositional Soviet art through the 1980s and its monumental representation in museum shows in the West thereafter. Most of what was seen in the Soviet underground of the 1970s was itself "installed" in some nongallery setting such as an apartment or open-air happening; the bulldozed art exhibition of the late Brezhnev era in this sense could be seen as the outer spatial limit of a wide range of site-specific work. The genre continued in Moscow conceptual art with what has been called "Aptart," which typically united a social scale of presentation based in everyday life with a diverse and often dissonant range of issues, materials, and strategies.[15] This work may often seem more of a cultural breeding ground for new ideas than a finished product, while Kabakov's installation art has all the finish and framing of the most professional work in the genre as it has developed in museum programs over the last twenty years in the West. Among his recent installations are *The Bridge*, which presents the evidence of a mysterious, catastrophic event that might have taken place had modern art been discussed in a Moscow apartment building's social club in 1984, shown at the Museum of Modern Art (1991);[16] *The Life of Flies*, an elaborate parody of late-Soviet metaphysics, with accompanying documentation in three languages (1992);[17] *Mental Institution*, a reconstructed example of Soviet institutional space, shown at the 1998 Whitney Biennial;[18] and the monumental *Palace of Projects*, which assembles innumerable miniature utopian projects for coping with reality, seen at the Reina Sofia Museum in Madrid and later in New York (1995–2000).[19] Kabakov's installation work thus records a movement from Soviet oppositional culture to Western postmodernism, as his work shifts from the millennial/dystopian horizons of the Soviet context to another kind of transcendence implied in the artist's showing, outside the Soviet Union, monumental works that publicly put on display its most interior reality.

Subjectivity in Kabakov's work is enacted in both formal and narrative terms: in the gaps between word and image, painting and installation, narrative and nonnarrative, transcendence and immanence. His formal strategies are elaborate negotiations between representation and conceptual art, while the narratives of his albums and installations are grounded in the everyday life of the era of stagnation, seen from its post-Soviet horizon. In *Ten Characters*, Kabakov invents the life histories of the dysfunctional fictional characters who live together in a communal apartment seen from both outside and within it, constructing a version of the apartment itself as the framework of the gallery installation. Transcendence really is the only option for social reality modeled on such living arrangements, which, from the revolution through the Khrushchev housing boom and into the present, typically crammed the urban working class into multifamily dwellings, often one family per room, where everyone shared the collective amenities and, according to the artist, life was open-ended verbal abuse. Kabakov's reconstruction creates a world of incommensurate, extreme personality types to be imagined as somehow impossibly sharing the same communal space, while inventing wildly adventurous behaviors and systems of belief to accommodate themselves to their world. The short narrative accounts accompanying the meticulously detailed individual installations (often typed and mounted on the walls near them) are as much mock disquisitions in *Lebensphilosophie* as anecdotes; they form a template through which the realities of Soviet systems of belief are represented as they would be experienced in everyday life. "Everyday life," translated as *byt* in the Soviet lexicon, is a central concern in Kabakov's work, as it was for both the realist and formalist traditions that preceded him.[20] The everyday life of the Brezhnev era of stagnation, the subject of much of his work, evinces from many post-Soviets an unutterable horror: "Our everyday life, you cannot imagine how boring it is!" remarked poet Alexei Parshchikov.[21]

There is a system of interlocking, mutually supporting beliefs in Kabakov's depiction of Soviet *byt*, an everyday habitus that is the reverse side of the monumental world of May Day parades, the Moscow Metro, and Soviet theme parks outside. For Kabakov, "The *kommunalka* presents a certain collective image, in which all the ill-assortedness and multi-leveledness of our reality is concentrated and vividly revealed," a reality figured as an "autonomous linguistic organism," "an extended childhood," "a repressive sea of words," "the madhouse," and so on.[22] Alternative dysfunctions for negotiating this social space are identified for each of the characters: one can either go into oneself ("Some of the inhabitants of the communal apartment lead a mysterious, even secretive existence"; 52) or "leap out of oneself," as Kabakov himself says he did ("While formally I haven't ceased to live inside myself, I observe what happens from repeatedly shifting positions"; 55). Beyond either possibility, "some powerful, lofty, and faraway sound is clearly audible," a higher voice perceptible to both artist and communal residents (54). Listening to the voice of that "beyond" will be one of the organizing metaphors of Kabakov's project — as it is simultaneously the voice of collective life and the position of transcendence from which the *kommunalka*'s individual voices may be heard. Both the compensatory fantasies of Kabakov's characters, and their encompassing horizons of imagined totality, become the answer of the Real of Soviet life to the impenetrable interlocutor Slavoj Žižek calls the big Other, which divides and hystericizes the subject — producing high-pitched frequencies of complaint, deformed ideological projections, and blank voids of nihilism, all symptoms of Soviet reality as constructed in the social space of the *kommunalka*.[23]

In "The Man Who Flew into His Picture," subjectivity is drawn as if by a magnet to a negating white space, a ground for pure projection (fig. 65): "Sitting alone in front of an enormous, poorly painted white board," the resident "sees before him an enormous, endless ocean of light, and at that moment he merges with the little, plain figure that he had drawn. . . . At the same time that he is following the departing figure with all his soul, the other half of his consciousness clearly realizes that he is sitting completely immobile in his lonely room." In this moment of self-defeat, however, "he comes to the conclusion that he needs some third person, some sort of witness [to be] present to watch him 'from the side'" (7). Such a witness is conveniently located as the case of delusions in the next room, where "The Man Who Collects the Opinions of Others," "standing behind the door, immediately writes down in his notebook everything which is said, no matter what." But this witness's quest for objectivity is only another structured fantasy:

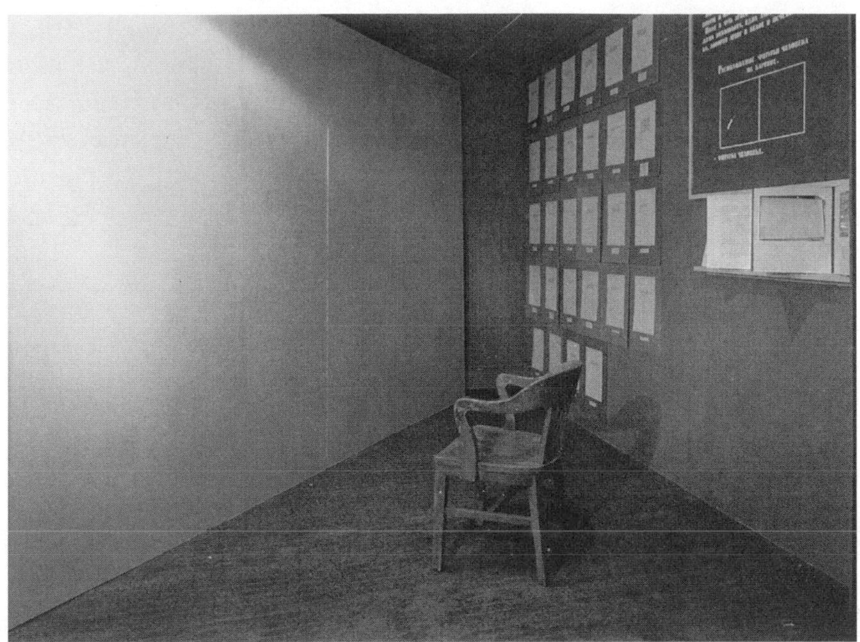

65. Ilya Kabakov, "The Man Who Flew into His Picture," detail from Ten Characters, *installation, 1989.*

> According to his view, opinions are arranged in circles. Beginning at any point, they then move centrifugally and as they move away from the centre they meet "opinions" moving from other centres. These waves are superimposed, one on top of another, according to him, the entire intellectual world is a gigantic network, a lattice of similar dynamic intersections of these waves. He compared all this to the surface of a lake, where 10–20 stones are randomly and uninterruptedly thrown all at once. (9)

"In talking about this, it was as though my neighbour actually saw these magical, shining circles" (10); Kabakov likewise visualizes them in his installation of tidy mock-ups of the character's notebook pages arranged around the "objects" that gave rise to the spreading "opinion waves." While this is clearly high satire of venerable Russian literary pedigree, there is an identification with these delusional modes of organizing reality that makes Kabakov's procedure unlike the realist mode of describing the subject positions of, say, the flophouse in Maxim Gorky's *Lower Depths* (cited as an influence in an interview).[24] Being an artist for Kabakov means to act in as delusional and obsessive a manner as his characters; the meticulous details of Kabakov's miniature mock-ups and full-scale realizations of the *kommunalka* reveal a complicity with the residents' hysterical obsessiveness, as do his characters' collections of objects and albums of kitsch postcards. It is Kabakov himself who assembled these Soviet versions of Trivial Pursuit, acting out his aesthetic strategies as an identification with the delusional structures of his personae.

In each of these works, the space of culture and everyday life is the opposite of the transcendental perspective and monumental organization of Soviet society's official self-presentation. This is forcefully presented in the dominant red of numerous kitsch posters covering the walls of "The Man Who Flew into Space from His Apartment," the central example of the delusional project of failed transcendence among the residents (fig. 66). In this installation (which was a separate installation before the rest of the *kommunalka* was realized), the resident schemes for years to construct a pseudoscientific device that will allow him to exceed the limits of gravity and leave this world behind. The resulting explosion, which rips a hole in the top floor of the communal apartment and sends its resident into orbit, blasts through the horizon of Soviet monumentalism as well — a parody of the orbits of Yuri Gagarin and followers as a state-sponsored transcendence purveyed to the masses at large. An intense desire to substitute material reality for ideological abstraction creates the displaced trajectory of his panicked flight: "His room was full of blueprints, some of them were glued on the wall. . . . On a table in the corner stood a model of our block, our street, and you could see our building. I asked him why there were metal bands attached to the model and leading upward from the roof our house. He suddenly said that it was the trajectory of his future flight" (13). Such kitsch futurism, as in the mechanical predictability of "We are Going to Communism," creates in the character a high metaphysics to explain how his contraption fits in with "objective reality":

> He imagined the entire Universe to be permeated by huge sheets of energy which "lead upwards somewhere." These gigantic upward streams he called "petals." . . . The Earth together with the sun periodically crosses through one of these enormous "petals." If you knew this precise moment, then you could jump from the orbit of the Earth onto this "petal," i.e., you could enter, join this powerful stream and be whirled upwards with it. (13)

66. *Ilya Kabakov, "The Man Who Flew into Space from His Apartment," detail from* Ten Characters.

Fabricating a contraption made of rubber "extension wires" and explosive charges, the resident realizes his objectives and blasts into orbit, creating a monumental void in the explanatory fabric of everyday life that others rationalize in a characteristic way: "Maybe he really did fly away, that sort of thing happens." In the ideological space vacated by monumental trajectories and transcendent goals one can see a cultural breeding ground for rumors, speculations, and theologies of all sorts — a space to be filled with all manner of cultural detritus. Žižek speaks of the ideological "hole" left by the fall of Eastern Bloc states in these terms: "When, for a brief, passing moment, the hole in the big Other, the symbolic order, becomes visible," it will be filled with delusions of all sorts. The duty of the post-Soviet intellectual, which Kabakov accepts, "is precisely to *occupy all the time*, even when the new order . . . renders invisible the hole itself, *the place of this hole*."[25]

Such systems of belief, orbiting as it were around a vacated belief, are made equivalent, in yet another irony, to the material culture that was supposed to provide them with normative expectations. An obsession with collecting, of the simple accumulation of bits and pieces of culture, becomes a metaphor for the activity of the artist; material reality replaces a more conventionally redemptive collective memory. In a number of his characters, Kabakov makes his art an inductive process whose compilation of oddments adds up to indeterminate, compensatory, but fascinating horizons that motivate his fractal characters. In "The Short Man," the character's project of accumulation and re-presenting cultural detritus in foldout albums is a parodic version of realism seen as representing the world "in little": "Everything that goes on in our communal kitchen, why, isn't that a subject, it's actually a readymade novel!" (20). However, the only people who can stoop so low as even to read this little world are, like its author, little — others invited in to view the work merely step over it as an obstacle. Social realism devolves into a micropolitics of trivia, leading to a community of one in which only a solipsist can read the work of the solipsistic man (as Louis Zukofsky wrote, "Strabismus may be a topic of interest between two strabismics; those who see straight look away!").[26] A substratum of material culture, reinterpreted as past not present reality, becomes a process of therapeutic recuperation in "The Man Who Never Threw Anything Away" (fig. 67): "A simple feeling speaks about the value, the importance of everything. This feeling is familiar to everyone who has looked through or rearranged his accumulated papers: this is the memory associated with all the events connected with each of these papers" (44). The

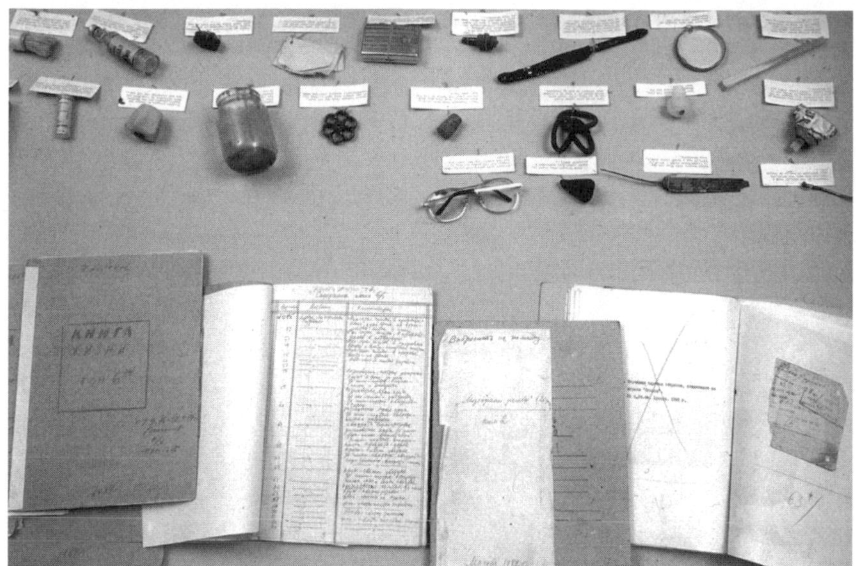

67. Ilya Kabakov, "The Man Who Never Threw Anything Away," detail from Ten Characters.

resident initiates a project of collecting, preserving, and labeling all the discarded items found in the *kommunalka*'s hallway in order to recover their memorial value: "An enormous past rises up behind these crates, vials, and sacks. . . . They cry out about a past life, they preserve it" (45). Such a collection of meaningless, material fragments ironically reverses Soviet culture's demand for a stabilizing poetics of memory, invalidating sentimental retrospection and leaving subjects no option but to face the compelling voids of futurity without recourse. Any attempt to substitute material culture for absent meaning only recycles the loss.

"The Person Who Describes His Life Through Characters" continues this process of induction to uncover a principle of individuation through his collected, collective subjects: "He undertook once to describe his life, mostly so that he could find out from this description who he himself was." In so doing, he realizes "that even these variegated fragments [of memory] belonged not to his single consciousness, his memory alone, but, as it were, to the most diverse and even separate minds, not connected with each other, rather strongly different from each other" (34) — producing what amounts to the delusional notion that there are, in fact, other people. Thus the character begins the process of constructing albums of the characteristics of his "ten characters" — precisely the early work that gave rise to

Kabakov's *kommunalka*, and situating him squarely within it. Such self-reference continues in "The Untalented Artist," who, ignoring the practical dictates of the state, makes a series of purposeless "painted notices" that combine his rudimentary technical skills as painter and propaganda poster letterer. The paradoxical success of his paintings (in the actual installation a beautiful group of large-scale parodies of everyday themes overlaid with irrelevant titling) is due equally to the artist's partly realized native talent and to the purposelessness of the assigned projects (various official notices and posters) he is commissioned to paint: "What results is a dreadful mixture of hackwork, simple lack of skill, and bright flashes here and there of artistic premonitions and 'illuminations'" (17) — a kind of suprasubjective intention realized in place of the unique signature of individual personality, yielding a figure of the artist as a social paradox (a likely reference to Kabakov's commercial work as an illustrator for Soviet journals as well).

In "The Collector," a similar suprasubjective horizon looms, as the dissociation of identity through collective processes proceeds. The character's arrangements of numerous color postcards on state tourist and memorial themes become "enormous, complex pictorial works which are worthy of a very great professional talent" (31), far beyond that of any individual artist. Recombining the strands of a fragmented culture, however, produces an effect of "the power of ORDER"; "This is the triumph of the victory of order over everything." There is a paradox here, however: while it is the artist who in fact created this order by making his arrangements of cultural materials, the voice of order points beyond individuality: "It seemed to me that in some terrible way, some kind of, how shall I say it, idea of COMMUNALITY, was expressed in [the arrangements], that very same thing which surrounded us all in our common overcrowded apartment" (32). Communality becomes the terrible absence between moments of material evidence, a voice of emptiness drawn from the incommensurability of its objects. This collective voice is further pursued in "The Composer Who Combined Music with Things and Images," whose staged mass productions in the *kommunalka* hallway, like miniature versions of Stalinist sports extravaganzas, trade the sovereignty of the artist who arranges reality for the totalizing horizon of a collective voice heard by all: "Gradually those who are reading the [arranged] texts begin to notice that beyond the sound of their voices is a faintly heard, special kind of sound" (27) — a transcendent moment of the metaphysics of communality.

We have come full circle, from an obsessively material collocation as an implicit satire on Soviet collective life to the question of utopian, transcendent, metaphysical perspectives. In "The Rope," a piece that serves as a comment on his characters, Kabakov defines the point at which materialism breaks off and spirituality begins: "So these empty ends of rope . . . represent the soul before and after 'our' life, and in the middle is depicted its life, so to speak, in its earthly segment" (48). Working out from these middles toward the open ends of the soul, Kabakov recuperates the multiple identities of his communal apartment in terms of a single, collective destiny, albeit otherworldly. His *kommunalka* project could not be less like Georges Perec's description of multiple lives in the same building in his novel *La Vie mode d'emploi*, where each life has a separate history, an individual meaning rendered in the reified space of owned or rented individual dwellings.[27] Kabakov, in his ironic rejection of Soviet culture, still maintains a totalizing attitude toward history — at the risk of virtual nihilism in regard to the things of this world, an attitude necessary, it would seem, to maintain the coherence of totality in relation to its determinate negation. In its derivation from material reality, Kabakov's nihilism exemplifies the Hegelian paradox "The spirit is a bone," or the coincidence in opposition of substance and spirit, from which Žižek derives the formula "limitation precedes transcendence."[28] The limitations of the lives of the characters are identical to the totality that transcends the meaninglessness of their material lives; "spirit" becomes the incommensurability of the material world, resulting in a horizon of "emptiness" as transcendental subjectivity.

In a short text on the status of the "beyond" in relation to material reality, Kabakov speaks of such an "emptiness" as a condition of his work: "First and foremost I would like to speak about a peculiar mold, a psychological condition of those people born and residing in emptiness. . . . Emptiness creates a peculiar atmosphere of stress, excitedness, strengthlessness, apathy, and causeless terror."[29] In the lived experience of the materialist state, in its anxiety and boredom, there is an inescapable horizon of totalizing "stateness":

> The stateness in the topography of this place is that which belongs to an unseen impersonality, the element of space, in short all that serves as an embodiment of emptiness. . . . A metaphor comes closest of all to a definition of that stateness: the image of a wind blowing interminably alongside and between houses, blowing through everything by itself an icy wind sowing cold and destruction. . . . What sort of goals does this wind,

> this stateness, set for itself, if they exist at all? These goals always bear in mind the mastery of the scope of all territory occupied by emptiness as a SINGLE WHOLE. (58)

From this single whole of Soviet reality it is but one step to profound nihilism as a substitute for collective ideology (not merely an individual attitude, this nihilism has become a significant fact of post-Soviet life): "Nothing results from anything, nothing is connected to anything, nothing means anything, everything hangs and vanishes in emptiness, is borne off by the icy wind of emptiness" (59). These collective emptinesses interpret the nonexistent fullnesses, the pasts and futures at both ends of Kabakov's individual, material rope. Ernst Bloch's millennial horizons of hope, having devolved through the course of their progressive unfolding in the history of the Soviet state, here reach their antithesis in negativity.[30] With evidence of similar phenomena in the West in the same period, this is not simply a post-Soviet phenomenon; what seems specifically post-Soviet is Kabakov's sense of the lack of any mediation for these compelling voids.[31] What would provide the social resolution for post-Soviet nihilism — the New Russian economy, mafia-organized primitive accumulation, or neofascist nationalism — was entirely in doubt at the time.

Values for transcendence in the project would thus seem to refer importantly to two diverse registers: the this-worldly perspective of the artist-as-character who organizes reality in some compensatory way, and the otherworldly vision of the collective/individual subject, who would seem to have no other option than to await the dystopian millennium. Kabakov, speaking from beyond Soviet reality in commenting on his installation for the Museum of Modern Art, explicitly resolves these two versions of transcendence:

> The installation as a genre is probably a way to give new correlations between — old and familiar things. By entering an installation, these various phenomena reveal their dependence, their "separateness," but they may reveal as well their profound connection with each other, which was perhaps lost long ago, which they at some time had, and which they always needed. And particularly important is the restoration of that whole that had fallen into its parts [the separation of art from the "mystical"] I had spoken of.[32]

This mystical union of restored parts within a formal whole would be one that Kabakov had induced from the ideological horizons of his characters but which, as artist working as it were "outside" the *kommunalka*, he can realize in his chosen form. There is an explicit self-contradiction here, as when Kabakov says in an interview, "Upon discharge from the madhouse, I cease to exist. I exist only insofar as I am the resident of a *kommunalka*. I know no other self."[33] It is clear that Kabakov's "outside" position as installation artist in the Museum of Modern Art, as an artist but also a quasi-Soviet émigré (he maintains studios in France and in Moscow), can only be another version of the transcendence strategized from within the confines of collective life. Resited within the museum's horizon, however, this insistence on wholeness becomes reinterpreted as tragic separation and loss, as the Fall of Communism celebrated in the curator's introduction to *Dislocations:*

> Kabakov's reconstruction of the Tenants' Club of Moscow Housing Project No. 8 gives one a sense of the dreary mediocrity of Soviet society. . . . This unwelcome gathering place has been set up for an official lecture on the demerits of unofficial art, examples of which are propped against the drab gray walls between oxblood banners. Although the work of artists outside the system, the paintings nonetheless exemplify some of the bleakness and awkwardness of mainstream Soviet life to which they are the oppositional exception.[34]

Nothing in Kabakov's work could be construed as endorsing such a view of opposition; indeed, its explicit purpose is to induce a metaphysical wholeness that reinterprets "the unity of opposites we learned about in school." How then to understand the central conceit of *The Bridge*, Kabakov's MOMA installation, that "apparently, someone or something was to appear in the city that evening, and not just anywhere, but right in the middle of the club hall"? The appearance and disappearance of this person occurs: "There is no single description of what happened — the reports of various witnesses maintain the most adamant discrepancies," and lead to a vision of dystopian chaos: "After all the commotion had subsided, the entire floor in the center of the hall was littered with groups of little white people, constantly exchanging places."[35] It is entirely too easy to view this moment as an allegory for a collapse of central authority leading to a negative social space in which the masses circulate aimlessly, without direction. The easy availability of this reading does seem to indicate an influence of the museum's interpretative horizons, trading Soviet history for the representative installation of Kabakov's allegory of totality — as evident in the triumphalism of the museum curator's subsequent framing of his work:

> The Union of Soviet Socialist Republics is a lost civilization. At its tumultuous beginning, it was inhabited by shining phantoms of the New Man who mingled imperceptibly with a grimly determined general population. In its darkest hours, many among that population became ghosts. All have now faded into the past, or been reborn without preparation into the post-utopian age.[36]

It is precisely Kabakov's project to insist on the co-occurrence of the utopian past in the "post-utopian age," however much he may have misled the museum curator. His integration of the ghosts of the past within the postmodern present occurs precisely in the literal materialization of his position outside the totality it organizes, in the experience of emigration and of the installation of his work in Western museums. Here there is an inevitable entropic undoing of superseded totality as Kabakov's partial, metaphysically sited narratives are displaced in a grand narrative of impossible destiny "after the Fall." However, it may be said here, as it has been elsewhere, that nothing is lost, even in translation, for the likewise evident effect of Kabakov's work is to make each of the other installations in the mainstream extravaganza — by Adrian Piper, Chris Burden, David Hammons, Louise Bourgeois, Bruce Nauman, and Sophe Calle, indeed the entire permanent collection of MOMA used by Calle as the site for her work — interpretable as the compensatory fantasies of the dysfunctional residents of an expanded communal apartment on Fifty-third Street in New York called "The Museum of Modern Art." This sovietization of cultural horizons — an opening of the oppositional politics of the Cold War to the reality of a shared historical horizon — provides a good reason to reject Kabakov's integration into the MOMA show as an imperial trophy collected under the banner of Western postmodernism.[37]

POST-SOVIET/POSTMODERN

To distinguish the post-Soviet from the postmodern, we will need to consider both formal and cultural dimensions of the representative work. Leslie Scalapino's experimental prose text *Orion* (1991), written after the author's travel to the Soviet Union in the early 1990s, provides a counterexample to the work of Dragomoshchenko and Kabakov for its fascination and horror with multinational moments of depthlessness and pastiche.[38] A formally disruptive, nonnarrative essay on the dispersed position of global isolation and homelessness, it combines fragmented perspectives from the

West, the Soviet Union, and the Third World. The overarching analytic framework (responsible as well for the work's dissociative form) is the alienation of consumer society in the West: "The conception of this [social isolation] does not exist for those who are from the highly organized civilization which is based in the view that being free is having consumer goods. . . . We see as in this – the comic book – one frame at a time" (151). The highly organized West produces and sees itself in the sequential frames of a "comic book" in which agency becomes a depthless image, the type of the postmodern simulacrum. On the other hand, society in the Soviet Union is not fragmented but totalized and static, a grotesque of collectivism:

> This other civilization, which they are viewing (who are from the highly organized civilization), does not have order. There is no order. A bus driver is a function, who might drive until running out of gas. Not knowing where he is going, and seemingly not even wondering. It is not a matter of where the bus is to be going. Not merely from not being organized. Though it is repressive.
>
> Consuming is not the ideal. . . .
>
> Went to the arcade
>
> but only alone
>
> that is the department store. It was in a city which had a high glass-domed ceiling, tiers, hundreds of compartments with only a few goods, interior bridges.
>
> The crowd pressing into the cells. The crowd waiting in line outside one cell. (151–52)

The GUM department store in Moscow, as a tourist destination, is seen as entirely outside of the fragmented perspective of the postmodern: "The people from the highly organized civilization – coming to the other civilization which had no order, though repressed – were hungry ghosts" (154). This confrontation is a direct contrast to the position of the postmodern consumer who, like Baudelaire in the arcades of modernity, experiences loss of self in the crowd. "Baudelaire's discovery of not being in experience / in the crowd" (162) becomes the serial form of dissociation known as the "comic book": "to have no other self / than in the comic book / and so for one not to be in rapport with it – or with experience – as being Baudelaire's discovery" (155).[39] The people from the organized civilization, the West, thus experience more than merely the shock of modernity in the encounter with the collective society of the Soviet Union as unordered and repressed. The persistence of the crowd, to which the reification of capitalism was the nonsolution in the first place, occurs as the failure of a defense — and they suffer the direct experience of collective existence as the Real, which can only be answered in the disordered hail of fragments of Scalapino's prose. "Our collective sense of not making connections which is seen as fragmentary series is not a given" (154): beyond reification is a condition where both order and disorder, comic book and mass civilization, are one and the same. Such a suspension of the meaning of difference for a depthless surface is one of the hallmarks of the postmodern; Scalapino's text marks its precise location in relation to its cultural other. At the same time, global capitalism's homogenization of cultural difference is strikingly paralleled in a moment of depthless confrontation, rendered as a pastiche of the Same.

The postmodern moment thus seems to be a process the West must go through, in losing the defense of reification in confrontation with its privileged other, collectivity, but this would certainly not be a primary motivation for the works of post-Soviet artists. While Dragomoshchenko's "Nasturtium as Reality" approaches the nonexistence of the flower through a fragmenting of perspectives, they are not primarily effects of reification. The nasturtium becomes the "transcendental object" of the Kantian tradition; as "object cause of desire" (for the organization of self, the continuity of culture, the knowledge of nature) it creates the energetic effects of its final figure, "The nasturtium bearing fire."[40] But this nature as unknowable leads in the opposite direction from postmodern pastiche; rather, subjectivity is constituted in its immanent horizons of lyric continuity, collective memory, and scientific objectivity. The entire activity of Dragomoshchenko's poem — its creation of new meaning in and of itself — is central to its implicit thesis that subjectivity, while everywhere in its own undoing, is produced in a movement from the transcendental object toward the horizons of an immanent unfolding. The formal dimensions of Dragomoshchenko's work — nonnarrative, fractal, predicative, and continually self-referring — become an instance of a "world-making" poetics that organizes a continuity of fabricated worlds only as they will be superseded. Central to these constructions is their conveyance of futurity: the lyric voice will constitute the authority of present address at a point in the distant future, when both collective memory and objective truth will have been revealed. Simultaneously, it is exactly the authority invested in the creation of new meaning that cancels out the empirical ground against which stable condensations of memory and culture may occur. While Dragomoshchenko's work seems to argue for a stability of archaic subtexts (of the collective body of nationality or church; of linguistic substrata such as Ukrainian; of individual memory), it is through its present-tense skepticism, presented exactly as a problem of "description," that it generates the unstable forms of post-Soviet subjectivity that must be resolved in futurity. The basis for such a reconstructed subject, after the fall of the New Man, is situated precisely on the fault line between the loss of cultural memory and the epistemological inadequacies of Soviet science. Georg Lukács once remarked that one of Stalin's greatest crimes was to think of social engineering as scientific.[41] The position of nature as unknowable in Dragomoshchenko's poetics clearly means to undermine the authority of any such thing as a "scientific" socialism as it discloses the traces of the past in our immediate experience, toward a future realization.

In Kabakov's installation of the *kommunalka*, a converse construction of subjectivity takes place, one perhaps more amenable to the international horizons of postmodernism, which dislocates state transcendence in the experience of post-Soviet emigration. This displacement of subjectivity and authority is literally embodied in Kabakov's shows in the high-rent collective apartments of the West, through which he takes part in that undermining of Soviet authority through foreign contacts that the Stalinist state did so much to prohibit. This new horizon is nothing if not self-canceling and ironic, even as it is sited toward its further, dialectical resolution. The emptying out of the dysfunctional "fullness" of the collective apartment into the nihilism of a post-Soviet "stateness" illustrates an eerily dystopian moment, but one that still conveys its displaced utopian ideals. In the *kommunalka*, every response of the individual to the interpellation of the state results in a compensatory behavior diametrically opposed to the elimination of antagonism at the end of history, even as the form of utopia is preserved in material processes of collecting, arranging, and performing the trash of culture. Rather than founding decentered subjectivity on the reification of a rationalized lifeworld, as in the West, post-Soviet subjects reenact a contradiction between the materiality of everyday life and a metaphysics of higher reality that they must internalize and reproduce. It is clearly to the point of Kabakov's construction of his characters that such modes of social reproduction can only yield an ideologically deformed result, even as each particular symptomatology still conveys a positive mode of social existence in some way. Indeed, Kabakov's subsequent *Palace of Projects* celebrates his characters' (and his own) compensatory behaviors in a capacious display. Here, society as the sum of its projects is clearly greater than any of its parts.

The difference between post-Soviet subjectivity and Western discourses of the postmodern, with their suspension of rational critique as a consequence of the subjective destitution of reified culture, should be apparent here. In fact, the historical emergence of an unstable post-Soviet subjectivity makes Western postmodernism appear even more qualified in its imagination of totality, which begins to come undone without the antagonism of the Soviet state. Here the construction of the postmodern as an effect of Cold War antagonism — hinted at by Fredric Jameson's seeing it as consequence of the "era of national revolutions" and the Vietnam War[42] — shows the cultural specificity rather than global necessity of Western postmodernism when compared to the post-Soviet horizons of Second-World subjectivity. The postmodern is thus not a one-size-fits-all form of social organization at the moment of devolution from the organizing stabilities of modern society — pointing to the still-unresolved differences between the First and Second Worlds. While the postmodern and the post-Soviet may have a great deal to say to each other, the historical conditions of their emergence finally mark them as incommensurate.

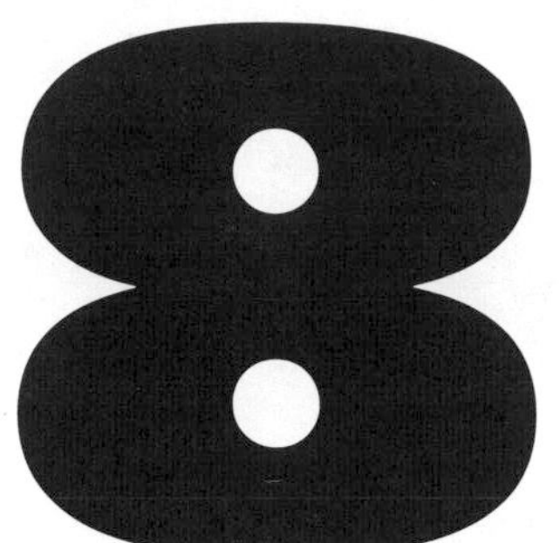

ZONE
THE POETICS OF SPACE IN POSTURBAN DETROIT

Le Détroit, a photographic/cinematic installation by Canadian photographer Stan Douglas, was exhibited by the Art Gallery of Windsor, Ontario, in 1999. This essay was delivered in the gallery space, surrounded by Douglas's photographs of the urban terrains of Detroit. Due to the presence of his images, it was written not so much as a critical commentary on them but as a kind of prelude and fantasia on their copresence in the gallery. In the essay, I wanted to derive the spatial form of postmodernism from its "origins" in Charles Olson's early work on space, and after his inaugural use of the term itself. This derivation was accompanied by a series of Douglas's photographs, one per zone of the essay, that I wished not so much to interpret as enhance in reading their representation of social space in Detroit. This representation, focusing as it does on the disused sites, abandoned and decaying houses, unkempt borders, and collapsing infrastructure within the larger context of urban depopulation and decline since the 1960s, turned out to be controversial in Detroit (indeed, the work was seen across the border in Windsor, not in Detroit). Certainly, Douglas's photographs were not intended to create an increase in urban tourism (except for selected art tourists who travel to Detroit precisely as a site for negativity). Nor were they meant as a dismissal of Detroit as a city in any kind of judgmental way. The question of negativity — aesthetic and social — is more broadly put in this work than as a record of social history, critique of capitalist social relations, or dismay at present politics, even if Detroit supplies abundant materials that can be used for such critiques. It is the position of the negative in the social reproduction of modernity, and its relation to the mode of inquiry that goes under the rubric of postmodernism in the arts, that is Douglas's concern. These are not pictures "of" Detroit, and ought not to be seen simply as such. They are disquisitions on the spaces made by human forms of destruction and undoing that, in the tradition of the sublime, turn us back to our fundamental purposes and ourselves. In the essay written for the occasion, I wanted to construct

68. Stan Douglas, Collapsed House, *1998. C-print, 18 × 36 inches.*

ten intersecting zones or nodal points of argument that would, in a radial manner, connect to Douglas's images on display. Here, without the copresence of the photographs, I have added two sections, one dealing more thoroughly with the formal argument of Douglas's work, and a conclusion on the difficult politics of representing Detroit. However, I have kept to my initial intention to rough out ideas in no more than two paragraphs in each zone, an economy allowing me to propose and dispose of the argument of each semiautonomous zone in its turn. The form of the essay is thus meant to stay close to my first responses to Douglas's work, and their inner logic, as a baseline critical practice prior to further development.

ZONE 1: THE POSTMODERN TURN

The postmodern in American literature originated as a spatial fantasy. The poet Charles Olson is credited with the first use of the term *postmodern* in literature, in a letter of 1951 from Black Mountain College: "And had we not, ourselves (I mean postmodern man), better just leave such things [the relics of history] behind us — and not so much trash of discourse, & gods?"[1] In its oblique and contorted syntax — the preferred style of the postmodern for Olson — the postmodern is a strange leaving behind that trashes its own discourse as it invokes the gods. That which is to be left behind, the modern, is condensed into objects, the dead "relics of history" against which the push of "outward man" will be made. But the terms for Olson's push beyond the modern episteme were given even earlier, in the opening pages of his 1947 study of Melville, *Call Me Ishmael*:

> I take SPACE to be the central fact to man born in America, from Folsom cave to now. I spell it large because it comes large here. Large, and without mercy.
>
> It is geography at bottom, a hell of wide land from the beginning. That made the first American story (Parkman's) exploration. . . .
>
> PLUS a harshness we still perpetuate, a sun like a tomahawk, small earthquakes but big tornadoes and hurrikans, a river north and south in the middle of the land running out of the blood.
>
> The fulcrum of America is the plains, half sea half land, a high sun as metal and obdurate as the iron horizon, and a man's job to square the circle.[2]

Olson's assumption of space is stated as a fact of possession at the outset: he takes space as the ground of his discourse, the site of its unfolding — which will be "without mercy."

For those schooled in the discourse, the spatial push is easily recognizable as one of the canonical themes of American studies. Sailing on the wide seas of the prairies, as in Cooper's novel of the same name, the restlessness of Western Man would assault the horizon as its limit, a spatial fantasy that converted millennial redemption into migration. In the period that produced *Call Me Ishmael*, America as Western Man had extended its oceanic fantasies into the Pacific, had converted the metaphor of the prairie as ocean into global domination. For Olson, Melville was "long-eyed enough to understand the Pacific as part of our geography, another West, prefigured in the plains, antithetical." The postmodern turn thus has, in one of its originary moments, an American discourse of spatial mastery, in an antiurbanist reconfiguration of the condensations and displacements of metropolitan European modernism as either progressive or cosmopolitan. "Big catches: he brought back holds full of the oil of the sperm, the light of American and European communities up to the middle of the 19th century." American productivity is atavistic, its correlative the "sperm" of the whale, in a return to sources beyond "logic and calculation": "It was an older sense than the European man's, more to do with magic than with culture." The postmodern originated in an atavistic return to fantasmatic space.

ZONE 2: THE OBJECT OF SPATIAL FANTASY

Every spatial fantasy correlates with an object. As corollary to Olson's fantasy of spatial domination, consider American investment in the machine. This is, as well, a part of the canon of American studies. For Olson, Ahab's spatial mastery is abetted by the technology of "one of most successful machines Americans had perfected up to that time — the whaleship" — as the vehicle of deathward fantasy. Technology per se is illusory mastery in the turn to the postmodern: in specifying the enabling conditions for American geopolitical mastery circa 1947, Olson cautions: "Americans still fancy themselves such democrats. But their triumphs are of the machine. It is the only mastery of space the average person ever knows, oxwheel to piston, muscle to jet. It gives trajectory." Victory over space, the propulsions of the piston and the jet were made on war production lines in American cities like Detroit. But this is not originary mastery, which precedes Western Man's illusory identification of the machine with the freedoms of space, Ahab's imaginary possession of the Pacific, if not the whale. What is required is a return to a more primitive condition of trajectory: "to the origins

69. *Stan Douglas,* Sections 5 and 8 of Herman Gardens, *1999. C-print, 45.7 × 55.9 cm.*

of things, the first day, the first man, the unknown sea, Betelgeuse, the buried continent. From passive places, his imagination sprang a harpoon." Such a magical act ought to spur Americans, after Melville, to their true aim: "to compel men or non-human forces to do one's will . . . lordship over nature." Technology is our revenge over nature in asserting spatial domination; insofar as it leads to postmodern fantasy, technology must be dissociated from its disavowal in the modern.

Technology as a magical transformation is to be distinguished from its humanist disavowal in relation to an object. Rather than producing an object correlative to an acknowledged cultural order, technology goes mad in its search for an impossible object, one that it will produce and destroy at the same time. This, for Melville in Olson's view, is Ahab's white whale: a condensation of the space that technology wants to dominate: "This Ahab had gone wild. The object of his attention was something unconscionably big and white. He had become a specialist: he had all space concentrated into the form of a whale called Moby-Dick." All space concentrated in the whale: the object of technology in the form of the whaling ship, which, internalized as an atavistic return, springs a harpoon. From madness, a harpoon: its object Moby-Dick. The object, nonexisting, leading onward across the wide seas. Spatial fantasy in the negativity of the object: Moby-Dick leads onward, fomenting harpoons which spring from the brain of Ahab as he goes forward, in a destructive rage, to penetrate space. At this hour, we are bombing . . . fill in the blanks: Tokyo, Hanoi, Baghdad, Yugoslavia, Afghanistan. The Pacific War gave Olson his reading of Melville, who becomes, more directly than Whitman, the privileged guide to space: "Whitman appears, because of his notation of the features of American life and his conscious identification of himself with the people, to be the more poet. But Melville had the will. He was homeless in his land, his society, his self." The isolato confronts the democrat, and becomes the preferred type of the American in his destructive, willful rage. The space of "the people," Whitman's America as gigantic man composed of as many parts as there are types, occupations, states, yields to a singular dysfunction of purpose. The object is not man's reflection of himself in the mirror but a negative compulsion.

ZONE 3: THE MODERN AS SPATIAL FANTASY

The organization of space is the primary fantasy of the modern. In critical theory, there is currently a widespread call for a return to space as a central category for analysis — a return to the inaugural concerns of the postmodern. At the moment of the breakdown of the modern, space is asserted over time: the space of lived experience and contradiction rather than the illusory unfolding of rationalized progress and domination. This spatial turn is particularly strong among feminist and postcolonial cultural critics, who depart from a center/periphery model of cultural expansion and control that is rightfully invoked as the bequest of the Enlightenment. But though there is a common point of departure in "Western Man," the distance between the feminist/postcolonial return to space and the inaugural moment of the postmodern is great. Olson's spatiality becomes a form of hyperdomination, a fantasy reducing the epochal tasks of the modern to the willful and destructive acts of an isolated individual. Olson's fantasy is unselfconscious and blind to its sources in social negativity, while in the critical return to space, it is the modern itself which is described as a form of fantasy. Olson cannot comprehend what kind of object the white whale is, and why it springs a harpoon, even as he pursues its spatial unfolding.

For the historian Teresa Brennan, in her psychoanalytic account of modernity, the fantasy of the modern may be elucidated in a historicist reading of Jacques Lacan's well-known use of the master-slave dialectic.[3] In the struggle for recognition by the lord or master, an order exceeding the subject that, in the analytic encounter and more generally in the unfolding of temporal experience, does not answer back, the subject as bondsman or slave is "captated" as a moment of *mis*recognition in the imaginary mirror. Brennan projects this moment outward "to a dialectic working between space in the environment and in the psyche" in which the imaginary becomes identified with the "other" as aggressively fixed in place. The struggle to be a self thus involves a fantasy of domination in which the other is held fixed, the exploded dynamics of the "ego's era" of the modern:

> The aggressive imperative involved in making the other into a slave, or object, will lead to spatial experience (territorial imperialism). This is because the objectification of the other depends on establishing a spatial boundary by which the other and the self are fixed. But this fixing of the other leads to the fear that the other will retaliate, which in turn leads to a feeling of spatial *constriction*[, one that] is related to the physical environment. These changes have physical effects on the psyche, which in turn alter the psychical perception of the environment, and of one's own boundaries. With spatial constriction, one's boundaries are threatened, and the resultant fear increases the need to control the object. (My emphasis, 9)

The modern is accurately described as the ego's era, then, insofar as the ego is caught up in a drama of recognition that directly leads to its "need for fixity and technological domination." The feminist turn of Brennan's analysis next appears: the ego's necessary positioning of the other is linked to the status of the "psychical fantasy of woman," with the placement of woman as a moment of domination and undoing at the ego's boundaries. In seeking to reread this fantasy as a consequence of capitalist social relations, Brennan goes on to recode its positioning of women as a splitting of the subject in relation to the commodity itself as object cause of desire. As a counter to the conservative implications of Lacan's positioning of women, she proposes a "foundational fantasy" that explains how psychical fantasies of space are simultaneously gendered and tied directly to economics:

> *The subject is founded by a hallucinatory fantasy in which it conceives itself as the locus of active agency and the environment as passive; its subjectivity*

> *is secured by a projection outward onto the environment, apparently beginning with the mother, which makes her an object which the subject in fantasy controls.* (11)

In the modern, the ego's era, the subject is identical to a hallucination at its own spatial limits, which are the site of a compelling negativity that must be dominated and denied. This moment of limit, or denial, has everything to do with a demand for the feminine.

ZONE 4: BOUNDARIES AS SUBJECT

Boundaries occur where the subject encounters its limits in the modern. Brennan's analogy between Lacanian imaginary and the politics of social space, even if wildly speculative (particularly in its goal of a return to an unconstrained "energetics" of psychic flux), suggests a mechanism for constructing social boundaries in modernity.[4] The fantasy of spatial domination, unleashed from its humanist moorings in the postmodern moment, turns out to be constitutive but denied in the modern. The spatial boundary is precisely where the self is stabilized in its objectification of the other; because this is an imaginary identification, it must be policed by a regime of mastery that exceeds it. In default to the imagination of some greater order of knowledge and control, subjects attempt to reproduce themselves as a form of spatial mapping onto the world they think they know, as imaginary, but therefore cannot control. Such a projection is aggressive: here we have the example of the colonial encounter, with European man projecting his own instability, under the misread orders of church and state, onto what will become subject peoples, who are thus constituted as others in an act of aggression. To control the consequences of this aggression, the ego shuts down its mechanism for spatial projection and tries to control its borders in what Brennan calls the "sadodispassionate" epistemology of Western science, the false neutrality of the positivist objectification of fact. This act of denial is primarily one of control, due to the fear, not only that the projection of ego's stability onto the other is imaginary, but that the other will retaliate and strike back. The more insecure the subject's domination, the more its boundaries are policed and disavowed.

Olson's production of spatial fantasy in the quest for control over the denying object — in other words, Ahab's quest for Moby-Dick over the wide seas of territorial expansion — thus appears as the typical mechanism for the construction of modern boundaries, where the object is in turn

70. Stan Douglas, Lafayette Park, *1999. C-print, 45.7 × 55.9 cm.*

denied. What Brennan adds to the genealogy of postmodernism, then, is the demand for the feminine (originally, the mother) in the construction of spatial limits. Something is troubling at the border: a lack, an insufficiency, the possibility of denial, which must be fixed in place. An example of such construction of boundaries, after the explosion of the postmodern, can be seen in an experimental novel by LeRoi Jones (later Amiri Baraka), *The System of Dante's Hell*, written in 1960–61 and published in 1965. Jones turns the spatial hierarchy of Dante's system on its head by locating the ever-constricting circles of hell in the social space he emerged from — Newark, New Jersey. In Jones's account of growing up insane in a world divided by race and class, if the ego (as a spatial configuration) has not yet stabilized, this is precisely a question of the construction of boundaries:

> NEWARK ST. (snakes writhe in the ditch, binding our arms. Our minds
> are strong. Our minds) . . .
>
> Its boundaries were Central Ave. To Sussex Ave. (1 block.) This is center I mean. Where it all, came on. The rest is suburb. The rest is outside this hole. Snakes die past this block. Flames subside.

(Add Sussex Ave. To Orange St. . . . because of Jim Jam & Ronnie & the cross-eyed girl who asked all new jersey to "do nasty."

(The slum LeRoy lived there also. 3 other Leroys. Two Griffiths (who sd they were cousins. One, the tall dark one, had a brother Robert who went from wet cowardice — which never completely subsided — to hipster violence. THE GEEKS. As some liaison or at least someone who wdn't get done in. Like Murray. THE DUKES.[5]

Jones writes in a form of associational fantasy, here addressed to the boundaries of any territory that can be identified with the limits of the self: "This is center I mean." If Jones follows Olson in his mode of postmodern fantasy as spatially unfolding and stylistically disjunct, he is also contained, from the outset, by the boundaries of a racial/cultural order that exceeds him and within which all acts of the imagination will be rendered suspect. Race and class are experienced as forms of spatial constriction, a shutting down or closing off of the inhabitable world, but Jones is explaining, in the exploded form of his experimental fiction, how the subject is not simply the object of such determination but is constructed in its own act of projection within it. The constricted, and therefore constructed, subject polices its own borders within the hell of a social space delimited by other people who are outside and white. Inside, territories unfold along with identity positions that are unstable or only provisionally stabilized: there are at least "3 other Leroys" as well as the author; "the cross-eyed girl . . . asked all new jersey to 'do nasty'"; and the violence of identity is figured in gangs such as "THE GEEKS" and "THE DUKES," names inscribed at the limits of their territories. Importantly, the sexual energy of "the cross-eyed girl" is associated with the drive to control boundaries in the construction of identity. Jones's fantasy space is internalized, within borders, at the same time that it is projective.

ZONE 5: SOCIAL SPACE AND NEGATIVITY

Spatial fantasies create boundaries by means of a negative object. We may now begin to consider the construction of boundaries in Detroit, their relation to the lived experience of social negativity. This prospect, while transparently evident to many outside Detroit, is controversial and contested by many living within its borders. And it is true that there has been a concerted effort to represent Detroit, particularly in liberal venues such as the *New York Times*, as an impossible aporia of racial and class division, not only the paradigm of failed urbanism but an agony of social dysfunction. Such a view of a Detroit, which embeds it within a larger national narrative as a symptom of intractable alterity, is rightly resented by those who live here — those occupying the manifold subject positions possible within its fragmented whole, who have an experience and a stake in its complex history. All this is granted — yet it is still true that Detroit has been the site of cataclysmic social trauma, one that is readily apparent in the gaps and elisions of its social terrain. For one coming from outside Detroit, a perception of visual negativity intersects readily with the sense of a social space divided into mutually exclusive, competing zones. At the macroscopic level, the border between the East Side and the Grosse Pointes, or the traditional racial and cultural divide of Eight Mile Road, can be seen from a satellite one hundred miles in space: even at that distance, the grass (and trees and landscaping) is greener on *one* side of the road — indicating a stupefying disparity of resources. At the same time, there is a microscopic politics of terrain that, while not as visually evident, is a persistent cultural fact. As with Jones's gangs, "the Geeks" and "the Dukes," social space is divided into competing and relatively autonomous turfs — and this is true, and perceptible, at many social levels and environments. (Want to know how business gets done in Detroit? I'll have to ask my cousin about that, and get back to you with a price on Monday.)

In the system of the Big Three's hell, the constriction of space at the borders of antagonistic zones re-creates the psychic dynamic that reinvests borders. Detroit becomes, at least in part, a negative object for those who live there, impossible to totalize or represent as a whole — and yet live here one does. Its representation in the local media, for instance, is a hopelessly impoverished mélange, a hodgepodge of fragmented human interest stories and industrial accidents, with social service spots thrown in for a consideration. And yet at the same time, one witnesses again and again an assertion on the part of those who live here of the adequacy of their terrain and its proper concerns, coinciding with an ironic denial of information coming from outside that would contest their worldview, as irrelevant. In a phenomenon much like the interpretive delusions at the boundaries of the Second World, developments elsewhere assume the form of a betrayal of that which one lives — and it is the necessary response to betrayal, perceived as an act of denial or criticism, that intensifies the obscure ergonomics of boundary formation. Boundaries between terrains are benign if not "sadodispassionate" in one sense, even if they are rigid and stultifying in another. Modernity re-creates its own orders in a negativity of the built world; by virtue of a special accident of history and geography, this is simply laid bare in Detroit. To restate the argument up to this point: the postmodern unleashes destructive spatial fantasies that are held in check in the modern. These fantasies occur as if at the limits of the formation of the ego, at a moment of misrecognition projected onto the other; in order to preserve stability, the fantasies are denied, thus reinvesting the limits of the self. The negativity experienced at the border of the self is the object cause of its reinforcement. Consider, for example, the denial of the events of 1967, the Detroit riots and concomitant white/middle-class flight to the suburbs, in their iterated reinforcements.[6] A comment frequently heard in the suburbs concerning Detroit, until just recently, was "I haven't been there in twenty years." Conversely, for many living in Detroit, the suburbs are a zone of nonexistence: the betrayers who elect to live there are well beyond the pale.

ZONE 6: GAPS BETWEEN TERRAINS

Social negativity is the unstable boundary between spaces of fantasy. While eminently a type and symptom of the modern, Detroit complicates the ascription of a single model for subjectivity in modernity. Such a singular subject might be represented, for instance, as the Renaissance Center — that dominating, phallic object from which the limits of the metropolitan area may be observed and policed. In Detroit, however, as in any social space of modernity, there is not one subject of domination but many subject positions, each with its own territorial claims. The negativity of the social totality, the entirety of metropolitan Detroit, occurs in the nonrecognition of the encompassing cultural order (which may also be assigned to that "nature" which eludes domination). Here the fantasmatic space of Detroit is subject to the same "white world" of nonrecognition, the unseeing Other positioned outside its limits that encloses Newark in Jones's novel, even as multiple zones are projected internally within its limits. A border or dividing line between terrains, then, becomes a privileged site of negativity within the encompassing and denying whole. At the boundary between one projected social space and another, in other words, occurs that denial — of the obdurate resistance of the other, in one sense, and of the disavowed limits of the same, in another — which intensifies the violence of social fantasy. The evident history of the dividing line in Detroit is, in this sense, anything but a secret: it is everywhere one looks, seen as the

71. Stan Douglas, Eastern Border of Indian Village, *1998. C-print, 45.7 × 55.9 cm.*

continually reexperienced locus of negativity that gives the whole its structure and limits, distributed at regular intervals within it.

In the Detroit metropolitan area, one is continually reminded of this logic of negativity experienced as the boundaries between terrains. As a result of its depopulation — over 40 percent since the riots of 1967 and their acceleration of the then-ongoing process of white migration — many neighborhoods in Detroit are visually marked by gaps between homes, public buildings, and production sites. A litany of its "damned demographics" provides a rough but accurate portrait of the larger dynamics of the Detroit metropolitan area:[7] from 1900 to 1950 the population of Detroit grew from under 285,700 to over 1.8 million, while from 1950 to 2000 it decreased from over 1.8 million to 951,270. There were no building permits issued in Detroit in 1988. Seventy-nine percent of the city is African-American, while 78 percent of the surrounding suburbs are "white"; average income of the city is 47 percent that of the suburbs. Neighborhoods in Detroit are overwhelmingly single-family dwellings, but in the 1990s, 1 percent of its housing stock was lost every year due to arson or "Devil's Night."[8] Even as the larger pattern is clear, the inexorable logic of depopulation and demolition is hard to imagine or accept. What results is a checkerboard spatial array of dysfunction, a steady erosion of the built world. Areas as well as buildings range from viable to disused: there are many relatively intact, functioning areas; many areas in transition to potential dysfunctional status; and many zones of negativity between viable terrains. Some of these areas, zones of disuse bordered by viable zones, are being returned to nature in biologically dissociated forms of industrial grassland or distressed woodland. Coyotes and wild dogs rumored to have jumped from freight trains; pheasants and geese; rabbits and groundhogs have established new populations in certain areas. Boundaries are also readily perceptible between the city limits proper and what were formerly known as its suburbs, but which should now be considered part of a larger metropolitan whole.[9] Negativity in Detroit, in general, is directly perceptible at the boundary lines between disjunct spaces and in the radical distinction between viable and dysfunctional zones. But rather than characterizing Detroit as a whole as negative, I am claiming that the metropolitan region as a whole is rifted with moments of negativity, and that these moments, rather than being footnotes to a positive account, are central to Detroit's reproduction of its own orders. This is especially evident at the moment of renewal in Detroit, which is everywhere being articulated as a willing embrace of a necessary destruction and removal before the proposed refunctioned totality can arise, phoenixlike, from its demolition site.

ZONE 7: ART AND NEGATIVITY

Aesthetic negativity is the unstable border between modernism and the modern. Artists have been concerned, since the dawn of aesthetic modernism, with the presentation of the negative as a source of aesthetic effects and the production of new forms in addition to nature. The representation of negative terrains in Detroit, then, intersects with a wide range of aesthetic strategies for the employment of the negative. While a Kantian account of aesthetic experience would require that negativity be positioned at the site of the sublime, which calls the percipient back to himself and demands a higher order of self-understanding, a modernist account following Heidegger would locate the negative as a moment of unveiling or disclosure and hence crucial for an authentic experience of Being.[10] Finally, a psychoanalytic account of fantasy, as I am primarily pursuing here, sees the negative as the object cause of desire that produces or enables fantasmatic affects that are in turn reconstructed, as pleasurable rather than destructive, in the art experience. The relations between these dynamics — of sublimity, disclosure, and fantasy — point, in turn, to a wide range of aesthetic strategies based on negativity, from the origins of modern art (in David's *Death of Marat*, for one critic; from Poe's "The Man of the Crowd" and Baudelaire's poetry and art criticism, for numerous others) to our postmodern present (as in the Situationists' strategy of urban disclosure known as the *dérive*).[11] Sublimity, to begin with, is a hallmark not only of aesthetic approaches to a distant and overwhelming nature but to the huge and incomprehensible urban landscape as well. Think, for instance, of Wordsworth's "Lines Composed above Tintern Abbey": the sublime experience the poet records is not the continuity of nature, memory, and desire but the five years of urban hell in London he has just left behind. It is a legacy of the romantic account of the imagination that we continue to locate the city as a source of negative effects that will be recuperated, later, in a beauteous and redemptive work of art, one that will return us to our original senses before their cataclysmic dissociation in the city.

In the 1970s, on my own and encountering San Francisco as a site of the urban sublime, I drew a diagonal line through a map of the city and spent several weeks photographing innumerable dissociated spaces on the southern (lower, working-class, minority, industrial) side of the line, producing not only a poetic record of urban dissociation but six hundred slides that I presented as a performance piece.[12] Later, at New Langton Arts in San Francisco, I helped organize a group show of artists working in various media titled "Urban Site."[13] It was interesting indeed to send out a call for work and receive a series of photographic or installation projects that relied heavily on the disjunct spaces of the city for their romantic effects. One artist, Nancy Rubins, for instance, built a colossal structure of junked camper tops in a disused lot right next to the San Francisco Art Commission Gallery. Vito Acconci used an empty lot across the street from Langton, where he fabricated a shelter out of four wrecked taxi bodies that was designed to be inhabited by the homeless, and was. Mark Pauline staged a performance under a freeway ramp that sent spectators scurrying as demonic machines spit flames and hurled boulders from slingshots (the gallery was later sued by a spectator who was injured by shattered chips from the freeway overpass that hit him in the arm). Writers, it is well to note, were less compelled by strictly romantic negativity: Ron Silliman staged a group reading of his poem *Tjanting* in the Civic Center Muni Metro station, where the voices of the twenty or so readers blended with the daily hum of the commute.[14] The urban theorist Manuel Castells presented an analysis of negativity in urban spaces that showed the functional relations between disused zones, human detritus, and capital.[15] Later, one of the gallery directors hinted that his Marxist analysis was all right, but perhaps a bit far from what we should be doing. It was precisely his rigorous account of totality that inspired me, as art.

ZONE 8: NEGATIVITY AND SOCIAL SPACE

Postmodernity is the border between the modern and aesthetic negativity. Within the visual arts, as opposed to the literary tradition, the discourse of the postmodern has primarily addressed the construction of the built world, and has been modeled on a primarily American experience of urban dystopia, from the antiurbanism of the Los Angeles freeway system to the theatrical hodgepodge of the Las Vegas strip. In its positive moment, at the intersection between social space and criticality, the discourse of the postmodern has insisted on a radical dissociation of simulacral surfaces within canceled progressive horizons. Whether this critical/stylistic use of surfaces itself partakes of a foundational negativity, or whether it participates in a higher-order dialectic of progress from a negative moment that is merely the present, remains to be seen. However, it would be hard to dissociate a celebration or investigation of negativity as the privileged locus of any totality from what the postmodern has meant or will come to mean. Before the gaudy speculations of Robert Venturi or Jean Baudrillard, who may be read as inverting the discourse of progressive modernity and substituting examples of negativity, dissociation, and nonnarration for moments of domination and control, consider the lure of Los Angeles to modernist critic Reyner Banham in the 1960s. His book, *Los Angeles: The Architecture of Four Ecologies*, was the first investigation between the built world and the kinds of fantasy structure one might call postmodern.[16] Arguably influenced by Los Angeles conceptualism, particularly Edward Ruscha's depictions of Los Angeles as a geometric grid of pre-postmodern blank apartment buildings, imitation tar-pit parking lots, carcinogenic sunsets, and dislocated palm trees, Banham's book reveals the primary position of fantasy in modern thinking on architecture. It is interesting, too, that some of Banham's fantasy structures may still be preserved as positive contributions to an evolving ethics and aesthetics of the built world. On the one hand, he insists on the dissociation of surfaces (the billboard over Johnny's diner on Wilshire Boulevard, in which the signage has a structural/functional importance equal to that which it advertises) as the necessity for going beyond the center/periphery model of the modern (the downtown area is identified only as a defunct and empty space, superseded by the intersections of the grid). On the other hand, Banham's fantasies betray a particular blind spot in terms of the geography of Los Angeles: while spaces at the periphery (the beaches, the hills) become the sites for fantasmatic investment, the interior becomes the dead zone of the underclass. Banham, in fact, titles his chapter dealing with Watts and Compton "The Plains of Id," in a particular arrogance of postmodern subject-centered unreason. The negative, then, is displaced from the border to the center, where it generates the fantasmatic exuberance of the yuppie culture to come. It is important that work on Los Angeles after Banham, from Mike Davis's *City of Quartz* to Charles Jencks's recent *Heterotopia*, and also including the postmodern geography of Edward Soja, has focused on repositioning its working-class, racialized social spaces within the larger social logic of the postmodern.[17]

The potential importance of the postmodern aesthetic and social theorizing of Los Angeles for a comparable account of Detroit has not yet been fully articulated. It is true that Los Angeles and Detroit have a great deal to say to each other, and that the two regions have been carrying on a profound social and cultural dialogue (sadly) over most of this century. If the preeminent use of Los Angeles for postmodern critique would seem to imply an import-export model of critical theory, with Los Angeles supplying the form and Detroit the as-yet unassimilated content, we might also consider that Detroit, in the form of the auto industry and its cultural hegemony within the metropolitan region, has arguably set the stage for what will become the postmodern in Los Angeles. But there is one crucial difference: Detroit, as an urban space, remains a moment of negativity to the postmodern fantasy built in Los Angeles, roughly as lunchbucket is negative to tinsel. Detroit's export to the world of fantasy in the 1960s, for instance, the Motown sound, emigrated to Los Angeles and has a minimal presence in Detroit at the present time.[18] While Los Angeles has provided central paradigms for the discourse of the postmodern (Fredric Jameson's use of John Portman's Bonaventura Hotel; Baudrillard's fascination with Disney and the desert; Michelangelo Antonioni's prescient account of Los Angeles postmodernity in *Zabriskie Point*), the debt Los Angeles owes to its modern origins in Detroit has scarcely been acknowledged. Detroit's negativity, here, is marked: it is the site for that destructive mode of productive organization, the rapacious and totalizing Fordism, that is the enabling condition for the

72. Stan Douglas, House with Wood-Grain Tile, *1998. C-print, 45.7 × 55.9 cm.*

genealogy of the postmodern, as Terry Smith's study of modern design, *The Making of the Modern,* which centers on Detroit, shows.[19] In "Postmodernism Ground Zero; or, Going to the Movies at the Grand Circus Park," Jerry Herron charts the rise of movie theaters as a kind of consumer index to the success of Fordist production, identifying the aporia of production precisely with the decline of the grand theaters (one of which, the Michigan Theater, was turned into a parking lot). But Herron avoids any direct connection to Los Angeles as a site of production, locating its product squarely in the consumerist half of exchange. This is due in part to the tradition in postmodern critical theory (after Jameson, particularly) that has tended to universalize Los Angeles as the site for the postmodern, and in part to a kind of "Detroit exceptionalism," where the city becomes a kind of hyperrealization of inherent tendencies of American culture as a whole: "Detroit, of course, is America's first postmodern city, and its old movie palaces model the necessary absence — as it might be called — on which postmodernism is 'founded.'"[20] Movies, in his cultural topography of imaginary absence, are imported from an elsewhere/nowhere that produces a simulacral cultural afterimage covering over the painful negativity of Detroit's effaced history. But the actual history of Detroit and the movies is one of regional exchange: Detroit sent Los Angeles cars, while the movies have a pride of place in the mass culture the Fordist assembly line invented. Stan Douglas's image of cars parked *inside* the former Michigan Theater, which Herron also describes, is a perfect conjunction of both. The methodological question to be asked here, and I am asking it, concerns the historicity of the negative within postmodern fantasy: the relation of the vertiginous space of the postmodern to that which it first denied.

ZONE 9: FOR A CRITICAL REGIONALISM

The discourses of the modern and the postmodern call for a critical regionalism. In its dialogue with Los Angeles, Detroit is the producer of that decentered, postmodern social space that goes beyond the center/periphery model of the modern. Later, in the collapse of its own urban center and the novalike expansion of its suburbs fleeing the energetic disturbances of a dying sun, Detroit will reclaim the implications of the forms of industrial production and individual, antisocial mobility it unleashed on the world. It is indeed remarkable that there has been so little investigation into Detroit as a region of the modern. This is so because in consumer-centered models of cultural critique, Detroit remains a producer; its contributions to culture, while many, are not organized either in modern or postmodern terms. The agony of the Detroit Institute of Arts, for instance, as a zone of culture within a terrain of productivist negativity, adheres to neither a modern nor a postmodern model: it cannot compel the modernist cultural capital and prestige of the Museum of Modern Art, nor can it articulate a cultural perspective that aligns it with the emerging social organization of the postmodern.[21] At the basis of the aporia of culture in Detroit are the central and compelling historical and social facts of negativity that shoot through its terrain like versions of Walter Benjamin's chips of millennial time: an urban center that nearly died about 1993, when the last major retail concerns closed their doors; the pulsing of abandonment and reinvestment that alternately destroys and revives the urban terrain; racial and class divisions, leading to the politics of boundary and turf and an overall cultural xenophobia. The specific history of Detroit demands an account, and not simply of a local and positive history. Rather, Detroit should be aligned with the unfolding discourses of cultural topology as one of postmodernity's major sites: as prime example of the fantasmatic undoing of the modern orders it invented and promulgated.

In a politics of critical regionalism that takes into account the supersession of modernity's center/periphery model, as well as the displaced shards of postmodern negativity, Cheryl Herr's *Critical Regionalism and Cultural Studies* provides a point of departure for a critical thinking to come.[22] To begin with, accounts of modern culture have been embarrassed by the claims of specific regions to attention, against the model of the metropolitan urbanism of its primary examples. One need only remember the way Faulkner and the Southern Agrarians insisted on the universality of their particular social conditions; in retrospect, this is clearly a fantasy of the modern in light of the abjection of cultural particulars that it cannot take into account, the specific history of the South. The scene in Quentin Compson's bedroom at Harvard where he tells his roommate, "I don't hate the south" is a quintessential moment of such modernist denial of region.[23] Opening the discourse of the modern to questions of region, however, is not simply to insist on a local and occluded history. Or better, it is to bring a local and occluded history, of those who have been placed at the margins of the modern as a source of negativity, directly to an analysis of the dynamics of a modern cultural order. Such an investigation leads, in turn, to a sense of the postmodern that is not locked into a fetishized or inert negativity, the kind of psychotopography indicated by the amorphous spatiality (as ego) of Deleuze and Guattari's concept "The Body without Organs" (as capitalism, the white world, and so on). Herr's account of a critical regionalism thus would supplant the dissociation of the center/periphery model with a series of interlocking terms that would specify the position within an overarching modernity of specific cultural regions, employing "a methodology of cross-cultural inquiry that seeks to align historical record, aesthetic representation, political economy, and cultural psychology" toward a reconciliation of the local and the global. She outlines several practical steps to be taken toward such a goal, among them:

- Pursue a negative dialectics that addresses cross-regional specificity on the basis of pairings, twinnings, and their often uncanny textual apparati.
- Imagine a comparative history/sociology that is both structural and interpretive.
- Scrutinize utopian views of the future that enter into dialogue with real local conditions.

- Study the location and interpretation of assemblages and spaces-between in a variety of organizational arenas and at a variety of organizational levels. (24)

A critical regionalism moves beyond the center/periphery model that distorts the perception of the border as negativity and threat; rather, the border (between city and suburb, say, or ethnic/racial groups) becomes an *internal* limit within an encompassing whole.

ZONE 10: SITE AND NONSITE

The negativity of the border becomes the site for a critique of regions. As an aesthetic practice, the overturning of the modern in an investigation of boundaries between center and periphery, leading to an expanded account of regions, is the central legacy of the work of environmental sculptor Robert Smithson.[24] Smithson's dialectic of site and nonsite exploded the metropolitan spatial imaginary of the visual arts at a particular moment of social and cultural upheaval, the late 1960s and early 1970s. Smithson's *nonsites,* it will be remembered, imported materials from areas of the natural world that would have been normally relegated to the margins of modernism's domain. It is important that these materials — salt, coal, iron ore — were equally raw materials, the basis of industrial processes of production. In turn, Smithson's *sites* were art works located in environments far from the metropolitan center, in spaces either considered inutile (the Great Salt Lake) or degraded (Smithson's proposal to redeem an Ohio mining site). In his dialectic of site and nonsite, Smithson was clearly engaging a postmodern fantasy of space in relation to a moment of negativity between terrains, as with the borders of the art world and the modern world of production: the gap between the two orders of aesthetic inquiry, a splitting of the modern subject precisely as a spatial dislocation. This dislocation, as inherent to the order of art, becomes for Smithson the engine of a dialectic. The mechanism of spatial fantasy is laid bare in the dialectic of site and nonsite — which thus aligns perfectly with a revised border as an internal limit, as an entailment of critical regionalism.

I now turn to the work of Stan Douglas, in a small sample of photographic images from the exhibition.[25] Everything that has been said so far has been a reading of his gallery exhibit, *Le Détroit.* Many of the specific connections between this critique and that work, however, I will leave in the space between two discourses: mine and his. The border between spaces,

73. Stan Douglas, View of the I-94 and Downtown Detroit, *1998. C-print, 45.7 × 55.9 cm.*

in this sense, is preserved and made the site of a critique. Both are predicated on a fundamental concern for the necessity of negativity as a moment of productive cultural and aesthetic unfolding (rather than as an aggravated instance of a romantic reinvestment in the social sublime). This is evident, even redundant, in the film installation that accompanied the display of photographs, which uses the device of a double projection of positive and negative images on a translucent screen. The film is a loop in which an African-American woman drives up to an abandoned housing project in the dark, climbs the stairs, walks through a series of damaged apartments, following only the beam of her flashlight, and, finding nothing, summarily leaves. The film technique thus uses literal processes of negativity to parallel its dark theme, as the vehicle for an elegant presentation of the denied affect (or postmodern gothic) in the destroyed spaces of Detroit. The positive and negative images nearly cancel themselves out, leaving the visual field populated with ghosts and afterimages: an uncanny mode of knowing in Detroit, where the empty fields of neighborhoods reduced to grassland

and the grassy fields of the cemetery blend in easily with one another. A binary logic of site and nonsite, representation and social collapse, is dismantled in the film's flickering oppositions and in the eternal return of the loop. Beyond the darkened room of Douglas's film installation, bright gallery lights illuminate a lucid series of urban portraits of Detroit in the late 1990s; in the photographs, as well, the dismantling of the modern in its form of center and periphery takes place as an eternal return to a more primary condition. For example, there is often a self-conscious positioning of buildings and site lines around Cartesian perspectives, but these are immediately absorbed by unorganized spaces that cannot be subsumed by them. Passages of water and sky are particularly active in these urban landscapes, engulfing the built world within a more encompassing totality that extends beyond them. In these images, a binary logic occurs between what has been built and organized and its undoing at the moment it encounters what cannot be dominated by it, the sky over all. This is the site of photographic pleasure: the recuperation of destruction by an order that enfolds it.

ZONE 11: DOUGLAS'S *LE DÉTROIT*

Photography is a site of desire and fantasy in a form of aesthetic negativity. This binary logic of site and nonsite is everywhere distributed in and through Stan Douglas's photographs, a part of their more complex installation. To begin with, the photographs themselves initiate an expanding series of contrasting oppositions, figured as terms of the social incommensurability of their subject. Then there is the boundary between media and genres to consider: photography and cinema. The film installation further explores the gap between alternative perspectives in the use of the translucent screen, superimposing negative and positive images over each other. The endless loop of the represented action becomes an eternal return in which the abandoned spaces of the city are emptied and replenished again and again. Finally, the exhibition itself, across the river from Detroit, beyond the boundary of nation, works a binary opposition between failed representation and pure presentation of a negativity that cannot be perceived within the social fabric of modernity — until it is disclosed. The negativity of the boundary becomes the site for constructed effects, by a direct presentation of the thing which cannot be named and the resulting syntax of displacement. If, as Benjamin observed, photography is the site of a loss of aura in modernity, these works attempt to locate the social origin of that effect, and to mobilize its energy otherwise.[26] In the film installation, the ghosting of the image becomes a gothic memorial to the lives of those who had lived in the abandoned housing project that is its site (Harmon Gardens); the buildings themselves are a kind of crypt in which the aura has been left to rot. This confrontation with the remains of a living social body turns out to be the site of powerful energetic disturbances, solar eruptions, neurological tremors. The temporal mechanics of the film projection (two continuous film loops projected onto the translucent screen) mimics these effects, while the fixed spatial display of photographs in the next room becomes a site of machinic investments of another order.

The photographs, as a series, manufacture and distribute negativity as the source of energetic effects that mimic the return of the aura at the site of its destruction. They are, in other words, a source of psychological effects — by no means simply a document of social reality. As critique, the photographs instantiate and replenish the loss of affect they record; the panoramic vista of the destroyed single-family house that frames the exhibition, in the best tradition of the sublime view, releases a visceral level of affect that becomes distributed throughout the constructed image (fig. 68). It is the formal arguments articulated in the components of the image itself that permit this: while the binary logic of symmetry on either side of the house — the use of the horizon line to split the image between human and natural world, and the division between natural world and human ruin itself — is self-consciously aesthetic, it is also analytic in locating incommensurate elements to be brought into an affective dialogue. The house itself, as object cause of desire, is the answer of the Real, of Detroit's social devolution, to the objectifying gaze of the photographer as Other, on the other side of the transferential divide. Yet the image is beautiful, stunning in its evocation of what is precisely missing from the picture: here, the opening onto social negativity evokes an aura of presence that photography purportedly destroyed. What this means for modernity may be seen in the image of a social space in the process of being returned to nature, a field of weeds, broken glass, and trees in various stages of disease (fig. 69). The atavistic moment framed at the outset of the postmodern, in Olson's fantasy of spatial domination beyond technology, returns as the violence that founded it. Space becomes the locus of a profound loss of sociality, site of a missing plenitude that might have been a city but is only a few buildings of a housing project on the other side of the lot. The modern as a built environment is thereby qualified by the social violence that subtends it, as in the Cartesian parallels, regular progression of urban apartments, and constructivist play space of the Mies van der Rohe urban townhouses of Lafayette Park (fig. 70). This regular and regulated environment could be completely evacuated, on the evidence of the surrounding images; its internal logic is laid bare as a predication of negativity and absence, anything but a transparent construction. It is the region between these two states — negativity and construction — that Douglas's photographs traverse; so the barely legible border between Detroit and the Grosse Pointes is marked, on the one side, by broken concrete, sprawling foliage, and power lines, but on the other, by a return to civic order with the substantial brick building to the back (fig. 71). The border is precisely a wild space of negative affects; in Detroit social space, this is always countered by the unit values of individual stability that make up its primarily single-family housing stock. The image of a boarded-up cabin in the African-American resort of Idlewild comments on this logic of placement and displacement: where a city is not, so housing will be (fig. 72). Social positivity always occurs within a bounded space, as a result of the logic of boundaries. An entire social terrain unfolds as a patchwork of contained spaces, of both productive and disused zones, within the limits that contain them. An elevated view of the social space of the city, only a few miles from downtown, gives evidence of a binary split between population and evacuation, utility and stasis (fig. 73). It is hard to tell which is more active in the photograph: the small industrial building or the vacant lot on either side of the photograph's central dividing line. In a final comment on the energetic effects that created Detroit's social space of utility and displacement, the infamous parking lot that was once the Michigan Theater shows a relationship between the forms of mobile agency and desire that created and destroyed Detroit, and the result (fig. 74). Sociality is a baroque impediment when compared to the need for parking space. In Douglas's photographs, social reality put into production creates psychotropic effects.

ZONE 12: POSTURBAN DETROIT

Modernity is best represented by those who imagine themselves outside it. Detroit, in an ongoing but mostly unnoticed discourse among urban planners, architects, artists, poets, and cultural critics, has become the focus of a discussion about the nature of modernity in its postmodern devolution, a site constructed and explored as a negative example.[27] Most of this discussion has taken place outside the boundaries of the metropolitan area of Detroit, and often from quite remote perspectives. The reception of Detroit

74. Stan Douglas, Michigan Theater, *1998. C-print, 45.7 × 55.9 cm.*

techno occurs likewise primarily in Europe; the music is still little known in Detroit, and is not part of an acknowledged narrative of identity. This reception can be distinguished from the marketing of Detroit automobiles, which obviously have had worldwide distribution. There is, in this sense, a necessarily negative relationship between the two phenomena: marketing and critique. The superinduction of the means of production (the redundancy of supply; the rationalization of technology; the circularity of markets; the transparency to the mode of exchange itself) works precisely by forcing out expensive suppliers, inefficient producers, and misdirected consumers. A seamless effect results in a unity of production and consumption (a form of equivalence, not identity, manufactured in Detroit).[28] Critical distance, on the other hand, is precisely that which undoes the redundancy that makes such an equivalence function. Put simply, it is impossible to criticize the auto industry in Detroit: what is good for the Big Three is good for everyone. (The only possible site of negativity, the situation of organized labor, has become a functioning part of production itself; thus it is not uncommon to see the UAW logo on the sides of factory buildings, alongside the company name.) Criticism of cultural phenomena is similarly atrophied in Detroit; there is no effective feedback system for cultural institutions simply because production and consumption are seen as the same (a situation, paradoxically, similar to that obtaining in the Second World, where the entire social totality was identified with production). As a result, the distance of critique can only be seen as negative, destructive, or simply impossible. There is a recurrent sense in Detroit that "it does not register"; this is a part of the functional logic of the market. The decay of the social fabric that evidently occurred — which Douglas's photographs document — could only have taken place in a situation where such direct evidence is seen as inadmissible, impossible, or nonexistent.

This identification with production, in both positive and negative senses, is why Detroit is an important site for thinking through the problem of modernity (in order to transform it into other forms), and likewise why this thinking has taken place largely outside the city. The critique of Detroit, as a result of the painful experience of exclusion and denial at the border, has polarized into two stereotypical forms: a genealogical positivism, where the disparate elements of the city's history and geography are celebrated as an object of knowledge;[29] and an aesthetic negativism, where the gap between terrains, their incommensurate logics, becomes an object of fascination and horror.[30] In the former, a recycled cultural identity is marketed in the form of T-shirts that read, "Detroit: Where the Weak are Killed and Eaten"; in the latter, tourists on an art adventure marvel at examples of the postmodern sublime. More theoretically put, the positivists want to celebrate incommensurate elements in the form of a reconstructed discourse, while the negativists want to return to the scene of discursive effects at the site of destruction. This binary logic, if not distorted to its extremes, is the framework of Douglas's responsible critique. It is the necessity of the great divide between incommensurate zones, as well as the divide between approaches to them, that is essayed in his work; in his reproduction of post-urban Detroit, Douglas dissociates modernity from its stabilizing control of space by relocating its dispersed moments of constitutive negation. Following this elegant solution, we will end by restating the theme: at the heart of modernity is an internal limit identified as the primary splitting of the border — as a loss of preexisting wholeness rather than any historical divide separating racial groups or social classes. The border described here is not constitutively a matter of the separation of black and white at Eight Mile Road, nor the separation of working-class industrial city from leisure-class suburb, with its private waterfront park. Rather, it is the process by which modern, industrial Detroit has created its own negation, and, in a cunning of capitalist unreason, the conditions of its reproduction — as brutal as they may be. If we follow the Marxist economist Ernest Mandel in seeing zones of disuse and unprofitability as particularly motivated in late capitalism — precisely because they are where superprofits can be made — we can see how, in the long run of history, the downtown area of Detroit has been prepared for profitable reinvestment, now certainly under way.[31] We see, then, not only the dismantling of the city through the brutal dialectic of profit and loss, but conditions for its rebuilding in a new form of brutality, where the fantasy of the quick buck becomes reality and Detroit feasts on its own negative history. Destruction here is ever and always construction; the bulldozers are piling up new piles of debris even as we speak. Douglas's unveiling of Detroit shows us a fantasy that has been there all along: the negativity of profit *as* loss.

NOTES

INTRODUCTION (pp. xv–xxxii)

Epigraphs from Vladimir Mayakovsky, *The Bedbug and Selected Poetry*, trans. Max Hayward and George Reavey (Bloomington: Indiana University Press, 1975), 71; William Carlos Williams, *Imaginations*, ed. Webster Schott (New York: New Directions, 1970), 105.

1 These formal and contextual aspects of construction provide a basis for approaching the wider horizon of social construction as it is currently understood: the constructedness of knowledge, subjectivity, and aesthetic experience. While I cannot develop that possibility here, an overview of debates on social construction may be found in Ian Hacking, *The Social Construction of What?* (Cambridge, Mass.: Harvard University Press, 1999).

2 Williams's text, as is well known, was edited to exclude the prose sections from its republication in the 1938 *Collected Poems* through the 1966 *Collected Shorter Poems.* The appearance in 1970 of a pirated edition that restored the prose to the original text had a profound (perhaps the original?) revisionary effect; William Carlos Williams, *Spring and All*, 2nd ed. (1923; Buffalo, N.Y.: Frontier Press, 1970); it led forthwith to the publication of the original text in Williams, *Imaginations.* On Williams and the Language School, see Alan Golding, "'What about All This Writing?': Williams and Alternative Poetics," *Sagetrieb* (forthcoming 2003).

3 Vladimir Mayakovsky, *How to Make Verse*, trans. Valentina Coe (Willimantic, Conn.: Curbstone Press, 1985), 29–30.

4 "There ought to be a wedding / a wedding, a wedding! / There ought to be a wedding / between Russia and the United States"; William Carlos Williams, "Jingle," in *The Collected Poems*, ed. Christopher MacGowan, vol. 2, *1938–1962* (New York: New Directions, 1988), 227–28.

5 For a recent account of 1930s Soviet design and its relation to the earlier avant-garde, see Margitt Rowell and Deborah Wye, eds., *The Russian Avant-Garde Book, 1910–1934* (New York: Museum of Modern Art, 2002).

6 On *Nachträglichkeit*, see Jean Laplanche, *Essays on Otherness* (New York: Routledge, 1999).

7 George Kubler, *The Shape of Time: Remarks on the History of Time* (New Haven, Conn.: Yale University Press, 1962).

8 Marshall Berman, *All That Is Solid Melts into Air: The Experience of Modernity* (Middlesex, Eng.: Penguin, 1988); on uneven development and profitability, see Ernest Mandel, *Late Capitalism*, trans. Joris De Bres (London: Verso, 1978).

9 On the material text, see Jerome J. McGann, *The Textual Condition* (Princeton, N.J.: Princeton University Press, 1991); McGann, *Black Riders: The Visible Language of Modernism* (Princeton, N.J.: Princeton University Press, 1993); and McGann, *Radiant Textuality: Literature after the World-Wide Web* (New York: Palgrave, 2001).

10 Cary Nelson, *Repression and Recovery: Modern American Poetry and the Politics of*

Cultural Memory, 1910–1945 (Madison: University of Wisconsin Press, 1989); Nelson, *Revolutionary Memory: Recovering the Poetry of the American Left* (London: Routledge, 2001); Walter Kalaidjian, *American Culture between the Wars: Revisionary Modernism and Postmodern Critique* (New York: Columbia University Press, 1993).

11 Michael Davidson, *Ghostlier Demarcations: Modern Poetry and the Material Word* (Berkeley: University of California Press, 1997).

12 Rachel Blau DuPlessis, *Genders, Races, and Religious Cultures in Modern American Poetry, 1908–1934* (Cambridge: Cambridge University Press, 2001).

13 Barrett Watten, *Total Syntax* (Carbondale: Southern Illinois University Press, 1985); Watten, "Social Formalism: Zukofsky, Andrews, and Habitus in Contemporary Poetry," *North Dakota Quarterly* 55, no. 4 (1987): 356–82.

14 Astradur Eysteinsson, *The Concept of Modernism* (Ithaca, N.Y.: Cornell University Press, 1990).

15 Daniel Belgrad, *The Culture of Spontaneity: Improvisation and the Arts in Postwar America* (Chicago: University of Chicago Press, 1998).

16 Kalaidjian, *American Culture between the Wars;* Rita Felski, *The Gender of Modernity* (Cambridge, Mass.: Harvard University Press, 1995); Janet Lyon, *Manifestoes: Provocations of the Modern* (Ithaca, N.Y.: Cornell University Press, 1999); Aldon Lynn Nielsen, *Black Chant: Languages of African-American Postmodernism* (Cambridge: Cambridge University Press, 1997).

17 Stephen Greenblatt, *Shakespearean Negotiations: The Circulation of Social Energy in Renaissance England* (Berkeley: University of California Press, 1988).

18 Kathleen Stewart, *A Space on the Side of the Road: Cultural Poetics of an "Other" America* (Princeton, N.J.: Princeton University Press, 1996).

19 Leslie Kurke, *Cultural Poetics in Ancient Greece: Cult, Performance, Politics* (Cambridge: Cambridge University Press, 1993).

20 J. G. A. Pocock, *The Machiavellian Moment: Florentine Political Thought and the Atlantic Republican Tradition* (Princeton, N.J.: Princeton University Press, 1975).

21 Marjorie Perloff, *The Futurist Moment: Avant-Garde, Avant Guerre, and the Language of Rupture* (Chicago: University of Chicago Press, 1986).

22 James F. Murphy, *The Proletarian Moment: The Controversy over Leftism in Literature* (Urbana: University of Illinois Press, 1991).

23 Norman Finkelstein, *The Utopian Moment in Contemporary American Poetry*, 2nd ed. (Lewisburg, Pa.: Bucknell University Press, 1993).

24 Rachel Blau DuPlessis and Peter Quartermain, eds., *The Objectivist Nexus: Essays in Cultural Poetics* (Tuscaloosa: University of Alabama Press, 1999).

25 Paul Maltby, *The Visionary Moment: A Postmodern Critique* (Albany, N.Y.: SUNY Press, 2002); Charles J. Stivale, "The 'MLA' Moment," *Profession* (1999): 248–57; Robert Pollack, *The Missing Moment* (Boston: Houghton Mifflin, 1999).

CHAPTER 1: New Meaning and Poetic Vocabulary (pp. 1–44)

Epigraph from Jackson Mac Low, "56th Light Poem: for Gretchen Berger — 29 November 1978," in *Representative Works: 1938–1985* (New York: Roof Books, 1986), 226.

1 Owen Barfield, *Poetic Diction: A Study in Meaning* (1928; Middletown, Conn.: Wesleyan University Press, 1973), 58.

2 See Barfield's discussion of poetic "strangeness" and his initial example of poetic diction without poetic form: "Thlee-piecee bamboo, two-piecee puff-puff, walk-along inside, no-can-see" — i.e., "Pidgin English for a three-masted screw steamer with two funnels." A true linguistic imperialist contemplating a species of exoticism, Barfield comments, "Detached from all historical associations and poetic tradition, [these words] present, as it were, the lowest common denominator of our subject"; ibid., 43, 46.

3 Mary Louise Pratt, *Toward a Speech Act Theory of Literary Discourse* (Bloomington: Indiana University Press, 1977), 3–37.

4 Michael J. Reddy, "The Conduit Metaphor: A Case of Frame Conflict in Our Language about Language," in Andrew Ortony, ed., *Metaphor and Thought* (Cambridge: Cambridge University Press, 1979), 284–324.

5 In the French case, the poem is determined by the rules of a language game (arriving at Joseph M. Conte's notion of "procedural form") rather than constructed from a preestablished lexicon; *Unending Design: The Forms of Postmodern Poetry* (Ithaca, N.Y.: Cornell University Press, 1991). The Oulipian technique called "N + 7," in which words to be used as, say, end words in a sestina are derived from the dictionary by skipping from an arbitrarily determined starting point in increments of seven words (example: begin with *input*; go to *inquisition*; go to *inroad*; go to *insatiable*, and so on), uses rules for selecting words from a source text but does not treat the source text as itself a vocabulary (as would be the case with BASIC English or the Dolch words).

6 Zukofsky translates Guido Cavalcanti's canzone "Donna mi prega" (which had earlier been translated, in light of a different epistemology of translation, as part of Ezra Pound's Canto 36). Albiach's translation influenced the contemporary French reception of American modernism and postmodernism; see the central placement of Zukofsky's work in Michel Deguy and Jacques Roubaud's anthology *Vingt Poètes américains* (Paris: Gallimard, 1981), as well as work in Claude Royet-Journaud's ephemeral magazine from the 1980s, *Zuk*.

7 It should be noted that such a theorizing of language as objectified does not only take place in relation to poetic form. Zora Neale Hurston, for example in "Story in Harlem Slang," foregrounds the differential opacity of African-American dialect in a way that is as modernist as, for example, Gertrude Stein's material texts; *The Complete Stories* (New York: HarperCollins, 1995).

8 I. A. Richards, *Principles of Literary Criticism* (New York: Harcourt, Brace, 1925).

9 I. A. Richards, *Basic English and Its Uses* (New York: Norton, 1943), 23.

10 C. K. Ogden, *Basic English: International Second Language*, rev. ed. of Ogden, *The System of Basic English* (1934; New York: Harcourt, Brace, and World, 1968), 15; Tom McArthur, ed., *The Oxford Companion to the English Language* (Oxford: Oxford University Press, 1992), s.v. "linguistic typology."

11 McArthur, *Oxford Companion*, s.v. "Basic English."

12 For the direct line of development linking the poetics of language in Coleridge to Richards's "semasiology" and beyond to leftist critiques such as Raymond Williams's

concept of "keywords," see A. C. Goodson, *Verbal Imagination: Coleridge and the Language of Modern Criticism* (Oxford: Oxford University Press, 1988).

13 For contemporary debates on BASIC during its period of international ascendance, when both Winston Churchill and Franklin Delano Roosevelt advocated it as a lingua franca, see Julia Johnson, ed., *Basic English* (New York: H. W. Wilson, 1944). BASIC is situated in the range of attempts to establish English as the international language in Robert Phillipson, *Linguistic Imperialism* (Oxford: Oxford University Press, 1967).

14 Such utopianism has survived, however, in the competing international language of the period, Esperanto, maintained by a network of enthusiasts with cultic overtones. Ogden argued strenuously for BASIC against Esperanto as an international language; C. K. Ogden, *Basic English versus the Artificial Languages* (London: Kegan Paul, Trench, Trubner, 1935).

15 McArthur, *Oxford Companion*, s.v. "Basic English."

16 Laura (Riding) Jackson and Schuyler B. Jackson, *Rational Meaning: A New Foundation for the Definition of Words and Supplementary Essays*, ed. William Harmon (Charlottesville: University of Virginia Press, 1997).

17 James Joyce, from "Work in Progress," trans. into BASIC English, with a note, by Joyce and C. K. Ogden, in *In "transition": A Paris Anthology* (London, 1990).

18 For "Language Control," see the overview in I. A. Richards, *Richards on Rhetoric: Selected Essays, 1929–1974*, ed. Ann E. Berthoff (Oxford: Oxford University Press, 1991).

19 Conte, *Unending Design*, 167–266.

20 Kit Robinson, *The Dolch Stanzas* (San Francisco: This Press, 1976), n.p.

21 On culturally embedded semantic frames, see Charles J. Fillmore, *Language Form, Meaning, and Practice* (Stanford, Calif.: CSLI Publications, 2002), and Paul Kay, *Words and the Grammar of Context* (Stanford, Calif.: CSLI Publications, 1997).

22 Such a hypertrophic sequence of semantic frames suggests a parodic paradigm of communicative action drawn from the vocabulary of George Herriman's existential cartoon series "Krazy Kat," in which Ignatz the mouse invites Krazy Kat to inspect one of his famous bricks ("come here / said the one / take a look at these"). Ignatz condenses interpretative frame into performative event as he bonks Krazy Kat on the head, thus accomplishing a kind of non-speech act with evident relish in its infelicity. The brick of meaning Ignatz throws at Krazy Kat is brought together, in such an imagined scenario, with the iteration of its repeated performance, suggesting Herriman's insight, throughout his oeuvre, into the simultaneity of interpretative frame and performative event.

23 For overviews of the *Biographia*, see Frederick Burwick, ed., *Coleridge's "Biographia Literaria": A Study in Meaning*, 3rd ed. (Columbus: Ohio State University Press, 1989).

24 Cited by Barfield in the introduction to *Poetic Diction*, 39.

25 On reading Coleridge in relation to textual disunity, see Jack Stillinger, *Coleridge and Textual Instability: The Multiple Versions of the Major Poems* (Oxford: Oxford University Press, 1994).

26 Paul Hamilton, *Coleridge's Poetics* (Oxford: Basil Blackwell, 1983), 148; hereafter *CP*.

27 John Keats, *The Letters of John Keats*, ed. Hyder Edward Rollins, 2 vols. (Cambridge, Mass.: Harvard University Press, 1958), 1:193.

28 Such a negative investment reveals the source of much of the interpretive paranoia surrounding the historical reception of open forms. Keats's call for "negative capability" in the poet as subject can be seen as a negative response to the open horizons for meaning in the poem as object. Identifying with Coleridge as aggressor may be one way out of Keats's dilemma of authority, which would rather remain content with the identity of subject and object in his "own" work. But Keats will always be happier with himself and his "own" work than he will be with Coleridge, implying not an anxiety of influence but the unwarranted synonymy that Coleridge sees as the basis of ideological rejections of another's expression in the reception of Wordsworth's poetry; see discussion below.

29 Samuel Taylor Coleridge, *Biographia Literaria; or, Biographical Sketches of My Literary Life and Opinions*, ed. James Engell and W. Jackson Bate (Princeton, N.J.: Princeton University Press, 1983), 85–86; hereafter *BL*.

30 For another reading of this passage, see Jerome Christensen, "The Romantic Movement at the End of History," *Critical Inquiry* 20, no. 3 (1994): 452–76. Christensen sees Coleridge's note as a failure to do anything but reproduce the antagonistic relation between the subject's investment in the disease of misrecognition (the ideological consequence of poetry's indeterminacy) and the subject's desire for a cure by critical mediation. It is the very opacity of the note that fails to bridge the gap (a reading perhaps supported by investment in the possibility of a transcendence that would jump over this chasm?).

31 For Eve S. Sweetser, the dynamics of semantic change would certainly be more complex than the splitting of Coleridge's paramecium, a guiding metaphor for romantic conceptions of linguistic origins that leads back to the abstract paternity of an "original" Indo-European; *From Etymology to Pragmatics: Metaphorical and Cultural Aspects of Semantic Structure* (Cambridge: Cambridge University Press, 1990).

32 Hamilton, *Coleridge's Poetics*, 93–96.

33 C. K. Ogden and I. A. Richards, *The Meaning of Meaning: A Study of the Influence of Language upon Thought and of the Science of Symbolism* (1923; New York: Harcourt, Brace, Jovanovich, 1989), 15.

34 Here, it is relevant that Sweetser advocates the study of semantic change through the study of the metaphorical structures of simple words precisely because of their culturally specific linguistic complexity; *From Etymology to Pragmatics*, 48: "The fact is, then, that we need to continue investigating the *least* surprising etymologies we can find. . . . The boring semantic histories are really the most interesting ones."

35 Ogden and Richards, *Meaning of Meaning*, 207.

36 Louis Zukofsky, "Thanks to the Dictionary," in *Collected Fiction* (Elmwood Park, Ill.: Dalkey Archive Press, 1990), 270–300; 275.

37 There may be evidence of Zukofsky's knowledge of and wry comment on BASIC in his spelling of *visiter*, which would follow BASIC rules for adding *-er* to nouns.

38 Zukofsky, "Thanks to the Dictionary," 296.

39 Peter Quartermain arrives at related conclusions about the textual processes of "Thanks to the Dictionary": "It thus plays a narrative with pre-existent meaning

against a writing which invites the reader to make meaning; a narrative the meaning of which we already know (for we have a traceable history of its interpretation) against a narrative whose meaning is not known. . . . The work exploits, then, the tension between two views of language: language as arbitrary (in which meaning is in the system and the context) and language as motivated (in which meaning is in the words). Either words have 'real' meanings (Adam was the perfect man because he knew the real name of things), or they don't. Either there is a necessary and inherent 'natural' connection between the word and its meaning, so that words *of themselves* tell you something of what they say, or there isn't." In his merging of cultural and linguistic texts, Zukofsky seems to claim a relation between nature and community at the problematic core of such a "natural" reference, one that stands as both extension and critique of BASIC's epistemology of language. Peter Quartermain, "The Poetics of Procedural Composition: The Case of Louis Zukofsky," paper delivered at "The First Postmodernists: American Poets of the 1930s Generation," University of Maine, 1993, 15–16; see also Quartermain, *Disjunctive Poetics: From Gertrude Stein and Louis Zukokfsky to Susan Howe* (Cambridge: Cambridge University Press, 1992).

40 Louis Zukofsky, from "Thanks to the Dictionary" (Buffalo, N.Y.: Gallery Upstairs Press, c. 1968). Unfortunately, it was not possible to reproduce the broadside here.

41 Louis Zukofsky, "Poetry," in *Prepositions: The Collected Critical Essays*, expanded ed. (Berkeley: University of California Press, 1981), 6–7; hereafter *P.* He goes on to write: "To think clearly then about poetry it is necessary to point out that its aims and those of science are not opposed or mutually exclusive. . . . It should be said rather that the most complicated standards of science — including definitions, laws of nature and theoretic constructions — are poetic. . . . Aware of like tolerances the poet can realize the standards of a scientific definition of poetry."

42 Louis Zukofsky, "Definition," in *Prepositions*, 173–74.

43 Louis Zukofsky, "BASIC," in ibid., 157.

44 Indeed, economy of expression, in the tradition of the Imagist movement and specifically Pound's portable definition "Dichtung = condensare," is the dominant literary value promoted in Zukofsky's *Test of Poetry*, e.g.: "Writing presents the finished matter, *it does not comment*. . . . Poetry is information: the effectiveness of the cadence is usually in direct proportion to the definiteness of the words used in that line. Cadence plus definite language equal the full meaning"; Louis Zukofsky, *A Test of Poetry* (1948; New York: C. Z. Publications, 1980), 84.

45 See Paul Mariani's account of Zukofsky's editorial suggestions for Williams's poems; *William Carlos Williams: A New World Naked* (New York: McGraw-Hill, 1981).

46 Louis Zukofsky, *"A"* (Berkeley: University of California Press, 1978); Zukofsky and Celia Zukofsky, *Catullus* (London: Cape Goliard, 1969).

47 See Barry Ahearn, *Zukofsky's "A": An Introduction* (Berkeley: University of California Press, 1983), esp. 231–42, for some key considerations.

48 Zukofsky, *"A,"* 106.

49 This "antiexpressivist" point proved to be controversial when presented in a short note on Zukofsky's *Catullus* at an evening in memory of Zukofsky organized by the San Francisco Poetry Center, November 1979; Barrett Watten, "Zukofsky's *Ca-*

tullus," *This* 4 (1976). Robert Duncan rebutted that Zukofsky could not translate Catullus because he could not identify with his passions, particularly his eroticism.

50 From Zukofsky and Zukofsky, *Catullus*, Carmen 80.

51 The facing page layout and Latin text is unfortunately not preserved in Louis Zukofsky, *Complete Short Poetry* (Baltimore: The Johns Hopkins University Press, 1991).

52 Jackson Mac Low to Barrett Watten, 11 November 2001.

53 Louis Zukofsky, *Bottom: On Shakespeare* (1963; Berkeley: University of California Press, 1987). Zukofsky's formulation "The words are my life" restages a resynonymy at the heart of what his language-centered poetics seemed originally to contest; as such, it appears as a transparent moment of "double-voiced discourse" in Zukofsky's work. Where Coleridge claims that the *I* and the *me* of identity and identification are collapsed in deficient aesthetic judgment, and where his dissociation of the two terms is central to his argument for desynonymy, Zukofsky seems to have reenacted the cardinal sin of organic form, here displaced outward onto language itself ("the words") as a form of identity with "my life." But the poems resulting from that resynonymy convey little of organic form.

54 Barrett Watten, "Poetic Vocabulary: A Conversation with Jackson Mac Low," *Aerial* 8 (1995): 107–20.

55 Mac Low, *Representative Works*, 19.

56 Coleridge, *Biographia Literaria*, 85.

57 Mac Low, *Representative Works*, 17.

58 Ibid., xv.

59 On representation in the history of German romanticism, see Azade Seyhan, *Representation and Its Discontents: The Critical Legacy of German Romanticism* (Berkeley: University of California Press, 1992); on political notions of representation, see Hanna Fenichel Pitkin, *The Concept of Representation* (Berkeley: University of California Press, 1967). See also George Hartley, *The Abyss of Representation: Marxism and the Postmodern Sublime* (Durham, N.C.: Duke University Press, forthcoming in 2003), which combines the critique of representation after romanticism with a discussion of its politics.

60 Mac Low, *Representative Works*, 40.

61 Jackson Mac Low, *The Pronouns: A Collection of Forty Dances for the Dancers, 3 February–22 March 1964* (Barrytown, N.Y.: Station Hill Press, 1979).

62 According to the author, "*all* the actions in *The Pronouns* were drawn in 1964 by a deterministic diastic reading-through method from a card pack entitled '56 sets of actions [made from words] drawn by chance operations from the Basic English list in Spring 1961.' . . . The titles of the *Pronouns* poems are all in that form but the ings were changed to declarative sentences in composing the bodies of the poems. . . . In making this action pack, I used one action as the seed text for a following group of actions that were incorporated into the poems until that seed text 'got used up.' Then I would use the next single action as the seed for the following actions until it got used up, etc. . . . Because I was more interested in making the poems than in documenting their making, I didn't [document] exactly how I ob-

tained the words from the [BASIC] list to make each action 'ing' and how many such action ings were to be inscribed on each card of the list"; Jackson Mac Low to Barrett Watten, 25 April 2002.

63 Mac Low, *Representative Works*, 132.

64 Richards, *Principles of Literary Criticism*, 226.

65 Watten, "Poetic Vocabulary," 108.

66 Particularly strong collections of Jackson Mac Low's "intentional" works are *Bloomsday* (Barrytown, N.Y.: Station Hill Press, 1984); and *Pieces o' Six* (Los Angeles: Sun and Moon, 1992).

CHAPTER 2: The Secret History of the Equal Sign (pp. 45–102)

1 George Hartley, *The Abyss of Representation: Marxism and the Postmodern Sublime* (Durham, N.C.: Duke University Press, forthcoming 2003).

2 On the notion of tendency in avant-garde poetry, see Steve Benson et al., "Aesthetic Tendency and the Politics of Poetry," *Social Text* 19–20 (1998): 261–75.

3 Paul Mann, *The Theory Death of the Avant-Garde* (Bloomington: Indiana University Press, 1991); hereafter *TD*.

4 On the concept of *posthistoire*, see Lutz Niethammer, *Posthistoire: Has History Come to an End?* (London: Verso, 1992).

5 Paul Mann, *Masocriticism* (Albany, N.Y.: SUNY Press, 1999), x.

6 Matei Calinescu, *Five Faces of Modernity: Modernism, Avant-Garde, Decadence, Kitsch, Postmodernism* (Durham, N.C.: Duke University Press, 1987); Renato Poggioli, *The Theory of the Avant-Garde* (Cambridge, Mass.: Harvard University Press, 1968); Peter Bürger, *The Theory of the Avant-Garde*, trans. Jochen Schülte-Sasse (Minneapolis: University of Minnesota Press, 1984).

7 Rosalind Krauss, *The Originality of the Avant-Garde and Other Modernist Myths* (Cambridge, Mass.: MIT Press, 1985); Donald Kuspit, *The Cult of the Avant-Garde Artist* (Cambridge: Cambridge University Press, 1993).

8 On affirmative culture, see Max Horkheimer and Theodor Adorno, *Dialectic of Enlightenment*, trans. John Cumming (New York: Continuum, 1998).

9 On the legacy of the Russian Formalism in mass-cultural forms such as advertising and film, see Victor Shklovsky, *Third Factory*, trans. Richard Sheldon (Ann Arbor, Mich.: Ardis, 1977), which describes his response to the social command of mass culture and transition from the "second factory" of literary theory to the "third factory" of social production, specifically the 1920s Soviet film industry. The influence of the Formalists can be traced through El Lissitzky's work in typography and design, and its importance for Bauhaus aesthetics, as well as in the development of modernist film syntax in the work of Sergei Eisenstein and Dziga Vertov. Matthew Teitelbaum, ed., *Montage and Modern Life, 1919–1942* (Cambridge and Boston, Mass.: MIT Press and Institute for Contemporary Art, 1992), is a collection of essays that supports the connection between avant-garde theory and mass-cultural forms in the period. For the connection between surrealism and the fashion industry, see Richard Martin, *Fashion and Surrealism* (New York: Rizzoli, 1987); for its relation to Lacanian psychoanalysis, see David Macey, *Lacan in Contexts* (London: Verso,

1998); and Carolyn J. Dean, *The Self and Its Pleasures: Bataille, Lacan, and the History of the Decentered Subject* (Ithaca, N.Y.: Cornell University Press, 1992).

10 In 1979, after my reading at the Poetry Center at San Francisco State University, poet George Oppen was heard to complain, "That's just rehashed surrealism"; Tom Mandel, personal communication. In 1980, when asked to present a series of lectures at the San Francisco artists space 80 Langton Street, I titled one of them, "Life among the Surrealists," after the book by Matthew Josephson; see "The Politics of Poetry: Surrealism and *L=A=N=G=U=A=G=E*," in Barrett Watten, *Total Syntax* (Carbondale: Southern Illinois University Press, 1985), 31–64. More recently, a reviewer of *Bad History* wrote: "Watten is a dialectical surrealist of the political unconscious"; [Steve Evans], review of Barrett Watten, *Bad History*, *Publisher's Weekly* (1998): 55.

11 Robert Rauschenberg's career, from innovative practitioner to mainstream spectacle, with three major museums filled with his work in New York in late 1997, exemplifies the paradoxes of such a recuperation.

12 For a concise attack on the politics of identity in relation to avant-garde practice, see Charles Bernstein, "Stein's Identity," *Modern Fiction Studies* 42, no. 3 (1996): 485–88; for the reconciliation of identity with recognition, see Marjorie Perloff, "Language Poetry and the Lyric Subject: Ron Silliman's Albany, Susan Howe's Buffalo," *Critical Inquiry* 25, no. 3 (1999): 405–34.

13 Bob Perelman, *The Marginalization of Poetry: Language Writing and Literary History* (Princeton, N.J.: Princeton University Press, 1996), 35.

14 Ron Silliman, ed., "The Dwelling Place: 9 Poets," *Alcheringa* 1, no. 2 (1975): 104–20. Note also Silliman's holistic epigraph from Charles Olson: "That which exists / through itself / is what is called meaning." The minianthology was followed by an essay, "Surprised by Sign: Notes on Nine." See also Steve McCaffery, ed., "The Politics of the Referent," *Open Letter* (3rd ser.) 7 (1977): 60–107, a series of essays published in the Canadian journal that anticipates the writing of *Legend.*

15 Jerome Rothenberg, "Notes and Comments," *Alcheringa* 1, no. 2 (1975): 131.

16 The first article to my knowledge that could be described as undertaking "Language bashing" (and there have been many) is Alan Soldofsky, "Language and Narcissism," *Poetry Flash* 74 (May 1979): n.p.

17 In a recent controversy, some twenty years after the naming of the journal, poet Ray DiPalma has disputed the originality of the name and its design, saying the idea came from him. The extent to which the equal signs were motivated by a politics or aesthetics of equivalence may be debated; Bernstein's partner Susan Bee designed the logo. Given the entire context of Language School aesthetics, it seems reductive to characterize the use of the equal signs as a graphic device that merely interrupts or spaces signification.

18 Bruce Andrews and Charles Bernstein, interview with Andrew Ross, in Ross, ed., "Reinventing Community: A Symposium on/with Language Poets," *Minnesota Review* (new ser.) 32 (1989): 27–50.

19 Marjorie Perloff, "The Word as Such: L=A=N=G=U=A=G=E Poetry in the Eighties," *American Poetry Review* 13 (May/June 1984): 405–34; Jerome McGann,

"Contemporary Poetry, Alternate Routes," in Robert Von Hallberg, ed., *Politics and Poetic Value* (Chicago: University of Chicago Press, 1987), 253–76.

20 Benson et al., "Aesthetic Tendency,"; the coauthors are Carla Harryman, Lyn Hejinian, Bob Perelman, Ron Silliman, and myself. The subtitle "A Manifesto" was added by the journal's editor.

21 Andrew Ross, "The New Sentence and the Commodity Form: Recent American Writing," in Cary Nelson and Lawrence Grossberg, eds., *Marxism and the Interpretation of Culture* (Urbana: University of Illinois Press, 1988), 361–80.

22 As we will see, Ann Vickery begins her discussion of the politics of the Language School by recuperating its formation in a third city, Washington, D.C.; *Leaving Lines of Gender: A Feminist Genealogy of Language Writing* (Middletown, Conn.: Wesleyan University Press, 2000).

23 For a history of the San Francisco Renaissance, see Michael Davidson, *The San Francisco Renaissance: Poetics and Community at Mid-Century* (Cambridge: Cambridge University Press, 1989); for the New York School, see David Lehman, *The Last Avant-Garde: The Making of the New York School* (New York: Doubleday, 1998); and William Watkin, *In the Process of Poetry: The New York School and the Avant-Garde* (Lewisburg, Pa.: Bucknell University Press, 2001).

24 It is in this sense that the paradigm of the "New York School" both succeeds and appropriates the art-historical convention of the "School of Paris" in its consolidation of cultural capital. Following this convention, the name "Language School," in its location of the avant-garde in place called "language" not identified with any metropolitan center, is my preferred, if ironic, name for the historical location of "so-called language-centered writing." In its positive content, of course, the name still must contend with the burden of self-canceling that attended its emergence; just so, a major publisher of "Language writing" recently told me he would never publish a book with the words "Language poetry" on its cover — although, somewhat later, he did.

25 When asked in a casual forum in the *Poetry Project Newsletter*, "What does the term 'school' imply when used for a group of writers," Charles Bernstein replied, "That the person using it hasn't read much of what he or she is talking about. Or: Schools are made to be broken"; *Poetry Project Newsletter* (New York) 128 (April/May 1988).

26 Barrett Watten, interview with Andrew Ross, in Ross, ed., "Reinventing Community: A Symposium on/with Language Poets," *Minnesota Review* (new ser.) 32 (1989): 30–39.

27 Julia Kristeva, *Revolution in Poetic Language*, trans. Margaret Waller (New York: Columbia University Press, 1984); hereafter *RPL*. For an overview of Kristeva's work, see Kelly Oliver, *Reading Kristeva: Unraveling the Double Bind* (Bloomington: Indiana University Press, 1993).

28 On *Tel Quel*, see Danielle Marx-Scouras, *The Cultural Politics of "Tel Quel": Literature and the Left in the Wake of Engagement* (University Park: Pennsylvania State University Press, 1996).

29 Alice Jardine, *Gynesis: Configurations of Women and Modernity* (Ithaca, N.Y.: Cornell University Press, 1985); Rachel Blau DuPlessis, *The Pink Guitar: Writing as Feminist*

Practice (New York: Routledge, 1990); and Marianne DeKoven, *Rich and Strange: Gender, History, Modernism* (Princeton, N.J.: Princeton University Press, 1991).

30 Indeed, Rosemary Hennessy, *Materialist Feminism and the Politics of Discourse* (New York: Routledge, 1993) and others have found Kristeva's reliance on the historical avant-garde to be a fatal weakness for her cultural politics.

31 For a recent positive discussion of the politics of Kristeva's textuality, see John Mowitt, *Text: The Genealogy of an Anti-Disciplinary Object* (Durham, N.C.: Duke University Press, 1992), 104–16.

32 Michel Foucault, *The Archeaology of Knowledge and the Discourse on Language*, trans. A. M. Sheridan Smith (New York: Pantheon, 1972), esp. 187–98; hereafter *AK*. On Foucault's historical context, see Didier Eribon, *Michel Foucault*, trans. Betsy Wing (Cambridge Mass.: Harvard University Press, 1991).

33 Behind Foucault's concept of discourse lies Nietzsche's watershed essay, "On the Advantages and Disadvantages of History for Life"; Michel Foucault, "Nietzsche, Genealogy, and History," in *Aesthetics, Method, and Epistemology*, ed. James D. Faubion, vol. 2 of *Essential Works of Michel Foucault, 1954–84*, ed. Paul Rabinow (New York: The New Press, 1998), 369–92.

34 On the history of structuralist linguistics, see F. W. Galan, *Historic Structures: The Prague School Project, 1928–1946* (Austin: University of Texas Press, 1984).

35 Ernesto Laclau and Chantal Mouffe, *Hegemony and Socialist Strategy: Toward a Radical Democratic Politics* (London: Verso, 1985).

36 Slavoj Žižek, "Beyond Discourse Analysis," in Ernesto Laclau, *New Reflections on the Revolution of Our Time* (London: Verso, 1990).

37 "Organized violence in language," it will be recalled, was Russian Formalist Viktor Shklovsky's account of rhyme, where unlike semantic fields (say, *moon* and *June*) are bound together by the likeness of their sounds (which, at another level, can only be perceived as parallel in denial of their minor differences, as opposed to their similarity). As Victor Erlich puts it, for Shklovsky, "juxtaposition on the basis of partial similarity of two otherwise dissimilar notions is the omnipresent principle of poetic creation"; *Russian Formalism: History–Doctrine*, 3rd ed. (New Haven, Conn.: Yale University Press, 1981), 225.

38 Charles Bernstein, *A Poetics* (Cambridge, Mass.: Harvard University Press, 1992).

39 Bruce Andrews, *I Don't Have Any Paper So Shut Up (or, Social Romanticism)* (Los Angeles: Sun and Moon, 1992); Andrews, *Paradise and Method: Poetics and Praxis* (Evanston, Ill.: Northwestern University Press, 1996).

40 Barrett Watten, "The Bride of the Assembly Line," *Impercipient Lecture Series* 8 (October 1997).

41 See Steven Clay and Rodney Philips, *A Secret Location on the Lower East Side: Adventures in Writing, 1960–1980* (New York: New York Public Library/Granary Books, 1998).

42 A comparison of language as place in postmodern poetics with a politics of region in modernism (as the site of counterhegemony) cannot be developed further here.

43 Bruce Andrews et al., *Legend* (New York: L=A=N=G=U=A=G=E/Segue, 1980); hereafter *L*.

44 Roman Jakobson, "The Dominant," in Ladislav Matejka and Krystyna Pomorska,

eds., *Readings in Russian Poetics: Formalist and Structuralist Views* (Ann Arbor: Michigan Slavic Publications, 1978), 82–90.

45 Ron Silliman gave his talk "The New Sentence" in the San Francisco Talk Series on 17 September 1979; it was collected in Bob Perelman, ed., *Talks*, special issue of *Hills* 6/7 (1980); and in Silliman, *The New Sentence* (New York: Roof Books, 1987).

46 Kristeva, *Revolution in Poetic Language*, 43–56.

47 On metalepsis, see Gérard Genette, *Narrative Discourse: An Essay on Method*, trans. Jane E. Lewin (Ithaca, N.Y.: Cornell University Press, 1980), 235.

48 For a working distinction between the two terms, see Anthony Easthope, *Poetry as Discourse* (London: Methuen, 1983).

49 For example, see Bruce Andrews, "Writing Social Work & Political Practice," *L=A=N=G=U=A=G=E* 9/10 (October 1979).

50 Kristeva, *Revolution in Poetic Language*, 13–14.

51 Bernstein, for instance, rereads the entirety of Ron Silliman's anthology *In the American Tree* in a pair of poems titled "Reading the Tree," arguably transforming a multiauthored discourse into the voice of a single author; Charles Bernstein, *Rough Trades* (Los Angeles: Sun and Moon, 1991), 31–41. Andrews's refusal of the distinction between poetry and poetics also works toward an encompassing social text that brings together many voices, which are sampled in the construction of the text; Bruce Andrews, *Paradise and Method;* and Andrews, *Lip Service* (Toronto: Coach House Press, 2001).

52 V. N. Voloshinov, *Marxism and the Philosophy of Language*, trans. Ladislav Matejka and I. R. Titunik (Cambridge, Mass.: MIT Press, 1973).

53 For skepticism on Kristeva's notion of the pre-Oedipal, see John Brenkman, *Straight Male Modern: A Cultural Critique of Psychoanalysis* (London: Routledge, 1993). In my work on Gertrude Stein, I avoid the concept, even though it has been much used in Stein criticism; Barrett Watten, "An Epic of Subjectivation: *The Making of Americans*," *Modernism/Modernity* 5, no. 2 (1998): 95–121.

54 Kristeva, *Revolution in Poetic Language*, 57.

55 For alternate approaches to the construction of homosocial bonds, see Eve Kosofsky Sedgwick, *Between Men: English Literature and Male Homosocial Desire* (New York: Columbia University Press, 1985); Wayne Koestenbaum, *Double Talk: The Erotics of Male Literary Collaboration* (New York: Routledge, 1989); David Savran, *Taking It Like a Man: White Masculinity, Masochism, and Contemporary American Culture* (Princeton, N.J.: Princeton University Press, 1998).

56 Kristeva, *Revolution in Poetic Language*, 48.

57 My reading is based on Sigmund Freud's inaugural paper in the large literature on narcissism, "On Narcissism: An Introduction," in *Collected Papers*, ed. and trans. Joan Rivière, 5 vols. (New York: Basic Books, 1959), 4:30–59.

58 Žižek, "Beyond Discourse Analysis"; Laclau and Mouffe, *Hegemony and Socialist Strategy.*

59 Toril Moi, *Sexual/Textual Politics* (London: Routledge, 1985); Hennessy, *Materialist Feminism.*

60 Kristeva, *Revolution in Poetic Language*, 47.

61 For a negative assessment of avant-garde technique as a form of fetishistic disavowal

of the feminine, see Marcia Ian, *Remembering the Phallic Mother: Psychoanalysis, Modernism, and the Fetish* (Ithaca, N.Y.: Cornell University Press, 1993). *Legend* in this sense may be compared to the recently published discussions of sexuality among (almost entirely male) surrealists, in José Pierre, ed., *Investigating Sex: Surrealist Research, 1928–1932*, trans. Malcolm Imrie (London: Verso, 1992).

62 Hennessy, *Materialist Feminism*, 53.

63 Carla Harryman to Ann Vickery, n.d.

64 See Bob Perelman's discussion of the "Brat Guts" aesthetic in *Marginalization of Poetry*, 32–33. The canonical example of surrealist collaboration in generating automatic texts is André Breton and Philippe Soupault, *The Magnetic Fields*, trans. David Gascoyne (London: Atlas Press, 1985), though there are many others.

65 Steve Benson, *As Is* (Berkeley, Calif.: The Figures, 1978); Barrett Watten, *1–10* (San Francisco: This Press, 1980).

66 Steve Benson, *Blindspots* (Cambridge, Mass.: Whalecloth Press, 1981).

67 Steve Benson, "Johnny Guitar," in *As Is*, 50–52.

68 A middle position between the breaking apart of subject position and its reconfiguration in the form of the poem occurs in section 10 of *Legend* (McCaffery, DiPalma, Silliman), titled "(grey) Probe Continues (grey)." In this section, horizontal displacement of aleatorical materials mimics the citationality of Kristeva's "phenotext," while the vertical axis of capitalized words creates an organizing principle, structured on the repetition and displacement that evidences the articulation of drives within language, Kristeva's "genotext"; Kristeva, *Revolution in Poetic Language*, 86–89. In "Non-Events," the horizontal axis of dissociation is called to order in a vertical integration of drives. This gives the intertextuality of both poems their effects of productivity, Benson's laterally open and improvisatory, mine vertically constrained and ironic. This integration, in turn, gives rise to a new thetic position that Kristeva sees as the beneficiary of avant-garde poetry's revolution, here the simultaneous authorial self-canceling and assertion of the poem itself as intertextual "Non-Event."

69 Vickery, *Leaving Lines of Gender*.

70 Ibid., 28, 36, 150, 261.

71 Gertrude Stein, *Tender Buttons* (1914), in *Selected Writings*, ed. Carl Van Vechten (New York: Random House, 1946), 407–52.

72 Texts of San Francisco Poets Theater from the late 1970s and early 1980s by Bob Perelman, Kit Robinson, Alan Bernheimer, Eileen Corder, Stephen Rodefer, and Carla Harryman can be found in Bob Perelman, ed., "Plays from San Francisco Poets Theater," in "Plays and Other Writing," *Hills* 9 (1983): 5–93; Harryman, *Animal Instincts: Prose Plays Essays* (Berkeley, Calif.: This Press, 1989); and Harryman, *Memory Play* (Oakland, Calif.: O Books, 1994). Production notes for a Poets Theater play by Kit Robinson appear in *Poetics Journal* 5; Kit Robinson, Eileen Corder, and Nick Robinson, "Poets Theater," in "Non/Narrative," *Poetics Journal* 5 (1985): 122–38.

73 Michael Davidson et al., *Leningrad: American Writers in the Soviet Union* (San Francisco: Mercury House, 1992).

74 Sections of Carla Harryman and Lyn Hejinian's *Wide Road* have appeared in Cam-

ille Norton and Lou Robinson, eds., *Resurgent: New Writing by Women* (Urbana: University of Illinois Press, 1992); Leslie Scalapino, ed., *O III Anthology* (Oakland, Calif.: O Books, 1993); and in *Aerial* 6 (1991); a draft of its ending section was published in the Montréal journal *Tessera;* and in Harryman and Hejinian, excerpt from *The Wide Road,* in "Feminist(s) Project(s)/Projets Des Féministes," *Tessera* 15 (1993): 56–64. See also *Sight,* a multiauthored poem by Lyn Hejinian and Leslie Scalapino (Washington, D.C.: Edge Books, 1999).

75 From the unpublished MS.

76 Harryman and Hejinian, *Wide Road,* 61–62.

77 The Poetics Listserv was set up by Charles Bernstein, with the assistance of Loss Pequeño Glazier; its archives are available on-line, dating back to March 1994. Bernstein continues to function as list owner, which gives him a quasi-official role in its conversations — a distinction that has been the site of considerable internal debate. Chris Alexander, as list administrator, also has a quasi-official role, which has polarized discussion around questions of the right to exclude individuals from the list.

78 Joel Kuszai, ed., *Poetics@* (New York: Roof Books, 1999).

79 Roman Jakobson, "Concluding Statement: Linguistics and Poetics," in Thomas A. Sebeok, ed., *Style in Language* (Bloomington: Indiana University Press, 1960), 350–77.

80 This may be compared to more hypotactic organization of the British Poets Listserv, where there is often a greater subordination under topic headings.

81 I will number the posts in the archive for April 1999 in the order in which they are listed, not necessarily the order in which they are posted but the order in which they would have been received, either as individual posts or in the digest form.

82 For an excellent report on the conference, see Linda Russo's post 285, "A Barnard Report," at the Listserv's archive. Debates on the conference continued through the month, and many women authors were the subject of discussion, not only Hejinian.

83 Lyn Hejinian, *Writing Is an Aid to Memory* (Berkeley, Calif.: The Figures, 1978).

CHAPTER 3: The Bride of the Assembly Line (pp. 103–46)

Epigraph from Gertrude Stein, *Everybody's Autobiography* (1937; Cambridge, Mass.: Exact Change, 1993), 240.

1 Some notable examples include John Dos Passos, *The Big Money;* Jack Conroy, *The Disinherited;* and, more recently, the novels of Elmore Leonard and Loren Estleman.

2 Barrett Watten, *Total Syntax* (Carbondale: Southern Illinois University Press, 1985), 68.

3 Ron Silliman, *Ketjak* (San Francisco: This Press, 1978); Silliman, *Tjanting* (Berkeley, Calif.: The Figures, 1981).

4 Barrett Watten, *Progress* (New York: Roof Books, 1985); Bob Perelman, *Primer* (San Francisco: This Press, 1981); Perelman, *To the Reader* (Berkeley, Calif.: Tuumba Press, 1984); Perelman, *The First World* (Berkeley, Calif.: The Figures, 1986); Steve Benson, *Blue Book* (Berkeley, Calif./New York: The Figures/Roof Books, 1988); Carla Harryman, *The Middle* (San Francisco: Gaz, 1983); Harryman, *Vice* (Elmwood, Conn.: Potes and Poets, 1987).

5 The discussion of *literaturnost* is adapted here from Barrett Watten, "What Is Literature? From Material Text to Cultural Poetics," in Romana Huk, ed., *Assembling Alternatives* (Middletown, Conn.: Wesleyan University Press, 2003).

6 On Russian Formalism, see Victor Erlich, *Russian Formalism: History–Doctrine*, 3rd ed. (New Haven, Conn.: Yale University Press, 1981); Lee T. Lemon and Marion J. Reis, ed. and trans., *Russian Formalist Criticism: Four Essays* (Lincoln: University of Nebraska Press, 1965); Ladislav Matejka and Krystyna Pomorska, eds., *Readings in Russian Poetics: Formalist and Structuralist Views* (Ann Arbor: Michigan Slavic Publications, 1978); and Peter Steiner, *Russian Formalism: A Metapoetics* (Ithaca, N.Y.: Cornell University Press, 1984).

7 Steiner, *Russian Formalism*, 50.

8 Ibid., 23.

9 F. W. Galan, *Historic Structures: The Prague School Project, 1928–1946* (Austin: University of Texas Press, 1984).

10 Erlich, *Russian Formalism*, 181.

11 In Yury Tynyanov's 1929 statement, "The boundaries of literature and life are fluid," implying that genres previously considered as nonliterary in relation to cultural context may be seen as literary. This statement may be compared to the marked relativism of, even an indifference toward, context in Roman Jakobson's 1941 claim that "today anything can serve as material for a poem" — and so literature, by virtue of its independence from context, becomes a more static and fixed concept; Erlich, *Russian Formalism*, 183.

12 Perhaps the importance of Jakobson's codification of Formalist insights was not so much the "structure-in-dominance" of the autonomous work of art but his extension of the material organization of art to the forms of a given culture. It is this reciprocity, on the one hand, that allows for a notion of language to emerge as the central concern of the human sciences in French Structuralism, and, on the other, that will eventually permit the work of art to be seen as the site for a cultural reflexivity.

13 Lemon and Reis, *Russian Formalist Criticism*, 23.

14 A world car is transparent to all contexts: it can be produced at an assembly point in any country and satisfy the regulatory and import/export requirements of all countries. The literary obverse of a world car would be opaque in all contexts and thus generalize all forms of regulation in its univocal denial of them.

15 Stephen Greenblatt, "Resonance and Wonder," in *Learning to Curse: Essays in Early Modern Culture* (New York: Routledge, 1990), 161–83: "By resonance I mean the power of the object displayed to reach out beyond its formal boundaries to a larger world, to evoke in the viewer the complex, dynamic cultural forces from which it has emerged. . . . By wonder I mean the power of the object displayed to stop the viewer in his tracks, to convey an arresting sense of uniqueness, to evoke an exalted attention" (170).

16 Stephen Greenblatt, "The Circulation of Social Energy," in *Shakespearean Negotiations: The Circulation of Social Energy in Renaissance England* (Berkeley: University of California Press, 1988), 1–20; 19.

17 On the other end of the spectrum from the "social energy" of a cultural poetics

stands a legislative ordering in which poetry is given its place in relation to larger cultural discourses: "Poesy then is a piece of a much larger whole encompassed by the term *literature*, a term whose modern equivalent would be *cultural poetics* in the sense of the sum of written discourses through which we apprehend and act upon the world and, more particularly, the discourses through which we distinguish between the imaginary and the real." The horizon of *cultural poetics* succeeds what had been known as *literature*, which would then include in "the sum of written discourses" not only Shakespeare but English law. Greenblatt views literature as administrative, even corrective, a form of cultural power that entitles its bearer to a particular social advantages — until the placeholder previously known as the author and now reformulated as a kind of transcultural genius thunders out like the ghost of Hamlet's father, providing an experience of resonance and wonder. Stephen Greenblatt, "What Is the History of Literature?" *Critical Inquiry* 23, no. 2 (1997): 460–81; 471.

18 The anecdote is often seen as the Achilles' heel of the New Historicism, but as a moment of textual overdetermination it works precisely to bridge the gap between the questions of power and social energy Greenblatt discusses. See chapter 5 below.

19 Charles Bernstein, "Poetics of the Americas," *Modernism/Modernity* 3, no. 3 (1996): 1–21; 20; reprinted in Bernstein, *My Way: Speeches and Poems* (Chicago: University of Chicago Press, 1999), 113–37; hereafter *PA*.

20 Ibid., 4. In rhyming with Stanley Cavell's title, *This New Yet Unapproachable America*, Bernstein reveals his Emersonian agenda but does not account for notions of liberal polity contained within its ideal of "this unrepresentable yet ever presenting collectivity," which could be Language poets at the MLA but which is also a notion of liberal society as a horizon "open" to the determinations of interest.

21 To be fair, Bernstein's politics of nonidentity derive from his impatience with "characterization," as in his essay of the same name, "Characterization," in *Content's Dream: Essays, 1975–1984* (Los Angeles: Sun and Moon, 1986) 428–62. But to oppose a poetics of nonidentity (either Language writing or its multinational variants) to someone who is, in turn, characterized as a coercive "authentic" identity, and to derive the value of the former in opposition to the latter, only reproduces the problem.

22 For the development of political calypso, see the following compilations: *Calypso Calaloo: Early Carnival Music in Trinidad*, Rounder 1105; *Calypso Carnival: 1936–1941*, Rounder 1077; *Calypsos from Trinidad: Politics, Intrigue, and Violence in the 1930s*, Arhoolie 7004; *Calypso War: Black Music in Britain, 1956–1958*, Sequel Records 232.

23 The antirealist account of modernism fits very well with an Emersonian politics that, self-consciously from the mid 1960s, helped give the postmoderns a way in to the Great Tradition of American literature — in moving from a subordination of social differences to the transcendental author. This Emersonian moment recalls, indeed, the debacle over the work of Louis Zukofsky in the notorious evening devoted to his work in San Francisco in 1979. Robert Duncan ended his presentation with a claim that Zukofsky's often discrepant particularity had meaning "so that we can be American!" which, at the time, seemed an unimpressive goal. My presen-

tation of Zukofsky's "material text" that followed meant to emphasize his politics of difference as precisely that, a politics. I *really* had an experience of opposition, and of what it feels like to be included in an "impossible" America, then.

24 On rethinking the opposition between modernism and realism, see Astradur Eysteinsson, "Realism, Modernism, and the Aesthetics of Interruption," in *The Concept of Modernism* (Ithaca, N.Y.: Cornell University Press, 1990), 179–241.

25 Michael Denning, *The Cultural Front: The Laboring of American Culture in the Twentieth Century* (London: Verso, 1997), esp. 212: "The figure who best exemplifies this radical modernism is William Carlos Williams," precisely because he goes beyond the modernist/realist distinction.

26 Michael North, *The Dialect of Modernism: Race, Language, and Twentieth-Century Literature* (Oxford: Oxford University Press, 1994).

27 The exemplarity of Stein is important, here, in other senses. Writers trying to extend Stein's "constructive" aesthetics, particularly in the expatriate magazine *transition*, provide another, if less successful, example in that their work did not reflexively engage new social meanings as much as Stein's.

28 This may seem true if one looks at just surface things like language. But if there is a telos in Stein, it is precisely in her dealing with teleology in the great watershed of her work, *The Making of Americans*. In moving from narrative portraits in *Three Lives* to nonnarrated ones in *Tender Buttons*, Stein produced a massively material text in *The Making of Americans*, at once psychologically invested and culturally mimetic, but whose formal necessities are not to be found solely in the surface effects of language; Barrett Watten, "An Epic of Subjectivation: *The Making of Americans*," *Modernism/Modernity* 5, no. 2 (1998): 95–121.

29 As I've been saying all along, Russian Formalism, which was misread in the historical development of Anglo-American "formalist" criticism, precisely accounts for a dynamic relation of text to context in central concepts such as "stepwise construction" and "the canonization of peripheral forms," as well as in its overall historicism.

30 This is very close to an argument Ron Silliman made in an article in *Socialist Review*, which was immediately contested by Leslie Scalapino; the debate is continued in Silliman and Scalapino, "What / Person? From an Exchange," in "The Person," *Poetics Journal* 9 (1991): 51–68.

31 To qualify the claim of universalist politics in Bernstein's own terms: "an exploration of the space between identities" may lead to "new collective identities," even if only hinted at, "impossible," or "virtual." Their value, however, will be "to presume a realm of social truths against the one truth of technorationality and its schizoid doubles, triumphalist capitalism and religious fundamentalism" (*Poetics of the Americas*, 19). My response, finally, is to question the form in which this struggle will take place: either as an aesthetic confederation of nonstandard, ideolectical practice, something like *transition*'s "Revolution of the Word," or in a literary politics more like the dialogue between modernism and realism in the same period. The arguments of our collectively written intervention, Steve Benson et al., "Aesthetic Tendency and the Politics of Poetry," *Social Text* 19–20 (1998): 261–75, and what follows, delineate the latter mode.

32 Charles Altieri, "What Is Living and What Is Dead in American Postmodernism:

Establishing the Contemporaneity of Some American Poetry," *Critical Inquiry* 22, no. 4 (1996): 764–89; reprinted in Altieri, *Postmodernisms Now: Essays on Contemporaneity in the Arts* (University Park: Pennsylvania State University Press, 1998), 23–49; hereafter "WIL."

33 After Monty Python's "Proust Paraphrase Contest" (the goal of which is to reduce *A la Recherche du temps perdu* to a one-sentence summary), this is my paraphrase of the argument of Charles Altieri's *Painterly Abstraction in Modernist American Poetry: The Contemporaneity of Modernism* (1989; University Park: Pennsylvania State University Press, 1995).

34 Lyn Hejinian, *The Cell* (Los Angeles: Sun and Moon, 1992).

35 In this sense, Lyn Hejinian's later long poem *A Border Comedy* is highly readable for its social reflexivity, precisely the border of its comedy; *A Border Comedy* (New York: Granary Books, 2001).

36 Alice B. Toklas, *What Is Remembered* (San Francisco: North Point Press, 1985), 95, 105; Linda Wagner-Martin, *"Favored Strangers": Gertrude Stein and Her Family* (New Brunswick, N.J.: Rutgers University Press, 1995), 150, 190.

37 Stein, *Everybody's Autobiography*, 48.

38 On the "two modernities," see Matei Calinescu, *Five Faces of Modernity: Modernism, Avant-Garde, Decadence, Kitsch, Postmodernism* (Durham, N.C.: Duke University Press, 1987); and Andreas Huyssen, *After the Great Divide: Modernism, Mass Culture, Postmodernism* (Bloomington: Indiana University Press, 1986). In a recent lecture, Huyssen indicated that he had substantially changed his earlier position; "High / Low in an Expanded Field," *Modernism / Modernity* 9, no. 3 (September 2002): 363–74.

39 Michael Davidson, "The Romance of Materiality: Gertrude Stein and the Aesthetic," in *Ghostlier Demarcations: Modern Poetry and the Material Word* (Berkeley: University of California Press, 1997), 35–63.

40 Wagner-Martin, *"Favored Strangers,"* 136.

41 Gertrude Stein, from "Work Again," in *Geography and Plays* (1922; Madison: University of Wisconsin Press, 1993), 399.

42 Dianne Souhami, *Gertrude and Alice* (London: Pandora Press, 1991), 143.

43 Janet Hobhouse, *Everybody Who Was Anybody: A Biography of Gertrude Stein* (New York: Doubleday, 1975), 114.

44 Gertrude Stein, "Scenes from the Door," in *Useful Knowledge* (1928; Barrytown, N.Y.: Station Hill Press, 1988), 78.

45 Stein, *Everybody's Autobiography*, 240–41.

46 James R. Mellow, *Charmed Circle: Gertrude Stein and Company* (Boston: Houghton Mifflin, 1974), 269.

47 Gertrude Stein, *The Autobiography of Alice B. Toklas* (1933; New York: Vintage Books, 1990), 152.

48 Hobhouse, *Everybody Who Was Anybody*, 114.

49 On Stein and genius, see Bob Perelman, *The Trouble with Genius: Reading Pound, Joyce, Stein, and Zukofsky* (Berkeley: University of California Press, 1994); and Barbara Will, *Gertrude Stein: Modernism and the Problem of Genius* (Edinburgh: Edinburgh University Press, 2000).

50 Ulla B. Dydo discusses the letter in "*Stanzas in Meditation*: The Other Autobiog-

raphy," in Richard Kostelanetz, ed., *Gertrude Stein Advanced* (Jefferson, N.C.: McFarland, 1990), 112–27.

51 The theory of the "two modernities" is nearly ubiquitous in Stein's reception. As an example, Jerome McGann writes that "Stein allowed herself to be transformed into a kind of circus animal" during her 1934 tour, even as "paradoxically, she never imagined that her work was meant for anything but a wide and even a popular audience"; *Black Riders: The Visible Language of Modernism* (Princeton, N.J.: Princeton University Press, 1993), 19–20, Of course, Stein's own discussion of the relation between "identity" and "entity" in *The Geographical History of America; or, The Relation of Human Nature to the Human Mind* (1936; New York: Vintage Books, 1973), bears directly on her distinction between "real writing" and "audience writing," though her motives for making the distinction need not be taken at face value.

52 "As I have said the essence of being a genius is to be able to talk and listen to listen while talking and talk while listening but and this is very important very important indeed talking has nothing to do with creation"; Gertrude Stein, *What Are Masterpieces* (Los Angeles: The Conference Press, 1940), 84.

53 Robert Grenier, "On Speech," *This* 1 (1971): n.p.; reprinted in Ron Silliman, ed., *In the American Tree*, 1st ed. (Orono, Maine: National Poetry Foundation, 1985), 496–97; 2nd ed., 477–78. The first citation of Grenier's one-liner as "originary" was made by Silliman in the introduction to his anthology (xv; xvii). Silliman qualifies his claim in a subsequent essay, "The Dysfunction of Criticism: Poets and the Critical Tradition of the Anti-Academy," in "Knowledge," *Poetics Journal* 10 (1998): 179–94. Bob Perelman's discussion is in *The Marginalization of Poetry: Language Writing and Literary History* (Princeton, N.J.: Princeton University Press, 1996), 39–57; hereafter *MP*.

54 Libbie Rifkin, *Career Moves: Olson, Creeley, Zukofsky, Berrigan, and the Ameican Avant-Garde* (Madison: University of Wisconsin Press, 2000), 136–45; Ann Vickery, *Leaving Lines of Gender: A Feminist Genealogy of Language Writing* (Middletown, Conn.: Wesleyan University Press, 2000), 150–66.

55 On Ford and the development of the assembly line, see Terry Smith, *Making the Modern: Industry, Art, and Design in America* (Chicago: University of Chicago Press, 1993); hereafter *MM*, and Ray Batchelor, *Henry Ford: Mass Production, Modernism, and Design* (Manchester: Manchester University Press, 1994).

56 On Grenier's "I hate speech" seen in the context of the late 1960s, see Barrett Watten, "The Turn to Language and the 1960s," *Critical Inquiry* 29, no. 1 (autumn 2002): 139–83.

57 Robert Grenier, *Sentences* (Cambridge, Mass.: Whale Cloth Press, 1978). The work is now available online at <www.whalecloth.org>.

58 There is an as yet untheorized genre of massive, obdurate, and unavailable works that establish the genius of a given author but which are unavailable, at least in their entirety; such a genre would include *The Making of Americans*, Robert Duncan's *Passages* during the fifteen years he refused to publish (1969–84), Coolidge's "longwork," Grenier's *Sentences*, and Ron Silliman's *The Alphabet*, among others. On Grenier's *Sentences*, see chapter 6 below.

59 Ron Silliman, introduction to *In the American Tree*, xv; xvii.

60 André Breton, *Manifestoes of Surrealism*, trans. Richard Seaver and Helen R. Lane (Ann Arbor: University of Michigan Press, 1972), 21.

61 On the work of Hannah Weiner, see Vickery, *Leaving Lines of Gender*, 204–16; Judith Goldman, "Hannah=hannaH: Politics, Ethics, and Clairvoyance in the Work of Hannah Weiner," in Steve Evans, ed., "After Patriarchal Poetry: Feminism and the Avant-Garde," *differences* 12, no. 2 (2001): 121–68.

62 Bob Perelman, "Seeing What Gertrude Stein Means," in *Trouble with Genius*, 129–69. For Perelman, Steinian genius is moment of reification analogous both to the ineffable meanings of her work and to the vulgarity of her public persona: "In all cases, there is a double insistence: (1) genius is unique, a fact that Stein states emphatically and demonstrates in various ways in the writing itself; and (2) genius is unavoidably perceptible and valuable, a fact that she also states emphatically that is demonstrated, in however suspect or tautological a sense, by her fame" (143).

63 The poem, to my knowledge, appeared only in *This*, and not in any later collection.

64 L. S. Vygotsky, *Thought and Language*, trans. Eugenia Hanfmann and Gertrude Vakar (Cambridge, Mass.: MIT Press, 1962), chap. 7.

65 Altieri, "What Is Living," 777.

66 A test of whether there is such a thing as progress in art might be made in relation to the idea of flatness as it resolutely turns into lyrical fullness time and again, from the indifference supposedly manifest in Marcel Duchamp's *Bottle Rack*, which ends up being high art, until just about now.

67 This reading of the politics of New York School abstraction is supported by revisionist accounts such as Serge Guilbaut, *How New York Stole the Idea of Modern Art* (Cambridge, Mass.: MIT Press, 1983).

68 Marshall Berman, *All That Is Solid Melts into Air: The Experience of Modernity* (Middlesex, Eng.: Penguin, 1988), chap. 2.

69 For such an analysis, see John Brenkman, "The Concrete Utopia of Poetry," in *Culture and Domination* (Ithaca, N.Y.: Cornell University Press, 1987), 102–40.

70 On serial form, see Joseph M. Conte, *Unending Design: The Forms of Postmodern Poetry* (Ithaca, N.Y.: Cornell University Press, 1991).

71 Grenier felt Creeley was going too far in the direction of reference, that his words were too much in the world and not enough in his head, and that he was still referring to what he was doing, rather than simply doing it; Robert Grenier, review of *Pieces* and *A Quick Graph: Collected Notes and Essays*, by Robert Creeley, *This* 1 (1971): n.p. "On Speech" was sandwiched between these two reviews.

72 Silliman, at least, notices the argument of the total form of *This* 1; "Dysfunction of Criticism," 181.

73 Libbie Rifkin's discusses the "slippery deictic 'this,'" from Olson's famous maxim "polis is *this*," in *Career Moves*, 47–49.

74 In a proposed anthology, *The Annotated "This,"* I hope to develop more this sense of the "feedback system" among writers as the journal went forward in time.

75 Clark Coolidge, *The Maintains* (San Francisco: This Press, 1974); excerpted in Silliman, *In the American Tree*, 243–48; 237–43; hereafter *TM*.

76 Clark Coolidge, *Own Face* (Lenox, Mass.: United Artists, 1978); Coolidge, *Solution Passage: Poems, 1978–1981* (Los Angeles: Sun and Moon, 1986); Coolidge, *Sound as Thought: Poems, 1982–1984* (Los Angeles: Sun and Moon, 1990).

77 Clark Coolidge, *Polaroid* (Bolinas, Calif.: Big Sky Books, 1975); excerpted in Silliman, *In the American Tree*, 249–52; 244–47.

78 Katharine M. E. Murray, *Caught in the Web of Words: James A. H. Murray and the Oxford English Dictionary* (Oxford: Oxford University Press, 1977).

79 H. L. Mencken, *The American Language: An Inquiry into the Development of English in the United States*, ed. Ravin I. McDavid Jr., 4th ed., rev (New York: Knopf, 1995), 16; Michael P. Kramer, *Imagining Language in America: From the Revolution to the Civil War* (Princeton, N.J.: Princeton University Press, 1992), 35.

80 The parallel between Webster and Ford as innovators was marked by none other than Ford himself, who rebuilt Webster's house in his Greenfield Village historical park. What Ford admired was the setting of national standards, in both Webster's spelling book and dictionary, but there is a comparison as well between the way Ford and Webster's rigid authoritarianism was realized in the editing out of inessentials (in streamlining of manufacturing, for Ford, or in spelling, for Webster).

81 Coolidge's jazz-based rhythmic drive is another social register in the poem, as Aldon L. Nielsen points out, that radically disrupts the corrective monomania of Webster's dictionary as a way of making the dead letter of national language come alive. On Coolidge and jazz, see "Whose Blues?" in Nielsen, *Writing between the Lines: Race and Intertextuality* (Athens: University of Georgia Press, 1994), chap. 7.

82 For a reading of Coolidge's "meter-making argument" that orients semantic ambiguity toward its organization of sound (and silence), see Herman Rapaport, "Poetic Rests: Ashbery, Coolidge, Scalapino," in "Knowledge," *Poetics Journal* 10 (1998): 155–64.

83 My "Factors Influencing the Weather" (in *This* 4) diverges, in this sense, from Coolidge's turn to "sound as thought" in wanting to keep the meaning-bearing units of language as central to poetic construction. The lyric form of Larry Eigner's concatenated assembly of phrasal units was important in this period as well; Barrett Watten, *Frame: 1971–1990* (Los Angeles: Sun and Moon, 1997), 290–95.

84 There will be more discussion of the politics of such interactions in *The Annotated "This."*

85 Watten, *Frame*, 196. This section of "The Word" is a modern translation of a riddle from Michael Alexander, *Old English Riddles from the Exeter Book* (London: Anvil, 1980). The answer is given in the poem, but as the missing word remains "other."

86 Cf. Marcel Duchamp, *The Essential Writings of Marcel Duchamp*, ed. Michel Sanouillet and Elmer Peterson (London: Thames and Hudson, 1973); Barrett Watten, "Mimesis," in *Frame*, 45–47.

87 Smith, *Making the Modern*, chaps. 1–4. This is one of the most important revisions of American modernism of the last fifteen years. See also, on industrial processes leading to the assembly line, Siegfried Giedion, *Mechanization Takes Command: A Contribution to Anonymous History* (1948; New York: Norton, 1969); on scientific management, Ford, and culture, Martha Banta, *Taylored Lives: Narrative Productions in the Age of Taylor, Veblen, and Ford* (Chicago: University of Chicago Press, 1993); on Ford, Batchelor, *Ford;* on the history of the auto business, James J. Flink, *The Automobile Age* (Cambridge, Mass.: MIT Press, 1990).

88 On the metaphor of the machine in modernism (e.g., Dada, cubism, constructivism,

Dos Passos, the poetic uses of the machine in Williams, Crane, Zukofsky, and Moore), see Lisa M. Steinman, *Made in America: Science, Technology, and American Modernist Poets* (New Haven, Conn.: Yale University Press, 1987); and Cecilia Tichi, *Shifting Gears: Technology, Literature, Culture in Modernist America* (Chapel Hill: University of North Carolina Press, 1987).

89 See Gilles Deleuze and Felix Guattari, "Balance-Sheet Program for Desiring Machines," *Semiotext(e)* 2, no. 3 (1977): 117–35; Deleuze and Guattari, *Anti-Oedipus: Capitalism and Schizophrenia*, trans. Robert Hurley, Robert Seem, and Helen R. Lane (Minneapolis: University of Minnesota Press, 1983), part 1.

90 Smith, *Making the Modern*, 28.

91 Barrett Watten, *Under Erasure* (La Laguna, Sp.: Zasterle Press, 1992), 30–31.

92 Ben Hamper, *Rivethead: Tales from the Assembly Line* (New York: Time Warner, 1992), 209.

93 Watten, *Progress*, 84–85.

CHAPTER 4: The Constructivist Moment (pp. 147–96)

Epigraph from Victor Shklovsky, *Third Factory*, trans. Richard Sheldon (Ann Arbor, Mich.: Ardis, 1977), 53. As presented to audiences, this essay was accompanied by both visual and audio materials; the figures reproduced here are taken from a wider range of visual images. "Techno breaks" by Detroit artists (Kenny Larkin, Underground Resistance, Theorem, Derrick May, Carl Craig, Kevin Saunderson, Jeff Mills, and Mike Banks) were also played at regular intervals.

1 While General Motors' move should not be seen as a cause of the reversal of Detroit's long trend of deurbanization from the 1960s to the 1990s, relocating the headquarters of one of the Big Three into John Portman's 1977 Renaissance Center complex is of more than merely symbolic value. While Ford money was crucial in financing the Renaissance Center in order to forestall Detroit's urban decline as early as 1971, its headquarters is just outside Detroit in Dearborn, the traditional center of Ford operations, while DaimlerChrysler's is more than twenty-five miles from downtown in Auburn Hills.

2 *New York Times*, 20 July 1997; *Detroit News*, 17 September 1997.

3 Viktor Shklovsky reflects on his dictum, cited above, in a passage important for its politics: "But artistic form carries out its own unique rape of the Sabine women. The material ceases to recognize its former lord and master. Once processed by the law of art, it can be perceived apart from its place of origin"; *Third Factory*, 53. Ann Jefferson discusses the gendered assumptions of Shklovsky's metaphor of dominance; "Literariness, Dominance, and Violence in Formalist Aesthetics," in Peter Collier and Helga Geyer-Ryan, eds., *Literary Theory Today* (Ithaca, N.Y.: Cornell University Press, 1990), 125–41. Shklovsky's memoir of the revolution and civil war, *A Sentimental Journey: Memoirs, 1917–1922*, trans. Richard Sheldon (Ithaca, N.Y.: Cornell University Press, 1970), reveals many points of contact between social violence and modernist aesthetics; his notion of "device," for one thing, is figured as a bomb that goes off in his hands.

4 On modernism and shock, see Georg Simmel, "The Metropolis and Mental Life," in Charles Harrison and Paul Wood, eds., *Art in Theory, 1900–1990* (London: Black-

well, 1992); Sigmund Freud, *Beyond the Pleasure Principle*, ed. and trans. James Strachey (New York: Norton, 1989); Walter Benjamin, *Charles Baudelaire: A Lyric Poet in the Age of High Capitalism*, trans. Harry Zohn (London: Verso, 1976); Paul Virilio, *Pure War* (New York: Semiotexte, 1983); and, on Benjamin, Leo Bersani, "Boundaries of Time and Being: Benjamin, Baudelaire, Nietzsche," in *The Culture of Redemption* (Cambridge, Mass.: Harvard University Press, 1990), 47–101; Susan Buck-Morss, *The Dialectics of Seeing: Walter Benjamin and the Arcades Project* (Cambridge, Mass.: MIT Press, 1991); and Peter Osborne, *The Politics of Time: Modernity and Avant-Garde* (London: Verso, 1995).

5 On the work of Iakov Chernikhov, see Catherine Cooke, ed., "Russian Constructivism and Iakov Chernikhov," *Architectural Design* 59, no. 7/8 (1989); Cooke, "Chernikhov: The Construction of Architectural and Machine Forms," *Architectural Design* 47 (1983): 73–80; Cooke, *Russian Avant-Garde: Theories of Art, Architecture, and the City* (London: Academy Editions, 1995); and Carlo Olmo and Alessandro de Magistris, eds., *Iakov Tchernikhov*, Documents et reproductions des archives de Aleksei et Dimitri Tchernikhov (Paris: Somogy, 1995).

6 Causes for this lack of interest in the avant-garde after the rise of Cultural Studies are many: a Hegelian historicism that yokes avant-garde agency to a rigid teleology; a ready-made institutional critique in which avant-garde urinals turn into fixtures such as the Museum of Modern Art; and critiques of race and gender in modernism after which the mythic originality of the avant-garde appears as *the* primary symptom of social dysfunction. Approaches to the avant-garde that do not adequately address its relation to Cultural Studies, in my view, include Renato Poggioli, *The Theory of the Avant-Garde* (Cambridge, Mass.: Harvard University Press, 1968); Matei Calinescu, *Five Faces of Modernity: Modernism, Avant-Garde, Decadence, Kitsch, Postmodernism* (Durham, N.C.: Duke University Press, 1987); Peter Bürger, *The Theory of the Avant-Garde*, trans. Jochen Schülte-Sasse (Minneapolis: University of Minnesota Press, 1984); Rosalind Krauss, *The Originality of the Avant-Garde and Other Modernist Myths* (Cambridge, Mass.: MIT Press, 1985); Donald Kuspit, *The Cult of the Avant-Garde Artist* (Cambridge: Cambridge University Press, 1993). On the other hand, Astradur Eysteinsson, *The Concept of Modernism* (Ithaca, N.Y.: Cornell University Press, 1990), stands out as a theoretical account of modernism that includes an important place for the avant-garde.

7 Cary Nelson and Lawrence Grossberg, eds., *Marxism and the Interpretation of Culture* (Urbana: University of Illinois Press, 1988); Cary Nelson, Lawrence Grossberg, and Paula Treichler, eds., *Cultural Studies* (New York: Routledge, 1992).

8 Cary Nelson, "Literature as Cultural Studies: 'American' Poetry of the Spanish Civil War," in Nelson and Dilip Parameshwar Gaonkar, eds., *Disciplinarity and Dissent in Cultural Studies* (New York: Routledge, 1996); Nelson, *Revolutionary Memory: Recovering the Poetry of the American Left* (London: Routledge, 2001).

9 Paul Mann, *The Theory Death of the Avant-Garde* (Bloomington: Indiana University Press, 1991), 32. The negativity of avant-garde is presumed, here, to be a purely formal one (in the logical sense) that bears little relation to the negativity of social experience. Even so, the radical negativity of the avant-garde — even at the moment of its "theory death" — is central to notions such as "foregrounding" in Russian

Formalism and "automatism" in surrealism, which anticipate both poststructuralist and Lacanian critical theory in the concepts of "markedness" in structuralism and "the agency of the letter" in Lacan. Insofar as these concepts are historical, they partake of the forms of the avant-garde.

10 Andreas Huyssen, *After the Great Divide: Modernism, Mass Culture, Postmodernism* (Bloomington: Indiana University Press, 1986).

11 For example, Catherine Gallagher describes a politics of "left formalism" where radical formal agency is simply by virtue of its negativity thought to have a coherent politics, and thus becomes a kind of bad object the critic should abject. "It was against such claims for the automatic subversiveness of art . . . that new historicists directed their critiques"; "Marxism and the New Historicism," in Aram Veeser, ed., *The New Historicism* (New York: Routledge, 1989), 37–48; 41, 44.

12 In this sense, the materialist feminism of Rosemary Hennessy singles out the avant-garde out as a form of duplicity: "The avant-garde text served the dominant ideology by providing it with something to replace what it lacked, but without directly calling into question the role of signification and the subject in its system of reproduction"; *Materialist Feminism and the Politics of Discourse* (New York: Routledge, 1993), 52–53. Avant-garde literary agency and cultural form are often seen to be a masculine preserve, as for Nancy Armstrong: "Modernism's antagonism toward both mass culture and women is all too well known"; "Modernism's Iconophobia and What It Did to Gender," *Modernism/Modernity* 5, no. 2 (1998): 47–76. The sense of antagonism here draws from, but distorts, the gendering of the great divide between a masculine modernism and a feminine mass culture.

13 The following recently published studies offer new approaches to the cultural politics of the avant-garde: Daniel Belgrad, *The Culture of Spontaneity: Improvisation and the Arts in Postwar America* (Chicago: University of Chicago Press, 1998); Margaret Cohen, *Profane Illumination: Walter Benjamin and the Paris of Surrealist Revolution* (Berkeley: University of California Press, 1993); Maria Damon, *The Dark End of the Street: Margins in American Vanguard Poetry* (Minneapolis: University of Minnesota Press, 1993); Rachel Blau DuPlessis, *Genders, Races, and Religious Cultures in Modern American Poetry, 1908–1934* (Cambridge: Cambridge University Press, 2001); Walter Kalaidjian, *American Culture between the Wars: Revisionary Modernism and Postmodern Critique* (New York: Columbia University Press, 1993); Janet Lyon, *Manifestoes: Provocations of the Modern* (Cornell University Press: 1999); Aldon Lynn Nielsen, *Black Chant: Languages of African-American Postmodernism* (Cambridge: Cambridge University Press, 1997); Libbie Rifkin, *Career Moves: Olson, Creeley, Zukofsky, Berrigan, and the American Avant-Garde* (Madison: University of Wisconsin Press, 2000); Tricia Rose, *Black Noise: Rap Music and Black Culture in Contemporary America* (Hanover, N.H.: Wesleyan University Press/University Press of New England, 1994); Kristin Ross, *The Emergence of Social Space: Rimbaud and the Paris Commune* (Minneapolis: University of Minnesota Press, 1988); Reva Wolf, *Andy Warhol, Poetry, and Gossip in the 1960s* (Chicago: University of Chicago Press, 1997).

14 Cited in Tony Pinkney, introduction to Raymond Williams, *The Politics of Modernism* (London: Verso, 1989), 25; hereafter *PM*.

15 Pierre Bourdieu, *The Rules of Art: Genesis and Structure of the Literary Field*, trans.

Susan Emanuel (Stanford, Calif.: Stanford University Press, 1996), 83; Raymond Williams, *The Sociology of Culture* (Chicago: University of Chicago Press, 1995); hereafter *SC*.

16 M. M. Bakhtin and P. M. Medvedev, *The Formal Method in Literary Scholarship: A Critical Introduction to Sociological Poetics*, trans. Albert J. Wehrle (Cambridge, Mass.: Harvard University Press, 1985); V. N. Voloshinov, *Marxism and the Philosophy of Language*, trans. Ladislav Matejka and I. R. Titunik (Cambridge, Mass.: Harvard University Press, 1986).

17 However, this is precisely the social experience that in fact led me to identify myself as a member of a literary avant-garde after the 1960s.

18 One may mention, here, the different configurations of negativity in women avant-garde artists — to begin with, high modernists such as Gertrude Stein, Laura Riding, Mina Loy, and Mary Butts — as well as the postmodern aesthetics of a "third space" of transnational social hybridity, theorized by Homi Bhabha and Paul Gilroy and exemplified by contemporary writers such as Nathaniel Mackey and Theresa Hak Kyung Cha.

19 Bourdieu, *Rules of Art*.

20 For accounts of Lissitzky's career, see Sophie Lissitzky-Küppers, ed., *El Lissitzky: Life/Letters/Text* (Greenwich, Conn.: New York Graphic Society, 1968), hereafter *EL*; *El Lissitzky, 1890–1941*, exhibition catalogue (Eindhoven, Neth.: Municipal Van Abbemuseum, 1990); and Victor Margolin, *The Struggle for Utopia: Rodchenko, Lissitzky, Moholy-Nagy, 1917–1946* (Chicago: University of Chicago Press, 1997); hereafter *SU*.

21 Yve-Alain Bois, "El Lissitzky: Radical Reversibility," *Art in America* (April 1988): 161–80.

22 Vladimir Markov, *Russian Futurism: A History* (Berkeley: University of California Press, 1968); and Camilla Gray, *The Russian Experiment in Art, 1863–1922*, rev. and enlarged ed. (London: Thames and Hudson, 1986) are examples of studies that locate the "end" of Russian modernism in the early 1920s, with the beginnings of the dialogue between avant-garde art and its social command; Stephanie Barron and Maurice Tuchman, eds., *The Avant-Garde in Russia, 1910–1930: New Perspectives*, exhibition catalogue (Cambridge, Mass.: MIT Press, 1980) see the "end" of the avant-garde in the consolidation of socialist realism around 1930; while *The Great Utopia: The Russian and Soviet Avant-Garde, 1915–1932*, exhibition catalogue (New York: Guggenheim Museum, 1992), follows the development of the avant-garde in social production to the end of the 1930s, seeing its "end" not even with the Moscow Trials but with the war. For post-Soviet artists and writers with whom I spoke in Leningrad in 1989, the avant-garde survived, apart from isolated individuals, mainly in Western art criticism after the war.

23 Benjamin H. D. Buchloh, "From Faktura to Factography," in Annette Michelson et al., eds., *"October": The First Decade, 1976–1986* (Cambridge, Mass.: MIT Press, 1987). On Mayakovsky's social command, see Vladimir Mayakovsky, *How to Make Verses*, trans. Valentina Coe (Willimantic, Conn.: Curbstone Press, 1985); Viktor Shklovsky, *Mayakovsky and His Circle*, ed. and trans. Lily Feiler (New York: Dodd, Mead, 1972).

24 *Webster's Collegiate Dictionary*, 10th ed., dates the term at 1900. *Webster's Third New International Dictionary* defines it as "an atom or group of atoms [as triphenyl methyl or hydroxyl] characterized by the presence of at least one unpaired electron and held to participate in many reactions (as polymerization and reactions in biological systems)." One wonders whether Freud's "trimethylamine" in "The Dream of Irma's Injection" is a free radical in this sense, as well as in Freud's association of it with sexuality.

25 On "rested totality," see Louis Zukofsky, "An Objective," in *Prepositions: The Collected Critical Essays*, expanded ed. (Berkeley: University of California Press, 1981), 12–18. I described the work of contemporary poet Robert Grenier, on the other hand, as an example of an "unrested totality"; Barrett Watten, "Grenier's *Sentences*," in Bruce Andrews and Charles Bernstein, eds., *The L=A=N=G=U=A=G=E Book* (Carbondale: Southern Illinois University Press, 1984), 235–37.

26 Alexander Gelley, ed., *Unruly Examples: On the Rhetoric of Exemplarity* (Stanford, Calif.: Stanford University Press, 1995).

27 The example is generally understood in a positivist sense of mimesis, as may be seen in the following dictionary definitions: *Webster's Third International*, s.v. "example": "a particular single item, fact, incident, or aspect that may be taken fairly as typical or representative"; it may also provide "a pattern or representative action or series of actions tending or intended to induce one to imitate or emulate." Cf. "exemplum": "an anecdote or short narrative used (as in a medieval sermon) to point a moral or sustain an argument."

28 For Jenny Holzer's work in the language of advertising, see *Writing/Schriften*, ed. Noemi Smolik (Ostfilden-Ruit, Ger.: Cantz, 1996); and David Joselit et al., eds., *Jenny Holzer* (New York: Phaidon, 1998).

29 Alexander Gelley, "Introduction," in *Unruly Examples*, 1–26; 14.

30 Michael J. Reddy, "The Conduit Metaphor: A Case of Frame Conflict in Our Language about Language," in Andrew Ortony, ed., *Metaphor and Thought* (Cambridge: Cambridge University Press, 1979).

31 Yulia Latinina, "Folklore and 'Novoyaz,'" in "The Person," *Poetics Journal* 9 (June 1991): 116–26; George Lakoff, *Moral Politics: What Conservatives Know That Liberals Don't* (Chicago: University of Chicago Press, 1996).

32 Kalaidjian, *American Culture between the Wars.*

33 J. Hillis Miller, "Parabolic Exemplarity: The Example of Nietzsche's *Thus Spake Zarathustra*," in Gelley, *Unruly Examples*, 62–74; 172.

34 Yve-Alain Bois offers a slightly different periodization of Lissitzky's career in three stages: (L1) the moment of high modernism, identified with painterly concerns and influence of Chagall; (L2) the overturning of the modernist paradigm after the influence of Malevich and the invention of the *Prouns;* and (L3) the turn to social production, from the *Pressa* exhibition to work on *USSR in Construction*, and including advertising and design; "El Lissitzky," 161–80.

35 Hal Foster, "Some Uses and Abuses of Russian Constructivism," in *Art into Life: Russian Constructivism, 1914–1932*, exhibition catalogue (New York: Rizzoli, 1990), 241–53; 244.

36 Margolin, *Struggle for Utopia*, 78.

37 Christina Lodder, *Russian Constructivism* (New Haven, Conn.: Yale University Press, 1983), 75; Margolin, *Struggle for Utopia*, 85.

38 Alexei Gan, excerpts from *Constructivism*, and Osip Brik, "From Pictures to Textile Prints," in John E. Bowlt, ed., *Russian Art of the Avant-Garde: Theory and Criticism*, rev. and enlarged ed. (London: Thames and Hudson, 1988), 214–24; 244–49.

39 Lissitzky also imagined that the *Prouns* could be rotated and be seen with any of their four sides at the top; thus their "horizon" is solely their own and does not depend on any preexisting one; Bois, "El Lissitzky," 172.

40 Cited in Margolin, *Struggle for Utopia*, 32.

41 El Lissitzky, "Proun" (1920), cited in Yve-Alain Bois, "From $-\infty$ to 0 to $+\infty$: Axonometry, or Lissitzky's Mathematical Paradigm," in *El Lissitzky, 1890–1941*, exhibition catalogue (Eindhoven, Neth.: Municipal Van Abbemuseum, 1990), 33; hereafter *A*; the same passage appears in Lissitzky, "New Russian Art: A Lecture" (1922), in Lissitzky-Küppers, *Lissitzky*, 330–40; 334.

42 Ilya Ehrenburg and El Lissitzky, "The Blockade of Russia Moves towards Its End," introduction to *Veshch* 1 (Berlin, 1922), in Lissitzky-Küppers, *Lissitzky*, 340–41. He insists on the relation of avant-garde form to revolution: "*We cannot imagine a creation of new forms in art unrelated to the change of social form*"; his emphasis, 341.

43 In his retrospective account of the 1920s, *Russia: An Architecture for World Revolution*, trans. Eric Dluhosch (Cambridge, Mass.: MIT Press, 1984), Lissitzky distinguishes between a merely technical revolution, occasioned by "the birth of the machine," and the social revolution of 1917, "to which the basic elements of Russian architecture are tied." Lissitzky's preference for the transformative *object* over that of the *machine* may be compared to Iakov Chernikhov's position: "A machine, whenever exposed, speaks for itself. A machine cannot but be constructive because it embodies all the aspects and principles of constructivism"; "The Constitution, Study, and Formation of Constructivism," in Stephen Bann, ed., *The Tradition of Constructivism*, reprint ed. (New York: Da Capo, 1974), 156.

44 El Lissitzky, "Prouns" (1921), cited in Margolin, *Struggle for Utopia*, 32.

45 El Lissitzky, "A. and Pangeometry," in Lissitzky, *Russia*, 142–49; 145; also in Lissitzky-Küppers, *Lissitzky*, 348–54; and Harrison and Wood, *Art in Theory, 1900–1990*, 303–7.

46 Bois, "El Lissitzky," 172.

47 Slavoj Žižek, *The Sublime Object of Ideology* (London: Verso, 1989), esp. chap. 5.

48 "To mention the final example, the famous MacGuffin, the Hitchcockian object, the pure pretext whose sole role is to set the story in motion but which is in itself 'nothing at all' — the only significance of the MacGuffin lies in the fact that it has some significance for the characters — that it must seem to be of vital importance to them"; ibid., 163.

49 Quoted in Margolin, *Struggle for Utopia*, 32.

50 For further historical contextualization of the transition from the modernist 1920s to the Stalinist 1930s, see Paul Wood, "The Politics of the Avant-Garde," in *Great Utopia*.

51 "Futurist negativity" is central to Bakhtin/Medvedev's critique of Russian Formalism; Bakhtin and Medvedev, *Formal Method in Literary Scholarship;* and also Chris-

topher Pike, ed., *The Futurists, the Formalists, and the Marxist Critique*, trans. Pike and Joe Andrew (London: Ink Links, 1979).

52 Shklovsky, *Mayakovsky and His Circle.*

53 Margolin, *Struggle for Utopia*, 11; emphasis mine.

54 On Lissitzky as Jew, see ibid., chap. 1.

55 Louis Zukofsky, *All: The Collected Short Poems, 1923–1958* (New York: Norton, 1965), 26; also in Zukofsky, *Complete Short Poetry* (Baltimore: The Johns Hopkins University Press, 1991), 23–24.

56 For recent readings of the "social" Zukofsky, see Mark Scroggins, ed., *Upper Limit Music: The Writing of Louis Zukofsky* (Tuscaloosa: University of Alabama Press, 1997).

57 Rachel Blau DuPlessis, "'Wondering Jews': Melting-Pots and Mongrel Thoughts," in *Genders, Races, and Religious Cultures*, 135–74.

58 Jean Day, *The Literal World* (Berkeley: Atelos Press, 1998), 53.

59 Ron Padgett, *Triangles in the Afternoon* (New York: Sun, 1979).

60 Conversation with the author.

61 The attendance figure is certainly exaggerated, though all three festivals were surprisingly well attended by enthusiastic audiences, given the continuing lack of media support for the genre. On the DEMF, see Liz Copeland, interview with Carl Craig, "High-Voltage Mastermind," *Metro Times*, 24 May 2000; Melissa Giannini, "Electric Heaven: Could It Be, Would It Be, the Festival of Our Dreams?" *Metro Times*, 22 May 2001; Carleton S. Gholz, "Techno Coup d'Etat," *Metro Times*, 5 June 2001, available at "MetroTimes.com," <www.metrotimes.com>.

62 Cited from the home page of Transmat Records (1997; unavailable 2002). For a basic history of Detroit techno, see Dan Sicko, *Techno Rebels: The Renegades of Electronic Funk* (New York: Billboard Books, 1999), as well as the two-part series by Hobey Echlin, "The History of Detroit Techno," parts 1 and 2, *Metro Times* (17–23, 24–30 May 1995) available at <www.metrotimes.com>; and Sicko, "Technorebels: Detroit's Agent of Change," *Urb* (August–September 1996): 56–65. A good current source (2002) for techno history is "World Techno Nation: Detroit Artists," <www.worldtechnonation.com/pages/detroit.htm>.

63 On "facelessness" in electronic dance music, see Robert Christgau, "Another Bleep World," *Village Voice* (16 February 1993): 69–70.

64 Asa Watten, in conversation.

65 "Somewhere in Detroit," <www.submerge.com>; the 2002 version of the site has changed considerably, providing interfaces in five languages and focusing entirely on product marketing rather than cultural politics. The 2002 Underground Resistance site, on the other hand, has been redesigned to register the fantasy of underground politics as a series of virtual bunkers; "Underground Resistance," <www.undergroundresistance.com>.

66 Scott Sterling, lecture presented at Cranbrook Museum, Bloomfield Hills, Michigan, 18 June 1997.

67 Cited in Echlin, "History of Detroit Techno," part 2.

68 Dick Hebdidge, *Subculture: The Meaning of Style* (London: Methuen, 1979), 100–112.

69 Erik Hanson, "Serious Groove: Roland and the Dance Music Phenomenon," *Roland User's Group: The Magazine for Electronic Musicians* 15, no. 2 (1997): 48–53.

70 Sterling, lecture at Cranbrook Museum.

71 Mike Banks, 11 March 1998, "Somewhere in Detroit" web site.

72 Dennis Teichman to Carla Harryman.

73 On the relation between orality and technology in the use of samples in African-American dance music, see Rose, *Black Noise*, chap. 3.

74 Sicko, "Technorebels," 59.

75 On the spatial metaphor of breaking through Eight Mile Road, see the "Purpose of Underground Resistance" page on its 2002 web site: "Underground Resistance is a label for a movement. / A movement that wants change by sonic revolution. / We urge you to join the resistance and help us combat / the mediocre audio and visual programming / that is being fed to the inhabitants of the earth. / This programming is stagnating the minds of the people; / building a wall between races and preventing world peace. / It is this wall we are going to smash. / By using the untapped energy potential of sound, / we are going to destroy this wall, / much the same as certain frequencies shatter glass. . . ."

76 One of Banks's recording labels is Red Planet Records, and he has used a recognizable 4/4 beat as an electronic motif to indicate his Native American influences (and heritage).

77 Banks, in conversation.

78 On recent Western European and American music subcultures, see Sarah Thornton, *Club Cultures: Music, Media, and Subcultural Capital* (Middletown, Conn.: Wesleyan University Press, 1996).

79 Scott Sterling, "Turntable Alchemy," *Sweater* 4 (October 1997): 36–41.

80 Web sites that were active at the time of writing (1997) and that continue to operate in the present (2002) include "Somewhere in Detroit"; "Plus 8," redesigned as "Plus 8 Classics (NovaMute)," <www.mute.com/mute/novamute/plus8/plus8.htm>; "Planet E," redesigned as "Planet E Communications," <www.planet-e.net>; and "Underground Resistance." All are substantially concerned with marketing records, even as avant-garde aesthetics and utopian politics are also evident. Sites previously active that are now unavailable include "2030 Home Page"; "Transmat Records"; "Tresor Records"; "Theorem"; "The History of Rave"; and "Ele_mental."

81 For an outstanding account of the relation of new music technologies to a "producer-centered" horizon, see Paul Théberge, *Any Sound You Can Imagine: Making Music/Consuming Technology* (Middletown, Conn.: Wesleyan University Press, 1997).

82 Sterling, lecture at Cranbrook Museum.

83 See Ed Luna's account of the relations between the historical avant-garde, from Varèse and Schoenberg to Cage and Stockhausen, to Detroit techno, from the no-longer-available 1997 "Ele_mental" site. This "high art" connection must be seen as a particular fan interest somewhat outside the discourse of the Detroit scene, however.

84 Lissitzky, *Russia*, 136–38.

85 Reproduced in Cooke, "Chernikhov," 80.

86 From the 1997 "Theorem" and "Planet E" sites, now unavailable.

87 For an opposite politics of repetition in music, see Jacques Attali, *Noise: The Political Economy of Music*, trans. Brian Massumi (Minneapolis: University of Minnesota Press, 1985), 87–132: "Literally speaking, 'taking power' is no longer possible in a repetitive society."

88 For the Turing test, see Andrew Hodges, *Alan Turing: The Enigma of Intelligence* (London: Unwin, 1983); Stacy Pullen, in sampling references to the "Replicants" of Ridley Scott's *Blade Runner* (1982) as a motif in his mix album *DJ Kicks*, evidences such a concern with relation between repetition and authenticity.

89 Melissa Giannini, "Better Grooming through Technology: Adult. Converts Neat-freak Style into Modern-Danceable Grooves," *Metro Times*, 27 March 2002: 13. On Craig's role in the politics of the DEMF, see Giannini, "Electric Heaven," and Gholz, "Techno Coup d'Etat."

CHAPTER 5: Nonnarrative and the Construction of History (pp. 197–237)

First epigraph from Robert Smithson, *The Writings of Robert Smithson*, ed. Nancy Holt (New York: New York University Press, 1979); second epigraph quoted in Michael Davidson et al., *Leningrad: American Writers in the Soviet Union* (San Francisco: Mercury House, 1992), 35. Arkadii Dragomoshchenko, then living in Leningrad, is a post-Soviet writer of intense "linguistic subjectivity" in an environment of defunct narratives; see his *Description*, trans. Lyn Hejinian and Elena Balashova (Los Angeles: Sun and Moon, 1990). For other post-Soviet poets, see "Mapping Codes: A Collection of New Writing from Moscow to San Francisco," *Five Fingers Review* 8–9 (1990); and Kent Johnson and Stephen M. Ashby, eds., *Third Wave: The New Russian Poetry* (Ann Arbor: University of Michigan Press, 1992).

1 Paul Ricoeur, *Time and Narrative*, 3 vols. (Chicago: University of Chicago Press, 1984–88), for example, forcefully argues the necessary reinforcements between the two.

2 See Jerome Rothenberg, ed., *Revolution of the Word: A New Gathering of American Avant-Garde Poetry* (New York: Seabury Press, 1974).

3 On narrative and the postmodern, see Jean-Francois Lyotard, *The Postmodern Condition: A Report on Knowledge*, trans. Geoff Bennington and Brian Massumi (Minneapolis: University of Minnesota Press, 1984); Fredric Jameson, *Postmodernism; or, The Cultural Logic of Late Capitalism* (Durham, N.C.: Duke University Press, 1991); hereafter *PM*; and Fred Pfeil, *Another Tale to Tell: Politics and Narrative in Postmodern Culture* (London: Verso, 1990).

4 Hayden White, *The Content of the Form* (Chicago: University of Chicago Press, 1987).

5 Sande Cohen, *Historical Culture: On the Recoding of an Academic Discipline* (Berkeley: University of California Press, 1986), 1.

6 Claude Lévi-Strauss, *The Savage Mind* (Chicago: University of Chicago Press, 1962), originates a series of positions in which "there is thus a sort of fundamental antipathy between history and systems of classification" seen as synchronic (242); cf. Seymour Chatman, *Coming to Terms: The Rhetoric of Narrative in Fiction and Film* (Ithaca, N.Y.: Cornell University Press, 1990), 9: "Nonnarrative text-types do not have an internal time sequence, even though, obviously, they take time to read,

view, or hear. Their underlying structures are static or atemporal — synchronic not diachronic."

7 Hayden White offers a Lacanian account of the imaginary unity of transcendental perspective in "The Question of Narrative in Contemporary Historical Theory," in *Content of the Form*, 36: "What is 'imaginary' about any narrative representation is the illusion of a centered consciousness capable of looking out on the world, apprehending its structure and processes, and representing them to itself as having all the formal coherency of narrativity itself." Such imaginary coherence — be it fictional, millennial, or simply transparent — constitutes and is constituted by the specific transcendental overview.

8 "When I am *in* my painting, I'm not aware of what I'm doing. It is only after a sort of 'get acquainted' period that I see what I have been about. I have no fears about making changes, destroying the image, etc., because the painting has a life of its own"; Jackson Pollock, quoted in Francis V. O'Connor, *Jackson Pollock* (New York: Museum of Modern Art, 1967), 40. It is interesting to imagine what Pollock means when he says he is "in" his painting rather than standing "over" it, as evidently he was.

9 For the debates over Serra's sculpture, see Harriet F. Senie, *The Tilted Arc Controversy* (Minneapolis: University of Minnesota Press, 2001).

10 Barrett Watten, "The Word," in *Conduit* (San Francisco: Gaz, 1988), 39. Carla Harryman, "Toy Boats," in *Animal Instincts: Prose Plays Essays* (Berkeley, Calif.: This Press, 1989), 107.

11 Since this essay was first written, there has been a further development of narrative theory addressed to the nonsequential forms of hypertext; see George P. Landow, ed., *Hyper/Text/Theory* (Baltimore: The Johns Hopkins University Press, 1994); and Landow, *Hypertext 2.0: The Convergence of Contemporary Critical Theory and Technology* (Baltimore: The Johns Hopkins University Press, 1997).

12 Lyn Hejinian, "Exit," *This* 12 (1982).

13 The way that such moments of narrative closure establish community is suggested in Mary Louise Pratt's early work, where she synthesizes the work of William Labov on the structural framework of oral narratives with the notion of the "cooperative principle" between interlocutors from Paul Grice's pragmatics; *Toward a Speech Act Theory of Literary Discourse* (Bloomington: Indiana University Press, 1977).

14 Theories of open reading practices, as in Umberto Eco, Wolfgang Iser, and others, have been frequently assimilated to the reading of language-centered writing; see Linda Reinfeld, *Language Poetry: Writing as Rescue* (Baton Rouge: Louisiana State University Press, 1992).

15 For Hejinian's account of nonnarration and closure, see Lyn Hejinian, "The Refusal of Closure," in *The Language of Inquiry* (Berkeley: University of California Press, 2000), 40–58.

16 Jackson Mac Low, "Wall Rev," *This* 12 (1982). See also Mac Low, *Representative Works: 1938–1985* (New York: Roof Books, 1986).

17 Roman Jakobson, "Concluding Statement: Linguistics and Poetics," in Thomas A. Sebeok, ed., *Style in Language* (Bloomington: Indiana University Press, 1960), 350–77.

18 "The Formalists differentiated between 'fable' (*fabula*) and 'plot' (*sjuzet*). . . . 'Fable' stood for the basic story stuff, the sum-total of events to be related in the work of fiction, in a word, 'the material for narrative construction'. Conversely, 'plot' meant the story as actually told or the way in which the events are linked together"; Victor Erlich, *Russian Formalism: History–Doctrine*, 3rd ed. (New Haven, Conn.: Yale University Press, 1981), 240.

19 Francis Fukuyama, *The End of History and the Last Man* (New York: The Free Press, 1992), xi.

20 Joel Fineman, "The History of the Anecdote: Fiction and Fiction," in Aram Veeser, ed., *The New Historicism* (New York: Routledge, 1989); hereafter *HA*.

21 Louis O. Mink, "Narrative Form as Cognitive Instrument," in Robert H. Canary and Henry Kozicki, ed., *The Writing of History: Literary Form and Historical Understanding* (Madison: University of Wisconsin Press, 1978), 129–49; 140; hereafter *NF*.

22 An example of a New Historicist anecdote that makes an argument out of the performative value of its disjunct date is to be found in Simon During, "The Strange Case of Monomania: Patriarchy in Literature, Murder in *Middlemarch*, Drowning in *Daniel Deronda*," *Representations* 23 (1988): 86–104.

23 Pratt, *Toward a Speech Act Theory*, 45–46.

24 Raymond Williams, *Television: Technology and Cultural Form* (New York: Schocken, 1975), esp. 96–108.

25 Hayden White, "The Value of Narrativity in the Representation of Reality," in *Content of the Form*, 1–25.

26 Umberto Eco, *The Open Work*, trans. Anna Cancogni (Cambridge, Mass.: Harvard University Press, 1989).

27 Barrett Watten, "Seyed Alavi," *Artweek* (14 March 1991).

28 Fredric Jameson, *The Political Unconscious: Narrative as a Socially Symbolic Act* (Ithaca, N.Y.: Cornell University Press, 1981), 13, 19–20; hereafter *PU*.

29 Ibid.; Jameson, *Postmodernism*, 25. George Hartley sums up the presuppositions in Jameson's periodization of this and other instances of postmodern culture in "Jameson's Perelman," in *Textual Politics and the Language Poets* (Bloomington: Indiana University Press, 1989), 42–52; Bob Perelman responds in "Exchangeable Frames," in "Non/Narrative," *Poetics Journal* 5 (1985): 168–76.

30 Hayden White, "Jameson's Defense of Narrative," in *Content of the Form*, 149.

31 Jameson, *Political Unconscious*, 82.

32 Cohen, *Historical Culture*, 69.

33 If we advance the critique of nonnarrativity beyond its relation to Universal History, however, we arrive at the recent interest among historians in the avant-garde for its aesthetics of interruption, as in Peter Osborne, *The Politics of Time: Modernity and Avant-Garde* (London: Verso, 1995).

34 Jerome McGann, "Contemporary Poetry, Alternate Routes," in Robert Von Hallberg, ed., *Politics and Poetic Value* (Chicago: University of Chicago Press, 1987), 253–76. For statements by a number of contemporary writers on the question of narrative and nonnarrative in their work, see "Non/Narrative," *Poetics Journal* 5 (1985).

35 Michael André Bernstein discusses the American epic tradition in *The Tale of the*

Tribe: Ezra Pound and the Modern Verse Epic (Princeton, N.J.: Princeton University Press, 1980); Joseph M. Conte, *Unending Design: The Forms of Postmodern Poetry* (Ithaca, N.Y.: Cornell University Press, 1991), treats a range of "serial" forms that reject the epic vocation but insist on an experience of temporality.

36 Charles Olson, *Selected Writings*, ed. Robert Creeley (New York: New Directions, 1966); Olson, *The Maximus Poems*, ed. George F. Butterick (Berkeley: University of California Press, 1983); Butterick, *A Guide to the "Maximus Poems" of Charles Olson* (Berkeley: University of California Press, 1978); "Olson in Language: The Politics of Style," in *Total Syntax* (Carbondale: Southern Illinois University Press, 1985), 115–39.

37 Cohen, *Historical Culture*, 105.

38 These appear against the background of another form, the primary process Freud located in the unconscious with his analytic method of "evenly hovering attention," which has been imitated in language writing from Gertrude Stein to the present and which I am not privileging here as an instance of nonnarrative form. Jameson, of course, would see this as the primary instance of nonnarrative form.

39 *Erik Bulatov*, exhibition catalogue (London: Institute of Contemporary Art, 1989). For other post-Soviet visual artists, see Matthew Cullerne Brown, *Contemporary Russian Art* (New York: Philosophical Library, 1989); David A. Ross, ed., *Between Spring and Summer: Soviet Conceptual Art in the Era of Late Communism* (Cambridge/Boston, Mass.: MIT Press/Institute of Contemporary Art, 1990); and Margarita Tupitsyn, *Margins of Soviet Art: Socialist Realism to the Present* (Milan: Giancarlo Politi Editions, 1989).

40 Eric Naiman, paper given at the Department of History, University of California, Berkeley, 1992.

41 Andrew Solomon, *The Irony Tower: Soviet Artists in a Time of Glasnost* (New York: Knopf, 1991).

42 On monumental history, see Friedrich Nietzsche, *On the Advantage and Disadvantage of History for Life*, trans. Peter Preuss (Indianapolis: Hackett, 1980).

43 On cultural memory and memorials, see James E. Young, "The Biography of a Memorial Icon: Nathan Rapoport's Warsaw Ghetto Monument," in Randolph Starn and Natalie Zemon Davis, ed., "Memory and Counter-Memory," *Representations* 26 (1989): 69–106. To illustrate Soviet memorial culture, I presented this essay along with slides of a number of memorials to the liberation of the Ukraine in the vicinity of Kiev.

44 On the "Real," see Slavoj Žižek, *The Sublime Object of Ideology* (London: Verso, 1989), chap. 5, and chapter 6 below.

45 Robert Smithson, "Entropy and the New Monuments," in *Writings*, presents a metaphor of "crystallization" in discussing contemporary minimalist sculpture that is related to this model of States 1 and 2.

46 After visiting Leningrad in August 1989, I wrote about the social space of Soviet memorial culture at length in Davidson et al., *Leningrad*, 72–73.

47 Erik Bulatov, interview, in *Arts* (1989): 85.

48 On the originary use of "kitsch" in American art history, see Clement Greenberg, "Avant-Garde and Kitsch," in Charles Harrison and Paul Wood, eds., *Art in Theory*,

1900–1990: An Anthology of Changing Ideas (London: Blackwell, 1992), 529–41: "If kitsch is the official tendency of culture in Germany, Italy, and Russia, it is not because their respective governments are controlled by philistines, but because kitsch is the culture of the masses in these countries, as it is everywhere else," 539.

49 Conversation with Moscow poet Alexei Parshchikov.

50 Boris Kagarlitsky, *The Thinking Reed: Intellectuals and the Soviet State from 1917 to the Present*, trans. Brian Pearce (London: Verso, 1988). Kagarlitsky's account itself is significant in terms of its negotiation of narrative; while not wanting to abandon Marxist-Leninist dialectic, particularly because of its explanatory force in the actual Soviet state, Kagarlitsky wishes to complicate matters by adding a Bakhtinian multiplicity to the historical process, by which he means to take account of culture as in a mutually constitutive but open-ended dialogue with the political. He writes: "We have to understand the culture of the past as a whole, as an independent System, and development not as a process of steady advance but as a more complex accumulation of historical experience through a dialogue of cultures" (280). Such a more complex accumulation would account for the wildly divergent belief systems rationalized by the modern Soviet state, but it would probably not find the formal moment of Bulatov's *I Am Going* to be more significant than one cultural strand among many, including Marxism.

51 Andrei Ikonnikov, *Russian Architecture of the Soviet Period*, trans. Lev Lyapin (Moscow: Progress Publishers, 1988), 387–88.

52 Claude Jolies and Viktor Misiano, "Interview with Erik Bulatov and Ilya Kabakov," in *Erik Bulatov*, 38–48.

53 A Moscow artist of the same period who deals with the kitsch side of memorial culture (an important component of Soviet pop culture) is Ilya Kabakov; see his *Ten Characters* (London: Institute of Contemporary Art, 1989), published in conjunction with the exhibition "Ilya Kabakov: The Untalented Artist and Other Characters," ICA (London), February 1989.

54 John Bushnell, *Moscow Graffiti: Language and Subculture* (Boston: Unwin Hyman, 1990).

55 *Little Vera*, dir. Vassili Pitchul, 1988.

56 Kagarlitsky, *Thinking Reed*, 216–37. Central to this reading is his discussion of neo-Slavophile "spiritual freedom" in relation to modernist "legal culture": "The Russian people [are] the bearer not of 'law' but of 'grace.' Law . . . means 'spiritual slavery,' whereas grace 'is the embodiment of spiritual freedom'" (224–25). Kagarlitsky would see this opposition united at many levels of Soviet culture, for instance in the figure of Stalin: "A similar contempt for law as something beneath consideration is characteristic also of Stalinism" (225), and this simultaneity of law and grace also could be read in Bulatov.

57 Barbara Kruger, *We Won't Play Nature to Your Culture* (London: Institute of Contemporary Art, 1983).

58 If there are different uses of nonnarrative between cultures, there are also different meanings for alternative or emergent cultures in them as well. Kagarlitsky suggests that the at-times fluid boundary between oppositional and official cultures in the post-Stalin Soviet Union is a way that "legal culture" organizes culture as a whole.

If Bulatov's intervention in the culture of memory and representation can be seen in the Brezhnev era as a kind of "social learning" developing from a dialogue of official and unofficial practices, its political horizons have greatly changed after Bulatov's emigration to the West. The alternative cultural practices of artists in the West, on the other hand, are quite various: Kruger is a mainstream gallery and museum artist, and the scale of her work in the early 1990s had become vast and socially comprehensive, while the collective practice of the New Sentence in the writers of the Language School developed through a network of alternative presses, distribution schemes, and art spaces.

59 Barrett Watten, *Opera — Works* (Bolinas, Calif.: Big Sky, 1975).

60 The quote is from Charles Olson, "The Kingfishers," in *Selected Writings*, 167–73.

61 From Stanley Karnow, *Vietnam: A History* (Harmondsworth, Eng.: Penguin, 1983).

62 The Vietnam memorial may be experienced as a narrative, but it is not structured as one — a central distinction of this essay. In fact, its capacity to engender more narrative approaches to it in historical time — unlike monuments to World War I casualties in many American town squares, which tend to restrict meanings and not develop them — is one of its great successes as a work.

63 Marita Sturken, "The Wall, the Screen, and the Image: The Vietnam Veterans Memorial," *Representations* 35 (1991): 118–42. Lyric and narrative possibilities for remembering Vietnam are discussed in David E. James, "Rock and Roll in Representations of the Invasion of Vietnam," *Representations* 29 (1990): 78–98. For Chris Burden's "other" Vietnam memorial, see Robert Storr, *Dislocations* (New York: Museum of Modern Art, 1991).

64 For the range of these practices, see two anthologies: Ron Silliman, ed., *In the American Tree*, 1st ed. (Orono, Maine: National Poetry Foundation, 1985); and Douglas Messerli, ed., *"Language" Poetries* (New York: New Directions, 1986).

65 I discuss the relation between surrealist methods and those of the postwar American avant-garde in "The Politics of Poetry: Surrealism and *L=A=N=G=U=A=G-E*," Watten, *Total Syntax*, 31–64.

66 Bruce Andrews et al., *Legend* (New York: L=A=N=G=U=A=G=E/Segue, 1980), 10–13; this section was written by Silliman and Ray DiPalma.

67 Gérard Genette, *Narrative Discourse: An Essay in Method*, trans. Jane E. Lewin (Ithaca, N.Y.: Cornell University Press, 1980), 195.

68 Ron Silliman, *The New Sentence* (New York: Roof Books, 1987).

69 Ron Silliman, *Tjanting* (Berkeley, Calif.: The Figures, 1980), 125.

70 If Ann Banfield's "sentence of narration" is a "now in the past," the New Sentence is a "now in the present"; see *Unspeakable Sentences: Narration and Representation* (Boston: Routledge, 1982).

71 Jameson, *Political Unconscious*, 98.

72 John Carman, "ABC Honcho Says He's Having Fun," *San Francisco Chronicle* (17 July 1992).

73 Bill Carter, "Behind Letterman Turmoil, an Icy Clash with His Boss," *New York Times* (4 March 2002); Jim Rutenberg, "Koppel's 'Nightline' Caught in Cross-Fire," *New York Times* (4 March 2002).

74 Ted Koppel, "Network News Is Still Serious Business," *New York Times* (5 March

2002); Jim Rutenberg, "Koppel Writes That 'Nightline' Still Fills a Need and Is Relevant," *New York Times* (5 March 2002).

75 Laura M. Holson, "Disney Woes Force Leader to Confront Hard Questions," *New York Times* (6 March 2002).

76 Jim Rutenberg and Bill Carter, "Future of 'Nightline' Remains Uncertain," *New York Times* (6 March 2002).

77 At this date (12 April 2002), Letterman has announced he will stay on CBS, and Koppel will keep his job at ABC for at least two more years. What closure this provisional ending may really bring, however, can only be gauged by the reader in present time.

CHAPTER 6: Negative Examples (pp. 238–90)

1 On antagonism, see Ernesto Laclau and Chantal Mouffe, *Hegemony and Socialist Strategy: Toward a Radical Democratic Politics* (London: Verso, 1985); Slavoj Žižek, "Beyond Discourse Analysis," in Laclau, *New Reflections on the Revolution of Our Time* (London: Verso, 1990); and Žižek, *The Sublime Object of Ideology* (London: Verso, 1989); here after *SO*.

2 On negativity, see Diana Coole, *Negativity and Politics: Dionysus and Dialectics from Kant to Poststructuralism* (New York: Routledge, 2000); and George Hartley, *The Abyss of Representation: Marxism and the Postmodern Sublime* (Durham, N.C.: Duke University Press, forthcoming 2003).

3 A key moment in the genealogy of negativity occurs with a benchmark definition of the "positive" in Hegel's biography, when, as his biographer puts it, "What had been the ideal of 'elevation of the infinite' in love increasingly became a 'positive' religion based on the authority of the teacher and on belief in a God who became increasingly and necessarily conceived not as an object of love but merely as a master who commands"; Terry Pinkard, *Hegel: A Biography* (Cambridge: Cambridge University Press, 2000), 143. See also Pinkard, *Hegel's Dialectic: The Explanation of Possibility* (Philadelphia: Temple University Press, 1988).

4 Theodor W. Adorno, *Negative Dialectics*, trans. E. B. Ashton (New York: Continuum, 1995); and for a shorter version of the problematic, Adorno, "Progress," in Gary Smith, ed., *Benjamin: Philosophy, Aesthetics, History* (Chicago: University of Chicago Press, 1989), 84–101. For the intellectual history of the concept, see Susan Buck-Morss, *The Origin of Negative Dialectics: Theodor W. Adorno, Walter Benjamin, and the Frankfurt Institute* (New York: The Free Press, 1977).

5 Žižek, *Sublime Object*, xii.

6 Ibid.; Slavoj Žižek, *For They Know Not What They Do: Enjoyment as a Political Factor* (London: Verso, 1991); Žižek, *Tarrying with the Negative: Kant, Hegel, and the Critique of Ideology* (Durham, N.C.: Duke University Press, 1993); Žižek, *The Plague of Fantasies* (London: Verso, 1997); Žižek, *The Ticklish Subject: The Absent Centre of Political Ontology* (London: Verso, 1999); hereafter *TS*. I am bracketing here Žižek's work in gender and film studies, though both are additional components to his critique of ideology: *Looking Awry: An Introduction to Jacques Lacan through Popular Culture* (Cambridge, Mass.: MIT Press, 1992); *Enjoy Your Symptom:*

Jacques Lacan in Hollywood and Out (New York: Routledge, 1992); and *The Metastases of Enjoyment: Six Essays on Woman and Causality* (London: Verso, 1994).

7 On the devolution of Yugoslavia, see Misha Glenny, *The Fall of Yugoslavia: The Third Balkan War* (London: Penguin Books, 1992).

8 Žižek discusses *Rear Window* in *Sublime Object*, 182–83; *Looking Awry*, 91–97; and *Tarrying with the Negative*, 64–65, 196–97.

9 *New York Times*, 19 February 2000.

10 Jacques Lacan, *The Four Fundamental Concepts of Psychoanalysis*, trans. Alan Sheridan, seminar of Jacques Lacan, Book XI, ed. Jacques-Alain Miller (New York: Norton, 1981), chaps. 5–8; see the discussion in Jonathan Scott Lee, *Jacques Lacan* (Boston: Twayne, 1990), as well as in-depth analysis in Richard Feldstein, Bruce Fink, and Maire Jaanus, eds., *Reading Seminar XI: Lacan's Four Fundamental Concepts of Psychoanalysis* (Albany, N.Y.: SUNY Press, 1995).

11 Lacan, *Four Fundamental Concepts*, chap. 7; Feldstein, Fink, and Jaanus, *Reading Seminar XI*.

12 This is my difference with Žižek: the film's happy ending is the right one.

13 Slavoj Žižek, "The 'Night of the World,'" in *Ticklish Subject*, 7–69.

14 Heidegger's encounter with Kant's faculty of the imagination is extensive, and is a major concern of the two series of lectures that coincided with and immediately followed the writing of *Being and Time*: Martin Heidegger, *Kant and the Problems of Metaphysics*, trans. Richard Taft, 5th ed., enlarged (Bloomington: Indiana University Press, 1982); Heidegger, *The Basic Problems of Phenomenology*, trans. Albert Hofstadter, rev. ed. (Bloomington: Indiana University Press, 1982).

15 On the "fantasm" in the Lacanian tradition, see Herman Rapaport, *Between the Sign and the Gaze* (Ithaca, N.Y.: Cornell University Press, 1994).

16 For Žižekian approaches to poetics, see Barrett Watten, "Laura Riding's Horizon Shifts," paper given at "Laura Riding and the Promise of Language," Cornell University, Ithaca, N.Y., October 1988; Watten, "FDR's Panic Attack: State Power and Cultural Poetics from Kenneth Fearing to Ezra Pound," paper given at "Cultural Poetics," University of Southampton, July 1966; Watten, "The Lost America of Love: A Genealogy," *Genre* 33, no. 3.4 (Fall/Winter 2000): 279–318.

17 Jean-Francois Lyotard, *The Postmodern Condition: A Report on Knowledge*, trans. Geoff Bennington and Brian Massumi (Minneapolis: University of Minnesota Press, 1984), 78; hereafter *PC*.

18 Wallace Stevens, *The Palm at the End of the Mind: Selected Poems and a Play*, ed. Holly Stevens (New York: Vintage Books, 1990), 54.

19 Žižek, *Sublime Object*, 169.

20 Ibid., 171–72.

21 Laura (Riding) Jackson, *The Poems of Laura Riding*, new ed. (1938; New York: Persea Press, 1980), 44.

22 Žižek, *Sublime Object*, 136–44.

23 The fourth in the series of "29 Poems," originally collected in *55 Poems* (Prairie City, Ill.: Decker, 1941), in Louis Zukofsky, *Complete Short Poetry* (Baltimore: The Johns Hopkins University Press, 1991), 23–24; see the reading of the whole poem in chap. 4.

24 Žižek, *Sublime Object*, 124.
25 Žižek, *Looking Awry*, 94.
26 Lucy Lippard, *Six Years: The Dematerialization of the Art Object . . .*, 2nd ed. (1973; Berkeley: University of California Press, 1997), 31.
27 Ann Goldstein and Anne Rorimer, eds., *Reconsidering the Object of Art, 1965–1975* (Cambridge, Mass.: MIT Press, 1995), 153.
28 Ron Padgett, *Great Balls of Fire* (Chicago: Holt, Rinehart, and Winston, 1969), 5; the poem is anthologized in Paul Hoover, ed., *Postmodern American Poetry: A Norton Anthology* (New York: Norton, 1994), 401.
29 Žižek, *Sublime Object*, 135.
30 Žižek, *Tarrying with the Negative*, 36.
31 Bill Berkson, *Blue Is the Hero (Poems 1960–1975)* (Kensington, Calif.: L Publications, 1976), 98.
32 Originally published in Barrett Watten, *Decay* (San Francisco: This Press, 1977); collected in Watten, *Frame: 1971–1990* (Los Angeles: Sun and Moon, 1997), 247.
33 Originally published in Barrett Watten, *1–10* (San Francisco: This Press, 1980); collected in Watten, *Frame*, 35–39.
34 For a recent example of such a dialectics of recuperation, see Andrew Epstein, "Verse vs. Verse: The Language Poets Are Taking Over the Academy, but Will Success Destroy Their Integrity?" *Lingua Franca* (September 2000): 45–54.
35 The questioning of this reference is meant as a point of entry into reading Heidegger, against the grain, as a social text. For social critiques of Heidegger, see Karl Löwith, *Martin Heidegger and European Nihilism*, ed. and trans. Richard Wolin and Gary Steiner (New York: Columbia University Press, 1995); Theodor W. Adorno, *The Jargon of Authenticity*, trans. Kurt Tarnowski and Fred Will (Evanston, Ill.: Northwestern University Press, 1973); Fred Dallmayr, *Life-World, Modernity, and Critique: Paths between Heidegger and the Frankfurt School* (Cambridge: Polity Press, 1991); Dallmayr, *The Other Heidegger* (Ithaca, N.Y.: Cornell University Press, 1993); and Pierre Bourdieu, *The Political Ontology of Martin Heidegger*, trans. Peter Collier (Stanford, Calif.: Stanford University Press, 1988).
36 Jaspers's work remains unpublished in English, though sections from it appear in Karl Jaspers, *Basic Philosophical Writings: Selections*, ed. Edith Ehrlich, Leonard H. Ehrlich, and George B. Pepper (Athens: Ohio University Press, 1986).
37 Martin Heidegger, "Comments on Karl Jaspers's 'Psychology of Worldviews,'" in *Pathmarks*, ed. William McNeill (Cambridge: Cambridge University Press, 1998), 1–38; 24, 21; hereafter "KJ"; my emphasis.
38 On projective anxiety, see Sianne Ngai, "Moody Subjects/Projectile Objects: Anxiety and Intellectual Displacement in Hitchcock, Heidegger, and Melville," *Qui Parle* 12, no. 2 (spring/summer 2001): 15–56.
39 Indeed, his biographer describes his lectures in the early 1920s as "avant-garde" provocations; Rüdiger Safranski, *Martin Heidegger: Between Good and Evil*, trans. Ewald Osers (Cambridge, Mass.: Harvard University Press, 1998), 99, 146.
40 Ibid., 118.
41 Jaspers, *Basic Philosophical Writings*, 96–97.
42 William D. Blattner, "Heidegger's Debt to Jaspers's Concept of the Limit Situation,"

in Alan M. Olson, ed., *Heidegger and Jaspers* (Philadelphia: Temple University Press, 1994), 153–66; 155.

43 André Breton, *Manifestoes of Surrealism*, trans. Richard Seaver and Helen R. Lane (Ann Arbor: University of Michigan Press, 1972), 37–38. For a culturally inflected reading of the surrealist image, see Margaret Cohen, *Profane Illumination: Walter Benjamin and the Paris of Surrealist Revolution* (Berkeley: University of California Press, 1993), as well as the discussion of the avant-garde and Benjamin in Peter Osborne, *The Politics of Time: Modernity and Avant-Garde* (London: Verso, 1995).

44 This Lacanian matheme translates as "the barred subject placed in relation to the object cause of desire," the formula for fantasy that is the basis of Slavoj Žižek's use of Lacan's *objet a* in ideology criticism; Žižek, *Sublime Object*, esp. chap. 5. "The Lacanian formula for this object is of course *objet petit a*, this point of Real in the very heart of the subject which cannot be symbolized, which is produced as a residue, a remnant, a leftover of every signifying process, a hard core embodying horrifying *jouissance*, enjoyment, and as such an object which simultaneously attracts and repels us — which *divides* our desires and thus provokes shame" (180).

45 See my account of "old Hegelian" notions of avant-garde opposition and recuperation in chapter 2 above.

46 Robert Grenier, *Sentences* (Cambridge, Mass.: Whale Cloth Press, 1978), unpaginated. The poems thus can be read in any order, and can be read spatially as well as sequentially. Grenier frequently displayed the work on walls or bulletin boards as he was composing it, making provisional sequences or arrays of cards. I have described the form of this work as a primitive hypertext; Barrett Watten, "Beyond the Demon of Analogy: www.poetics," paper read at "E-Poetry," SUNY Buffalo, April 2001.

47 Fredric Jameson, *Postmodernism; or, The Cultural Logic of Late Capitalism* (Durham, N.C.: Duke University Press, 1991); George Hartley, "Jameson's Perelman: Reification and the Material Signifier," in *Textual Politics and the Language Poets* (Bloomington: Indiana University Press, 1989), 42–52.

48 Heidegger, "Comments," 4.

49 The retrograde technology of Grenier's work brings to mind Heidegger's intervention on the question, "The Question Concerning Technology," in *Basic Writings*, ed. David Farrell Krell (New York: Harper and Row, 1977), 238–318.

50 Robert Grenier, *What I Believe / Transpiration/Transpiring / Minnesota* (Oakland, Calif.: O Books, n.d.).

51 Heidegger, "Comments," 26.

52 Robert Grenier, *12 from r h y m m s* (Scotia, N.Y.: Pavement Saw Press, 1996). Grenier's use of the beaches of San Mateo County in Northern California as a site equivalent to a "limit situation" began in the late 1960s and continued through the writing of his first large-scale serial work, *A Day at the Beach*, later published in revised and edited form; *A Day at the Beach* (New York: Roof Books, 1984).

53 Sites displaying Robert Grenier's visual poetry in 2002: "For Larry Eigner," <www.concentric.net/~lndb/grenier/lgloo.htm>; "Greeting," <www.thing.net/~grist/l&d/grenier/rggrt01.htm>; "Pond I," <www.thing.net/~grist/l&d/grenier/rgpnd01.

htm>; and "10 Pages from *r h y m m s*," <www.thing.net/~grist/l&d/grenier/lgrenaoo.htm>.

54 Ron Silliman, ed., *In the American Tree: Language, Realism, Poetry*, 2nd ed. (Orono, Maine: National Poetry Foundation, 2002).

55 David Wojnarowicz, *Close to the Knives: A Memoir of Disintegration* (New York: Vintage, 1991), esp. 138–62.

56 Barrett Watten, "The Turn to Language and the 1960s," 1993. *Critical Inquiry* 29, no. 1 (autumn 2002): 139–83.

57 Robert Grenier, "On Speech," *This* 1 (1971), n.p. Grenier speaks of forms of writing that may reflect particular ethnic markers, "e.g., Norwegian/American dialect," but "there is no value in the linguistic vehicle per se, i.e. spoken noises and written letters are signs of the reality of words in the head (of which some few are 'interesting'/get written down, of those few are printed/become widely known/are read aloud to crowds)." In this impossible politics, public speech and national identity are precluded to the barred subject.

58 On the politics of authenticity in Central Europe, see Martin Prochazka, "Prisoner's Predicament: Public Privacy in Havel's *Letters to Olga*," *Representations* 43 (1993): 126–54.

59 For a sense of Grenier's position, see Robert Grenier, "On the Empty/Sublime," <socrates.berkeley.edu/~moriarty/2/grenier.htm>; and Grenier, "Realizing Things: Talk at SUNY/Buffalo, October 22, 1998," <epc.buffalo.edu/authors/grenier/rthings.html>.

60 I cannot think of a Cultural Studies argument against "uniqueness" per se; rather, the argument is cast in terms of the normative assumptions of the unique subject as white, male, European, bourgeois, aesthetic, and so on. It would be an interesting inquiry to compare the Cultural Studies prejudice against the sovereign subject with its survival in recent feminist work on the avant-garde, particularly in the genre of the lyric. Of course, Adorno's *Jargon of Authenticity* stands as the definitive rejection, within Critical Theory, of Heidegger's claims to individuating uniqueness.

61 For an account of Foucault's work that is attentive to Heidegger's influence but that elides moments of negativity in Foucault in favor of questions of power and norms, as typical of his American reception, see Hubert L. Dreyfuss and Paul Rabinow, *Michel Foucault: Beyond Structuralism and Hermeneutics*, 2nd ed. (Chicago: University of Chicago Press, 1983).

62 For Foucault and *Tel Quel*, see Danielle Marx-Scouras, *The Cultural Politics of "Tel Quel": Literature and the Left in the Wake of Enlightenment* (University Park: Pennsylvania State University Press, 1996).

63 Indeed, it is scarcely mentioned even in Simon During's Cultural Studies–based account, *Foucault and Literature: Toward a Genealogy of Writing* (London: Routledge, 1996).

64 On the avant-garde in Detroit, see chapters 4 above and 8 below.

65 As in Raymond Williams, *The Politics of Modernism: Against the New Conformists* (London: Verso, 1989); see also the critical account of socially "negative" cults in Paul Mann, *Masocriticism* (Albany, N.Y.: SUNY Press, 1999).

66 For women experimental writers, see Mary Margaret Sloan, ed., *Moving Borders:*

Three Decades of Innovative Writing by Women (Jersey City, N.J.: Talisman House, 1998); and Maggie O'Sullivan, ed., *Out of Everywhere: Linguistically Innovative Poetry by Women in North America and the U.K.* (London: Reality Street, 1996).

67 Marjorie Welish, *The Annotated "Here" and Selected Poems* (Minneapolis: Coffee House Books, 2000), 50.

68 Carla Harryman, *Memory Play* (Oakland, Calif.: O Books, 1994), 18–19.

69 Michel Foucault, *The Order of Things: An Archaeology of the Human Sciences* (New York: Vintage Books, 1973), xv.

70 It is precisely the refusal of mediation, of understanding the materiality of the fact of language, that Adorno criticizes in Heidegger, and such a criticism could be applied, as well, to Grenier; Adorno, *Jargon of Authenticity.*

71 For an Adornean discussion of the avant-garde, see Steve Evans, "'A World Unsuspected': The Dynamics of Literary Change in Hegel, Bourdieu, and Adorno," *Qui Parle* 12, no. 2 (spring/summer 2001): 57–106.

CHAPTER 7: Post-Soviet Subjectivity in Arkadii Dragomoshchenko and Ilya Kabakov (pp. 291–320)

Epigraphs from Michael Davidson et al., *Leningrad: American Writers in the Soviet Union* (San Francisco: Mercury House, 1992), 23 and 34–35.

1 For a history of oppositional cultures in the postwar period, see Boris Kagarlitsky, *The Thinking Reed: Intellectuals and the Soviet State from 1917 to the Present*, trans. Brian Pearce (London: Verso, 1988); for a specific history of emerging forms of visual art, see David A. Ross, ed., *Between Spring and Summer: Soviet Conceptual Art in the Era of Late Communism* (Cambridge/Boston, Mass.: MIT Press/Institute of Contemporary Art, 1990); and Andrew Solomon, *The Irony Tower: Soviet Artists in a Time of Glasnost* (New York: Knopf, 1991); and for an account of new developments in poetry, see Mikhail Epshtein, *After the Future: The Paradoxes of Postmodernism and Contemporary Russian Culture* (Amherst: University of Massachusetts Press, 1995).

2 Dmitrii Prigov, "Conceptualism and the West," trans. Michael Molnar, in "Elsewhere," *Poetics Journal* 8 (1989): 12–16; 12.

3 For an anthology of post-Soviet poetry, see Kent Johnson and Stephen M. Ashby, eds., *Third Wave: The New Russian Poetry* (Ann Arbor: University of Michigan Press, 1992).

4 Michael Molnar, introduction to Arkadii Dragomoshchenko, *Description*, trans. Lyn Hejinian and Elena Balashova (Los Angeles: Sun and Moon, 1990), 7.

5 Arkadii Dragomoshchenko, "Nasturtium as Reality," in Dragomoshchenko, *Description*, 93–112; hereafter "NR."

6 *Lieu de mémoire* is a term for a memorial site coined by French historian Pierre Nora; see his *Rethinking France/Les Lieux de mémoire*, trans. Mary Trouille (Chicago: University of Chicago Press, 2001).

7 V. N. Voloshinov, *Marxism and the Philosophy of Language*, trans. Ladislav Matejka and I. R. Titunik (Cambridge, Mass.: MIT Press, 1973).

8 Arkadii Dragomoshchenko, "I(s)," trans. Lyn Hejinian and Elena Balashova, in "The Person," *Poetics Journal* 9 (1991): 127–37, 130 (my emphasis); see also Drago-

moshchenko, "Syn/Opsis/Taxis," trans. Hejinian and Balashova, in "Elsewhere," *Poetics Journal* 8 (1989): 5–8.

9 Andrei Tarkovsky, *Sculpting in Time: Reflections on the Cinema*, trans. Kitty Hunter-Blair (Austin: University of Texas Press, 1986), 65.

10 Watten, in Davidson et al., *Leningrad*, 43.

11 Mikhail Dziubenko, "'New Poetry' and Perspectives for Philosophy," trans. Lyn Hejinian and Elena Balashova, in "Elsewhere," *Poetics Journal* 8 (1989): 224–31, 27.

12 Wilhelm von Humboldt, *On Language: The Diversity of Human Language-Structure and Its Influence on the Mental Development of Mankind*, trans. Peter Heath (Cambridge: Cambridge University Press, 1988).

13 Kabakov's career is well documented in Amei Wallach, *Ilya Kabakov: The Man Who Never Threw Anything Away* (New York: Harry N. Abrams, Inc., 1996), which contains a detailed biography and documentation of his installation projects to date.

14 Ilya Kabakov, *Ten Characters* (London: Institute of Contemporary Art, 1989).

15 On the genres of late-Soviet art, see Ross, *Between Spring and Summer;* and Margarita Tupitsyn, *Margins of Soviet Art: Socialist Realism to the Present* (Milan: Giancarlo Politi Editions, 1989).

16 Robert Storr, *Dislocations* (New York: Museum of Modern Art, 1991).

17 Ilya Kabakov, *Das Leben der Fliegen/Life of Flies/Zhizn mukh* (Ostfildern bei Stuttgart, Ger.: Cantz, 1992).

18 Wallach, *Ilya Kabakov*, 184–87.

19 Ilya Kabakov, *Dvoretz proiektov/The Palace of Projects, 1995–1998* (London: Artangel, 1998).

20 Two traditions of "everyday life" thus may be brought to Kabakov's work: the Russian use of the concept of *byt* from the nineteenth century through the Russian Formalists, and the "critique of everyday life" of Henri Lefebvre and the Situationists. On everyday life in the Soviet context, see Svetlana Boym, *Common Places: The Mythology of Everyday Life in Russia* (Cambridge, Mass.: Harvard University Press, 1994).

21 Personal conversation, late 1980s.

22 Victor Tupitsyn, "From the Communal Kitchen: A Conversation with Ilya Kabakov," trans. Jane Bobko, *Arts* 66, no.2 (1991), 50–54.

23 Slavoj Žižek, *The Sublime Object of Ideology* (London: Verso, 1989), 180–81.

24 Tupitsyn, "Conversation with Kabakov," 50.

25 Slavoj Žižek, *Tarrying with the Negative: Kant, Hegel, and the Critique of Ideology* (Durham, N.C.: Duke University Press, 1993), 2–3.

26 Louis Zukofsky, *Prepositions: The Collected Critical Essays*, expanded ed. (Berkeley: University of California Press, 1981), 12.

27 Georges Perec, *Life, a User's Manual*, trans. David Bellos (Boston: David Godine, 1987).

28 Žižek, *Tarrying with the Negative*, esp. 33–39.

29 Ilya Kabakov, "On Emptiness," in Ross, *Between Spring and Summer*, 55.

30 Ernst Bloch, *The Utopian Function of Art and Literature*, trans. Jack Zipes and Frank Mecklenburg (Cambridge, Mass.: MIT Press, 1988).

31 See, for example, Bill Buford, *Among the Thugs* (London: Secker and Warburg, 1991), and compare to the emergence of nihilist behavior among soccer fans in John Bushnell, *Moscow Graffiti: Language and Subculture* (Boston: Unwin Hyman, 1990).
32 Ilya Kabakov, artist's statement and text for installation, *Dislocations*, Museum of Modern Art, 1991.
33 Tupitsyn, "Conversation with Ilya Kabakov," 54.
34 Storr, *Dislocations*, 16–17.
35 Ibid.
36 Robert Storr, introduction to Wallach, *Ilya Kabakov*, 7.
37 Kabakov himself expressed doubts about the effectiveness of his installation, feeling outdone by the technical expertise of Louise Bourgeois's enormous erotic sculpture, and Bruce Nauman's aggressive use of technology; Wallach, *Ilya Kabakov*, 82–83. But he neglects the dialogic impact of his installation on the space of the museum itself — an effect that was also noticeable in his installation of *Mental Institution* at the 1998 Whitney Biennial.
38 Leslie Scalapino, *The Return of Painting, The Pearl, and Orion: A Trilogy* (San Francisco: North Point Press, 1991); see also references to "Moscow" that appear in Leslie Scalapino, *New Time* (Middletown, Conn.: Wesleyan University Press, 1999).
39 One of the formal framing devices of Scalapino's text is a series of essays on the comic book as a response to Walter Benjamin, *Charles Baudelaire: A Lyric Poet in the Age of High Capitalism*, trans. Harry Zohn (London: Verso, 1976).
40 On the transcendental object in relation to the *objet a*, see Žižek, *Tarrying with the Negative*, 17–18.
41 Georg Lukács, *Record of a Life*, trans. Rodney Livingstone (London: Verso, 1971).
42 Fredric Jameson, *Postmodernism; or, The Cultural Logic of Late Capitalism* (Durham, N.C.: Duke University Press, 1991), ix–xxii.

CHAPTER 8: Zone (pp. 321–48)

1 Charles Olson to Robert Creeley, 20 October 1951, in Creeley and Olson, *The Complete Correspondence*, ed. George F. Butterick, vol. 8 (Santa Rosa, Calif.: Black Sparrow, 1987), 79; cited in Creeley and Olson, *Correspondence*, xxv.
2 Charles Olson, *Call Me Ishmael* [1947], in *Collected Prose*, ed. Donald Allen and Benjamin Friedlander (Berkeley: University of California Press, 1977), 1–106; 17.
3 Teresa Brennan, *History after Lacan* (London: Routledge, 1993).
4 Brennan herself realizes the analytic disparity between her Lacanian analysis of the ego's limits and her quasi-Reichian account of energy and flux; in *Exhausting Modernity: Grounds for a New Economy* (New York: Routledge, 2000), she returns to the site of her Lacanian analysis and radically revises it, employing the work of Melanie Klein to account for the aggressivity Lacan cites as constitutive of the imaginary.
5 LeRoi Jones, *The System of Dante's Hell* (New York: Grove Press, 1965), 76; reprinted in Amiri Baraka (LeRoi Jones), *The Fiction of LeRoi Jones/Amiri Baraka* (Chicago: Lawrence Hill Books, 2000).
6 An excellent account of the psychodynamics of the 1967 Detroit riots, particularly in terms of the investment in racial boundaries by deficient ego structures, may be

found in John Hersey, *The Algiers Motel Incident* (1968; Baltimore: The Johns Hopkins University Press, 1998).

7 The phrase "damned demographics" is former mayor Coleman Young's.

8 Georgia Daskalakis, Charles Waldheim, and Jason Young, eds., *Stalking Detroit* (Barcelona: Actar, 2001), 14–15, citing U.S. Census figures.

9 On the question of urban/suburban divide versus a politics of metropolitan regions, see David Rusk, *Cities without Boundaries*, 2nd ed. (Washington, D.C.: Woodrow Wilson Center Press, 1995); and Joel Garreau, *Edge City: Life on the New Frontier* (New York: Doubleday, 1991), who cites the following as emerging or "edge" cities: Auburn Hills; Troy; Farmington Hills; the 696/Telegraph, Prudential Town Center, and Northland Mall areas of Southfield; and Fairfield Village (99–138). In my discussion, Detroit projects an internal boundary within the larger metropolitan region. The boundaries between Detroit and the metropolitan region and that region and other global regions (as well as "nature") are differently constituted.

10 For a discussion of Heideggerian aesthetics, see Herman Rapaport, *Is There Truth in Art?* (Ithaca, N.Y.: Cornell University Press, 1997). See also Sianne Ngai, "Moody Subjects/Projectile Objects: Anxiety and Intellectual Displacement in Hitchcock, Heidegger, and Melville," *Qui Parle* 12, no. 2 (spring/summer 2001): 15–56.

11 T. J. Clark, *Farewell to an Idea: Episodes from a History of Modernism* (New Haven, Conn.: Yale University Press, 1999); Walter Benjamin, *Charles Baudelaire: A Lyric Poet in the Era of High Capitalism*, trans. Harry Zohn (London: Verso, 1976); Guy Debord, "Theory of the Dérive," in Ken Knabb, ed. and trans., *Situationist International: An Anthology* (Berkeley, Calif.: Bureau of Public Secrets, 1981).

12 "Reverse Maps," slide performance, 80 Langton Street, 21 December 1979; see "Barrett Watten: Writer in Residence," in *80 Langton Street: June 1979–April 1980*, gallery catalogue (San Francisco: 80 Langton Street, 1980), 58–61; Bob Perelman, "Barrett Watten: December 19–22, 1979," in *Artists and Writers in Residence*, residency catalogue (San Francisco: 80 Langton Street, 1980), 26–52.

13 "Urban Site: Art in the City: August 16–September 30, 1983," in *The Last 80 Langton Street Catalogue* (San Francisco: 80 Langton Street, 1984), 61–75. The literature portion of the program was curated by Ron Silliman.

14 Ron Silliman, *Tjanting* (Berkeley, Calif.: The Figures, 1980). In 1978, Silliman read his long poem *Ketjak* (San Francisco: This Press, 1978) on the corner of Powell and Market Streets, San Francisco — a much more chaotic urban space, a kind of Hyde Park corner occupied by missionaries, Hare Krishna followers, and political activists. His choice of the Muni Metro station for the later reading thus involved an element of institutional critique.

15 Works by Manuel Castells available at the time were *The Urban Question: A Marxist Approach* (Cambridge, Mass.: MIT Press, 1977); *City, Class, and Power* (New York: St. Martin's Press, 1978); *The Economic Crisis and American Society* (Princeton, N.J.: Princeton University Press, 1980). See also Castells, *The Informational City: Information Technology, Urban Restructuring, and the Urban-Regional Process* (Oxford: Basil Blackwell, 1989).

16 Reyner Banham, *Los Angeles: The Architecture of Four Ecologies* (New York: Harper and Row, 1971).

17 Mike Davis, *City of Quartz: Excavating the Future in Los Angeles* (Cambridge, Mass.: MIT Press, 1990); Charles Jencks, *Heterotopia: Los Angeles, the Riots, and the Strange Beauty of Hetero-Architecture* (London: Academy Editions, 1993); Edward Soja, *Postmodern Geographies: The Reassertion of Space in Critical Social Theory* (London: Verso, 1989).

18 Suzanne E. Smith, *Dancing in the Street: Motown and the Cultural Politics of Detroit* (Cambridge, Mass.: Harvard University Press, 1999).

19 Terry Smith, *Making the Modern: Industry, Art, and Design in America* (Chicago: University of Chicago Press, 1993).

20 Jerry Herron, "Postmodernism Ground Zero; or, Going to the Movies at the Grand Circus Park," in *AfterCulture: Detroit and the Humiliation of History* (Detroit: Wayne State University Press, 1993), 117–53.

21 On the cultural politics of the DIA, see Jeffrey Abt, *A Museum on the Verge: A Socioeconomic History of the Detroit Institute of Arts, 1882–2000* (Detroit: Wayne State University Press, 2002).

22 Cheryl Temple Herr, *Critical Regionalism and Cultural Studies: From Ireland to the American Midwest* (Gainesville: University Press of Florida, 1996).

23 William Faulkner, *Absalom, Absalom!* (New York: Vintage, 1990).

24 Robert Smithson, *The Writings of Robert Smithson*, ed. Nancy Holt (New York: New York University Press, 1979); Robert Hobbs, *Robert Smithson: Sculpture* (Ithaca, N.Y.: Cornell University Press, 1981); and Smithson, *Collected Writings* (Berkeley: University of California Press, 1996).

25 The complete installation of *Le Détroit* (involving both photographic images and film installation) was shown at the Art Gallery of Windsor, 1999; Art Institute of Chicago, 2000; Kunsthalle Basel, 2001; and the Serpentine Gallery, London 2002; selections from the photographs were seen at the David Zwirner Gallery, New York, in 1998. Other recent catalogues include *Stan Douglas* (London: Phaedon, 1998); *Stan Douglas* (Vancouver, B.C.: Vancouver Art Gallery, 1999); and *Stan Douglas: Journey into Fear* (Basel: Walter Konig, 2002).

26 Walter Benjamin, "The Work of Art in the Age of Mechanical Reproduction," in *Illuminations* (London: Jonathan Cape, 1970), 219–54.

27 Two notable contributions to the critical literature on Detroit are Camilo José Vergara, *American Ruins* (New York: The Monacelli Press, 1999), which sees Detroit in relation to numerous other examples of urban decline; and, specifically focusing on Detroit, Daskalakis, Waldheim, and Young, *Stalking Detroit*.

28 The so-called Treaty of Detroit of 1948 established a relationship between auto producers and auto workers that would raise wages so workers could afford the product they made (and the lifestyle that went with it); see Nelson Lichtenstein, *Walter Reuther: The Most Dangerous Man in Detroit* (Urbana: University of Illinois Press, 1995).

29 Lowell Boileau's outstanding web site "The Fabulous Ruins of Detroit" still at times succumbs to preservationist discourse that risks advertising Detroit as an urban tourist site, complete with tours, as suggested in the affirmation coded into its url: <yesdetroit.com>.

30 European art tourists making a beeline to Tyree Guyton's Heidelberg Project, a site-

specific installation on the east side of Detroit that converts both occupied and disused housing into enormous assemblages, exemplify this attitude, as does Vergara's "serious proposal" to create a monumental site of urban ruin in downtown Detroit, which Herron attacks; see "Three Meditations on the Ruins of Detroit," in Daskalakis, Waldheim, and Young, *Stalking Detroit*, 32–41. Vergara's project, however, is politically responsible and can in no sense be reduced to a form of voyeurism of urban negativity.

31 Ernest Mandel, *Late Capitalism*, trans. Joris De Bres (London: Verso, 1978).

BIBLIOGRAPHY

Abt, Jeffrey. *A Museum on the Verge: A Socioeconomic History of the Detroit Institute of Arts, 1882–2000*. Detroit: Wayne State University Press, 2002.

Adorno, Theodor W. *The Jargon of Authenticity*. Trans. Kurt Tarnowski and Fred Will. Evanston, Ill.: Northwestern University Press, 1973.

———. *Negative Dialectics*. Trans. E. B. Ashton. New York: Continuum, 1995.

———. "Progress." In Gary Smith, ed., *Benjamin: Philosophy, Aesthetics, History*, 84–101. Chicago: University of Chicago Press, 1989.

Ahearn, Barry. *Zukofsky's "A": An Introduction*. Berkeley: University of California Press, 1983.

Alexander, Michael. *Old English Riddles from the Exeter Book*. London: Anvil, 1980.

Altieri, Charles. *Painterly Abstraction in Modernist American Poetry: The Contemporaneity of Modernism*. University Park: Pennsylvania State University Press, 1995.

———. *Postmodernisms Now: Essays on Contemporaneity in the Arts*. University Park: Pennsylvania State University Press, 1998.

———. "What Is Living and What Is Dead in American Postmodernism: Establishing the Contemporaneity of Some American Poetry." *Critical Inquiry* 22, no. 4 (1996): 764–89.

Andrews, Bruce. *I Don't Have Any Paper So Shut Up (or, Social Romanticism)*. Los Angeles: Sun and Moon, 1992.

———. *Lip Service*. Toronto: Coach House Press, 2001.

———. *Paradise and Method: Poetics and Praxis*. Evanston, Ill.: Northwestern University Press, 1996.

———. "Writing Social Work & Political Practice," *L=A=N=G=U=A=G=E* 9/10 (October 1979).

Andrews, Bruce, and Charles Bernstein. Interview with Andrew Ross. *Minnesota Review* 32 (1989): 27–50.

———, eds. *The L=A=N=G=U=A=G=E Book*. Carbondale: Southern Illinois University Press, 1984.

Andrews, Bruce, Charles Bernstein, Ray DiPalma, Steve McCaffery, and Ron Silliman. *Legend*. New York: L=A=N=G=U=A=G=E/Segue, 1980.

Armstrong, Nancy. "Modernism's Iconophobia and What It Did to Gender." *Modernism/Modernity* 5, no. 2 (1998): 47–76.

Attali, Jacques. *Noise: The Political Economy of Music*. Trans. Brian Massumi. Minneapolis: University of Minnesota Press, 1985.

Bakhtin, M. M., and P. M. Medvedev. *The Formal Method in Literary Scholarship: A Critical Introduction to Sociological Poetics*. Trans. Albert J. Wehrle. Cambridge, Mass.: Harvard University Press, 1985.

Banfield, Ann. *Unspeakable Sentences: Narration and Representation*. Boston: Routledge, 1982.

Banham, Reyner. *Los Angeles: The Architecture of Four Ecologies*. New York: Harper and Row, 1971.

Bann, Stephen, ed. *The Tradition of Constructivism*. Reprint ed. New York: Da Capo, 1974.

Banta, Martha. *Taylored Lives: Narrative Productions in the Age of Taylor, Veblen, and Ford*. Chicago: University of Chicago Press, 1993.

Baraka, Amiri (LeRoi Jones). *The Fiction of LeRoi Jones/Amiri Baraka*. Chicago: Lawrence Hill Books, 2000.

———. *The System of Dante's Hell*. New York: Grove Press, 1965.

Barfield, Owen. *Poetic Diction: A Study in Meaning*. Middletown, Conn.: Wesleyan University Press, 1973.

Barron, Stephanie, and Maurice Tuchman, eds. *The Avant-Garde in Russia, 1910–1930: New Perspectives*. Exhibition catalogue. Cambridge, Mass.: MIT Press, 1980.

Batchelor, Ray. *Henry Ford: Mass Production, Modernism, and Design*. Manchester: Manchester University Press, 1994.

Belgrad, Daniel. *The Culture of Spontaneity: Improvisation and the Arts in Postwar America*. Chicago: University of Chicago Press, 1998.

Benjamin, Walter. *Charles Baudelaire: A Lyric Poet in the Age of High Capitalism*. Trans. Harry Zohn. London: Verso, 1976.

———. "The Work of Art in the Age of Mechanical Reproduction." In *Illuminations*, 219–54. London: Jonathan Cape, 1970.

Benson, Steve. *As Is*. Berkeley, Calif.: The Figures, 1978.

———. *Blindspots*. Cambridge, Mass.: Whalecloth Press, 1981.

———. *Blue Book*. Berkeley, Calif./New York: The Figures/Roof Books, 1988.

Benson, Steve, Carla Harryman, Lyn Hejinian, Bob Perelman, Ron Silliman, and Barrett Watten. "Aesthetic Tendency and the Politics of Poetry." *Social Text* 19–20 (1998): 261–75.

Berkson, Bill. *Blue Is the Hero (Poems 1960–1975)*. Kensington, Calif.: L Publications, 1976.

Berman, Marshall. *All That Is Solid Melts into Air: The Experience of Modernity*. Middlesex, Eng.: Penguin, 1988.

Bernstein, Charles. *Content's Dream: Essays, 1975–1984*. Los Angeles: Sun and Moon, 1986.

———. *My Way: Speeches and Poems*. Chicago: University of Chicago Press, 1999.

———. *A Poetics*. Cambridge, Mass.: Harvard University Press, 1992.

———. "Poetics of the Americas." *Modernism/Modernity* 3, no. 3 (1996): 1–21.

———. *Rough Trades*. Los Angeles: Sun and Moon, 1991.

———. "Stein's Identity." *Modern Fiction Studies* 42, no. 3 (1996): 485–88.

Bernstein, Michael André. *The Tale of the Tribe: Ezra Pound and the Modern Verse Epic*. Princeton, N.J.: Princeton University Press, 1980.

Bersani, Leo. *The Culture of Redemption*. Cambridge, Mass.: Harvard University Press, 1990.

Bloch, Ernst. *The Utopian Function of Art and Literature*. Trans. Jack Zipes and Frank Mecklenburg. Cambridge, Mass.: MIT Press, 1988.

Bois, Yve-Alain. "El Lissitzky: Radical Reversibility." *Art in America* (April 1988): 161–80.

———. "From $-\infty$ to 0 to $+\infty$: Axonometry, or Lissitzky's Mathematical Paradigm." In *El Lissitzky, 1890–1941*, exhibition catalogue. Eindhoven, Neth.: Municipal Van Abbemuseum, 1990.

Bourdieu, Pierre. *The Political Ontology of Martin Heidegger*. Trans. Peter Collier. Stanford, Calif.: Stanford University Press, 1988.

———. *The Rules of Art: Genesis and Structure of the Literary Field*. Trans. Susan Emanuel. Stanford, Calif.: Stanford University Press, 1996.

Bowlt, John E., ed. *Russian Art of the Avant-Garde: Theory and Criticism*. Rev. and enlarged ed. London: Thames and Hudson, 1988.

Boym, Svetlana. *Common Places: The Mythology of Everyday Life in Russia*. Cambridge, Mass.: Harvard University Press, 1994.

Brenkman, John. *Culture and Domination*. Ithaca, N.Y.: Cornell University Press, 1987.

———. *Straight Male Modern: A Cultural Critique of Psychoanalysis*. London: Routledge, 1993.

Brennan, Teresa. *Exhausting Modernity: Grounds for a New Economy*. New York: Routledge, 2000.

———. *History after Lacan*. London: Routledge, 1993.

Breton, André. *Manifestoes of Surrealism*. Trans. Richard Seaver and Helen R. Lane. Ann Arbor: University of Michigan Press, 1972.

Breton, André, and Philippe Soupault. *The Magnetic Fields*. Trans. David Gascoyne. London: Atlas Press, 1985.

Brown, Matthew Cullerne. *Contemporary Russian Art*. New York: Philosophical Library, 1989.

Buchloh, Benjamin H. D. "From Faktura to Factography." In Annette Michelson et al., eds., *"October": The First Decade, 1976–1986*. Cambridge, Mass.: MIT Press, 1987.

Buck-Morss, Susan. *The Dialectics of Seeing: Walter Benjamin and the Arcades Project*. Cambridge, Mass.: MIT Press, 1991.

———. *The Origin of Negative Dialectics: Theodor W. Adorno, Walter Benjamin, and the Frankfurt Institute*. New York: The Free Press, 1977.

Buford, Bill. *Among the Thugs*. London: Secker and Warburg, 1991.

Bulatov, Erik. Interview. In *Arts* (1989): 85.

Bürger, Peter. *The Theory of the Avant-Garde*. Trans. Jochen Schülte-Sasse. Minneapolis: University of Minnesota Press, 1984.

Burwick, Frederick, ed. *Coleridge's "Biographia Literaria": A Study in Meaning*. 3rd ed. Columbus: Ohio State University Press, 1989.

Bushnell, John. *Moscow Graffiti: Language and Subculture*. Boston: Unwin Hyman, 1990.

Butterick, George. *A Guide to the "Maximus Poems" of Charles Olson*. Berkeley: University of California Press, 1978.

Calinescu, Matei. *Five Faces of Modernity: Modernism, Avant-Garde, Decadence, Kitsch, Postmodernism*. Durham, N.C.: Duke University Press, 1987.

Castells, Manuel. *City, Class, and Power*. New York: St. Martin's Press, 1978.
———. *The Economic Crisis and American Society*. Princeton, N.J.: Princeton University Press, 1980.
———. *The Informational City: Information Technology, Urban Restructuring, and the Urban-Regional Process*. Oxford: Basil Blackwell, 1989.
———. *The Urban Question: A Marxist Approach*. Cambridge, Mass.: MIT Press, 1977.
Chatman, Seymour. *Coming to Terms: The Rhetoric of Narrative in Fiction and Film*. Ithaca, N.Y.: Cornell University Press, 1990.
Christensen, Jerome. "The Romantic Movement at the End of History." *Critical Inquiry* 20, no. 3 (1994): 452–76.
Clark, T. J. *Farewell to an Idea: Episodes from a History of Modernism*. New Haven, Conn.: Yale University Press, 1999.
Clay, Steven, and Rodney Philips. *A Secret Location on the Lower East Side: Adventures in Writing, 1960–1980*. New York: New York Public Library/Granary Books, 1998.
Cohen, Margaret. *Profane Illumination: Walter Benjamin and the Paris of Surrealist Revolution*. Berkeley: University of California Press, 1993.
Cohen, Sande. *Historical Culture: On the Recoding of an Academic Discipline*. Berkeley: University of California Press, 1986.
Coleridge, Samuel Taylor. *Biographia Literaria; or, Biographical Sketches of My Literary Life and Opinions*. Ed. James Engell and W. Jackson Bate. Princeton, N.J.: Princeton University Press, 1983.
Conte, Joseph M. *Unending Design: The Forms of Postmodern Poetry*. Ithaca, N.Y.: Cornell University Press, 1991.
Cooke, Catherine. "Chernikhov: The Construction of Architectural and Machine Forms." *Architectural Design* 47 (1983): 73–80.
———. *Russian Avant-Garde: Theories of Art, Architecture, and the City*. London: Academy Editions, 1995.
———, ed. "Russian Constructivism and Iakov Chernikhov," *Architectural Design* 59, no. 7/8 (1989).
Coole, Diana. *Negativity and Politics: Dionysus and Dialectics from Kant to Poststructuralism*. New York: Routledge, 2000.
Coolidge, Clark. *The Maintains*. San Francisco: This Press, 1974.
———. *Own Face*. Lenox, Mass.: United Artists, 1978.
———. *Polaroid*. Bolinas, Calif.: Big Sky Books, 1975.
———. *Solution Passage: Poems, 1978–1981*. Los Angeles: Sun and Moon, 1986.
———. *Sound as Thought: Poems, 1982–1984*. Los Angeles: Sun and Moon, 1990.
Creeley, Robert, and Charles Olson. *The Complete Correspondence*. Ed. George F. Butterick. Vol. 8. Santa Rosa, Calif.: Black Sparrow, 1987.
Dallmayr, Fred. *Life-World, Modernity, and Critique: Paths between Heidegger and the Frankfurt School*. Cambridge: Polity Press, 1991.
———. *The Other Heidegger*. Ithaca, N.Y.: Cornell University Press, 1993.
Damon, Maria. *The Dark End of the Street: Margins in American Vanguard Poetry*. Minneapolis: University of Minnesota Press, 1993.

Daskalakis, Georgia, Charles Waldheim, and Jason Young, eds. *Stalking Detroit.* Barcelona: Actar, 2001.

Davidson, Michael. *Ghostlier Demarcations: Modern Poetry and the Material Word.* Berkeley: University of California Press, 1997.

———. *The San Francisco Renaissance: Poetics and Community at Mid-Century.* Cambridge: Cambridge University Press, 1989.

Davidson, Michael, Lyn Hejinian, Ron Silliman, and Barrett Watten. *Leningrad: American Poets in the Soviet Union.* San Francisco: Mercury House, 1992.

Davis, Mike. *City of Quartz: Excavating the Future in Los Angeles.* Cambridge, Mass.: MIT Press, 1990.

Dean, Carolyn J. *The Self and Its Pleasures: Bataille, Lacan, and the History of the Decentered Subject.* Ithaca, N.Y.: Cornell University Press, 1992.

Debord, Guy. "Theory of the Dérive." In Ken Knabb, ed. and trans., *Situationist International: An Anthology.* Berkeley, Calif.: Bureau of Public Secrets, 1981.

Deguy, Michel, and Jacques Roubaud. *Vingt poètes américains.* Paris: Gallimard, 1981.

DeKoven, Marianne. *Rich and Strange: Gender, History, Modernism.* Princeton, N.J.: Princeton University Press, 1991.

Deleuze, Gilles, and Felix Guattari. *Anti-Oedipus: Capitalism and Schizophrenia.* Trans. Robert Hurley, Robert Seem, and Helen R. Lane. Minneapolis: University of Minnesota Press, 1983.

———. "Balance-Sheet Program for Desiring Machines." *Semiotext(e)* 2, no. 3 (1977): 117–35.

Denning, Michael. *The Cultural Front: The Laboring of American Culture in the Twentieth Century.* London: Verso, 1997.

Dragomoshchenko, Arkadii. *Description.* Trans. Lyn Hejinian and Elena Balashova. Los Angeles: Sun and Moon, 1990.

———. "I(s)." Trans. Lyn Hejinian and Elena Balashova. In "The Person," *Poetics Journal* 9 (1991): 127–37.

———. "Syn/Opsis/Taxis." Trans. Lyn Hejinian and Elena Balashova. In "Elsewhere," *Poetics Journal* 8 (1989): 5–8.

Dreyfuss, Hubert L., and Paul Rabinow. *Michel Foucault: Beyond Structuralism and Hermeneutics.* 2nd ed. Chicago: University of Chicago Press, 1983.

Duchamp, Marcel. *The Essential Writings of Marcel Duchamp.* Ed. Michel Sanouillet and Elmer Peterson. London: Thames and Hudson, 1973.

DuPlessis, Rachel Blau. *Genders, Races, and Religious Cultures in Modern American Poetry, 1908–1934.* Cambridge: Cambridge University Press, 2001.

———. *The Pink Guitar: Writing as Feminist Practice.* New York: Routledge, 1990.

DuPlessis, Rachel Blau, and Peter Quartermain, eds. *The Objectivist Nexus: Essays in Cultural Poetics.* Tuscaloosa: University of Alabama Press, 1999.

During, Simon. *Foucault and Literature: Toward a Genealogy of Writing.* London: Routledge, 1996.

———. "The Strange Case of Monomania: Patriarchy in Literature, Murder in *Middlemarch*, Drowning in *Daniel Deronda*." *Representations* 23 (1988): 86–104.

Dydo, Ulla B. "*Stanzas in Meditation*: The Other Autobiography." In Richard Kostelanetz, ed., *Gertrude Stein Advanced*, 112–27. Jefferson, N.C.: McFarland, 1990.

Dziubenko, Mikhail. "'New Poetry' and Perspectives for Philosophy." Trans. Lyn Hejinian and Elena Balashova. In "Elsewhere," *Poetics Journal* 8 (1989): 224–31.

Easthope, Anthony. *Poetry as Discourse*. London: Methuen, 1983.

Eco, Umberto. *The Open Work*. Trans. Anna Cancogni. Cambridge, Mass.: Harvard University Press, 1989.

El Lissitzky, 1890–1941. Exhibition catalogue. Eindhoven, Neth.: Municipal Van Abbemuseum, 1990.

Epshtein, Mikhail. *After the Future: The Paradoxes of Postmodernism and Contemporary Russian Culture*. Amherst: University of Massachusetts Press, 1995.

Epstein, Andrew. "Verse vs. Verse: The Language Poets Are Taking Over the Academy, but Will Success Destroy Their Integrity?" *Lingua Franca* (September 2000): 45–54.

Eribon, Didier. *Michel Foucault*. Trans. Betsy Wing. Cambridge, Mass.: Harvard University Press, 1991.

Erik Bulatov. Exhibition catalogue. London: Institute of Contemporary Art, 1989.

Erlich, Viktor. *Russian Formalism: History–Doctrine*. 3rd ed. New Haven, Conn.: Yale University Press, 1981.

Evans, Steve. "'A World Unsuspected': The Dynamics of Literary Change in Hegel, Bourdieu, and Adorno." *Qui Parle* 12, no. 2 (spring/summer 2001): 57–106.

Eysteinsson, Astradur. *The Concept of Modernism*. Ithaca, N.Y.: Cornell University Press, 1990.

Feldstein, Richard, Bruce Fink, and Maire Jaanus, eds. *Reading Seminar XI: Lacan's Four Fundamental Concepts of Psychoanalysis*. Albany, N.Y.: SUNY Press, 1995.

Felski, Rita. *The Gender of Modernity*. Cambridge, Mass.: Harvard University Press, 1995.

Fillmore, Charles J. *Language Form, Meaning, and Practice*. Stanford, Calif.: CSLI Publications, 1997.

Fineman, Joel. "The History of the Anecdote: Fiction and Fiction." In Aram Veeser, ed., *The New Historicism*. New York: Routledge, 1989.

Finkelstein, Norman. *The Utopian Moment in Contemporary American Poetry*. 2nd ed. Lewisburg, Pa.: Bucknell University Press, 1993.

Flink, James J. *The Automobile Age*. Cambridge, Mass.: MIT Press, 1990.

Foster, Hal. "Some Uses and Abuses of Russian Constructivism." In *Art into Life: Russian Constructivism, 1914–1932*, 241–53. Exhibition catalogue. New York: Rizzoli, 1990.

Foucault, Michel. *Aesthetics, Method, and Epistemology*. Ed. James D. Faubion. Vol. 2 of *Essential Works of Michel Foucault, 1954–84*, ed. Paul Rabinow. New York: The New Press, 1998.

———. *The Archaeology of Knowledge and the Discourse on Language*. Trans. A. M. Sheridan Smith. New York: Pantheon, 1972.

———. *The Order of Things: An Archaeology of the Human Sciences*. New York: Vintage Books, 1973.

Freud, Sigmund. *Beyond the Pleasure Principle*. Ed. and trans. James Strachey. New York: Norton, 1989.

———. *Collected Papers*. Ed. and trans. Joan Rivière. 5 vols. New York: Basic Books, 1959.

Fukuyama, Francis. *The End of History and the Last Man*. New York: The Free Press, 1992.

Galan, F. W. *Historic Structures: The Prague School Project, 1928–1946*. Austin: University of Texas Press, 1984.

Garreau, Joel. *Edge City: Life on the New Frontier*. New York: Doubleday, 1991.

Gelley, Alexander, ed. *Unruly Examples: On the Rhetoric of Exemplarity*. Stanford, Calif.: Stanford University Press, 1995.

Genette, Gérard. *Narrative Discourse: An Essay in Method*. Trans. Jane E. Lewin. Ithaca, N.Y.: Cornell University Press, 1980.

Giedion, Siegfried. *Mechanization Takes Command: A Contribution to Anonymous History*. New York: Norton, 1969.

Glenny, Misha. *The Fall of Yugoslavia: The Third Balkan War*. London: Penguin Books, 1992.

Golding, Alan. "'What about All This Writing?': Williams and Alternative Poetics." *Sagetrieb* (forthcoming 2003).

Goldman, Judith. "Hannah=hannaH: Politics, Ethics, and Clairvoyance in the Work of Hannah Weiner." In "After Patriarchal Poetry," Steve Evans, ed., *differences* 12, no. 2 (2001): 121–68.

Goldstein, Ann, and Anne Rorimer, eds. *Reconsidering the Object of Art, 1965–1975*. Cambridge, Mass.: MIT Press, 1995.

Goodson, A. C. *Verbal Imagination: Coleridge and the Language of Modern Criticism*. Oxford: Oxford University Press, 1988.

Gray, Camilla. *The Russian Experiment in Art, 1863–1922*. Rev. and enlarged ed. London: Thames and Hudson, 1986.

The Great Utopia: The Russian and Soviet Avant-Garde, 1915–1932. Exhibition catalogue. New York: Guggenheim Museum, 1992.

Greenblatt, Stephen. *Learning to Curse: Essays in Early Modern Culture*. New York: Routledge, 1990.

———. *Shakespearean Negotiations: The Circulation of Social Energy in Renaissance England*. Berkeley: University of California Press, 1988.

———. "What Is the History of Literature?" *Critical Inquiry* 23, no. 2 (1997): 460–81.

Grenier, Robert. *12 from r h y m m s*. Scotia, N.Y.: Pavement Saw Press, 1996.

———. *A Day at the Beach*. New York: Roof Books, 1984.

———. "On Speech." *This* 1 (1971): n.p.

———. *Sentences*. Cambridge, Mass.: Whale Cloth Press, 1978.

———. *What I Believe / Transpiration/Transpiring / Minnesota*. Oakland, Calif.: O Books, n.d.

Guilbaut, Serge. *How New York Stole the Idea of Modern Art*. Cambridge, Mass.: MIT Press, 1983.

Hacking, Ian. *The Social Construction of What?* Cambridge, Mass.: Harvard University Press, 1999.

Hamilton, Paul. *Coleridge's Poetics*. Oxford: Basil Blackwell, 1983.

Hamper, Ben. *Rivethead: Tales from the Assembly Line.* New York: Time Warner, 1992.

Harrison, Charles, and Paul Wood, eds. *Art in Theory, 1900–1990: An Anthology of Changing Ideas.* London: Blackwell, 1992.

Harryman, Carla. *Animal Instincts: Prose Plays Essays.* Berkeley, Calif.: This Press, 1989.

———. *Memory Play.* Oakland, Calif.: O Books, 1994.

———. *The Middle.* San Francisco: Gaz, 1983.

———. *Vice.* Elmwood, Conn.: Potes and Poets, 1987.

Harryman, Carla, and Lyn Hejinian. From *The Wide Road,* in "Feminist(s) Project(s) Projects Des Féministes," *Tessera* 15 (1993): 56–64.

Hartley, George. *The Abyss of Representation: Marxism and the Postmodern Sublime.* Durham, N.C.: Duke University Press, forthcoming 2003.

———. *Textual Politics and the Language Poets.* Bloomington: Indiana University Press, 1989.

Hebdidge, Dick. *Subculture: The Meaning of Style.* London: Methuen, 1979.

Heidegger, Martin. *The Basic Problems of Phenomenology.* Trans. Albert Hofstadter. Rev. ed. Bloomington: Indiana University Press, 1982.

———. *Basic Writings.* Ed. David Farrell Krell. New York: Harper and Row, 1977.

———. *Being and Time.* Trans. Joan Stambaugh. Albany, N.Y.: SUNY Press, 1996.

———. *Kant and the Problems of Metaphysics.* Trans. Richard Taft. 5th ed., enlarged. Bloomington: Indiana University Press, 1982.

———. *Pathmarks.* Ed. William McNeill. Cambridge: Cambridge University Press, 1998.

Hejinian, Lyn. *A Border Comedy.* New York: Granary Books, 2001.

———. *The Cell.* Los Angeles: Sun and Moon, 1992.

———. *The Language of Inquiry.* Berkeley: University of California Press, 2000.

———. *Writing Is an Aid to Memory.* Berkeley, Calif.: The Figures, 1978.

Hejinian, Lyn, and Leslie Scalapino. *Sight.* Washington, D.C.: Edge Books, 1999.

Hennessy, Rosemary. *Materialist Feminism and the Politics of Discourse.* New York: Routledge, 1993.

Herr, Cheryl Temple. *Critical Regionalism and Cultural Studies: From Ireland to the American Midwest.* Gainesville: University Press of Florida, 1996.

Herron, Jerry. *AfterCulture: Detroit and the Humiliation of History.* Detroit: Wayne State University Press, 1993.

Hersey, John. *The Algiers Motel Incident.* Baltimore: The Johns Hopkins University Press, 1998.

Hobbs, Robert. *Robert Smithson: Sculpture.* Ithaca, N.Y.: Cornell University Press, 1981.

Hobhouse, Janet. *Everybody Who Was Anybody: A Biography of Gertrude Stein.* New York: Doubleday, 1975.

Hodges, Andrew. *Alan Turing: The Enigma of Intelligence.* London: Unwin, 1983.

Holzer, Jenny. *Writing/Schriften.* Ed. Noemi Smolik. Ostfilden-Ruit, Ger.: Cantz, 1996.

Hoover, Paul, ed. *Postmodern American Poetry: A Norton Anthology.* New York: Norton, 1994.

Horkheimer, Max, and Theodor Adorno. *Dialectic of Enlightenment.* Trans. John Cumming. New York: Continuum, 1998.

Humboldt, Wilhelm von. *On Language: The Diversity of Human Language-Structure and Its Influence on the Mental Development of Mankind.* Trans. Peter Heath. Cambridge: Cambridge University Press, 1988.

Hurston, Zora Neale. *The Complete Stories.* New York: HarperCollins, 1995.

Huyssen, Andreas. *After the Great Divide: Modernism, Mass Culture, Postmodernism.* Bloomington: Indiana University Press, 1986.

———. "High / Low in an Expanded Field." *Modernism / Modernity* 9, no. 3 (September 2002): 363–74.

Ian, Marcia. *Remembering the Phallic Mother: Psychoanalysis, Modernism, and the Fetish.* Ithaca, N.Y.: Cornell University Press, 1993.

Ikonnikov, Andrei. *Russian Architecture of the Soviet Period.* Trans. Lev Lyapin. Moscow: Progress Publishers, 1988.

Jackson, Laura (Riding). *The Poems of Laura Riding.* New ed. New York: Persea Press, 1980.

Jackson, Laura (Riding), and Schuyler B. Jackson. *Rational Meaning: A New Foundation for the Definition of Words and Supplementary Essays.* Ed. William Harmon. Charlottesville: University of Virginia Press, 1997.

Jakobson, Roman. "Concluding Statement: Linguistics and Poetics." In Thomas A. Sebeok, ed., *Style in Language,* 350–77. Bloomington: Indiana University Press, 1960.

———. "The Dominant." In Ladislav Matejka and Krystyna Pomorska, eds., *Readings in Russian Poetics: Formalist and Structuralist Views,* 82–90 Ann Arbor: Michigan Slavic Publications, 1978.

James, David E. "Rock and Roll in Representations of the Invasion of Vietnam." *Representations* 29 (1990): 78–98.

Jameson, Fredric. *The Political Unconscious: Narrative as a Socially Symbolic Act.* Ithaca, N.Y.: Cornell University Press, 1981.

———. *Postmodernism; or, The Cultural Logic of Late Capitalism.* Durham, N.C.: Duke University Press, 1991.

Jardine, Alice. *Gynesis: Configurations of Women and Modernity.* Ithaca, N.Y.: Cornell University Press, 1985.

Jaspers, Karl. *Basic Philosophical Writings: Selections.* Ed. Edith Ehrlich, Leonard H. Ehrlich, and George B. Pepper. Athens: Ohio University Press, 1986.

Jefferson, Ann. "Literariness, Dominance, and Violence in Formalist Aesthetics." In Peter Collier and Helga Geyer-Ryan, eds., *Literary Theory Today,* 125–41. Ithaca, N.Y.: Cornell University Press, 1990.

Jencks, Charles. *Heterotopia: Los Angeles, the Riots, and the Strange Beauty of Hetero-Architecture.* London: Academy Editions, 1993.

Johnson, Julia, ed. *Basic English.* New York: H. W. Wilson, 1944.

Johnson, Kent, and Stephen M. Ashby, eds. *Third Wave: The New Russian Poetry.* Ann Arbor: University of Michigan Press, 1992.

Joselit, David, et al., eds. *Jenny Holzer.* New York: Phaidon, 1998.

Joyce, James. From *Finnegans Wake.* In *In "transition": A Paris Anthology.* London: 1990.

Kabakov, Ilya. *Das Leben der Fliegen/Life of Flies/Zhizn mukh.* Ostfildern bei Stuttgart, Ger.: Cantz, 1992.

———. *Dvoretz proiektov/The Palace of Projects, 1995–1998.* London: Artangel, 1998.

———. *Ten Characters.* London: Institute of Contemporary Art, 1989.

Kagarlitsky, Boris. *The Thinking Reed: Intellectuals and the Soviet State from 1917 to the Present.* Trans. Brian Pearce. London: Verso, 1988.

Kalaidjian, Walter. *American Culture between the Wars: Revisionary Modernism and Postmodern Critique.* New York: Columbia University Press, 1993.

Karnow, Stanley. *Vietnam: A History.* Harmondsworth, Eng.: Penguin, 1983.

Kay, Paul. *Words and the Grammar of Context.* Stanford, Calif.: CSLI Publications, 1997.

Keats, John. *The Letters of John Keats.* Ed. Hyder Edward Rollins. 2 vols. Cambridge, Mass.: Harvard University Press, 1958.

Koestenbaum, Wayne. *Double Talk: The Erotics of Male Literary Collaboration.* New York: Routledge, 1989.

Kramer, Michael P. *Imagining Language in America: From the Revolution to the Civil War.* Princeton, N.J.: Princeton University Press, 1992.

Krauss, Rosalind. *The Originality of the Avant-Garde and Other Modernist Myths.* Cambridge, Mass.: MIT Press, 1985.

Kristeva, Julia. *Revolution in Poetic Language.* Trans. Margaret Waller. New York: Columbia University Press, 1984.

Kruger, Barbara. *We Won't Play Nature to Your Culture.* London: Institute of Contemporary Art, 1983.

Kubler, George. *The Shape of Time: Remarks on the History of Time.* New Haven, Conn.: Yale University Press, 1962.

Kurke, Leslie. *Cultural Poetics in Ancient Greece: Cult, Performance, Politics.* Cambridge: Cambridge University Press, 1993.

Kuspit, Donald. *The Cult of the Avant-Garde Artist.* Cambridge: Cambridge University Press, 1993.

Kuszai, Joel, ed. *Poetics@.* New York: Roof Books, 1999.

Lacan, Jacques. *The Four Fundamental Concepts of Psychoanalysis.* Trans. Alan Sheridan. Seminar of Jacques Lacan, Book XI, ed. Jacques-Alain Miller. New York: Norton, 1981.

Laclau, Ernesto, and Chantal Mouffe. *Hegemony and Socialist Strategy: Toward a Radical Democratic Politics.* London: Verso, 1985.

Lakoff, George. *Moral Politics: What Conservatives Know That Liberals Don't.* Chicago: University of Chicago Press, 1996.

Landow, George P. *Hypertext 2.0: The Convergence of Contemporary Critical Theory and Technology.* Baltimore: The Johns Hopkins University Press, 1997.

———, ed. *Hyper/Text/Theory.* Baltimore: The Johns Hopkins University Press, 1994.

Laplanche, Jean. *Essays on Otherness.* New York: Routledge, 1999.

Latinina, Yulia. "Folklore and 'Novoyaz.'" In "The Person," *Poetics Journal* 9 (June 1991): 116–26.

Lee, Jonathan Scott. *Jacques Lacan.* Boston: Twayne, 1990.

Lehman, David. *The Last Avant-Garde: The Making of the New York School.* New York: Doubleday, 1998.

Lemon, Lee T., and Marion J. Reis, ed. and trans. *Russian Formalist Criticism: Four Essays.* Lincoln: University of Nebraska Press, 1965.

Levi-Strauss, Claude. *The Savage Mind.* Chicago: University of Chicago Press, 1962.

Lichtenstein, Nelson. *Walter Reuther: The Most Dangerous Man in Detroit.* Urbana: University of Illinois Press, 1995.

Lippard, Lucy. *Six Years: The Dematerialization of the Art Object. . . .* 2nd ed. Berkeley: University of California Press, 1997.

Lissitzky, El. *Russia: An Architecture for World Revolution.* Trans. Eric Dluhosch. Cambridge, Mass.: MIT Press, 1984.

Lissitzky-Küppers, Sophie, ed. *El Lissitzky: Life/Letters/Text.* Greenwich, Conn.: New York Graphic Society, 1968.

Lodder, Christina. *Russian Constructivism.* New Haven, Conn.: Yale University Press, 1983.

Löwith, Karl. *Martin Heidegger and European Nihilism.* Ed. and trans. Richard Wolin and Gary Steiner. New York: Columbia University Press, 1995.

Lukács, Georg. *Record of a Life.* Trans. Rodney Livingstone. London: Verso, 1971.

Lyon, Janet. *Manifestoes: Provocations of the Modern.* Ithaca, N.Y.: Cornell University Press, 1999.

Lyotard, Jean-Francois. *The Postmodern Condition: A Report on Knowledge.* Trans. Geoff Bennington and Brian Massumi. Minneapolis: University of Minnesota Press, 1984.

Mac Low, Jackson. *Bloomsday.* Barrytown, N.Y.: Station Hill Press, 1984.

———. *Pieces o' Six.* Los Angeles: Sun and Moon, 1992.

———. *The Pronouns: A Collection of Forty Dances for the Dancers, 3 February–22 March 1964.* Barrytown, N.Y.: Station Hill Press, 1979.

———. *Representative Works: 1938–1985.* New York: Roof Books, 1986.

Macey, David. *Lacan in Contexts.* London: Verso, 1998.

Maltby, Paul. *The Visionary Moment: A Postmodern Critique.* Albany, N.Y.: SUNY Press, 2002.

Mandel, Ernest. *Late Capitalism.* Trans. Joris De Bres. London: Verso, 1978.

Mann, Paul. *Masocriticism.* Albany N.Y.: SUNY Press, 1999.

———. *The Theory Death of the Avant-Garde.* Bloomington: Indiana University Press, 1991.

Margolin, Victor. *The Struggle for Utopia: Rodchenko, Lissitzky, Moholy-Nagy, 1917–1946.* Chicago: University of Chicago Press, 1997.

Mariani, Paul. *William Carlos Williams: A New World Naked.* New York: McGraw-Hill, 1981.

Markov, Vladimir. *Russian Futurism: A History.* Berkeley: University of California Press, 1968.

Martin, Richard. *Fashion and Surrealism.* New York: Rizzoli, 1987.

Marx-Scouras, Danielle. *The Cultural Politics of "Tel Quel": Literature and the Left in the Wake of Engagement.* University Park: Pennsylvania State University Press, 1996.

Matejka, Ladislav, and Krystyna Pomorska, eds. *Readings in Russian Poetics: Formalist and Structuralist Views.* Ann Arbor: Michigan Slavic Publications, 1978.

Mayakovsky, Vladimir. *The Bedbug and Selected Poetry*. Trans. Max Hayward and George Reavey. Bloomington: Indiana University Press, 1975.

———. *How to Make Verse*. Trans. Valentina Coe. Willimantic, Conn.: Curbstone Press, 1985.

McArthur, Tom, ed. *The Oxford Companion to the English Language*. Oxford: Oxford University Press, 1992.

McCaffery, Steve, ed. "The Politics of the Referent." *Open Letter* (3rd ser.) 7 (1977): 60–107.

McGann, Jerome. *Black Riders: The Visible Language of Modernism*. Princeton, N.J.: Princeton University Press, 1993.

———. "Contemporary Poetry, Alternate Routes." In Robert Von Hallberg, ed., *Politics and Poetic Value*, 253–76. Chicago: University of Chicago Press, 1987.

———. *Radiant Textuality: Literature after the World-Wide Web*. New York: Palgrave, 2001.

———. *The Textual Condition*. Princeton, N.J.: Princeton University Press, 1991.

Mellow, James R. *Charmed Circle: Gertrude Stein and Company*. Boston: Houghton Mifflin, 1974.

Mencken, H. L. *The American Language: An Inquiry into the Development of English in the United States*. Ed. Ravin I. McDavid, Jr. 4th ed., rev. New York: Knopf, 1995.

Messerli, Douglas, ed. *"Language" Poetries*. New York: New Directions, 1986.

Mink, Louis O. "Narrative Form as Cognitive Instrument." In Robert H. Canary and Henry Kozicki, ed., *The Writing of History: Literary Form and Historical Understanding*, 129–49. Madison: University of Wisconsin Press, 1978.

Moi, Toril. *Sexual/Textual Politics*. London: Routledge, 1985.

Mowitt, John. *Text: The Genealogy of an Anti-Disciplinary Object*. Durham, N.C.: Duke University Press, 1992.

Murphy, James F. *The Proletarian Moment: The Controversy over Leftism in Literature*. Urbana: University of Illinois Press, 1991.

Murray, Katharine M. E. *Caught in the Web of Words: James A. H. Murray and the Oxford English Dictionary*. Oxford: Oxford University Press, 1977.

Nelson, Cary. "Literature as Cultural Studies: 'American' Poetry of the Spanish Civil War." In Nelson and Dilip Parameshwar Gaonkar, eds., *Disciplinarity and Dissent in Cultural Studies*. New York: Routledge, 1996.

———. *Repression and Recovery: Modern American Poetry and the Politics of Cultural Memory, 1910–1945*. Madison: University of Wisconsin Press, 1989.

———. *Revolutionary Memory: Recovering the Poetry of the American Left*. London: Routledge, 2001.

Nelson, Cary, and Lawrence Grossberg, eds. *Marxism and the Interpretation of Culture*. Urbana: University of Illinois Press, 1988.

Nelson, Cary, Lawrence Grossberg, and Paula Treichler, eds. *Cultural Studies*. New York: Routledge, 1992.

Ngai, Sianne. "Moody Subjects/Projectile Objects: Anxiety and Intellectual

Displacement in Hitchcock, Heidegger, and Melville." *Qui Parle* 12, no. 2 (spring/summer 2001): 15–56.
Nielsen, Aldon Lynn. *Black Chant: Languages of African-American Postmodernism.* Cambridge: Cambridge University Press, 1997.
———. *Writing between the Lines: Race and Intertextuality.* Athens: University of Georgia Press, 1994.
Niethammer, Lutz. *Posthistoire: Has History Come to an End?* London: Verso, 1992.
Nietzsche, Friedrich. *On the Advantage and Disadvantage of History for Life.* Trans. Peter Preuss. Indianapolis: Hackett, 1980.
Nora, Pierre. *Rethinking France/Les Lieux de mémoire.* Trans. Mary Trouille. Chicago: University of Chicago Press, 2001.
North, Michael. *The Dialect of Modernism: Race, Language, and Twentieth-Century Literature.* Oxford: Oxford University Press, 1994.
Norton, Camille, and Lou Robinson, eds. *Resurgent: New Writing by Women.* Urbana: University of Illinois Press, 1992.
O'Connor, Francis V. *Jackson Pollock.* New York: Museum of Modern Art, 1967.
Ogden, C. K. *Basic English: International Second Language.* Rev. ed. of Ogden, *The System of Basic English.* New York: Harcourt, Brace, and World, 1968.
———. *Basic English versus the Artificial Languages.* London: Kegan Paul, Trench, Trubner, 1935.
Ogden, C. K., and I. A. Richards. *The Meaning of Meaning: A Study of the Influence of Language upon Thought and of the Science of Symbolism.* New York: Harcourt, Brace, Jovanovich, 1989.
Oliver, Kelly. *Reading Kristeva: Unraveling the Double Bind.* Bloomington: Indiana University Press, 1993.
Olmo, Carlo, and Alessandro de Magistris, eds. *Iakov Tchernikhov.* Documents et reproductions des archives de Aleksei et Dimitri Tchernikhov. Paris: Somogy, 1995.
Olson, Alan M., ed. *Heidegger and Jaspers.* Philadelphia: Temple University Press, 1994.
Olson, Charles. *Collected Prose.* Ed. Donald Allen and Benjamin Friedlander. Berkeley: University of California Press, 1977.
———. *The Maximus Poems.* Ed. George F. Butterick. Berkeley: University of California Press, 1983.
———. *Selected Writings.* Ed. Robert Creeley. New York: New Directions, 1966.
Osborne, Peter. *The Politics of Time: Modernity and Avant-Garde.* London: Verso, 1995.
O'Sullivan, Maggie, ed. *Out of Everywhere: Linguistically Innovative Poetry by Women in North America and the U.K.* London: Reality Street, 1996.
Padgett, Ron. *Great Balls of Fire.* Chicago: Holt, Rinehart, and Winston, 1969.
———. *Triangles in the Afternoon.* New York: Sun, 1979.
Perec, Georges. *Life, a User's Manual.* Trans. David Bellos. Boston: David Godine, 1987.
Perelman, Bob. "Barrett Watten: December 19–22, 1979." In *Artists and Writers in Residence*, 26–52. San Francisco: 80 Langton Street, 1980.

———. "Exchangeable Frames." In "Non Narrative," *Poetics Journal* 5 (1985): 168–76.
———. *The First World.* Berkeley, Calif.: The Figures, 1986.
———. *The Marginalization of Poetry: Language Writing and Literary History.* Princeton, N.J.: Princeton University Press, 1996.
———. *Primer.* San Francisco: This Press, 1981.
———. *To the Reader.* Berkeley, Calif.: Tuumba Press, 1984.
———. *The Trouble with Genius: Reading Pound, Joyce, Stein, and Zukofsky.* Berkeley: University of California Press, 1994.
———, ed. "Plays from San Francisco Poets Theater." In "Plays and Other Writing," *Hills* 9 (1983): 5–93.
Perloff, Marjorie. *The Futurist Moment: Avant-Garde, Avant Guerre, and the Language of Rupture.* Chicago: University of Chicago Press, 1986.
———. "Language Poetry and the Lyric Subject: Ron Silliman's Albany, Susan Howe's Buffalo." *Critical Inquiry* 25, no. 3 (1999): 405–34.
———. "The Word as Such: L=A=N=G=U=A=G= E Poetry in the Eighties." *American Poetry Review* 13 (May/June 1984): 405–34.
Pfeil, Fred. *Another Tale to Tell: Politics and Narrative in Postmodern Culture.* London: Verso, 1990.
Phillipson, Robert. *Linguistic Imperialism.* Oxford: Oxford University Press, 1967.
Pierre, José, ed. *Investigating Sex: Surrealist Research, 1928–1932.* Trans. Malcolm Imrie. London: Verso, 1992.
Pike, Christopher, ed. *The Futurists, the Formalists, and the Marxist Critique.* Trans. Pike and Joe Andrew. London: Ink Links, 1979.
Pinkard, Terry. *Hegel: A Biography.* Cambridge: Cambridge University Press, 2000.
———. *Hegel's Dialectic: The Explanation of Possibility.* Philadelphia: Temple University Press, 1988.
Pinkney, Tony. Introduction to Raymond Williams, *The Politics of Modernism.* London: Verso, 1989.
Pitkin, Hanna Fenichel. *The Concept of Representation.* Berkeley: University of California Press, 1967.
Pocock, J. G. A. *The Machiavellian Moment: Florentine Political Thought and the Atlantic Republican Tradition.* Princeton, N.J.: Princeton University Press, 1975.
Poggioli, Renato. *The Theory of the Avant-Garde.* Cambridge, Mass.: Harvard University Press, 1968.
Pollack, Robert. *The Missing Moment.* New York: Houghton Mifflin, 1999.
Pratt, Mary Louise. *Toward a Speech Act Theory of Literary Discourse.* Bloomington: Indiana University Press, 1977.
Prigov, Dmitrii. "Conceptualism and the West." Trans. Michael Molnar. In "Elsewhere," *Poetics Journal* 8 (1989): 12–16.
Prochazka, Martin. "Prisoner's Predicament: Public Privacy in Havel's *Letters to Olga.*" *Representations* 43 (1993): 126–54.
Quartermain, Peter. *Disjunctive Poetics: From Gertrude Stein and Louis Zukokfsky to Susan Howe.* Cambridge: Cambridge University Press, 1992.
———. "The Poetics of Procedural Composition: The Case of Louis Zukofsky."

Paper delivered at "The First Postmodernists: American Poets of the 1930s Generation," University of Maine, 1993.

Rapaport, Herman. *Between the Sign and the Gaze.* Ithaca, N.Y.: Cornell University Press, 1994.

———. *Is There Truth in Art?* Ithaca, N.Y.: Cornell University Press, 1997.

———. "Poetic Rests: Ashbery, Coolidge, Scalapino." In "Knowledge," *Poetics Journal* 10 (1998): 155–64.

Reddy, Michael J. "The Conduit Metaphor: A Case of Frame Conflict in Our Language about Language." In Andrew Ortony, ed., *Metaphor and Thought.* Cambridge: Cambridge University Press, 1979.

Reinfeld, Linda. *Language Poetry: Writing as Rescue.* Baton Rouge: Louisiana State University Press, 1992.

Richards, I. A. *Basic English and Its Uses.* New York: Norton, 1943.

———. *Principles of Literary Criticism.* New York: Harcourt, Brace, 1925.

———. *Richards on Rhetoric: Selected Essays, 1929–1974.* Ed. Ann E. Berthoff. Oxford: Oxford University Press, 1991.

Ricoeur, Paul. *Time and Narrative.* 3 vols. Chicago: University of Chicago Press, 1984–88.

Rifkin, Libbie. *Career Moves: Olson, Creeley, Zukofsky, Berrigan, and the Ameican Avant-Garde.* Madison: University of Wisconsin Press, 2000.

Robinson, Kit. *The Dolch Stanzas.* San Francisco: This Press, 1976.

Robinson, Kit, Eileen Corder, and Nick Robinson. "Poets Theater." In "Non/Narrative," *Poetics Journal* 5 (1985): 122–38.

Rose, Tricia. *Black Noise: Rap Music and Black Culture in Contemporary America.* Middletown, Conn.: Wesleyan University Press 1994.

Ross, Andrew. "The New Sentence and the Commodity Form: Recent American Writing." In Cary Nelson and Lawrence Grossberg, eds., *Marxism and the Interpretation of Culture*, 361–80. Urbana: University of Illinois Press, 1988.

Ross, David A., ed. *Between Spring and Summer: Soviet Conceptual Art in the Era of Late Communism.* Cambridge/ Boston, Mass.: MIT Press/Institute of Contemporary Art, 1990.

Ross, Kristin. *The Emergence of Social Space: Rimbaud and the Paris Commune.* Minneapolis: University of Minnesota Press, 1988.

Rothenberg, Jerome. "Notes and Comments." *Alcheringa* 1, no. 2 (1975): 131.

———, ed. *Revolution of the Word: A New Gathering of American Avant-Garde Poetry.* New York: Seabury Press, 1974.

Rowell, Margitt, and Deborah Wye, eds. *The Russian Avant-Garde Book, 1910–1934.* New York: Museum of Modern Art, 2002.

Rusk, David. *Cities without Boundaries.* 2nd ed. Washington, D.C.: Woodrow Wilson Center Press, 1995.

Safranski, Rüdiger. *Martin Heidegger: Between Good and Evil.* Trans. Ewald Osers. Cambridge, Mass.: Harvard University Press, 1998.

Savran, David. *Taking It Like a Man: White Masculinity, Masochism, and Contemporary American Culture.* Princeton, N.J.: Princeton University Press, 1998.

Scalapino, Leslie. *New Time.* Middletown, Conn.: Wesleyan University Press, 1999.
———. *The Return of Painting, The Pearl, and Orion: A Trilogy.* San Francisco: North Point Press, 1991.
———. ed. *O III Anthology.* Oakland, Calif.: O Books, 1993.
Scroggins, Mark, ed. *Upper Limit Music: The Writing of Louis Zukofsky.* Tuscaloosa: University of Alabama Press, 1997.
Sedgwick, Eve Kosofsky. *Between Men: English Literature and Male Homosocial Desire.* New York: Columbia University Press, 1985.
Senie, Harriet F. *The Tilted Arc Controversy.* Minneapolis: University of Minnesota Press, 2001.
Seyhan, Azade. *Representation and Its Discontents: The Critical Legacy of German Romanticism.* Berkeley: University of California Press, 1992.
Shklovsky, Victor. *Mayakovsky and His Circle.* Ed. and trans. Lily Feiler. New York: Dodd, Mead, 1972.
———. *A Sentimental Journey: Memoirs, 1917–1922.* Trans. Richard Sheldon. Ithaca, N.Y.: Cornell University Press, 1970.
———. *Third Factory.* Trans. Richard Sheldon. Ann Arbor, Mich.: Ardis, 1977.
Sicko, Dan. *Techno Rebels: The Renegades of Electronic Funk.* New York: Billboard Books, 1999.
———. "Technorebels: Detroit's Agent of Change." *Urb* (August–September 1996): 56–65.
Silliman, Ron. "The Dysfunction of Criticism: Poets and the Critical Tradition of the Anti-Academy." *Poetics Journal* 10 (1998): 179–94.
———. *Ketjak.* San Francisco: This Press, 1978.
———. *The New Sentence.* New York: Roof Books, 1987.
———. *Tjanting.* Berkeley, Calif.: The Figures, 1980.
———, ed. "The Dwelling Place; 9 Poets." *Alcheringa* 1, no. 2 (1975): 104–20.
———. *In the American Tree.* 1st ed. Orono, Maine: National Poetry Foundation, 1985.
Silliman, Ron, and Leslie Scalapino. "What / Person? From an Exchange." In "The Person," *Poetics Journal* 9 (1991): 51–68.
Simmel, Georg. "The Metropolis and Mental Life." In Charles Harrison and Paul Wood, eds., *Art in Theory, 1900–1990.* London: Blackwell, 1992.
Sloan, Mary Margaret, ed. *Moving Borders: Three Decades of Innovative Writing by Women.* Jersey City, N.J.: Talisman House, 1998.
Smith, Suzanne E. *Dancing in the Street: Motown and the Cultural Politics of Detroit.* Cambridge, Mass.: Harvard University Press, 1999.
Smith, Terry. *Making the Modern: Industry, Art, and Design in America.* Chicago: University of Chicago Press, 1993.
Smithson, Robert. *Collected Writings.* Berkeley: University of California Press, 1996.
———. *The Writings of Robert Smithson.* Ed. Nancy Holt. New York: New York University Press, 1979.
Soja, Edward. *Postmodern Geographies: The Reassertion of Space in Critical Social Theory.* London: Verso, 1989.
Soldofsky, Alan. "Language and Narcissism." *Poetry Flash* 74 (1979): n.p.

Solomon, Andrew. *The Irony Tower: Soviet Artists in a Time of Glasnost.* New York: Knopf, 1991.

Souhami, Dianne. *Gertrude and Alice.* London: Pandora Press, 1991.

Stan Douglas. London: Phaedon, 1998.

Stan Douglas. Vancouver, B.C.: Vancouver Art Gallery, 1999.

Stan Douglas: Journey into Fear. Basel: Walter Konig, 2002.

Stein, Gertrude. *The Autobiography of Alice B. Toklas.* New York: Vintage Books, 1990.

———. *Everybody's Autobiography.* Cambridge, Mass.: Exact Change, 1993.

———. *The Geographical History of America; or, The Relation of Human Nature to the Human Mind.* New York: Vintage Books, 1973.

———. *Geography and Plays.* Madison: University of Wisconsin Press, 1993.

———. *Selected Writings.* Ed. Carl Van Vechten. New York: Random House, 1946.

———. *Useful Knowledge.* Barrytown, N.Y.: Station Hill Press, 1988.

———. *What Are Masterpieces.* Los Angeles: The Conference Press, 1940.

Steiner, Peter. *Russian Formalism: A Metapoetics.* Ithaca, N.Y.: Cornell University Press, 1984.

Steinman, Lisa M. *Made in America: Science, Technology, and American Modernist Poets.* New Haven, Conn.: Yale University Press, 1987.

Stevens, Wallace. *The Palm at the End of the Mind: Selected Poems and a Play.* Ed. Holly Stevens. New York: Vintage Books, 1990.

Stewart, Kathleen. *A Space on the Side of the Road: Cultural Poetics of an "Other" America.* Princeton, N.J.: Princeton University Press, 1996.

Stillinger, Jack. *Coleridge and Textual Instability: The Multiple Versions of the Major Poems.* Oxford: Oxford University Press, 1994.

Stivale, Charles J. "The 'MLA' Moment." *Profession* (1999): 248–57.

Storr, Robert. *Dislocations.* New York: Museum of Modern Art, 1991.

Sturken, Marita. "The Wall, the Screen, and the Image: The Vietnam Veterans Memorial." *Representations* 35 (1991): 118–42.

Sweetser, Eve S. *From Etymology to Pragmatics: Metaphorical and Cultural Aspects of Semantic Structure.* Cambridge: Cambridge University Press, 1990.

Tarkovsky, Andrei. *Sculpting in Time: Reflections on the Cinema.* Trans. Kitty Hunter-Blair. Austin: University of Texas Press, 1986.

Teitelbaum, Matthew, ed. *Montage and Modern Life, 1919–1942.* Cambridge and Boston, Mass.: MIT Press and Institute for Contemporary Art, 1992.

Théberge, Paul. *Any Sound You Can Imagine: Making Music/Consuming Technology.* Middletown, Conn.: Wesleyan University Press, 1997.

Thornton, Sarah. *Club Cultures: Music, Media, and Subcultural Capital.* Middletown, Conn.: Wesleyan University Press, 1996.

Tichi, Cecilia. *Shifting Gears: Technology, Literature, Culture in Modernist America.* Chapel Hill: University of North Carolina Press, 1987.

Toklas, Alice B. *What Is Remembered.* San Francisco: North Point Press, 1985.

Tupitsyn, Margarita. *Margins of Soviet Art: Socialist Realism to the Present.* Milan: Giancarlo Politi Editions, 1989.

Tupitsyn, Victor. "From the Communal Kitchen: A Conversation with Ilya Kabakov." Trans. Jane Bobko. *Arts* 66, no. 2 (October 1991): 48–55.

"Urban Site: Art in the City: August 16–September 30, 1983." In *The Last 80 Langton Street Catalogue*, 61–75. San Francisco: 80 Langton Street, 1984.
Veeser, Aram, ed. *The New Historicism*. New York: Routledge, 1989.
Vergara, Camilo José. *American Ruins*. New York: The Monacelli Press, 1999.
Vickery, Ann. *Leaving Lines of Gender: A Feminist Genealogy of Language Writing*. Middletown, Conn.: Wesleyan University Press, 2000.
Virilio, Paul. *Pure War*. New York: Semiotexte, 1983.
Voloshinov, V. N. *Marxism and the Philosophy of Language*. Trans. Ladislav Matejka and I. R. Titunik. Cambridge, Mass.: Harvard University Press, 1986.
Vygotsky, L. S. *Thought and Language*. Trans. Eugenia Hanfmann and Gertrude Vakar. Cambridge, Mass.: MIT Press, 1962.
Wagner-Martin, Linda. *"Favored Strangers": Gertrude Stein and Her Family*. New Brunswick, N.J.: Rutgers University Press, 1995.
Wallach, Amei. *Ilya Kabakov: The Man Who Never Threw Anything Away*. New York: Harry N. Abrams, Inc., 1996.
Watkin, William. *In the Process of Poetry: The New York School and the Avant-Garde*. Lewisburg, Pa.: Bucknell University Press, 2001.
Watten, Barrett. *1–10*. San Francisco: This Press, 1980.
———. "Beyond the Demon of Analogy: www.poetics." Paper read at "E-Poetry," SUNY Buffalo, April 2001.
———. *Conduit*. San Francisco: Gaz, 1988.
———. *Decay*. San Francisco: This Press, 1977.
———. "An Epic of Subjectivation: *The Making of Americans*." *Modernism/Modernity* 5, no. 2 (1998): 95–121.
———. "FDR's Panic Attack: State Power and Cultural Poetics from Kenneth Fearing to Ezra Pound." Paper given at "Cultural Poetics," University of Southampton, July 1966.
———. *Frame: 1971–1990*. Los Angeles: Sun and Moon, 1997.
———. Interview with Andrew Ross. In "Reinventing Community: A Symposium on/with Language Poets," Ross, ed. *Minnesota Review* (new ser.) 32 (1989): 30–39.
———. "Laura Riding's Horizon Shifts." Paper given at "Laura Riding and the Promise of Language," Cornell University, Ithaca, N.Y., October 1988.
———. "The Lost America of Love: A Genealogy." *Genre* 33, no. 3.4 (2000): 279–318.
———. *Opera — Works*. Bolinas, Calif.: Big Sky, 1975.
———. "Poetic Vocabulary: A Conversation with Jackson Mac Low." *Aerial* 8 (1995): 107–20.
———. *Progress*. New York: Roof Books, 1985.
———. "Seyed Alavi." *Artweek* (14 March 1991).
———. "Social Formalism: Zukofsky, Andrews, and Habitus in Contemporary Poetry." *North Dakota Quarterly* 55, no. 4 (1987): 356–82.
———. *Total Syntax*. Carbondale: Southern Illinois University Press, 1984.
———. "The Turn to Language and the 1960s." *Critical Inquiry* 29, no. 1 (autumn 2002): 139–83.
———. *Under Erasure*. La Laguna, Sp.: Zasterle Press, 1992.
———. "What Is Literature? From Material Text to Cultural Poetics." In Romana

Huk, ed., *Assembling Alternatives*, Middletown, Conn.: Wesleyan University Press, 2003.
———. "Zukofsky's *Catullus*." *This* 4 (1976).
Welish, Marjorie. *The Annotated "Here" and Selected Poems*. Minneapolis: Coffee House Books, 2000.
White, Hayden. *The Content of the Form*. Chicago: University of Chicago Press, 1987.
Will, Barbara. *Gertrude Stein: Modernism and the Problem of Genius*. Edinburgh: Edinburgh University Press, 2000.
Williams, Raymond. *The Politics of Modernism: Against the New Conformists*. London: Verso, 1989.
———. *The Sociology of Culture*. Chicago: University of Chicago Press, 1995.
———. *Television: Technology and Cultural Form*. New York: Schocken, 1975.
Williams, William Carlos. *The Collected Poems*. Ed. Christopher MacGowan. Vol. 2, *1938–1962*. New York: New Directions, 1988.
———. *Imaginations*. Ed. Webster Schott. New York: New Directions, 1970.
———. *Spring and All*. 2nd ed. Buffalo, N.Y.: Frontier Press, 1970.
Wojnarowicz, David. *Close to the Knives: A Memoir of Disintegration*. New York: Vintage, 1991.
Wolf, Reva. *Andy Warhol, Poetry, and Gossip in the 1960s*. Chicago: University of Chicago Press, 1997.
Wood, Paul. "The Politics of the Avant-Garde." In *The Great Utopia: The Russian and Soviet Avant-Garde*. Exhibition catalogue. New York: Guggenheim Museum, 1992.
Young, James E. "The Biography of a Memorial Icon: Nathan Rapoport's Warsaw Ghetto Monument." In Randolph Starn and Natalie Zemon Davis, ed., *Representations* 26 (1989): 69–106.
Žižek, Slavoj. "Beyond Discourse Analysis." In Ernesto Laclau, *New Reflections on the Revolution of Our Time*. London: Verso, 1990.
———. *Enjoy Your Symptom: Jacques Lacan in Hollywood and Out*. New York: Routledge, 1992.
———. *For They Know Not What They Do: Enjoyment as a Political Factor*. London: Verso, 1991.
———. *Looking Awry: An Introduction to Jacques Lacan through Popular Culture*. Cambridge, Mass.: MIT Press, 1992.
———. *The Metastases of Enjoyment: Six Essays on Woman and Causality*. London: Verso, 1994.
———. *The Plague of Fantasies*. London: Verso, 1997.
———. *The Sublime Object of Ideology*. London: Verso, 1989.
———. *Tarrying with the Negative: Kant, Hegel, and the Critique of Ideology*. Durham, N.C.: Duke University Press, 1993.
———. *The Ticklish Subject: The Absent Centre of Political Ontology*. London: Verso, 1999.
Zukofsky, Louis. *"A."* Berkeley: University of California Press, 1978.
———. *All: The Collected Short Poems, 1923–1958*. New York: Norton, 1965.

———. *Bottom: On Shakespeare.* Berkeley: University of California Press, 1987.
———. *Collected Fiction.* Elmwood Park, Ill.: Dalkey Archive Press, 1990.
———. *Complete Short Poetry.* Baltimore: The Johns Hopkins University Press, 1991.
———. *Prepositions: The Collected Critical Essays.* Expanded ed. Berkeley: University of California Press, 1981.
———. *A Test of Poetry.* New York: C. Z. Publications, 1980.
Zukofsky, Louis, and Celia Zukofsky. *Catullus.* London: Cape Goliard, 1969.

INDEX

Page numbers in italics refer to illustrations.

BARRETT WATTEN is Associate Professor of English at Wayne State University and the author of *Total Syntax* (1985), essays on avant-garde poetics. He was the editor of *This* (1971–82) and co-editor of *Poetics Journal* (1982–98). Recent collections of his literary work include *Frame (1971–1990)* (1997), *Bad History* (1998), and, forthcoming, *Progress/Under Erasure.*